"Where many see the Old Testament as disconnected and disjointed, Kevin Chen demonstrates that its unity can be demonstrated through attention to key passages. His close reading of core passages convincingly shows the unity of the Old Testament's message and the hope that emerges through it. Chen thus provides us with a map that helps us read the Old Testament well."

David Firth, tutor in Old Testament at Trinity College, Bristol

"What Kevin Chen offers here may be described as a stargazer of the entire heavens (the text of the Old Testament) discovering among the vast array ten particularly bright-shining, powerfully gravitational 'nexus' passages. This constellation provides the framework for seeing how all the parts of the Old Testament cohere and connect together."

Ray Lubeck, professor of Old Testament at Multnomah University

"In *Wonders from Your Law*, Kevin Chen identifies ten key nexus passages in the Old Testament, resulting in an integrative and intertextual approach that honors the literary, textual, and theological unity of the Old Testament. Readers will discover the themes of creation, deliverance, the temple, the Messiah, and his kingdom as well as wisdom, which are all weaved together to form God's story with Israel. The book contributes creatively to Old Testament theology from an evangelical perspective. It invites us to get on the 'subway' of the Old Testament and to be awed by its 'transfer stations' and, ultimately, its destination."

Chloe T. Sun, professor of Old Testament and program director of the Chinese Studies Center, Fuller Theological Seminary

"Kevin Chen's *Wonders from Your Law* establishes an exegetically grounded Old Testament theology that highlights how significant parts of the canon work together in subtle but significant conversations through connecting texts. The reader who wonders how Moses and the prophets read Scripture and understood the Messiah will find many treasures and wonders explained, clarified, and proclaimed. If you treasure the Old Testament, biblical theology, or the Old Testament's depiction of the Messiah, then you need to join Chen on this important journey through the Old Testament."

Peter Link Jr., professor of Christian studies at Charleston Southern University

WONDERS FROM YOUR LAW

NEXUS PASSAGES AND THE PROMISE OF AN EXEGETICAL INTERTEXTUAL OLD TESTAMENT THEOLOGY

KEVIN S. CHEN

FOREWORD BY
STEPHEN G. DEMPSTER

An imprint of InterVarsity Press
Downers Grove, Illinois

InterVarsity Press
P.O. Box 1400 | Downers Grove, IL 60515-1426
ivpress.com | email@ivpress.com

©2024 by Kevin S. Chen

All rights reserved. No part of this book may be reproduced in any form without written permission from InterVarsity Press.

InterVarsity Press® is the publishing division of InterVarsity Christian Fellowship/USA®. For more information, visit www.intervarsity.org.

All Scripture quotations, unless otherwise indicated, are translated by the author.

The publisher cannot verify the accuracy or functionality of website URLs used in this book beyond the date of publication.

Cover design: David Fassett
Interior design: Daniel van Loon
Image Credits: © duncan1890 / DigitalVision Vectors / Getty Images, © ZU_09 / DigitalVision Vectors / Getty Images, © Grafissimo / DigitalVision Vectors / Getty Images, Bigmouse108 / iStock / Getty Images Plus

ISBN 978-1-5140-0320-6 (print) | ISBN 978-1-5140-0321-3 (digital)

Printed in the United States of America ∞

Library of Congress Cataloging-in-Publication Data
Names: Chen, Kevin S., 1979- author.
Title: Wonders from your law : Nexus passages and the promise of an exegetical intertextual Old Testament theology / Kevin S. Chen.
Description: Downers Grove, IL : IVP Academic, [2024] | Includes bibliographical references and index.
Identifiers: LCCN 2024008264 (print) | LCCN 2024008265 (ebook) | ISBN 9781514003206 (print) | ISBN 9781514003213 (digital)
Subjects: LCSH: Bible Old Testament–Criticism, interpretation, etc. | BISAC: RELIGION / Biblical Studies / Old Testament / General | RELIGION / Christian Theology / Systematic
Classification: LCC BS1171.3 .C446 2024 (print) | LCC BS1171.3 (ebook) | DDC 221.6–dc23/eng/20240401
LC record available at https://lccn.loc.gov/2024008264
LC ebook record available at https://lccn.loc.gov/2024008265

---

31 30 29 28 27 26 25 24 | 13 12 11 10 9 8 7 6 5 4 3 2 1

For Kristina

As you grow up

may you come to know the wonders of God's law

and the wonders of his love

CONTENTS

FOREWORD BY STEPHEN G. DEMPSTER	IX
ACKNOWLEDGMENTS	XIII
INTRODUCTION	XV
ABBREVIATIONS	XXIX

1 NEXUS PASSAGES AND THE STORY OF OLD TESTAMENT
   THEOLOGY AS A DISCIPLINE — 1

2 GENESIS 1–3
   Creation and Wisdom (Literature) — 45

3 EXODUS 15:1-18
   The Exodus According to the Song of the Sea — 77

4 NUMBERS 24
   The Star from Jacob and a Deuteroevangelium — 104

5 DEUTERONOMY 32
   A Song for the Ages — 142

6 2 SAMUEL 7
   Who Is the Son Worthy to Build the Lord's House? — 167

7 ISAIAH 52:13–53:12
   The Suffering Servant — 189

8 JONAH 2
   Exodus 1.5 — 216

9 PSALM 72
   A Messianic Peak in the Middle of the Psalter — 242

10 PROVERBS 8:22-31
   Wisdom, the Beginning of the Lord's Way — 265

11 DANIEL 9
   Daniel, Student of Scripture — 286

CONCLUSION | 311	BIBLIOGRAPHY | 317
GENERAL INDEX | 337	SCRIPTURE INDEX | 347

FOREWORD
STEPHEN G. DEMPSTER

THE RESURRECTED JESUS JOINS two of his very depressed disciples incognito on the Emmaus road. It is the third day after his crucifixion. They are convinced he is still dead, his lifeless corpse sealed in a dark tomb in Jerusalem. He listens to their laments about their dashed hopes in a messiah who was to deliver Israel. But the traveling stranger gives them a lesson in biblical hermeneutics, reprimanding their lack of ability to connect the dots of their own Scriptures, which predicted the recent events. If they only knew how to read their Bibles.

> "So thick-headed! So slow-hearted! Why can't you simply believe all that the prophets said? Don't you see that these things had to happen, that the Messiah had to suffer and only then enter into his glory?" Then he started at the beginning, with the Books of Moses, and went on through all the Prophets, pointing out everything in the Scriptures that referred to him. . . . Then he said, "Everything I told you while I was with you comes to this: All the things written about me in the Law of Moses, in the Prophets, and in the Psalms have to be fulfilled." (Lk 24:25-27, 44 MSG)

Was Jesus right or wrong? In the last few centuries of biblical criticism, which have resulted in a plethora of methodologies to study the Bible, there has been a strong consensus that Israel's Scriptures do not have a coherent message. It is impossible that a vast, heterogeneous collection of literature with multiple genres written over a long span of time could have any expected coherence. It is more like a ragbag than a book, appearing like a tangled mess that needs to be carefully dissected and deconstructed to hear its many messages. But I am reminded of Jesus' reply to his depressed followers: "All things written about me [in your Bible] have to be fulfilled."

Such an answer assumes there is a way of reading Scripture correctly, which assumes an intensive knowledge of the details and an overall knowledge of how these details connect to one another to show a larger story. It's a matter of reading rightly.

Kevin Chen's *Wonders from Your Law* is the result of taking Jesus' hermeneutic seriously. It is an intensive study of the Scriptures, the result of a profound reflection on their content, and a conviction in their authority and claim to be divine revelation. The result is that the concept of the Messiah is not a late construction embraced toward the end of the biblical period as a means of dealing with the disenchantment and disillusion of the Jewish people. Nor is it an invention of early Christianity superimposed on the biblical texts, the result of cognitive dissonance coming to terms with the shock of the death of Jesus. No. There is a story line and a metanarrative in Israel's Scriptures. The Messiah is not just obliquely present but connects many of the details of Israel's Scriptures. He is there from the beginning and throughout the texts as a central theme.

Chen creatively takes his readers on a journey to show how this is true, displaying the unity and pervasiveness of this theme in the Old Testament. After an informative introduction discussing the history of Old Testament theology and laying out his evangelical presuppositions, Chen discusses texts from each of the major divisions of the Hebrew Bible: four from Torah, three from the Prophets, and three from the Writings: Genesis 1–3, Exodus 15, Numbers 24, Deuteronomy 32, 2 Samuel 7, Isaiah 53, Jonah 2, Psalm 72, Proverbs 8, and Daniel 9.

These texts are what he calls nexus passages, because they specifically connect with other texts, developing the messianic theme throughout the Scriptures. Continuing with theme of a journey, Chen creatively uses the analogy of a map in a subway to illustrate the importance and function of nexus passages. At first sight the subway map seems like a bewildering puzzle, with all the intersecting lines and dots. But the dots that represent transfer stations connect the various lines and relate them to one another so that one can get to the desired destination:

Foreword

It is easy to think of the Old Testament as a hodgepodge of diverse material that bears little coherence. If its constituent books are like differently colored subway lines, these lines often seem like they are going in different directions but without much connection to one another. However, this book argues that nexus passages are to the literary, textual, and theological cohesion of the Old Testament what transfer stations are to subway systems.

Readers can evaluate the success of Chen's project for themselves. But I find his study convincing and stimulating. For example, detailed comparison of the Abrahamic covenant in Genesis 15 and the Davidic covenant in 2 Samuel 7 shows striking similarities. The most important one is that the predictive elements focus on a particular descendant "who will go out from your loins" (אֲשֶׁר יֵצֵא מִמֵּעֶיךָ; see Gen 15:4; 2 Sam 7:12). Since such a construction only occurs in these two texts, it points to a relationship between them concerning a descendant from the line of Abraham who will bless the nations, continued in the line of David. Other texts such as Genesis 12:3 and Psalm 72, which emphasize the two seeds resulting in universal blessing, reinforce this link.

Another arresting example is an example of "braiding," when two disparate texts are meshed together, such as in Isaiah 54:3, which appears after the Suffering Servant atones for sin. The result is that Israel's seed will burst forth from its limited confines to the right and to the left (יָמִין וּשְׂמֹאול תִּפְרֹצִי) and inherit the nations (וְזַרְעֵךְ גּוֹיִם יִירָשׁ). These texts originate in Genesis 28:14 and Genesis 22:17-18 and are braided together to show the continuity and development of the messianic theme.

If only we knew how to read our Bibles. As you travel in the subway of God's Word, enjoy the transfer stations. In Psalm 119:18 the psalmist prays to the Lord, "Open my eyes, that I might behold wonders from your law." While the prayer is offered directly to God, one of the ways God opens our eyes is to provide gifted interpreters to his church. This book by Kevin Chen is one such gift for you "to take up and read" and see those wonders of the law for yourself.

ACKNOWLEDGMENTS

IT IS A DREAM COME TRUE for me to work with IVP Academic on a second book together. I had it in my heart to write on both the Pentateuch and Old Testament theology several years ago, and to see this desire fulfilled is very special. Thank you to Jon Boyd (again), who took on this project in the initial stages, believed in it, and helpfully shaped both the subtitle and conclusion of this book. Rachel Hastings took over shortly before the initial manuscript was due and guided me through the revision process and many other details leading up to publication. She has played the diverse roles of editor, dialogue partner, encourager, and project manager with skill and grace. Many thanks, Rachel! Two peer reviewers deeply engaged with my manuscript and provided encouragement and expert feedback that have made this book much better than it would have been. A big thank you to you both. Thank you to Stephen Dempster, whose outstanding scholarship is matched by his great kindness, for your special effort in writing such an engaging and gracious foreword. Thank you to my good friend Seth Postell for brainstorming potential nexus passages with me early on and for pointing me to several helpful sources. Thank you also to Jonathan Shelton, who read several chapters of this book and provided helpful feedback, especially on chapter six.

I see the kind providence of God through both the unexpected opportunity to have written on Psalm 110 as a nexus passage and the two (Chinese) institutions that invited me to teach Old Testament theology.[1] Without such space to wrestle with this difficult subject, this book never would have been written. Thank you to my Old Testament Theology students at Christian Witness Theological Seminary, with whom I shared

---

[1] See Kevin Chen, "Psalm 110: A Nexus for Old Testament Theology," *CTR* 17, no. 2 (Spring 2020): 49-65.

some of these ideas and who prayed for this book project when the proposal was being evaluated. Thank you to our librarian, Jane Chang, for filling the many interlibrary loan requests that I made while researching for this book.

Although he has been with the Lord for several years now, I would like to acknowledge again Dr. John Sailhamer, who first sparked my interest in Old Testament theology and whose approach I continue to follow. Whether we his students were aware of it or not, his teaching was practically always dealing with Old Testament theology because his exegetical method and view of the Tanak simultaneously accounted for both individual passages and Old Testament theology. For me, time and more research have further confirmed his seminal insights.

Finally, thank you to my family and friends, who have encouraged, supported, and prayed for me and this book. You know who you are, and I appreciate each of you. I decided to dedicate this book to my daughter Kristina as soon as the proposal was accepted in November 2020. At the time, she was only five years old. Years have passed, but my desire and prayer for her young life and mind remain the same.

INTRODUCTION

Every passage in the Bible is connected to other passages in the Bible, but some passages are much more highly connected than others. For example, "In the beginning God created the heavens and earth" (Gen 1:1) is a far more highly connected text (see Is 65:17, "Behold, I am creating a new heavens and a new earth"; Rev 21:1) than, say, "These are the sons of Dishan: Uz and Aran" in Genesis 36:28, or the like. In this book, such a highly connected passage is called a nexus passage. Through its purposeful use of words, themes, imagery, plot structure, coordination with another allusion, literary form, and/or syntax, a nexus passage connects not only to the passages immediately before and after it but also to others further away in the literary context. The passages to which it connects may be found in another part of the same biblical book or in another biblical book altogether. The large number of significant connections between a nexus passage and other passages is precisely what makes it a *nexus* passage. As the example above illustrates, a high level of connection correlates with the ability to link and integrate different parts of the Old Testament together. This means that the identification and study of nexus passages will enhance our appreciation of the literary, textual, and ultimately theological unity of the Old Testament.

As I am using them, the terms *literary* and *textual* have significant overlap, but the former emphasizes the Old Testament and its books as coherent works of literature, whereas the latter focuses on the Old Testament text itself and especially the phenomenon of (authorially intended) intertextuality. While recognizing that other definitions exist, I define Old Testament theology as the study and presentation of the intrinsic, historical meaning of the Old Testament based on the intrinsic, historical meaning of each Old Testament book and these books' interrelationship. With this working definition, an appreciation of the literary, textual, and theological unity of the Old Testament is at the heart of the study of Old Testament theology. In this book, I approach Old Testament theology through ten nexus passages from across the Tanak (Law, Prophets, Writings) and show that the theological unity they set forth centers on the eschatological Messiah and his kingdom.

IMAGINING THE INTERCONNECTIVITY OF THE OLD TESTAMENT: A SUBWAY SYSTEM AND ITS TRANSFER STATIONS

Since the concept of nexus passages may be unfamiliar, I offer an illustration to help readers visualize and imagine the interconnectivity of the Old Testament, which I will argue for more rigorously later. This can also be considered a thought experiment, a concept made famous in modern physics, useful for such purposes as illustration (e.g., Schrödinger's cat) and hypothesis, sometimes leading to eventual breakthrough (e.g., Einstein chasing a beam of light). Even though these thought experiments are not actualized, such imaginative exercises can help us think about reality in new and creative ways, which can be helpful in resolving perennial problems not only in science but in Old Testament theology. This is because the ruts in which disciplines sometimes find themselves are often related to entrenched ways of thinking that are partially correct but ultimately insufficient to account for all the data (e.g., Newtonian physics). If the oft-lamented fragmentation of biblical studies is any indication, there continues to be a need for robust working models, along with accompanying theories, for understanding the interconnectivity and unity of the Old Testament.[1]

The present work builds on productive scholarship concerning intertextuality, allusion, and inner-biblical interpretation for the purpose of evangelical Old Testament theology. While such models and theories would not necessarily be expected in critical scholarship broadly, they are appropriate within evangelical scholarship, which holds to the divine authorship,

---

[1] Regarding this fragmentation, see, e.g., Craig Bartholomew, "Biblical Theology and Biblical Interpretation: Introduction," in *Out of Egypt: Biblical Theology and Biblical Interpretation*, ed. Craig Bartholomew et al. (Grand Rapids, MI: Zondervan, 2004), 4. He refers to "the endless fragmentation of the Bible that historical criticism led to."

Introduction   xvii

inspiration, and resultant unity of Scripture. Although many modern evangelical works on biblical theology highlight intertextuality, fuller-scale models for understanding the interconnectivity of the Old Testament that leverage intertextuality for understanding biblical authors, the composition of their books, and the meaning of these books are uncommon.[2] I first propose the following illustration of the model, with methodological issues explained later in this introduction.

My illustration for the interconnectivity of the Old Testament is that of a complex subway system or metro transit network. Such transit systems are found in many major cities across the world, including New York City, London, Paris, Tokyo, Beijing, and others. A mere glance at the maps of such transit systems reveals an incredible, even bewildering, amount of complexity: differently colored lines going every which way, these lines sometimes straight but often curving, angling, or intersecting with other lines, and hundreds of stations, each represented by a dot labeled with its own sometimes peculiar name.

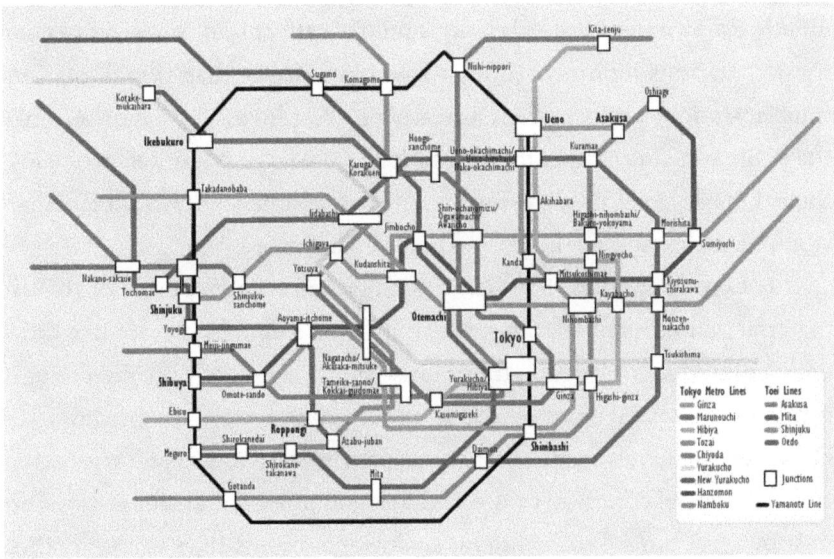

Figure I.1. Subway map with transfer stations

---

[2] The work of John Sailhamer is one exception.

Despite the initial shock that one feels when seeing such a map, there is a method to this tangled madness. As both residents and visitors can attest, these metro transit systems can get them (almost) everywhere they need to go on a daily basis. This is not necessarily because they live near one station on one line and only travel on that line, nor merely because of the aggregate reach of all lines put together, but because there are transfer stations that allow riders to conveniently travel on other lines and hence access the entire transit network. Without these transfer stations, the many lines would still cross one another but would remain independent and disconnected, much to the disadvantage of riders. City planners, of course, thought of this ahead of time and designed these transit networks with both reach and interconnectivity in mind.

Every station is connected to the stations immediately before and after it (unless it is at the end of a line), but transfer stations are especially highly connected. By their very nature, they link otherwise independent lines together. The great thing about having a transfer station for two lines that cross is that it essentially doubles the reach for riders, who can now conveniently use two lines instead of just one. This effect multiplies as lines and transfer stations multiply. Though fewer in number than typical stations, transfer stations play an essential and irreplaceable role for the cohesion of the entire network. If the transfer stations were to go out of service or lose their transfer capability, the entire network as a *network* would fall apart. Without such stations, there is no network anymore.

It is easy to think of the Old Testament as a hodgepodge of diverse material that bears little coherence. If its constituent books are like differently colored subway lines, these lines often seem like they are going in different directions but without much connection to one another. However, this book argues that nexus passages are to the literary, textual, and theological cohesion of the Old Testament what transfer stations are to subway systems. Producing much stronger bonds than primarily theological, salvation-historical, or thematic approaches, nexus passages hold the Old Testament together literarily, textually, and theologically, even as their authors drew on major themes and effected this unity as a historical act.³ In this case, the city planners who understood and designed this intricate, interconnected system are the authors of the Old Testament. Careful study of their work reveals that the books of the Old Testament and the Old Testament itself are not the tangled mess that they might appear to be at first glance but a beautifully constructed "web of words."⁴

Sometimes transfer stations link more than two lines together. At the time of writing, Châtelet station in central Paris links five, King's Cross/St. Pancras station in London six, and Times Square–42nd Street station in New York City twelve (these numbers do not even include transfers to buses and longer-distance trains).

Such major transfer stations are necessarily very large. Passengers who have used them before know that it can be a long walk to make a transfer in such a large station. Likewise, the nexus passages chosen for analysis in this book connect with multiple passages (sometimes including other nexus passages) and even multiple Old Testament books. It will accordingly take considerable effort to explore a nexus passage within the literary context of its own book and in relation to other books that it alludes to (or is alluded to by). By its very nature, a transfer station is part of two or more lines. Likewise, a nexus passage has its primary literary context in its own book but often also has significant relationships to other books with which it interconnects.

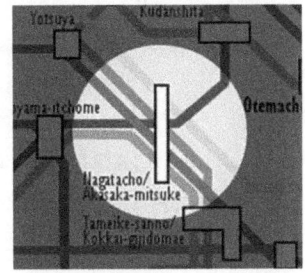

Figure I.2. Transfer station that links multiple lines

Nexus passages show that the Hebrew Bible is not a jumble of ancient religious documents but a literary, textual, and theological wonder. The Old Testament does not merely describe the wonders that God performed in history, such as during the exodus. Rather, the way in which the Hebrew

---

³For an argument for understanding *historical* not just in a historical-critical way but, even more importantly, in relation to the canonical text, see Christopher R. Seitz, *Prophecy and Hermeneutics: Toward a New Introduction to the Prophets*, Studies in Theological Interpretation (Grand Rapids, MI: Baker Academic, 2007), 46, 70-72, 90-92.

⁴Meir Sternberg, *The Poetics of Biblical Narrative* (Bloomington: Indiana University Press, 1985), 141. For more on OT authors, see Kevin Chen, "Psalm 110: A Nexus for Old Testament Theology," *CTR* 17, no. 2 (Spring 2020): 65.

Bible was written is also a wonder, bearing the marks of divine genius and derived human genius working together in harmony. We should therefore imitate the psalmist's prayer in Psalm 119:18, "Uncover my eyes, that I may see wonders from your law."[5] In addition to drawing together and thus integrating multiple texts, some nexus passages even show how the major Old Testament themes found in these texts (e.g., creation, Abrahamic covenant, exodus, wisdom) feed into the greater theme of the eschatological Messiah and his kingdom. In these cases, the literary and textual unity achieved by nexus passages serves a specifically Christocentric theological purpose. Studying nexus passages can thus result in greater faith and knowledge of the Messiah.

NEXUS PASSAGES AS A TEXT-CENTERED APPROACH THAT SEEKS AUTHORIAL INTENT

Since nexus passages focus on the literary and textual unity of the Old Testament for theological ends, the approach of this book is self-evidently a text-centered approach. Support for such an approach comes from the inspiration of Scripture, as taught in 2 Timothy 3:16 ("all Scripture is inspired [θεόπνευστος]"). Although every historical event falls under the sovereign rule of God and some biblical events involve divine action and/or speech, strictly speaking events are not inspired in this sense. Furthermore, there is a fundamental distinction between the respective natures of a written text and of the historical events it describes. This distinction does not impugn in any way the historical reliability of the biblical record but concerns the fact that a written text and a historical event, whether biblical or otherwise, are inherently different things. A text consists of words, follows the grammatical and syntactical rules of a language, is written by an author, and bears authorial meaning in the context of a biblical book. This meaning in turn requires attention to the composition of the whole book and its compositional strategy, which includes factors such as repetition, themes, intertextuality, the arrangement

---

[5]"Law" (תּוֹרָה) here need not refer to legal material per se but instead to Scripture, as in Ps 1:2.

and ordering of passages, and literary macrostructure.[6] In contrast, an event can include speech but is essentially nonverbal and arises independently of an author, authorial intent, and compositional strategy. Instead, a historical event is a unique space-time occurrence that happens once in particular, unrepeatable circumstances. A text can be a reliable, accurate record of an event, but the inherently different natures of text and event mean that a text should not be confused or fully equated with the event it describes.

Related to their containing a practically infinite amount of information, events do not bear determinate meaning (e.g., Acts 3:12; 14:11), but the Scriptures helpfully provide a selective, authoritative record and interpretation of biblical events. Thus, though text and event are distinct by nature, the historical reliability of the Bible means that the text of Scripture is unbreakably bound to biblical events as a trustworthy account of historical realities on which the Christian faith depends. The study of historical events plays a major role in many Old Testament theologies, but authors' intent is also at least as important to Old Testament theology (see chapter one). The study of nexus passages attempts to give consistent attention to this intent through its expression in the text. Research into Old Testament events definitely has historical and apologetic value, but for reasons given above as well as in chapter one, I prefer a text-centered approach to Old Testament theology. Limited historical reconstruction of biblical authors' circumstances only occasionally enters into the discussion (e.g., the Pentateuch) because of the frequent anonymity and/or uncertain date of many Old Testament books. Because Scripture itself cites the Old Testament as the Word of God and of human biblical authors without distinction (e.g., Mt 15:7; Heb 3:7), I view the divine author's intent and the human author's intent as one and the same.[7]

---

[6]John Sailhamer, *The Meaning of the Pentateuch* (Downers Grove, IL: InterVarsity Press, 2009), 11; see also Robert Polzin, *Samuel and the Deuteronomist: 1 Samuel* (Bloomington: Indiana University Press, 1993), 57, 59, which distinguishes between "crude" redaction and authorial (and "poetic," not "genetic") composition.

[7]For more on this issue, see Kevin Chen, *The Messianic Vision of the Pentateuch* (Downers Grove, IL: InterVarsity Press, 2019), 17-19.

IDENTIFYING NEXUS PASSAGES

If nexus passages are so helpful to understanding the Old Testament, we need to know how to find them. That is, we need criteria for identifying nexus passages, which are marked by their high interconnectivity to other passages both in their own book and in other Old Testament books. In keeping with the subway-system and transfer-station metaphor, we are especially interested not in interconnectivity that may be accidental but that which results from authorial activity and design. In other words, we are dealing not with intertextuality in a broad sense (as conceived of by Julia Kristeva) or mere textual parallels but with authorially intended intertextuality and allusion.[8]

Although studying intertextuality is as much an art as it is a science, the most objective indication of such intertextuality is lexical repetition (while accounting for differing word frequencies).[9] This criteria of shared language should coordinate with the criteria of shared themes, imagery, and/or plot structure. In some cases, a high amount of the latter can compensate for relatively less shared language (e.g., Gen 3:15 and Num 24:17). Shared syntax, the same literary form (e.g., poetry), and/or coordination with another allusion (e.g., braiding; see chapter four) also increase the likelihood of intertextuality. These criteria are applicable not only to single instances of authorially intended intertextuality or allusion but also to nexus passages, which have multiple instances of the same. As such, nexus passages are characterized by a high degree of dependence on other texts and/or other texts depending on them.[10]

Since the nature of a nexus passage is that it brings together other texts beginning in its own book, the analysis of each nexus passage in chapters two through eleven also involves showing its importance to the compositional strategy of its own book, whether in the literary macrostructure and/

---

[8]E.g., Robert de Beaugrande and Wolfgang Dressler, *Introduction to Text Linguistics* (New York: Longman, 1981), 10-11, 182; John Sailhamer, *Introduction to Old Testament Theology* (Grand Rapids, MI: Zondervan, 1995), 207-13; Peter Leithart, *Deep Exegesis: The Mystery of Reading Scripture* (Waco, TX: Baylor University Press, 2009), 117-18.

[9]Jeffery Leonard, "Identifying Inner-Biblical Allusions: Psalm 78 as a Test Case," *JBL* 127, no. 2 (2008): 246-48.

[10]Adapted from Leonard, "Identifying Inner-Biblical Allusions," 262.

or as a climactic passage of some kind. For example, Genesis 1–3 (chapter two) is the introduction to the Pentateuch, and the other three nexus passages from the Pentateuch (chapters three through five) deal with major poetic sections that are pillars of the Pentateuch's macrostructure (see chapter three). Second Samuel 7 (chapter six) is not an obvious feature in the macrostructure of 1–2 Samuel, but it is a climactic moment within the narrative. Likewise, Isaiah 53 (chapter seven) is not an obvious macrostructural element in Isaiah but is the last of the four Servant Songs, which play a major role in Isaiah 40–55 and hence the book of Isaiah. On the other hand, there are other Old Testament passages that also have many literary and textual connections but do relatively little thematic and/or theological integration (e.g., Deut 7:1-6). These passages may focus on a second-tier theme and bear less weight for Old Testament theology than the nexus passages in this book.

My focus on nexus passages relates to John Sailhamer's observations concerning literary seams, such as for the Tanak (Deut 34:10-12/Josh 1:8; Mal 4:4-6/Ps 1:2).[11] These texts bind the Tanak together at the boundaries of its three major divisions (Law, Prophets, Writings) in a coherent way. Deuteronomy 34:10-12 and Malachi 4:4-6 emphasize the eschatological restoration of prophecy, and Joshua 1:8 and Psalm 1:2 the need to meditate on Scripture.[12] Besides affecting how we view the Old Testament as a whole (see chapter one), these seams also exhibit intertextuality and can be considered nexus passages. Thus, there is some overlap between a seam and a nexus passage. However, whereas the term *seam* generally implies a key role in a work's literary macrostructure (like the Psalter's seams) and/or special authorial activity, the term *nexus passage* emphasizes high interconnectivity and the integration it achieves.[13]

---

[11] Sailhamer, *Meaning of the Pentateuch*, 217-18.
[12] See Stephen B. Chapman, *The Law and the Prophets: A Study in Old Testament Canon Formation* (Grand Rapids, MI: Baker Academic, 2020), 135-36, 140. Chapman adds the link between "the law of Moses, my servant," in Mal 4:4 and "Moses, my servant" and "the law" in Josh 1:2, 7 (see also Deut 34:5), as well as between the "sending" (שׁלח) of Moses in Deut 34:11 and Elijah in Mal 4:5.
[13] Gerald Wilson, *The Editing of the Hebrew Psalter* (Chico, CA: Scholars Press, 1985), 207-8; Sailhamer, *Meaning of the Pentateuch*, 23, 49, 50-51, 305-6, 313-14.

ANALYZING NEXUS PASSAGES BASED ON THE PRIORITY OF THE PENTATEUCH

Although the Mosaic authorship of the Pentateuch has been long abandoned by critical scholarship and is not necessarily agreed on by all evangelicals either, I hold to the Mosaic authorship of the Pentateuch based on biblical testimony (Deut 31:24; Josh 8:32; Neh 8:1), while leaving room for exceptional passages that appear to be added to the canonical Pentateuch by a later, Spirit-guided prophetic author (e.g., Deut 33:1; 34:5-12). Even in these rare cases, the text is still inspired (2 Tim 3:16), and Jesus' reference to a later canonical Pentateuch as being written by Moses (Jn 5:46-47) supports the Mosaic authorship of the Pentateuch and the retention of its original meaning in the canonical form. Furthermore, the essential Mosaic authorship of the Pentateuch implies its temporal priority compared to other Old Testament books. If Moses wrote the Pentateuch, then it was probably the first Old Testament book to be written.[14]

The temporal priority of the Pentateuch means that it was possible and even likely that later Old Testament authors knew the Pentateuch and engaged it in their books. References to the "law of Moses" throughout the Old Testament thus involve this Mosaic Pentateuch, in whatever protocanonical shape it was in at the time (e.g., Josh 1:7-8; 2 Kings 14:6; Mal 4:4) and not just, say, the book of Deuteronomy in isolation. Significantly, later references to the Pentateuch include not only such explicit citations of Moses' teaching or "the law" but also allusions, some of which exegete or interpret the Pentateuch. For example, Jeremiah 31:31-33 contrasts the new covenant written "on their heart" with "the covenant I made with their fathers when I took them by the hand to lead them out of the land of Egypt, my covenant which they broke." If Jeremiah knew the Pentateuch, as his disputes with corrupt leaders also suggest (Jer 2:8; 8:8), he appears to be pulling together and exegeting multiple passages from the Pentateuch concerning the Sinai covenant (Ex 19:5), Israel's breaking of that covenant (e.g., Ex 32:7-8, 19), and the new covenant (Deut 30:6).

---

[14]Throughout the book I will at times refer to the Pentateuch as a single book.

Whereas this allusion involves multiple passages in Pentateuch, Jeremiah 29:13 alludes specifically to Deuteronomy 4:29. The wording of the two passages is strikingly similar, and even the respective contexts concerning Israel's eschatological restoration after exile are the same.

> You will seek me and find me, for you will search for me with all your heart. (Jer 29:13)
>
> וּבִקַּשְׁתֶּם אֹתִי וּמְצָאתֶם כִּי תִדְרְשֻׁנִי בְּכָל־לְבַבְכֶם
>
> You will seek the Lord your God from there and you will find him, for you will search for him with all your heart and with all your soul. (Deut 4:29)
>
> וּבִקַּשְׁתֶּם מִשָּׁם אֶת־יְהוָה אֱלֹהֶיךָ וּמָצָאתָ כִּי תִדְרְשֶׁנּוּ בְּכָל־לְבָבְךָ וּבְכָל־נַפְשֶׁךָ

Although critical scholarship explains such phenomena in other ways, this example and many others like it suggest that prophetic authors read and interpreted the Pentateuch. Who better to have preserved, studied, and taught it to new generations? Furthermore, the similarity of thought and language between Deuteronomy 4:29 and Hosea 3:5 (see also Deut 4:30, which has "turn" [שׁוּב] and "in the last days" [בְּאַחֲרִית הַיָּמִים]) shows the importance of Deuteronomy 4:29 to both Hosea and Jeremiah, and thus Deuteronomy 4:29 serves as an illustrative example of a nexus passage. "Afterwards the sons of Israel will *turn* and *seek the Lord their God* [וּבִקְשׁוּ אֶת־יְהוָה אֱלֹהֵיהֶם] and David their king, and tremble before the Lord and his goodness *in the last days*" (Hos 3:5).

Some argue that the authorship of the Pentateuch does not greatly affect its interpretation and meaning, but the necessary connection between this issue and pentateuchal priority certainly affects how intertextual relationships within the Old Testament are understood. If the Pentateuch was not completed by the time the book of Jeremiah was written, then Jeremiah 29:13 cannot be explained as a reference to the Pentateuch as a completed book. It can be merely a reference to an incomplete version or isolated part of the Pentateuch, or a common tradition or

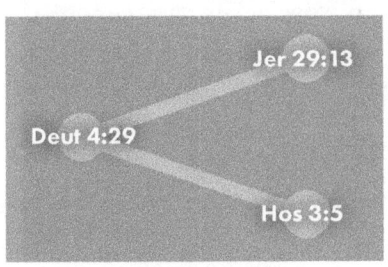

Figure I.3. Nexus connections to Deuteronomy 4:29-30

redaction that appears in both texts. Textual parallels in this case would not necessarily bear major significance for thoroughly constituting the literary, textual, and theological unity of the Old Testament. On the other hand, seeing these parallels as intentional references to the Pentateuch, often interpretive but still in accordance with its original meaning, means that later prophetic authors identified certain texts from the Pentateuch, sometimes linked them to other texts, and interpreted them authoritatively. Sailhamer refers to this phenomenon by characterizing the Hebrew Bible/Tanak as "text and commentary."[15]

Even though there are many allusions within the Old Testament that do not involve the Pentateuch and whose directionality can be more elusive, pentateuchal priority provides a historical, literary, textual, and theological foundation for this broader phenomenon in the Old Testament.[16] Indeed, even when an allusion does not directly involve the Pentateuch, the Pentateuch can still be treated as an existing historical reality and literary-theological influence on the biblical authors involved. Their books likely allude to the Pentateuch elsewhere. Every nexus passage examined in this work has demonstrable textual links to the Pentateuch. The purposes of allusion vary, but many nexus passages in the Old Testament use allusion for the purpose of interpretation.[17] As will be seen in the body of this work, the intent of the earlier text is often retained, reinforced, and reapplied in the newer text.

THE PLAN OF THIS BOOK

With this introduction having introduced what nexus passages are and methodological considerations for studying them, chapter one will situate this approach in relation to the fields of biblical theology and Old

---

[15]John Sailhamer, "The Messiah and the Hebrew Bible," *JETS* 44, no. 1 (2001): 13, 15-17.
[16]For further discussion of directionality, see Leonard, "Identifying Inner-Biblical Allusions," 257-64.
[17]Iain Provan, "The Messiah in the Books of Kings," in *The Lord's Anointed: Interpretation of Old Testament Messianic Texts*, ed. Philip Satterthwaite, Richard Hess, and Gordon Wenham (Grand Rapids, MI: Baker, 1995), 74, refers broadly to "narrative patterning," which can involve both similarities and differences. A subtype that ultimately emphasizes a contrast between two narratives is the inversion story. See Yair Zakovitch, "Through the Looking Glass: Reflections/Inversions of Genesis Stories in the Bible," *BibInt* 1 (1993): 139. For recent discussion and bibliography related to narrative analogies, see Seth Postell, "Reading Genesis, Seeing Moses: Narrative Analogies with Moses in the Book of Genesis," *JETS* 65, no. 3 (2022): 437-55.

Testament theology, especially the figures of Johann Philipp Gabler and J. C. K. von Hofmann. It will also discuss the issue of a center in the Old Testament and set forth the analysis of nexus passages as a constructive evangelical approach to Old Testament theology. Readers who are more interested in direct treatment of nexus passages may consider proceeding quickly to chapters two through eleven, which provide analysis of ten nexus passages from across the Tanak.

The distribution of four nexus passages from the Pentateuch, three from the Prophets, and three from the Writings is intentional and shows that such passages can be found in different parts of the Old Testament canon. The concern for canonical distribution also meant that I avoided choosing more than one nexus passage from the same book, except in the Pentateuch (a very long and important book), but even so the examples from the Pentateuch are spread out. I also tried to avoid unnecessary repetition of content between nexus passages. While every nexus passage treated in this book meets the criteria outlined above, evenness of distribution prevented me from choosing more than one from Genesis or Isaiah while also pushing me to choose one from the Minor Prophets (Jon 2). Likewise, avoiding repetition meant that choosing a nexus passage that is dominated by a major theme such as exodus (Ex 15) or the Davidic covenant (2 Sam 7) resulted in treating otherwise qualified nexus passages on the same theme in relation to another highlighted nexus passage rather than in their own chapters. Furthermore, I felt that at least one nexus passage was needed to integrate Wisdom literature (chapters two and ten), since this is a long-standing challenge in Old Testament theology, and at least two nexus passages focus on the eschatological Messiah (chapters four, seven, and nine). Thus, the ten nexus passages in this book are not the only ten, nor the top ten necessarily (though some of them should be included), but are a representative ten that account for distribution, avoidance of repetition, the need to deal with Wisdom literature, and the desire to demonstrate the Christocentric center of the Old Testament. The existence of additional nexus passages actually reinforces the basic premise of their usefulness to integrate the Old Testament material.

CONCLUSION

Nexus passages are a promising way to perceive the unity of the Old Testament text. Beginning on the literary and textual level, they show the interconnectivity of the Old Testament in a way that ultimately demonstrates its theological, even Christocentric, unity. Like transfer stations in subway systems, nexus passages link together multiple passages from other parts of the same book and even from other books. As a thoroughly text-centered approach that seeks the author's intent and emphasizes texts with high connectivity, the study of nexus passages aims to make a unique contribution to the study of Old Testament theology.

ABBREVIATIONS

1QIsaᵃ	Isaiahᵃ
4QMMT	Miqṣat Maʿaśê ha-Torah
AB	Anchor Bible
ApOTC	Apollos Old Testament Commentary
ASV	American Standard Version
BBR	*Bulletin for Biblical Research*
BDB	Brown, Francis, S. R. Driver, and Charles A. Briggs. *A Hebrew and English Lexicon of the Old Testament*
BHS	*Biblia Hebraica Stuttgartensia*
BibInt	*Biblical Interpretation*
BSac	*Bibliotheca Sacra*
CBQ	*Catholic Biblical Quarterly*
CTR	*Criswell Theological Review*
EvQ	*Evangelical Quarterly*
FOTL	Forms of the Old Testament Literature
GKC	*Gesenius' Hebrew Grammar.* 2nd ed. Edited by Emil Kautzsch. Translated by Arther E. Cowley. Oxford: Clarendon, 1910
HALOT	*The Hebrew and Aramaic Lexicon of the Old Testament.* Ludwig Koehler, Walter Baumgartner, and Johann J. Stamm. Translated and edited under the supervision of Mervyn E. J. Richardson. 4 vols. Leiden: Brill, 1994–1999
ICC	International Critical Commentary
Int	*Interpretation*
JBL	*Journal of Biblical Literature*
JETS	*Journal of the Evangelical Theological Society*
JSOT	*Journal for the Study of the Old Testament*
KJV	King James Version
LXX	Septuagint
MSG	*The Message* by Eugene Peterson
MT	Masoretic Text
NA[28]	Novum Testamentum Graece, 28th ed. (Nestle-Aland)
NETS	New English Translation of the Septuagint
NICOT	New International Commentary on the Old Testament

NIV	New International Version
NPNF²	*A Select Library of Nicene and Post-Nicene Fathers of the Christian Church*. Edited by Philip Schaff and Henry Wace. Second series. 14 vols. 1886–1889. Reprint, Peabody, MA: Hendrickson, 1994
OTL	Old Testament Library
RSV	Revised Standard Version
SHBC	Smyth & Helwys Bible Commentary
SJT	*Scottish Journal of Theology*
TOTC	Tyndale Old Testament Commentaries
TJ	*Trinity Journal*
TynBul	*Tyndale Bulletin*
VT	*Vetus Testamentum*
WBC	Word Biblical Commentary
WTJ	*Westminster Theological Journal*
ZAW	*Zeitschrift für die alttestamentliche Wissenschaft*
ZTK	*Zeitschrift für Theologie und Kirche*

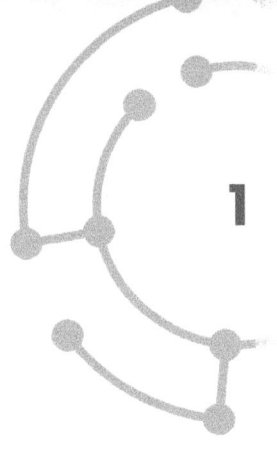

NEXUS PASSAGES AND THE STORY OF OLD TESTAMENT THEOLOGY AS A DISCIPLINE

THIS CHAPTER SITUATES THE STUDY of nexus passages in the context of Old Testament theology as a discipline. The ultimate purpose is to present the analysis of nexus passages as a constructive evangelical approach to Old Testament theology. In order to do this, it is necessary to show continuity with both the story of Old Testament theology as a discipline and evangelical theological commitments. Understanding this story in turn requires understanding the parent discipline of biblical theology, which has influenced both the origin and development of Old Testament theology. The analysis below is not a mere rehashing of the history of interpretation but engages key figures (e.g., Gabler, von Hofmann) and issues (e.g., the term *historical*, the existence of a center) for the sake of a better understanding of this discipline and how the analysis of nexus passages contributes to it.

OLD TESTAMENT THEOLOGY IN THE SHADOW OF JOHANN PHILIPP GABLER'S PROGRAM FOR BIBLICAL THEOLOGY

The discipline of Old Testament theology is a subset of the discipline of biblical studies and more specifically of biblical theology, which is commonly traced to Johann Philipp Gabler even if, strictly speaking, it did not begin with him.[1] His seminal treatise, *De justo discrimine theologiae biblicae*

---

[1] For a detailed treatment of the origins of biblical theology that goes beyond and often before Gabler, see John Sailhamer, *Introduction to Old Testament Theology* (Grand Rapids, MI: Zondervan,

et dogmaticae regundisque recte utriusque finibus (1787), concerns "the proper distinction between biblical theology and dogmatic theology."[2] Gabler argues that biblical theology is "of historical origin, conveying what the holy writers felt about divine matters." Dogmatic (or systematic) theology, on the other hand, is "of didactic origin, teaching what each theologian philosophises rationally about divine things, according to the measure of his ability or of the times, age, place, sect, school, and other similar factors." Citing examples from the history of theology, Gabler remarks, "Dogmatic theology is subject to a multiplicity of change along with the rest of the humane disciplines. . . . But the sacred writers are surely not so changeable that they should in this fashion be able to assume these different types and forms of theological doctrine." In his opening comments, Gabler had expressed his more general concern about "those who use the sacred words to tear what pleases them from its context in the sacred Scriptures" and "do not pay attention to the mode of expression peculiar to the sacred writers . . . [and] express something other than the true sense of these authors." In contrast, biblical theology emphasizes the Bible's historically situated meaning and is careful "to distinguish among each of the periods in the Old and New Testaments, each of the authors, and each of the manners of speaking which each used as a reflection of time and place, whether these manners are historical or didactic or poetic." Gabler's concern with the historical author's intended meaning appears yet again in his desire to avoid "new dogmas about which the authors themselves never thought."[3]

1995), 117-57. See also Joachim Schaper, "The Question of a 'Biblical Theology' and the Growing Tension Between 'Biblical Theology' and a 'History of the Religion of Israel': From Johann Philipp Gabler to Rudolf Smend, Sen.," in *Hebrew Bible/Old Testament: The History of Its Interpretation*, ed. Magne Saebø (Göttingen: Vandenhoeck & Ruprecht, 2013), 3.1:628-35. Scobie starts with the Bible itself and downplays Gabler but in so doing obscures the differences between biblical theology as a discipline and the more general task of accurately interpreting the whole Bible or a large portion thereof. This is because his concept of biblical theology goes beyond such as a discipline. See Charles Scobie, "The History of Biblical Theology," in *New Dictionary of Biblical Theology*, ed. T. Desmond Alexander and Brian Rosner (Downers Grove, IL: InterVarsity Press, 2000), 11-20.
[2]See English translation by John Sandys-Wunsch and Laurence Eldredge, "J. P. Gabler and the Distinction Between Biblical and Dogmatic Theology: Translation, Commentary, and Discussion of His Originality," *SJT* 33 (1980): 134-44, followed by commentary through 158.
[3]Sandys-Wunsch and Eldredge, "J. P. Gabler and the Distinction," 135-40.

Even as Gabler's treatise set forth a path for biblical theology, it also revealed the challenge of the task itself, including the classic problem of the unity of the Testaments. He remarks, "The sacred books, especially of the New Testament, are the one clear source from which all true knowledge of the Christian religion is drawn." While affirming that "all the sacred writers are holy men and are armed with divine authority," Gabler further asserts that "not all attest to the same form of religion; some are doctors of the Old Testament [i.e., 'basic elements,' Gal 4:9] . . . others are of the newer and better Christian Testament."[4] Whereas there is no questioning the importance of the New Testament for Christianity, Gabler thus goes further by his sharp distinction between Old Testament and New Testament forms of religion and what later became Old Testament theology and New Testament theology. Significantly, the role of Old Testament theology within biblical theology is left hanging. If the New Testament is "the newer and better Christian Testament," what place is there for an older, worse, less-Christian Old Testament?

Gabler's idea, citing Samuel Morus (a respected theologian of that time), was to search for "universal ideas" (or "notions") in various parts of the Scriptures, expressed in a way "consistent with its own era, its own testament, its own place of origin, and its own genius." Comparison of different passages would show "wherein the separate authors agree in a friendly fashion, or differ among themselves; then finally there will be the happy appearance of biblical theology, pure and unmixed with foreign things." John Sandys-Wunsch and Laurence Eldredge explain that Gabler's aim was to find those parts of Scripture that are "trans-historical" and to "isolat[e]" and "eliminate" the Bible's "purely historical characteristics . . . leav[ing] the truth exposed." An example of something having "purely historical characteristics" is the "Mosaic rites [or law]."[5]

Even if Gabler's project were to be followed through, it would set out to demonstrate the theological unity of Scripture without requiring literary and textual unity. By relying on universal ideas, Gabler has given up on any

---

[4]Sandys-Wunsch and Eldredge, "J. P. Gabler and the Distinction," 134, 139.
[5]Sandys-Wunsch and Eldredge, "J. P. Gabler and the Distinction," 141-42, 147-48.

unity based on the authorially intended meaning that he so values elsewhere. In the end, this meaning is important to Gabler and must be respected but is not the direct means by which biblical theology relates to the unity of Scripture. As Loren Stuckenbruck comments, "Biblical theology for Gabler only *begins* by determining the meaning of the text from the perspective of the biblical authors. . . . Herein lies an ambiguity which Gabler apparently never fully resolved. . . . Historical interpretation *does not define the task or goal of biblical theology so much as it involves a necessary starting point to be transcended.*" Indeed, Gabler above referred to a "pure" biblical theology ultimately based on universal ideas. Thus, although Gabler's approach "begins with the application of a historical method, [it] does not retain the historical as a check once a later stage of the analysis has been reached."[6] Robert Morgan relatedly sees "filtering" or "sifting" of biblical data at each step in Gabler's process, with the initial historical and exegetical step already being "neutraliz[ed]" in the next step, "despite his insistence that this must not happen."[7]

Gabler's use of universal ideas brings with it a certain externality to the biblical text itself. According to Sandys-Wunsch and Eldredge, this concept is "based on the philosophical doctrine that universal truths are more real than the particulars from which they are derived. . . . [Morus] compares the process of eliciting universal truth from Scripture with the process of eliciting universals from particulars in philosophy."[8] To be consistent, Gabler's rejection of imposing one's own ideas on the text should be equally applied to the potential imposition of universal ideas as unifying principles for biblical theology. Indeed, Stuckenbruck calls this a "synthetic, reductionary method. . . . From the outset, a value judgment within the biblical canon is operative."[9] Magne Sæbø likewise refers to Gabler's "way of

---

[6]Loren Stuckenbruck, "Johann Philipp Gabler and the Delineation of Biblical Theology," *SJT* 52 (1999): 143-44, 47, emphasis original. Again, "Once the exegetical process has been carried through, historical context no longer offers a check for the derived universal ideas" (152).
[7]Robert Morgan, "Gabler's Bicentenary," *Expository Times* 98, no. 6 (1987): 164-67.
[8]Sandys-Wunsch and Eldredge, "J. P. Gabler and the Distinction," 156, which footnotes Morus's *De notionibus universis in theologia*, 239. Gabler "hoped that modern rational methods would help him identify what is essential" (Morgan, "Gabler's Bicentenary," 165).
[9]Stuckenbruck, "Johann Philipp Gabler and the Delineation," 145.

reducing the biblical material . . . to its general theological concepts, whereby the emphasis is now on the latter." Furthermore, if the New Testament is basically in accord with these ideas, even embodying them, and the Old Testament much less so, how does one avoid imposing New Testament universals onto the Old?[10] Is there a substantive difference between biblical theology and New Testament theology (which can also invoke the OT as background) if the universals are the same?[11] What is the real value of the historical meaning of the Old Testament for Christians?

Gabler's aforementioned comments about the vast differences between the Testaments show that he did not believe authorial meaning to be consistent across Scripture. Furthermore, by focusing simply on the views of Moses, David, Solomon, the prophets, Jesus, and the apostles, Gabler does not clearly distinguish between the meaning of a character's words in specific parts of a biblical book and the authorial meaning of the book as a whole. For example, Jesus' words are of greatest importance to Christians, but methodologically speaking, he was not an author and must be distinguished from the respective authors of the Gospels. Even if a character within a book is also taken as the author of the whole book (e.g., Moses and the Pentateuch), the meaning of this character's words in a particular passage and the author's meaning as expressed through the whole book cannot simply be equated. The many examples of direct speech uttered by Moses in the Pentateuch, each with their own context and emphasis, are not equivalent to the meaning of the Pentateuch. Indeed, based on Gabler's comments, there does not seem to be a clear category for the authorial meaning of a biblical book. Such confusion also relates to confusion of the categories of text and event (e.g., a person's spoken words at a specific time in history but included in a biblical book that itself bears meaning), as discussed in the introduction.

---

[10] Magne Sæbø, "Johann Philipp Gablers Bedeutung für die Biblische Theologie," *ZAW* 99, no. 1 (1987): 9. Sæbø characterizes Gabler's "conceptual constancy of Scripture" ("begriffliche Konstanz der Schrift") as "probably above all that of the NT" ("wohl vor allem die des NT"; 9). All German and foreign-language translations are my own.

[11] E.g., Robert Morgan, "New Testament Theology as Implicit Theological Interpretation of Christian Scripture," *Int* 70, no. 4 (2016): 392: "Ideally a Christian biblical theology would perhaps be a New Testament theology that includes as much Old Testament theology as is implied by the newer religion's dependence on and critical reception of the older Testament."

Gabler's lower view of inspiration reveals what is likely a contributing factor to his position. In wanting to "investigate what in the sayings of the Apostles is truly divine, and what perchance merely human," and "whether some of [their opinions], which have no bearing on salvation, were left to their own ingenuity," it is clear that Gabler's conception of biblical theology cannot be adopted wholesale by those who hold to verbal plenary inspiration, even if he was thinking of the example of women wearing veils in the preceding context of his treatise. This may partially explain why Gabler wants to extract universal ideas from what is, for evangelicals, already a universal biblical text, inspired by God in its entirety. Elsewhere, Gabler relatedly remarks, "In the sacred books are contained the opinions not of a single man nor of one and the same era or religion."[12] While containing some elements of truth, this emphasis on diversity moves away from traditional views on the divine authorship of Scripture. Stuckenbruck accordingly observes that Gabler's emphasis on "particularity and historicality . . . relativizes the doctrine of inspiration."[13]

In relation to a unity of Scripture rooted in the biblical text, the impact is that once certain passages are sifted out (e.g., as not "truly divine . . . [and] perchance merely human"), the scope of the discussion has subtly but significantly changed from the canonical text to some subset of it. This is a fundamentally different starting point from believing that the canonical text in its entirety is inspired (2 Tim 3:16) and then pursuing the historically situated, authorially intended meaning of the text for biblical theology. At the same time, the problem of a canon within a canon has persisted in biblical theology even for evangelicals, but for different reasons (e.g., the inherent challenge of demonstrating the unity of such a vast corpus). Either way, the textual unity of Scripture based on historically situated, authorially intended meaning often has been left aside, seemingly ruled out at the outset in the task of biblical theology.[14] It is this de facto presupposition that needs to be reconsidered. Behind it lies a host of

---

[12]Sandys-Wunsch and Eldredge, "J. P. Gabler and the Distinction," 143, 139.
[13]Stuckenbruck, "Gabler and the Delineation," 145.
[14]E.g., Craig Bartholomew, "Biblical Theology and Biblical Interpretation: Introduction," in *Out of Egypt: Biblical Theology and Biblical Interpretation*, ed. Craig Bartholomew et al. (Grand Rapids,

assumptions about the nature and meaning of Scripture, its constituent books, and its countless passages. The literary, textual, and theological unity of Scripture should be treated as an open question, beginning with the Old Testament.

To be sure, the demonstration of such a unity is an overwhelmingly large task, involving the determination of the historically situated, authorially intended meaning of every Old Testament book, along with their varied unifying interrelationships. Such thoroughgoing unity must be hard-won, that is, demonstrated exegetically, examining one piece of evidence at a time. With respect to these interrelationships, nexus passages are especially useful and illuminating.

OLD TESTAMENT THEOLOGY FROM ITS BEGINNINGS TO J. C. K. VON HOFMANN TO TODAY

Old Testament theology: Early decades. "Biblical theology," in the "modern sense of the description of the theology of the Bible in the Bible's own terms," was not a term coined by Gabler in his 1787 treatise but had been used already in G. T. Zachariae's recently published five-volume work, *Biblische Theologie*.[15] Gabler commends Zachariae's work in his treatise while at the same time suggesting it can be improved on.[16] Gabler's work did not immediately result in the recognition of biblical theology as a distinct discipline, but over time his influence exceeded all others.[17] Ludwig Diestel's classic work on the history of (Christian) Old Testament interpretation names George Lorenz Bauer as the first to investigate Old Testament theology separately from biblical theology (1796).[18] Although his

---

MI: Zondervan, 2004), 1: "In large swathes of the academy we have in practice, if not in theory, given up on our attempts to articulate the unity of the Bible on its own terms."

[15] Sandys-Wunsch and Eldredge, "J. P. Gabler and the Distinction," 138niii, 149. See note 1 above.

[16] Sandys-Wunsch and Eldredge, "J. P. Gabler and the Distinction," 138. On 151-55, Sandys-Wunsch and Eldredge further argue for Gabler's direct dependence on and revision of Zachariae. For discussion of Zachariae's work, see Stuckenbruck, "Johann Philipp Gabler and the Delineation," 141-42; John Sandys-Wunsch, "G. T. Zachariae's Contribution to Biblical Theology," *ZAW* 92, no. 1 (1980): 12-21.

[17] Sandys-Wunsch and Eldredge, "J. P. Gabler and the Distinction," 149; Saebø, "Johann Philipp Gablers Bedeutung," 15.

[18] Ludwig Diestel, *Geschichte des Alten Testamentes in der christlichen Kirche* (Jena: Mauke, 1869), 709, 712. See also Brevard Childs, *Biblical Theology: A Proposal* (Minneapolis: Fortress, 1993), 5; Sandys-Wunsch and Eldredge, "J. P. Gabler and the Distinction," 150.

ideas developed independently from Gabler, Bauer was coming from "the same intellectual background" and "tackled the same problems," such that this separation is not surprising.[19] As mentioned above, Gabler believed that the two Testaments represented different religions and characterized the New Testament as "the newer and better Christian Testament." The history of Old Testament theology has been treated at length many times over, and what follows is a selective treatment that highlights aspects that provide helpful background for current issues in evangelical biblical theology and for my approach.[20]

According to Diestel, Bauer organized his material under the two main categories of theology proper and anthropology. Bauer warned against imposing ideas from later times and instead recommended comparison with ancient Near Eastern and Greek concepts. However, Diestel characterizes Bauer's treatment of the Old Testament in fourteen or fifteen sections, which included separating Genesis from rest of the Pentateuch and concluding with the later psalms, "a tearing of the material" ("eine Zerreissung des Stoffes"). Even worse, Diestel sees the same underlying deistic rationalism as continuing with Gottlob Philipp Christian Kaiser (1812), whose comparative, religious-historical treatment of Judaism is a "shocking caricature" ("abschreckenden Carricatur"), guided by and classified under a universalist framework. Kaiser emphasizes a "world-God" (*Weltgott*) in contrast to national gods (e.g., Israel's), which miss an alleged universalist monotheism. He detects this world-God in the older books of the Old Testament (e.g., the Pentateuch) but as coming from a very late editor (*Bearbeiter*) influenced by Persian thought and mythology rather than Abraham, Jacob, or Moses. As Diestel observes, Kaiser has accepted "a full uniformity of Old Testament ideas with pagan conceptions and myths."[21]

---

[19] Schaper, "Question of a 'Biblical Theology,'" 640.
[20] E.g., Sailhamer, *Introduction to Old Testament Theology*, 117-57; Gerhard Hasel, *Old Testament Theology: Basic Issues in the Current Debate*, 4th ed. (Grand Rapids, MI: Eerdmans, 1991), 10-27; John Hayes and Frederick Prussner, *Old Testament Theology: Its History and Development* (Atlanta: John Knox, 1985).
[21] Diestel, *Geschichte des Alten Testamentes*, 712-14.

Without endorsing the extremes to which later scholars sometimes went, Gabler's program for biblical theology did have in it the seeds for the history of religions.[22] His aforementioned belief that the Old Testament and New Testament espouse two religions is already a basic framework for the history of the Jewish and Christian religions. Furthermore, if these two religions are, in Gabler's words, not from "the same era," then it is easy to understand why Bauer sought ancient parallels from the regions surrounding Israel for better understanding. A similar extrabiblical move is hinted at in Gabler's own treatise. In calling for the consideration of the ideas of Moses, David, Solomon, the prophets, Jesus, and the apostles for biblical theology, he also says, "For many reasons we ought to include the apocryphal books for this same purpose."[23] Even though Sandys-Wunsch maintains the distinctiveness of biblical theology based on its attachment to some form of revelation or ongoing authority in the Bible, the boundary between biblical theology and history of religions was undefined from the outset, and the sense in which biblical theology is biblical (i.e., focused on the biblical text) likewise muddled, whether by extrabiblical apocryphal books or by sources for other ancient religions.[24]

In this regard, the titles of early works on Old Testament theology are telling.[25] Bauer's 1796 *Theology of the Old Testament or Outline of the Religious Concepts of the Ancient Hebrews. From the Most Ancient Times Until the Beginning of the Christian Epoch* equates Old Testament theology with tracing Hebrew religious thought in a way that goes beyond the scope of

---

[22] Sandys-Wunsch, "G. T. Zachariae's Contribution to Biblical Theology," 23, calls Zachariae, who influenced Gabler, "the father not only of biblical theology but also ultimately of the history of biblical religion."

[23] Sandys-Wunsch and Eldredge, "J. P. Gabler and the Distinction," 140.

[24] Sandys-Wunsch, "G. T. Zachariae's Contribution to Biblical Theology," 17: "The assumption that there is some sort of revelation or at least ongoing authority in the Bible is what distinguishes biblical theology from a history of biblical religion." See Schaper, "Question of a 'Biblical Theology,'" 625-50. Gerhard Ebeling writes that "limitation to the canon of scripture has also become problematic" because of the need to consider religious background for comparison, and more importantly, an account of the "historical development" requires it (e.g., pre-Christian Judaism, contemporaneous extracanonical books). Ebeling, "The Meaning of 'Biblical Theology,'" *Journal of Theological Studies* 6, no. 2 (1955): 221; see also Charles Scobie, *The Ways of Our God: An Approach to Biblical Theology* (Grand Rapids, MI: Eerdmans, 2003), 85.

[25] The titles below have been translated from Diestel, *Geschichte des Alten Testamentes*, 712-14 nn 13, 15, 18.

the Old Testament text itself ("Until the Beginning of the Christian Epoch"). Likewise, Kaiser's 1812 *The Biblical Theology or Judaism and Christianity According to the Grammatical-Historical Method of Interpretation and According to a Frank Position in the Comparative-Critical Universal History of Religions and in the Universal Religion* implicitly equates biblical theology with Judaism and Christianity, explicitly subordinated to a universalist, history-of-religions framework. Similarly, the next work mentioned by Diestel in his survey is C. P. W. Gramberg's *Critical History of the Religious Ideas of the Old Testament* (1829), which, though more detailed and objective than Kaiser, still treats the Old Testament as "only an aggregate of 'religious ideas.'"[26]

Such approaches to biblical theology often subdivided the Old Testament into additional historical periods. This periodization accords with the spirit of Gabler's proposal, which, as noted above, emphasizes that Old Testament and New Testament religion are not from "the same era" and recommends "distinguish[ing] among each of the periods in the Old and New Testaments, each of the authors, and each of the manners of speaking which each used as a reflection of time and place."[27] For example, W. M. L. de Wette divides the religion of the Old Testament into an earlier Hebraism and later, degenerated (!) Judaism after Ezra. Influenced by de Wette, Gramberg divided the Old Testament and its "religious ideas" into seven periods (excluding everything pre-Davidic because of its uncertainty) and the apocryphal books into six periods.[28] Hans Frei notes that the use of distinct historical periods to understand the Bible can be traced back to Johannes Cocceius in the seventeenth century, who used it in his covenant theology and "became the remote progenitor of the so-called *heilsgeschichtliche Schule* of the nineteenth century."[29] This salvation-historical school and its influence will receive extended attention in the following section.[30]

---

[26]Diestel, *Geschichte des Alten Testamentes*, 714.
[27]Sandys-Wunsch and Eldredge, "J. P. Gabler and the Distinction," 139.
[28]Diestel, *Geschichte des Alten Testamentes*, 714-15. The second and third periods run parallel (respectively, from after Hezekiah until shortly before the exile, and from Uzziah to Josiah).
[29]Hans Frei, *The Eclipse of Biblical Narrative* (New Haven, CT: Yale University Press, 1974), 46.
[30]For examples of periodization among evangelicals, see Geerhardus Vos, *Biblical Theology: Old and New Testaments* (Edinburgh: Banner of Truth, 1948), vii-x (e.g., the Mosaic epoch and the prophetic epoch of revelation); Charles Ryrie, *Dispensationalism Today* (Chicago: Moody, 1965),

The early decades of Old Testament theology as a discipline saw a variety of external, often philosophical, frameworks used by scholars. Diestel notes the special influence of the philosophy of Jakob Friedrich Fries on de Wette's work.[31] Brevard Childs characterizes de Wette and others as "introducing a heavily philosophical reading under the influence of Kant and de Fries, which again focused on symbolic interpretation of ethical concepts from the Bible."[32] On the other hand, Kaiser's aforementioned views involved a universalist framework as well as accounting for mythological influence. Childs's summary assessment of this period is that "there went a search for a new philosophical framework by which to integrate the biblical material over and above a straightforward historical reading," whether idealism, idealism mixed with Romanticism, or historical evolution.[33] Morgan likewise remarks that Gabler's original proposal "was overtaken by more ambitious schemes which fused historical criticism and theological interpretation."[34] As Sandys-Wunsch explains, "It may well be that one of the limitations of biblical theology as a whole is that it is inextricably bound up with the philosophical outlook of the times when it was written."[35]

This leads to the realization of a great irony in the discipline of biblical theology: since Gabler, biblical theology sought a distinction and greater freedom from the external, unifying control of dogmatic theology but often substituted other external, unifying systems in its place. An absolute, presuppositionless freedom was in fact never possible, but such substitutions, no matter what kind, still easily lapse into imposing meaning onto the biblical text, the very thing Gabler was trying to avoid. He identified the intruding influence of ever-changing dogmatic systems on biblical interpretation, but the subsequent course of biblical theology would also

---

57-63 (seven dispensations); Graeme Goldsworthy, *Gospel-Centered Hermeneutics* (Downers Grove, IL: InterVarsity Press, 2006), 247-48, 253-56 (three stages: creation to David/Solomon, prophetic eschatology, Christ).

[31]Diestel, *Geschichte des Alten Testamentes*, 715.

[32]Childs, *Biblical Theology: A Proposal*, 5.

[33]Childs, *Biblical Theology: A Proposal*, 6-7.

[34]Morgan, "Gabler's Bicentenary," 164. Brian Rosner, "Biblical Theology," in Alexander and Rosner, *New Dictionary of Biblical Theology*, 4-5, also emphasizes theological interpretation in contrast with an objectivist approach.

[35]Sandys-Wunsch, "G. T. Zachariae's Contribution to Biblical Theology," 17.

be influenced by changing philosophical systems.³⁶ The underlying problem is that biblical theology simultaneously wants both a historical treatment of the biblical text *and* a means to unify it, but the inability of this historical method to produce unity then requires a supplementary method that is not historical and undermines this fundamental emphasis. Historical-critical methodology instead tends to fragment the biblical text (e.g., sources, literary strata) and thus shifts the ground of historical meaning, which then must account for potentially varying dates for different portions of the same passage and accordingly determine for each what literary context is relevant and what is not. Historical meaning itself thus disintegrates under the same historical-critical method used to discover it.³⁷ Indeed, a little over a century after Gabler's seminal treatise, George Gilbert assessed his impact through (critical) scholars who "have brought out with hitherto unknown clearness the rich variety of Scripture" and "helped to destroy that idea of the unity of the Bible which prevailed before the Reformation."³⁸

J. C. K. von Hofmann's salvation-history approach. A nineteenth-century scholar worth extended consideration because of his influence on contemporary evangelical biblical theology is J. C. K. von Hofmann, one of the key representatives of a "salvation history" (*Heilsgeschichte*) approach.³⁹ Even though von Hofmann's ideas are not adopted wholesale today, his salvation-historical framework is sometimes treated as axiomatic among evangelicals. For example, while acknowledging that there are different definitions of biblical theology historically, Peter Gentry and Stephen Wellum define its current usage in terms of salvation history and favorably cite Geerhardus Vos's evangelical redemptive-historical approach as a "legitimate" approach to biblical theology.⁴⁰ While there are certainly ways of using salvation history less as a guiding framework and

---

³⁶Sandys-Wunsch and Eldredge, "J. P. Gabler and the Distinction," 137-38.
³⁷See Brevard Childs, "The Sensus Literalis of Scripture: An Ancient and Modern Problem," in *Beiträge zur Alttestamentlichen Theologie. Festschrift für Walther Zimmerli zum 70. Geburtstag*, ed. H. Donner (Göttingen: Vandenhoeck & Ruprecht, 1977), 90-91.
³⁸George Gilbert, "Biblical Theology: Its History and Its Mission. II.," *The Biblical World* 6 (1895): 358.
³⁹John Sailhamer, "The Messiah and the Hebrew Bible," *JETS* 44, no. 1 (2001): 6, 8-10.
⁴⁰Peter Gentry and Stephen Wellum, *Kingdom Through Covenant: A Biblical-Theological Understanding of Covenants* (Wheaton, IL: Crossway, 2012), 27-28, 30, 32.

more as one aspect among many, its use as a framework is sufficiently widespread to merit attention here.[41]

Noting the influences on von Hofmann's approach and scholarly responses to it provide helpful context for his ideas. Hans-Joachim Kraus passingly mentions both theological influences on von Hofmann's *Heilsgeschichte* (e.g., Cocceius, Johann Albrecht Bengel, Friedrich Schleiermacher) and influences from the study of history (Georg Wilhelm Friedrich Hegel, Leopold von Ranke).[42] In a lengthy article about von Hofmann's thought, Ernst-Wilhelm Wendebourg concludes that von Hofmann "basically remains rooted in romantic thought. . . . It is therefore understandable that Hofmann is seen again and again in close proximity to idealism . . . a child of romantic and idealistic historical speculation."[43] When Diestel's magisterial work was published in 1869, he referred to von Hofmann's approach as a "new school," since it had begun to be set forth relatively recently in 1841 in the first volume of *Weissagung und Erfüllung im alten and im neuen Testamente* ("Prophecy and Fulfillment in the Old and New Testaments").[44]

Von Hofmann saw his prophecy-fulfillment scheme as especially able to encompass the biblical material.[45] This scheme is based on knowing "the

---

[41]E.g., James Hamilton, *God's Glory in Salvation Through Judgment: A Biblical Theology* (Wheaton, IL: Crossway, 2010), 41, 43, 46-47. Benjamin Gladd writes, "At the heart of biblical theology is the unfolding nature of God's plan of redemption as set forth in the Bible," which is not a "'flat' biblical theology." See Gladd, "Series Preface," in *Exodus Old and New: A Biblical Theology of Redemption*, by L. Michael Morales (Downers Grove, IL: InterVarsity Press, 2020), ix-x. On the popular level (Crossway, 9Marks, Gospel Coalition), note the emphasis on tracing progressive revelation, the divine "saving plan," and the story of creation, fall, redemption, and new creation in Chris Bruno, "10 Things You Should Know About Biblical Theology," Crossway, February 10, 2017, www.crossway.org/articles/10-things-you-should-know-about-biblical-theology/. Likewise, Graeme Goldsworthy acknowledges the debate concerning what biblical theology is but ultimately emphasizes a historical process and favorably cites Vos' definition oriented toward progressive revelation and salvation history. See Goldsworthy, "What Is the Discipline of Biblical Theology," 9Marks, February 26, 2010, www.9marks.org/article/what-discipline-biblical-theology/. Though not as emphatic, see the reference to "the biblical story of redemptive history" in "Biblical Theology," Gospel Coalition, accessed June 1, 2020, www.thegospelcoalition.org/topics/biblical-theology/.
[42]Hans-Joachim Kraus, *Geschichte der historisch-kritischen Erforschung des Alten Testaments*, 3rd ed. (Neukirchen-Vluyn: Neukirchener, 1982), 226.
[43]Ernst-Wilhelm Wendebourg, "Die Heilsgeschichtliche Theologie J. Chr. K. v. Hofmanns in ihrem Verhältnis zur romantischen Weltanschauung," ZTK 52, no. 1 (1955): 103-4. Original: "Im Grunde bleibt er dem romantischen Denken verhaftet. . . . Es ist darum verständlich, daß Hofmann immer wieder in großer Nähe zum Idealismus gesehen ist . . . ein Kind der Romantik und der idealistischen Geschichtsspekulation."
[44]Diestel, *Geschichte des Alten Testamentes*, 699.
[45]J. C. K. von Hofmann, *Weissagung und Erfüllung im alten und im neuen Testamente* (Nördlingen: Beck, 1841), 1:1.

starting point and endpoint of [salvation] history."[46] He explains, "If it is true that all things, big and small, serve to bring about the unification of the world under its head, Christ [see Eph 1:10], then there is nothing in world history in which is not something divine [note the Romantic impulse], nothing for which the promise must remain necessarily foreign." In particular, he boldly asserts, "Israel in all its institutions and in its history is a prophecy of the future."[47] Kraus describes von Hofmann as seeing a "congruence" between revelation and history, as well as a close relationship between "act-revelation" (*Tatoffenbarung*) and "word-revelation" (*Wortoffenbarung*).[48] It is probably no coincidence that these two types of revelation are also foundational to Vos's evangelical redemptive-historical approach.[49]

Significantly, von Hofmann is working with a broader definition of *prophecy* that goes beyond predictive statements made in direct speech and includes historical parallels, similar to typology.[50] He generalizes that "a future event can also be depicted in an earlier one and presented in advance," like a Roman triumphal procession did for Caesar Augustus.[51] Salvation history and typology are also frequently linked in modern evangelical biblical theology. Citing von Hofmann, Graeme Goldsworthy makes this connection in his own salvation-historical approach. Goldsworthy further links typology on the hermeneutical level to *sensus plenior*.[52]

Salvation history and typology are in turn intertwined with the concept of progressive revelation, which is not simply about revelation taking place gradually over time and climaxing in Christ but emphasizes the increase in substantially new revelatory knowledge resulting in significantly greater

---

[46] Von Hofmann, *Weissagung und Erfüllung*, 3. The original reads "that history" (*jener Geschichte*), where "that" refers to the "history of the works of salvation" (*Geschichte des Heilswerkes*) in the previous sentence.

[47] Von Hofmann, *Weissagung und Erfüllung*, 7.

[48] Kraus, *Geschichte der historisch-kritischen Erforschung*, 227-28.

[49] Vos, *Biblical Theology*, 6-7. Vos engages Gabler, rationalism, and the influence of evolutionary theory (9-11), but the index of subjects and names does not include von Hofmann.

[50] Regarding the connection to typology, see Diestel, *Geschichte des Alten Testamentes*, 699, 720; Eberhard Hübner, *Schrift und Theologie: Eine Untersuchung zur Theologie Joh. Chr. K. von Hofmanns* (Munich: Chr. Kaiser, 1956), 89-90, 92-95.

[51] Von Hofmann, *Weissagung und Erfüllung*, 15. The preceding context uses the example of Abraham's justification in Gen 15:6 being fulfilled by his obedience (Jas 2:23).

[52] Goldsworthy, *Gospel-Centered Hermeneutics*, 242-44, 247, 243-56.

clarity concerning Christ and the gospel. The concept of progressive revelation itself has been attributed to Johann Albrecht Bengel (1687–1752). He explains, "Gradually God advances in laying open the mysteries of his kingdom, whether the things themselves or the times. What was kept concealed initially was then later understood openly. What is given in whatever age, the saints should embrace it, taking no more, accepting no less."[53] Bengel's statement expresses not only the self-evidently gradual nature of revelation but also the relative obscurity of revelation in earlier stages. Such initial concealment suggests that the Old Testament is inherently insufficient and unclear, especially its earlier portions.

The significance of Bengel's principle was felt already in the nineteenth century, with Gustav Friedrich Oehler calling it "at that time . . . quite new," and Franz Delitzsch appreciating it as "one of the most precious utterances of Bengel's."[54] Although predating von Hofmann (1810–1877) by over a century, Bengel himself can be seen as another precursor of a salvation-historical approach, as shown through his interest in (linear) biblical chronology.[55] Bengel's special attention to the book of Revelation as the crown jewel of Scripture accords with his views on progressive revelation and salvation history.[56] The confluence of progressive revelation with salvation history is thus quite natural for Bengel, as it is today.

---

[53]Johann Alberti Bengel, *Ordo Temporum* (Stuttgart: J. B. Mezler, 1770), 257 (§8.1). Original: "Gradatim Deus in patefaciendis regni sui mysteriis progreditur, sive res ipsae spectentur, sive tempora. Opertum tenetur initio, quod deinde apertum cernitur. Quod quavis aetate datur, id sancti debent amplecti, non plus sumere, non minus accipere." See Sailhamer's translation in *Introduction to Old Testament Theology*, 125. Relatedly, see Johann Albrecht Bengel, *Sechzig erbauliche Reden über die Offenbarung Johannis*, 2nd ed. (Stuttgart: J. C. Erhard, 1758), 505. Bengel writes, "God deals with his secrets sacredly: he does not give to all everything at once, but each one at the right time in the right order and measure, to whom it belongs, according to his will." Original: "Gott gehet mit seinen Geheimnissen heiliglich um: er gibt nicht allen alles auf einmal, sondern ein jedes zu rechter Zeit in rechter Ordnung und Maasse, denen, für die es gehöret, nach seinem Willen."
[54]Gustav Friedrich Oehler, *Theology of the Old Testament*, rev. trans. George Day (New York: Funk & Wagnalls, 1883), 31n3; Franz Delitzsch, *Messianic Prophecies in Historical Succession*, trans. Samuel Ives Curtiss (repr., Eugene, OR: Wipf & Stock, 1997), 38n1. Delitzsch uses it to explain why the protoevangelium in Gen 3:15 "should be first recognized so late, and should be first fully and completely disclosed through the New Testament" (38).
[55]Charles Fritsch, "Bengel, the Student of Scripture," *Int* 5, no. 2 (1951): 205, 212-14; Frei, *Eclipse of Biblical Narrative*, 4, 175-76.
[56]Ernst Benz, *The Mystical Sources of German Romantic Philosophy*, trans. Blair Reynolds and Eunice Paul (Allison Park, PA: Pickwick, 1983), 30-33; Julien Lambinet, "Les principes de la méthode exégétique de J. A. Bengel (1687–1752), piétiste du Württemberg," *Ephemerides Theologicae*

Back to von Hofmann, like Gabler he also departs from a traditional view of inspiration but in a different way, saying, "Every working of the Spirit on men in his service may be called inspiration." His broadened view of inspiration includes the example of the Spirit coming on Samson and enabling him tear a lion into pieces like a young goat (Judg 14:6), such that "wherever a man says or does something, which is willed by God for an extraordinary purpose, there is a wonder and inspiration." This understanding of inspiration to include both what someone "says or does" corresponds to the aforementioned categories of "word-revelation" (*Wortoffenbarung*) and "act-revelation" (*Tatoffenbarung*). In the same context, von Hofmann explicitly rejects the traditional limitation of inspiration to the writing of Scripture as a "willful limitation of a word of far-reaching significance."[57]

Together with his Christian interpretation of history, von Hofmann's broadened definitions of both prophecy and inspiration correspondingly encompass certain historical events or acts. Thus, von Hofmann argues, "All progress of the history of this people [i.e., Israel] is thereby explained as the progress of the history of salvation, since its result was the circumstances of the birth of Jesus." Unlike other national histories, "the history of Israel serves as preparation for Christ." For its part, the Old Testament "is a pre-depiction of Christ and his transfigured community." For this purpose of presenting Christ in the world are "history and prophecy at the same time," even "prophesying history" ("weissagenden Geschichte") and the work of the Spirit.[58] Von Hofmann thus blurs the line between prophecy and history.

By now it should be apparent how von Hofmann's salvation-historical approach to biblical theology worked, including its dependence on broadened conceptions of prophecy and inspiration. Diestel characterizes von Hofmann thus: "History, above all that of the OT, is the outworking of the divine economy; this kingdom-history is understood as the main theological purpose, not in its natural conditionality and concrete reality,

---

Lovanienses 89, no. 4 (2013): 253, 257-58, 265-68; Martin Brecht, "Johann Albrecht Bengels Theologie der Schrift," *ZTK* 64, no. 1 (1967): 105-9, 111-16.

[57] Von Hofmann, *Weissagung und Erfüllung*, 25-26.
[58] Von Hofmann, *Weissagung und Erfüllung*, 36, 39-40.

which is indeed only a shell, but only in so far as the individual events are somehow predepictions of Christ." This approach is obviously a far cry from historical-critical approaches, which center on historical-critical results ("reality") while often offering much less in relation to Christ as seen above. Diestel, himself a critical scholar, sees von Hofmann as disinterested in historical facts, valuing only symbols, types, and prophecy, and pejoratively characterizes him as a "theosopher [who] does not want to know that the OT is also a tradition."[59] Though not a traditional conservative either, von Hofmann, for his part, subtitled his work "A Theological Approach" ("Ein theologischer Versuch"), which contrasts with critical approaches.[60]

Accusations of theosophy aside, it is true that what drives von Hofmann is not the authorially intended, historically situated meaning of the Old Testament text. Instead, says Diestel, "The entire Old Testament is only important as a long chain of divine acts and divine speech." He sees von Hofmann's approach as naive and focusing on "only witnesses of revelation" rather than "of religious faith" (e.g., Gabler).[61] Sailhamer, who also engages von Hofmann at length, highlights the subtle but significant "tendency to reduce Scripture to the role of witness to revelation, rather than the source of revelation . . . [i.e.,] the orthodox notion that revelation rests in the written words of Scripture."[62] Arlis John Ehlen relatedly says of von Hofmann, "It is the *Heilsgeschichte* itself that is primary. The Scriptures are secondary, the faithful deposit of the historical development of revelation."[63]

Although evangelicals would never go this far, those who embrace salvation history as a framework for biblical theology still need to discern this

---

[59] Diestel, *Geschichte des Alten Testamentes*, 699, 705.
[60] Von Hofmann, *Weissagung und Erfüllung*, 1. Regarding von Hofmann's merely relative theological conservatism, see John Rogerson, *Old Testament Criticism in the Nineteenth Century* (Philadelphia: Fortress, 1985), 104. Rogerson writes, "Delitzsch . . . stayed much closer to Confessional orthodoxy than did Hofmann."
[61] Diestel, *Geschichte des Alten Testamentes*, 699.
[62] Sailhamer, *Introduction to Old Testament Theology*, 65.
[63] Arlis John Ehlen, "Old Testament Theology as *Heilsgeschichte*," *Concordia Theological Monthly* 35, no. 9 (1964): 532. Similarly, he sees in Wizenmann, an eighteenth-century precursor of von Hofmann, the belief that "history is the primary thing, and the testimony to it given by the Scriptures is already one step removed; theology must be interested primarily in the former rather than the latter" (528-29). See also Gustav Weth, *Die Heilsgeschichte: Ihr universeller und ihr individueller Sinn in der offenbarungsgeschichtlichen Theologie des 19. Jahrhunderts* (Munich: Chr. Kaiser, 1931), 87.

inherent tension, lest it lead to confusing the relationship between revelation and Scripture (i.e., all Scripture is revelation), and correspondingly that between salvation history and Scripture, which should be distinguished.⁶⁴ Sailhamer further characterizes von Hofmann thus: "It was not the text of Scripture that was messianic. It was history itself that was messianic. It was not Israel's historical writings that were messianic but the history that Israel itself experienced."⁶⁵ Whereas biblical theology is concerned with exegesis of authorial meaning, von Hofmann's approach instead focuses on "witnesses of [divine] revelation" within the Old Testament and construes them in a unifying salvation-historical framework.

Von Hofmann's salvation-historical framework is certainly preferable for evangelicals compared to many other frameworks discussed above. His Christocentrism is naturally also quite appealing for many evangelicals. Nevertheless, what must be borne in mind is that von Hofmann's framework relies heavily on the New Testament and is not rigorously based on an exegesis of the Old Testament text. The aforementioned critique of the use of external, often philosophical systems to achieve unity in biblical theology thus applies again to this extrinsic salvation-historical framework. Martin Brecht's assessment of Bengel applies to salvation-historical approaches generally: "Scripture as a system . . . is not detached from chronology. . . . The system of chronological-economic thought has for Bengel the same significance as metaphysics for orthodoxy. It is the framework of his thought structure. . . . Chronology thus constitutes the unity of Scripture."⁶⁶

As suitable as it can be as a Christian philosophy of history or even as a provisional framework for biblical theology, the problem with using chronology to organize Scripture is that at best it produces a weak unity because chronology can unify just about anything historical. Putting things

---

⁶⁴Sailhamer, *Introduction to Old Testament Theology*, 67. An example of this confusion can be found in Richard Gaffin, "The Redemptive-Historical View," in *Biblical Hermeneutics: Five Views*, ed. Stanley Porter and Beth Stovell (Downers Grove, IL: InterVarsity Press, 2012), 91-93. Despite his affirmation that "Scripture is itself revelation," he also calls it "a witness to revelation," which confuses the issue. Of similar effect is his use of the category of "deed revelation" alongside "word revelation."
⁶⁵Sailhamer, "Messiah and the Hebrew Bible," 8.
⁶⁶Brecht, "Johann Albrecht Bengels Theologie der Schrift," 115.

on a timeline automatically yields a kind of temporal-sequential unity. Certainly salvation history also provides a high-level framework and story line that includes creation, fall, redemption, and consummation. Nevertheless, it does not deal adequately with the many-sided features of the Old Testament text and can be reductionistic with respect to exegesis of the Old Testament. Salvation history as a kind of unifying historical-theological principle for Scripture cannot be disproven (for the Christian), but it does not prove much about the literary and textual unity of Scripture either. Though writing about the biblical theology movement (see below), Childs aptly points out, "By stressing history, the fragmentation of the Bible which was associated with literary criticism was overcome. Behind all the sources and redactions was the one continuing line that joins the Old and the New Testament."[67] In other words, emphasis on historical continuity enables one to overcome fragmentation of the text of Scripture. The same could be said of evangelical reliance on salvation history as a unifying framework, even if the nature of this fragmentation has less to do with critical scholarship and more with the inherent difficulty of perceiving the unity of Scripture on rigorously exegetical grounds. Either way, the literary and textual unity of Scripture remains unaddressed.

Although von Hofmann's approach may still be considered biblical insofar as it accords with certain important aspects of biblical teaching, salvation history for him remains first and foremost a historical-theological framework, not a rigorously exegetical one that gives full voice to the meaning of each book and its constituent passages. After analyzing examples of von Hofmann's exegesis, Eberhard Hübner concludes that von Hofmann "is committed to theological exegesis" and recognizes historical issues (some of which are historical-*critical*) but subordinates them to theological interests.[68] These theological interests are not only salvation historical but sometimes from systematic theology.[69] Thus, his exegesis "is

---

[67] Childs, *Biblical Theology in Crisis*, 40; see also Scobie, *Ways of Our God*, 84.
[68] Hübner, *Schrift und Theologie*, 94, followed by Kraus, *Geschichte der historisch-kritischen Erforschung*, 229.
[69] For salvation-historical influences, see Hübner, *Schrift und Theologie*, 84-90. For systematic theology, see 82 (analogy of faith), 91.

not in the first place determined by historical and philological factors but theological ones."[70] The problem is not that von Hofmann's exegesis naturally involved presuppositions (as all exegesis does), even theological ones, but that the fundamental distinctiveness of biblical theology from a priori theological frameworks is compromised in his salvation-historical "theological exegesis." Even if some historical-critical issues are largely excluded for evangelicals, the above discussion still relates to some evangelical use of salvation history for biblical theology.

While having merit for a Christian view of history and a theologically based Christocentrism, its linear, chronological nature as a framework for biblical theology is also reductionistic because Old Testament books and especially the Old Testament canon in their final form(s) do not fit smoothly into a linear-chronological framework, even if this framework is combined with a major biblical theme such as salvation or redemption (i.e., salvation/redemptive history). In order for the Old Testament material to be made to fit this framework, the Old Testament canon must be broken apart (because the books are not in chronological order), its books rearranged, and then the material within each book sometimes also rearranged (e.g., Psalms, Daniel).[71] The Christocentric witness of the Old Testament would also be better demonstrated from first principles, that is, exegesis.

It is true that Scripture tells of a clear beginning and end to history and as such has an important linear element in its *message*, but its canonical *form* in both Old and New Testaments is a mixture of chronological and nonchronological, even cyclical elements (e.g., Kings in relation to the

---

[70]Hübner, *Schrift und Theologie*, 88. Original: "ist nicht in erster Linie an historischen und philologischen, sondern an theologischen Tatbeständen gemessen." Likewise, Hübner says regarding another example on 89, "Hofmann's biblical exegesis stands under an entire determined heuristic principle" ("Hofmanns Schriftauslegung einem ganz bestimmten heuristischen Prinzip untersteht"). See also Wendebourg, "Heilsgeschichtliche Theologie J. Chr. K. v. Hofmanns," 73; Kraus, *Geschichte der historisch-kritischen Erforschung*, 228.

[71]Brevard Childs, *Introduction to the Old Testament as Scripture* (Philadelphia: Fortress, 1979), 77: "To work from the final form is to resist any method which seeks critically to shift the canonical ordering. Such an exegetical move occurs whenever an overarching category such as *Heilsgeschichte* subordinates the peculiar canonical profile, or a historical-critical reconstruction attempts to refocus the picture according to its own standards of aesthetics or historical accuracy." See also Christopher Seitz, *Prophecy and Hermeneutics: Toward a New Introduction to the Prophets* (Grand Rapids, MI: Baker, 2007), 30-31, 72, 92; Sailhamer, *Meaning of the Pentateuch*, 170, who cites the examples of Ruth and Chronicles as chronologically displaced in the Tanak.

preexilic prophetic books and Chronicles, as well as the four Gospels).[72] Since biblical theology emphasizes the categories of the Bible itself, this form must be thoroughly respected, even as we abstract its message from its form and contents. Certainly, this canonical form has major linear elements (e.g., Genesis–Kings; Revelation) and is more linear than it is cyclical, but a linear chronological framework still cannot do justice to the full scope of biblical material as we have it in its canonical form. Christopher Seitz thus distinguishes between canonical Scripture's own presentation of history and historical-critical linear presentations.[73]

Salvation history as a unifying framework ultimately depends not on exegeting the authorial meaning of the Old Testament but on a Christian view of history more broadly. Even though evangelicals (including myself) affirm this view of history, there remains a crucial difference between affirming the *reality* of salvation history and using salvation history as a *unifying framework* for biblical theology. Likewise, a Christian philosophy of history that encompasses the biblical witness (i.e., from the top down), even if it is supported by select key passages, should not be equated with demonstrating the literary, textual, and ultimately theological unity of the Old Testament from the ground up.[74] Using salvation history as a unifying framework for biblical theology thus runs the risk of missing significant parts of the historical meaning of the Old Testament text because it does not arise organically from exegesis. It is as though the theological systems that concerned Gabler, as well as the universal ideas that he essentially substituted for them and the philosophical systems used by others, were in turn replaced by von Hofmann by a salvation-historical framework. None of these frameworks should be confused with a unity thoroughly based on exegesis of the historical meaning of biblical authors.

---

[72]See Stephen Dempster, *Dominion and Dynasty: A Theology of the Hebrew Bible* (Downers Grove, IL: InterVarsity Press, 2003), 159, who refers to the "suspension" of the canonical story line in the Latter Prophets and in the Writings until its resumption in the book of Daniel. Scobie also draws attention to cyclical and/or nonlinear elements in the Bible (*Ways of Our God*, 152-53, 192).

[73]Seitz, *Prophecy and Hermeneutics*, 69-72. However, for Seitz the figural version of history in the canon does not rely much on predictive prophecy, as its views of providence and divine sovereignty focus on "retrospective accordance and typological fit" (69).

[74]Sailhamer, *Introduction to Old Testament Theology*, 56.

To be sure, modern evangelical approaches to biblical theology that employ salvation history often combine it with extensive, fruitful exegetical work.[75] The continuing issue, however, is that when salvation history is used as a major unifying principle, the priority of the historical author's meaning can get confused. Exegetical fruit from such eclectic approaches is always a helpful contribution to our knowledge of the Bible, but insofar as biblical theology seeks an exegetically derived unity of Scripture, the classic problems remain, whether we look at modern approaches, von Hofmann, Gabler, Bengel, or many others. Moreover, it is probably no coincidence that the concepts of salvation history, typology, and progressive revelation favor the New Testament over the Old Testament, in accordance with the views of von Hofmann, Gabler, and Bengel.[76] The aforementioned vague relationship between biblical theology and the study of history is thus reflected not only in a history-of-religions approach (later shaped by Julius Wellhausen) but also in that of salvation history.

Old Testament theology during the last hundred years. In the twentieth century, the influence of history of religions and salvation history on biblical theology continued in the well-known works of both Walter Eichrodt and Gerhard von Rad. Defining the "concern" of Old Testament theology as being "to construct a complete picture of the OT realm of belief," Eichrodt relates this task to "a double aspect" of "comparative study of religions" (even "constant reference" thereto) and of "looking on towards the New Testament . . . [in] historical development," the latter involving a

---

[75]E.g., Bruce Waltke, *An Old Testament Theology* (Grand Rapids, MI: Zondervan, 2007); Hamilton, *God's Glory in Salvation*; G. K. Beale, *A New Testament Biblical Theology: The Unfolding of the Old Testament in the New* (Grand Rapids, MI: Baker Academic, 2011). Hasel refers to Eduard König's esteem for the reliability of the OT and call for the use of the grammatical-historical method of interpretation but still characterizes König's work as a "hybrid" that includes "a history of the development of Israelite religion" (*Old Testament Theology*, 25).

[76]Oehler, *Theology of the Old Testament*, 31n3: "Bengel himself wrote nothing on the Old Testament, except as his *Ordo Temporum* includes the Old Testament. . . . Disjointed suggestive hints in connection with the Old Testament are to be found scattered everywhere in his numerous writings." Andrew Helmbold notes that early in his career Bengel worked with Hochstetter on a German Bible "wherein the punctuation was made to conform to the Hebrew acccents [sic]" and "wr[o]te an essay on the Hebrew accents," and later in life, he wrote a preface to his son-in-law's commentary on the Minor Prophets. See Helmbold, "J. A. Bengel:—'Full of Light,'" *Bulletin of the Evangelical Theological Society* 6, no. 3 (1963): 73.

"movement [which] does not come to rest until the manifestation of Christ, in whom the noblest powers of the OT find their fulfilment."⁷⁷ These two aspects broadly align with history of religions and salvation history. Eichrodt adds that the unity of the Testaments is not only historical but also consists of "a mighty living reality" of "the irruption of the Kingship of God into this world and its establishment here."⁷⁸

Von Rad does not attempt a complete picture of Israel's faith but instead focuses on the "credal statements," viewed in relation to "those contexts in the saving history [n.b.] in which it was arranged by Israel." Over time, these statements "grow into . . . enormous masses of traditions" and "are completely tied up with history." Elsewhere, von Rad relatedly identifies the subject matter of Old Testament theology as "Israel's own explicit assertions about Jahweh." These statements focus on the relationship between Yahweh and Israel specifically with respect to "continuing divine activity in history," that is, "divine acts in history," as regarded by Israel's faith. Von Rad has in mind not something "systematically arranged" but "many traditions which little by little combined into ever larger complexes of tradition. Theologically, these accumulations were in a state of constant flux."⁷⁹ In their respective ways, the works of Eichrodt and von Rad thus show the influence of history of religions and salvation history. Even von Rad's typical association with tradition history can be related to the history of religion.⁸⁰ It is true that von Rad contrasts his approach with

---

⁷⁷Walter Eichrodt, *Theology of the Old Testament*, trans. J. A. Baker (Philadelphia: Westminster, 1961), 1:25-26.
⁷⁸Eichrodt, *Theology of the Old Testament* 1:26.
⁷⁹Gerhard von Rad, *Old Testament Theology*, trans. D. M. G. Stalker (Peabody, MA: Hendrickson, 2005), 1:vi, 105-6, 112.
⁸⁰Rolf Rendtorff discusses the relationship between von Rad and a "comparative" (*vergleichende*) approach to *Religionsgeschichte*, including his references to elements of neighboring religions. See Rendtorff, "Gerhard von Rad und Religionsgeschichte," in *Theologie in Israel und in den Nachbarkulturen*, ed. Manfred Oeming et al. (Münster: LIT, 2004), 18-21. For the relationship of *Traditionsgeschichte* to *Religionsgeschichte*, see Henning Paulsen, "Traditionsgeschichtliche Methode und religionsgeschichtliche Schule," *ZTK* 75, no. 1 (1978): 26, commenting on Gunkel (whose influence can be seen in von Rad, *Old Testament Theology* 1:v), "The distinction and convergence [of tradition-historical method] with religion-history are altogether not obvious. . . . The effect of a certain interchangeability of religion-history and tradition-history can arise" ("Unterschied und Konvergenz mit der Religionsgeschichte werden durchaus nicht ersichtlich. . . . der Eindruck einer gewissen Austauschbarkeit von Religions- und Traditionsgeschichte enstehen konnte").

the critical reconstruction of Israel's religion, but his interest in Israel's historical traditions is still a diachronic retracing of the development of these religious ideas.[81]

The uncertain relationship between biblical theology and the study of history appears again in the so-called biblical theology movement, also of the twentieth century. This movement emphasized that the Bible was a theological book and a unity, while also making "God's revelation of himself in history central to biblical theology."[82] There is some resemblance to von Hofmann's approach here.[83] Craig Bartholomew notes that this movement's "emphasis on God's acts in history," though seemingly solving some problems, ultimately was criticized by James Barr and Langdon Gilkey, who exposed its attempt to strike a middle course between church and academy, orthodoxy and liberalism.[84] Relatedly, the uncertain relationship between the biblical text and extrabiblical sources as material for biblical theology has persisted.[85]

From an evangelical perspective, an article by Elmer Martens that surveys the field from 1978–2007 beginning with Walter Kaiser brings us closer to the present day. Martens characterizes Kaiser's scheme as "giving progressive revelation through history a prominent place in his outline." Even as canonical and narrative approaches have arisen (e.g., Brevard Childs and John Goldingay, respectively), Martens notes the continuing problem of "how 'history' as a category should function within an OT theology." Reminiscent of the nineteenth-century scholars discussed above, he points out the strengths of a historical-chronological approach

---

[81] For von Rad's use of the term *religion*, see von Rad, *Old Testament Theology* 1:v, 112. According to Rendtorff, modern *Religionsgeschichte* tends more toward "the reconstruction of the history of religion of *Israel* . . . with only sporadic sidelong glances at other ANE religions" "Gerhard von Rad und Religionsgeschichte," 22; ("die Rekonstruktion der Geschichte der Religions Israels . . . mit nur sporadischen Seitenblicken auf andere altorientalische Religionen").
[82] Bartholomew, "Biblical Theology and Biblical Interpretation," 5.
[83] Childs highlights the movement's emphasis on "the revelation of God in history," which was not new and became "the central characteristic of the Erlangen Theology of the mid-nineteenth century" (*Biblical Theology in Crisis*, 39). Von Hofmann taught at Erlangen during this time. Wendebourg refers to him as "Der Erlanger Theologe" ("Die heilsgeschichtliche Theologie J. Chr. K. v. Hofmanns," 64), and Hübner calls him the "bedeutendste Vertreter der sog. Erlanger Schule" (*Schrift und Theologie*, 9).
[84] Bartholomew, "Biblical Theology and Biblical Interpretation," 4-10.
[85] Childs, *Biblical Theology: A Proposal*, 8-9.

as "the ease with which one can then organize material into eras" and the formation of a "bridge from the OT to the NT [that] is then easy to cross." He also observes that since von Hofmann, "Conservatives have had a penchant for the category of history as a way of ordering the OT," which he characterizes as a "linear approach." Martens himself further believes that history should be "given an important but not an exclusive place" in Old Testament theology. Although he mentions challenges to a historical approach, such as critical interpretations of history and the difficulty of deriving theology from history, he remains committed to the "historical dimension" and "historic progression" in Old Testament theology. Among other things, Martens ultimately calls for a nuanced "deference to 'history'" and attention to "the dynamic movement in the biblical message" (cf., Eichrodt as cited above), whatever the approach. His comments show preference for a nuanced historical approach, even as he sees possible additional potential for the canonical approach, the viability of a "qualified thematic approach," and "large possibilities" for a narrative approach.[86]

Of course, a narrative approach has some natural resonances with Martens's interests, since history is naturally conceived of as a narrative. What Martens apparently does not see as a significant problem are the aforementioned issues with an exegetically extrinsic linear-chronological framework for biblical theology as it relates to the exegesis of the Old Testament and its literary and textual unity. Brittany Kim and Charlie Trimm's recent work, *Understanding Old Testament Theology*, engages many more recent works and somewhat similarly classifies approaches to Old Testament theology as emphasizing history (whether events or narrative), theme (whether single or multiple), and/or contexts such as canon.[87] In any case, the aforementioned fundamental challenges to biblical theology still remain, such as its distinction from systematic theology and other external frames of reference, the nature of historical methodology, and the quest for the unity of Scripture.

---

[86] Elmer Martens, "Old Testament Theology Since Walter C. Kaiser, Jr.," *JETS* 50, no. 4 (2007): 673, 675-77, 690.
[87] Brittany Kim and Charlie Trimm, *Understanding Old Testament Theology* (Grand Rapids, MI: Zondervan, 2020). In addition to canonical context, this work also discusses approaches based on the reader's context, such as Jewish biblical theology and postmodern approaches.

THE DEBATE OVER THE CENTER OF THE OLD TESTAMENT AND OLD TESTAMENT THEOLOGY

As seen above, works on Old Testament theology often deal with themes. In some cases, a single theme or set of related themes is used as an organizing principle, or center, especially in the writing and presentation of Old Testament theology. Richard Davidson lists fifty (!) such centers that have been proposed by various Old Testament and/or biblical theologies.[88] Davidson and Martens both raise the issue of how a particular organizing theme is chosen and verified as correct.[89] Occasionally, proposals are made for *a* center (or something merely central), not *the* center.[90] Still, there appears to be a high level of subjectivity in the choice of any kind of center. When a single theme is insisted on as the center, there is the additional risk of reductionism, which leads Gerhard Hasel to seek a "multiplex approach with the multitrack treatment of longitudinal themes."[91] Proposals involving formulas or complex/multiple themes as a center (e.g., James Hamilton's "God's glory in salvation through judgment" involves three or four concepts) provide broader coverage but can still be charged with reductionism.[92] We might ask how many major themes there are in the Old Testament (ten to thirty?) and what they are.

To move the discussion beyond unnecessary either-or dichotomies, we should first recognize that these major themes are interrelated. After all, we can probably agree that such themes as God, promise, covenant, Israel, God's glory, God's kingdom, salvation, wisdom, temple, and so on are all major themes and are interrelated, even if these interrelationships can be

---

[88]Richard M. Davidson, "Back to the Beginning: Genesis 1–3 and the Theological Center of Scripture," in *Christ, Salvation, and the Eschaton: Essays in Honor of Hans K. LaRondelle*, ed. Daniel Heinz, Jiří Moskala, and Peter M. van Bemmelen (Berrien Springs, MI: Old Testament Dept., Seventh-day Adventist Theological Seminary, Andrews University, 2009), 5-9.

[89]Davidson, "Back to the Beginning," 10; Martens, "Old Testament Theology," 676.

[90]E.g., Dane Ortlund, "Is Jeremiah 33:14-26 a 'Centre' to the Bible? A Test Case in Inter-canonical Hermeneutics," *EvQ* 84, no. 2 (April 2012): 120. Ortlund argues that this passage is a center but not the center to the Bible. Andrew Abernethy and Gregory Goswell call the theme of God's kingship "central" but not "the center." See Abernethy and Goswell, *God's Messiah in the Old Testament* (Grand Rapids, MI: Baker Academic, 2020), 5.

[91]Hasel, *Old Testament Theology*, 205.

[92]Regarding formulas, see Hasel, *Old Testament Theology*, 143-45, 151-53. Hamilton, *God's Glory in Salvation through Judgment*.

construed in different ways.⁹³ It is also still possible that one or a few themes are more central or even the center. To be sure, knowledge of major themes is often arrived at through works that emphasize one or a small number of them as *the* center, but as more and more major themes are discerned and set forth as such, the actual benefit may be a deeper awareness of major themes in the Old Testament, simply because it is impossible for all of the proposals for a single center to be correct.

In view of this, a logical next step would be to discern the overall configuration of major themes and whether a true center can be demonstrated. Without such a perspective, it will be difficult for biblical theologians who use this approach to get beyond various proposals of a small number of these themes vying for preeminence. At the same time, whether an eschatological Messiah is a major theme in the Old Testament is highly disputed, and this question affects the overall configuration of major themes. While attempting no definitive list of what these major themes are, the present work will argue that the eschatological Messiah is not only a major theme but the integrative center of the Old Testament (see below), since he often appears in compositionally strategic passages (e.g., nexus passages) as the climactic expression of major Old Testament themes, starting in the Pentateuch and across the Tanak. There is thus a relationship between the literary and textual integration achieved by nexus passages and the exegetically derived, theological integration of the Old Testament in the eschatological Messiah. Significantly, this center is supported by exegesis that is also sensitive to the composition of Old Testament books and of the Tanak.

Even as I hold to the eschatological Messiah as center, it is important to recognize that scholars seem to be working with different definitions of what a center is. Hasel himself contrasts "an organizational center on the basis of which the OT can be systematized" with "a theological center." Elsewhere he refers to an "organizational center" as a "central concept," "central idea," or "central element." He nevertheless objects to making "a

---

⁹³For a recognition of multiple major themes, minor themes, and their grouping, see Scobie, *Ways of Our God*, 87, 91.

single concept or a certain formula into an abstract divining-rod with which all OT expressions and testimonies are combined into a unified system," since "the multiplex and multiform nature of the OT resists such handling of its materials and thoughts." On the other hand, Hasel's theological center "functions as a unifying aspect despite its richness and variety, but it is not capable of being used as an organizing or systematizing principle or criterion for writing an OT theology." As for this theological center, "God/Yahweh is the dynamic, unifying center of the OT." He emphasizes that this "dynamic, unifying center" is not "a static organizing principle on the basis of which an OT theology can be structured," while still ultimately relating to the Old Testament's "hidden inner unity."[94] Thus, Hasel's standard discussion includes at least two definitions of *center*.

In the buildup to these conclusions, Hasel also treats some proposals that imply still other conceptions of what a center is. For example, his discussion of von Rad's later views on the centrality of the Deuteronomistic theology of history seems to concern another kind of center: the center of the Old Testament and its theology as yet another (component) theology, that is, the Deuteronomistic theology of history.[95] Even though Hasel classifies von Rad under the category of "a single concept, theme, motif, or idea as the center of the OT," von Rad's use of the Deuteronomistic theology of history as a center remains distinct and considerably more complex than other views in this category. Perhaps Hasel's preference for a theological center has influenced his lumping all other proposals together as "organizational center[s]."[96] In any case, von Rad's center still raises questions of how the Deuteronomistic theology of history is determined, what it is, and why it should be preferred.

Hasel also cites Siegfried Herrmann's view that Deuteronomy itself is the center of the Old Testament because it captures so many key Old Testament issues and ideas.[97] Proposing a biblical book as center is yet another

---

[94]Hasel, *Old Testament Theology*, 163, 139, 141-42, 144-45, 168, 171, 206.
[95]Hasel, *Old Testament Theology*, 146-50, which use the language of a "secret center" and "historico-theological center."
[96]Hasel, *Old Testament Theology*, 151, 160, 163.
[97]Hasel, *Old Testament Theology*, 156-57.

conception of what *center* can mean, distinct from defining it as a single or small number of concepts (e.g., covenant), a theological center (i.e., God), or a component theology (e.g., the Deuteronomist's). This kind of center may be called a textual center and can consist of a text of any length, whether a book or a passage. Davidson, for example, proposes Genesis 1–3 instead.[98] Like von Rad taking the Deuteronomistic theology of history as center, taking a biblical book such as Deuteronomy as center requires additional explanation as to what precisely the nature of such a center is. Ironically, there is a certain recursiveness to both types of centers, in which the original question concerning the center of the Old Testament (a text) and of Old Testament theology has led to proposals of centers that require us to determine what an embedded component theology is or what a constituent text means. The precise meanings of these centers are not self-evident, unlike single- or few-concept centers (e.g., covenant) or Hasel's theological center (i.e., God/Yahweh).

Thus, the center of the Old Testament can refer to a single- or few-concept center, a theological center, a component theology, a textual center, or perhaps something else still. Thus, productive discussion concerning the existence and nature of a center of the Old Testament and Old Testament theology should include clear explanations of what kind of center is meant. An additional distinction should be made between a central concept that attempts to systematize the Old Testament from the top down and a thread that can merely be found in the material itself without necessarily systematizing it.[99] A similarly weaker conception would be that of a "common denominator" in the Old Testament material.[100] Moreover, whereas salvation history has been considered a center, von Hofmann's classic formulation predates the efforts to derive a center from the Old Testament during the last century and instead is focused on a historical-theological framework involving a Christian philosophy of history.[101]

---

[98]Davidson, "Back to the Beginning," 11-19. Even though Davidson calls his proposal a "theological center" (by which he means "center," it seems; see 5, 9-11), this should not be confused with Hasel's specialized use of the same phrase. See also Ortlund, "Is Jeremiah 33:14-26 a 'Centre,'" 119-38.
[99]Hasel, *Old Testament Theology*, 165-66.
[100]Hasel, *Old Testament Theology*, 162, 168.
[101]Davidson cites Cullmann as an example of a scholar who holds to salvation history as the center of Scripture ("Back to the Beginning," 6). Scobie further adds von Rad, Goppelt, and Ladd (*Ways*

Despite my recognition of more kinds of centers than Hasel, his distinction between an organizational center and a nonorganizational center (e.g., his theological center) is still useful because it highlights the relationship between a proposed center and the writing and presentation of Old Testament theology. He repeatedly points out that proposals for an organizational center cannot do justice to the Old Testament material in all its variety. What Hasel seems to have in mind would be an Old Testament theology whose table of contents organizes the Old Testament material in terms of a static single or few central concept(s), a formula, or the like.[102] Citing David Baker with approval, he believes that there is a unity to the Old Testament but not through a single concept.[103] Hasel thus seems to be objecting to what could also be called punctiliar (e.g., systematizing the entire OT under a single concept) or linear (e.g., a table of contents for an OT theology doing the same) conceptions of a center.[104]

Although Hasel does not use spatial ideas to express his views, other scholars do, such as George Fohrer's "dual concept" around which the Old Testament material can be grouped.[105] Fohrer uses two-dimensional, spatial imagery of the two foci of an ellipse to describe his center (the rule of God and the communion between God and humankind). Baker, in an older

---

of Our God, 86). For earlier discussion of a center, or principle (*Prinzip*), from de Wette to Eichrodt, see Rudolf Smend, *Die Mitte des Alten Testaments: Exegetische Aufsätze* (Tübingen: Mohr Siebeck, 2002), 30-40, where this principle is referred to Israel's religion, religious ideas, and religious history. Such a center is obviously quite different from the one that we attempt to derive exegetically in this work.

[102] E.g., Hasel, *Old Testament Theology*, 160 ("the organizing principle for the writing of an OT theology"), 163 ("an organizational center on the basis of which the OT can be systematized"), 168 ("an organizing or systematizing principle or criterion for writing an OT theology"). For his use of *static* in this way, see references to a "static organizing principle" on 170-71.

[103] Hasel, *Old Testament Theology*, 167. See also David L. Baker, *Two Testaments, One Bible*, 1st ed. (Downers Grove, IL: InterVarsity Press, 1976), 385: "The Old Testament is a unity and has some unifying factor which makes it such. . . . [But] no one unifying factor can adequately embrace the whole." Also, "There is indeed a unity in the Old Testament but it cannot be expressed by a single concept" (386). See also David L. Baker, *Two Testaments, One Bible*, 3rd ed. (Downers Grove, IL: InterVarsity Press, 2010), 152: "No single concept can sum up the meaning of the whole Old Testament." Baker does believe in the Bible's "unity in diversity" (230-36) and "the centrality of Jesus, the Christ of the Old Testament and the New" (281).

[104] See Hasel, *Old Testament Theology*, 154. There he criticizes single-center proposals for being based on an "unspoken presupposition which has its roots in philosophical premises going back to scholastic theology of medieval times." He extends this critique to dual centers on 157.

[105] Georg Fohrer, "Das Alte Testament und das Thema 'Christologie,'" *Evangelische Theologie* 30, no. 6 (1970): 295.

edition of one of his works, uses a three-dimensional elliptical cylinder with Christ as center, two foci as God/Yahweh and Israel, concentric layers of the cylinder as election, promise, covenant, kingdom, and so on, and the cylinder's length corresponding to historical time.[106] Adapting Baker's model, Davidson uses a circular cylinder (i.e., no foci) to explain his view of Genesis 1–3 (and its seven major themes) as center.[107] Scott Duvall and Daniel Hays use the spatial imagery of a spiderweb to illustrate what they set forth as the "cohesive center" for the Bible (i.e., God's relational presence), which connects to other major themes but not necessarily always directly.[108]

What these different conceptions of a center suggest is that there still may be a way to describe and envision a satisfactory center for Old Testament theology. It may not be an organizational center in the way that Hasel conceives of it, but neither need it be his theological center, that is, God/Yahweh, which Charles Scobie says is "to state the obvious."[109] As a sort of (lowest) common denominator, the unity that this theological center achieves is naturally weak. The exegetical-compositional, integrative center that I propose is neither organizational nor theological according to Hasel's categories.

Due to their strategic role within their books and within the Old Testament, nexus passages, which should not be confused with textual centers (see above), will help us begin to see an exegetically derived, integrative center of the Old Testament. As I will show first in chapter four, the convergence and use of major themes to prophesy of the eschatological Messiah suggests that he is the exegetical and compositional center of the Pentateuch and its theology.[110] The Pentateuch and its

---

[106] Baker, *Two Testaments, One Bible*, 1st ed., 386.
[107] Davidson, "Back to the Beginning," 26-28. He also uses a many-faceted diamond as an illustration (11, 14, 23, 26). Though it is illustrating a hermeneutical framework for biblical theology rather than a center, see the analogy of a two-dimensional map for three-dimensional reality in Christopher J. H. Wright, "Mission as Matrix for Hermeneutics and Biblical Theology," in Bartholomew et al., *Out of Egypt*, 138-40.
[108] J. Scott Duvall and J. Daniel Hays, *God's Relational Presence: The Cohesive Center of Biblical Theology* (Grand Rapids, MI: Baker, 2019), 4-5. They contrast this with a wheel, whose spokes all directly connect to the hub.
[109] Scobie, *Ways of Our God*, 94.
[110] Sailhamer, *Meaning of the Pentateuch*; Kevin Chen, *The Messianic Vision of the Pentateuch* (Downers Grove, IL: InterVarsity Press, 2019).

theology in turn are both foundational to the whole Old Testament and have affected the writing and theology of other Old Testament passages and books.[111] As Sailhamer argues, this pentateuchal hope is reinforced by the seams of the Tanak (Deut 34/Josh 1; Mal 4/Ps 1; 2 Chron 36), which provide an overarching structure for the Old Testament and reinforce the same center.[112] He points out that the conclusions of both the Pentateuch and the Prophets look forward to the return of prophecy (Deut 34:10-12 [see also Deut 18:15-18]; Mal 4:5), the opening passages of both the Prophets and the Writings commend meditation on Scripture (Josh 1:8; Ps 1:2-3; see also Mal 4:4), and the one who is to "go up" and build the temple in 2 Chronicles 36:23 can be understood as the messianic son of David (see 1 Chron 22:10-11). Several other Old Testament books emphasize this Messiah's coming to an equal or even greater degree as compared with the Pentateuch (e.g., Samuel, Isaiah, the Twelve, Psalms, Daniel), and still others show the clear impact of the Pentateuch's messianic hope (e.g., Jeremiah, Ezekiel, Chronicles) through direct prophecy of this Messiah reinforced by mediating themes such as the Davidic covenant and/or new covenant.

Even though this center is not the center of every Old Testament book when considered individually and hence is not an organizational center, these books still orbit and are within the gravitational pull of the messianic center via the Pentateuch and the Tanak's seams.[113] Since the Old Testament is not one-dimensional, its center and the relationship of this center to the whole can also be envisioned in multiple dimensions. Analogous to the solar system, there is no inherent reason why the distance between each book and this center must be equal, so long as (1) the messianic center itself is sufficiently supported by the Pentateuch, a critical mass of

---

[111]E.g., Kevin Chen, "Psalm 110: A Nexus for Old Testament Theology," *CTR* 17, no. 2 (Spring 2020): 49-65.

[112]Sailhamer, "Messiah and the Hebrew Bible," 11-23; Sailhamer, *Meaning of the Pentateuch*, 56, 152, 169, 217-18.

[113]Given the reality of shorter books and books with special emphases (e.g., Song of Songs, Lamentations, Esther, Ezra-Nehemiah), it is a lot to ask for any proposed center to be the center of every book without exception. Hamilton also uses solar-system and gravity language and imagery to describe the center of biblical theology without playing it out as I do here (*God's Glory in Salvation*, 53, 355, 512, 555).

additional Old Testament books, and the Tanak's overarching structure; and (2) the remaining books are genuinely connected to this center.

This connection can be immediate or mediated. If immediate, a book may have, in descending order of strength, the same center as the Old Testament, the center of the Old Testament as an explicit major theme (e.g., through prominent messianic prophecies), or the center of the Old Testament as an explicit minor theme (still through messianic prophecy). If mediated, a book may relate to the center of the Pentateuch/Old Testament through relatively indirect intentional foreshadowing of the Messiah (e.g., Judg 5; see chapter 4), mediating themes (e.g., Davidic covenant, new covenant, kingdom, wisdom), and/or historical continuity (e.g., Pentateuch and Joshua through Kings). Moreover, every Old Testament book has the Pentateuch as its literary, textual, and theological foundation, is intertextually related with the Pentateuch, and has the Tanak and its seams as a literary-theological framework. Even though some Old Testament books are not overtly messianic, they are still framed by the Pentateuch's prophecies of exile and the subsequent arrival of the Messiah "in the last days" (Gen 49:1, 8-12; Num 24:14-19; Deut 4:25-28; 31:16-29). In many cases, this eschatological hope is cast in terms of history (e.g., the exodus), which reinforces the unity of Old Testament by linking history and eschatology.[114]

Like the planets in our solar system, each book has its unique character and also exerts its own gravitational pull (e.g., Wisdom literature, Song of Songs), just as Earth and other planets do on their moons and other orbiting objects. This three-dimensional conception of the center of the Old Testament is both dynamic (e.g., planetary and lunar motion) and respects the uniqueness of each book (e.g., its genre). Considered by itself, each planet or book can be investigated for its unique composition and center, even as the eschatological messianic theology of the Pentateuch and the seams of the Tanak (reinforced by other key books and passages) hold the entire dynamic corpus together.

---

[114]See von Rad, *Old Testament Theology* 2:112-18, 299-300, 365.

PARAMETERS FOR EVANGELICAL APPROACHES TO OLD TESTAMENT THEOLOGY

Given the inherent challenges to defining and doing biblical theology, as seen above, carving out a space for evangelical Old Testament theology is not straightforward. The influence of Gabler means that biblical theology has strong roots in critical scholarship, including its rejection of a traditional view of inspiration. Moreover, while having a historical emphasis, biblical theology has ambiguous relationships to the study of history and history of religions. Whether from an evangelical perspective or not, biblical theology often also depends on a working solution to the problem of the unity of the Testaments, which is reflected in some proposals for biblical theology favoring the New Testament. Furthermore, there is the related problem that the unifying framework used, whether philosophical or otherwise, is frequently extrinsically imposed on the biblical text, analogous to the dogmatic categories that Gabler wanted to avoid. In this case, the distinction between biblical and systematic theology that he argued for is severely weakened.

Evangelical approaches to Old Testament theology are characterized first and foremost by a high view of biblical inspiration. Sailhamer remarks, "The notion of an inspired text of Scripture has played an important, indeed central, role in the growth and development of OT theology," be it through belief in traditional verbal inspiration or varying degrees of rejection of this doctrine.[115] Indeed, this is the fundamental difference between evangelical biblical scholarship and critical scholarship more broadly, and it is an important one for biblical theology. Evangelical approaches naturally also distinguish between biblical and systematic theology in some way (while sometimes also attempting some integration) and correspondingly follow biblical theology's classic historical emphasis.

Although evangelicals basically agree on the historical accuracy of the biblical record (including miracles) and God's sovereignty over and direct involvement in history, the ambiguous nature of what it means for

---

[115]Sailhamer, *Introduction to Old Testament Theology*, 152.

biblical theology to be historical carries over from the broader discipline to evangelical approaches. A salvation-historical approach is obviously historical, but *historical* refers here to the unfolding of a historical process and a linear-chronological historical framework for biblical theology. On the other hand, the word *historical* can be used to describe a biblical author's original, historical meaning. This usage concerns what the Bible itself teaches, compared to what meanings might be imposed on it by philosophical or theological frameworks. Here, *historical* does not refer primarily to a historical sequence of events but the historical situatedness of authorial intent. As seen above, Gabler himself used the word in this way when he referred to "a biblical theology, of historical origin, conveying what the holy writers felt about divine matters," in contrast to "a dogmatic theology of didactic origin." Likewise using *historical* with reference to the (authorial and textual) meaning of the Bible itself, he remarks, "Biblical theology, as is proper to historical argument, is always in accord with itself when considered by itself."[116] Gabler's classic proposal was not focused on the historical succession of events recorded in Scripture (e.g., salvation history) but rather on sifting the results of exegesis through universal ideas (or notions), which can then be properly used by dogmatic (systematic) theology.[117]

Within this broader context of biblical theology as a discipline, evangelical biblical theology can thus be historical in more than one way. Salvation-historical approaches are certainly historical, but so are those approaches that thoroughly prioritize historical, authorial meaning without relying on a salvation-historical framework, as in this book. As shown above, this kind of historical emphasis can be traced back to Gabler himself. Sailhamer sees a similar use of the term *historical* earlier in Johann August Ernesti (1707–1781) and even earlier in the seventeenth century (e.g., Salomon Glassius) in connection with the grammatical or literal

---

[116] Sandys-Wunsch and Eldredge, "J. P. Gabler and the Distinction," 137. More clearly, biblical theology "deals only with those things which holy men perceived about matters pertinent to religion, and is not made to accommodate our point of view" (144).

[117] Sandys-Wunsch and Eldredge, "J. P. Gabler and the Distinction," 141-44. Gabler was attentive to the respective eras of biblical authors, but for the purpose of exegesis (139-40).

sense (*sensus literalis*).¹¹⁸ The "literal, that is historical, sense" (*sensus literalis sive historicus*) is found still earlier, in Martin Luther.¹¹⁹

The implication that salvation history should be seen as only one evangelical approach to biblical theology is important because of the strong influence of Vos's evangelical redemptive-historical approach. As mentioned above, Gentry and Wellum hold him in high esteem, even calling him "the evangelical pioneer of a legitimate approach to biblical theology." In their reckoning, biblical theology as a discipline can be traced through two paths, one legitimate and one illegitimate, tied to the Enlightenment, Gabler, and other critical scholars.¹²⁰ Wellum and Gentry are right to highlight the major impact that the doctrine of inspiration has on biblical theology, but the problem with their "two [distinct] paths" accounting of biblical theology is that it does not show enough awareness of the likely influence of some ideas from critical scholarship on Vos himself, who conceived of biblical theology as "History of Special Revelation."¹²¹ He explains, "Biblical Theology deals with the material from the historical standpoint, seeking to exhibit the organic growth or development of the truths of Special Revelation from the primitive pre-redemptive Special Revelation given in Eden to the close of the New Testament canon."¹²² This conception of biblical theology along with the above discussion of Gabler and von Hofmann shows that Vos's redemptive-historical approach shares

---

[118] John Sailhamer, "Johann August Ernesti: The Role of History in Biblical Interpretation," *JETS* 44 (2001): 195, 198, 201-2, 205-6.

[119] Diestel, *Geschichte des Alten Testamentes*, 247: "Wherever Luther speaks of the significance of history is usually meant this literal, that is, historical sense." Gerhard Ebeling refers to the "sensus literalis bzw. [respectively] historicus" as a generally accepted foundation for exegesis and also refers to it as the "literal historical sense" (*sensus literalis historicus*). See Ebeling, "Die Anfänge von Luthers Hermeneutik," *ZTK* 48, no. 2 (1951): 182-83; see also Kraus, *Geschichte der historisch-kritischen Erforschung*, 9-11.

[120] Gentry and Wellum, *Kingdom Through Covenant*, 28-30; see also Hamilton, *God's Glory in Salvation*, 41-47. His tracing of biblical theology to Scripture itself resembles Scobie (see note 1 above).

[121] Vos, *Biblical Theology*, v. Ehlen says that the approaches of Beck and von Hofmann bear "the specific character of a history of revelation" ("Old Testament Theology as *Heilsgeschichte*," 530). See also Weth, *Heilsgeschichte*, 55, 81, 83, 85, 87.

[122] Vos, *Biblical Theology*, v-vi. He also writes, "Biblical Theology is that branch of Exegetical Theology which deals with the process of the self-revelation of God deposited in the Bible" (5). See also Geerhardus Vos, "The Idea of Biblical Theology as a Science and as a Theological Discipline," in *Redemptive History and Biblical Interpretation: The Shorter Writings of Geerhardus Vos*, ed. Richard Gaffin (Phillipsburg, NJ: Presbyterian and Reformed, 1980), 7.

some fundamental categories with nonevangelical approaches, including Gabler's historical emphasis and von Hofmann's emphasis on salvation history, tendency to treat Scripture as witness to past instances of revelation and as a history of revelation, and categorization of revelation into word-revelation and act-revelation.

The influence of Vos on evangelical biblical theology today is well-documented and acknowledged by evangelical scholars themselves.[123] This means that there is a probable trail of influence all the way back to von Hofmann, even if he is only sometimes recognized. Goldsworthy is aware of von Hofmann but still proceeds to say, "That biblical theology is salvation history is a commonly held evangelical position."[124] Without relying on Vos but likewise emphasizing the historical element in terms of historical events, the organization of biblical material into eras, and development over time, Martens's requirement that Old Testament theology emphasize "the historical dimension" and "historic progression" fits well with salvation history. Though he does allow for other approaches to history in Old Testament theology such as canon and story, he still sees canonical approaches (for Martens, those that follow a canonical ordering of the Old Testament books) as problematic because the "dynamic nature of God's interaction with humans is at risk when historic progression is set aside" and because such canonical approaches are "prone to some choppiness."[125] Nevertheless, the major contributions of Sailhamer, Paul House, and Stephen Dempster, for example, still stand on their own merits even though salvation history is not prominent in their work.[126]

Vos deserves credit both for carving out space within the discipline of biblical theology for evangelicals and for leading the way for many subsequent evangelical scholars to follow his general path. Nevertheless, his

---

[123] Beale, *New Testament Biblical Theology*, 9, 19-21; Gentry and Wellum, *Kingdom Through Covenant*, 31n20, 32n26; Hamilton, *God's Glory in Salvation*, 43 (including n35).

[124] Graeme Goldsworthy, *Christ-Centered Biblical Theology* (Downers Grove, IL: InterVarsity Press, 2012), 57; see also Martens, "Old Testament Theology," 676.

[125] Martens, "Old Testament Theology," 677.

[126] Sailhamer, *Introduction to Old Testament Theology*; Paul House, *Old Testament Theology* (Downers Grove, IL: InterVarsity Press, 1998), 53-57. Dempster recognizes a large block of commentary (Latter Prophets, Ruth through Lamentations) within the narrative story line of the Tanak (*Dominion and Dynasty*, 159).

undeniable impact does not mean that salvation history should be equated with evangelical biblical theology. He set forth an influential way for evangelicals to approach biblical theology, but there is no reason to conclude that it is the only (general) way for evangelicals to approach the topic, nor even that its framework is a required part of an evangelical approach. Neither should such a narrow conception of what it means for biblical theology to be historical (e.g., salvation-historical) be used as a criticism of other approaches that are historical in terms of rigorously holding to the author's historical meaning, especially because both share common ground concerning the historical accuracy of Scripture and God's sovereignty over and direct involvement in history. As argued above, the focus on the historical author's intent is traceable to Gabler himself and is more faithful to what the Bible itself teaches (i.e., the exegesis of passages and books) because it does not invoke an exegetically extrinsic framework such as salvation history.

Neither should progressive revelation be treated as an axiom in evangelical biblical theology, or biblical interpretation for that matter. Taking Bengel's view as the classic understanding, we need to distinguish between the self-evident realities that revelation did not happen all at once and climaxed in the first coming of Christ, on the one hand, and the supposed nature of progress in this stream of revelation, on the other. For Bengel, this progress was related to revelation in earlier times being obscure and concealing certain things. When applied to the Old Testament, such an approach is ambiguous and opens the door for unsubstantiated assumptions that affect Old Testament interpretation. If all that is meant is that divine revelation climaxes in Christ (Heb 1:1-2; see also Jn 1:1, 14), then there is no problem. But if, along with this, the possibility is excluded a priori that an exegesis of the Old Testament that seeks the author's intent can show a messianic vision within the Old Testament itself, then progressive revelation has unfairly biased the exegesis of the Old Testament before it has even begun.

If Bengel's concept of progressive revelation is to be thoroughly supported, the Old Testament material itself suggests some major difficulties. For example, if Moses was the greatest prophet who ever lived (besides

Jesus himself) related to his uniquely face-to-face relationship with the Lord (Num 12:6-8; Deut 34:10), and if he wrote the Pentateuch, then why would subsequent books of the Old Testament, written by prophets with a less intimate knowledge of God than Moses, necessarily *exceed* the Pentateuch in the quality and scope of their revelatory content? How do we know that the relationship between their respective writings is not the other way around, or equal?[127] Relatedly, if Isaiah 52:13–53:12 is the clearest messianic prophecy in the Old Testament (for the sake of argument), how do Old Testament passages and books written subsequently progress beyond this climactic passage? Such questions contrast with Vos's position that progressive revelation is organic and can be likened to a seed that eventually becomes a full-grown tree.[128] Could not the prophecies of the Lion of Judah in Genesis 49:8-12, the star from Jacob in Numbers 24:17-19, and the Suffering Servant in Isaiah 52:13–53:12 all reveal the tree rather than just a seed (or seedling)? Furthermore, does a coherent chronological ordering of the Old Testament material even exist that suggests such progressive revelation over time, even if this progression need not be uniform?

Bengel's greater interest in the New Testament and especially the book of Revelation suggests that these more detailed questions about Old Testament interpretation were not the primary drivers of his concept of progressive revelation. Instead, this concept gives the impression of lumping the Old Testament material together simplistically. In the end, there is no disputing the climactic coming of Christ and *additional*, helpful revelation over time, but progressive revelation, in its common usage and thoroughly applied to the Old Testament material, remains unsubstantiated.[129] Thus, Scobie remarks concerning progressive revelation, "Many rightly utter words of caution."[130]

---

[127]Joseph Blenkinsopp, *The Pentateuch* (New York: Doubleday, 1992), 232; Blenkinsopp, *Prophecy and Canon* (Notre Dame, IN: Notre Dame University Press, 1977), 41, 44, 86-87, 89-91, 94.
[128]Vos, *Biblical Theology*, 7.
[129]For a response to the idea that Old Testament authors could not have known much about the Messiah, see Chen, *Messianic Vision of the Pentateuch*, 19-20.
[130]Scobie, *Ways of Our God*, 91.

Based on evangelical works on biblical theology, parameters for evangelical Old Testament theology include a high view of biblical inspiration, a distinction between biblical and systematic theology, and a genuine attempt at some kind of historical approach. This historical aspect certainly includes belief in the historical accuracy of the Bible, God's sovereignty over history, his direct involvement in history, and even the reality of salvation history itself. However, the use of salvation history as a unifying framework for biblical theology is not essential to an evangelical historical approach. Attention to the authorial meaning and what the Bible itself teaches, which evangelical approaches broadly embrace, is also historical but can be rigorously carried through methodologically such that it reveals the literary, textual, and theological unity of Scripture, rendering exegetically extrinsic frameworks such as salvation history unnecessary to this end. Likewise, neither is the use of progressive revelation necessary to evangelical biblical theology. I argue elsewhere that the common use of typology is not necessary either.[131] Within this broader framework, evangelicals have exercised the freedom to emphasize various themes and/or present results topically, book by book (including in different orderings), or otherwise.

For the sake of clarity, it should be noted that the word *canonical* is used with different meanings by scholars, including evangelicals. As pointed out above, Martens uses it with reference to the presentation of Old Testament theology book by book in a (Hebrew) canonical ordering. Hamilton also follows this usage, as does Dempster.[132] However, Bruce Waltke calls his own approach "canonical" related to his belief in the unity of the Old and New Testaments, even though his organization does not follow such an ordering.[133] Sailhamer's canonical approach, set forth in a methodology-focused work, proposes a Hebrew canonical ordering but was never fully worked out for the entire Old Testament.[134] He actually preferred to

---

[131]Chen, *Messianic Vision of the Pentateuch*, 12-23.
[132]Hamilton, *God's Glory in Salvation*, 64-65 (including n113); Dempster, *Dominion and Dynasty*, 33-35, 47-51.
[133]Waltke, *Old Testament Theology*, 10.
[134]Sailhamer, *Introduction to Old Testament Theology*, 197-252. His *Meaning of the Pentateuch* deals with OT theology but focuses on the Pentateuch.

describe his approach as "compositional."[135] On the other hand, Childs's canonical approach is a *critical* approach that attempts to overcome the (textual) fragmentation of historical criticism through the unifying effect of the canon and the continuing use of canonical Scripture by the church.[136] Significantly, his proposal does not depend on a traditional view of inspiration and still allows for some use of historical criticism.[137]

The unity achievable by evangelicals, however, is more far-reaching because the verbal plenary inspiration of Scripture implies both its historical accuracy and its divinely authored, organic unity. In other words, a high view of inspiration sees strong bonds between the divine author and the human author, as well as between these authors and Scripture as the Word of God written. The biblical text is in turn historically accurate with respect to the historical events it records. Though distinct entities, (biblical) text and (historical) event are in harmony and linked strongly together. Furthermore, as the product of a single divine mind, Scripture as a text is coherent and interconnected for readers to perceive. The arrows in figure 1.1 represent these continuous relationships among the divine author, the human author, Scripture (including its intrinsic interconnectedness), and history, all of which are rooted in inspiration (the result of the two arrows on the left). The figure reinforces the fundamental importance of inspiration, and how fragmentation results when it is abandoned.[138] In the present work, I attempt to show that the divinely authored unity of Scripture is literary, textual, and ultimately theological.

---

[135] E.g., Sailhamer, *Meaning of the Pentateuch*, 48, 149, 160, 219, passim. See also Kevin Chen, "Gleanings from the John H. Sailhamer Papers at Southeastern Baptist Theological Seminary," *Southeastern Theological Review* 9, no. 1 (2018): 108.

[136] Childs, *Biblical Theology in Crisis*, 91-92, 99-100, 112-13. The effect of canon is not static but was a "canonical process," including canonical shaping and redaction. See Brevard Childs, *Biblical Theology of the Old and New Testaments* (Minneapolis: Fortress, 1993) 70-71, 73.

[137] Childs sees inspiration as concerning "the uniqueness of the canonical context of the church" (*Biblical Theology in Crisis*, 104). Regarding historical criticism, see 106-8, 112-13.

[138] The weakness of Childs's approach is also implied. He effectively wants to leave off the arrows that concern inspiration and the connection between text and event, and instead "Scripture" ← "readers" (church) to attain the unity of Scripture. His canonical unity arises from a canonical process and the church rather than from divine inspiration.

Figure 1.1. Inspiration, dual authorship, historical reliability, and unity of Scripture

OLD TESTAMENT THEOLOGY THROUGH ITS NEXUS PASSAGES

The approach to Old Testament theology in this work follows within the broader evangelical stream outlined above. I affirm the verbal plenary inspiration of Scripture, the historical accuracy of Scripture, the historical reality of biblical events, the sovereignty of God over history, and his direct and sometimes supernatural involvement in it. Along with others, I distinguish between biblical theology and systematic theology in that biblical theology begins by asking what the Bible itself teaches considered on its own terms, in contrast with primarily using other categories. Where my approach differs from other approaches that also emphasize exegesis of the author's historical meaning is that this priority is maintained throughout the entire task of Old Testament theology. In other words, there is no appeal to an exegetically extrinsic framework to unify the biblical material, whether Gabler's universal ideas, von Hofmann's salvation history, or otherwise. This is because I believe that exegesis of the author's intent can demonstrate the literary, textual, and theological unity of the Old Testament. Inherent to the Old Testament text itself, nexus passages are especially useful to this end.

In the search for authorial intent, I believe it is best to keep hermeneutical first principles to a minimum so as to avoid imposing meaning on the biblical text as much as possible.[139] I limit these first principles to inspiration, the existence of authorial intent, and the communication of this intent through entire books of Old Testament. There is even a sense in which the coherence of each biblical book is not truly a first principle but something that can be supported inductively from exegesis of these books. Treating salvation history, progressive revelation, and/or typology as hermeneutical first principles easily compromises the priority placed on exegesis and authorial intent in biblical theology, and so is excluded. The fewer presuppositions the better, lest any of them prove unreliable.

Even Christocentric theology does not need to be a first principle. To be sure, the Christocentric nature of Scripture is important, but this reality is far more striking and persuasive when it is the result of exegesis rather a presupposition of it. Likewise, the *regula fidei* is important not simply because it is the historic tradition of the church but because it arises from the proper interpretation of the Scriptures. This is not to suggest that it is possible for interpreters to completely avoid influences from our theology, the New Testament, or our varied life experiences, since such influences exist even when we are not conscious of them. Nevertheless, given such influences, the fundamental issue is still whether the Scriptures, especially the Old Testament, bear an authorially intended witness to Christ. Building on existing work in this area, I believe that the Old Testament can be shown to bear such witness to Christ, its exegetical-compositional, integrative center. In other words, that "in him [i.e., Christ] all things hold together" (Col 1:17) can be demonstrated to be true not only of creation generally (Col 1:15-16) but also of the Old Testament itself on the literary and textual level.

---

[139] Sandys-Wunsch warns, "Our axioms of exegetical procedure may only appear to be axioms because we have not looked hard enough at the idea of truth on which they are based" ("Zachariae's Contribution to Biblical Theology," 17). He continues, "In some respects we are less competent in philosophy and the critical analysis of our presuppositions than the scholars of the eighteenth century. Having fallen into a pragmatic approach to our discipline, we tend to forget the non-biblical origin of so many of our concepts such as 'history of salvation,' 'existential awareness,' 'authenticity' and so on'" (23).

CONCLUSION

This chapter positions the study of nexus passages in the context of the academic discipline of Old Testament theology. Rather than attempt a comprehensive history of the discipline, I have selectively engaged key figures and issues that have shaped Old Testament theology to provide context for the present state of the discipline and for my approach. The study of nexus passages is an evangelical approach that also thoroughly holds to Gabler's original emphasis on the author's historical meaning. By arguing for the theological, even Christocentric, unity of the Old Testament based on literary and textual grounds, this approach does not rely on external unifying frameworks such as salvation history. The rest of this book attempts to validate this approach through examination of ten nexus passages from across the Tanak.

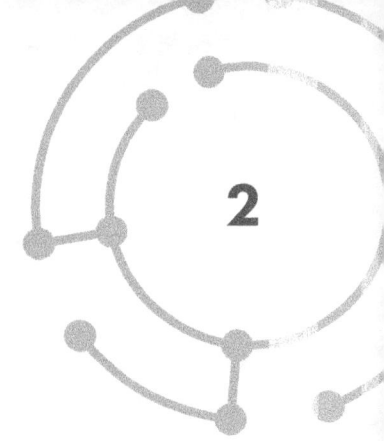

2

GENESIS 1–3

CREATION AND WISDOM (LITERATURE)

Genesis 1–3 is one of the most important nexus passages in the Bible. This is because of both its extremely high connectivity to other passages in the Pentateuch, the Old Testament, and the New Testament, and its unique position as the foundational text in the foundational book of the Bible, the Pentateuch. Unlike other chapters in this book, which deal with shorter nexus passages in more detail, this chapter focuses on showing that so-called Wisdom literature (Proverbs, Ecclesiastes, and Job) is rooted in and integrated with Genesis 1–3, especially its wisdom elements. Whereas detailed exegesis of Genesis 1–3 and analysis of its interconnectedness would require a lengthy book, this chapter attempts to show that Wisdom literature is by no means alien to Old Testament theology because it is textually and theologically dependent on and intertwined with the foundational passage of the Old Testament itself. Genesis 1–3 also highlights my proposed compositional, integrative center of the Old Testament, the eschatological Messiah, through its prophecy of the seed of the woman in Genesis 3:15. Although this mention is brief, it is both climactic in the narrative context and compositionally strategic within the Pentateuch. I will return to Genesis 3:15 and its strategic role in the Pentateuch when discussing Numbers 24 in chapter four.

The importance of Genesis 1–3 is self-evident to even the casual reader of the Bible. With its opening phrase, "In the beginning" (בְּרֵאשִׁית), this passage presents itself as the first part of the long story that follows in the Pentateuch, the Old Testament, and even the New Testament. It is also often pointed out that Genesis 1–3 deals with such major biblical themes as creation, fall, and redemption. Such thematic connections can be more closely analyzed on the textual level, as Gordon Wenham does in showing that the Garden of Eden is a sanctuary.[1] With focused attention on literary techniques, Seth Postell likewise explores Genesis 1–3 as introduction to the Pentateuch and the Tanak.[2] His work is directed specifically toward how Adam's failure in Eden and subsequent exile prefigures Israel's failure at Mount Sinai and predicted exile from the Promised Land.[3] Many, including me, have naturally investigated the seed of the woman in Genesis 3:15 and how this crucial text relates to other proposed messianic texts in the Old Testament.[4] Productive work in these areas, however, does not exhaust Genesis 1–3 as a nexus passage. With the problem of Wisdom literature for Old Testament theology in mind, I argue below that seeing Genesis 1–3 as a nexus passage specifically related to Wisdom literature ties these Old Testament books literarily, textually, and theologically to this foundational text of the Old Testament and hence constructively integrates them into Old Testament theology.

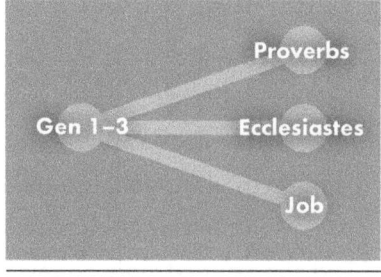

Figure 2.1. Nexus connections between Genesis 1–3 and Wisdom literature

---

[1]Gordon Wenham, "Sanctuary Symbolism in the Garden of Eden Story," in *Proceedings of the Ninth World Congress of Jewish Studies, Division A: The Period of the Bible* (Jerusalem: World Union of Jewish Studies, 1986), 19-25; contra Daniel Block, *Covenant: The Framework of God's Plan of Redemption* (Grand Rapids, MI: Baker, 2021), 27-30. Block sees royal themes rather than priestly ones and explains the parallels in terms of (later) "temple theology" reflecting "creation theology" but not vice versa (with respect to Gen 1–3). In response, if the Pentateuch is a coherent literary work produced essentially by one author, then tabernacle theology is not necessarily later than the creation theology of Gen 1–3.
[2]Seth Postell, *Adam as Israel: Genesis 1–3 as the Introduction to the Torah and Tanakh* (Eugene, OR: Wipf & Stock, 2011). See also Gerald Klingbeil, ed., *The Genesis Creation Account and Its Reverberations in the Old Testament* (Berrien Springs, MI: Andrews University Press, 2015). The present chapter was written independently of "Genesis and Creation in the Wisdom Literature," which does overlap with my treatment at points but at others is more focused on creation themes in Wisdom literature.
[3]Postell, *Adam as Israel*, 3.
[4]E.g., Kevin Chen, *The Messianic Vision of the Pentateuch* (Downers Grove, IL: InterVarsity Press, 2019), 35-66; Jonathan Cheek, "Recent Developments in the Interpretation of the Seed of the Woman in Genesis 3:15," *JETS* 64 (2021): 215-36.

WISDOM LITERATURE, CREATION, AND GENESIS 1–3

The difficulty of integrating Wisdom literature into Old Testament theology involves textual, interpretive, and historical challenges that have sometimes been exacerbated for various reasons. To begin with the core issues, scholars have long recognized the strong experiential thrust of Wisdom literature, whether the sayings in Proverbs, the despair voiced in Ecclesiastes, or Job's suffering and subsequent struggles.[5] On the other hand, Old Testament theology, as a subfield of biblical theology, has inherited a historical emphasis (see introduction) that has frequently found a specifically *salvation*-historical expression. However, salvation history and other themes such as covenant, Israel, law, prophecy, and priesthood, which are so important elsewhere in the Old Testament and often emphasized in Old Testament theology, are not as apparent in Wisdom literature.[6] To complicate matters further, the experiential emphasis of biblical Wisdom literature combined with the discovery of similar wisdom literature in the ancient Near East (e.g., the Instruction of Amenemope) has led some to conclude that wisdom literature as a category is secular rather than the result of revelation.[7] However, even if there was some interaction between broader wisdom literature and biblical Wisdom literature, my traditional position on the inspiration of Scripture still leads me to affirm the distinctness of biblical Wisdom literature.

Even as scholars have struggled with integrating Wisdom literature with the rest of the Old Testament, they notice its relationship to creation. In a seminal article, Walther Zimmerli famously remarks, "Wisdom thinks resolutely within the framework of a theology of creation."[8] Tremper Longman agrees: "Though the sages spoke sparingly of creation directly, it was indeed

---

[5] E.g., Gerhard von Rad, *Wisdom in Israel*, trans. James D. Martin (Nashville: Abingdon, 1972), 3-10.
[6] Tremper Longman, *The Fear of the Lord Is Wisdom: A Theological Introduction to Wisdom in Israel* (Grand Rapids, MI: Baker Academic, 2017), xiv, 128.
[7] Von Rad, *Wisdom in Israel*, 9-10.
[8] Walther Zimmerli, "The Place and Limit of the Wisdom in the Framework of the Old Testament Theology," *SJT* 17, no. 2 (1964): 148. As supporting evidence, he cites Ecclesiastes' use of the more generic terms *God*, *Maker*, and *Creator*, rather than "God of Israel," "God of the Fathers," or "Yahweh of hosts." Writing in 2017, Longman calls Zimmerli's quote "perhaps the most quoted single sentence concerning wisdom literature over the past forty years" (*Fear of the Lord*, 127).

crucial to their worldview."⁹ Wisdom has thus been seen as rooted within creation and creation theology, which connects naturally with Wisdom literature's experiential emphasis since the created order is the arena for human experience. Creation itself is also a public display of divine wisdom. Nevertheless, the linkage of wisdom to creation and general human experience still contrasts with salvation history and its emphasis on divine intervention and Israel's particular historical experiences of salvation.¹⁰ As Zimmerli boldly asserts, "Wisdom has no relation to the history between God and Israel."¹¹ Instead, wisdom has an "international character" and "has to do with man [אָדָם]."¹² Zimmerli further argues that "people" (עַם) are mentioned in Proverbs but not "as the elect of Yahweh," and likewise "king" in Proverbs and Ecclesiastes but not as "the anointed king of God's people Israel and the son of David."¹³ He concludes that both the historical writing of the Deuteronomist and the words of the prophets are very different from that of the wise man. Zimmerli raises multiple issues that will be addressed below, but his statement about the term *king* seems to be contradicted by Proverbs 1:1, which refers to "Solomon, son of David, king of Israel" and exerts a controlling influence on the book of Proverbs (see also Eccles 1:1).¹⁴ In any case, Zimmerli bifurcates (Israel's) salvation history and wisdom/creation.

On the other hand, Gerhard von Rad, who also relates creation and wisdom, sets forth creation as the starting point of salvation history and sees parallels between them (e.g., God's power over waters at creation and in the exodus) while still subordinating creation to salvation history. However, in his treatment of "more comprehensive statements about the creation of the world," he excludes Genesis 2:4b–3:24, since its supposed author, the Yahwist (J), does not "treat of the creation of the world at all," and von Rad begins instead with Deutero-Isaiah, the Priestly source (and

---

⁹Longman, *Fear of the Lord*, 145.
¹⁰Richard Belcher Jr., *Finding Favour in the Sight of God: A Theology of Wisdom Literature*, New Studies in Biblical Theology 46 (Downers Grove, IL: InterVarsity Press, 2018), 5.
¹¹Zimmerli, "Place and Limit," 147.
¹²Zimmerli, "Place and Limit," 147. "The explicit rule of life is built upon to [sic] the observation of facts" (150).
¹³Zimmerli, "Place and Limit," 147.
¹⁴Zimmerli calls the "Solomonic origin" of Ecclesiastes "fiction" and seems to imply the same for Proverbs ("Place and Limit," 147).

thus Gen 1), and selected psalms, with the former two each a "chief witness about Creation."¹⁵ In contrast, my approach deals with Genesis 1–3 as a whole, including creation, wisdom, and still other aspects, and as a strategic part of the compositional strategy of the Pentateuch. While not excluding other intertextual relationships, I see Wisdom literature as especially influenced by Genesis 1–3, even as such influence does not require that Genesis 1–3 itself be considered Wisdom literature.

Some scholars have already proposed helpful ways in which Wisdom literature can be better integrated into the Old Testament. John Goldingay discusses the "complementarity of salvation-history and wisdom" in terms of God's redemption of humans that he created, humanity's need for redemption after being created, and the goal of redemption as new life still within the created order.¹⁶ Roland Murphy provides nuance to the distinctive emphases of Wisdom literature by pointing out that its experiential nature is still historical (even if not salvation historical) and is not secular since it is concerned with *God's* creation, God himself, and faith in God.¹⁷ Regarding divinely instituted order in creation, Longman observes, "When we think of wisdom's connection to creation theology, it is wrong-minded to think only of Gen. 1–2. To the extent that wisdom is related to creation theology, it does not return us to Eden but recognizes that we live in a troubled, disordered world [of Gen 3]." He believes that the distinctiveness of Wisdom literature, though having some merit, has been "overemphasized to the point of distortion." For all its emphasis on experience, Longman points out that Wisdom literature is still theological and based ultimately on revelation, since it is rooted in the fear of the Lord.¹⁸ Will Kynes objects to the category of Wisdom literature itself and proposes a multidirectional intertextual integration of this corpus into the Old Testament.¹⁹

---

¹⁵Gerhard von Rad, *Old Testament Theology*, trans. D. M. G. Stalker (Peabody, MA: Prince, 2005), 1:136-37.

¹⁶John Goldingay, "The 'Salvation History' Perspective and the 'Wisdom' Perspective Within the Context of Biblical Theology," *EvQ* 51 (1979): 201-7.

¹⁷Roland Murphy, *The Tree of Life: An Exploration of Biblical Wisdom Literature*, 2nd ed. (Grand Rapids, MI: Eerdmans, 1996), 113-15, 125-26.

¹⁸Longman, *Fear of the Lord*, 142, xvi, 119-20, 161, 163.

¹⁹Will Kynes, *An Obituary for "Wisdom Literature": The Birth, Death, and Intertextual Reintegration of a Biblical Corpus* (Oxford: Oxford University Press, 2019).

There is much constructive work in these various proposals and even some overlap between my approach and the respective views of Longman and Kynes. Even so, I pursue these things further from the perspective of Genesis 1–3 as a nexus passage. As explained in the introduction, my approach takes seriously the final form of biblical books, holds to the Pentateuch as the first Old Testament book to be written, sees sufficient historical and textual reasons for believing that later biblical authors understood and alluded to the Pentateuch in their own books, and attempts to demonstrate the literary, textual, and ultimately theological unity of the Old Testament along these lines.[20]

Applied to the problem of Wisdom literature in Old Testament theology, taking Genesis 1–3 as a nexus passage especially in relation to Wisdom literature is a promising path. Indeed, Craig Bartholomew and Ryan O'Dowd believe that this corpus is established within the tradition of "the imagery and theology of the creation account in Genesis," and further remark, "Old Testament wisdom, unsurprisingly, has myriad connections with Genesis 1–3."[21] If the authors of Proverbs, Ecclesiastes, and Job were not only aware of the Pentateuch but engaged human experience (and possibly ancient Near Eastern wisdom tradition sometimes; see 1 Kings 4:30, 34; 10:1-3) especially through the lens of Genesis 1–3, this explains not only the presence of intertextuality and theological coherence between Genesis 1–3 and Wisdom literature but also the relative absence in Wisdom literature of themes common elsewhere in the Old Testament, such as the patriarchal promises, the covenant, Israel's salvation history (e.g., the exodus), prophets, the Sinai law, and religious rituals.[22] Genesis 1–3 does not directly deal with these either because they have not yet arisen in the Pentateuch's sequential storyline. It is too early in the unfolding narrative to speak of them. This would also explain Longman's assessment that "wisdom literature lacks

---

[20]See Charles Scobie, *The Ways of Our God: An Approach to Biblical Theology* (Grand Rapids, MI: Eerdmans, 2003), 149, 183. Scobie argues for the fundamental importance of creation (including Gen 1–3) based on its initial position in canonical Scripture.

[21]Craig Bartholomew and Ryan O'Dowd, *Old Testament Wisdom Literature: A Theological Introduction* (Downers Grove, IL: InterVarsity Press, 2011), 29, 269.

[22]This listing has been adapted from Longman, *Fear of the Lord*, 128. See also Belcher, *Finding Favour in the Sight*, 3, who mentions an emphasis on the individual compared to the nation (of Israel). For ancient Near Eastern wisdom and parallels with biblical Wisdom literature, see Longman, *Fear of the Lord*, 148-60.

explicit interaction" with biblical history from Genesis 12 onward.²³ On the other hand, like Wisdom literature, Genesis 1–3 is concerned with creation, wisdom, order, the individual person, and general human experience as represented by Adam, whose very name means "humanity" (אָדָם). What better extant (and authoritative) text for the authors of Wisdom literature to engage than Genesis 1–3, which tells that part of Adam's story most representative of humanity?

One reason the creation account in Genesis 1–3 has not been used more frequently to integrate Wisdom literature into the Old Testament and Old Testament theology may be the continuing impact of source criticism along with the dates assigned to these sources relative to Wisdom literature. This impact is evident in von Rad above, who first accepts the division of Genesis 1–3 into Genesis 1:1–2:4a (P) and Genesis 2:4b–3:24 (J), and then prioritizes Genesis 1:1–2:4a along with Deutero-Isaiah and select psalms. Even so, Richard Belcher Jr. explains that some object to *starting* with Genesis 1 "because it is a late, mature product of Israelite creation theology. The critical reconstruction of Israel's history that Wellhausen popularized is still common even if source criticism and the way he presented Israel's history are not followed."²⁴ If Genesis 1 is treated as late creation theology, then the search for creation theology would not begin with any material in Genesis 1–3 at all, even if it includes Genesis 1 later in the process.

Thus, entrenched beliefs concerning the sources of Genesis 1–3 and their dating, combined with a diachronic interest in the origin and development of wisdom in Israel, have at times led to searching for a creation theology guided by critical reconstructions and by biblical texts only as they fit these reconstructions. While affirming the relationship between wisdom and creation, my approach instead leads to grounding Wisdom literature first in the canonical account of creation and Eden in Genesis 1–3, which itself is rich with wisdom themes.

---

²³Longman, *Fear of the Lord*, 128.
²⁴Belcher, *Finding Favour in the Sight*, 12. See also Hans-Jürgen Hermisson, "Observations on the Creation Theology in Wisdom," trans. Barbara Howard, in *Israelite Wisdom: Theological and Literary Essays in Honor of Samuel Terrien*, ed. John Gammie (Missoula, MT: Scholars Press, 1978), 47-53. Hermisson focuses instead on Ps 104, followed by Ps 89; 93; Job 38–41.

WISDOM IN GENESIS 1–3

Wisdom themes and language are an important part of the textual fabric of Genesis 1–3. Genesis 1 starts with the fundamental truth that God is Creator (Gen 1:1). In the midst of desolation and mighty waters (Gen 1:2), God speaks light into darkness, sees this light as "good" (טוֹב), separates (בָּדַל) light from darkness, and names (קָרָא) the light and darkness (Gen 1:3-5). The repeated acts of separation (Gen 1:4, 6-7, 14, 18) and naming (Gen 1:5, 8, 10), along with the making of plants and animals according to "kind" (Gen 1:11-12, 21, 24-25), give a strong impression of an ordered world. As a text, Genesis 1:1–2:3 itself follows a discernible literary pattern punctuated by "there was evening and there was morning— the [*n*th] day." The creation of "humanity" (אָדָם) as male and female in the "image" (צֶלֶם) and "likeness" (דְּמוּת) of God naturally has universal application to all humans (Gen 1:26-28). As seen previously, creation, order, and humanity are important elements of Wisdom literature.

Whereas Genesis 1 might be said to have wisdom overtones via creation, wisdom themes and language are explicit in Genesis 2–3. The two trees highlighted in Genesis 2:9, one leading to life and the other to death (Gen 2:17; 3:22), correspond to the theme of "two ways" common to Wisdom literature (e.g., Prov 1:7; 9:1-6, 13-18; see also Deut 30:15; Ps 1). The name of the latter tree as "the tree of the *knowledge* of good and evil [or 'bad']" (עֵץ הַדַּעַת טוֹב וָרָע) makes wisdom an explicit theme in this context (see Prov 1:7, "the fear of the Lord is the beginning of knowledge [דַּעַת]"). Longman believes that "wisdom . . . is clearly at play in the story of Adam and Eve's rebellion against God," particularly as it concerns this tree.[25] Whereas in a real sense this tree is a tree of *death* (Gen 2:17), its setting forth a (false) hope for wisdom reappears in Genesis 3:5, when the serpent concludes his enticement with the promise of "be[ing] like God, knowing good and evil" (יֹדְעֵי טוֹב וָרָע). After Adam and Eve have eaten the forbidden fruit, the Lord's words that they have "become like one of us, knowing good and evil" (לָדַעַת טוֹב וָרָע) foregrounds this tree's association with

---

[25]Longman, *Fear of the Lord*, 94.

wisdom for a fourth time (Gen 3:22; see also Gen 2:9, 17; 3:5). Given Adam and Eve's rebellion against God to gain this knowledge and the consequences of shame, banishment, and death, these words of the Lord in Genesis 3:22 suggest that the serpent had mixed truth with lies in Genesis 3:5.

Meanwhile, the characterization of the serpent as "more *shrewd* [עָרוּם] than all other animals of the field" at the beginning of the fall narrative (Gen 3:1) sets up the entire temptation as a contest for wisdom: Who is wiser, God or the serpent? How is wisdom gained? What is wisdom anyway? God had already commanded regarding the tree of the knowledge of good and evil that its promise of (godless) wisdom was to be avoided (Gen 2:17). But along comes a very intelligent, talking serpent, who casts doubt on and confuses God's word, "Did God really say that you should not eat *from any tree of the garden* [מִכֹּל עֵץ הַגָּן]?" (Gen 3:1). In fact, God had said the opposite, "*From any tree of the garden* [מִכֹּל עֵץ הַגָּן] you may freely eat," with only one exception (Gen 2:16-17). In the serpent's second statement, he is emboldened and flatly contradicts the woman's claim and God's original statement (Gen 2:17, "you will surely die") that eating the forbidden fruit will result in death (Gen 3:4, "you will not surely die"). At this point, the serpent, who indeed is wiser than other animals (Gen 3:1), has implied that he is also wiser than God.

The serpent proceeds to play up the promise of wisdom offered by the tree of the knowledge of good and evil: "In the day that you [plural] eat it, your eyes will be opened, and you will be like God, knowing good and evil" (Gen 3:5). Of course the Lord has already explained what would happen "in the day that you eat it" (Gen 2:17), but the serpent substitutes positive outcomes of wisdom and being like God for the actual negative outcome of certain death. Ironically, humanity is already like God in the sense of being created in his image and likeness (Gen 1:26-27). Human worth and dignity is thus divinely bestowed at creation in relationship to God and in connection with obedience to the noble calling to rule and to fill the earth. The serpent, however, promises a Godlikeness and wisdom to be gained independently from God and in rebellion against him. The serpent's implicit claim in Genesis 3:5 to know what "God knows" (יֹדֵעַ אֱלֹהִים) and insinuation that God is withholding knowledge with ill intent from Eve brings the contest for wisdom to a climax: God knows, but the serpent knows better, and so can Eve if she wants. When Eve succumbs, Genesis 3:6 makes clear that she was motivated by physical desires ("the tree was good for food") and the tree's attractive appearance ("it was pleasing to the eyes"; see Gen 2:9) as well as its being "desirable to gain wisdom" (וְנֶחְמָד הָעֵץ לְהַשְׂכִּיל). Or so she thought.

The immediate consequences of Adam and Eve's rebellion unmask their futile grasp for wisdom and the serpent's bait-and-switch (Gen 3:7). Adam and Eve's eyes are indeed "opened" (פָּקַח), as the serpent predicted (Gen 3:5), but what they "knew" (יָדַע) was not enlightenment but their own nakedness and shame (Gen 3:7). Their grasp for Godlike wisdom ends in embarrassing failure. Ingrid Faro points out the connection between "seeing" and "knowing" in Genesis 3:5 ("your *eyes* will be *opened* [פָּקַח] . . . *knowing* [יָדַע] good and evil") and Genesis 3:7 ("the *eyes* of both of them were *opened* [פָּקַח] and they *knew* [יָדַע] that they were naked") and explains, "The reference is to a knowledge that comes from seeing differently."[26] Indeed, Adam and Eve had already been "naked" (עֲרוּמִּים) but were unashamed (Gen 2:25), but now they knew that they were "naked" (עֵירֻמִּם, Gen 3:7; different word) and were ashamed of it and what they had done (Gen 3:7-11). The "shrewd" (עָרוּם) serpent had only led them to experience this latter "nakedness" (עֵירֻמִּם).

As created beings, they would never be fully like God in infinite wisdom as they might have thought (Gen 3:5), but they did know "evil/bad" (רַע) in a new, personal way through their rebellion and its consequences (Gen 3:22). Whereas creation in Genesis 1 is "good" (טוֹב), even "very good" (טוֹב מְאֹד), "evil" (רַע) will henceforth characterize the very makeup of the human heart (Gen 6:5; 8:21). God and his wisdom are proven right, and the serpent, Adam, and Eve are wrong. Human wisdom, even at its

---

[26]Ingrid Faro, *Evil in Genesis: A Contextual Analysis of Hebrew Lexemes for Evil in the Book of Genesis* (Bellingham, WA: Lexham, 2021), 113, emphasis removed. For similar collocations involving יָדַע and רָאָה, see Deut 29:4; Is 6:9.

best and by design, is thus incomplete and derivative of God's, based not on what finite human beings think (Prov 14:12; 16:25) but on humility, faith, and the fear of the Lord (Prov 3:5-6; 15:33).

GENESIS 1–3 AND PROVERBS

Like Genesis 1–3, Wisdom literature affirms the perfect wisdom of God and the futility of seeking wisdom apart from God. As many observe, biblical authors of Wisdom literature often articulate this foundational truth in terms of "the fear of the Lord." Proverbs 9:10 says, "The fear of the Lord is the beginning of wisdom." Job 28:28 similarly asserts, "The fear of the Lord—it is wisdom." Ecclesiastes 12:13 calls "the end of the matter" (סוֹף דָּבָר) to "fear God and keep his commandments." There is even a rough symmetry in describing the fear of the Lord in these three passages as the "beginning" of wisdom, wisdom itself, and the "end" of the matter. Given that Proverbs 1–9 is the first major section in Proverbs and serves as a long introduction to the rest of the book, I have chosen to limit my analysis to Proverbs 1–3 as representative of this larger section.[27] If Raymond Van Leeuwen is right that the primary message of Proverbs 1–9 involves a created world where wisdom, good, and life contrast with folly, evil, and death, then the discussion below will show that Proverbs 1–3 indeed is a fair representation.[28] As seen above, this contrast is also at the heart of Genesis 1–3. A subsequent chapter will return to Proverbs 1–9 when analyzing Proverbs 8 (chapter ten).

As the prologue of Proverbs begins (Prov 1:1-7), its wisdom message has clear parallels to Genesis 1–3, which could indicate an allusion. Following its title, "The proverbs of Solomon" (Prov 1:1), which recalls the wise king who sought to "discern between good and evil" (1 Kings 3:9), the explanation of the book's purpose uses language parallel to Genesis 2–3: "to *know* [לָדַעַת] wisdom and correction" (Prov 1:2; see Gen 2:9, 17; 3:5, 7, 22),

---

[27] Roland E. Murphy calls Prov 1–9 "a kind of 'introduction' to chapters 10–31." See Murphy, *Proverbs*, WBC (Nashville: Thomas Nelson, 1998), xix. See also Longman, *Fear of the Lord*, 25; Bartholomew and O'Dowd, *Old Testament Wisdom Literature*, 79, 82.

[28] Raymond Van Leeuwen, "Liminality and Worldview in Proverbs 1–9," *Semeia* 50 (1990): 111, 116, 130. He is followed by Craig Bartholomew, "Qohelet as a Master of and Mastered by Metaphor," in *Networks of Metaphors in the Hebrew Bible*, ed. Danilo Verde and Antje Labahn (Leuven: Peeters, 2020), 344.

"to take the correction of *insight* [הַשְׂכֵּל]" (Prov 1:3; see Gen 3:6), and to give "intelligence" (עָרְמָה; see Gen 3:1) and "knowledge" (דַּעַת, Prov 1:4).[29] Likewise, each word (or a cognate thereof) in the book's motto, "The fear of the Lord is the beginning of knowledge" (יִרְאַת יְהוָה רֵאשִׁית דָּעַת, Prov 1:7), is found in Genesis 1–3. The terms translated "the Lord" and "knowledge" can be seen, for example, in Genesis 2:9, and "beginning" (רֵאשִׁית) in Genesis 1:1 ("beginning" will be revisited in chapter ten), but here I note the contrast between "the fear of the Lord" and Adam's "fear" (יָרֵא) and hiding after foolishly eating the fruit (Gen 3:10). Whereas "the fear of the Lord" involves "turn[ing] from evil" (רַע; Job 1:1; Prov 3:7), Adam chose evil and as a result was later afraid. Positively, fearing the Lord is often related to trusting him (Prov 3:5-7; see Gen 22:8, 12, 14; Ex 14:31; Ps 40:3; 115:11).

In the context of an appeal to heed parental instruction in Proverbs 1:8-9 reminiscent of Deuteronomy (Deut 6:6-9), the rest of Proverbs 1 sets forth the two ways of wisdom and folly (Prov 1:10-33).[30] This theme is a direct link to the choice between the tree of life and the tree of the knowledge of good and evil in Genesis 2:9. This thematic link involves the repetition of the term "knowledge" (דַּעַת) in Proverbs 1:22, 29 ("fools hate knowledge"; "they hated knowledge and did not choose the fear of the Lord") already found in Proverbs 1:2, 4, 7 (see also Prov 2:5-6, 10), which strengthens the connection back to Genesis 2–3 (where Adam and Eve are also mistaken about knowledge). Furthermore, the warning against sinners who may "entice" (פָּתָה) in Proverbs 1:10 recalls the serpent's enticement of Eve. Lady Wisdom even says of those who reject her, "Let them *eat from the fruit of their way*" (וְיֹאכְלוּ מִפְּרִי דַרְכָּם, Prov 1:31), reminiscent of Adam and Eve both literally and figuratively (Gen 3:2-3, 6, 16-19, 23-24).

---

[29]For analysis of parallels between Adam and Solomon, see John A. Davies, "'Discerning Between Good and Evil': Solomon as a New Adam in 1 Kings," *WTJ* 73 (2011): 39-43, who discusses themes (and occasional language) of rule, paradise conditions, sanctuary/temple, obedience/disobedience, expulsion/exile, the River Gihon, plants/animals, life, blessing, and the image of God as prophet, priest, and king.

[30]E.g., C. F. Keil and Franz Delitzsch believe that Prov 1:7–9:18 echoes the Shema in Deut 6:4-9 and "savours of the Book of Deuteronomy." See Keil and Delitzsch, *Proverbs, Ecclesiastes, Song of Solomon*, Commentary on the Old Testament 6 (repr., Peabody, MA: Hendrickson, 1996), 25.

On the other hand, those who heed Lady Wisdom will "dwell securely" (יִשְׁכָּן־בֶּטַח, Prov 1:33; see Deut 33:12, 28; Jer 23:6, 33:16). The respective destinies of the wise/righteous and the foolish/wicked are similarly expressed in Proverbs 2:21-22 in terms of "inhabit[ing] the land" (יִשְׁכְּנוּ אָרֶץ) versus "be[ing] cut off from the land" (מֵאֶרֶץ יִכָּרֵתוּ; see Deut 11:31). Scholars have noticed another connection to Deuteronomy here, but within the Pentateuch, the theme of living in the land does not begin with Deuteronomy, or even the patriarchal narratives, but with Adam and Eve in the Garden of Eden.[31] The contrast between "the wise *inherit* [נָחַל] glory" and "fools bear shame [קָלוֹן]" in Proverbs 3:35 also fits with this land theme and Adam and Eve's shame.

While Proverbs 1–3 also deals with other matters, the preceding shows that thematically and conceptually it has much in common with Genesis 1–3. Although there are some lexical links as well, a closer look at a few more passages will show more definitively that the author of Proverbs was probably consciously engaging Genesis 1–3. After Lady Wisdom's call in Proverbs 1:20-33, Proverbs 2 urges "my son" to seek wisdom diligently for his own good (Prov 2:11), especially in keeping him from corrupt people (Prov 2:12-15) such as the wayward woman (Prov 2:16-19). Proverbs 3 continues this appeal with direct calls to trust the Lord (Prov 3:5), fear the Lord (Prov 3:7), honor the Lord with one's wealth (Prov 3:9), and receive the Lord's fatherly correction (Prov 3:11-12; see Gen 5:1-2).

In such a literary context, the continuing appeal to seek wisdom in Proverbs 3:13-18 concludes, "She [i.e., wisdom] is a *tree of life* to those who lay hold of her, and those who take hold of her are blessed" (Prov 3:18). This reference to "a tree of life" (עֵץ־חַיִּים) fits smoothly into the matrix of aforementioned links between Proverbs 1–3 and Genesis 1–3 (e.g., wisdom/knowledge, two ways, fruit/eating, living in the land), while the use of a nearly identical phrase ("*the* tree of life" [עֵץ הַחַיִּים] in Gen 2:9; 3:22, 24 and nowhere else in the OT) suggests intentional engagement

---

[31]John Sailhamer, *Genesis Unbound* (repr., Eugene, OR: Wipf & Stock, 2001), 14-15, 50-54. Sailhamer also believes Gen 1:2-31 concerns the preparation of the land for human beings. For the connection between Prov 2:21 and Deuteronomy, see, e.g., Duane Garrett, *Proverbs, Ecclesiastes, Song of Songs*, New American Commentary (Nashville: Broadman, 1993), 77.

with Genesis 1–3. Although the phrase "a tree of life" also appears three times elsewhere (Prov 11:30; 13:12; 15:4), the lack of context in these sayings is limiting, whereas the additional links to Genesis 1–3 in the preceding context of Proverbs 3:18 suggest an allusion to the Garden of Eden here and all along.[32] The absence of the ה-article ("the") in Proverbs is not a major issue since this article is uncommon in Proverbs generally and *the* tree of life in Eden is unique.

Although several interpreters see the tree of life in Proverbs 3:18 as merely a metaphor with a weak connection to Genesis 2–3, Bartholomew and O'Dowd, citing this connection and the focus on creation in Proverbs 8:22-31, argue, "The wisdom tradition picks up these themes and language from Genesis 1–3."[33] The literary context of Proverbs 3:18 provides still more evidence for an allusion. While steering clear of Genesis 1 (maybe because of its later date in critical estimation), Christine Roy Yoder takes Proverbs 3:18 as an allusion to Genesis 2–3 and observes, "The tree of life is but one stitch in a thick tapestry of intertextual connections between the poem [i.e., Prov 3:13-20] and Genesis 2–3."[34] The term אָדָם ("man"), used twice in Proverbs 3:13 ("the man [אָדָם] who gets discernment"), appears repeatedly in Genesis 1–3. Certainly this word can be used in the generic sense of "humanity" (Prov 3:4, 30; Gen 1:26-27), but in Proverbs 3:13-18 אָדָם is suggestively

---

[32] Regarding the varied amount of context for these four passages in Proverbs, see Christine Roy Yoder, "Wisdom Is the Tree of Life: A Study of Proverbs 3:13-20 and Genesis 2–3," in *Reading Proverbs Intertextually*, ed. Katharine Dell and Will Kynes (London: T&T Clark, 2019), 11-12. For an integrated treatment of these passages, see Christopher Ansberry, "Arbors Among Aphorisms: The Anatomy of the Tree in the Book of Proverbs," in Verde and Labahn, *Networks of Metaphors*, 264-70.

[33] Bartholomew and O'Dowd, *Old Testament Wisdom Literature*, 29; contra Graeme Goldsworthy, *The Tree of Life: Reading Proverbs Today* (Sydney: Anglican Information Office Press, 1993), 59. Goldsworthy writes, "Probably not a reference to the tree in Eden ... though the author would have known of it." William R. Osborne recognizes echoes of Gen 2–3 but ultimately calls its use in Prov 3:18 a "stock image, or even dead metaphor." Osborne, "The Tree of Life in Proverbs and Psalms," in *The Tree of Life*, ed. Douglas Estes (Leiden: Brill, 2020), 105-7. See "spring of life" in Prov 10:11; 13:14; 14:27; 16:22.

[34] Yoder, "Wisdom Is the Tree," 12 (including n6). At the outset of her article, she refers to the "nearly half a millennium" that elapsed between the mention of the tree of life in Gen 2–3 and in Proverbs (p. 11). In n1 on the same page, she references the common critical view of Gen 2–3 as a "Yahwist text, which suggests a date rather early in Israel's history." She acknowledges the ongoing debate and those who would say it is exilic or early postexilic. In any case, diachronic intertextuality applies for her here because she believes that Prov 1–9 "arguably dates to the early post-exilic period."

used of a person "who finds wisdom" (Prov 3:13) and lays hold of "a tree of life" (Prov 3:18), in contrast with the failed attempt at wisdom by Adam (אָדָם) and his banishment from the tree of life in Genesis 3. The curses in Genesis 3:14, 17 also contrast with the statements of blessing for the wise that frame Proverbs 3:13-18 ("Blessed [אַשְׁרֵי] is the man [אָדָם] who finds wisdom," Prov 3:13; "those who take hold of her are blessed [מְאֻשָּׁר]," Prov 3:18).

In Proverbs 3:14-15, the greater value of wisdom compared to "silver" (כֶּסֶף), "gold" (חָרוּץ), and "rubies" (פְּנִינִים) not only recalls a similar comparison in Proverbs 2:4 (see Job 28:15-19) but also the mentions of "gold" (זָהָב), "bdellium" (בְּדֹלַח), and "onyx" (שֹׁהַם) in Genesis 2:11-12 with respect to the river(s) of Eden. Ezekiel 28:13 also directly links gold, onyx, and other precious things to the Garden of Eden. Yoder further observes that the theme of desire is another link between Proverbs 3:13-18 and Genesis 2–3 (e.g., Eve's desire in Gen 3:6 and wisdom's superiority to "all your desires" [כָּל־חֲפָצֶיךָ] in Prov 3:15).[35] Yoder points out the parallel between Eve desiring and "taking" (לָקַח) from the wrong tree in Genesis 3:6 and the appeal to "take hold of" (*hiphil* תָּמַךְ/חָזַק) wisdom in Proverbs 3:18 (see her fruit in Prov 8:19 and "*take* correction" [לָקַח] in Prov 1:3).

In Proverbs 3:16, wisdom/a tree of life is described as having "length of days" in her right hand, which recalls "the tree of life" in Genesis 3:22 bearing fruit that allows one to "live forever" (וְחַי לְעֹלָם). Although some may regard "length of days" (אֹרֶךְ יָמִים) as merely referring to long life in keeping with Proverbs' this-worldly perspective, several statements in Proverbs suggest something more (e.g., Prov 10:30; 12:19, 28; see also Prov 10:2, 30; 11:4, 28, 31; 12:3, 7). If the concept of eternal life is deemed inconceivable or anachronistic for the book of Proverbs, we may recall that it is already explicit in Genesis 3:22 and hence accessible to all who read or heard that passage (see "life forever" [חַיִּים עַד־הָעוֹלָם] in Ps 133:3). Besides its two appearances in Proverbs 3:2, 16, the phrase "length of days" appears most frequently in the Psalms (four times), where its usage generally suggests living forever (Ps 21:4; 23:6; 91:16; 93:5; see also Job 12:12; Lam 5:20).

---

[35]Yoder, "Wisdom Is the Tree," 12, 15-16.

The "riches and glory" (עֹשֶׁר וְכָבוֹד) in wisdom's left hand in Proverbs 3:16 tie back to the precious metals and gems in Proverbs 3:14-15 and Proverbs 2:4 as well as contrasting with Adam and Eve's nakedness and loss in Genesis 3. Their hiding from God and to some extent from each other in Genesis 3:7-8 also contrasts with the promise of finding "favor . . . in the eyes of God and man" in Proverbs 3:4. In their godless attempt "to gain wisdom" (לְהַשְׂכִּיל; Gen 3:6), they had forfeited the "good insight" (שֵׂכֶל־טוֹב) that is also promised in Proverbs 3:4. In Proverbs 3:17, the pleasant and peace-filled "ways" (דֶּרֶךְ) of wisdom recall "the way of the tree of life" in Genesis 3:24. Yoder also sees a contrast here with the "enmity" (אֵיבָה) and "pain" (עֶצֶב/עִצָּבוֹן) described in Genesis 3:15-17.[36]

Table 2.1. Tree of life in Genesis 2–3 and Proverbs 3:13-18

	Genesis 2–3	**Proverbs 3:13-18**
Tree of life	"the tree of life" (Gen 2:9; 3:22, 24)	"a tree of life" (Prov 3:18)
Wisdom language	"knowledge of good and evil" (Gen 2:9, 17; 3:21), "shrewd" (Gen 3:1), "gain wisdom" (Gen 3:6)	"wisdom," "discernment" (Prov 3:13)
Man (אָדָם)	"the man" (repeatedly in Gen 2–3)	"Blessed is the *man* . . . and the *man* . . ." (Prov 3:13)
Blessing or cursing	"Cursed are you" (Gen 3:14) "Cursed is the ground" (Gen 3:17)	"*Blessed* is the man . . ." (Prov 3:13)
Precious metals or stones	gold, bdellium, onyx (Gen 2:11-12)	silver, gold, rubies, riches (Prov 3:14-16)
Taking something desirable	Eve "took" fruit that was "desirable" for gaining wisdom (Gen 3:6)	blessing to those who "take hold of" wisdom (Prov 3:18), which is superior to "all your desires" (Prov 3:15)
Eternal (or at least long) life	"eat [from the tree of life] and live forever" (Gen 3:22)	"length of days is in her right hand" (Prov 3:16)
Nakedness or glory	"they knew that they were *naked*" (Gen 3:7; see also Gen 3:10-11)	"in her left hand are riches and *glory*" (Prov 3:16)

The lexical and thematic coherence between the presentation of wisdom as a tree of life in Proverbs 3:13-18 with Genesis 2–3 suggests

---

[36]Yoder, "Wisdom Is the Tree," 17.

that not only is Proverbs 1–3 conceptually congruent with Genesis 1–3 but also that it is consciously engaging these opening chapters of the Old Testament. Even though the way back to the original tree of life has been barred, it is as though there remains hope in a fallen world to access another tree of life and recover the blessing that was lost (Prov 3:13, 18). This tree of life is available to all humanity (אָדָם). The way to a restored Eden is thus to desire, seek, find, and lay hold of wisdom through fear of the Lord. Similarly, if Adam and Eve had faithfully obeyed the Lord, this would have been their wisdom ("the fear of the Lord is to hate evil," Prov 8:13). The tree of the knowledge of good and evil offered only godless wisdom that brings death (see 1 Tim 6:20; Jas 3:15), but wisdom gained in the fear of the Lord is indeed a tree of life, as it would have been in Eden also. Whereas the former tree seems to conflate "good" (טוֹב) and "evil/bad" (רַע), Proverbs 1–3 makes a clear distinction between the two (see Deut 30:15). Wisdom brings knowledge of "every good path" (Prov 2:9), delivers from "the way of evil" (Prov 2:12), keeps one from "those rejoicing to do evil" (Prov 2:14; see also Prov 1:16) and instead on "the way of good people" (Prov 2:20), gives "good insight" (Prov 3:4), involves "turn[ing] from evil" (Prov 3:7), and has "good" value (Prov 3:14). Indeed, from the all-important perspective of God's command in Genesis 2:17, there is no question which tree was bad no matter what it was called.

Besides the reference to a tree of life in Proverbs 3:18, another strong piece of evidence for the author of Proverbs' intentional engagement with Genesis 1–3 is the very next verse, Proverbs 3:19. This verse links to the preceding context by repeating "wisdom" (חָכְמָה) and "discernment" (תְּבוּנָה) from Proverbs 3:13 and by its focus on creation, which accords with the dual mention of אָדָם in Proverbs 3:13.[37] The rich engagement with Genesis 1–3 found in Proverbs 3:13-18 is continued in striking fashion in Proverbs 3:19, which reads like Genesis 1:1 reworked into a poetic parallelism emphasizing wisdom:

---

[37]Yoder, "Wisdom Is the Tree," 13-14.

יְהוָה בְּחָכְמָה יָסַד־אָרֶץ כּוֹנֵן שָׁמַיִם בִּתְבוּנָה

The Lord founded the earth with wisdom; he established the heavens with understanding. (Prov 3:19)

בְּרֵאשִׁית בָּרָא אֱלֹהִים אֵת הַשָּׁמַיִם וְאֵת הָאָרֶץ

In the beginning God created the heavens and earth. (Gen 1:1)

The links between these two texts are lexical, thematic, and syntactical. Genesis 1:1 and Proverbs 3:19 each concern the creation of the "heavens" (שָׁמַיִם) and the "earth" (אָרֶץ). Whereas these two terms are found in both verses, a slight difference is the fronted subject and covenant name "Lord" (יְהוָה) in Proverbs 3:19 instead of "God" (אֱלֹהִים) in Genesis 1:1. Genesis 1 uses "God" throughout, whereas this word appears a mere five times in Proverbs. Likewise, instead of "create" (בָּרָא) in Genesis 1:1, Proverbs 3:19 uses "founded" (יָסַד) and "established" (כּוּן), two terms that sometimes are used to describe creation in poetic texts (e.g., Deut 32:6; Ps 8:3; 24:2; 78:69; 89:11, 37; 104:5; Job 31:15; 38:4).[38] The clearest difference in meaning between the two verses concerns "in the beginning" (בְּרֵאשִׁית) in Genesis 1:1 versus "with wisdom" (בְּחָכְמָה) and "with understanding" (בִּתְבוּנָה) in Proverbs 3:19, which frame most of the verse. These forms are syntactically parallel (note the use of בְּ), but it is as though wisdom terminology has been substituted for "beginning" (רֵאשִׁית). Suggestively, the terms "wisdom" (חָכְמָה) and "beginning" (רֵאשִׁית) are closely related in Psalm 111:10 ("the fear of the Lord is the *beginning* of *wisdom*"; see Prov 1:7; 4:7) and Proverbs 8, where Wisdom (Prov 8:12) says, "The Lord acquired me, the *beginning* of his way" (Prov 8:22). These issues will be discussed in further detail in chapter ten.

The connection between Genesis 1:1 and Proverbs 3:19 has long been noticed by Jewish interpreters, who also note the connection to the building of the tabernacle led by Bezalel, who was filled "with wisdom" (בְּחָכְמָה), "with understanding" (בִּתְבוּנָה), and "with knowledge" (בְּדַעַת;

---

[38]Raymond Van Leeuwen further points out the parallel to Prov 24:3-4 in support of taking Prov 3:19-20 as an example of creation cast in terms of building and architecture. Van Leeuwen, "Cosmos, Temple, House: Building and Wisdom in Ancient Mesopotamia and Israel," in *From the Foundations to the Crenellations: Essays on Temple Building in the Ancient Near East and Hebrew Bible*, ed. Mark Boda and Jamie Novotny (Münster: Ugarit-Verlag, 2010), 407-12.

Ex 31:3; 35:31; see also 1 Kings 7:14), just like the Lord at creation (Prov 3:19-20; see also Prov 2:6).[39] The "depths" (תְּהוֹמוֹת) in Proverbs 3:20 recall the "deep" (תְּהוֹם) in Genesis 1:2, while their "break[ing] forth" (בָּקַע) along with precipitation from clouds uses similar language to the onset of the flood in Genesis 7:11. Yoder also notes the connection to rain (from above) and mist from the ground (from below) in Genesis 2:5-6.[40]

Taken together, the reference to a tree of life in Proverbs 3:18 and the wisdom-inspired reworking of Genesis 1:1 in Proverbs 3:19 provide solid evidence that Proverbs 1–3 intentionally engages Genesis 1–3 on both the thematic and lexical levels. The strong links from Proverbs 3:13-20 to creation and Eden in Genesis 1–3 do not stand in isolation but are reinforced by the additional thematic and lexical links involving Proverbs 1–3 discussed above. If Proverbs 1–9 provides the central outlook and guiding framework for rest of the book (Prov 10–31), then the preceding is a constructive step toward demonstrating that Proverbs is not only conceptually coherent with Genesis 1–3 but rooted in it on the textual and literary levels.[41]

GENESIS 1–3 AND ECCLESIASTES

In my attempt to show that Wisdom literature is textually, literarily, and theologically grounded in Genesis 1–3 as a nexus passage, I now turn to Ecclesiastes. This difficult book has been interpreted in various and sometimes contradictory ways, as Kynes's helpful survey shows.[42] For the sake of brevity, I simply state my belief in a positive overall message of the book based on its conclusion, "The end of the matter, everything has been heard: fear God and keep his commandments" (Eccles 12:13). Despite the despair and frustration voiced frequently in Ecclesiastes, there is still hope because ultimately "God will bring every work into judgment, including every hidden thing whether good or evil" (Eccles 12:14). Likewise, although

---

[39] E.g., Fragmentary Targum and Targum Neofiti (on Gen 1:1); Bereshit Rabbah 1.4; Midrash Tanhuma (on Gen 1:1 and Pekudei 3:3, 16); Rashi (on 1 Kings 7:14), Ramban (on Gen 1:1-2).

[40] Yoder, "Wisdom Is the Tree," 14.

[41] In Prov 10–29, a few sayings directly relate to Gen 1–3, such as those referring to the "Maker" of humanity (Prov 14:31; 17:5; 20:12; 22:2; see also Prov 29:13). Others assume the fallen world of Gen 3 (e.g., Prov 13:23; 14:20; 17:8).

[42] Kynes, *Obituary for "Wisdom Literature,"* 180-84.

human effort is often futile, God's work is beautiful and endures (Eccles 3:11, 14). Below I attempt to show that the theology of Ecclesiastes is rooted in Genesis 1–3 thematically and conceptually, and sometimes even lexically.

Zimmerli says Ecclesiastes "emerges from an explicit theology of creation" and "knew even the combined text of Gen. 1–3 and for that matter, I suppose, also the whole Pentateuch."[43] He sees Ecclesiastes 3:11 ("He has made everything beautiful in its/his time") as reflecting Genesis 1 and the central fact that God created the world. Indeed, the reference to God as "your creator" (בּוֹרְאֶיךָ) in Ecclesiastes 12:1 is the only place in Wisdom literature that uses the same verb (בָּרָא, "create") that appears in Genesis 1:1, 21, 27; 2:3. Just a few years before Zimmerli, Charles Forman concluded his seminal article with the "contention that the early chapters of Genesis [i.e., Gen 1–11] represent the most important single influence in the ideas of Ecclesiastes regarding the nature and destiny of man, the character of human existence, and the fact of God."[44] Though some believe this influence to be present but weaker, scholars have continued to explore Ecclesiastes along these lines.[45] When broader scholarship has done so, it often holds to a very late date for Ecclesiastes (i.e., later than Genesis and P), which is common in critical scholarship. In contrast, Proverbs has sometimes been dated earlier.[46] Relatedly, in critical scholarship, an influence of Genesis on Ecclesiastes often entails agreement in thought, but not always.[47] There is likely underlying skepticism about the unity of

---

[43]Zimmerli, "Place and Limit," 155.
[44]Charles Forman, "Koheleth's Use of Genesis," *Journal of Semitic Studies* 5, no. 3 (1960): 263. Zimmerli's original article in German was published in 1963.
[45]For recent surveys of literature on this issue, see Katharine J. Dell, "Exploring Intertextual Links Between Ecclesiastes and Genesis 1–11," in *Reading Ecclesiastes Intertextually*, ed. Katharine J. Dell and Will Kynes (London: Bloomsbury, 2014), 3. Dell questions many of these links. More positively, see Matthew Seufert, "The Presence of Genesis in Ecclesiastes," *WTJ* 78 (2016): 75-78. He classifies his own position as seeing the presence of Genesis as "widespread" in Ecclesiastes, in contrast with others, who on the one side see it as "extremely widespread" or on the other as either "limited" or "extremely limited" (78).
[46]Bernd Schipper discusses the dating of Proverbs to the postexilic period and alternatively at least parts of it to the monarchic period. Schipper, "'Teach Them Diligently to Your Son!': The Book of Proverbs and Deuteronomy," in Dell and Kynes, *Reading Proverbs Intertextually*, 21-22. Murphy thinks Prov 1–9 is postexilic and Prov 10–31 preexilic (*Proverbs*, xix-xx).
[47]E.g., Forman, "Koheleth's Use of Genesis," 256: "Koheleth obviously knew Genesis and accepted some of its presuppositions while occasionally taking issue with others."

Scripture and inspiration at play here. On the other hand, speaking from an evangelical perspective, Duane Garrett refers to Ecclesiastes' "theological and literary dependence on the early chapters of Genesis" and calls Ecclesiastes "a collection of reflections on creation and the fall, or even reflections on the continuing significance of creation and the fall."[48]

Ecclesiastes itself provides significant evidence that its theology is not only rooted in creation theology broadly considered but in the creation account of Genesis 1 and in the Eden/fall account in Genesis 2–3, as Garrett asserts. Several passages in Ecclesiastes are striking in their conformity to the thought and language of Genesis 1–3. For example, Ecclesiastes 7:29 reads, "God made humanity upright but they sought many schemes." Practically every part of this sentence directly connects to Genesis 1–3. First, "God made humanity" (עָשָׂה הָאֱלֹהִים אֶת־הָאָדָם) in Ecclesiastes 7:29 uses the same words as Genesis 1:26, "And God said, 'Let us make man'" (וַיֹּאמֶר אֱלֹהִים נַעֲשֶׂה אָדָם).[49] The only other texts with these words used in this way are Genesis 5:1 and Genesis 9:6, which likely also refer to Genesis 1:26. Second, humanity's original, pristine state as "upright" in Ecclesiastes 7:29 (יָשָׁר) accords with God's creation of humanity in the image and likeness of God in Genesis 1:26 and the comprehensive assessment of "very good" in Genesis 1:31.

Third, humanity's subsequent pursuit of "many schemes" (חִשְּׁבֹנוֹת רַבִּים) in Ecclesiastes 7:29 accurately describes the fall of the representative man in Genesis 3 as well as the repeated failures described in Genesis 4 and onwards. The "many schemes" (חִשְּׁבֹנוֹת רַבִּים) in Ecclesiastes 7:29 even lexically parallels the increase of human evil prior to the flood in Genesis 6:5 ("the wickedness of humanity [אָדָם] was *great* [רַבָּה] on the earth, and every form of the *thoughts* [מַחְשְׁבֹת] of their hearts was only evil all the time"; see Eccles 9:3). Just a few verses earlier, Ecclesiastes 7:20 also describes fallen humanity in a way that agrees with both Genesis 6:5 and Genesis 3, "There is no righteous man [אָדָם] on earth who does good and

---

[48] Garrett, *Proverbs, Ecclesiastes, Song of Songs*, 278-79.
[49] Forman also makes the connection to Gen 1:26 without specifically mentioning lexical links ("Koheleth's Use of Genesis," 259).

does not sin." Thus, Forman remarks, "Koheleth [i.e., the preacher] acknowledges the problem of evil in human nature" and that "something went wrong with man."[50]

Another example of Ecclesiastes' literary and theological dependence on Genesis 1–3 involves descriptions of death in terms of "returning" (שׁוּב) to the ground and/or dust from which a living being came.[51] Adam had been "formed of dust from the ground [עָפָר מִן־הָאֲדָמָה]" (Gen 2:7) and was sentenced to death accordingly, that is, to "return to the ground [שׁוּבְךָ אֶל־הָאֲדָמָה], for from it [מִמֶּנָּה] you were taken. For dust [עָפָר] you are, and to dust you will return [וְאֶל־עָפָר תָּשׁוּב]" (Gen 3:19). Though also including animals, Ecclesiastes 3:20 uses many of the same words, "all are from the dust [מִן־הֶעָפָר], and all return to the dust [שָׁב אֶל־הֶעָפָר]." Likewise, Ecclesiastes 12:7 describes human death thus, "the dust returns [וְיָשֹׁב הֶעָפָר] to the earth as it was before."

The preceding example brings up the theme of death, which is common to both Genesis 2–3 and Ecclesiastes, where it dominates. It is the unescapable reality of death that leads the Preacher to despair. Having already tried various forms of pleasure, accomplishment, and then wisdom (Eccles 2:1-13), he found only limited value for wisdom because both the wise and the fool ultimately have the same fate (Eccles 2:14). From this perspective, wisdom has no purpose (Eccles 2:15). The wise will die and be forgotten all the same (Eccles 2:16). The Preacher's revulsion at this is voiced in Ecclesiastes 2:17-18, "I hated life.... I hated all my toil... which I must leave to a man who will be after me." Death is implied early in Ecclesiastes (Eccles 1:4, "a generation comes, and a generation goes") and is explicit throughout the book (e.g., Eccles 3:2, 19-21; 4:2; 5:15; 6:3-6, 12; 7:1-2, 15-17; 8:8; 9:2-5, 10; 12:1-7).[52]

Ecclesiastes, however, does not only see life in terms of impending death but also sees God as playing an active role in bringing about this frustrated

---

[50]Forman, "Koheleth's Use of Genesis," 258-59.
[51]Forman mentions this connection briefly ("Koheleth's Use of Genesis," 258).
[52]David Clemens points out connections between Eccles 1:1-11 and Eccles 11:7–12:14 that strengthen this point by showing that death frames the book. Clemens, "The Law of Sin and Death: Ecclesiastes and Genesis 1–3," *Themelios* 19, no. 3 (1994): 5-6.

human existence. Ecclesiastes 1:13 describes "all that is done under the heavens" as a "grievous task" (עִנְיַן רָע) that "God has given to humanity" (see Eccles 2:26; 3:10; 4:8; 8:16). Ecclesiastes 7:13 implies the same: "See the work of God: For who can straighten what he has made crooked?" This is not to say that God necessarily bears sole or ultimate responsibility. In view of his making humanity originally upright (Eccles 7:29) and his justice (Eccles 3:17; 11:9; 12:14), sinful humanity must bear ultimate responsibility, and God must have just cause in all that he does, including bringing death and all its consequences. Ecclesiastes does not make this connection explicit for its readers, but its strong connection to Genesis 1–3 suggests the propriety of filling in this gap concerning the cause-and-effect relationship between sin and death.[53] After giving extensive evidence for the presence of Genesis in Ecclesiastes, Matthew Seufert concludes that Ecclesiastes should be understood "in light of Adam's fall into sin and God's subsequent judgment of death and toil."[54]

If this is true, then humanity's frustration with death stems not only from having "eternity in their heart" (Eccles 3:11) but also from their originally being created to live forever (Gen 3:22). In other words, the created order was never meant to be inherently futile for humanity but became that way because of sin and the subsequent divine death sentence. Additional support for this point can be found in William Anderson's demonstration that frustration of work is a major theme in both Genesis 3:17-19 and Ecclesiastes.[55] The "pain" or "painful toil" (עֶצֶב/עִצָּבוֹן, Gen 3:16-17; note the similar עֵץ in Gen 3:17 and עֵשֶׂב in Gen 3:18) to which Adam and Eve are sentenced in work and childbearing (see Gen 1:28; 2:5) parallels the frustrating "toil" (עָמָל) and "work" (מַעֲשֶׂה) frequently mentioned in Ecclesiastes (e.g., Eccles 1:3; 2:17).[56] Such wearisome labor "under the sun"

---

[53] Clemens, "Law of Sin and Death," 6.
[54] Seufert, "Presence of Genesis in Ecclesiastes," 91, emphasis removed. Contra Dell, who believes that Ecclesiastes is simply describing "the given nature of the human condition" ("Exploring Intertextual Links," 9).
[55] William Anderson, "The Curse of Work in Qoheleth: An Exposé of Genesis 3:17-19 in Ecclesiastes," *EvQ* 70, no. 2 (1998): 99-113.
[56] Anderson deals with this parallel but without reference to Eve and childbearing in Gen 3:16 ("Curse of Work in Qoheleth," 102).

(תַּחַת הַשָּׁמֶשׁ) further matches the themes and imagery of Genesis 3:19, "*by the sweat of your nose* [בְּזֵעַת אַפֶּיךָ] you will eat food." Even though life and work "under the sun" does not always imply physical labor (e.g., Eccles 1:9, 14), the negative consequences of Genesis 3:17-19 are naturally understood as also having broader application. Scholars also see connections in Ecclesiastes between "vanity" (הֶבֶל) and Abel, whose name is the same Hebrew word and whose life exemplifies it.[57]

Based on the above, I understand "there is nothing new under the sun" (Eccles 1:9) as a complaint about a world marred by sin and death. The "everything" (כָּל) that God originally made "very good" (טוֹב מְאֹד, Gen 1:31) tragically became "vanity" (הֶבֶל, Eccles 1:2).[58] Only a truly "new" (חָדָשׁ) work of God can change this (Is 65:17; Jer 31:31; Ezek 36:26) because only he can straighten what he himself made crooked (Eccles 7:13; see also Eccles 1:15).

More could be said, but the preceding shows the legitimacy and value of interpreting Ecclesiastes against the background of Genesis 1–3. As some scholars argue, links between the two texts are not occasional but extensive. These links are thematic and conceptual as well as lexical in some key places. In accordance with Genesis 1–3, Ecclesiastes recognizes the original goodness of humanity and wrestles with the presently fallen world of sin and death. The relationship between these two texts further demonstrates the interconnectivity of Genesis 1–3 as a nexus passage especially related to Wisdom literature.

GENESIS 1–3 AND JOB

To complete the discussion of Genesis 1–3 as a nexus passage especially related to Wisdom literature, I now turn to Job. Although the bulk of the book, involving Job's dialogue with his friends (Job 3–37), can be bewildering at times, key parts of the book, such as its opening section in Job 1–2, closing section in Job 38–42, and even some texts from the intervening

---

[57]E.g., Seufert especially highlights Eccles 7:15; 8:14 ("Presence of Genesis in Ecclesiastes," 86). For a discussion of *hebel* as an organizing "megametaphor" in Ecclesiastes, see Bartholomew, "Qohelet as a Master," 332-36.
[58]Bartholomew, "Qohelet as a Master," 332-33.

dialogue have conspicuous connections to Genesis 1–3. As the first and last sections of Job, Job 1–2 and Job 38–42 are especially important to the literary structure and meaning of Job. Indeed, scholars observe links to Genesis 1–3 in these two sections. For example, Bartholomew and O'Dowd see Job's wife's advice to "curse God and die" (Job 2:9) as an "echo" of Eve's influence on Adam in the Garden of Eden (Gen 3:6) and add, "Images of creation in Genesis 1–3 continue to emerge throughout Job."[59] Sam Meier has investigated connections between Genesis 1–3 and Job 1–2 and argues that they "are not accidental but instead result from a conscious adaptation of Genesis to the fabric of the new narrative." His critical stance is explicit in his reference to Genesis 1–3 as "P and J creation accounts" and his implicit belief in a late date for the book of Job.[60] Nevertheless, his observations are still useful within our framework of a protocanonical Mosaic Pentateuch that was written before other Old Testament books, including Job.

Meier points out that Job's "moral uniqueness" (see Job 1:8/Job 2:3, "there is none like him in the earth") parallels Adam's uniqueness as the first human. He also notes Job's comparison to "all the sons of the *east* [קֶדֶם]" (Job 1:3) in relation to Eden's location "in the east" (מִקֶּדֶם, Gen 2:8). Whereas Meier relates Uz to Genesis 10:23; 22:21; and 36:28, we may also note that Job's dwelling "in the land of Uz" (בְּאֶרֶץ־עוּץ, Job 1:1) connects to Adam's location "in the garden of Eden" (בְגַן־עֵדֶן, Gen 2:15) with "every *tree*" planted there (עֵץ, Gen 2:9), since Uz and *tree* are similar words in Hebrew. Meier further highlights Job "turning from evil" (Job 1:1, 8; 2:3) compared to Adam eating from the tree of the knowledge of good and evil and suggests that Job is "a second Adam in a repeat performance, a unique man in a pristine environment who is about to be confronted with a test from God." Meier points out the common theme of an "idyllic life" seen in Genesis 1 and Job's large family and numerous livestock in Job 1:2-3, which is also an apparent fulfillment of "be fruitful and multiply" and the command for humanity to rule animals in Genesis 1:22, 28.[61] Meier notes that the adversary's

---

[59] Bartholomew and O'Dowd, *Old Testament Wisdom Literature*, 134.
[60] Sam Meier, "Job I–II: A Reflection of Genesis I–III," *VT* 39, no. 2 (1989): 183, 193; see also 185n12.
[61] Meier, "Job I–II," 184-86.

remark that God "blessed" (בָּרַךְ) Job's work in Job 1:10 reinforces this. The broader theme of blessing and cursing is a major aspect of both Genesis 1–3 and Job 1–3 (see Gen 2:3; 3:14, 17; Job 1:5, 11, 21; 2:5, 9; 3:1).

Relatedly, Manfred Oeming has investigated the use of אָדָם ("Adam"/"humanity"/"man") in Job. He believes that Eliphaz's question to Job, "Were you the first man born?" (הֲרִאישׁוֹן אָדָם תִּוָּלֵד) in Job 15:7 is best understood in light of Genesis 2 (see Job 38:21). For Oeming, Eliphaz's confrontational question implies that Job is unlike the first man Adam especially because Adam had superior wisdom as one who enjoyed "direct communication with God."[62] Eliphaz's accusation in Job 15:5 that Job "chose the tongue of the crafty/shrewd [לְשׁוֹן עֲרוּמִים]" appears to be a coordinated allusion to the "shrewd" (עָרוּם) serpent and its speech in Genesis 3 (see also Gen 2:25).[63] Oeming also cites Zophar in Job 20:4-7, "Do you know this from of old, from when man was set upon the earth [מִנִּי שִׂים אָדָם עֲלֵי־אָרֶץ], that the joy of the wicked is short and the rejoicing of the godless is momentary? If his pride ascends to the heavens and his head reaches the clouds, he will perish forever like his dung." Oeming sees here a reference to Adam and the fall in Genesis 3 as well as the Tower of Babel in Genesis 11, both of which involve a wicked overreach that was quickly punished.

Last, Oeming cites Job's claim in Job 31:33 not to "have covered my transgressions like Adam/man, to hide in my bosom my guilt" as an allusion to Adam and Eve hiding in Genesis 3:8.[64] Taken together, he argues that these three texts in Job refer to Genesis 2–3. Like Meier's analysis above, this evidence suggests that Job is engaged with creation theology not only in the basic sense that God is Creator (e.g., Job 38:4-7) but specifically as presented in Genesis 1–3, which includes the temptation and fall.

---

[62]Manfred Oeming, "To Be Adam or Not to Be Adam: The Hidden Fundamental Anthropological Discourse Revealed in an Intertextual Reading of אָדָם in Job and Genesis," in *Reading Job Intertextually*, ed. Katharine J. Dell and Will Kynes (New York: Bloomsbury, 2013), 25.

[63]See Scott Noegel, *Janus Parallelism in the Book of Job* (Sheffield: Sheffield Academic Press, 1996), 21-22. Noegel cites Job 15:5 as an example of (the character) Job's "polysemy" and "word-manipulation" but without reference to Gen 2–3. John Briggs Curtis draws attention to Elihu's "smooth words" (Job 32:17), his serpentine crawling/slithering (חָל, Job 32:6), and use of the verb "grasp the heel" (עָקַב, Job 37:4), reminiscent of Gen 3:15. Curtis, "Word Play in the Speeches of Elihu (Job 32–37)," *Proceedings of the Eastern Great Lakes and Midwest Bible Societies* 12 (1992): 23-25.

[64]Oeming, "To Be Adam," 26-27.

Indeed, with language and themes that parallel Ecclesiastes (e.g., Eccles 1:3), Eliphaz, though wrong at other times, is right to say in Job 5:7, "Humanity is born to trouble" (אָדָם לְעָמָל יוּלָּד).

Meier's analysis includes still more examples that reinforce the likelihood that the author of Job thoughtfully engaged Genesis 1–3, including on a textual level. First, Job's trials as a sort of de-creation begin with animals (his livestock, Job 1:14-17), then humans (his children, Job 1:18-19), the latter effected by a "great wind" (רוּחַ גְּדוֹלָה, Job 1:19), which parallels "the Spirit of God" in Genesis 1:2 as well as animals and humanity later in Genesis 1.[65] Michael Fishbane relatedly sees Job 3:1-13 as a "reversal ... of creation" as described in Genesis 1:1–2:4a (e.g., "let there be darkness" in Job 3:4a).[66] Second, Meier draws attention to Job calling himself "naked" (עָרֹם) in Job 1:21, which parallels Genesis 2:25; 3:7, 10-11, and his going out from his mother's womb and "return[ing] there," which parallels Genesis 3:19.[67] Third, Meier argues that the adversary's striking Job's "bone and flesh" in Job 2:5 carries the double meaning of Job's body and his wife (Gen 2:23, "bone of my bones and flesh of my flesh"), who tempts Job using words that implicitly devalue the Lord's view of Job and resemble the adversary's words (i.e., Job 2:3/Job 2:9, God: "He still holds fast to his integrity"; wife: "Are you still holding fast to your integrity?"; Job 2:5/Job 2:9, adversary: "He will curse you"; wife: "Curse God").[68]

Despite broader scholarship's reluctance to relate the serpent in Genesis 3 or the adversary (הַשָּׂטָן) in Job 1–2 to Satan, these figures parallel each other, and the former two can still be understood as references to Satan, at least from an evangelical perspective.[69] On the one hand, the

---

[65] Meier, "Job I-II," 188.
[66] Michael Fishbane, "Jeremiah IV 23-26 and Job III 3-13: A Recovered Use of the Creation Pattern," *VT* 21 (1971): 153.
[67] Meier, "Job I-II," 188-89. He sees Job's nakedness as metaphorical since Job 1:20 shows that he was clothed.
[68] Meier, "Job I-II," 189-90.
[69] For this reluctance, see Gordon Wenham, *Genesis 1–15*, WBC (Waco, TX: Word, 1987), 72. Wenham comments on the traditional view of the snake as Satan, "Since there is no other trace of a personal devil in early parts of the OT, modern writers doubt whether this is the view of our narrator." David Clines claims that the adversary in Job 1–2 is only Job's adversary, not necessarily God's adversary or humanity's adversary. Clines, *Job 1–20*, WBC (Dallas: Word, 1989), 20.

serpent like Satan is an adversary of both God and humanity through its denial of God's word ("you will not surely die," Gen 3:4; cf. Gen 2:17) and luring of humanity into rebellion and death. On the other hand, the adversary in Job 1–2 likewise denies the Lord's positive assessment of Job, wants to ruin Job, and is quite shrewd in his tactics of both claiming that Job does not genuinely fear God and hiding his involvement from Job. Both the serpent and the adversary are arrogant liars (see Job 1:11, 2:5, "surely he will curse you to your face"). The introduction of both villains with the Hebrew article and little explanatory antecedent information ("*the* serpent" [הַנָּחָשׁ] in Gen 3:1 and "*the* adversary" [הַשָּׂטָן] in Job 1:6) hints to readers that they may already know the identity of each character. Presumably there was more than one serpent that existed in Eden, and "the serpent" in Genesis 3:1 refers not to the only serpent but to a unique one.

Another connection between Job and Genesis 1–3 is the theme of sea monsters, which relates to the themes of serpents and Satan discussed above. In Fishbane's aforementioned analysis of Job 3:1-13 and Genesis 1:1–2:4a, he sees Leviathan (לִוְיָתָן) in Job 3:8 as parallel to "the great sea creatures" (הַתַּנִּינִם הַגְּדֹלִים) created in Genesis 1:21.[70] These two terms are mentioned together in Psalm 74:13-14, where they are enemies defeated by the Lord in a maritime battle: "You broke the heads of the *great sea creatures* [תַּנִּינִים] on the waters; you crushed the heads of *Leviathan* [לִוְיָתָן]." Whereas references to Leviathan are usually in passing (see Is 27:1; Ps 104:26), the extended description of Leviathan in Job 41:1-34 is unique in the Old Testament, which will prove helpful below. Using the term found in Genesis 1:21, Job asks whether he is a threatening "sea creature" (תַּנִּין) over which the Lord has set a guard (Job 7:12). Furthermore, Job 9:13; 26:12 refer to a sea monster named Rahab (רַהַב). John Day believes that "Rahab may simply be an alternative name for Leviathan."[71]

The statement "by his understanding he [= God] crushes Rahab" in Job 26:12 is suggestively followed in Job 26:13 by "his hand pierces the fleeing serpent." This is the only place where the term נָחָשׁ ("serpent")

---

[70]Fishbane, "Jeremiah IV 23-26 and Job III 3-13," 154.
[71]John Day, "God and Leviathan in Isaiah 27:1," *BSac* 155 (1998): 431.

appears in Job (see Job 20:14, 16 for other words for snake: פֶּתֶן, אֶפְעֶה), suggesting an additional connection between sea monsters and snakes. The idea that sea monsters and snakes are in effect related species from the perspective of Old Testament authors is well-supported by the usage of relevant terms.[72] For example, when Moses throws his staff on the ground, the creature it becomes is called a "serpent" (נָחָשׁ) in Exodus 4:3 and Exodus 7:15 but is called a "sea creature" (תַּנִּין) in Exodus 7:9-10, 12. Likewise, Deuteronomy 32:33 refers to the "venom of sea creatures" (תַּנִּין) and the "poison of snakes" (פֶּתֶן) in two halves of a poetic parallelism. Similarly, Psalm 91:13 parallels "the lion and the snake" (פֶּתֶן) with "the young lion and the sea creature" (תַּנִּין). Even stronger evidence is Isaiah 27:1, which, like Job 26:12-13, predicts that the Lord will slay "Leviathan, the fleeing serpent [נָחָשׁ], Leviathan, the crooked serpent [נָחָשׁ] . . . the sea creature [תַּנִּין] which is in the sea." The phrase "fleeing serpent" (נָחָשׁ בָּרִחַ) is the same phrase as in Job 26:13 (נָחָשׁ בָּרִיחַ; full spelling of בָּרִיחַ here). These passages imply that readers of the Old Testament should think of sea creatures as serpentine and snakes as amphibious (like a water snake or eel?). Indeed, standard lexicons (BDB, *HALOT*) list "serpent" as a possible meaning of תַּנִּין and cite Amos 9:3 ("if they hide from my eyes on the ocean floor, from there I will command the serpent and it will bite them") as an example of נָחָשׁ referring to a sea creature.

The inherent connection between sea monsters and serpents, which can be sustained by the Pentateuch itself, as seen above in Exodus 7:9-10, 12 and Deuteronomy 32:33, suggests that the sea creatures of Genesis 1:21 and the serpent of Genesis 3 can also be linked, even though this is not obvious from Genesis 1–3 alone. Furthermore, this connection suggests that the common theme of sea monsters in Job and Genesis 1–3 involves not only "the great sea creatures" in Genesis 1:21 but also the serpent in Genesis 3 (see Job 26:12-13), which already has a separate connection to the adversary in Job 1–2. Thus, the adversary, sea monsters, serpents, and

---

[72]Stated differently, see Elaine Phillips, "Serpent Intertexts: Tantalizing Twists in the Tales," *BBR* 10, no. 2 (2000): 239-40; René A. López, "The Meaning of 'Behemoth' and 'Leviathan' in Job," *BSac* 173 (2016): 419-22.

Satan seem intertwined. Job seems aware of Leviathan as a powerful evil force (Job 3:8) and that God has power over and can crush such sea monsters (Job 7:12; 26:12-13; see Is 51:9), but ironically, he does not know or consider the role of evil beings in his suffering.

In the final section of the Lord's answer to Job (Job 41), however, there are direct indications to the reader and even hints to Job that his adversary is Leviathan, who has been involved all along. Like the adversary and the serpent, Leviathan is proud, even "the king over all the sons of pride" (Job 41:34; and hence a stranger to wisdom, Job 28:8, 14). The Lord's special ability to humble the proud (Job 40:11-12) applies by implication to this proud beast (see Job 38:13-15; 41:11, 33).[73] The distinctive superiority of this animal ("king") to other creatures parallels the serpent being "craftier than all the animals of the field that the Lord God made" (Gen 3:1). Leviathan's scaly exterior (Job 41:15-17) and its underparts leaving a trail in the mud (Job 41:30) resemble the serpent sentenced to crawl on its belly and eat dust in Genesis 3:14.

Furthermore, unlike other animals described in Job 38–39, which at most "cry out" for food (Job 38:41), "laugh" (Job 39:7, 18, 22), or say "Aha!" (Job 39:25), Leviathan's "tongue" (לְשׁוֹן) cannot be controlled (Job 41:1), and it will never "multiply supplications" (תַּחֲנוּנִים) or "speak gentle things" to Job (Job 41:3). Though many translations of Job 41:12 ("I will not keep silence") concern Leviathan's "limbs"/"parts" (בַּדָּיו) and its "mighty strength" (דְּבַר־גְּבוּרוֹת), these two terms could instead be interpreted as referring to its "boasting" and "proud talk," that is, arrogant speech (see Job 11:3, "Will your *boasting* silence men?" [בַּדֶּיךָ מְתִים יַחֲרִישׁוּ]).[74] While some may interpret Leviathan's speech as hyperbole, there remains a suggestive correspondence with the harsh words of the adversary in Job 1–2 and the talking serpent of Genesis 3. Like the serpent

---

[73]Eric Ortlund further notes the imagery of a divine warrior in Job 40:9-14 (see Gen 3:15; Ex 15:6-7), which suggests that the Lord's second speech in Job 40–41 deals with the supernatural realm and more directly addresses the issue of justice. Ortlund, "The Identity of Leviathan and the Meaning of the Book of Job," *TJ* 34 (2013): 26-29.

[74]There is also a text-critical issue regarding the first word of Job 41:12 (Kethib: לֹא; Qere: לוֹ ["would that" or "for/concerning it/him"]; see JPS).

and the adversary, Leviathan's mouth cannot be bridled (Job 41:13; see fire from its mouth, Job 41:19, 21), and as much as one may wish to wound its head, like the serpent it is at war/enmity with humanity (Gen 3:15; Job 41:7-8). It will never make a covenant with Job, nor be his "servant forever" (Job 41:4; contra Job 5:23; Gen 1:28; Ezek 34:25; Hos 2:18). Indeed, subduing Leviathan requires divine power (Job 7:12; 26:12-13; 40:9-13), just as restraining the adversary does (Job 1:12; 2:6).[75] This suggests that, despite Job's intense pain, the Lord who sets a limit for the sea and its "proud waves" (Job 38:8-11) had also set a limit on the activities of its most fearsome creature in advance of its final defeat (see Gen 3:15; Job 7:12; 26:12-13).

To summarize, though Job may not be obviously related to Genesis 1–3 at first glance, a closer look at Job 1–2; 38–41; and some passages in between suggests that the book of Job is deeply rooted Genesis 1–3 textually and theologically. In addition to explicit creation themes in Job 38–41, the many parallels between the blessedness and testing of Job and that of Adam in the Garden of Eden show how Satan's activity and testing of the faithful can look in a postfall world. Furthermore, the close correspondence between the serpent in Genesis 3, the adversary in Job 1–2, and Leviathan in Job 41 reinforces the connection between Job and Genesis 1–3 and even illuminates the meaning of the book of Job itself. As seen above, these parallels often are not only thematic but also verbal and theological.

CONCLUSION

Despite focusing on wisdom elements in Genesis 1–3, the preceding discussion has provided a taste of the rich interconnectivity of this nexus passage. Genesis 1–3 is thus not only the introduction to the Bible but also

---

[75]See Henry Rowold, "לְי־הוּא! מִי הוּא? Leviathan and Job in Job 41:2-3," *JBL* 105 (1986): 106. Rowold further interprets Job 41:10 ("Who is he to stand against me [מִי הוּא לְפָנַי יִתְיַצָּב]?") as referring to Leviathan rather than Job. As support, he cites the "adversative sense of לְפָנֵי יִתְיַצָּב" (Deut 7:24; 9:2; 11:25; Josh 1:5) and the conflict between God and Leviathan in Ps 74:12-14 and Is 27:1. Related to my argument linking Leviathan and the adversary, I observe that the sons of God and the adversary similarly "stand before" (יָצַב עַל) the Lord in Job 1:6; 2:1.

a text that directly links to and affects many other biblical texts. As relates to the longstanding challenge of Wisdom literature for Old Testament theology, the themes, language, and theology of Genesis 1–3 provide an anchor point for Wisdom literature in the Bible. Both Genesis 1–3 and Wisdom literature emphasize creation, wisdom, humanity, and experience, while giving less attention to salvation history, Israel, covenant, and other themes more common elsewhere in the Old Testament. This is because Wisdom literature is not some rogue corpus but has been especially influenced textually and theologically by Genesis 1–3.[76]

---

[76]Examples of treatments of Wisdom literature involving other intertexts include Schipper, "'Teach Them Diligently,'" 21-34; Scott Harris, *Proverbs 1–9: A Study of Inner-Biblical Interpretation* (Atlanta: Scholars Press, 1996).

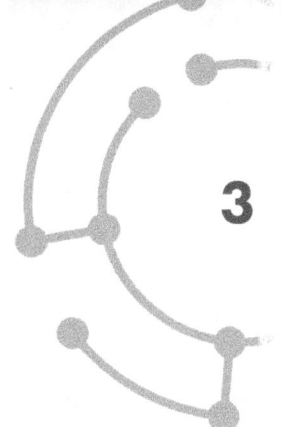

3

EXODUS 15:1-18

THE EXODUS ACCORDING TO THE SONG OF THE SEA

LIKE CREATION IN THE PREVIOUS CHAPTER, the exodus is one of the great themes in the Bible and interconnects extensively with the Pentateuch, Old Testament, and New Testament. Yair Zakovitch remarks, "No other event in the history of Israel is given so much attention by biblical writers as is the Exodus."[1] Michael Fishbane calls the exodus "the archetypal expression of [each Israelite generation's] own future hope . . . the consummate expression of divine power and national redemption."[2] As the preeminent example of historical salvation in the Old Testament, it serves in both the Old and New Testaments as a pattern that will be exceeded by eschatological salvation, a second exodus (e.g., Is 11:11-16; Jer 16:14-15; Mic 7:15-20).[3] Gerhard von Rad explains the relationship between eschatology and history insightfully: "The specific form of the new thing which they herald is not chosen at random; the new is to be effected in a way which is more or less analogous to God's former saving work."[4]

---

[1] Zakovitch adds, "The story of the Creation is no less vital." Yair Zakovitch, *"And You Shall Tell Your Son . . .": The Concept of the Exodus in the Bible* (Jerusalem: Magnes, 1991), 9; see also 97.
[2] Michael Fishbane, *Text and Texture* (New York: Schocken, 1979), 121.
[3] Some scholars distinguish between a "new exodus" (a broader term) and a "second exodus." E.g., Andrew Brunson, *Psalm 118 in the Gospel of John: An Intertextual Study on the New Exodus Pattern in the Theology of John* (Tübingen: Mohr Siebeck, 2003), 154n51.
[4] Gerhard von Rad, *Old Testament Theology*, trans. D. M. G. Stalker (Peabody, MA: Prince, 2005), 2:117. See also Zakovitch: "All the raw materials needed to construct scenarios of the future redemption are found in the tradition of the past redemption, the Exodus, sometimes amalgamated with elements borrowed from Creation traditions" (*"And You Shall Tell,"* 56-57).

Several other considerations reinforce the importance of the exodus. Miraculous events that take place in relation to it are often characterized as unprecedented (e.g., Ex 9:18, 24; 10:14; 11:6; see also Deut 34:10-12). The exodus narrative explains that the Lord's purpose in these signs was not only for Israel, including their future generations, to "know that I am the Lord" (Ex 10:2; see also Ex 13:8, 14) but also for the grander purpose "to declare my name in all the earth" (לְמַעַן סַפֵּר שְׁמִי בְּכָל־הָאָרֶץ, Ex 9:16).[5] This included Pharaoh, who declared early on, "Who is the Lord that I should obey his voice and let Israel go? I do not know the Lord" (Ex 5:2; see also Ex 8:10, 22), as well as the Egyptians who will also "know that I am the Lord" (Ex 7:5; 14:4, 18). The dispelling of ignorance through knowledge of the Lord relates thematically to the spread of the Lord's glory.[6] This theme is emphasized at the end of the exodus narrative with the Lord being "glorified" (*niphal* כָּבֵד) over Pharaoh and his army at the Re(e)d Sea in Exodus 14:4, 17-18 and the declaration, "Who is like you among the gods, Lord?" in Exodus 15:11 (see also Ex 15:14, "the peoples have heard").[7]

The literature on the exodus and/or second exodus is vast and cannot possibly be thoroughly engaged here.[8] In any case, my purpose in this chapter is not to treat the exodus merely as a theme, as rich and fruitful as that can be, but through an exodus-themed nexus passage. Naturally, there are many good options for such a nexus passage. I have chosen the Song of the Sea in Exodus 15:1-18 because it both climactically concludes the exodus narrative in Exodus 1–14 and plays a key role in the compositional

---

[5]John Durham, *Exodus*, WBC (Waco, TX: Word, 1987), 128.
[6]See L. Michael Morales, *Exodus Old and New: A Biblical Theology of Redemption* (Downers Grove, IL: InterVarsity Press, 2020), 40-43, 66.
[7]For yet another view of the Red Sea as wordplay meaning "Sea of End/Extinction," see Bernard Batto, "The Reed Sea: *Requiescat in Pace*," *JBL* 102, no. 1 (1983): 34-35. See also Walter Wifall, "The Sea of Reeds as Sheol," *ZAW* 92, no. 3 (1980): 325-32.
[8]In addition to what has been already cited above (and limiting ourselves to monographs), see, e.g., Bryan Estelle, *Echoes of Exodus: Tracing a Biblical Motif* (Downers Grove, IL: InterVarsity Press, 2018); Samuel E. Loewenstamm, *The Evolution of the Exodus Tradition*, trans. Baruch Schwartz (Jerusalem: Magnes, 1992); Fishbane, *Text and Texture*, 121-40; R. Michael Fox, ed., *Reverberations of the Exodus in Scripture* (Eugene, OR: Wipf & Stock, 2014); David Pao, *Acts and the Isaianic New Exodus* (Tübingen: Mohr Siebeck, 2000); Rikki E. Watts, *Isaiah's New Exodus in Mark*, Biblical Studies Library (Grand Rapids, MI: Baker Academic, 2000); William Webb, *Returning Home: New Covenant and Second Exodus as the Context for 2 Corinthians 6.14–7.1* (Sheffield: JSOT Press, 1993).

strategy of the Pentateuch.⁹ In this chapter, I begin with the narrative buildup to the Song of the Sea before focusing on Exodus 15:1-18 itself and its nexus connections to the Pentateuch and to the rest of the Old Testament. Even so, my analysis of the Song of the Sea in Exodus 15:1-18 and its connected passages will be necessarily selective because the connections are so numerous.

Before proceeding, I would like to remind the reader that the nexus passages in this book are often themselves interconnected. This is true of our first two nexus passages: Genesis 1–3 and Exodus 15:1-18. Sailhamer notices the common textual pattern of God preparing the land for humanity by dividing the waters, provisioning the land, and giving the land to his people.¹⁰ Thus, although I focus on other connections to the Song of the Sea, it should not be viewed in isolation from Genesis 1–3 or other nexus passages (see chapters five and eight). My discussion of Exodus 1–14 below shows some of its own intertextual connections that contribute to the plot development climaxing in Exodus 15.¹¹

EXODUS 1-14: LEAVING EGYPT

Exodus 1–15:21 is the larger literary unit that Exodus 15:1-18 concludes and as such provides essential context for the Song of the Sea. Exodus 1–14 itself has many intertextual connections, which suggest the importance of this entire section to the Pentateuch and the Old Testament. As I will show below, the exodus narrative is intertwined with themes of creation, the Abrahamic covenant, and conflict between Eve, the serpent, and their respective seed as described in Genesis 3:15. These themes in the narrative build toward their reappearance and resolution in Exodus 15:1-18. I conclude this section by comparing and contrasting

---

⁹The former claim holds up even from a source-critical perspective because the shared language between Ex 15:1-18 and its preceding narrative context "is almost evenly split between JE and P words," according to James W. Watts, *Psalm and Story: Inset Hymns in Hebrew Narrative* (Sheffield: JSOT Press, 1992), 58.

¹⁰John Sailhamer, *The Pentateuch as Narrative* (Grand Rapids, MI: Zondervan, 1992), 84.

¹¹Many other exodus-related intertextual connections exist. E.g., Sailhamer highlights parallels between Abram's sojourn in Egypt in Gen 12:10-20 and Israel's (e.g., famine, plagues, receiving possessions from the Egyptians; *Pentateuch as Narrative*, 141-43). Similarly, see Zakovitch, "And You Shall Tell," 18-20. He notes further parallels to Jacob's stay at Laban's house (46-48).

the (poetic) Song of the Sea with the narrative account of the Red Sea crossing in Exodus 14.

Following Joseph's death in Genesis 50:26, which closes the Joseph narrative in Genesis 37–50, the book of Exodus continues the story with the sons of Israel still in Egypt. The listing of "the names of the sons of Israel" in Exodus 1:1-5 serves as a link to the preceding narrative in which these sons were main characters while also preparing for a historical and narrative transition in Exodus 1:6, "Joseph died and all his brothers and all that generation." Whereas Jacob's descendants had earlier numbered seventy (Ex 1:5), the era of their long sojourn in Egypt involved tremendous numerical growth (Ex 1:7-12; see Gen 47:27).

This growth is described in ways that suggest an intentional reference to God's blessing to humanity at creation and to Abraham. Like Genesis 1:28, Exodus 1:7 states, "Now the sons of Israel were *fruitful* [פָּרָה] and increased greatly [שָׁרַץ] and *multiplied* [רָבָה] and became very, very strong. And the land was *filled* [מָלֵא] with them." The verb שָׁרַץ ("increased greatly") also appears in Genesis 1 describing creatures that "swarm" or "teem" in the water (Gen 1:20-21; see Ex 8:3) and is used in conjunction with commands to Noah and his family to be fruitful and multiply in Genesis 8:17; 9:7. As for the Abrahamic covenant, although common terms are not as obvious, Israel's dramatic numerical growth in Exodus 1:7-12 alludes to the promises to their forefather Abraham involving numerous descendants (e.g., Gen 12:2; 13:16; 15:5; 22:17), which themselves directly relate to Genesis 1:28; 9:1, 7.

Israel's "becoming strong" (עָצַם) in Exodus 1:7, even "too strong" for Pharaoh (עָצוּם מִמֶּנּוּ) in Exodus 1:9, suggestively recalls the Lord's characterization of Abraham's future descendants as "a great and *strong* [עָצוּם] nation" in Genesis 18:18 and Abimelech's request that Abraham's son Isaac move away because he had "become much too strong for us" (עָצַמְתָּ־מִמֶּנּוּ מְאֹד) in Genesis 26:16 (see Ex 1:20). Israel's great number and unstoppable multiplication permeates Exodus 1:7-12 (רַב in Ex 1:9; רָבָה also in Ex 1:10, 12; see also Ex 1:20). Even their "break[ing] forth" (פָּרַץ) in Exodus 1:12 can be traced back to the reaffirmation of the Abrahamic covenant promises to

Jacob in Genesis 28:14. The covenant with the forefathers is also explicitly cited in Exodus 2:24 and alluded to many times subsequently (see Ex 3:6, 15-16; 4:5; 6:8).

From its inception, the Abrahamic covenant was already linked to Israel's affliction and servitude in Egypt. During the formal institution of this covenant in Genesis 15:7-21, the Lord predicts that the Israelites will be slaves in a foreign country for four hundred years (Gen 15:13). Israel's enslavement in Exodus 1:11-14 not only fulfills this prophecy but does so in a way that links these two texts together lexically. Genesis 15:13 says that Israel will "serve" (עָבַד) foreigners, who will "afflict" (עָנָה) them, and Exodus 1:11-14 says twice that the Egyptians "afflict[ed]" (עָנָה) the Israelites (Ex 1:11-12) and forced them to "serve" (עָבַד, Ex 1:13-14; see עֲבֹדָה, "service"). Their "building" (בָּנָה) of "cities" (עִיר, Ex 1:11) and working with "mortar" (חֹמֶר) and "bricks" (לְבֵנָה, Ex 1:14) recalls the godless and futile construction of the Tower of Babel (Gen 11:3-4), which strikingly involves all four of these terms.[12] The implication is that Pharaoh follows in the footsteps of the proud, rebellious builders of Babel.

Likewise, his use of "sorcerers" (מְכַשְּׁפִים) and "magicians" (חַרְטֹם) with their "secret arts" (לָט) to oppose Moses and Aaron (Ex 7:11, 22; 8:7, 18) suggests Pharaoh's alignment with the demonic and hence the serpent and its seed in Genesis 3:15.[13] Reinforcing this point, Michael Morales notes the comparison of Pharaoh to a sea monster in Ezekiel 29:3; 32:2 as well as his "going out to the water" in Exodus 7:15; 8:20.[14] Thus, Pharaoh's enslavement of Israel can be seen as a prime example of the enmity mentioned in Genesis 3:15. The formal institution of the Abrahamic covenant in Genesis 15:7-21 also predicts the exodus itself (Gen 15:14) as well as hinting at it through what Morales calls an "exodus formula" in Genesis 15:7, "I am the Lord who brought you out of Ur of the Chaldeans to give you this land to inherit" (see Ex 20:2/Deut 5:6,

---

[12] See Kevin Chen, *The Messianic Vision of the Pentateuch* (Downers Grove, IL: InterVarsity Press, 2019), 147.
[13] For further discussion, see Chen, *Messianic Vision of the Pentateuch*, 157-58.
[14] Morales, *Exodus Old and New*, 56-59. For discussion of the relationship between serpents and sea monsters, see under "Genesis 1–3 and Job" in chapter two.

"I am the Lord your God who brought you out of the land of Egypt, out of the house of slaves").[15]

The contest between Pharaoh and the Lord not only involves the unseen realm and who has greater spiritual power (see Ex 8:19) but also is a contest of wisdom. Exodus 7:11 mentions Pharaoh's "wise men" (חֲכָמִים) alongside his sorcerers and magicians. Furthermore, at the outset of the exodus narrative, the new king of Egypt advises his own people, "Come, *let us act wisely* [נִתְחַכְּמָה] toward them" (Ex 1:10). If Pharaoh is indeed part of the seed of the serpent, he acts like the serpent here also by participating in a wisdom contest (see chapter two). Though the idea of enslaving Israel is put into effect, a later scheme to kill Israelite newborn boys (Ex 1:16) is outsmarted by two Hebrew midwives. The narrative says twice that Shiphrah and Puah "feared God" (Ex 1:17, 21; see Ex 14:31). Without direct calling them wise, this characterization along with their actions finds parallels with the theme of the wise woman in Proverbs (and elsewhere) and the conclusion of Ecclesiastes, "*Fear God* [אֶת־הָאֱלֹהִים יְרָא] and keep his commandments" (Eccles 12:13). The implied superior wisdom of the midwives, Moses (compared to Pharaoh's wise men), and the Lord himself shows the subtle presence of the theme of wisdom in Exodus 1–15, which may be further linked to Wisdom literature generally (see chapters two and ten). The magicians themselves later fail to match Moses and Aaron's signs and admit, "This is the finger of God" (Ex 8:18-19; see also Ex 9:11). The Lord's incomparability is also explicit in Exodus 8:10 and 9:14, a theme that peaks in the Song of the Sea in Exodus 15:11, "Who is like you among the gods, Lord?"

Echoing the contest for Adam and Eve's allegiance, the contest between Pharaoh and the Lord is about whom Israel will "serve" (עָבַד). The Lord called for the Israelites' release for the very reason that "they may serve me" (Ex 4:23; 8:1, 20; 9:1, 13; 10:3). After the Passover, when Pharaoh finally let them go to "serve the Lord" (Ex 12:31-32), he quickly regretted releasing Israel "from serving us" (Ex 14:5). The nature of

---

[15]Morales, *Exodus Old and New*, 21. The language and syntax used here are unique to these three passages.

service to Pharaoh and to the Lord radically differed (see Mt 11:28-30). Serving Pharaoh was bitter and harsh (Ex 1:14; 5:9-14; 6:9) and led to cries for help and groaning (Ex 2:23-24; 5:15). The Lord wanted to deliver Israel from such service (Ex 6:6) in this "house of slaves" (Ex 13:3, 14; 20:2). The narrative repeatedly references Israel's "burdens" (סְבָלוֹת, Ex 1:11, 2:11, 5:4-5) from which they need release (Ex 6:6-7; see Ps 81:7; Is 9:3; 10:27; 14:25).

Whereas service to Pharaoh was never-ending (Ex 5:5), serving the Lord involved offering sacrifices in the wilderness (Ex 3:18; 5:3; passim) and even celebrating a feast (Ex 5:1; 10:9), with further details to be specified by the Lord himself later (Ex 10:26; see also Ex 8:27). The mere mention of a sacrificial feast shows that serving the Lord is far better than serving Pharaoh.[16] Although celebrated initially in Egypt (see Num 9:1-5), the Passover instructions use the same language of service (Ex 12:25-26), sacrifice (Ex 12:27), and feast (Ex 12:14; see also Ex 13:5-6).[17] Accordingly, the "service" (עֲבֹדָה) of the Passover is nothing like service to Egypt, as the Passover does not depend on Israel's hard labor but rather on the Lord's power and mercy in saving their firstborns from death through the "sacrifice of the Passover" (Ex 12:25-27).

With many more instructions to come at Sinai concerning sacrifices, feasts, and obeying the Lord, the position of the Passover instructions suggests their fundamental importance. Time is reoriented based on Passover (Ex 12:2), which indicates a new beginning for Israel reminiscent of Genesis 1:1.[18] Of similar significance, the "law" (תּוֹרָה) that the Passover instructions set forth to be passed to the next generation is the gospel story

---

[16]R. Alan Cole interprets this feast as referring to "the great religious occasion of Sinai." Cole, *Exodus*, TOTC (Downers Grove, IL: InterVarsity Press, 1973), 80. Contra Durham, who interprets this as a "general destination" (*Exodus*, 40). There were certainly sacrifices offered at Sinai (Ex 24:5), but although Moses, Aaron, Nadab, Abihu, and the seventy elders "ate and drank" in the Lord's presence (Ex 24:9-11), whether or not this constitutes Israel celebrating a feast is uncertain. The Covenant Code did include direct instructions concerning the three annual feasts (Ex 23:14-17), including Passover (see Ex 12:14).

[17]The Passover has nexus connections of its own. See Chen, *Messianic Vision of the Pentateuch*, 90, 150-52. Morales also notes that a whole burnt offering signifies "utter consecration unto God," which shows "something of *how* the son of Abraham would bring about the salvation of humanity: through complete surrender and loyalty to God" (*Exodus Old and New*, 29, emphasis original).

[18]See Zakovitch, *"And You Shall Tell,"* 105.

of the Lord's salvation from Egypt (Ex 13:9). As the book of Exodus unfolds, the instructions concerning Sabbath rest further demonstrate the basic difference between serving the Lord and Pharaoh (compare the verb "to cease/rest" [שָׁבַת] in Ex 5:5 with Ex 16:30; 23:12; 34:21). One results in groaning, the other in the jubilant song of Exodus 15:1-18.

After the Passover, Pharaoh drove out the Israelites (Ex 12:31-32) but then changed his mind and pursued them in the direction of the Red Sea (Ex 14:5). The text says twice that the Lord "harden[ed] Pharaoh's heart" (Ex 14:4, 8; see also Ex 14:17) for his own glory. Despite the Israelites' fears (Ex 14:10, 13), Moses encouraged them that they would "see" the Lord's salvation (Ex 14:13), which they did (Ex 14:31). The waters were "split" (בָּקַע, Ex 14:16, 21), and the Israelites passed through (Ex 14:22, 29), whereas the Lord "looked down" (שָׁקַף) on the Egyptian army in pursuit and "confused" (הָמַם) them (Ex 14:24).[19]

One of the strongest emphases in Exodus 14 is on Pharaoh's army, which is evident through the terms "army" (חַיִל, Ex 14:4, 9, 17, 28), "chariot" (רֶכֶב, Ex 14:6-7, 9, 17-18, 23, 26, 28; see also מֶרְכָּבָה, Ex 14:25), "horse" (סוּס, Ex 14:9, 23), "horsemen" (פָּרָשׁ, Ex 14:9, 17-18, 23, 26, 28), "choice men" (בָּחוּר, Ex 14:7), and "officers" (שָׁלִישׁ, Ex 14:7). Some of this terminology carries over into the Song of the Sea (i.e., horse, rider, Ex 15:1; chariot, army, officer, Ex 15:4). The importance of the Lord's defeat of the Egyptian military is confirmed by the summary statement in Exodus 15:19 and Miriam's brief reprise in Exodus 15:21. Exodus 14 also emphasizes that Pharaoh and the Egyptians "pursue[d]" (רָדַף, Ex 14:4, 8, 9, 23) the Israelites, eventually "overtaking" them (נָשַׂג, Ex 14:9). Correspondingly, the Song of the Sea has the (generalized) "enemy" (אֹיֵב) saying, "Let me pursue, let me overtake" (אֶרְדֹּף אַשִּׂיג, Ex 14:9). Salvation terminology (יָשַׁע/יְשׁוּעָה) can also be found across Exodus 14–15 (Ex 14:13, 30; 15:2). "Spirit/wind" (רוּחַ) also appears in both texts, though the meaning changes from something encountered in the natural world in Exodus 14:21 ("east

---

[19]This corresponds to Gen 11:7 and the links between Pharaoh and Babel mentioned above. Note also the place name, Migdol, in Ex 14:2, which differs by only one vowel from the Hebrew word for "tower" (מִגְדָּל) in Gen 11:4-5.

wind") to the supernatural "breath/spirit" of the Lord in Exodus 15:8, 10 ("the breath of your nostrils," "you blew with your breath/spirit").

A more obvious difference between Exodus 14 and Exodus 15 is that the former explains Moses' role in lifting his staff or hand (Ex 14:16, 21, 26-27) and Israel's traversing the sea on "dry land" (יַבָּשָׁה, Ex 14:16, 22, 29; see also Ex 15:19), whereas the Song of the Sea does not. In fact, it is the Lord who "stretched out your right hand" in Exodus 15:12. Thus, even as Exodus 14 and preceding frequently credit the Lord and his hand for signs and wonders (e.g., Ex 3:20; 7:4-5; 9:3, 15; 14:14, 25, 30-31), the silence concerning any intermediary (including Moses and his hand, e.g., Ex 4:2, 4, 6-7; 14:16) in Exodus 15:1-18 makes it even clearer that the glory for the recent victory belongs entirely to the Lord.[20]

EXODUS 15:1-18 AS A STRATEGIC AND INTERCONNECTED TEXT WITHIN THE PENTATEUCH

The Song of the Sea in Exodus 15:1-18 is important not only as the climactic conclusion to the exodus narrative in Exodus 1–14 but also within the strategy and structure of the Pentateuch as a whole. In his study of psalms (i.e., poetry marked by praise) embedded in narrative, including Exodus 15:1-18, James Watts remarks, "Many of these poems occupy thematically climactic and structurally crucial positions in larger blocks of narrative, or even whole books." When at or near the end of a narrative section, these psalms help "bring the narrative to a climactic finale," not by advancing the plot but through their "thematic contents" and "theocentric emphasis." Accordingly, Watts sees the Song of the Sea as serving "thematic interests, concerns for large-scale narrative structure [for Ex 1–15], and a desire for close reader identification with the Israelites at the Reed Sea."[21]

Whereas Watts focuses on psalms in Old Testament narrative generally, treats other embedded poems more briefly, and does not pursue

---

[20]See Brevard Childs, *The Book of Exodus*, OTL (Louisville: Westminster, 1974), 249; Kevin Chen, *Eschatological Sanctuary in Exodus 15:17 and Related Texts* (New York: Lang, 2013), 65-67.
[21]Watts, *Psalm and Story*, 11, 187, 190, 60.

the question of the literary macrostructure of the Pentateuch, John Sailhamer argues that the Pentateuch should be viewed as one book (see 2 Chron 25:4) and is structured by means of a narrative-poetry-epilogue sequence that repeats four times and encompasses all of Genesis through Deuteronomy.[22] His proposal gives particular weight to the four major poetic sections (Gen 49:1-27 [Jacob blesses his sons]; Ex 15:1-18; Num 23:7-10, 18-24; 24:3-9, 15-24 [Balaam's oracles]; Deut 32–33 [Song of Moses and Moses blesses Israel]) not only for reasons of structure and shift in genre from narrative to poetry but also because of lexical, thematic, and plot features.

In immediate connection with all but one of these four major poetic sections (i.e., Ex 15:1-18), a main human character (i.e., Jacob, Balaam, or Moses) calls others together (קָבַץ, אָסַף, Gen 49:1-2; הָלַךְ, Num 24:14; קָהַל, Deut 31:28) to tell them ("declare," Gen 49:1; "counsel," Num 24:14; "speak/bear witness," Deut 31:28) what will happen "in the last days" (בְּאַחֲרִית הַיָּמִים, Gen 49:1; Num 24:14; Deut 31:29).[23] Coupled with a pause in the story line, these important messages subtly draw the reader into the audience as well.[24] If this is not accidental but a strategic aspect of the Pentateuch's literary macrostructure, then the implication is that, for all its attention to history and law, the Pentateuch also has eschatology at the core of its theology.[25] This eschatological element is communicated not only through these major poetic sections but also through other key texts in the Pentateuch (e.g., Gen 3:15; Deut 4:30). The same three poetic sections also involve the themes of blessing (Gen 49:25-26, 28; Num 22:6;

---

[22]Sailhamer, *Pentateuch as Narrative*, 35-37; John Sailhamer, *The Meaning of the Pentateuch* (Downers Grove, IL: InterVarsity Press, 2009), 36, 323-25.

[23]The meaning of this phrase is disputed, but there remains sufficient evidence for understanding it in the traditional, eschatological sense (see LXX, KJV). See discussion in chapter four and in Chen, *Messianic Vision of the Pentateuch*, 109-14. See also Stephen Dempster, "'At the End of the Days' (בְּאַחֲרִית הַיָּמִים)—An Eschatological Technical Term? The Intersection of Context, Linguistics and Theology," in *The Unfolding of Your Words Gives Light: Studies on Biblical Hebrew in Honor of George L. Klein*, ed. Ethan Jones (University Park, PA: Eisenbrauns, 2018), 118-41.

[24]Two scholars see a parallel between these poems and the use of songs in a musical play. See Watts, *Psalm and Story*, 187; Sailhamer, *Meaning of the Pentateuch*, 34, 242-43, 278, 322.

[25]Recall Gerhard von Rad's comment concerning history and eschatology at the beginning of this chapter.

24:1, 9-10; Deut 33:1) and wisdom (Gen 49:1-2; Num 23:7, passim [Balaam's proverbs; see chapter four]; Deut 31:19, 22; 32:1-2), suggesting that the Pentateuch's eschatology is intertwined with these two important themes.[26] Blessing, wisdom, and eschatology (Gen 3:15) also appear together in Genesis 1–3.

Moreover, the eschatological perspective of the Pentateuch is not some vague notion but is focused on the Messiah.[27] It is no accident that what Jacob says will happen "in the last days" (Gen 49:1) focuses on a king from the line of Judah who will rule his brothers and the nations (Gen 49:8-12) and that Balaam likewise warns Balak concerning an Israelite king who will crush Israel's enemies "in the last days" (Num 24:14-19). Both this "Lion of Judah" prophecy (Gen 49:8-12) and "star from Jacob" prophecy (Num 24:17-19) appear in major poetic sections, suggesting that a specifically *messianic* eschatology is central to the Pentateuch. Likewise, although I will not go into detail here about the obscure and disputed Deuteronomy 33:7 ("Hear, Lord, the voice of Judah, and bring him to his people.... Be a help against his adversaries"), a messianic interpretation can make sense of the verse itself, especially in relation to the parallel blessing of Judah in Genesis 49:8-12.[28] Even if Deuteronomy 33:7 were not heavily relied on, Genesis 49:8-12 and Numbers 24:14-17 would still be largely sufficient for demonstrating the messianic eschatology of the Pentateuch through its major poems.

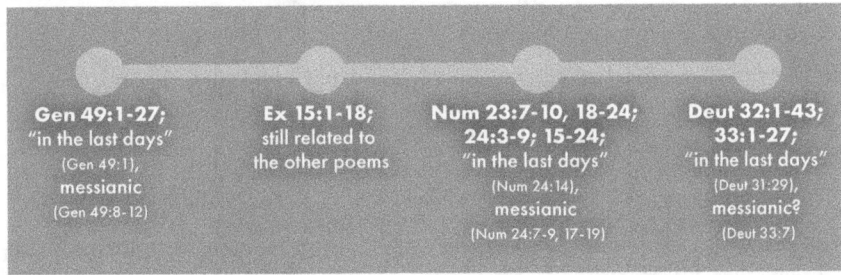

Figure 3.1. The major poems/poetic sections of the Pentateuch

---

[26]My student Sister Wang pointed out the theme of blessing in these passages to me.
[27]Sailhamer, *Meaning of the Pentateuch*, 36-37.
[28]Chen, *Messianic Vision of the Pentateuch*, 253-57.

The very poems that are the most important to Sailhamer's proposal for the messianic theology of the Pentateuch are treated more briefly by Watts as "other poems" because they do not meet his criteria of being psalms characterized by praise, even though he still sees Genesis 49:1-27 as serving a similar purpose and the poetry in Numbers 23–24 perhaps also.[29] Watts does treat Deuteronomy 32:1-43 at length and sees it as "creat[ing] a climactic effect at the end of Deuteronomy (and the Pentateuch)," but the gap between the two approaches remains.[30] Watts's interest in psalms in Old Testament narrative broadly leads him to recognize only a "theocentric" emphasis (which does fit Ex 15:1-18; Deut 32:1-43), whereas Sailhamer's focus on major poems (a broader category than psalms) in the Pentateuch leads to an eschatological, messianic emphasis. Sailhamer's argument for the messianic theology of the Pentateuch based on its major poetic sections has similarities to Brevard Childs's argument that the framing poems in 1 Samuel 2 and 2 Samuel 22 "establish a dominant eschatological, messianic perspective for the whole [of 1–2 Samuel]."[31] Whereas critical scholars have sometimes seen 2 Samuel 22–23 as a conscious imitation of Deuteronomy 32–33 within the framework of a so-called Deuteronomistic History, pentateuchal priority and textual evidence (Num 24:7/1 Sam 2:10/2 Sam 22:47; Num 24:2-4, 15-16/ 2 Sam 23:1-2) would suggest that this dependence extends to other poems in the Pentateuch.[32]

The messianic eschatology of the Pentateuch will be revisited in the next chapter, but the preceding shows the importance of Exodus 15:1-18 as a major poem within the macrostructure of the Pentateuch. Even though it

---

[29] Watts, *Psalm and Story*, 171-73, including n2.

[30] Watts, *Psalm and Story*, 80. Giving more weight to comparative evidence from the ancient Near East for Ex 15; Judg 5; and Deut 32 (i.e., Piye Stela, Ahiqar), Steven Weitzman derives the significance of these early examples of embedded poetry from these parallels, which later resulted in the revision of a few biblical texts to conform with them (Is 38:9-20; Prayer of Azariah in Dan 3 LXX; 1 Chron 16:7-36). See Weitzman, *Song and Story in Biblical Narrative: The History of a Literary Convention in Ancient Israel* (Bloomington: Indiana University Press, 1997). Though distinct from Watts's method and results, this critical approach does not begin with or eventually give attention to the literary macrostructure of the Pentateuch either.

[31] Brevard Childs, *Introduction to the Old Testament as Scripture* (Philadelphia: Fortress, 1979), 278; see also 272-75. He is followed by Watts, *Psalm and Story*, 115, who includes 2 Sam 23:1-7.

[32] For critical scholars, see Watts, *Psalm and Story*, 110-11, 116.

does not appear in conjunction with "in the last days" or contain a messianic prophecy, the Song of the Sea concludes a narrative section and has connections to the other three major poetic sections (Gen 49:1-27; Num 23–24; Deut 32–33). In Exodus 15:1, a main human character (Moses), though not gathering people together (they are already gathered), still declares an important message through poetry involving other characters in the narrative ("the sons of Israel"). Similarly, Miriam "the prophetess" follows her brother's song with a shorter version, in which she leads "all the women" (Ex 15:20-21). Whereas Exodus 15:1-12 in the Song of the Sea retrospectively celebrates the Lord's recent victory, the remainder of the song in Exodus 15:13-18 looks forward to how the Lord will lead his redeemed people through danger to "your holy dwelling" (נְוֵה קָדְשֶׁךָ, Ex 15:13) and "the mountain of your inheritance" (הַר נַחֲלָתְךָ, Ex 15:17). The arrival of the Lord's people at their destination depicts the fulfillment of the Abrahamic covenant promise of land, which was shown in the previous section to be central to the exodus narrative (Ex 3:6-8, 15-17).

The end of the song looks all the way to the everlasting reign of the Lord (Ex 15:18, "the Lord will reign forever and ever"; see Ps 146:10), which complements the prophecies of the Messiah's reign "in the last days" in the other major poems.[33] Whereas the everlasting nature of the Messiah's rule seems assumed in Genesis 49:1, 8-12 and Numbers 24:14, 17-19, it is explicit in Isaiah 9:7, which describes his kingdom as having "no end" (אֵין־קֵץ) and lasting "from now until forever" (מֵעַתָּה וְעַד־עוֹלָם). When viewed together, Daniel 2:44-45 ("the *God of heaven* will establish a kingdom which will never be destroyed. . . . It will stand forever") and Daniel 7:13-14 ("*his dominion* [i.e., the son of man's] is an everlasting dominion. . . . His kingdom is one that will not be destroyed") confirm that the Lord's everlasting kingdom and the Messiah's everlasting kingdom are the same kingdom.

Furthermore, the depiction of the Lord as "a man of war" (אִישׁ מִלְחָמָה, Ex 15:3) who defeats his "enemy" (אֹיֵב, Ex 15:6, 9) in the Song of the

---

[33] Sailhamer, *Pentateuch as Narrative*, 271: "As with the other poetic texts, Moses' central concern is with the future King who will reign over God's kingdom."

Sea resembles that of the Messiah who defeats his "enemies" (צָר/אֹיֵב; Num 24:8, 17-19; Deut 33:7; see also Gen 49:8) in the other major poems. In the literary context preceding Exodus 15, the root איב only appears in Genesis 3:15 ("enmity"); Genesis 22:17 ("gate of his enemies"); and Genesis 49:8 ("your hand will be on the neck of your enemies"), all key prophecies of messianic salvation.[34] Sailhamer observes that "Your right hand, Lord, *shatters the enemy*" (תִּרְעַץ אוֹיֵב) in Exodus 15:6 recalls the striking of the serpent's head in Genesis 3:15, which is a foundational text for the major poems (see chapter four).[35] It is as though the defeat of Pharaoh, likely a member of the serpent's seed (see above), is meant by the author of the Pentateuch to be a foretaste of the final victory of the seed of the woman over the serpent. Psalm 74:13 seems to confirm this: "You divided the sea by your strength; you broke the heads of the sea monsters on the waters."[36] The preceding also suggests that final victory is equally attributed to both the Lord and the seed of the woman.

Another suggestive connection between the Song of the Sea, the other major poems, and Genesis 1–3 involves "You will bring them and *plant them* [נָטַע]on the mountain of your inheritance" in Exodus 15:17. The only other texts in the Pentateuch where the Lord plants something are Genesis 2:8 and Numbers 24:6. In Genesis 2:8, the Lord God "plants" a garden in Eden. Furthermore, just as the Lord God "took" (לָקַח) the man and "gave rest" (*hiphil* נוּחַ) to him in the garden (Gen 2:15), so he "brings" his people and "plants" them on a mountain in Exodus 15:17. Ezekiel 28:13-14 even links "Eden, the garden of God" with "the holy mountain of God," strengthening this connection.[37] Exodus 15:17 thus seems to be saying that the Lord will bring his redeemed "people" (עַם, Ex 15:13, 16; they are not

---

[34]For more on Gen 3:15; 49:8, see chapter four. For Gen 22:17b, see T. Desmond Alexander, "Further Observations on the Term 'Seed' in Genesis," *TynBul* 48, no. 2 (1997): 363-67.

[35]Sailhamer, *Pentateuch as Narrative*, 271; Chen, *Messianic Vision of the Pentateuch*, 77 (fig. 2.1).

[36]Although it is hard to be sure, we may wonder whether Ps 74:13 and Ezek 29:3/Ezek 32:2 (see above) are reading the Pentateuch and linking Pharaoh to sea monsters based on the Pentateuch's casting of Pharaoh as a member of the seed of the serpent.

[37]If Gen 2:8 and Ex 15:17 are strategically related in the Pentateuch, they support the connection made in Ezek 28:13-14.

referred to as "Israel" in the song) back to the Garden of Eden, except now the people themselves are like trees also (see Ps 1:3). Sailhamer points out that God's acts of making and establishing a sanctuary with his own hands (Ex 15:17) are additional links to creation in Genesis 1–2.[38]

As will be discussed in chapter ten, Proverbs also describes creation as an act of divine building, using similar language and themes (compare יָסַד, כּוּן, עָשָׂה, אָמֵץ, עָזַז, and מוֹסָד in Prov 3:19; 8:26-29 to פָּעַל, מָכוֹן, and כּוּן in Ex 15:17). The divinely established sanctuary in Exodus 15:17 thus may involve *new* creation themes as well (see Ex 15:16, "the people which you *acquired* [קָנָה]"; Is 28:16, "Behold, I lay a foundation [יָסַד] stone in Zion").[39] Exodus 15:17 thus depicts the Lord as a builder-planter of a garden-sanctuary (see 2 Sam 7:10-13; Jer 1:10). Creation themes also feature in Exodus 1–14, as noted previously.

The planting in Numbers 24:6 fits seamlessly with the plantings of Genesis 2:8 and Exodus 15:17. It appears in a major poetic section in Balaam's third speech, which shifts attention to the Messiah (Num 24:7b-9; see chapter four). Balaam praises Israel's tents and dwellings (Num 24:5) and characterizes them in Edenic fashion, "like *gardens by the river* [גַּנֹּת עֲלֵי נָהָר], like aloes the Lord *planted* [נָטַע], like cedars by the water" (Num 24:6). Eden also had a river (Gen 2:10), and, recalling Exodus 15:17, the Lord "plants" Israel's tents like Edenic trees in a perfect location. Also linking Exodus 15 and Numbers 24 are the terms "possess/possession" (יְרֵשָׁה/יָרַשׁ). In Exodus 15:9, the enemy's attempt to "possess" is thwarted, but in Numbers 24:18, the Messiah makes enemies his "possession" in fulfillment of the Abrahamic covenant promises (Gen 15:4; 22:17; 24:60). The "peoples"/"nations" (גּוֹיִם/עַמִּים) are also found in both poetic sections, as well as others (Gen 27:29; 49:10; Ex 15:14; Num 24:8, 20; Deut 32:43; 33:3, 17, 19).

In addition to its strategic importance to the literary macrostructure of the Pentateuch and its interconnection with the other major poetic sections, the Song of the Sea in Exodus 15:1-18 is also important because

---

[38] Sailhamer, *Meaning of the Pentateuch*, 577.
[39] For more discussion of Ex 15:17, see Chen, *Eschatological Sanctuary in Exodus 15:17*.

it appears in conjunction with the faith theme in the Pentateuch.[40] Exodus 14:31 concluded the narrative account of the Red Sea crossing in a resoundingly positive way, "And the people feared the Lord and *believed* [אָמַן] in the Lord and in his servant Moses." Their great fear of the Egyptians (Ex 14:10; see also Ex 14:13) was no more, and they returned to the faith that they had shown in their better moments (Ex 4:31, "the people believed [אָמַן]"). Although the faith theme as expressed through the verb אָמַן does not appear frequently in the Pentateuch, Hans-Christoph Schmitt argues for the significance of this theme based on its appearance not only in Exodus 1–14 but also centrally in the patriarchal narratives (Gen 15:6), the Sinai narrative (Ex 19:9), and the wilderness narrative (Num 14:11; 20:12).[41] Considered along with the macrostructure of the Pentateuch, the Song of the Sea is the only major poetic section that also appears in conjunction with the faith theme as expressed through the verb אָמַן (see Deut 32:4, 20). Accordingly, Childs calls the Song of the Sea "the response of faith" by redeemed Israel (see Ps 106:12).[42]

There may not be a more positive moment for Israel's spiritual state in the recorded history of the Old Testament than Exodus 14:31. They saw the Lord's mighty hand, feared him, and believed in him. The song is thus likely intended as a paradigmatic expression of faith. Within the Pentateuch, it is also the only major poem voiced by a group. The only other "songs" (שִׁיר/שִׁירָה) in the Pentateuch are the brief one in Numbers 21:17-18 and the song that testifies of Israel's future rebellion in Deuteronomy 32:1-43 (see Deut 31:19-22, 30). Childs calls Exodus 15:1-18 a hymn and notes "striking parallels in form and content with those [hymns] of the Psalter" (e.g., Ps 77:14, 16; 89:14-15; 93:1-2; 95:3; 96:5; 98:2).[43] Suggestively, many of the parallels Childs cites are from Psalms 93–100, which

---

[40]For this theme, see Hans-Christoph Schmitt, "Redaktion des Pentateuch im Geiste der Prophetie," *VT* 32 (1982): 170-89.
[41]Schmitt, "Redaktion des Pentateuch," 176-77.
[42]Childs, *Book of Exodus*, 248. He is speaking in terms of the final form of the text, not the possible prehistory of Ex 15:1-18 "in its independent state." Ps 106:12 links Ex 14:31 and Ex 15:1 in exactly this way.
[43]Childs, *Book of Exodus*, 250.

emphasize the kingship of the Lord like Exodus 15:18 does. The majesty of the Lord or of the circumstances surrounding his mighty acts are a major theme in Exodus 15:1-18. He is "highly exalted" (גָּאֹה גָּאָה, Ex 15:1; see also Ex 15:21) and acted in "majesty" (גָּאוֹן, Ex 15:7). He himself is "majestic" (אָדַר, Ex 15:11), as is his right hand (Ex 15:6) as well as the waters (Ex 15:10). There is no one like him, "awesome in praises, doing wonders" (Ex 15:11). Whereas his enemies are thrown down (הָרַס) and sink like "stone"/"lead" into the bottom of the sea (Ex 15:4, 5, 7, 10), the Lord is lifted up by his people (Ex 15:2).[44]

The Song of the Sea thus proclaims the glory of the Lord in salvation and is unmatched as such within the Pentateuch. If the Lord's redeemed people glorifying him together in song is as important as the Psalter says, then the Song of the Sea provides both a strong formal and thematic link between the Pentateuch and the Psalter and a glimpse into the ultimate destiny of the Lord's people. We will praise him together forever (e.g., Ps 115:18; 145:1-2). In the context of Exodus 1–14, the sequence of suffering, outcry, divine response, and praise also maps to the same pattern in lament psalms.

The preceding shows the importance and interconnectivity of Exodus 15:1-18 within its own book, the Pentateuch. The Song of the Sea is a primary feature of the Pentateuch's literary macrostructure as the second of four major poetic sections. Although it lacks the phrase "in the last days" and an explicit messianic thrust, it still has significant connections to the other three major poetic sections. Exodus 15:1-18 also has its own distinct features through its combination with a climactic expression of the Pentateuch's faith theme (Ex 14:31) and extended proclamation of the Lord's glory in song. As a nexus passage, the Song of the Sea has numerous connections within the Pentateuch and to the rest of the Old Testament.

Recognizing that there are more passages than there is space to deal with, the following sections treat a few notable passages from other Old

---

[44]Danilo Verde, "'Who Is Like You Among the Gods, O YHWH?' (Exod 15,11): The Interweaving of Metaphors in the Song of the Sea," in *Networks of Metaphors in the Hebrew Bible*, ed. Danilo Verde and Antje Labahn (Leuven: Peeters, 2020), 16-17.

Testament books that are intertextually related to Exodus 15:1-18.[45] I am not simply looking for exodus themes generally but instead for literary and textual relationships to the Song of the Sea. This is why I will not treat, for example, the crossing of the Jordan in Joshua 3–4, which has obvious parallels to the crossing of the Red Sea (e.g., Josh 4:23-24) but is not strongly dependent on Exodus 15:1-18.[46]

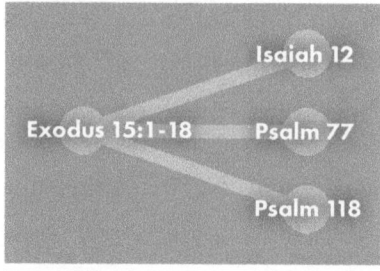

Figure 3.2. Select nexus connections from Exodus 15:1-18 to other Old Testament books

THE SONG OF THE SEA AND ISAIAH 12

Like Exodus 15:1-18, Isaiah 12 concludes the larger literary unit of which it is a part, Isaiah 6–12.[47] The predominance of poetry in Isaiah, on the other hand, means that the preceding context of Isaiah 12 is not a sequential narrative like Exodus 1–14 (though see narrative portions in Is 6–8). The poetry in Isaiah does not proceed in a uniformly linear fashion but includes sudden topic switches from judgment to salvation and vice versa (e.g., multiple topic switches in Is 1:26–2:6). However, Alec Motyer points out that the "song" in Isaiah 12, like others in Isaiah, is "placed with exactitude."[48] Proportionally, there is more space given to judgment than salvation in Isaiah 6–12, as in much of the book of Isaiah. While there certainly are salvation passages in the preceding context (e.g., Is 1:26b-27; 2:1-4; 4:2-5; 7:14-15; 9:1-7; 10:20-21), Isaiah 11–12 is notable as a lengthy one that climactically concludes Isaiah 6–12.

In addition to a strongly hopeful outlook and common vocabulary and themes, the repetition of "in that day" in Isaiah 11:10, 11; 12:1, 4 (see also Is 10:20, 27) seems to tie Isaiah 11:10–12:6 to the scene described in

---

[45]For texts that relate specifically to Ex 15:17 and to a certain extent Ex 15:13-18, see Chen, *Eschatological Sanctuary in Exodus 15:17*. In this chapter, I intentionally chose texts that I have not treated at length elsewhere.
[46]For discussion, see Fishbane, *Text and Texture*, 122-25.
[47]Occasionally scholars instead take Is 1–12 as a unit.
[48]J. Alec Motyer, *The Prophecy of Isaiah* (Downers Grove, IL: InterVarsity Press, 1993), 127. See also Hans-Peter Mathys, *Dichter und Beter: Theologen aus spätalttestamentlichere Zeit* (Göttingen: Vandenhoeck & Ruprecht, 1994), 184-85; Allan Harman, *Isaiah* (Fearn, UK: Christian Focus, 2005), 113. Harman believes that Is 12 is a fitting conclusion to Is 1–12.

Isaiah 11:1-9.[49] This scene centers on "a shoot from the stump of Jesse" (Is 11:1), on whom the Spirit of the Lord rests (Is 11:2). He judges righteously (Is 11:3-5) and brings a peace to creation that surpasses even what was experienced in Eden (Is 11:6-8). All of this takes place at the Lord's "holy mountain," and knowledge of him will finally fill the earth (Is 11:9). The Davidic king promised here would seem to be the same one as the "Prince of Peace" who sits "on the throne of David" in Isaiah 9:6-7. Whereas some scholars interpret these passages as referring to historical (preexilic) Davidic kings, the predictions of a perfect king and kingdom better suit the Messiah and the messianic kingdom.[50]

A messianic interpretation of Isaiah 11:1-9 fits the subsequent context, including Isaiah 12. The "root of Jesse" in Isaiah 11:10 (שֹׁרֶשׁ יִשַׁי), which continues the image of new growth from Jesse in Isaiah 11:1, is sought out not only by Israel but by the nations, similar to the way the nations seek the Lord in Isaiah 2:2-4.[51] In turn, the glory of the "resting place" of "the root of Jesse" in Isaiah 11:10 parallels the glory of the "branch of the Lord" in Isaiah 4:2. Following the messianic prophecies of Isaiah 11:1-10 are the prophecies of a second exodus in Isaiah 11:11-16. This connection can be seen not only through the repetition of "in that day" in Isaiah 11:10 and Isaiah 11:11 but also through the Lord lifting "a banner for the nations" (נֵס לַגּוֹיִם) in Isaiah 11:12 that has just been identified as the root of Jesse, who "stands as a banner of the peoples" (עֹמֵד לְנֵס עַמִּים) in Isaiah 11:10 (see the "banner" [נֵס] on which the bronze snake is set in Num 21:8-9). Thus the Lord's work of gathering his people "a second time" not only from Egypt but also from Assyria and many other places (Is 11:11) is centered on the Messiah, to whom Israel and the nations will rally (Is 11:12). The reality of a second exodus is clearest in Isaiah 11:15-16, where the Lord makes a "highway" (מְסִלָּה) through waters for "the remnant of his people" (see Is 11:11; 7:3; 10:20-22), "just as there was for Israel when he brought them up from the land of Egypt."

---

[49]Barry Webb, *The Message of Isaiah*, Bible Speaks Today (Downers Grove, IL: InterVarsity Press, 1996), 74, 77; Motyer, *Prophecy of Isaiah*, 120-21, 127.

[50]John Oswalt, *The Book of Isaiah: Chapters 1–39*, NICOT (Grand Rapids, MI: Eerdmans, 1986), 277-78. As an example of interpreting these texts as referring to historical kings, see Andrew Abernethy and Gregory Goswell, *God's Messiah in the Old Testament* (Grand Rapids, MI: Baker, 2020), 85, 98.

[51]Webb, *Message of Isaiah*, 76.

Isaiah 11:11-16 itself has connections to the Song of the Sea. In Isaiah 11:11, the Lord uses "his hand" a second time "to *acquire* [קָנָה] the remnant of his people [עַם]." The only other Old Testament passage that combines exodus themes with the Lord's acquisition of a people is Exodus 15:16, which refers to "the people that you acquired" (עַם־זוּ קָנִיתָ).[52] By implication, Exodus 15:16 shows that the exodus was the first time the Lord acquired his people. A worldwide scope is also common to both Isaiah 11:11-16 and the Song of the Sea. The gathering of the Lord's people from a listing of nations, even "the four corners of the earth" in Isaiah 11:11-12, parallels the reference to peoples, Philistia, Edom, Moab, and Canaan in Exodus 15:14-15 (see Is 11:14). The question "Who is like you among the gods, Lord?" (Ex 15:11) also has worldwide significance and expresses a sentiment similar to many passages in Isaiah (e.g., Is 2:8-22; 46:1-7).

Isaiah 12 is the response of the individual ("you [singular] will say in that day," Is 12:1) and of the Lord's people ("you [plural] will say in that day," Is 12:4) to the salvation described in the previous context. This broadly parallels Exodus 15:1-18, which is Moses and the Israelites' response to the Lord's salvation at the Red Sea. The strongest evidence for an intertextual relationship between these two texts is the nearly verbatim repetition of "Yah is my strength and song, and he has become my salvation" (עָזִּי וְזִמְרָת יָהּ וַיְהִי־לִי לִישׁוּעָה) from Exodus 15:2 in Isaiah 12:2 (which adds "the Lord" [יְהוָה] after "Yah"). Motyer remarks on Isaiah 12:2, "The words are from Exodus 15:2."[53] Harman sees both Isaiah 12:2 and Isaiah 12:5 ("Make music to the Lord, for he has done majestic things" [זַמְּרוּ יְהוָה כִּי גֵאוּת עָשָׂה]; cf. Ex 15:21) as alluding to the Song of the Sea.[54] Commentators further suggest that the drawing of water in Isaiah 12:3 relates to the Lord's provision of water in the subsequent wilderness narrative (e.g., Ex 15:22-27; 17:1-7).[55]

There are still more links between Isaiah 12 and Exodus 15:1-18. "Salvation" (יְשׁוּעָה) is mentioned twice more in Isaiah 12:2-3 (see Ex 14:13,

---

[52]Deut 32:6 also describes the Lord as having acquired Israel but without clear exodus themes.
[53]Motyer, *Prophecy of Isaiah*, 129. Webb calls this "an almost exact quotation" (*Message of Isaiah*, 77).
[54]Harman, *Isaiah*, 113.
[55]Motyer, *Prophecy of Isaiah*, 129; Oswalt, *Book of Isaiah: Chapters 1–39*, 294.

30) and elicits music and joy in both contexts (Ex 15:1-2, 20-21; Is 12:3, 5-6). Although Isaiah 12:1 refers to the Lord's anger turning away and Exodus 15:1 to the Lord's recent military victory, both texts use first-person singular verbs that express or directly relate to praising the Lord (Ex 15:1-2, "I will sing [אָשִׁירָה].... I will praise him [וְאַנְוֵהוּ].... I will exalt him [וַאֲרֹמְמֶנְהוּ]"; Is 12:1-2, "I will praise you [אוֹדְךָ].... I will trust and not be afraid [אֶבְטַח וְלֹא אֶפְחָד]").[56] Both texts use a less common term אֵל to refer to God (Ex 15:2; Is 12:2) and glorify the Lord and "his name" (שְׁמוֹ, Ex 15:3; Is 12:4) on an international scale (see "peoples" [עַמִּים] in Ex 15:14; Is 12:4). The Lord having "done majestic things" (גֵאוּת עָשָׂה) in Isaiah 12:5 seems to draw on his "doing wonders" (עֹשֵׂה פֶלֶא) in Exodus 15:11 and his majesty as expressed in Exodus 15:1, 7 (see גָּאוֹן/גָּאָה). The Lord who is "majestic in holiness [קֹדֶשׁ]" in Exodus 15:11 is likewise called "the Holy One [קְדוֹשׁ] of Israel" in Isaiah 12:6, as he often is in Isaiah. Both Exodus 15:1-18 and Isaiah 12 conclude similarly, with the Lord dwelling in the midst of Zion or a sanctuary (Ex 15:17; Is 12:6).

Table 3.1. Links between Exodus 15:1-18 and Isaiah 12

	Exodus 15:1-18	**Isaiah 12**
"Yah is my strength and my song, and he has become my salvation"	Ex 15:2	Is 12:2
Music and joy	"sing to the Lord" (Ex 15:1, 21), "song" (Ex 15:2), dancing (Ex 15:20)	"song" (Is 12:2), "joy" (Is 12:3), "Make music to the Lord" (Is 12:5a)
"Salvation"	Ex 15:2 (see also Ex 14:13, 30)	Is 12:2-3
"I will . . ."	"I will sing. . . . I will praise him. . . . I will exalt him" (Ex 15:1-2)	"I will praise you. . . . I will trust and not be afraid" (Is 12:1-2)
"God" (as אֵל) and "his name"	Ex 15:2-3	Is 12:2, 4
The Lord's majesty and majestic works	"he is highly exalted" (Ex 15:1), "majesty" (Ex 15:7), "doing wonders," "majestic in holiness" (Ex 15:11)	"done majestic things" (Is 12:5), "the Holy One of Israel" (Is 12:6)
Temple or Zion	"the sanctuary . . . your hands established" (Ex 15:17)	"shout for joy, inhabitant of Zion" (Is 12:6)

---

[56]Motyer links the turning away of divine wrath in Is 12:1 to the Isaiah's visionary experience of atonement in Is 6:1-7 (*Prophecy of Isaiah*, 127).

The overflowing joy expressed in Isaiah 12 along with its many links to Exodus 15:1-18 demonstrates that there is much in the Song of the Sea that typifies the Lord's salvation generally, including eschatological salvation. Furthermore, the "crossing over" (עָבַר) of the Lord's people as terrified peoples look on in Exodus 15:14-16 is not necessarily a simple prophecy of crossing the Jordan under Joshua. Norbert Lohfink notes that whereas the Song of the Sea is silent concerning Israel's passage through the Red Sea, it does emphasize their passage through the "peoples" (Ex 15:14; see Ex 15:16, "until your people, Lord, cross over, until the people you acquired cross over").[57] Whereas he sees the Song as "open-ended" and intended to encompass every act of the Lord's salvation, the people's trembling (רָגַז, רָעַד), writhing (חִיל), terror (בָּהַל, אֵימָה, פַּחַד), melting (מוּג), and becoming like a stone (יִדְּמוּ כָּאָבֶן) especially fit an eschatological context (Ex 15:14-16; see Is 13:7-8; 33:14; 64:1; Hab 3:7; Ps 2:5, 11; 48:5-6; 99:1).[58] Either way, the combination of praise, music, joy, and salvation suggests that Isaiah 12 is a sort of new song (Ps 96:1; 98:1) patterned after the Song of the Sea. As Barry Webb notes, the singing in Isaiah 12 follows an exodus (Is 11:15-16) just as the Song of the Sea does.[59] Thus, there appears to have been careful engagement not only with the Song of the Sea but also with its narrative context.

THE SONG OF THE SEA AND PSALMS 77; 118

Psalm 77 extensively draws on the Song of the Sea in the latter half of the psalm. In the first half, the psalmist cries out to the Lord in distress (Ps 77:1-4) and thinks on the past (Ps 77:5-6). In response to questions about the Lord's apparent rejection and failure to show love, grace, and compassion (Ps 77:7-9), the psalmist consoles himself by remembering the Lord's saving acts of the past (Ps 77:10-20), particularly the exodus (Ps 77:15-20). Close attention to Psalm 77:10-20 reveals that the psalmist is recalling the exodus especially through the lens of the Song of the Sea.

---

[57]Norbert Lohfink, *The Christian Meaning of the Old Testament*, trans. R. A. Wilson (Milwaukee: Bruce, 1968), 81-84.
[58]See Chen, *Eschatological Sanctuary in Exodus 15:17*, 49-52.
[59]Webb, *Message of Isaiah*, 77. See also discussion of Mic 7 in relation to Jon 2 in chapter eight.

The language used in Psalm 77:10-20 often parallels language that specifically characterizes Exodus 15:1-18. For example, the psalmist thinks back on "the years of the *right hand* [יְמִין] of the Most High" (Ps 77:10). Although the Lord's "hand" (יָד) appears frequently in Exodus 1–15, his "right hand" is unique to Exodus 15:6, 12. As he calls to mind "the deeds of *Yah* [יָהּ]" (Ps 77:12), he uses a title for the Lord that is unique to Exodus 15:2 within Exodus 1–15.

To these lexical links may be added "wonder"/"doing wonders" (עֹשֵׂה פֶלֶא/פֶּלֶא, Ps 77:11, 14; Ex 15:11), "work"/"made" (פָּעַל, Ps 77:12; Ex 15:17), "in holiness" (בַּקֹּדֶשׁ, Ps 77:13; Ex 15:11), "peoples" (עַמִּים, Ps 77:14; Ex 15:14), "strength" (עֹז, Ps 77:14; Ex 15:2, 13), "writh[ing]" (חִיל, Ps 77:16; Ex 15:14), "tremble" (רָגַז, Ps 77:16, 18; Ex 15:14), and "depths" (תְּהֹמוֹת, Ps 77:16; Ex 15:5, 8).[60] Although not involving terms exclusively traceable to the Song of the Sea, the similarities between "Who is a great god like God?" (מִי־אֵל גָּדוֹל כֵּאלֹהִים) in Psalm 77:13 and "Who is like you among the gods, Lord?" (מִי־כָמֹכָה בָּאֵלִם יְהוָה) in Exodus 15:11; "You redeemed your people with your arm" (גָּאַלְתָּ בִּזְרוֹעַ עַמֶּךָ) in Psalm 77:15 and "the people you redeemed" (עַם־זוּ גָּאָלְתָּ) in Exodus 15:13 (see "arm" in Ex 15:16); and "in many waters" (בְּמַיִם רַבִּים) in Psalm 77:19 and "in majestic waters" (בְּמַיִם אַדִּירִים) in Exodus 15:10 are also notable.

These extensive lexical and thematic links, along with the fact that the text involves a recollection of a past work of salvation by the Lord, strongly suggests that Psalm 77:10-20 is remembering the exodus specifically via the Song of the Sea. This does not exclude additional intertextual connections to passages such as Psalm 18:7-17 and Habakkuk 3:10-12.[61] Michael Wilcock is confident that Psalm 77 alludes in detail to the Song of the Sea.[62]

---

[60]Not only are the only two occurrences of "doing wonders" (עֹשֵׂה פֶלֶא) in these two texts (Ex 15:11; Ps 77:14), but Ps 78:12 suggestively has the similar "he did wonders" (עָשָׂה פֶלֶא). See Robert L. Cole, *The Shape and Message of Book III (Psalms 73–89)* (Sheffield: Sheffield Academic Press, 2000), 62. He also points out lexical links between Ps 76 and the Song of the Sea (p. 59), including "horse and rider" (Ex 15:1, 19, 21; Ps 76:6), and explains that these three psalms "share references to the exodus" (59-60). These references appear to be often mediated through the Song of the Sea.

[61]Regarding the common vocabulary between these two texts and Ps 77:16-19, see Marvin Tate, *Psalms 51–100*, WBC (Dallas: Word, 1990), 273-74.

[62]Without going into the detail I have here, see Michael Wilcock, *The Message of Psalms 73–150* (Downers Grove, IL: InterVarsity Press, 2001), 23. Wilcock writes, "The particular passage in his

Thus, the psalmist's acts of "remembering" (זָכַר, Ps 77:11), "meditating" (הָגָה, Ps 77:12), and "musing" (שִׂיחַ, Ps 77:12) likely have Scripture as their object, just as in Joshua 1:8; Psalms 1:2; 119:15, 23, 27, 48, 52, 78, 148.[63] The waters "seeing" and "writhing" (חִיל), along with the depths "trembling" (רָגַז) in Psalm 77:16, parallel the peoples "hearing," "trembling" (רָגַז), and being seized by "writhing" (חִיל) in Exodus 15:14. This supports the parallel within the Song of the Sea between the passage through the waters (Ex 15:8-10) and the passage through the nations (Ex 15:12-17) set forth by Lohfink.[64] Unlike Exodus 15:1-18, Psalm 77:19-20 directly explains that the Lord led his people through the waters.[65]

Psalm 118 also has clear links to the Song of the Sea. Like Isaiah 12:2, Psalm 118:14 cites Exodus 15:2, "Yah is my strength and my song, and he has become my salvation" (עָזִּי וְזִמְרָת יָהּ וַיְהִי־לִי לִישׁוּעָה). Yet not only does Psalm 118:14 cite Exodus 15:2 verbatim, but also Psalm 118:21 adds an allusive adaptation, "and you have become my salvation" (וַתְּהִי־לִי לִישׁוּעָה). Psalm 118 also repeatedly uses the less common title "Yah" (Ps 118:5, 14, 17-19), which is probably rooted in Exodus 15:2.[66] Jacques Trublet further connects "the Lord is *for me*" (יְהוָה לִי) in Psalm 118:7 to Psalm 118:14, 21 (which also have לִי) as a "refrain."[67] The latter half of Exodus 15:2, "This is *my God*, I will praise him; the God of my father, *I will exalt him*" (זֶה אֵלִי וְאַנְוֵהוּ אֱלֹהֵי אָבִי וַאֲרֹמְמֶנְהוּ) is also quite similar in thought, syntax, and terminology to Psalm 118:28, "You are *my God*, I will praise you; my God,

---

mind must be Moses' song after the crossing of the Red Sea, especially Exodus 15:11-18, to which he alludes in some detail." Focusing on Ps 77:13-15 and the Song of the Sea, see Helen Jefferson, "Psalm LXXVII," *VT* 13, no. 1 (1963): 87-91; John Kselman, "Psalm 77 and the Book of Exodus," *Journal of the Ancient Near Eastern Society* 15 (1983): 51-58. Kselman also discusses Ps 77:10, 20.

[63] See Cole, *Shape and Message of Book III*, 62. Cole further notes "day" and "night" in the first part of Ps 77 and sees a correspondence between the psalmist in Ps 77 and the blessed man in Ps 1.

[64] Lohfink, *Christian Meaning of the Old Testament*, 82-83.

[65] Though not as extensive an allusion, "they *believed in* his words; they *sang* his *praise*" (וַיַּאֲמִינוּ בִדְבָרָיו יָשִׁירוּ תְּהִלָּתוֹ) in Ps 106:12 also engages the text of Ex 14–15 (Ex 14:31, "they *believed in* the Lord" [וַיַּאֲמִינוּ בַּיהוָה]; Ex 15:1, "sang" [יָשִׁיר]; Ex 15:11, "awesome in *praises*" [נוֹרָא תְהִלֹּת]).

[66] Besides its forty appearances in the Psalter, "Yah" appears only in Ex 15:2; 17:16; Is 12:2; 26:4; 38:11. I have argued above that Is 12:2 alludes to Ex 15:2, and Is 26:4 is suggestively part of a "song" (Is 26:1) that may also be rooted in the Song of the Sea (see "majestic things" in Is 26:10 as in Is 12:5).

[67] Jacques Trublet, "Approche canonique des Psaumes du Hallel," in *The Composition of the Book of Psalms*, ed. Erich Zenger (Leuven: Peeters, 2010), 345.

I will exalt you" (אֵלִי אַתָּה וְאוֹדֶךָּ אֱלֹהַי אֲרוֹמְמֶךָּ). The Lord's mighty "right hand" (יָמִין) is mentioned exactly three times in both poems (Ex 15:6, 12; Ps 118:15-16).

In view of these extensive allusions and noting the theme of threatening nations in Psalm 118:10-16 (see Ex 15:14-16), Frank-Lothar Hossfeld and Erich Zenger argue, "The whole song in Exod 15:1-18 is the hermeneutical horizon within which Psalm 118 is to be understood."[68] Joy (Ex 15:1, 20; Ps 118:15, 24), salvation (Ex 15:2; Ps 118:14-15, 21, 25), deliverance from death (Ex 15:9-10; Ps 118:17-18), and temple (Ex 15:17; Ps 118:26-27) are additional thematic links. Hossfeld and Zenger further observe that "the arc of events that determines Exodus 15 as a whole may also be in the background of the composition of Psalm 118," since both begin with a rescue and end at a temple.[69] He believes the individual deliverance in Psalm 118 is an intentional "actualization," "continuation," and "transformation" of the exodus.[70] Ian Vaillancourt more pointedly remarks that the allusion in Psalm 118:14 "communicates that the new exodus is being accomplished."[71] Such perspectives accord with Psalm 118 concluding the Egyptian Hallel (Ps 113–118), which is bound together by its connection to the exodus and other indications of coherence.[72]

The link between a new (or second) exodus and the deliverance of the individual in Psalm 118 takes on even more significance in view of the New Testament's messianic interpretation of the rejected stone in Psalm 118:22 (see Mt 21:42; Mk 12:10; 1 Pet 2:7). Yet, the meaning of the stone within the context of Psalm 118 is not immediately clear. Hossfeld and Zenger see the stone metaphor as "fit[t]ing perfectly" the preceding description of the deliverance of an individual (Ps 118:5, "from distress I called to the Lord").[73]

---

[68] Frank-Lothar Hossfeld and Erich Zenger, *Psalms 3: A Commentary on Psalms 101–150*, trans. Linda Maloney, Hermeneia (Minneapolis: Fortress, 2011), 239.
[69] Hossfeld and Zenger, *Psalms 3*, 235. Trublet also sees an echo of Ex 15:11 in Ps 113:5 ("Who is like the Lord our God?"; "Approche canonique des Psaumes du Hallel," 357).
[70] Hossfeld and Zenger, *Psalms 3*, 234-35.
[71] Ian Vaillancourt, *The Multifaceted Saviour of Psalms 110 and 118: A Canonical Exegesis* (Sheffield: Sheffield Phoenix, 2019), 152.
[72] Vaillancourt, *Multifaceted Saviour*, 167-70; Michael Snearly, *The Return of the King: Messianic Expectation in Book V of the Psalter* (New York: T&T Clark, 2016), 110-13.
[73] Hossfeld and Zenger, *Psalms 3*, 242. Michael Snearly calls Ps 118:5 "a proper heading," with Ps 118:1-4, 29 serving as introduction and conclusion. Snearly, "Psalm 118: The Rejected Stone,"

This individual had conflict with "man/humanity" (אָדָם, Ps 118:6; see also Ps 118:8), "those who hate me" (שֹׂנְאָי, Ps 118:7), and even "all the nations" (כָּל־גּוֹיִם, Ps 118:10), whom he cut off in the Lord's name (Ps 118:10-12). Evidently, the speaker was involved in a major battle and was victorious through the Lord's help (Ps 118:7). The significance of this individual's deliverance to the community later in the psalm (i.e., Ps 118:15, 23-24, 26-27) suggests that this is no ordinary individual and explains why scholars tend to view the speaker as a king.[74] This deliverance apparently is also evidence of the Lord's steadfast love, or "covenant faithfulness" (חֶסֶד, Ps 118:1-4; see also Ps 107:1).[75] Michael Snearly further points out the parallel between "he who comes in the name of the LORD" in Psalm 118:26 and David, who does the same against Goliath in 1 Samuel 17:45 (see also Is 30:27; Hab 2:3).[76] Surprisingly, the speaker sees his affliction not only as coming from his enemies but also as discipline from the Lord (Ps 118:18).

Identifying a historical Israelite king who fought all the nations in the name of the Lord and fits the profile of Psalm 118 is difficult, but this profile does match the messianic king of Psalm 2 and Psalm 110 (see Ps 2:1-3, 8-9; 110:5-6).[77] Furthermore, the experience of suffering as inflicted simultaneously by both God and humanity recalls the Suffering Servant in Isaiah 53:3-5 (see Ps 22:1, 6-8). Likewise, the rejection and exaltation of the stone in Psalm 118:22 matches the experience of the Suffering Servant, who was despised by people but later highly exalted (Is 52:13; 53:3, 12; see Acts 4:11). Hossfeld and Zenger comment, "A stone thrown away by the builders is taken by YHWH, as the master builder, and is even placed as a very important stone in *his* building."[78] The common themes surrounding the stone laid as a foundation in Zion as a "precious cornerstone" in Isaiah 28:16 suggest that it is

---

in *The Moody Handbook of Messianic Prophecy*, ed. Michael Rydelnik and Edwin Blum (Chicago: Moody, 2019), 693.

[74]Vaillancourt remarks that most scholars "either support or at least favour the idea of the psalmist as a king" (*Multifaceted Saviour*, 131).

[75]Snearly connects this faithfulness to the Davidic covenant in Ps 89 ("Psalm 118: The Rejected Stone," 695-96).

[76]Snearly, "Psalm 118: The Rejected Stone," 696-97.

[77]Snearly, "Psalm 118: The Rejected Stone," 698: "The psalm itself, its immediate context in the Psalms, and the broader OT context all consistently point to the Messiah."

[78]Hossfeld and Zenger, *Psalms 3*, 241, emphasis original.

closely related to the stone that became "the head of the corner" in Psalm 118:22 (see 1 Pet 2:6-7). If Psalm 118 does indeed concern the deliverance of the messianic king who is at the center of the second exodus, it would fit the messianic prophecy in Numbers 24:8 ("God brings him out of Egypt"), which also depicts him at the center of the second exodus (see chapter four).

CONCLUSION

As a classic text that represents the exodus theme in the Old Testament, the Song of the Sea (Ex 15:1-18) both is a climactic conclusion to the preceding exodus narrative (Ex 1–14) and plays a key role as one of the four major poetic sections in the Pentateuch. Its status as a nexus passage is evident through its intertextual connections within the Pentateuch and to other Old Testament books. The sampling of passages discussed above demonstrates that later biblical authors who reflected on the exodus sometimes did so specifically via the Song of the Sea. In the case of Psalm 77, the psalmist reflected on the exodus with the help of Exodus 15:1-18. On the other hand, Isaiah 12 and Psalm 118 engage and cite the Song of the Sea with respect to a second exodus, which suggests that Exodus 15:1-18 is not only a celebration of past deliverance but relates to future salvation as well (Ex 15:13-18). In this sense, the song is also our song, since we await a future work of God that concludes with the Lord reigning over his people in an Edenic sanctuary (Ex 15:17-18). The Messiah's role in the second exodus will become even clearer in the next chapter, as will his place in the theology of the Pentateuch and of the Old Testament. The exodus he leads will involve a remnant from not only Israel but also the nations (Is 11:10, 12; Amos 9:12).[79]

---

[79] Fishbane sees Egypt as experiencing an "'exodus'-type event" of its own in Is 19:19-25, where the exodus "becomes the symbolic form through which a messianic moment is envisaged" (*Text and Texture*, 128-29). Among other things, he observes in Is 19:20 that it is Egypt who will have "oppressors" (לֹחֲצִים; see Ex 3:9), "cry out" (יִצְעֲקוּ; see Ex 2:23; 5:8, 15), and be delivered by the Lord (see Ex 14:13, 30). Humanity's exile, whether from Eden or the Tower of Babel, also suggests their participation in the second exodus. Regarding exile from Eden, see Seth Postell, *Adam as Israel: Genesis 1–3 as the Introduction to the Torah and Tanakh* (Eugene, OR: Pickwick, 2011), 120-34. Regarding the theme of exile and the Tower of Babel, Morales observes the repetition of the verb "scatter" (פּוּץ) in Gen 11:4, 8, 9 (see Cain's "wandering" [נוּד, Gen 4:12, 14; also "Nod," Gen 4:16]; *Exodus Old and New*, 13). Though the term does not always imply judgment (Ex 5:12), פּוּץ is used in several notable passages concerning Israel's exile (Deut 4:27; 28:64; 30:3; Is 11:12; Jer 30:11; Ezek 36:19; Neh 1:8).

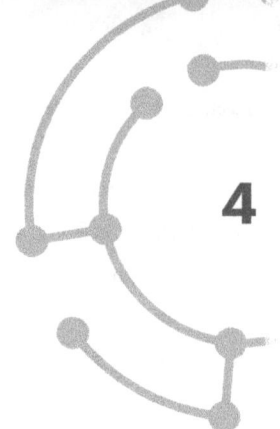

4

NUMBERS 24

THE STAR FROM JACOB AND A DEUTEROEVANGELIUM

THE PREVIOUS TWO CHAPTERS on Genesis 1–3 and Exodus 15 have naturally involved such key themes in the Pentateuch as creation and exodus. Our third nexus passage from the Pentateuch, Numbers 24, concerns what I believe to be the central theme of the Pentateuch and the Old Testament: the eschatological Messiah (Num 24:17-19). Although this center (or integrative center; see introduction) could have been discussed earlier in relation to the seed of the woman in Genesis 3:15, the focus on Genesis 1–3 in relation to Wisdom literature in chapter two led to reserving extensive discussion of the Messiah for the present chapter, which will still involve intertextuality between Genesis 3:15 and Numbers 21–24. Since I have written on the Messiah and the Pentateuch already, including Numbers 24, the discussion below will both draw on key points from prior research and add to it, especially by giving more attention to nexus connections.[1] If the eschatological Messiah really is the exegetically derived, compositional, integrative center of the Pentateuch and the Old Testament, then these nexus connections are especially important evidence. I begin by setting Numbers 24 within the context of Numbers 21–24. The coherence of this section contributes to the messianic message of Numbers 24. Afterward, I will consider the Balaam narrative in relation to both the Abrahamic covenant and the exodus. Next, the heart of this chapter will make

---

[1] Kevin Chen, *The Messianic Vision of the Pentateuch* (Downers Grove, IL: InterVarsity Press, 2019).

a detailed exegetical case for a messianic interpretation of Balaam's oracles in Numbers 24, which will be followed by discussion of their nexus connections to other Old Testament books.

NUMBERS 21–24: ON THE WAY TO THE PROMISED LAND (AGAIN)

Numbers 24 should be seen not only as the conclusion to the Balaam narrative in Numbers 22–24 but also in light of Israel's second approach to the Promised Land, which is repeatedly opposed by peoples whose territories Israel wants to cross. This approach began with their failed attempt to pass through Edom in Numbers 20:14-21 and was followed by the opposition of Sihon and Og in Numbers 21:21-35. The many references to Moab in Numbers 21 (Num 21:11, 13, 15, 20, 26) pave the way for Israel to be opposed by yet another people, Moab, in Numbers 22–24.

In addition to this narrative continuity, there are additional connections between the Balaam narrative in Numbers 22–24 and its preceding context, especially Numbers 21.[2] Moab's past defeat at the hands of Sihon (Num 21:26-29), who was just defeated by Israel (Num 21:23-25), foreshadows Moab's frustration by Balaam and eschatological defeat at the hands of "the star from Jacob" in Numbers 24:17 (see also Num 24:14; Jer 48:45-47). Moab's defeats are described through poetry, and both literary contexts have still more poetry in them (Num 21:14-15, 17-18; 24:3-9). Both Numbers 21 and Numbers 24 also emphasize Israel's "possession" (יָרַשׁ/יְרֵשָׁה) of their enemies (e.g., Sihon, Og, Edom) and their land (Num 21:24, 32, 35; 24:18), with reference to leaving no "survivor" (שָׂרִיד, Num 21:35; 24:19). Thus, the defeat of Sihon and Og can be seen as a picture not only of what the Israelites should do to the Canaanites (e.g., Deut 31:4) but also of their eschatological victory over all their enemies (Num 24:14, 17-19). Israel's arrival to "the top of Pisgah, which overlooks the face of Jeshimon," in Numbers 21:20 is also a precursor of two of the locations from which Balaam was supposed to curse Israel (Num 23:14, 28).

---

[2]For the importance of Num 21, see Baruch Levine, *Numbers 21–36*, AB (New York: Doubleday, 2000), 79. For connections, see Chen, *Messianic Vision of the Pentateuch*, 200-201.

The recounting of Moab's defeat by Sihon and the Amorites by "those who speak proverbs" (הַמֹּשְׁלִים, Num 21:27) provides yet another link to Numbers 22–24 through Balaam's sevenfold taking up (נָשָׂא) of "his proverb" (מָשָׁל, or *mashal*; Num 23:7, 18; 24:3, 15, 20-21, 23). Not counting the mocking proverb in Deuteronomy 28:37, these are the only such proverbs in the Pentateuch. That there are seven of them in Numbers 23–24 further hints at their completeness and importance (see seven altars, bulls, and rams in Num 23:1, 14, 29).³ Commentators often emphasize the broader use of מָשָׁל (e.g., "popular saying" in 1 Sam 10:12; "declaration" or "discourse" in Job 27:1; "taunt" in Is 14:4) with the effect of downplaying its significance here, but the poetic form and expression of Balaam's oracles, along with accompanying wisdom themes (see below), suggest some form of heightened discourse and/or comparative element.⁴ Regardless of how מָשָׁל is translated in Numbers 23–24, these features hint at both a connection to Genesis 1–3, Proverbs, and Wisdom literature (see "seven" in Prov 6:16; 9:1; 24:16; 26:16, 25) and the need for wisdom to understand Balaam's prophecies. Furthermore, the emphasis on Balaam speaking only what the Lord tells him (Num 22:35, 38; 23:5, 12, 16; 24:13; see also Num 23:26; 24:2) implies that his proverbs come directly from the Lord himself.⁵ The Lord thus chose here to communicate through "proverbs" (מְשָׁלִים) rather than more straightforward means.

John Sailhamer points out a similarly close relationship between prophecy and wisdom at the end of Hosea (Hos 14:9, "Who is wise? Let him understand these things. Who is discerning? Let him know them").⁶

---

³For other significant sevens, see Jacob Milgrom, *Numbers*, JPS Torah Commentary (Philadelphia: Jewish Publication Society, 1990), 194. He notices that there are seven oracles (209) but makes no further comment. See also Timothy Ashley, *The Book of Numbers*, NICOT (Grand Rapids, MI: Eerdmans, 1993), 465.

⁴See Ashley, *Book of Numbers*, 469; George Buchanan Gray, *A Critical and Exegetical Commentary on Numbers*, ICC (Edinburgh: T&T Clark, 1986), 344-45.

⁵Regarding the Lord having "put a word in the mouth of Balaam" in Num 23:5, 16 (see also Num 23:12), Milgrom remarks, "the Lord told him the exact words" (*Numbers*, 195). He takes the absence of this construction in relation to the third and fourth oracles as implying a distinction (198, 202), but the Spirit of God coming on Balaam in Num 24:2 does not suggest any decline in the quality and accuracy of the latter two oracles.

⁶John Sailhamer, *The Meaning of the Pentateuch* (Downers Grove, IL: InterVarsity Press, 2009), 51. See also Mark Boda, Russell Meek, and William Osborne, eds., *Riddles and Revelations: Explorations into the Relationship Between Wisdom and Prophecy in the Hebrew Bible* (New York: T&T

Citing Hosea 12:10 and Ezekiel 17:2, Rambam in the Middle Ages drew attention to prophets' use of "proverbs" (מְשָׁלִים) and the need for readers to understand these in order to fully grasp the prophets' meaning.[7] Balaam's origin from "Pethor" (פְּתוֹר, Num 22:5) is another hint at wisdom in the Balaam narrative, since the similar-looking verb "interpret" (פָּתַר) repeatedly appears in the Joseph narrative concerning his ability to explain dreams (Gen 40:8, 16, 22; 41:8, 12-13, 15; see "interpretation" [פִּתְרוֹן], Gen 40:5, 12, 18; 41:11; Joseph as "discerning and wise" [נָבוֹן וְחָכָם], Gen 41:39).[8]

The donkey episode (Num 22:21-35) likewise has implicit wisdom themes. Baruch Levine explains that its effect is to "mock Balaam. . . . The noted clairvoyant cannot see what his jenny saw!"[9] He is even confronted by his donkey (Num 22:28), who tries to reason with him (Num 22:30). Unlike the talking (and shrewd) snake in Genesis 3, the talking donkey was actually right! Like Israel in Isaiah 1:3, who does not "know" (יָדַע) or "understand" (בִּין) and has less sense than an ox or a "[male] donkey" (חֲמוֹר), so blind Balaam does not "know" (יָדַע, Num 22:34) and understands less than his "[female] donkey" (אָתוֹן; see Ps 32:9). His wish that there were "a sword in my hand" (חֶרֶב בְּיָדִי) to kill his donkey (Num 22:29) is especially foolish because the angel of the Lord opposing him actually does have a drawn sword in hand ready to slay Balaam (Num 22:23, 31, 33). The theme of wisdom will be further reinforced in Balaam's third and fourth proverbs (see below). Seth Postell further points out the parallel between Balaam's compulsion of the donkey to keep going forward and Balak's persistent attempts to get Balaam to curse Israel, as well as the Lord speaking respectively through the donkey and Balaam in response.[10]

Clark, 2018). The articles in this volume focus on relationships between the wisdom corpus and prophetic corpus.

[7] Rambam, *Guide for the Perplexed*, introduction, prefatory remarks, 9; see also 2.43, 47.

[8] Milgrom observes that this connection was made in early midrash (e.g., Targums Pseudo-Jonathan and Neofiti on Num 22:5; *Numbers*, 186, 319).

[9] Levine, *Numbers 21–36*, 154; see also Ashley, *Book of Numbers*, 457.

[10] Seth Postell, "Numbers 24:5-9: The Distant Star," in *The Moody Handbook of Messianic Prophecy: Studies and Expositions of the Messiah in the Old Testament*, ed. Michael Rydelnik and Edwin Blum (Chicago: Moody, 2019), 290-91. Similarly, Clinton Moyer, "Who Is the Prophet, and Who the Ass? Role-Reversing Interludes and the Unity of the Balaam Narrative (Numbers 22–24)," *JSOT* 37, no. 2 (2012): 174-75.

The most significant connection between Numbers 21 and Numbers 22–24 is the repetition of the root נחש in Numbers 21:6-7, 9 concerning the bronze "snake" (נָחָשׁ) and in Numbers 23:23 and Numbers 24:1 concerning the "omens" (נַחַשׁ) that Balaam had used in the past. As argue elsewhere, the root נחש in Numbers 21–24 both links this section together and ties it back to Genesis 3.[11] This is because the bronze snake passage not only uses the term "snake" (נָחָשׁ) five times, like Genesis 3 (Gen 3:1-2, 4, 13-14; the only two OT texts that do this), but also involves the theme of ultimate victory over "the snake" despite its poisonous bite (Num 21:7-9, lit.), much like Genesis 3:15. Another allusion to Genesis 3:15 is found in Numbers 24:17 ("he will crush the temples [i.e., sides of the head]/corners of Moab"), such that allusions to Genesis 3:15 frame Numbers 21–24. Together, the bronze snake (Num 21:4-9) and the star from Jacob (Num 24:17) are intended to remind readers of the "seed of the woman" prophecy and provide foretastes of his final triumph over the snake. Accordingly, Numbers 21–24, though certainly consisting of other elements also, can be thought of as a deutero-evangelium that is rooted in the protoevangelium of Genesis 3:15.[12]

Table 4.1. The protoevangelium of Genesis 3:15 and Deuteroevangelium of Numbers 21–24

	Genesis 3	**Numbers 21–24**
Snake/נָחָשׁ (five times)	Gen 3:1-2, 4, 13-14	Num 21:6-7, 9; also "omen"/ נַחַשׁ in Num 23:23; 24:1
Snake brings human suffering and death	deceives Adam and Eve into eating fruit that brings death (Gen 3:1-6), strikes the heel of the seed of the woman (Gen 3:15)	bites Israelites so that they die (Num 21:6)
Overcoming the snake	seed of the woman will crush the head of the snake (Gen 3:14-15)	"let him remove the snake from us" (Num 21:7); those bitten "live" if they look at the bronze snake (Num 21:8-9); also "there is no omen [נַחַשׁ] against Jacob" (Num 23:23)
Crush head(s) of enemy in a final battle	"he will crush your head" (Gen 3:15)	"in the last days" (Num 24:14), Israelite king will crush the heads of Moab (Num 24:17)

---

[11] Chen, *Messianic Vision of the Pentateuch*, 201-4.
[12] Kevin Chen, "The 'Deuteroevangelium' in Numbers 21–24," Cateclesia Institute, December 13, 2021, https://cateclesia.com/2021/12/13/the-deuteroevangelium-in-numbers-21-24/.

Both passages involved in this frame also emphasize the importance of seeing. Seeing the bronze snake results in healing and life (Num 21:8-9, נָבַט/רָאָה), and seeing the star reveals the eschatological savior (Num 24:17, שׁוּר/רָאָה; see also Num 22:31; 23:9). Correspondingly, if the repetition of נחשׁ is a cohesive device in Numbers 21–24, then Balaam's declaration that "there is no omen against Jacob" (לֹא־נַחַשׁ בְּיַעֲקֹב, Num 23:23) may also have a prophetic element ("there is no snake [נָחָשׁ] in/against Jacob"; see Num 21:6, "fiery snakes *among the people*" [בָּעָם]).[13] Thus, Numbers 21–24 intertwines with not only wisdom but also the Edenic snake, eschatological salvation, and creation (see reference to Adam in Num 23:19, to Seth in Num 24:17, and to Cain in Num 24:22). Like wisdom, these themes also appear in Balaam's proverbs. Because of the intrinsic relationship between wisdom and creation (chapter two), the appearance of both themes in Numbers 21–24 may not be accidental. Furthermore, closer consideration of Balaam's oracles (i.e., his third and fourth proverbs) below will demonstrate more clearly their messianic expectation.

THE BALAAM NARRATIVE AND THE ABRAHAMIC COVENANT

The Balaam narrative in Numbers 22–24 is not only directly linked to Numbers 21, the seed of the woman, and wisdom but further has clear links to Abrahamic covenant texts and the exodus. Thus, though not always given much attention, Numbers 22–24 strongly interconnects with such major themes in the Pentateuch as creation, Messiah, the Abrahamic covenant, and the exodus. Considering only these connections, the Balaam narrative, including Numbers 24, is already a nexus passage. Its links to Abrahamic covenant texts are apparent at the outset. The strategy of Balak king of Moab focuses on summoning Balaam to "curse [אָרָה] this people for me ... for I know that whoever you bless is blessed [תְּבָרֵךְ מְבֹרָךְ] and whoever you curse is cursed [תָּאֹר יוּאָר]" (Num 22:6).[14] This is a direct challenge to the Lord's determined purpose in the Abrahamic covenant to

---

[13]Chen, *Messianic Vision of the Pentateuch*, 215. Levine leaves open the possibility of a double meaning for בְּ as "in" and "against" but only with respect to "omen" (*Numbers 21–36*, 185).
[14]Gray, *Numbers*, 307; Milgrom, *Numbers*, 186.

bless Israel (Gen 12:2-3; 22:17-18). In Genesis 12:3 and 27:29, the Lord even uses similar language of blessing "those who bless you" and cursing "the one/those who curse you" (see Num 24:9).

As the Balaam narrative continues, Balak's persistent attempts to curse Israel (Num 22:11, 17; 23:7, 11, 13, 25, 27; 24:10; often using the verb קָבַב) make increasingly plain that he is an enemy of the Lord and his people. The Lord himself makes clear that Israel shall not be cursed, "for they are blessed" (Num 22:12), and Balaam informs Balak of the impossibility of cursing them (Num 23:8, 20). The inability to "count the dust [עֲפַר] of Jacob" or "the number of a fourth of Israel" (Num 23:10) is a direct reference to the Abrahamic covenant promises, especially Genesis 13:16 (see Gen 15:5; 22:17; 26:4; 28:14; 32:12). Along these lines, the parallel between "the *dust* of Jacob" in Balaam's first proverb (Num 23:10) and "the *star* from Jacob" in Balaam's fourth proverb (Num 24:17) nicely frames the four main proverbs in terms of the Abrahamic promise of descendants (Gen 13:16; 15:5).

The certainty of the Lord's purpose to bless Israel is especially apparent in the second proverb in Numbers 23:19: "God is not a man that he would lie, nor a son of man that he would change his mind. Will he speak and not act? Will he speak and not establish it?" Such constancy in the Lord's love for Israel recalls the formal institution of the Abrahamic covenant (Gen 15:7-21), emphatic statements of blessing (e.g., Gen 22:17), and other references to the Lord's faithfulness to his covenant (e.g., Deut 7:9; Ps 89:29, 33-34). The emphatic blessing in Genesis 22:17 uses an infinitive absolute construction, "I will surely bless you" (בָרֵךְ אֲבָרֶכְךָ), which appears only here in Genesis (see also Deut 15:4) and has direct parallels to Balak's complaints in Numbers 23:11 and Numbers 24:10, "you have surely blessed them" (בֵּרַכְתָּ בָרֵךְ; infinitive absolute last both times; see also Num 23:20, 25).[15]

In response to Balak's third and final attempt (Num 23:27), Balaam ends the third proverb in dramatic fashion, "Blessed are those who bless you,

---

[15] These are the only six appearances of the infinitive absolute of בָּרַךְ in the Pentateuch.

and cursed are those who curse you" (Num 24:9), another allusion to an Abrahamic covenant text (Gen 27:29; see further discussion below). Not only does this contradict yet again Balak's desire to curse Israel, but it even hints that Balak has set himself up to be cursed because of his intentions.[16] Balak's original confidence in Balaam that "whoever you bless is blessed, and whoever you curse is cursed" (Num 22:6) has been thrown back in his face. The experience of blessing or curse for the nations will depend instead on the conditions of Numbers 24:9.[17] At this point, Balak becomes angry and finally gives up (Num 24:10-11). His attempt to thwart the Abrahamic covenant, whether intended as such or not, is futile. The Abrahamic covenant and many of its key texts are thus a major part of the Balaam narrative. Furthermore, the prophecies of an eschatological king in Balaam's third and fourth proverbs in Numbers 24 draw on these texts in suggesting the Abrahamic covenant promises are ultimately fulfilled messianically.

THE BALAAM NARRATIVE AND THE EXODUS

The connection between the Balaam narrative and the exodus is equally clear. When messengers first summon Balaam, they tell him, "Behold, a people has gone out [יָצָא] of Egypt" (Num 22:5). This is both an obvious reference to the exodus and a common way of describing it (e.g., Ex 16:1, 3, 6, 32; 18:1; 19:1; 20:2). The exodus is referred to again in Numbers 22:11 ("the people who are going out [*qal* participle יָצָא] of Egypt") and Numbers 23:22 ("God brings them out [*hiphil* participle יָצָא] of Egypt"). Numbers 24:8 similarly seems to be referring to a future exodus (see below). Thus, the Balaam narrative is closely connected to the exodus even though in the literary context of the Pentateuch the exodus was narrated back in Exodus 14. Correspondingly, Deuteronomy 23:4 describes Israel's encounter with Balaam in Numbers 22–24 as having taken place "when you went out of Egypt."

---

[16]Milgrom, *Numbers*, 202, 205. See, though without mentioning Num 24:9, J. Gordon McConville, *Deuteronomy*, ApOTC (Downers Grove, IL: InterVarsity Press, 2002), 349. McConville sees in Deut 23:3-6 and the ban on Ammonites and Moabites entering the assembly "a turning back upon itself of the curse on Israel that Moab sought."
[17]Postell, "Numbers 24:5-9: Distant Star," 288, 290, 298.

As Exodus 3:16-17 and 6:6-8 explain, the exodus was never simply about leaving Egypt but also about entering the Promised Land. Accordingly, Israel's recent attempt to pass through Edom in Numbers 20:14-17 recalls the exodus as though they had almost reached their ultimate destination. Though not placed literarily at the end of the Pentateuch, Israel's subsequent defeat of Sihon and Og east of the Jordan (Num 21:21-35) is therefore treated as a precursor to what they should do to the Canaanites on the other side of the Jordan (Deut 3:21; 31:4; Josh 2:10-11; 9:9-10). Similarly, the historical summary of Israel's history to that point in Joshua 24:2-13 presents their confrontation with Moab in Numbers 22–24 as directly preceding their crossing of the Jordan (Josh 24:9-11).

Closer investigation reveals even more links to the exodus, as I have shown previously.[18] Hedwige Rouillard notes the use of dark spiritual powers against Israel by both Egypt and Moab (e.g., Ex 7:11, 22; Num 22:7; 23:23), as well as the phrase "covers the eye of [all] the land" (inflected form of עַיִן הָאָרֶץ + כָּסָה) in Exodus 10:5, 15 and Numbers 22:5, 11.[19] Taking it a step further, Sailhamer shows that the Balaam story in relation to Pharaoh's opposition to Israel in Exodus 1–2 is an example of how "one story parallels another." Both Pharaoh and Balak "were kings of large and powerful nations which represented a major obstacle to Israel's entering the Promised Land" and were threatened by Israel being too "numerous" (רַב) and "strong" (עָצוּם) for them (Ex 1:9; Num 22:3, 6). Sailhamer further points out that Pharaoh's three attempts to harm Israel in Exodus 1 (enslavement, Ex 1:11-14; command to midwives to kill newborn boys, Ex 1:15-21; command that every male infant be thrown into the Nile, Ex 1:22) parallel Balak's three attempts to curse Israel. In both cases, however, such opposition results only in greater blessing for Israel (Ex 1:12; Num 24:10).[20] Thus, the Balaam narrative has strong connections to the exodus also. Moreover, the prophecies in Numbers 24 suggest that there will be a greater exodus yet to come.

---

[18]Chen, *Messianic Vision of the Pentateuch*, 210-11.
[19]Hedwige Rouillard, *Le Pericope de Balaam (Nombres 22–24): La Prose et les "Oracles"* (Paris: J. Gabalda et Cie, 1985), 54-55.
[20]John Sailhamer, *The Pentateuch as Narrative* (Grand Rapids, MI: Zondervan, 1992), 406-7.

BALAAM'S PROVERBS IN NUMBERS 23-24 AS A MAJOR POETIC SECTION IN THE PENTATEUCH

In addition to the textual-thematic links to creation, wisdom, Messiah, Abrahamic covenant, and exodus, the Balaam narrative and especially its embedded poetic proverbs play a major role as a seam in the literary macrostructure of the Pentateuch. In chapter three, I discussed the structure of the Pentateuch as consisting of a narrative-poetry-epilogue sequence that repeats four times and encompasses the entire Pentateuch.[21] Within this literary macrostructure, Balaam's proverbs are the third major poetic section (Num 23:7-10, 18-24; 24:3-9, 15-24). Unlike the other major poetic sections, the poetry in Balaam's proverbs does not consist of a long section of continuous poetry (see Gen 49:1-27; Deut 32:1-43; 33:2-29) but rather four distinct, medium-length poems followed by three short poems (Num 24:20b, 21b-22, 23b-24), all within the same literary context. More importantly, the poetry in Numbers 23–24 appears in conjunction with the phrase "in the last days" (בְּאַחֲרִית הַיָּמִים), like the first and fourth poetic sections (Gen 49:1; Num 24:14; Deut 31:29).

Along with the only other appearance of this phrase in the Pentateuch (Deut 4:30), these texts work together to express the Pentateuch's eschatology. They focus on the coming of the Messiah (Gen 49:8-12; Num 24:17-19; see also Deut 33:7), Israel's preparatory experience of disaster because of idolatry (Deut 31:29), and Israel's ultimate repentance and restoration from exile because of the Lord's compassion and covenant faithfulness (Deut 4:29-31). Thus, the Pentateuch's eschatology is not some vague hope but specifically focused on the coming of the Messiah during the time of Israel's exile and acute need. This specifically messianic eschatology is thus intertwined with the literary macrostructure of the Pentateuch and arguably at the heart of the Pentateuch's compositional strategy and message. There are also other texts in the Pentateuch that do not use "in the last days" but still contribute to its messianic, eschatological vision. As we will see below, some of these texts are alluded to in

---

[21] Sailhamer, *Pentateuch as Narrative*, 35-37; Sailhamer, *Meaning of the Pentateuch*, 36, 323-25.

Numbers 24 (e.g., Gen 3:15; 22:17; 27:29; 49:9-10). Balaam's oracles in Numbers 24 are crucial to the messianic vision of the Pentateuch and receive extended attention in the next section.

BALAAM'S THIRD AND FOURTH PROVERBS AND THE MESSIANIC STAR IN NUMBERS 24

Balaam's third and fourth proverbs are distinguished from the first two by his not seeking "omens" (נְחָשִׁים) but instead experiencing "the Spirit of God" (רוּחַ אֱלֹהִים) coming on him (Num 24:1-2; see Gen 1:2). They are also properly called *oracles* because of the term נְאֻם in Numbers 24:3-4, 15-16, which does not appear in the first two proverbs. Baruch Levine makes a connection to "the spirit of prophecy" that came on the seventy elders in Numbers 11:17, 25-27 and argues that Balaam is "no longer a pagan diviner, he has become a prophet."[22] Whereas in Numbers 11:29 Moses (who is absent from the Balaam narrative) longed for the Spirit to come on "all the people of the Lord" (כָּל־עַם יְהוָה) so that they might be "prophets," here instead the Spirit surprisingly comes on a Gentile magician. At the same time, new-covenant themes hover in the background of both passages. Balaam's oracles are the only recorded, explicitly Spirit-bestowed prophetic messages in the Pentateuch. Certainly the Spirit was on Moses and Joshua (Num 11:17; 27:18), and Moses' words and interactions with the Lord on many occasions would surely be at least equal to Balaam's (e.g., Ex 3:1–4:17; 19:3-6, 20-24; 33:7-11), but Balaam's third and fourth proverbs (i.e., oracles) are still distinguished literarily by the Spirit's explicit involvement.

Balaam's special reception of divine revelation is confirmed by his testimony at the beginnings of the oracles themselves. He testifies in Numbers 24:3-4 that he is one whose "eye is opened [שְׁתֻם הָעָיִן] . . . [and] hears [שֹׁמֵעַ] the sayings of God, who sees a vision of the Almighty [מַחֲזֵה שַׁדַּי יֶחֱזֶה]; falling down and whose eyes are uncovered [נֹפֵל וּגְלוּי עֵינָיִם]." Numbers 24:15-16 repeats this testimony and further

---

[22]Levine, *Numbers 21–36*, 191.

adds that Balaam "knows the knowledge of the Most High" (יֹדֵעַ דַּעַת עֶלְיוֹן). Given that the first two proverbs contained no such testimony, the likely reason for this awakening of his senses is the Spirit coming on him. Accordingly, Numbers 24:2 says that Balaam "saw Israel dwelling according to their tribes," which suggests that he saw more than just Israel's "outskirts" (קָצֶה), as he saw on the previous two occasions (Num 22:41; 23:13). The combined references to seeing, hearing, and knowing, along with repetition between Numbers 24:3-4 and Numbers 24:15-16, give unusual emphasis to Balaam's experience of divine revelation and relate to the broader wisdom theme in the narrative. Furthermore, this divinely bestowed spiritual understanding strikingly matches Israel's need in Deuteronomy 29:4 for the Lord to give them "a heart to know, and eyes to see, and ears to hear" (לֵב לָדַעַת וְעֵינַיִם לִרְאוֹת וְאָזְנַיִם לִשְׁמֹעַ).

Balaam's testimony refers to his eye and/or seeing three times each in Numbers 24:3-4 and Numbers 24:15-16. Within the Balaam narrative, this emphasis is reinforced by Balaam's initial blindness to the angel of the Lord during his journey to Moab, after which "the Lord uncovered the eyes of Balaam" (וַיְגַל יְהוָה אֶת־עֵינֵי בִלְעָם) so that he "saw [רָאָה] the angel of the Lord" in Numbers 22:31. The terms "uncover" (גָּלָה), "eye" (עַיִן), and "see" (רָאָה) in Numbers 22:31 even match Balaam's testimony in Numbers 24:4 and especially Numbers 24:16-17 ("whose eyes are uncovered [וּגְלוּי עֵינָיִם] . . . I see him [אֶרְאֶנּוּ]"). Just as Balaam finally sees the angel on the third time (see Num 22:22, 24, 26, 28), his spiritual perception is heightened beginning with his third proverb, culminating in his seeing the star of Numbers 24:17.[23] Both times Balaam "bows down" (הִשְׁתַּחֲוָה) or "falls down" (נָפַל, Num 24:4, 16; see Gen 42:6; 44:14; 49:8). His seeing a "vision" (מַחֲזֶה) in Numbers 24:4, 16 also parallels the "vision" (מַחֲזֶה) Abram saw in Genesis 15:1 in connection with his great reward (Gen 15:1), the "seed" who will "inherit" (יָרַשׁ) all that is his (Gen 15:3-4; see Num 24:18), his gazing (נָבַט) at the stars (Gen 15:5; see Num 24:17), and

---

[23] Postell, "Numbers 24:5-9: Distant Star," 291-92. Milgrom observes that both times "Balaam's eyes are opened in the third scene" (*Numbers*, 192). He believes the repetition of *uncover* and *eyes* in these texts is deliberate.

the formal institution of the Abrahamic covenant (Gen 15:7-21). These are the only texts in the Pentateuch that use this word for vision, מַחֲזֶה (see מַרְאָה in Gen 46:2; Num 12:6; for the verb חָזָה, see Ex 18:21; 24:11).

The sudden opening of Balaam's eyes in Numbers 22:31 and Numbers 24 further recalls the temptation of Adam and Eve in Genesis 3. The serpent successfully enticed them by claiming, "God knows [יָדַע] that in the day that you eat from it, *your eyes will be opened* [וְנִפְקְחוּ עֵינֵיכֶם], and you will be like God, knowing [יָדַע] good and evil" (Gen 3:5). Indeed, after eating from the tree of the knowledge of good and evil (Gen 3:6), "both of their eyes [עַיִן] were opened [פָּקַח], and they knew [יָדַע] that they were naked" (Gen 3:7). In chapter two, I cited Ingrid Faro's observation concerning the close connection between seeing and knowing in these verses.[24] This connection is also found in the Balaam narrative (see Num 22:34, "I did not know"; Num 24:16, "who knows the knowledge of the Most High"). The obvious difference between the eye-opening experiences in Genesis 3 and Numbers 24 is that one resulted in knowing (and seeing) one's own shame and nakedness (Gen 3:7) and the other in genuine "knowledge [דַּעַת] of the Most High" and seeing "a star from Jacob" (Num 24:16-17). The epiphany promised by the serpent was a farce, but Balaam's came from the Spirit of God (Num 24:2). The so-called knowledge (דַּעַת) of good and evil brought death on humanity and banishment from Eden (Gen 2:17; 3:22-23), but the knowledge of the messianic star will bring salvation and the restoration of paradise.

From the perspective of the Pentateuch as a whole and its compositional strategy, this juxtaposition suggests that true knowledge of God (i.e., wisdom) is bestowed by the Spirit and focuses on the Messiah rather than being grasped at by humanity in rebellion against God. We have already seen above that allusions to Genesis 3:15 frame Numbers 21–24 and that the root נחשׁ is used to provide literary cohesion. Thus, the relationship between Genesis 3 and Numbers 21–24 appears to be manifold.

As the third and fourth proverbs continue, Balaam bears witness to an eschatological king. This is clearer and more direct in the fourth proverb,

---

[24]See chapter two, note 25.

whereas the third proverb first describes Israel in glowing terms. Israel's tents and dwellings are "good" (טוֹב as a verb), "like gardens by a river [כְּגַנֹּת עֲלֵי נָהָר], like aloes the Lord planted [נָטַע], like cedars by water [מָיִם]" (Num 24:5-6). The creation and Edenic themes, language, and imagery (see Gen 1:31; 2:8-14) blend Israel with creation and Eden themselves, and they further hint that access to Eden has been restored and that Balaam is describing eschatological Israel as seen in his vision. Indeed, the repeated references to water in Numbers 24:6-7 (river, waters) contrast with Israel's actual location in (or near) arid Jeshimon (Num 23:28; see Num 21:20; Deut 32:10). References to Israel's holiness and uprightness in the first two proverbs (Num 23:9-10, 21; contra Num 20:3-5; 21:5; 25:1) have already suggested their focus (though not exclusive) on a perfected, eschatological Israel.[25] I pointed out in chapter three that the Edenic theme of the Lord planting (Gen 2:8) links the Pentateuch's second and third major poetic sections (Ex 15:17; Num 24:6). Broader Edenic themes can also be found in the first and fourth major poetic sections (Gen 49:11-12; Deut 32:33, 42; 33:28).

The last section of Balaam's third proverb shifts the focus to a future king of Israel (Num 24:7-9). The second proverb briefly mentioned "the shout of a king among them" in Numbers 23:21 but immediately returned to describing Israel (Num 23:22). Numbers 24:7a MT is enigmatic: "Water will flow from his buckets, and his seed is in many waters." At the very least, this line seems to refer to the increase of Israel's seed. Numbers 24:7a LXX differs radically: "A man will go out from his seed and he will rule many nations" (ἐξελεύσεται ἄνθρωπος ἐκ τοῦ σπέρματος αὐτοῦ καὶ κυριεύσει ἐθνῶν πολλῶν). There are no references to water or buckets, seed is in the first clause instead of the second as in the MT, and there are references to a man who rules nations. Targum Onqelos is similar: "The anointed king from his sons will be great and rule over many nations" (יְסַגֵּי מַלְכָּא דְיִתְרַבָּא מִבְּנוֹהִי וְיִשְׁלוֹט בְּעַמְמִין סַגִּיאִין). These two readings match Numbers 24:17, "A star will tread from Jacob, and a scepter will arise from Israel."

---

[25]Chen, *Messianic Vision of the Pentateuch*, 213-15.

However Numbers 24:7a is understood, manuscript evidence for Numbers 24:7b unequivocally focuses on a future king of Israel. Still, there are significant textual variants, with the MT reading, "His king will be higher than Agag, and his kingdom will be exalted," and the LXX, "His [i.e., the man's from Num 24:7a] kingdom will be higher than Gog, and his kingdom will be exalted." Whether this future Israelite king will be greater than Agag or Gog greatly affects interpretation. If Agag, then this king is naturally taken as Saul (see Targum Pseudo-Jonathan). If the eschatological enemy Gog of Ezekiel 38–39, then this king would have to be an eschatological king also. The "Agag" reading has the support of the MT and the Targums, whereas "Gog" is supported by the Samaritan Pentateuch, the LXX, and the three later Greek versions (Aquila, Symmachus, and Theodotion) that in their respective ways revised the LXX to better conform to the Hebrew text.[26] Sailhamer further points out that Ezekiel 38:17 assumes that Gog has already been prophesied of "in former days through my servants the prophets" and traces this to Numbers 24:7, since this Gog is not mentioned elsewhere in the Hebrew Bible (see different Gog in 1 Chron 5:4; Amos 7:1 LXX; Num 24:23 LXX).[27]

As though to resolve the problem of Saul losing the kingdom and contradicting "his kingdom will be exalted" in the next line of Numbers 24:7b, Rashi takes "his kingdom" here to refer not to Saul's (i.e., the king in the previous clause) but to Israel's kingdom, which gains strength through David and Solomon. This reading also maintains consistency in the referent of "his," that is, Israel's ("his [= Israel's] king will be higher... his [= Israel's] kingdom will be exalted"). In contrast, the exalted kingdom in Numbers 24:7 LXX primarily belongs to the eschatological king who comes from Israel's seed, rules many nations, and is exalted over Gog ("a man will go out from his [= Israel's] seed and he [= the man] will rule many nations, and his [= the man's] kingdom

---

[26] Sailhamer, *Meaning of the Pentateuch*, 244–45. For an introduction to these three Greek translators, see Karen Jobes and Moisés Silva, *Invitation to the Septuagint*, 2nd ed. (Grand Rapids, MI: Baker, 2015), 26–30. Evidently, the "Gog" reading persisted into the second century AD, when they lived. In the medieval period, Ramban may have been aware of both readings. He discusses both Agag and Gog as a name used for every king or prince of Amalek or Magog, respectively. See Abraham Geiger, *Urschrift und Übersetzungen der Bibel in ihrer Abhängigkeit von der innern Entwicklung des Judentums* (Breslau: Julius Hainauer, 1857), 366.

[27] Sailhamer, *Meaning of the Pentateuch*, 245.

will be exalted over Gog, and his [= the man's] kingdom will increase"; see NETS).[28] Thus, intertwined with the Agag/Gog variant readings is the precise referent of "his" in "his kingdom" in the last clause of Numbers 24:7.

The divergence between Rashi's interpretation of Numbers 24:7 and the LXX continues in Numbers 24:8. In keeping with Rashi's reading of *"his* king" and *"his* kingdom" as meaning Israel's king/kingdom in Numbers 24:7b, he then naturally takes the opening clause of Numbers 24:8, "God brings *him* out of Egypt," as referring to Israel again. Numbers 24:8 LXX similarly reads, "God guided him out of Egypt," such that there is less textual difficulty this time (the verbs still differ; see Ex 15:13 LXX), but because Numbers 24:7 LXX ends with two references to "his kingdom" (βασιλεία αὐτοῦ; i.e., that of the eschatological king), "God guided *him* out of Egypt" in Numbers 24:8 LXX reads as though this king is brought out of Egypt, resembling but not identical to Israel being brought out of Egypt in Numbers 23:22 ("God brings them out of Egypt"; see NETS).[29] Working from the MT itself, Sailhamer argues that the distinction between "God brings *them* [plural] out of Egypt" in Numbers 23:22 MT and "God brings *him* [singular] out of Egypt" in Numbers 24:8 MT is significant, especially since "him" and "his" (singular) are used of Israel throughout Numbers 23:21-22 otherwise.[30] Postell argues that "them" in Numbers 23:22 makes clear that God brings out Israel here, not the king who is also mentioned in the immediately preceding line (Num 23:21).[31]

Rashi's interpretation of the Hebrew text has its merits, but it still results in a discontinuity between the exalted king and the exalted kingdom in Numbers 24:7b. The king is exalted, but not *his* kingdom. Such discontinuity fits James Kugel's broader characterization of rabbinic exegesis of parallelism.[32] Rashi's explanation that Numbers 24:7b concerns Israel's

---

[28]See Postell, "Numbers 24:5-9: Distant Star," 293.
[29]See Barnabas Lindars, *New Testament Apologetic: The Doctrinal Significance of the Old Testament Quotations* (London: SCM Press, 1961), 216-17.
[30]Sailhamer, *Meaning of the Pentateuch*, 331, 519-20.
[31]Postell, "Numbers 24:5-9: Distant Star," 295.
[32]James Kugel shows that rabbinic exegesis tended to distinguish the meanings of parallel lines, whether justified or not, and calls this the "forgetting" of parallelism. See Kugel, *The Idea of Biblical Poetry: Parallelism and Its History* (New Haven, CT: Yale University Press, 1981), 96-109.

king and Israel's kingdom notwithstanding, the more overt parallels between the two verbs concerning exaltation (רוּם, נָשָׂא) and between king/kingdom (מֶלֶךְ, מַלְכוּת) would suggest a greater continuity between the exaltation of king and kingdom in Numbers 24:7b. Indeed, if it were not for the mention of Agag and the problem of Saul's loss of the kingdom, "his kingdom" would naturally be understood as that of the king's (and by extension Israel's). Furthermore, the immediately preceding description of Israel's Edenic destiny in Numbers 24:5-6 better fits the coming of an eschatological king than a failed king, even if just briefly mentioned. Rashi's reading of the third and fourth proverbs involves multiple topic shifts (Num 24:7, Israel/Saul, then Israel/David/Solomon; Num 24:8-9, Israel; Num 24:17-18, David; Num 24:19, Messiah ["another ruler"]).

Though Numbers 24:8a and Numbers 23:22 are identical except for the object pronoun "him/them," the above provides evidence for an intentional distinction between the Lord bringing out Israel from Egypt in Numbers 23:22 and his bringing out their king from Egypt in Numbers 24:8. The continued used of singular pronouns in Numbers 24:9 provides additional evidence for taking Numbers 24:8 as concerning an individual, Israel's king. As Sailhamer emphasizes, Numbers 24:9 consists of a quotation of Genesis 49:9 ("He stoops down, he lies down like a lion, and like a lioness, who will raise him?") followed by a quotation of Genesis 27:29 ("Those who curse you are cursed, and those who bless you are blessed").[33] For Numbers 24:9a and Genesis 49:9b, the two lines differ only in the verb used for "lie down" (שָׁכַב/רָבַץ) and the word used for "lion" (אֲרִי/אַרְיֵה). For Numbers 24:9b and Genesis 27:29c, the order of the two clauses is reversed, but the two texts are otherwise identical.

Sailhamer believes that "such cross-referencing and quotation shows an author's [not necessarily Balaam's] conscious awareness of the strategic importance of these three poems."[34] The nearly verbatim correspondence of Numbers 24:9 to Genesis 27:29 and Genesis 49:9 strongly suggests authorially intended intertextuality at work. It is as though Numbers 24:9 has

---

[33]Sailhamer, *Pentateuch as Narrative*, 408-9.
[34]Sailhamer, *Meaning of the Pentateuch*, 36, 331, 475-78.

Numbers 24

pick up these two textual threads and deliberately braided them together to conclude Balaam's third oracle. Both Genesis 27:29 and Genesis 49:9 concern an individual king, suggesting the same for Numbers 24:9 (and Num 24:8).

The respective plot structures surrounding Genesis 27:29 and Genesis 49:9 increase the likelihood of intentional braiding, or citation of or allusion to multiple texts within the same text.[35]

Figure 4.1. Genesis 27:29 and Genesis 49:9 braided in Numbers 24:9

Both texts are found at high points in the narrative in which a patriarch blesses his son(s). In Genesis 27:27-29, Isaac blesses Jacob, and in Genesis 49:1-27, Jacob blesses his twelve sons. Within the story line, these fatherly blessings are not merely family affairs but solemn moments in which the Abrahamic covenant promises and blessings are passed down to the next generation. The aforementioned ongoing allusions to Abrahamic covenant texts in the Balaam narrative suggest that the use of Genesis 27:29 and Genesis 49:9 in Numbers 24:9 is intended to evoke the Abrahamic

---

[35]This is similar to what is called an "interpretive blend" in Gary Edward Schnittjer, *Old Testament Use of the Old Testament* (Grand Rapids, MI: Zondervan, 2021), xxxiii. See the passing use of "braiding" in Ron Haydon, "'The Law and the Prophets' in MT Daniel 9:3-19," *BBR* 24, no. 1 (2014): 20, unbeknownst to me when I started using the term. He nevertheless deserves credit for using it earlier than I did.

covenant also, especially those aspects that are common to the respective contexts of Genesis 27:27-29 and Genesis 49:8-12. It is as though, long after the patriarchal era (and after the giving of the law at Sinai), the messianic fulfillment of the Abrahamic covenant is being refocused in Numbers 24:9.

At the time that Isaac and Jacob gave these blessings, both patriarchs were aged and blind (Gen 27:1; 48:10). Likewise, Numbers 22:31 and Numbers 24:3-4, 15-16 imply that Balaam's usual state is also a kind of blindness (see Num 22:21-30). The immediately preceding contexts of the portions of Genesis 27:29 and Genesis 49:9 cited in Numbers 24:9 highlight an individual king and his brothers bowing down to him (Gen 27:29, "Let peoples serve you and nations bow down [הִשְׁתַּחֲוָה] to you. . . . Let the sons of your mother bow down to you"; Gen 49:8, "Let the sons of your father bow down [הִשְׁתַּחֲוָה] to you"). Thus, as Sailhamer points out, Genesis 27:29 and Genesis 49:8 are themselves related, with Judah's brothers bowing down to him being a likely reference to the earlier promise of Jacob's brothers bowing down to him.[36] Both immediate contexts also describe this king as ruling the nations (Gen 27:29; 49:10). Likewise, Balaam "falls down" while having a vision of the "star" who rules the nations (Num 24:16-19).

Numbers 24:9, then, most likely specifically evokes the Abrahamic covenant's promise of an eschatological king who will rule Israel and the nations (Gen 27:29; 49:8-10). Its own preceding context also concerns a king exalted over Israel and the nations (Num 24:7). Also, if the "him" in Numbers 24:9 is an eschatological king, then continuity of pronoun usage with Numbers 24:8 implies that the "him" whom God brings out of Egypt is likewise this individual, eschatological king. Thus, Numbers 24:8-9 presents the Messiah as both the fulfillment of the Abrahamic covenant and the center of an eschatological exodus, integrating these two major themes. Furthermore, if "Blessed are those who bless you, and cursed are those who curse you" in Numbers 24:9 not only alludes to Genesis 27:29

---

[36]Sailhamer, *Meaning of the Pentateuch*, 475.

but also fits its immediate context in the oracle, then Balaam's switch to second-person address ("you") opens up the possibility that he is in some sense speaking to this king directly.[37] At the same time, the source of this allusion in the blessing of Jacob in Genesis 27:29, though primarily concerning an individual king, does not entirely exclude a corporate element because of Jacob's representative status for national Israel (Gen 25:23).

Unlike the previous proverbs, Balaam's fourth proverb is unsolicited, as Balak was fed up and sent Balaam home (Num 24:10-11). Balaam reiterates his original commitment to say only what the Lord told him (Num 24:12-13; see Num 22:35, 38) but before leaving gives a parting message concerning "what this people will do to your people *in the last days*" (בְּאַחֲרִית הַיָּמִים, Num 24:14). This phrase appears four times in the Pentateuch and ten times in the Prophets (counting the Aramaic equivalent in Dan 2:28). Although the precise meaning of בְּאַחֲרִית הַיָּמִים has become controversial, with some believing it can refer to the future generally, there is a long history of understanding it eschatologically, starting from the LXX (using ἔσχατος each time except for Jer 48:47, which is not part of LXX Jeremiah), to the Vulgate (using *novissimus* usually, otherwise *extremus*), to Rashi in the Middle Ages (e.g., he associates it with "the end" [הקץ] in his comments on Gen 49:1; see Ramban but contra Radak), and on to earlier English translations (KJV, ASV, JPS). Modern English translations still generally translate this phrase eschatologically, especially in the Prophets (contra NIV). I argue elsewhere that the interpretation of this phrase has become unnecessarily convoluted, and I hold to its eschatological meaning, as well-supported by Deuteronomy 4:30; Isaiah 2:2/Micah 4:1; Jeremiah 48:47; 49:39; Ezekiel 38:16; Daniel 2:28; and Hosea 3:5.[38]

Balaam's fourth proverb focuses on an eschatological star and scepter that defeats Moab and Israel's enemies (Num 24:17-19). The "star" (כּוֹכָב)

---

[37] As such, this text has potential for prosopological exegesis. See Matthew Bates, *The Birth of the Trinity* (Oxford: Oxford University Press, 2016).

[38] Chen, *Messianic Vision of the Pentateuch*, 109-14. See also Stephen Dempster, "'At the End of the Days' (בְּאַחֲרִית הַיָּמִים)—An Eschatological Technical Term? The Intersection of Context, Linguistics and Theology," in *The Unfolding of Your Words Gives Light: Studies on Biblical Hebrew in Honor of George L. Klein*, ed. Ethan Jones (University Park, PA: Eisenbrauns, 2018), 118-41.

in Numbers 24:17 is another allusion to the Abrahamic covenant, which promises Abraham descendants as numerous as the stars (Gen 15:5; 22:17; 26:4). Just as Abraham went outside and saw (נָבַט) the stars in Genesis 15:5 related to his vision (Gen 15:1), so Balaam sees (שׁוּר/רָאָה) one star in Numbers 24:17 in a vision (Num 24:16). The stars represent Abraham's numerous offspring, and the individual star comes from them ("a star treads from Jacob") and is the greatest star of them all. To be sure, there are no other direct references to an individual star as representing one of Abraham's descendants, but Joseph's second dream, in which eleven "stars" (כּוֹכָבִים) represent his eleven brothers and the sun and moon represent his parents (Gen 37:9-10), associates Joseph himself with a star.[39] This association of Joseph with a star is relevant because his dreams of his brothers bowing down to him (הִשְׁתַּחֲוָה, Gen 37:7, 9) interconnect with Genesis 27:29 and Genesis 49:8, which have just been shown to be linked to Numbers 24:9.

Numbers 24:17 then describes this same figure as a "scepter" (שֵׁבֶט) who "will arise [קוּם] from Israel." This scepter represents a king and alludes to the scepter (שֵׁבֶט) that will not depart from Judah in Genesis 49:10. Numbers 24:9a had just alluded to Genesis 49:9b ("He stoops down, he lies down like a lion"), and these two allusions to the blessing of Judah in Genesis 49:8-12 in a short span suggest that Balaam's third and fourth proverbs are both describing the same eschatological king from Judah.[40] The repeated allusions to Genesis 49:8-12 show the dependence of Numbers 24 on the first major poetic section in the Pentateuch (Gen 49:1-27), itself also a messianic high point. Just as the blessing of Judah was given in the context of failures of Reuben, Simeon, and Levi (Gen 49:3-7), so the broader context of the Balaam narrative also recounts failures of members of these same three tribes (Num 16:1-10; 20:12; 25:14).

Adding to the connection between the star in Numbers 24:17 and Joseph's second dream, the scepter that "arises" (קוּם) from Israel in the next

---

[39]Levine briefly mentions Joseph's second dream and its stars as a relevant parallel among others (*Numbers 21-36*, 201).

[40]In his comments on Num 24:14, Ramban argues that the third oracle concerns Saul and David, whereas the fourth concerns the eschatological Messiah.

line also recalls Joseph's first dream. In Genesis 37:7, his "sheaf" (אֲלֻמָּה) "arose" (קוּם), and his brothers' sheaves bowed down to his. Attention to the imagery of a scepter arising from Israel in Numbers 24:17 is supported by Balaam's description of it as part of what he "sees" (שׁוּר/רָאָה). When combined with the hint at Joseph's second dream through the star in the preceding clause, this parallelism in Numbers 24:17 ("a star treads from Jacob, and a scepter will arise from Israel") suggests a coordinated allusion to Joseph's two dreams of rule in Genesis 37:6-10 and its own classification as a sort of dual-allusion parallelism. The alternation of Jacob and Israel in Numbers 24:17 even matches Genesis 37:1-3, 13, 33, such that Joseph/his sheaf can be said to arise from Israel also (i.e., the individual).

Just as Sailhamer shows that Joseph's dreams have been recast to depict the eschatological Messiah in Genesis 49:8, so it appears that these same dreams are being used again to depict the eschatological Messiah in Numbers 24:17.[41] In this way, Joseph's dreams contribute to the messianic theology of the Pentateuch twice through allusions in the two major poetic seams of Genesis 49 and Numbers 23–24. However, different aspects of these dreams are being used in each case. Genesis 49:8 highlights the act of brothers bowing down (הִשְׁתַּחֲוָה; see Gen 37:7, 9-10), whereas Numbers 24:17 omits this and focuses more on the one who is receiving this homage, whether represented by a star (Gen 37:9/Num 24:17) or sheaf/scepter that "arises" (קוּם, Gen 37:7/Num 24:17). At the same time, the exaltation of the scepter in Numbers 24:17 matches that of the Lion of Judah in Genesis 49:9, who "goes up" (עָלָה) and will be "raised up" (קוּם).[42]

After marching forth (דָּרַךְ) and then arising (וְקָם), this star/scepter "will crush the temples [i.e., sides of the head]/corners of Moab" (וּמָחַץ פַּאֲתֵי מוֹאָב, Num 24:17; note *weqatal* verb again). The word פֵּאָה means "corner" or "side," whether of the head (Lev 13:41; 19:27), a table (Ex 25:26), a building (Ex 26:18), land (Lev 19:9), or otherwise. This could suggest that Numbers 24:17 concerns the borders of Moab's land that are struck, but the dual form פַּאֲתֵי in Numbers 24:17 (i.e., "two sides of Moab") and the close

---

[41] Sailhamer, *Pentateuch as Narrative*, 235.
[42] For more on the exaltation theme in Genesis, see Chen, *Messianic Vision of the Pentateuch*, 103.

parallel in Jeremiah 48:45 ("the פְּאַת of Moab and the *forehead* of the sons of tumult"; see below) suggest that the sides of the head, or temples, are meant in Numbers 24:17. In addition to dramatically portraying Moab's doom, the image of an eschatological hero crushing his enemies' heads matches that of the seed of the woman crushing the serpent's head in Genesis 3:15. The terms for "crush" and "head" differ, but the imagery is the same.[43]

James Hamilton refers to "what appears to be the interpretation of Gen 3:15 in Num 24:17."[44] Although Genesis 3:15 directly concerns only the crushing of the head of the ultimate enemy, its mention of the seed of the serpent and Balak's hiring of Balaam to use evil spiritual power against Israel (including "omens" [נַחַשׁ]) suggest that the enemies in Numbers 24:17 are part of the serpent's seed. As noted above, the allusion to Genesis 3:15 in Numbers 24:17 brings Balaam's oracles and the "snake"/"omen" (נחשׁ) theme to a climax and concludes the deuteroevangelium in Numbers 21–24 with the same hope for the ultimate defeat of the serpent with which it began (Num 21:4-9).

Thus, just as Numbers 24:9 braided Genesis 27:29 and Genesis 49:9 at the end of Balaam's third proverb, so Numbers 24:17 braids Genesis 3:15; 37:6-10 (Joseph's dreams); and Genesis 49:10 (scepter) in the fourth proverb. The use of Genesis 3:15 in Numbers 24:17 is especially significant because it identifies the king hoped for in Numbers 24:9, 17 as the seed of the woman in Genesis 3:15. This makes it harder to interpret the star as David, as some have done (e.g., Rashi), because David would then also have to be seed of the woman who crushes the serpent's head. The use of Genesis texts in Balaam's third and fourth proverbs concerning the Abrahamic covenant and creation is thus coordinated in a way that suggests that the hopes set forth in Genesis 3:15; 27:27-29; 49:8-12 are the same messianic hope. This is evidence that the eschatological Messiah is the integrative center of the Pentateuch and Old Testament, since major themes

---

[43] See Sailhamer, *Pentateuch as Narrative*, 409.
[44] James Hamilton, "The Skull Crushing Seed of the Woman: Inner-Biblical Interpretation of Genesis 3:15," *Southern Baptist Journal of Theology* 10, no. 2 (2006): 34.

from creation (e.g., seed of the woman), the Abrahamic covenant, and the exodus (Num 24:8) find their ultimate expression in him.

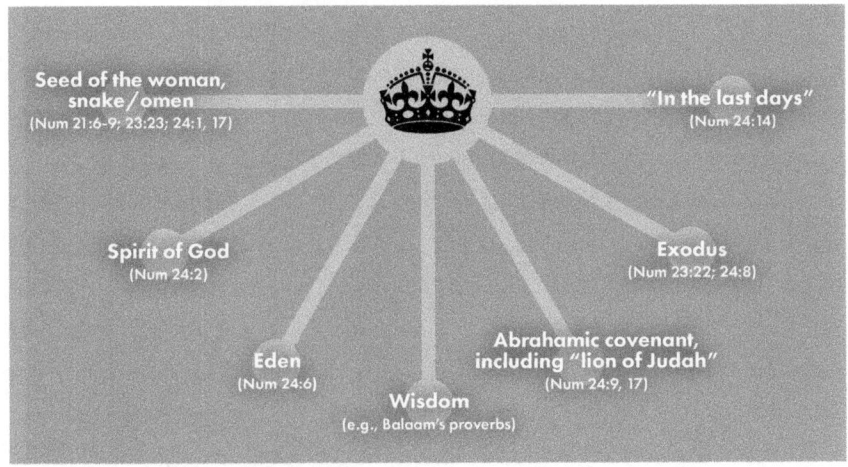

Figure 4.2. Major themes that feed into the messianic message of Numbers 24

The rest of Numbers 24:17-19 reinforces the links to creation and the Abrahamic covenant. After the mention of Moab in Numbers 24:17, which fits the Moabite and Midianite opposition of Numbers 22–24 (e.g., Num 22:3-4, 7-8, 10), the following mention of "the sons of Seth [שֵׁת]" at the end of Numbers 24:17 significantly expands the scope of the Messiah's victory. Seth was a second-generation human being (Gen 4:25), and although humanity was not all descended from him, he was an ancestor of Noah (Gen 5:6-8, 28-29), from whom the nations in Genesis 10 later came (Gen 10:1). Thus, "the sons of Seth" is best understood as referring to humanity, as Targum Onqelos and Rashi argue.[45]

The expansion of scope beyond Moab opens the door for still other nations to be mentioned. Numbers 24:18 proceeds to predict that "Edom will be a possession, and Seir, his enemies, will be a possession" (וְהָיָה אֱדוֹם יְרֵשָׁה וְהָיָה יְרֵשָׁה שֵׂעִיר אֹיְבָיו). Edom had recently opposed Israel in Numbers 20:14-21, but even they and their land would

---

[45]Contra Gordon Wenham, *Numbers*, TOTC (Downers Grove, IL: InterVarsity Press, 1981), 179-80. Wenham prefers "sons of Shut," referring to the Šutu in Egyptian texts.

eventually become Israel's through the Messiah. Furthermore, the expanded scope of the Messiah's victory through the phrase "the sons of Seth" hints that "Edom" (אֱדוֹם) in the next clause could likewise represent "humanity" (אָדָם; Gen 1:26-27), just as it does in Amos 9:12 and Obadiah (see below). In this case, Amos and Obadiah would be picking up on a wordplay already present in Numbers 24:18.

Furthermore, as I have shown previously, the clause "and Seir, his enemies, will be a possession" (וְהָיָה יְרֵשָׁה שֵׂעִיר אֹיְבָיו) in Numbers 24:18 strikingly plays on the clause "may your seed possess the gate of his enemies" (וְיִרַשׁ זַרְעֲךָ אֵת שַׁעַר אֹיְבָיו) in Genesis 22:17.[46] The term "enemies" (אֹיְבָיו) is repeated, "possession"/"possess" are cognates (יָרַשׁ/יְרֵשָׁה), and "Seir" plays on "gate" (שַׁעַר/שֵׂעִיר). The seed in this clause of Genesis 22:17 corresponds to the star and scepter of Numbers 24:17, suggesting again that this eschatological king is the fulfillment of the Abrahamic hope expressed in Genesis 22:17b-18. The braiding in Numbers 24:17-19 thus continues, adding Genesis 22:17 to Genesis 3:15; 37:6-10; and 49:10. The context of Genesis 22:17 is even an emphatic blessing following Abraham's near-sacrifice of Isaac, and Desmond Alexander has led the way in arguing that this last clause in Genesis 22:17 and the following Genesis 22:18 are messianic.[47] Because Genesis 24:60 similarly states, "May your seed *possess* the *gate* of those who hate him" (וְיִירַשׁ זַרְעֵךְ אֵת שַׁעַר שֹׂנְאָיו), this text should be linked to Genesis 22:17 and Numbers 24:18 also. Israel's triumph at the end of Numbers 24:18 has evidently come through their eschatological king, who defeats all enemies and takes possession of the whole earth.

The closing prayer in Numbers 24:19, "May he rule from Jacob," concerns the same star "from Jacob" (מִיַּעֲקֹב; see Is 65:9) and scepter "from Israel" (מִיִּשְׂרָאֵל) in Numbers 24:17. The verb "rule" (רָדָה) is notably used also in Genesis 1:26, 28, when humanity received the initial divine mandate to rule the earth (see Ps 72:8). There are four unrelated uses of this verb elsewhere in the Pentateuch (i.e., Lev 25:43, 46, 53; 26:17), but the

---

[46]Chen, *Messianic Vision of the Pentateuch*, 46, 222; see also Postell, "Numbers 24:5-9: Distant Star," 304.

[47]T. Desmond Alexander, "Further Observations on the Term 'Seed' in Genesis," *TynBul* 48, no. 2 (1997): 364-68.

messianic use in Numbers 24:19 is likely coordinated with God's original charge to humanity in Genesis 1:26, 28. Thus Numbers 24:17-19 probably braids Genesis 1:26-28 as well.

Numbers 24:17-19 serves as a fitting climax to Balaam's four main proverbs and the Balaam narrative, while at the same time being a remarkable example of braiding. While predicting the coming of an eschatological Messiah who will defeat all of his and Israel's enemies and rule the earth, Numbers 24:17-19 braids Genesis 1:26-28; 3:15; 22:17; 24:60; 37:6-10; 49:10.

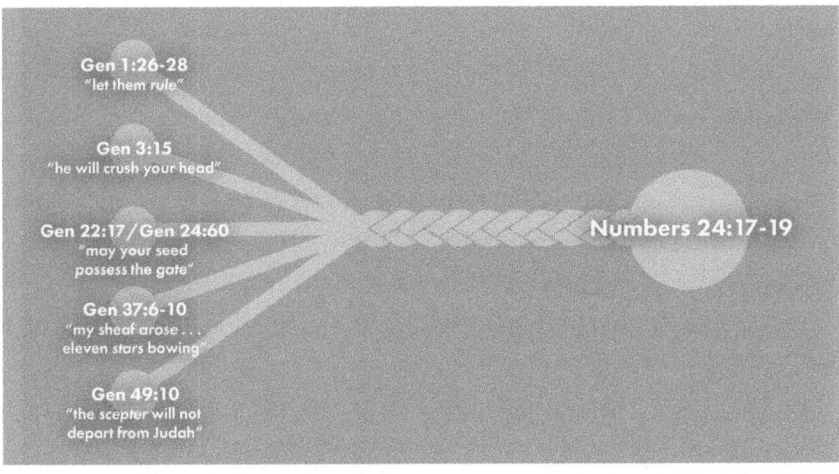

Figure 4.3. Braiding in Numbers 24:17-19

Though Alexander focused on only Genesis 3:15 and Genesis 49:8-12, it is as though what he calls "the messianic ideology of Genesis" has been fleshed out and sharpened in the poetry of Numbers 24 in condensed form.[48] Sailhamer also strongly advocates for close attention to the Pentateuch's poems and their interrelationship, including Genesis 3:15; 27:27-29; 49:8-12; those in Numbers 24; and others. Recall that Numbers 24:17-19 interconnects with Numbers 24:9, which itself braids Genesis 27:29 and

---

[48]T. Desmond Alexander, "Messianic Ideology in the Book of Genesis," in *The Lord's Anointed: Interpretation of Old Testament Messianic Texts*, ed. Philip Satterthwaite, Richard Hess, and Gordon Wenham (Grand Rapids, MI: Baker, 1995), 19-39.

Genesis 49:9, and that Numbers 24:8 ties in the theme of exodus. Thus, Balaam's oracles in Numbers 24 provide significant evidence for the eschatological Messiah as the compositional, integrative center of the Pentateuch and the Old Testament.

NEXUS CONNECTIONS TO OTHER BIBLICAL BOOKS

Scholars have noticed quotations and allusions to Balaam's oracles (i.e., third and fourth proverbs). When these are collected, we see a surprising number of later prophetic authors who paid special attention to the two oracles in Numbers 24. In other words, Numbers 24 not only braids important Genesis texts but is in turn alluded to. Sometimes Numbers 24 is itself braided with other Old Testament texts. This suggests that later Old Testament authors recognized the importance of Numbers 24, including its interconnectivity. I begin below with examples that are relatively well-established among scholars before adding others that fewer have noticed.

Amos 9:11-12 and Obadiah 17-21. The first two examples concern the possession of Edom as predicted in Numbers 24:18. Amos 9:11-12 connects the possession of Edom with the restoration of the Davidic house, "I will raise up the fallen tabernacle of David . . . so that they may possess the remnant of Edom." According to C. F. Keil, "possess" (יָרַשׁ) "is chosen with reference to the prophecy of Balaam (Num. 24:18), that Edom should be the possession of Israel."[49] Walter Kaiser agrees.[50] Obadiah likewise predicts Israel's possession of Edom (Obad 18-19, 21). According to Jacob Milgrom, Numbers 24:19, which includes the clause "and he will destroy the survivor from the city" (וְהֶאֱבִיד שָׂרִיד מֵעִיר), "was clearly incorporated into Obadiah's prophecy (1:17-18) against Edom: 'The house of Jacob shall dispossess [יָרַשׁ] . . . and no savior [sic?] shall be left [וְלֹא־יִהְיֶה שָׂרִיד] of the House of Esau' (see Amos 9:12)."[51] Daniel Block sees "echoes" of

---

[49]C. F. Keil and F. Delitzsch, *The Minor Prophets*, Commentary on the Old Testament 10 (repr., Peabody, MA: Hendrickson, 1996), 222. See also Michael Shepherd, *A Commentary on the Book of the Twelve* (Grand Rapids, MI: Kregel, 2018), 202-3.
[50]Walter Kaiser, "The Davidic Promise and the Inclusion of the Gentiles (Amos 9:9-15 and Acts 15:13-18): A Test Passage for Theological Systems," *JETS* 20, no. 2 (1977): 103. He does not cite Keil, but his comments are very similar.
[51]Milgrom, *Numbers*, 208.

Numbers 24:18-19 in "Obadiah's vocabulary of possession [יָרַשׁ, vv. 17, 19-20], survivors [שָׂרִיד, v. 18], and doing valiantly [cf. v. 11b]."⁵² Accordingly, Keil calls both Amos 9:12 and Obadiah 17-21 "declarations of the prophets . . . [which have] an unmistakeable allusion to this prophecy."⁵³ For these scholars, the common theme of Israel's possession of Edom and accompanying terminology (at least *possess* and *Edom*) justify perceiving these allusions to Numbers 24.

Thus, no matter how obscure Numbers 24:18-19 may seem to today's readers, evidently this text was not obscure to these two prophets, both of whom rely on it in the climactic conclusions to their respective books. Moreover, if the sequencing of Amos and Obadiah in the Masoretic edition of the Twelve is not accidental and based at least in part on allusions to this same text, then it appears that the compositional strategy of the Pentateuch, which features Balaam's oracles as part of a compositional seam, has influenced the composition of the Twelve, since Amos and Obadiah are consecutive in the MT and as such also involve a compositional seam. As Sailhamer notes, the compositional seams of other Old Testament books frequently followed the pattern of the Pentateuch's compositional seams.⁵⁴ If the Twelve is one such book, then we may add its final composer as a third prophetic author to this list of those who saw the importance of Balaam's oracles.

Jeremiah 48:45. In the context of the Lord coming to Moab for "the year of their visitation" (Jer 48:44), Jeremiah 48:45 says that fire will consume "the temple of Moab and the skull of the sons of tumult" (פְּאַת מוֹאָב וְקָדְקֹד בְּנֵי שָׁאוֹן). The similarity to the "temples of Moab" (פַּאֲתֵי מוֹאָב) and the "skull [קַרְקַר, obscure but similar-looking to קָדְקֹד] of all the sons of Seth" in Numbers 24:17 is striking, and Gordon Wenham thinks that Jeremiah 48:45 is quoting Numbers 24:17.⁵⁵ Similarly, John

---

⁵²Daniel Block, *Obadiah: The Kingship Belongs to Yahweh*, Hearing the Message of Scripture (Grand Rapids, MI: Zondervan, 2013), 93 (including n68).
⁵³C. F. Keil and Franz Delitzsch, *The Pentateuch*, Commentary on the Old Testament 1 (repr., Peabody, MA: Hendrickson, 1996), 784.
⁵⁴Sailhamer, *Meaning of the Pentateuch*, 203. See also Seth Postell, "Messianism in Light of Literary Strategy," *BSac* 177 (2020): 329-50.
⁵⁵Wenham, *Numbers*, 179.

Bright sees Jeremiah 48:45-47 as "composed in good part of snatches of very ancient poems" (Jer 48:45b/Num 21:28a; Jer 48:45c/Num 24:17c; Jer 48:46/Num 21:29).⁵⁶ To strengthen the case still further, the oracle concerning Moab closes with "in the last days" (בְּאַחֲרִית הַיָּמִים, Jer 48:47), like Numbers 24:14. For Wenham and Bright, the common theme of the judgment of Moab and accompanying terminology justify a dependence of Jeremiah 48 on Numbers 24 (see Num 21:28-29).

However, whereas only the judgment of Moab is mentioned in Numbers 24:17, the judgment of Moab in Jeremiah 48 ends with a brief but strong note of hope in Jeremiah 48:47, "I will restore the fortunes of Moab in the last days." This difference parallels Edom's judgment *and* salvation in Amos 9:12 (possessed, yet called by the Lord's name) compared to the focus on their eschatological judgment in Numbers 24:18. Nevertheless, in the broader scheme of the Pentateuch and the spread of Abrahamic blessing to the nations (Gen 12:3; 18:18; 22:18; 28:14), the eschatological judgment and salvation of the nations is not unusual. Moreover, "possess" (יָרַשׁ) seems to be used in a positive, salvific sense in Amos 9:12, which could affect our understanding of its usage in Numbers 24:18 and Obadiah.

Other texts noticed by scholars (Dan 11:30; Ps 110; 2; Ezek 38:17?; Hos 11:1?). Some other examples from broader scholarship may be considered more briefly. Although I did not discuss the "ships from Kittim" in Numbers 24:24 above, Wenham thinks that Daniel 11:30 quotes this portion of Balaam's prophecies.⁵⁷ Likewise, George Gray thinks that Daniel 11:30 "appear[s] to allude" to Numbers 24:24.⁵⁸ Wenham also thinks that "Psalm 110 contains enough verbal parallels with Numbers 24:15-19 to make it probable that the psalmist knew Balaam's oracle and was consciously alluding to it."⁵⁹ Previously I considered these and other intertextual connections to Psalm 110 as a nexus passage

---

⁵⁶John Bright, *Jeremiah*, AB (Garden City, NY: Doubleday, 1965), 322; likewise, John A. Thompson, *The Book of Jeremiah*, NICOT (Grand Rapids, MI: Eerdmans, 1980), 713.
⁵⁷Wenham, *Numbers*, 183.
⁵⁸Gray, *Numbers*, 378.
⁵⁹Wenham, *Numbers*, 183 (including n1).

itself.⁶⁰ Gary Schnittjer also notes a possible link between Psalm 2:8-9 ("you will shatter them with a scepter [שֵׁבֶט]") and Numbers 24:17-19.⁶¹ If Psalms 1–2 are taken as the introduction to the Psalter, then this allusion coordinates the Psalter's composition at least in part with the Pentateuch's. Psalm 2 and Psalm 110 themselves have much in common, with both depicting global opposition to the Lord and his chosen king.

At this point, we can already see that scholars have recognized references to Balaam's oracles in Jeremiah, Amos, Obadiah, Psalms, and Daniel. Assuming that these five books have different authors, this means that these five later Old Testament authors, plus the final composer of the Twelve, all not only knew these oracles but saw their importance and incorporated them into their own books in significant ways. This number does not count broader references to the Balaam narrative that are not specifically directed to the oracles (e.g., Josh 24:9-10; Judg 11:25; Mic 6:5; Neh 13:2).

Seeing this many prophetic authors draw on Balaam's oracles makes one wonder whether there are still more. If the "Gog" reading in Numbers 24:7 is adopted (see LXX, Aquila, Symmachus, Theodotion), then Ezekiel can be added to the list (Ezek 38:18). Though a minority view, Sailhamer argues that Hosea 11:1 ("out of Egypt I called my son") alludes to Numbers 24:8 ("God brings him out of Egypt").⁶² If he is right, then Hosea could be added also. Besides these more debated examples, there are additional ones that could garner wider agreement.

2 Samuel 23:1-5 and Proverbs 30:1-4. Scholars have observed that the introductory formula to Balaam's oracles is very similar to the ones found in 2 Samuel 23:1 and Proverbs 30:1.⁶³

---

⁶⁰Kevin Chen, "Psalm 110: A Nexus for Old Testament Theology," *CTR* 17, no. 2 (Spring 2020): 49-65.

⁶¹Schnittjer, *Old Testament Use of the Old Testament*, 57.

⁶²Sailhamer, "Hosea 11:1 and Matthew 2:15," *WTJ* 63 (2001): 87-96; Dan McCartney and Peter Enns, "Matthew and Hosea: A Response to John Sailhamer," *WTJ* 63 (2001): 97-105. This interaction is discussed in Michael Shepherd, *The Twelve Prophets in the New Testament* (New York: Lang, 2011), 19-22; Kevin Chen, "(Mis)Understanding Sailhamer," *Journal for the Evangelical Study of the Old Testament* 7, no. 1 (2021): 45-48. See also Lindars, who argues that Matthew interpreted Hos 11:1 with the help of Num 24:7-8 LXX (*New Testament Apologetic*, 216-17).

⁶³E.g., A. A. Anderson, *2 Samuel*, WBC (Dallas: Word, 1989), 267-68; Roland Murphy, *Proverbs*, WBC (Nashville: Thomas Nelson, 1998), 226.

The oracle of Balaam son of Beor, and the oracle of the man who eye is opened. (Num 24:3, 15)

נְאֻם בִּלְעָם בְּנוֹ בְעֹר וּנְאֻם הַגֶּבֶר שְׁתֻם הָעָיִן

The oracle of David son of Jesse, and the oracle of the man raised up [on high?]. (2 Sam 23:1)

נְאֻם דָּוִד בֶּן־יִשַׁי וּנְאֻם הַגֶּבֶר הֻקַם עָל

The words of Agur son of Jakeh, the prophecy, the oracle of the man to Ithiel, to Ithiel and Ucal/is consumed. (Prov 30:1)

דִּבְרֵי אָגוּר בִּן־יָקֶה הַמַּשָּׂא נְאֻם הַגֶּבֶר לְאִיתִיאֵל לְאִיתִיאֵל וְאֻכָל

All three texts begin with "the oracle/words of *x* son of *y*" (using the term *oracle*, this formula appears only in Num 24:3, 15 and 2 Sam 23:1) and continue in the next clause with the phrase "the oracle of the man" (נְאֻם הַגֶּבֶר; found only in these three texts). Numbers 24:3, 15 and 2 Samuel 23:1 are especially alike because they both begin with "oracle" (נְאֻם) and end with constructions involving passive verbs. Proverbs 30:1 may also end with a passive verb ("consumed"?), and even its different first term, "words" (דִּבְרֵי), matches the "last *words* [דִּבְרֵי] of David" in the first part of 2 Samuel 23:1. Also, if Agur and Jakeh in Proverbs 30:1 are Gentiles, as many scholars think, then there is a parallel to the Gentile Balaam in Numbers 24.[64] These three passages are also the only "oracles" (נְאֻם) from a human speaker.[65] Based on these lexical, syntactic, and thematic parallels (and others), we may consider whether 2 Samuel 23:1-5 and Proverbs 30:1-4 also allude to Numbers 24.

As seen above, the formula in 2 Samuel 23:1 especially resembles the one in Numbers 24:3, 15. Additional lexical and thematic connections further strengthen the likelihood of an allusion. The prefacing of 2 Samuel 23:1-7 as David's "last" (הָאַחֲרֹנִים) words recalls not only the patriarchal, messianic blessings of Isaac and Jacob (Gen 27:27-29; 49:1, 8-12; see Deut 32–33) but also Balaam's mention of the "last/end of" (אַחֲרִית) days in Numbers 24:14 and that Balaam's oracles are also his "last [recorded] words." Like Balaam, who had the Spirit of God come on him

---

[64]Lindsay Wilson, *Proverbs*, TOTC (Downers Grove, IL: InterVarsity Press, 2018), 306.
[65]Gary Rendsburg also counts the obscure Ps 36:1, but the speaker is "transgression." Rendsburg, "The Northern Origin of 'The Last Words of David' (2 Sam 23,1-7)," *Biblica* 69, no. 1 (1988): 115.

(Num 24:2), "the Spirit of the Lord" spoke through David (2 Sam 23:2), who is thus cast as a prophet (see Acts 2:30). Like Balaam's oracles, David's oracle also focuses on a perfect, eschatological king (2 Sam 23:3-4). David describes this king as fulfilling the Davidic covenant (2 Sam 23:5). This latter description parallels Balaam's oracles, which describe this king's exaltation (Num 24:7), fulfillment of the *Abrahamic* covenant (Num 24:9, 17-18), and defeat of enemies in an eschatological battle (Num 24:17-19). Interestingly, the form וְיָרֹם in Numbers 24:7 ("and let [his king] be exalted") has parallels in two other important poems in Samuel (וְיָרֵם in 1 Sam 2:10, "and let [the horn of his messiah] be exalted"; וְיָרֻם in 2 Sam 22:47, "and let [the God of the rock of my salvation] be exalted"), raising the possibility that all three poems in 1 Samuel 2:1-10 and 2 Samuel 22–23 allude to Numbers 24.[66]

Back to 2 Samuel 23:1-7 itself, Ralph Klein further points out its "wisdom flavor" through the contrast between the righteous king and the wicked, as well as the characterization of the righteous king as "ruling in the fear of God."[67] This parallels the wisdom elements in the Balaam narrative, including the oracles (see above). Without intending to make a connection to Balaam's proverbs, Kyle McCarter Jr. calls 2 Samuel 23:3b-4 a *mashal* (מָשָׁל).[68] Second Samuel 23:3 LXX even reads the first instance of מוֹשֵׁל in the verse as "parable" (παραβολὴν), as though its consonantal *Vorlage* was meant to be read as מָשָׁל, whether the direct object of the preceding (Brenton's translation) or following (NETS). Either way, the content of the oracle in the LXX is explicitly a proverb or parable.

Compositionally, 2 Samuel 23:1-7 also is a major poem in the macrostructure of 1-2 Samuel (see 1 Sam 2:1-10; 2 Sam 1:18-27; 2 Sam 22–23:7).[69]

---

[66]Jonathan Shelton pointed out this repetition of רום and allusion of 1 Sam 2:10/2 Sam 22:47 to Num 24:7 to me in personal correspondence. See also Postell, "Messianism in Light of Literary Strategy," 335-36 (including n20).

[67]Ralph Klein, "The Last Words of David," *Currents in Theology and Mission* 31, no. 1 (2004): 16.

[68]P. Kyle McCarter Jr., *II Samuel*, AB (New York: Doubleday, 1984), 480, 483. Hans Wilhelm Hertzberg refers to those who believe that the poem's language "has close affinity with the [*mashal*]." Hertzberg, *I & II Samuel*, trans. John Bowden, OTL (Philadelphia: Westminster, 1964), 400.

[69]See Benjamin Thompson, "Pride and Kingship: A Literary Reading of 1 and 2 Samuel Considering the Role of the Poetry in the Characterisation of the Kings" (PhD diss, Queen's University, 2021), 24-30.

The compositional factor recalls the discussion of the Amos-Obadiah connections above. The combined compositional, lexical, syntactic, and thematic links involving 2 Samuel 23:1-5 are at least as strong as the links for the above passages identified by scholars as alluding to Numbers 24. Despite Hans Hertzberg's claim that the similar introductory formula "is not a case of literary borrowing, but of stylistic form," the additional links from 2 Samuel 23:1-7 to Numbers 24 that go beyond this formula suggests that David's oracle does allude to Balaam's oracles.[70] For the same reasons, an allusion to Numbers 24:3, 15 seems more likely than David Toshio Tsumura's related suggestion that, based on similar titles in Egyptian poetry, "David had learned the Egyptian literary practices indirectly from the Jebusite court in Jerusalem, which had a close relationship with Egypt during the Amarna age."[71]

As mentioned above, Proverbs 30:1, despite textual difficulties in Proverbs 30:1b ("for Ithiel, for Ithiel and Ucal/is consumed" [אֻכָל]), also has similarities to Numbers 24:3, 15 (prophetic message of "x son of y," "the oracle of the man" [נְאֻם הַגֶּבֶר], Gentile speakers). Like the poetic oracles in Numbers 24 and 2 Samuel 23:1-7, Proverbs 30 occupies an important position in the macrostructure of the book, that is, the conclusion to the book of Proverbs in Proverbs 30–31. Sailhamer takes this as one of many examples showing that Old Testament authors of prophetic and Wisdom books "were well-versed in the Mosaic Pentateuch as a literary text" and that

> the compositional seams of books such as Proverbs often were modeled after and built on the compositional seams of the Pentateuch. The introductory words about Agur in Proverbs 30:1-2 are clearly linked to Balaam's introduction in Numbers 24:3. Prophecy becomes wisdom until the return of a future prophet—a common theme found along the seams of the OT canon [see Josh 1:8; Ps 1:2].[72]

---

[70]Hertzberg, *I & II Samuel*, 400. For critical scholars, there would also be the issue of dating these two texts. See Levine, *Numbers 21–36*, 230-32. Tony Cartledge refers to broader scholarship's wide acceptance of the "great antiquity of the Balaam texts" and the common belief that 2 Sam 23:1-7 is from the Davidic era, if not David himself. He calls 2 Sam 23:1 "strongly reminiscent" of Num 24:3, 15. Cartledge, *1 & 2 Samuel*, SHBC (Macon, GA: Smyth & Helwys, 2001), 669.
[71]David Toshio Tsumura, *The Second Book of Samuel*, NICOT (Grand Rapids, MI: Eerdmans, 2019), 323.
[72]Sailhamer, *Meaning of the Pentateuch*, 203.

Additional considerations support an allusion to Numbers 24 in Proverbs 30:1-4. Like Numbers 24, Proverbs 30:1-4 naturally also has wisdom language (discernment, Prov 30:2; learn, wisdom, knowledge, know, Prov 30:3). The term "foolish" (בַּעַר) in Proverbs 30:2 can further be connected via wordplay to Balaam, the son of Beor (בְּעוֹר).[73] Most uses of this word for "foolish" (בַּעַר) even match the characterization of Balaam during the donkey episode (i.e., as someone who did not "know," Ps 73:22; 92:6; as like an animal, Ps 73:22; as hating correction, Prov 12:1). The ultimate focus of Proverbs 30:1-4 on the Lord ("What is his name?"), and his seemingly equally glorious son ("What is the name of his son?") in Proverbs 30:4 hints tantalizingly at a messianic interpretation (for further discussion, see chapter ten), which, though brief, would match Numbers 24. Although Numbers 24 does not refer to the Messiah as son, other messianic passages in the Pentateuch do (Gen 27:27; 49:9). The Solomonic origin of (much of) the book of Proverbs also legitimizes a connection from Proverbs 30:4 to the Davidic covenant text 2 Samuel 7:14 and its emphasis on divine sonship. These considerations suggest that Proverbs 30:1-4 also alludes to Numbers 24.

Judges 5:26-27. Though not frequently noticed, the poetic description of Jael killing Sisera in Judges 5:26-27 also appears to allude to Balaam's oracles, though in a different way from the previous passages analyzed. Whereas other texts use Balaam's prophecies for their own prophecies, Judges 5:26-27 draws on his prophecies and those of Genesis 3:15; 49:8-12 to describe a *past* event. Such a description hints that this past victory is a foretaste and glimpse of the actual fulfillment of these same prophecies. Hamilton highlights the common theme of "crushing the head" between Genesis 3:15; Judges 4–5; and other texts, as well as a possible allusion in Judges 5:26 to Numbers 24:17 through the verb "crush" (מָחַץ).[74] Judges 5 is also the lone lengthy poem in the book,

---

[73]Targum Jonathan; Seth Postell, Eitan Bar, and Erez Soref, *Reading Moses, Seeing Jesus: How the Torah Fulfills Its Goal in Yeshua*, 2nd ed. (Wooster, OH: Weaver, 2017), 76n1. See also Milgrom, *Numbers*, 186, 319.

[74]Hamilton, "Skull Crushing Seed," 35. See also Stephen Dempster, *Dominion and Dynasty: A Theology of the Hebrew Bible* (Downers Grove, IL: InterVarsity Press, 2003), 132.

compositionally analogous to the four major poetic sections in the Pentateuch and the poems in Samuel.

Judges 5:26-27 and its immediate context have significant lexical and thematic parallels that increase the likelihood of allusions to Genesis 3:15; 49:8-12; Numbers 24:8-9, 17.[75] Language and themes of a "woman" (אִשָּׁה, Gen 3:15/Judg 5:24) and crushing an enemy's "head" (רֹאשׁ, Gen 3:15/Judg 5:26) provide a strong connection to Genesis 3:15. Judges 5:26-27 is linked to Genesis 49:8-12 through the common terms "milk" (חָלָב, Gen 49:12/Judg 5:25), "stoop down" (כָּרַע, Gen 49:9/Judg 5:27), and "between his/her feet" (בֵּין רַגְלָיו/רַגְלֶיהָ, Gen 49:10/Judg 5:27), as well as the related terms "lie down" (שָׁכַב/רָבַץ, Gen 49:9/Judg 5:27) and the similarly spelled "ruler's staff"/"annihilate" (מְחֹקֵק/מָחֲקָה, Gen 49:10/Judg 5:26). In addition to the connection between Judges 5:26 and Numbers 24:17 through the word "crush" (מָחַץ), which also links to Numbers 24:8, Jael's crushing of Sisera's "temple" (רַקָּה) in Judges 5:26 recalls the crushing of Moab's "temples" (פֵּאָה) in Numbers 24:17. Moreover, although Sisera's stooping down (כָּרַע), falling (נָפַל), and lying down (שָׁכַב) in Judges 5:27 do parallel Genesis 49:9 (which has כָּרַע and רָבַץ also in sequenced *qatal* third-person masculine singular forms), the link to Numbers 24:9 is stronger because this text uses the same term not only for "stoop down" (כָּרַע) but also for "lie down" (שָׁכַב). The surrounding context of Numbers 24:9 even has "fall down" (נָפַל), referring to Balaam's response to the revelation (Num 24:4, 16).[76] Certainly, the way some of these terms are used is different from Genesis 49:8-12 and Numbers 24:8-9, 17, but their use still recalls these two texts, while the crushing of the enemy's head provides the primary, stronger link to Genesis 3:15 and Numbers 24:17. We should also notice here how the description in Judges 5:26-27 serves the purposes of the poem in Judges 5 while at the same time braiding Genesis 3:15; 49:9-10, 12; Numbers 24:8-9, 17. Judges 11:25 further refers to the Balaam narrative, and the preceding evidence is sufficient to support

---

[75]The following builds on my previous work in Chen, *Messianic Vision of the Pentateuch*, 52, 130.
[76]See George Moore, *A Critical and Exegetical Commentary on Judges*, ICC (Edinburgh, T&T Clark, 1989), 166. Moore notes the parallel between "he stoops down" and "he lies down" in Judg 5:27 and Num 24:9 but makes no comment.

a prior allusion in Judges 5:26-27 specifically to Balaam's oracles in Numbers 24. Jael's victory over Sisera thus is presented as a foretaste of the eschatological victory of the seed of the woman.

Isaiah 63:1-3. The book of Isaiah may also be added to this lengthy list of Old Testament books that allude to Balaam's oracles in Numbers 24. Sailhamer argues that the figure in Isaiah 63:1-3 who comes from Edom with bloodstained clothes has been intentionally presented in terms of Genesis 3:15 and Genesis 49:11-12. He believes that Isaiah has begun with the image of the king whose clothes are stained by grapes in Genesis 49:11. Sailhamer also believes that Isaiah draws on Genesis 3:15 (presumably the crushing of the serpent's head) to fill out the picture from Genesis 49:11 "into one of a warrior treading in the wine presses of divine wrath."[77] Isaiah 63:2 asks, "Why is your garment red and your clothes *like one who treads the winepress*?" Previously, I further argued that the bruising of the seed's heel in Genesis 3:15 and an allusion in Genesis 49:11 to Joseph's bloodstained robe in Genesis 37:31-33 suggest that the blood on the king's garments may also include his own.[78]

There appears to be yet another intertextual layer to Isaiah 63:1-3. This text clearly concerns the judgment of "Edom" (Is 63:1), cast as "treading [דָּרַךְ] the winepress" (Is 63:2). In Numbers 24:17, the "star *treads* [דָּרַךְ] from Jacob," and it possesses "Edom" in Numbers 24:18. The collocation of "Edom"/"tread" is rare (see Amos 9:12-13), and this suggests that Isaiah 63:1-3 has drawn on not only

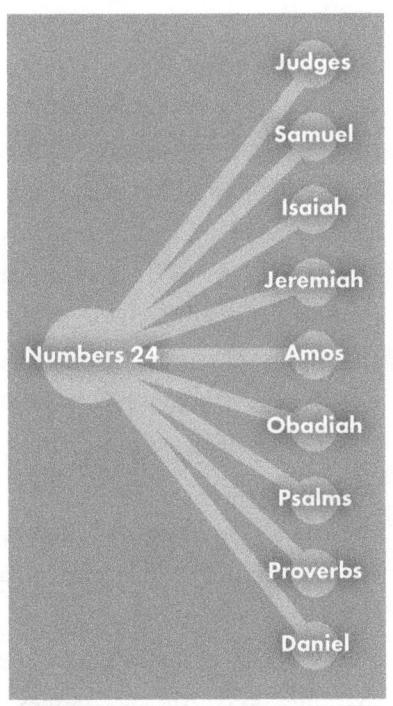

Figure 4.4. Nexus connections from Numbers 24 to other Old Testament books

---

[77]Sailhamer, *Meaning of the Pentateuch*, 239.
[78]Chen, *Messianic Vision of the Pentateuch*, 136-37.

Genesis 3:15 and Genesis 49:11-12 but also Numbers 24:17-18. Amazingly, the same three passages are also braided in Judges 5:26-27. My previous analysis of Psalm 110 also links these three passages among others to this psalm.[79] Thus, the preliminary list gathered simply by surveying broader scholarship (Jeremiah, Amos, Obadiah, Psalms, and Daniel) can be expanded to include Judges, Samuel, Isaiah, Proverbs, and possibly even Ezekiel and Hosea. Even if some readers assign less weight to some of these examples, this list remains impressive by any measure and demonstrates that Numbers 24 is a nexus passage.

NUMBERS 24, MESSIAH, AND THE CENTER OF THE OLD TESTAMENT

As a nexus passage, Numbers 24 both is highly connected to other key texts within the Pentateuch and occupies a key position in its macrostructure and compositional strategy. Furthermore, Numbers 24 is just as highly connected to many other Old Testament books, with later biblical authors often not only alluding to it but doing so at key compositional junctures in their own books. If we were searching simply for a textual center of the Old Testament (see introduction), Numbers 24 would be a good candidate. However, as pointed out earlier, the problem with stopping here is that the proposed textual center still has to be explained. What does it mean? In the case of Numbers 24, the focus of its oracles is the coming of Israel's eschatological king. Thus, Numbers 24 is a *messianic* nexus passage.

Although by itself not a banner example of a major pentateuchal theme such as creation or exodus (see chapters two and three), the preceding has shown that Numbers 24 brings together key creation texts, Abrahamic covenant texts, and exodus texts to cast a vision of the Messiah, eschatological Israel, and eschatological salvation and judgment. To a greater extent than any other passage in the Pentateuch (to my knowledge), Numbers 24 shows that these key texts and themes in the Pentateuch ultimately have a messianic purpose. Such a messianic synthesis suggests that the Pentateuch's

---

[79] Chen, "Psalm 110," 51-57, 59-60.

exegetically derived center is this eschatological king. Allusions to Numbers 24 in other Old Testament books also highlight the Messiah and eschatology.

Even though the Messiah is not mentioned every time (and need not be), his appearance in several intertexts outside the Pentateuch (e.g., 2 Sam 23:3-4; Is 63:1-3; Amos 9:11-12; Ps 110; see also Judg 5:26-27) and his centrality to Numbers 24 (itself central to the Pentateuch's macrostructure) suggest that this eschatological king is not only the exegetical and compositional center of the Pentateuch but even of the Old Testament, which has the Pentateuch as its historical and theological foundation. I have argued at length for the former in a previous work, and whereas the latter would take multiple works by multiple scholars to demonstrate thoroughly, the above discussion of nexus connections to other Old Testament books and some of the subsequent chapters in the present work provide supporting evidence.

CONCLUSION

As part of one of the Pentateuch's key poetic sections and the finale of Numbers 21–24, Numbers 24 is the climax of the latter's deuteroevangelium, which builds on the protoevangelium of Genesis 3:15. Drawing together numerous pentateuchal texts concerning creation, wisdom, Abrahamic covenant, and exodus for a messianic purpose, Numbers 24 shows how literary and textual unity can achieve theological, even Christocentric, unity. The importance of this text is further supported by the number of Old Testament books that refer to it, especially Balaam's oracles. The evidence above has shown that the authors of Judges, Samuel, Isaiah, Jeremiah, possibly Ezekiel, possibly Hosea, Amos, Obadiah, Psalms, Proverbs, and Daniel were not only aware of these oracles but made use of them as an important part of their own writings. Even if some prefer a more conservative count, the number of Old Testament books that allude to Balaam's oracles still confirms their importance to the Old Testament and its theology. Thus, frequent inattention to Numbers 24 and the moderate attention given to it by the New Testament (NA[28] lists only three allusions) belies its importance to the Old Testament as a nexus passage.

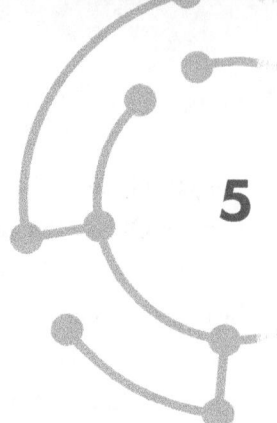

5

DEUTERONOMY 32

A SONG FOR THE AGES

THE SONG OF MOSES in Deuteronomy 32:1-43 has long been recognized for its numerous connections to prophetic literature. Carl Cornhill's classic characterization of the song as "largely a compendium of prophetic theology" is still quoted to the present day.[1] Writing from a critical perspective, he believed that Deuteronomy 32:1-43 was late and "through and through full of reminiscences of the older prophets," such as Hosea, (Proto-)Isaiah, Micah, Jeremiah, and Deutero-Isaiah.[2] Though agreeing with Cornhill's basic point, S. R. Driver emphasizes "greater affinities with prophets of the Chaldaean age [i.e., Jeremiah, Ezekiel], than with the earlier prophets."[3] More recently, Stephen Chapman acknowledges Cornhill and concludes that the song is "a pastiche of prophecy."[4]

While recognizing the prophetic element, Gerhard von Rad places Deuteronomy 32:1-43 "in the sphere of Wisdom literature."[5] James Boston's

---

[1] Carl Heinrich Cornhill, *Einleitung in das Alte Testament* (Freiburg: Mohr, 1891), 71. Original: "gewissermaassen ein Compendium der prophetischen Theologie." Quotations can be found as early as Driver (1896) and relatively recently in McConville (2002).
[2] Cornhill, *Einleitung in das Alte Testament*, 71. Original: "durch und durch voll Reminiscenzen an ältere Propheten."
[3] S. R. Driver, *Deuteronomy*, ICC (repr., Edinburgh: T&T Clark, 1986), 347. For the argument that Deut 32 is a "covenant lawsuit" arising from prophetic circles, see G. Ernest Wright, "The Lawsuit of God: A Form-Critical Study of Deuteronomy 32," in *Israel's Prophetic Heritage*, ed. Bernhard Anderson and Walter Harrelson (New York: Harper, 1962), 26-67.
[4] Stephen Chapman, *The Law and the Prophets* (Grand Rapids, MI: Baker, 2020), 158-64. Building on Weinfeld, Chapman emphasizes the song's connection to Jeremiah (163). See Moshe Weinfeld, *Deuteronomy and the Deuteronomic School* (Winona Lake, IN: Eisenbrauns, 1992), 361, citing Deut 32:37-38/Jer 2:28; Deut 32:9/Jer 10:16; Deut 32:22/Jer 15:14/Jer 17:4.
[5] Gerhard von Rad, *Deuteronomy*, trans. Dorothea Barton, OTL (Philadelphia: Westminster, 1966), 200.

article cites the introduction of the song (Deut 32:1-3), overt wisdom language (Deut 32:6, 15, 21, 28), and other vocabulary shared with Wisdom literature as evidence for "wisdom influence" in addition to "prophetic influence" on Deuteronomy 32:1-43. He concludes, "The line between prophet and wise man must not be drawn too sharply."[6] From an evangelical perspective, these connections are not hard to explain if later Old Testament authors read the Pentateuch and memorized the Song of Moses as the Lord predicted future generations would (Deut 31:19-21, 30). This is all the more significant given that Israel will forget the Lord despite being commanded not to do so (Deut 6:12; 32:18). If even rebellious generations of Israelites also knew this song, then the prophets were wise to use it as common ground.[7] Today, this suggests that we should keep this song in mind when reading the prophets.

The preceding brief survey shows that Deuteronomy 32:1-43 is a well-established candidate for a nexus passage, with connections to the prophets and to wisdom, if not more. Indeed, Alan Cooper points out that Deuteronomy 32:1-43 provides "the plan of Jewish history."[8] He discusses Ramban's comments on Deuteronomy 32:40, which include, "Now this Song, which is our true and faithful testimony, tells us clearly all that will happen to us [i.e., conquest, idolatry, exile].... It is known that all this has been fulfilled, and it was so."[9] The predictions of entrance into Canaan,

---

[6] James R. Boston, "The Wisdom Influence upon the Song of Moses," *JBL* 87, no. 2 (1968): 202.
[7] See Jeffrey Tigay, *Deuteronomy*, JPS Torah Commentary (Philadelphia: JPS, 1996), 511. For the historical plausibility of Israel memorizing this song, see George A. F. Knight, *The Song of Moses: A Theological Quarry* (Grand Rapids, MI: Eerdmans, 1995), 4-6. Since I hold to the Mosaic authorship of the Pentateuch, I do not follow his broader proposal of the song's origin.
[8] Alan Cooper, "The Song of Moses (Deuteronomy 32:1-43) as the Plan of Jewish History," in *Ve-'Ed Ya'aleh (Gen 2:6): Essays in Biblical and Ancient Near Eastern Studies Presented to Edward L. Greenstein*, ed. Peter Machinist et al. (Atlanta: SBL Press, 2021), 2:989-1005. He explains that for Ramban this history includes not only biblical and postbiblical history but "Jewish history in its entirety" from "initial election" to "ultimate redemption" (994). Knight draws attention to "days of old" in Deut 32:7 and the term אַחֲרִית, or "end" (*Song of Moses*, 34-35). The latter is found in Deut 31:29; 32:20, 29.
[9] Cooper, "Song of Moses," 992. For this translation of Ramban, see https://www.sefaria.org/Deuteronomy.32.40?lang=en&with=Ramban&lang2=en. Josephus writes that the song "contained a prediction of what was to come to pass afterward; and in agreement all things have happened all along, and do still happen to us" (*Antiquities of the Jews* 4.8.44; trans. William Whiston, *The New Complete Works of Josephus* [Grand Rapids, MI: Kregel, 1999]). Cooper also cites Sifre Devarim 333 (trans. Louis Finkelstein): "How great is this song, for it includes present, past and future, and this world and the world to come."

rebellion, and exile (not to mention final salvation) not only link to the Major and Minor Prophets but also to the historical books that narrate this sequence of events. From yet another part of the Tanak, Psalm 135:14 looks forward to future salvation and cites Deuteronomy 32:36 verbatim, "For the Lord will vindicate his people and have compassion on his servants" (כִּי־יָדִין יְהוָה עַמּוֹ וְעַל־עֲבָדָיו יִתְנֶחָם; see Ps 90:13).[10] Like Deuteronomy 32:31, 37-39, Psalm 135 also contrasts the Lord with idols (Ps 135:5, 15-18). Psalm 81 has multiple allusions to the Song of Moses (e.g., Ps 81:1/Deut 32:43; Ps 81:8/Deut 32:1; Ps 81:9/Deut 32:12; Ps 81:14-15/Deut 32:41, 43; Ps 81:16/Deut 32:14).[11] Thus, George Knight believes that Deuteronomy 32:1-43 was for future generations a "'quarry' that was easily hewed, which has in fact been done throughout the whole of the Scriptures."[12]

As if this were not enough, we have seen already that Deuteronomy 32–33 is one of four major poetic sections in the Pentateuch (see chapter three) and hence a pillar in its macrostructure. The importance of Deuteronomy 32:1-43 within the Pentateuch is already indisputable given the aforementioned divine command to recite it from generation to generation and the divine prediction (and hence guarantee) that the song would not be "forgotten" (שָׁכַח, Deut 31:21). Through strategic repetition of the phrase "in the last days" in three of these poetic sections (Gen 49:1; Num 24:14; Deut 31:29; see also Deut 4:30), the Song of Moses in Deuteronomy 32:1-43, along with Jacob's blessing (Gen 49:1-27) and Balaam's oracles (Num 24:3-9, 14-19), explicitly involves prophetic eschatology and provides an eschatological framework for the Pentateuch and its theology. Whereas the glimpses of the last days in Genesis 49 and Numbers 24 effectively transport readers' imaginations instantaneously to the messianic era, Deuteronomy 32:1-43 provides a unique description of the

---

[10] See Adolf Kamphausen, *Das Lied Moses. Deut. 32, 1–43* (Leipzig: F. A. Brockhaus, 1862), 181.
[11] See Derek Kidner, *Psalms 73–150*, TOTC (Downers Grove, IL: InterVarsity Press, 1975), 293, 295-96.
[12] Knight, *Song of Moses*, 13; see also 33, 38, 43, 46, 111, 129-30. Throughout the book, he lists examples, such as the prophets, Job, and Paul (26); Deutero-Isaiah and Ezekiel (85); Isaiah (95, 102); and Judges (96); and asserts that Jeremiah would have known this song "possibly even by heart" (89).

long buildup to this climax, in addition to describing eschatological judgment and salvation themselves. I continue below with a discussion of the Song of Moses in connection with Deuteronomy and the Pentateuch before proceeding to analyze several of its nexus connections to other Old Testament books.

THE SONG OF MOSES IN DEUTERONOMY AND THE PENTATEUCH

As one of the last passages in Deuteronomy, the Song of Moses in Deuteronomy 32:1-43 naturally plays an important role in the Pentateuch. Tina Dykesteen Nilsen calls it a "triple conclusion" to the life of Moses, Deuteronomy, and the Pentateuch.[13] As part of the last major poetic section in the Pentateuch, Deuteronomy 32:1-43 is also a fourth conclusion to this series of pillars in the macrostructure of the Pentateuch and draws together many key themes from the previous three poetic sections. Knight references the view of the song as "a 'living' interpretation of the Torah" that emphasizes the first commandment against worshiping other gods.[14] In relation to the Pentateuch's story line, Moses' final instructions to the Israelites are largely finished, and his death, the leadership transition to Joshua, and Israel's crossing the Jordan are imminent (Deut 31:1-8, 13-15; 34:1-9). However, Moses' focus in Deuteronomy 32:1-43 is not so much on this imminent future but Israel's rebellion and exile in the more distant future. Whereas Deuteronomy 4:25-28 had already predicted this and Deuteronomy 30:1 assumes it, Deuteronomy 31–32 is emphatic through the extended attention it gives to Israel's future idolatry, punishment, and ultimate redemption.

In Deuteronomy 31:16-18, the Lord predicts that after Moses' death the Israelites will "whore [זָנָה] after foreign gods of the land" (31:16) and incite the Lord's wrath. The Lord then commands Moses to "write down for yourselves this song and teach it to the sons of Israel, set it in their mouth

---

[13]Tina Dykesteen Nilsen, *The Origins of Deuteronomy 32: Intertextuality, Memory, Identity* (New York: Lang, 2018), 3. Working from within a critical framework, she adds that it is also "an introduction to the rest of the Deuteronomistic History."
[14]Knight, *Song of Moses*, 2.

so that this song will be a witness for me against the sons of Israel" (Deut 31:19).[15] Later, when Israel grows complacent in the land (i.e., "gets fat," דָּשֵׁן), commits idolatry, and is punished for it, the song will bear witness against them (Deut 31:20-21). Moses obediently writes down the song and teaches it to Israel (Deut 31:22, 30), and the Song of Moses itself is found in Deuteronomy 32:1-43.

Echoing the Lord's prediction in Deuteronomy 31:16, Moses reiterates in Deuteronomy 31:27, 29 the Israelites' "rebellion" (מְרִי; see also מָרָה, Deut 9:7, 24) and "stiff neck" (עָרְפְּךָ הַקָּשֶׁה), which he knows will only get worse after his death. His characterization of Israel as corrupt (שָׁחַת) in Deuteronomy 31:29 is repeated in Deuteronomy 32:5, which recalls the corrupt flood generation (Gen 6:11-12) and Israel's sin with the golden calf (Ex 32:7). Israel's choice to do "evil" (רַע) instead of "good" (Deut 6:18; 12:28; 30:15) will bring "calamity" (רָעָה) on themselves "in the last days" (Deut 31:29). Such an eschatological time frame is likewise linked with Israel's punishment (and restoration) in Deuteronomy 4:30. The assembling of elders and officers (Deut 31:28) and Moses speaking "in the ears of the whole congregation of Israel" (Deut 31:30) show again that this song is to be taken with utmost seriousness.

As the Song of Moses begins, its wisdom flavor becomes immediately apparent (Deut 32:1-2). Moses calls heaven and earth to heed "the sayings of my mouth" (אִמְרֵי־פִי) in Deuteronomy 32:1, a phrase that can refer to speech generally (Ps 54:2; Prov 6:2) but can also be used of wise speech in particular (Ps 78:1; Prov 4:5; 8:8). More directly related to wisdom, he then refers to "my teaching" (לִקְחִי) and "my speech" (אִמְרָתִי) in Deuteronomy 32:2, which also have wisdom affinities. While acknowledging other uses, Boston argues that the double appeal to listen in Deuteronomy 32:1 ("give ear [אָזַן] ... hear [שָׁמַע]") best fits a wisdom context.[16]

In relation to the major poetic sections of the Pentateuch, the previous chapters have briefly noted the theme of wisdom linking the three

---

[15] The language of "teaching" (לָמַד) and instruction in the "mouth" (פֶּה) in Deut 31:19 and Deut 31:21-22 picks up on themes from passages such as Deut 6:1; 11:19; 18:18; 30:14; though without the new-covenant overtones of the latter two texts.

[16] Boston, "Wisdom Influence upon the Song," 199-201. He acknowledges poetic and prophetic uses.

eschatological poetic sections in Genesis 49; Numbers 23–24; and Deuteronomy 32–33. Interestingly, Boston's listing of double appeals, which allow for variation in vocabulary and word order, includes Genesis 49:2 ("hear [שְׁמַע] ... hear [שְׁמַע]") and Numbers 23:18 ("hear [שְׁמַע] ... give ear [אֲזֵן]"; see also Ex 15:26; Judg 5:3; Is 1:2). Although he does not classify these two contexts as wisdom, the appeal to the sons of Jacob to listen to their father in Genesis 49:1-2 strongly resembles appeals to "my son" in Proverbs (Prov 1:8, 10, 15; 2:1; passim), and wisdom themes appear throughout the Balaam narrative (see chapter four). In Numbers 23:18, although there is no father-son relationship, Balaam still calls Balak "*son* of Zippor." Deuteronomy 32:1-43 repeatedly complains about the Lord's foolish "sons," Israel (Deut 32:5-6, 18-20).

The word "sayings" (אִמְרֵי) in Deuteronomy 32:1 further parallels "the sayings of God" (אִמְרֵי־אֵל) in Balaam's oracles (Num 24:4, 16), the only other places this word appears in the Pentateuch besides possibly Genesis 49:21 (Vulgate *eloquia*) in the first major poetic section. The effect is to bind Genesis 49; Numbers 23–24; and Deuteronomy 32–33 even more closely together, on the basis of not only their poetic form and a main character calling others together to tell them what will happen "in the last days" (Gen 49:1; Num 24:14; Deut 31:29) but also wisdom. This further suggests that wisdom in the Pentateuch ultimately means understanding and living in light of its prophetic, messianic eschatology (see Ps 2:10-12). The double appeals to listen in Genesis 49:1 and Deuteronomy 32:1 stand at the beginning of both poems, and the appeal in Numbers 23:18 is followed by Balaam's eschatological oracles in Numbers 24 not long after. As shown in chapter two, wisdom themes are also a major element of Genesis 1–3, thus forming an *inclusio* with Deuteronomy 32:1-43 around the Pentateuch also.

The pairing of heavens and earth in Deuteronomy 32:1 not only continues their role as witness from Deuteronomy 31:28 (see Deut 30:19) but also harks back to Genesis 1:1 (see also Gen 2:1, 4; 14:19, 22). Other repeated terms increase the likelihood of Deuteronomy 32:1-43 alluding to the opening chapters of Genesis and contributing to an *inclusio* encompassing the Pentateuch. The rare term "hover" (רָחַף) in Deuteronomy 32:11 is found elsewhere in the Pentateuch only in Genesis 1:2 ("the Spirit of God hovered over the waters"). Likewise, "wasteland" (תֹּהוּ) in Deuteronomy 32:10 appears elsewhere in the Pentateuch only and famously in Genesis 1:2 ("the land was empty"). These striking parallels between Deuteronomy 32:10-11 and Genesis 1:2 cast the Lord's guidance of Israel in the wilderness in terms of creation (see Ex 19:4).[17] Another term, "grass" (דֶּשֶׁא), in Deuteronomy 32:2 is found elsewhere in the Pentateuch only in Genesis 1:11-12. Both texts also use the relatively more common term "vegetation" (עֵשֶׂב). Deuteronomy 32:24, 33, and 42 will add allusions to Genesis 3 (see below).

Beyond the opening chapters of Genesis, the combination of heavens and earth with positive precipitation imagery in Deuteronomy 32:1-2 (including "dew"/טַל) recalls Genesis 27:28, part of an important poem that relates to the major poem in Genesis 49:1-27 (see also 2 Sam 23:4; Ps 72:6).[18] Likewise, the reference to Israel's wayward "inclination" (יֵצֶר) in Deuteronomy 31:21 uses a term found elsewhere in the Pentateuch only in Genesis 6:5 and Genesis 8:21, of the flood generation and the evil inclination/intention of the (thoughts of) their hearts (see "evil" [רַע/רָעָה] in Gen 6:5; 8:21; Deut 31:18, 21, 29). Along with Israel's characterization as corrupt (Gen 6:11-12; Deut 31:29; 32:5; see above), this lexical repetition reinforces their similarity to the flood generation and the reality that Israel is no better than humanity generally, since all are characterized by the same waywardness. The reference to the Lord as Israel's "father who *acquired* you [קָנָה]" and "*made* [עָשָׂה] you" in Deuteronomy 32:6 seems to draw on Genesis 1:26 ("let us make [עָשָׂה] humanity in our image") and Genesis 14:19, 22 ("*possessor* [קָנָה] of heaven and earth"; see also Ex 15:16).

As the Song of Moses proceeds, Moses gives several of its main ideas in Deuteronomy 32:3-4, that is, to proclaim "the name of the Lord" (שֵׁם יְהוָה), show his "greatness" (גֹּדֶל), demonstrate that his "work" (פֹּעַל) is "perfect"

---

[17]See Knight, *Song of Moses*, 46.
[18]John Sailhamer, *The Pentateuch as Narrative* (Grand Rapids, MI: Zondervan, 1992), 191, 235; Sailhamer, *The Meaning of the Pentateuch* (Downers Grove, IL: InterVarsity Press, 2009), 472, 475.

(תָּמִים) and "just" (מִשְׁפָּט), and display his character as "faithful" (אֱמוּנָה), "righteous" (צַדִּיק), and "upright" (יָשָׁר). The Lord's name (שֵׁם) and its proclamation (קָרָא) recall especially the revelation of this name to Moses in Exodus 3:13-15 and "calling on" (קָרָא + בְּ) this name in Exodus 34:5-7, which was also accompanied by a listing of divine attributes. Knight points out that this name "differentiates him from all the divinities" that humanity has ever worshiped.[19] The goodness of the Lord and his ways contrasts with the wickedness of his "children" Israel (Deut 32:5-6).

In the larger movement of the song, the perfection of the Lord's "work" (פֹּעַל) in Deuteronomy 32:4 is important because it includes his use of the nations to punish Israel (Deut 32:21, 25, 30) while not giving them free rein either (see Habakkuk; see below).[20] In Deuteronomy 32:27, the Lord will not let enemies say (forever), "Our hands [יָדֵינוּ] are exalted, and the Lord has not done [פָּעַל] all this." The point is that the Lord *has* done this, and the repetition of the root פעל in Deuteronomy 32:4, 27 implies that the Lord's perfect work involves both his using the nations to judge Israel and his preventing the nations from boasting. The likelihood that the nations will ultimately acknowledge the Lord's work is also suggested by their own judgment and salvation in Deuteronomy 32:34-43 (for salvation, note "rejoice, O nations" in Deut 32:43). Moreover, Deuteronomy 7:9-10 links the Lord's "repayment" (שָׁלַם) of his "haters" (שָׂנֵא) to his covenant faithfulness ("faithful God"/הָאֵל הַנֶּאֱמָן), which suggests that his "vengeance" (נָקָם) and "repayment" (שָׁלַם) of his "adversaries"/"haters" (שָׂנֵא/צַר) in Deuteronomy 32:35, 41, 43 likewise coordinates with his "faithfulness" (אֱמוּנָה) in Deuteronomy 32:4. The connection between the Lord's covenant faithfulness and his defeat of enemies recalls both the Ten Commandments (Ex 20:5; Deut 5:9) and the Abrahamic covenant (e.g., Gen 12:3; 22:17; 24:60; Num 23:19-20).[21]

---

[19] Knight, *Song of Moses*, 16.
[20] See J. Gordon McConville, *Deuteronomy*, ApOTC (Downers Grove, IL: InterVarsity Press, 2002), 453. McConville says this "'work' . . . will be elaborated in this song." Likewise, Tigay sees the song as elaborating on the themes of Deut 32:4-6 (*Deuteronomy*, 300).
[21] See the Melchizedek episode in Gen 14:18-20, which has in common with Deut 32:41-43 "Salem/ repayment" (שָׁלַם), priestly language (כֹּהֵן; כִּפֶּר in Deut 32:43), and "adversaries" (צַר). Additional

Like Deuteronomy 32–33, the second and third major poetic sections in the Pentateuch also emphasize the Lord's work using the root פָּעַל, which appears outside these poetic sections only once (Lev 19:13; see Deut 33:11). The Song of the Sea climaxes with a reference to "an established place for your dwelling *you made* [פָּעַלְתָּ]" in Exodus 15:17, and Israel's triumph in Numbers 23:23 will result in others speaking of "what God has done [פָּעַל]." Exodus 15:17 also has a *polel* form of כּוּן ("establish"), which appears elsewhere in Genesis through Kings only in Deuteronomy 32:6 and 2 Samuel 7:13, 24. The Lord is the subject each time, establishing a sanctuary, a people, or a throne.

The focus on the Lord's work in the song can also be traced through the word "hand" (יָד). The "work" (מַעֲשֶׂה; different term) of Israel's "hands" (יָד) is what incites the Lord's anger in the first place (Deut 31:29). When used negatively, the phrase "work of [human] hands" often refers to idols (Deut 4:28; 27:15; 2 Kings 19:18; 22:17). As mentioned above, though the Lord uses the nations to punish Israel, he will not allow them to "exalt" (רוּם) their hand (Deut 32:27). Related to this, he will judge the nations in turn and deliver his people "when he sees that their *hand* [יָד; i.e., strength] is gone" (Deut 32:36). The abasement of human hands, whether the enemies' or Israel's, sets the stage for the exaltation of the Lord's own "hand" (יָד). He powerfully declares, "I, I am he, and there is no god besides me.... None can deliver from my *hand*" (Deut 32:39). He solemnly "lifts" (נָשָׂא) his hand to heaven (Deut 32:40) and swears that he will take vengeance with his hand (Deut 32:41). Moses' other song, the Song of the Sea, likewise emphasizes the Lord's hand, right hand, and arm (Ex 15:6, 12, 16-17), along with the defeat and silencing of the "enemy"/"Pharaoh" (פַּרְעֹה/אוֹיֵב; Ex 15:4, 6, 9; see Deut 32:27, 42 [note פְּרָעוֹת = "locks"/"leaders" looks like an irregular plural, "Pharaohs"]).[22] This is fitting since the two

---

terms shared with the Song of Moses are "wine" (יַיִן; Deut 32:33, 38), "Most High" (עֶלְיוֹן; Deut 32:8), "acquire" (קָנָה; Deut 32:6), and "heavens" and "earth" (Deut 32:1).

[22]Other links include "sword" (חֶרֶב; Ex 15:9; Deut 32:41-42; see also Deut 33:29), "inherit(ance)" (נַחֲלָה; Ex 15:17 [see also יָרַשׁ, Ex 15:9]; Deut 32:8-9), "stone"/"rock" (צוּר/אֶבֶן; Ex 15:5, 16; Deut 32:4, passim), "acquire" (קָנָה; Ex 15:16; Deut 32:6), "guide" (נָחָה; Ex 15:13; Deut 32:12), "seize" (אָחַז; Ex 15:14-15; Deut 32:41), and "father" (אָב; Ex 15:2; Deut 32:6-7, 17). Regarding

songs emphasize the Lord's "salvation" (יְשׁוּעָה, Ex 15:2; Deut 32:15), both past and future (Ex 15:13-18; Deut 32:34-43). Besides Exodus 14:13, the only other appearance of this term in the Pentateuch is in Genesis 49:18 ("I wait for your *salvation*, Lord"), the first major poetic section. Taken together with the above, we can see how the Song of Moses draws together many key terms and themes from the previous three poetic sections (e.g., "in the last days," wisdom, covenant faithfulness, the Lord's work/hand, salvation, song). The song also has messianic elements that draw mostly on Genesis 3 but also on Numbers 24, as will be seen later.

Table 5.1. Links between Deuteronomy 32:1-43 and the other three major poetic sections

	Genesis 49; Exodus 15; Numbers 23–24	Deuteronomy 32
The Lord's "work" or what he "does/makes" (פֹּעַל)	Ex 15:17; Num 23:23	Deut 32:4
Exaltation of the Lord's "hand," "right hand," or "arm"	Ex 15:6, 12, 16-17	Deut 32:39-41
The Lord's "salvation"	Gen 49:18; Ex 15:2	Deut 32:15
"In the last days"	Gen 49:1; Num 24:14	Deut 31:29
"Give ear" and/or "listen"	Gen 49:2; Num 23:18	Deut 32:1
"Song" associated with Moses	Ex 15:1	Deut 31:30

Another notable emphasis in the Song of Moses is food. In the buildup to the song itself, the Lord will bring Israel into a land "flowing with milk and honey" (זָבַת חָלָב וּדְבָשׁ), but Israel "will eat, be satisfied, grow fat [וְאָכַל וְשָׂבַע וְדָשֵׁן], and turn to other gods" (Deut 31:20). The former phrase is a common way of describing the abundance of the land (e.g., Ex 3:8, 17; Lev 20:24; Num 14:8; Deut 6:3), and Israel eating and being satisfied is also mentioned several times earlier in Deuteronomy (Deut 14:29; 23:24; 26:12). Sometimes this is linked with the danger of forgetting the Lord (Deut 6:11-12; 8:10-14; 11:15-16), just as it is here in Deuteronomy 31:20 and 32:15. Like in Deuteronomy 31:20, Israel's

---

"Pharaohs" in Deut 32:43, see Kevin Chen, *The Messianic Vision of the Pentateuch* (Downers Grove, IL: InterVarsity Press, 2019), 158-59; Knight, *Song of Moses*, 128.

rebellion is described in terms of eating and getting fat in Deuteronomy 32:15 (שָׁמֵן, עָבָה; different terms). This verse follows a description of the Lord's abundant provision in Deuteronomy 32:13-14 using an array of food language ("eat," "produce" [תְּנוּבָה], "nurse" [יָנַק], "honey," "oil" [שֶׁמֶן], "curds" [חֶמְאָה], "milk," "fat" [חֵלֶב], "wheat" [חִטָּה], "grape" [עֵנָב], "wine" [חָמֶר]).[23]

The phrase "blood of the grape" (דַּם־עֵנָב) in Deuteronomy 32:14 appears nowhere else in the Old Testament but has a nearly identical parallel in Genesis 49:11, "the blood of grapes" (דַּם־עֲנָבִים). Both Deuteronomy 32:13-14 and Genesis 49:11-12 emphasize the Lord's abundant material provision in agrarian terms (e.g., "milk"/חָלָב), though Genesis 49:11-12 describes the messianic era and Deuteronomy 32:13-14 a provision that will be ultimately forgotten by Israel. Interestingly, both the Song of Moses in Deuteronomy 32:1-43 and the Lion of Judah prophecy in Genesis 49:8-12 end with references to "blood" (דָּם; Gen 49:11; Deut 32:42-43) and to metaphorical drunkenness (Deut 32:42, "I will make my arrows drunk with blood"; Gen 49:12, "his eyes are darkened from wine"). Genesis 49:11-12 also uses the term "wine" (יַיִן). The repeated references to the Lord's enemies' and his servants' "blood" in Deuteronomy 32:42-43 suggestively appear alongside his priestly "atonement" (כָּפַר, Deut 32:43) for his people. Psalm 110 has a similar combination of war and priesthood. Indeed, I have argued previously that Genesis 3:15 involves both battle and cleansing (related to the unclean serpent; see Gen 49:11-12), and the Lord's eschatological atonement in Deuteronomy 32:43 accordingly resolves the core problem of the people's "corruption" (שָׁחַת) in Deuteronomy 32:5 (see also Deut 4:25; 31:29; Ezek 16:47, 63).[24]

Corresponding to the abundant material provision of Deuteronomy 32:13-14, one of Israel's punishments is famine in Deuteronomy 32:24.

---

[23] Pete Link pointed out to me in personal correspondence that the important combination of "curds and honey" in Is 7:15, 22 is also found here.

[24] Chen, *Messianic Vision of the Pentateuch*, 57-59, 134-36. Thank you to Yohanan Stanfield for pointing out the connection between corruption and atonement in Deut 32:5, 43. He also notes a link to the same two terms in relation to the golden calf (Ex 32:7; 30; see Gen 6:11-14). See his forthcoming work, mentioned below in note 43.

Continuing the food theme, the "vine" (גֶּפֶן), "grapes" (עֵנָב), "clusters" (אֶשְׁכּוֹל), and "wine" (יַיִן) of idol-worshiping enemies are described negatively in Deuteronomy 32:31-33. Israel is rebuked for trusting in an idolatrous "rock" (צוּר) and partaking of the "*fat* of their sacrifices" and "*wine* of their drink offerings" (Deut 32:37-38). These pale in comparison to the true Rock and his provision (Deut 32:4, 13-14).[25] This food theme is another parallel with the opening chapters of Genesis through the tree of life and the tree of the knowledge of good and evil. Like Adam and Eve, Israel foolishly eats the wrong food (Deut 32:38).

Along with Deuteronomy 32:26-27, the last section of the song in Deuteronomy 32:34-43 is significant because it shows that the song's scope encompasses not only Israel's idolatry and punishment by the nations but also the judgment of these nations and the salvation of the Lord's people. In other words, despite the song's preceding context only mentioning judgment (Deut 31:16-30), the content of the song also concerns eschatological salvation.[26] If I am correct that the eschatological Messiah is the integrative center of the Pentateuch (chapter four), then we would expect that he would prominently feature in the Pentateuch's climactic poetic section, which synthesizes key elements from the previous three poetic sections. It is true that messianic elements are not as obvious in the Song of Moses as they are in Genesis 49 and Numbers 24, but the song's allusions to the defeat of the serpent and his seed in Genesis 3:15 and Numbers 24:17 suggest, as discussed below, that such elements are still present.

Repeated references to snakes, snake poison, and crushing the enemy in the second half of the Song of Moses suggest multiple allusions to Genesis 3 that both coordinate with the other allusions to the first chapters of Genesis and bring to mind the seed of the woman of Genesis 3:15. As one of Israel's afflictions, Deuteronomy 32:24 mentions "the poison of crawling things of the dust" (i.e., snakes, see Mic 7:17), which Knight links to the wilderness/*tohu* theme in Deuteronomy 32:10.[27] Both themes originate in

---

[25] McConville, *Deuteronomy*, 459.
[26] See N. T. Wright, *Paul and the Faithfulness of God* (Minneapolis: Fortress, 2013), 1:130-31, 2:1077, 1165, 1463. Wright discusses Josephus's eschatological understanding of the song.
[27] Knight, *Song of Moses*, 46.

Genesis 1–3. Snake poison reappears in Deuteronomy 32:33a ("poison of snakes" [חֲמַת תַּנִּינָם]), using another less common term (תַּנִּין) that is translated "sea creature" in Genesis 1:21 and "snake" in Exodus 7:9-10, 12. Deuteronomy 32:33b follows with "the poison of vipers is cruel" (וְרֹאשׁ פְּתָנִים אַכְזָר). Apart from snakes, poison or bitterness is also found in Deuteronomy 32:24a ("destruction of bitterness" [קֶטֶב מְרִירִי]) and Deuteronomy 32:32b ("grapes of poison" [עִנְּבֵי־רוֹשׁ], "clusters of bitterness" [אַשְׁכְּלֹת מְרֹרֹת]). The unusual emphasis on snakes and poison in Deuteronomy 32:24, 32-33 not only evokes Genesis 3 but also reminds us of Israel (and humanity's) need for deliverance from the same (see Num 21:4-9).

In connection with this snake theme, the latter part of the Song of Moses also refers to the head of the enemy and striking a blow to this head. In Deuteronomy 32:33b, "the poison of vipers is cruel" can also be read as "the *head* of vipers is cruel" (רֹאשׁ פְּתָנִים אַכְזָר) because the spelling of the word translated "poison" (רֹאשׁ) is identical to the common term for "head." This double meaning links to the head of the serpent in Genesis 3:15 as well as to this serpent as a sort of head of his seed (i.e., vipers, snakes in Deut 32:33; see also Hab 3:13). The *striking* of the enemy's head is found at the climactic conclusion of the Song of Moses. In Deuteronomy 32:42, the Lord's arrows and sword will strike blood, flesh, and "the *head* of the locks/leaders [/Pharaohs?] of the enemy" (רֹאשׁ פַּרְעוֹת אוֹיֵב; see LXX: κεφαλῆς ἀρχόντων ἐχθρῶν).[28] The Lord's "sword" (חֶרֶב) likewise strikes "Leviathan, the fleeing serpent" (נָחָשׁ) in a final battle in Isaiah 27:1. These considerations suggest that Deuteronomy 32:42 is predicting the same victory that Genesis 3:15 does. If the "Pharaohs" wordplay (פַּרְעוֹת) is valid in Deuteronomy 32:42, then "head of the 'Pharaohs' of the enemy" has ingeniously fused the archetypal serpent of Eden with the preeminent human enemy in the Pentateuch, Pharaoh, along with all other Pharaohs who would come after him.

Certainly in Deuteronomy 32:42 (and Is 27:1) it is the Lord who strikes the head of the enemy, not the Messiah. However, if the Pentateuch is a

---

[28]Chen, *Messianic Vision of the Pentateuch*, 158-59, 250.

coherent work with a unifying strategy, then the Lord striking the head of the "enemy" (אֹיֵב) in Deuteronomy 32:42 should be seen within the contours of Edenic "enmity" (אֵיבָה) and the Messiah striking the head of the enemy in Genesis 3:15 and Numbers 24:17. Deuteronomy 32:42 uses an existing picture of messianic victory to depict the Lord's eschatological salvation of his people (see Ex 15:6).[29] These texts imply that both the Lord and the Messiah are central actors in the eschatological defeat of the enemy serpent, with Deuteronomy 32:42 overlaying Genesis 3:15. Given the other allusions of the Song of Moses to the opening chapters of Genesis, Deuteronomy 32:42 thus suggests another important allusion that specifically highlights the Pentateuch's central message of messianic, eschatological salvation.

Portrayals of the Lord and of the Messiah that resemble one another are also found in relation to Numbers 24. The parallels between the messianic warrior of Numbers 24 and the divine warrior of Deuteronomy 32:39-43 (see Ex 15:6) reinforce the likelihood of a messianic backdrop for Deuteronomy 32:39-43 and the close relationship, and perhaps even identification, between the Lord and the Messiah.[30] Both the Lord in Deuteronomy 32:41-43 and the Messiah in Numbers 24:8 fight with "arrows" (חֵץ) against "adversaries" (צָר). This collocation and usage appears only in these two Old Testament texts.[31] Thus, both the Messiah's victory in Numbers 24:8, 17 and the Lord's victory in Deuteronomy 32:41-43 "in the last days" (Num 24:14; Deut 31:29) culminate with striking the head(s) of the enemy, shooting adversaries with arrows, and "consuming" (אָכַל, Num 24:8; Deut 32:42) them.

The power of both the Lord and the Messiah in each context (Deut 32:39; Num 24:8, 17) is displayed through the act of "striking" (מָחַץ; see also

---

[29]Regarding the use of an existing textual picture/image in another text, see Kevin Chen, "The 'Deuteroevangelium' in Numbers 21–24," Cateclesia Institute, December 13, 2021, https://cateclesia.com/2021/12/13/the-deuteroevangelium-in-numbers-21-24/.

[30]See Chen, *Messianic Vision of the Pentateuch*, 96-97, for an exegetical argument for the Messiah's divinity on the basis of his reception of worship in Gen 27:29. If the Messiah is divine, then there is no conflict between Deut 32:42 and Gen 3:15/Num 24:17 whether "the Lord" in the song is taken as the Trinity or as the Messiah himself.

[31]"Arrows" only appears elsewhere in the Pentateuch in Gen 49:23 and Deut 32:23 (major poems), and "adversaries" (צָר) only in Gen 14:20; Num 10:9; Deut 32:27; 33:7.

similarly spelled חָץ), a verb that appears elsewhere in the Pentateuch only in Deuteronomy 33:11. The use of מָחַץ in Numbers 24:8, 17 appears to be carefully planned, with "striking" (מָחַץ) Moab's heads in Numbers 24:17 connecting *back* to striking (שׁוּף) the serpent's head in Genesis 3:15 and "striking" (מָחַץ) with arrows in Numbers 24:8 connecting *forward* to Deuteronomy 32:39, 42. With respect to the nations, Numbers 24:8 says that the Messiah "consumes the nations his enemies" (יֹאכַל גּוֹיִם צָרָיו), and Deuteronomy 32:43, as a result of the Lord's vengeance, says with great hope using similar syntax, "Rejoice, O nations, his people" (הַרְנִינוּ גוֹיִם עַמּוֹ).[32]

Table 5.2. Deuteronomy 32:1-43 draws together messianic elements from Genesis 3 and Numbers 24

	Genesis 3 and Numbers 24	Deuteronomy 32
Snake(s), snake poison	Gen 3:1-2, 4, 13-15 (see Num 21:6; 24:1 ["omens"])	Deut 32:24, 32-33
Wounding enemy's "head"	Gen 3:15; Num 24:17 (see also Ex 15:6)	Deut 32:42
Shooting "arrows" at "adversaries" and "consuming" them	Num 24:8	Deut 32:41-43
"Strike" (מָחַץ)	Num 24:8, 17 (see Gen 3:15)	Deut 32:39
"Nations" affected	Num 24:8 (see Gen 22:17)	Deut 32:43 (see Gen 22:18)

This bright ray of hope in Deuteronomy 32:43 immediately follows the striking of the head of the enemy in Deuteronomy 32:42 (see Gen 49:18).[33] The same sequence is implied with the striking of the head of the serpent in Genesis 3:15, which presumably brings salvation to humanity. The vengeance and atonement that are the reasons for the nations' joy in Deuteronomy 32:43 can also be traced to Genesis 3:15 (see above discussion). Although Deuteronomy 32:43 is the only reference to joy in what is

---

[32]Additional common terminology reinforces the bond between Num 24 and Deut 32:1-43. Besides its use in the phrase "in the last days" (Num 24:14; Deut 31:29), both contexts have two uses of "last/end" (אַחֲרִית) regarding the fate or destiny of a people (Num 23:10 [also Balaam's end]; Num 24:20; Deut 32:20, 29). Both contexts describe the defeat of enemies using the phrase "blood of the slain" (דַּם חָלָל/חֲלָלִים; Num 23:24; Deut 32:42), which only appears elsewhere in the OT in 2 Sam 1:22. More parallels are *hithpael* נחם ("change one's mind," "relent") in Num 23:19/Deut 32:36; "rock" (צוּר) in Num 23:9/Deut 32:4, passim; the root פאה in Num 24:17/Deut 32:26; and *hiphil* שׁוּב (first-person *yiqtol*) in Num 23:20/Deut 32:41.

[33]Regarding a related sequence in Gen 49:18, see Chen, *Messianic Vision of the Pentateuch*, 54.

otherwise a somber song, its final position sounds a strong positive note that affects the tenor of the whole song. A "new song" of salvation would seem to naturally follow (Ps 96:1; 98:1-2). Thus, the Song of Moses (Deut 32:1-43) ends in the spirit of the Song of the Sea (Ex 15:1-18) but with all the nations, not just Israel, celebrating the Lord's salvation and doing so forever. It is probably no coincidence that the following poem in Deuteronomy 33:1-29 also ends with an allusion to Eden and eschatological restoration. As Sailhamer points out, whereas the Lord God "drove out the man" (וַיְגָרֶשׁ אֶת־הָאָדָם) from Eden after the fall and "stationed" (וַיַּשְׁכֵּן) cherubim to guard the way back (Gen 3:24), Deuteronomy 33:27-28 describes Israel's future Edenic blessedness in reverse fashion: "He drove out the enemy from before you" (וַיְגָרֶשׁ מִפָּנֶיךָ אוֹיֵב) so that "Israel dwelled securely" (וַיִּשְׁכֹּן יִשְׂרָאֵל בֶּטַח) in a fruitful land.[34]

To sum up the relationship of the Song of Moses to the messianic vision of the Pentateuch, whereas Genesis 3:15; 49:8-12; and Numbers 24:17 directly predict the coming of the messianic victor, the song presents the Lord's eschatological salvation in a way that suggests the Messiah's involvement and perhaps even identification with the Lord himself. In other words, the song may not be messianic in the usual sense, but it does have christological implications. When the song is not read in isolation or only as part of Deuteronomy but within its compositional context in the Pentateuch, readers can infer that the seed of the woman and star of Jacob is directly involved in the eschatological victory described in Deuteronomy 32. There is evidence of the Song of Moses being treated in this very way in 1 Samuel 2:1-10.

THE SONG OF MOSES AND THE SONG OF HANNAH (1 SAM 2:1-10)

Scholars have long noticed parallels between Hannah's poetic prayer in 1 Samuel 2:1-10 and Deuteronomy 32:1-43. For example, Ernest Wright remarks, "The themes in the final speech of Yahweh [Deut 32:39-42] are

---

[34]Sailhamer, *Pentateuch as Narrative*, 478.

closely paralleled in various places, for example, in the Song of Hannah."³⁵ More specifically, Gerhard von Rad notes the parallel between Deuteronomy 32:39b, "I put to death [אָמִית], and then I make alive [וַאֲחַיֶּה]; I struck and I will heal," and 1 Samuel 2:6, "The Lord puts to death [מֵמִית] and makes alive [וּמְחַיֶּה]; he brings down to Sheol and then brings up [וַיָּעַל]."³⁶ Verbal syntax (וַיָּעַל is a *wayyiqtol*) further suggests that these paired actions involve a death-to-life sequence and are not simply parallel demonstrations of power (see Jn 5:21).³⁷ In their respective contexts, this sequence matches the humiliation ("death") of Israel/Hannah followed by salvation (e.g., Deut 32:22-25; 1 Sam 1:1-16).

Another example is the divine title "rock" (צוּר) used repeatedly in Deuteronomy 32:4, 13, 15, 18, 30, 31 (see also Deut 32:37) and 1 Samuel 2:2 (see also 2 Sam 22:3, 32, 47; 23:3). As a divine title, this term appears mostly in the Psalms and Isaiah but nowhere else in the Pentateuch (see stone in Gen 49:24) or in Joshua through Kings. Not only does the use of this title unite the Song of Moses and Hannah's prayer in 1 Samuel 2:1-10, but so does its comparison of the true rock, the Lord, to other rocks, idols.³⁸ Deuteronomy 32:31 says, "Their rock [i.e., an idol] is not like our rock," and Deuteronomy 32:37 asks of Israel's idols, "Where are their gods, the rock in which they took refuge [חָסָה]?" Likewise, Hannah declares in 1 Samuel 2:2, "There is no rock like our God" (see 2 Sam 22:32, "Who is a rock besides our God?"). Hannah's immediately preceding statements ("There is none holy like the Lord, for there is none besides you") are also

---

³⁵Wright, "Lawsuit of God," 57. See also P. Kyle McCarter Jr., *I Samuel*, AB (New York: Doubleday, 1980), 75-76, including n6.
³⁶Von Rad, *Deuteronomy*, 199.
³⁷The first half of 1 Sam 2:6 has a participle followed by another seemingly parallel participle, but then the second half has a participle followed by *wayyiqtol*. For *wayyiqtol* denoting sequence and following a participle, see *GKC* §111a, u (n.b., Job 12:4, perhaps also Amos 9:5; Nah 1:4; Prov 20:26). Diethelm Michel lists Ps 18:33, 48 (n.b., substantival participles); Ps 107:40; 136:10-11 as four examples of *wayyiqtol* after a (hymnic) participle denoting a consequence (*Folge*). See Michel, *Tempora und Satzstellung in den Psalmen* (Bonn: H. Bouvier, 1960), 41. Also suggesting a sequence, the first part of Deut 32:39b has *yiqtol* followed by *weyiqtol*, and the second has *qatal* followed by *yiqtol*. See also Ethan Jones, "1 Samuel 2:6: Time and *Wayyiqtol* in Hannah's Song," *VT* 72, no. 1 (2022): 26-46. Jones seems to assume sequence (37, 39) but tries to prove that the *wayyiqtol* here is past tense ("narrated past event," 34"). *Sheol* also appears in Deut 32:22.
³⁸See David Toshio Tsumura, *The First Book of Samuel*, NICOT (Grand Rapids, MI: Eerdmans, 2007), 143.

similar to Deuteronomy 32:39 ("There is no god besides me"). Thus, the Lord's identity as rock is central to both songs.

Hannah's extended attention to the Lord humbling the proud but saving the humble (1 Sam 2:3-9) also matches a major emphasis of the Song of Moses. As noted above, Israel is punished for their pride (Deut 32:15), enemy pride is held in check by the Lord (Deut 32:27), and his people are saved when they are humbled and their idols exposed (Deut 32:36-38). Another parallel is Hannah being "provoked" (כָּעַס; 1 Sam 1:6-7, 16) by her "adversary" (צָרָה; 1 Sam 1:6), which recalls the Lord being provoked by Israel and foreign nations (Deut 32:16, 19, 21, 27).

At the same time, Hannah's joy in the Lord's "salvation" (יְשׁוּעָה) in 1 Samuel 2:1 more closely parallels Israel's celebration of salvation in the first part of the Song of the Sea in Exodus 15:1-2 (see Gen 49:18; Deut 32:15). Both passages also use first-person verbs and the term "exalt" (רוּם; Ex 15:2; 1 Sam 2:7, 8, 10; see also Deut 32:27). The uncommon description of enemies "being silent" (דָּמַם) in 1 Samuel 2:9 and Exodus 15:16 is another strong link to the Song of the Sea. Furthermore, the "exaltation" (רוּם) of a horn in 1 Samuel 2:1, 10 not only frames Hannah's prayer but links to yet another major poetic section in the Pentateuch, Numbers 24. Hannah's prayer climaxes in 1 Samuel 2:10 with jussives, "May he give strength to *his king*" (וְיִתֶּן־עֹז לְמַלְכּוֹ; see "strength" in Ex 15:2, 13) and "Let the horn of his Messiah *be exalted*" (וְיָרֵם קֶרֶן מְשִׁיחוֹ), which alludes to one of the high points in Balaam's oracles in Numbers 24:7 by disassembling the line "May *his king be exalted* above Agag" (וְיָרֹם מֵאֲגַג מַלְכּוֹ).[39] As Numbers 24:9 suggests, this king is the Lion of Judah in Genesis 49:9. Just as Genesis 49:8-12 foretold, 1–2 Samuel shows that the Messiah whom Hannah longs for in 1 Samuel 2:10 will come from Judah, specifically through David.[40]

Thus, Hannah's prayer strongly suggests that she not only knew the Song of Moses but also knew the Pentateuch's other major poems and

---

[39] If *braiding* refers to one text citing multiple texts, then *disassembly* can refer to the effective division of a cited text into discrete components. First Samuel 2:10 alludes to "his king" and "exalt" in one line of Num 24:7 but uses these two terms in different lines. See Chen, "'Deuteroevangelium' in Numbers 21–24."

[40] Jonathan Shelton helped me see this and other connections to Gen 49.

understood Deuteronomy 32:1-43 in relation to them. Her knowledge of the Song of Moses accords with the above observation that the Lord predicted that even rebellious generations of Israelites would not forget this song (Deut 31:21). How much more the godly Hannah! She is also the first person in the biblical record to refer to the Messiah as "Messiah" (מָשִׁיחַ, 1 Sam 2:10). Although some see Hannah rejoicing like a triumphant warrior as disconnected from her giving birth to a son, the combination of birth and military, even messianic (1 Sam 2:10), victory is attested in Genesis 3:15 and Isaiah 9:6-7.[41] As the first major poem in 1–2 Samuel that is programmatic for the book (1 Sam 2:10/2 Sam 22:51), elements of the Song of Moses have further affected 1–2 Samuel through 1 Samuel 2:1-10.[42]

DEUTERONOMY 32:1-43 AND ISAIAH

Scholars have also noticed connections between the Song of Moses and Isaiah, and perhaps the most important example is the link between Deuteronomy 32:1-43 and Isaiah 1.[43] This link is significant because of both the strength of the evidence and the role of Isaiah 1 as an introduction to the book of Isaiah, which suggests a ripple effect like 1 Samuel 2:1-10 has on 1–2 Samuel.[44] Like Deuteronomy 32:1 ("*Give ear, O heavens*, and I will speak; and *hear, O earth*, the sayings of my mouth"), Isaiah's "vision" (חָזוֹן, Is 1:1) begins, "*Hear, O heavens, and give ear, O earth*, for the Lord has spoken" (Is 1:2). The Lord complains against "sons" (בָּנִים) whom he

---

[41] For the supposed disconnect, see Henry Preserved Smith, *The Books of Samuel*, ICC (Edinburgh: T&T Clark, 1977), 14; Randall Bailey, "The Redemption of YHWH: A Literary Critical Function of the Songs of Hannah and David," *BibInt* 3, no. 2 (1995): 214.

[42] See McCarter, *I Samuel*, 76; Tsumura, *First Book of Samuel*, 135. Note the similarity of Deut 32:4, "The Rock, his work is perfect," and 2 Sam 22:31, "God, his way is perfect."

[43] Ronald Bergey uses computer analysis to trace "language elements in common with Deuteronomy 32" and remarks that within Is 1–36, "Isaiah ch. 1 has no rival in this regard." Bergey, "The Song of Moses (Deuteronomy 32.1-43) and Isaianic Prophecies: A Case of Early Intertextuality?," *JSOT* 28, no. 1 (2003): 36. See also Nilsen, *Origins of Deuteronomy 32*, 158. Tigay refers to Is 1:2-4 as "a summary of Deuteronomy 32:1-18" (*Deuteronomy*, 511). Yohanan Stanfield has a forthcoming work on Deut 32:1-43 and Isaiah that argues that the song is foundational to Isaiah and is alluded to throughout Isaiah. The work is to be published in Hebrew by Magnes Press with the title להאזין להאזינו, and there are also plans for an English translation, *Listen to the Song*.

[44] Bergey, along with Is 1, analyzes parallels in Is 5; 28; and 30 and notes "the key initial and intermediary positions they hold in their respective major textual blocks" ("Song of Moses [Deuteronomy 32.1-43]," 36).

raised but who "rebelled against me," are "corrupt" (שִׁחֵת), and "forsook the Lord" (Is 1:2, 4), just like Deuteronomy 32:5-6, 18-20 (see "reject"/[נָאַץ], Deut 31:20/Is 1:4). The description of Israel in Isaiah 1:3 as foolish ("does not know . . . does not understand") matches the same emphasis in Deuteronomy 32:6 ("foolish nation, not wise") and elsewhere (Deut 32:15, 28-29). Their unfavorable comparison to farm animals who know their "owner" (קֹנֵה) in Isaiah 1:3 also parallels Deuteronomy 32:6 (the Lord "who acquired you" [קָנֶךָ]) and perhaps also their getting fat and unruly kicking in Deuteronomy 32:15.

As in the Song of Moses, the result of Israel's foolishness is destruction by enemies that would have been utterly devastating if not for the Lord's restraint (Is 1:7-9; Deut 32:27; note "except"/לוּלֵי in both texts, as well as Sodom and Gomorrah in Is 1:9-10; Deut 32:32). Continuing in the footsteps of Deuteronomy 32:1-43, despite an indefinite period of severe judgment, there is hope for forgiveness of sins/atonement (Is 1:18; see Deut 32:43), vengeance against the Lord's "adversaries"/"enemies" (Is 1:24; see Deut 32:35, 41), a "turning" (*hiphil* שׁוּב) of the Lord in connection with his "hand" (Is 1:25-26; see Deut 32:40-41, though used differently), mention of whether his people are faithful (נֶאֱמָנָה, Is 1:21, 25; see Deut 32:20), and their redemption by "justice" (Is 1:27; see Deut 32:4, 41; note "captives"/"penitent ones" [וְשָׁבֶיהָ] in Deut 32:42/Is 1:27).[45]

Another clear connection to the Song of Moses has been identified in Isaiah 43.[46] In the context of calling for blind and deaf Israel (Is 43:8), the Lord reminds them of his knowledge of all things, including the future (Is 43:9), so that they will "know" (יָדַע), "believe" (אָמַן), and "*discern* that *I am he*" (וְתָבִינוּ כִּי־אֲנִי הוּא, Is 43:10). Likewise, the Lord longs that Israel will be able to "discern" in Deuteronomy 32:29 and declares, "I am he," in Deuteronomy 32:39 (note witnesses in Deut 31:19, 21, 26;

---

[45]Mostly overlapping but with some differences, see Bergey, "Song of Moses (Deuteronomy 32.1-43)," 39-42.
[46]Thomas Keiser, "The Song of Moses: A Basis for Isaiah's Prophecy," *VT* 55, no. 4 (2005): 486, 490-92, 495-96, 498. His thesis is that there is "a direct and conscious dependency between Isaiah xl–xlviii and the Song of Moses theologically, thematically and literarily" (487). He also highlights Is 44 on the basis of "rock," Jeshurun, and Eloah (489-90).

Is 43:9-10). Like Deuteronomy 32:37-39 (see also Num 23:20), Isaiah 43:10-13 continues, "Before me there was no god formed, and after me there will not be. I, I am the Lord [אָנֹכִי יְהוָה], and there is no savior besides me. . . . I am God [וַאֲנִי־אֵל]. . . . I am he, and none can deliver from my hand [אֲנִי הוּא וְאֵין מִיָּדִי מַצִּיל]; I act [אֶפְעַל], and who will turn it back?" Unmistakably emphasizing the Lord's glory and divine work, Deuteronomy 32:39 uses the independent personal pronoun "I" (אֲנִי) four times, and Isaiah 43:10-13 uses "I" (אֲנִי/אָנֹכִי) six times (see Is 43:3-5, 15). The broader relationship between the Song of Moses and Isaiah 40–55 bears on the interpretation of Isaiah 53 (chapter seven).

THE SONG OF MOSES AND HABAKKUK

Whereas many have noticed the connection between the Song of Moses and Isaiah, its relationship to Habakkuk has received less attention. Nevertheless, the connection between Deuteronomy 32:1-43 and Habakkuk provides significant evidence for the song as a nexus passage and, via issues relating to Habakkuk 2:4 ("the righteous will live by faith"), enriches our understanding of justification by faith.

As mentioned above, both the Song of Moses and Habakkuk focus on the Lord's use of ungodly nations to punish Israel for their sins. Whereas Deuteronomy 32:1-43 predicts this as a matter of fact, Habakkuk struggles to accept it (Hab 1:12–2:4). At the same time, the prophet's struggle fits the Lord's use of a "foolish nation" (גּוֹי נָבָל) to "provoke" (כָּעַס) his people and "make them jealous" (אַקְנִיאֵם) in Deuteronomy 32:21. Furthermore, the song itself actually implies that the Lord's "justice" (מִשְׁפָּט; Deut 32:4) is not fully manifested until the end of time (Deut 32:41; see Hab 1:4, 7, 12). In the words of Deuteronomy 32:35a, there will be "vengeance," and "at the appointed time [לְעֵת] their foot will slip." This matches the main point of Habakkuk 2:2-20, especially Habakkuk 2:3a, "The vision is still for the appointed time [לַמּוֹעֵד] and hastens [פֻּחַ] to the end." Likewise, Deuteronomy 32:35b proclaims, "The day of their calamity [יוֹם אֵידָם] is near, and it will hasten [חָשׁ], ready for them." Habakkuk 2:3b accordingly teaches the faithful, "If it tarries, wait for it, for it [he?] will surely come and not delay" (see Deut 7:10). At the conclusion of Habakkuk, the prophet waits "for the day of distress" (לְיוֹם צָרָה) to come on the enemy (Hab 3:16; see Jer 46:21; Obad 12-15; Nah 1:7; Zeph 1:15).

The connection between the Song of Moses and Habakkuk becomes even more convincing when we consider key shared terminology: "work/do" (פעל), "faithfulness/believe" (אָמַן/אֱמוּנָה), "rock" (צוּר), "strike" (מָחַץ), and "head" (רֹאשׁ). As mentioned above, Deuteronomy 32:4 declares, "The Rock [הַצּוּר], his work [פָּעֳלוֹ] is perfect," and Deuteronomy 32:27 implies that the affliction of Israel by idolatrous nations is something the Lord has "done" (פָּעַל). In his response to Habakkuk's complaint about the failure of "law" (תּוֹרָה) and "justice" (מִשְׁפָּט; Hab 1:4), the Lord declares, "Look *in the nations* [בַגּוֹיִם] and see, and be totally amazed, for I am *doing a work* [פֹּעַל פֹּעֵל] in your days; you will not *believe* [אָמַן] when it is told" (Hab 1:5). This work is the Lord's use of the fierce, idolatrous Chaldeans to punish Israel (Hab 1:6-11; 2:13, 16), which matches the Lord's use of a boastful nation to slaughter Israel in Deuteronomy 32:21, 25, 27 (see also Is 28:21). Furthermore, just as the Lord does not allow the enemy's ignorance to persist concerning what the Lord has "done" (פָּעַל) in Deuteronomy 32:27, so the prophet Habakkuk ultimately overcomes his crisis of faith and testifies, "I am in awe of *your work* [פָּעָלְךָ], Lord" (Hab 3:2). Truly, he has done "all this" (כָּל־זֹאת; Deut 32:27), and "Is it not indeed from the Lord of Hosts? For the earth will be filled with the knowledge of the glory of the Lord" (Hab 2:13-14). The difficulty of understanding the Lord's work (of salvation) as it relates to the suffering of his people at the hands of the wicked further connects to Joseph (Gen 45:5-8; 50:20), Israel's enslavement in Egypt, and David (e.g., 2 Sam 22). While perhaps not fully resolving this existential difficulty, the Lord's own suffering along the way as Rock who did everything for Israel in Deuteronomy 32:4, 10-19 can be a profound comfort.[47]

---

[47] For connections to water from the rock through Deut 32:13, see Chen, *Messianic Vision of the Pentateuch*, 177-82. Interestingly, the salvation brought by water from the rock in Deut 8:15 concerns a desert characterized not only by thirst but also "fiery serpents." It is as though Deut 8:15 is connecting water from the rock in Num 20:2-13 to the bronze snake incident in Num 21:4-9, which also involves water and manna (Num 21:5; Deut 8:15-16).

As Habakkuk 1:5 suggests ("you will not believe when it is told"), Habakkuk's struggle was a test of *faith* (אָמַן; see the general application of Hab 1:6 in Acts 13:41). Whereas Habakkuk 1–2 shows his faith experiencing growing pains, Habakkuk 3 reflects a newfound, hard-won faith. While still facing the reality of invaders (Hab 3:16), he focuses on the Lord's glory and victory (Hab 3:2-15). The object of the prophet's faith is the vision (Hab 2:3) of eschatological salvation for the Lord's people and "day of distress" for his enemies (Hab 3:16), that is, the same message as is in Deuteronomy 32:35-36, 39-42. Could the Song of Moses be a central part of the "visions" (חָזוֹן) of Habakkuk 2:2-3 and Isaiah 1:1 applied to their respective historical contexts? Even in devastation (Hab 3:16-17), Habakkuk can rejoice and be glad in the Lord (Hab 3:18-19). It is as though the rejoicing commanded in Deuteronomy 32:43 does not have to wait entirely until the final judgment.

Faith, and/or faithfulness, is also famously part of Habakkuk 2:4, "The righteous will live by *his faith/faithfulness*" (אֱמוּנָתוֹ). Though not identical, (human) faith and faithfulness are inseparable in Psalm 78:8, 22, 32, 37, a psalm that begins in much the same way as Deuteronomy 32:1-43 ("give ear," Ps 78:1). In the context of the Lord's second speech to Habakkuk (Hab 2:2-20) and of the book of Habakkuk as a whole, Habakkuk 2:4 reads like an indirect call to the prophet (and the reader) to faith and faithfulness, a call Habakkuk understood and heeded (see Hab 1:6; 3:2, 16-19). "Faithfulness" (אָמַן/אֱמוּנָה) is also an important part of the Song of Moses and links up with the faith theme (*Glaubensthematik*) in the Pentateuch (e.g., Gen 15:6; Ex 14:31; Num 14:11; 20:12).[48] Deuteronomy 32:4 extols the Lord as a "God of faithfulness" (אֵל אֱמוּנָה, which connects to his work; see discussion of Deut 7:9-10 above), and Deuteronomy 32:20 describes Israelites who will be judged as "sons in whom there is no *faithfulness*" (אָמַן). Their lack of *faith* can be easily inferred from the context (e.g., Deut 32:15-18) and contrasts with the faith/faithfulness of the righteous in

---

[48]Hans-Christoph Schmitt focuses on the construction *hiphil* אָמַן + בְּ. See Schmitt, "Redaktion des Pentateuch im Geiste der Prophetie," *VT* 32 (1982): 170-89. I suggest broadening this to include אָמַן/אֱמוּנָה in Deut 32, which would further link two major compositional elements together: Schmitt's faith theme and the major poetic sections (see Ex 14:31).

Habakkuk 2:4 (see also Is 26:2). Furthermore, if the Song of Moses is as influential on Habakkuk as it appears, then the song's emphasis on divine glory, human helplessness (including *un*faithfulness) and need for grace, and unmediated divine action (Deut 32:27, 36, 39-42) should inform the interpretation of faith/faithfulness in Habakkuk 2:4 and any derivative soteriology.[49] Also, whether in the Song of Moses, Habakkuk, or Paul, the context of faith/faithfulness is eschatological judgment and salvation.

By themselves, the similarity of content and coordinated use of "work/do" and "faith/faithfulness" are already strong arguments for a large-scale dependence of Habakkuk on the Song of Moses.[50] Yet there is also Habakkuk's use of the divine title "rock" in Habakkuk 1:12, which is uncommon in the prophets outside Isaiah. Additionally, the battle scene in Habakkuk 3:7-15, including the Lord's arrows (Hab 3:11; Deut 32:42), the "flash" (בָּרָק) of his spear/sword (Hab 3:11; Deut 32:41), the judgment of the nations and salvation of his people (Hab 3:12-13; Deut 32:41-43), and the "striking" (מָחַץ) of the "head" (רֹאשׁ) of the enemy (Hab 3:13-14; Deut 32:39, 42), matches the eschatological battle described in Deuteronomy 32:39-43. As was the case in Hannah's prayer (1 Sam 2:10), Habakkuk relates the Song of Moses to the Lord's "m/Messiah" (Hab 3:13).

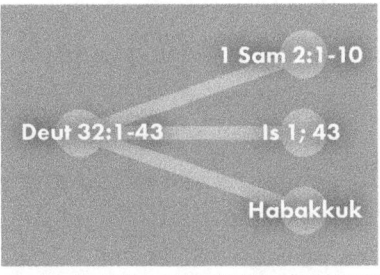

Figure 5.1. Select nexus connections from Deuteronomy 32:1-43 to other Old Testament books

CONCLUSION

The Song of Moses in Deut 32:1-43 has long been recognized for its relationship to the prophets, wisdom, the unfolding of Israel's history, and more. This chapter has also emphasized its role as part of the last major

---

[49]E.g., Wright, *Paul and the Faithfulness of God* 2:1229n639, 1463-71. Wright recognizes the importance of Deut 32 to Paul and some issues in the literary context of Hab 2:4 but does not pursue it in either case. He does discuss Deut 32 and grace on 1228.

[50]Such closely coordinated use is difficult to find elsewhere in the OT. Passages that come close are Is 43:10, 13; Ps 92:2, 4; 111:3, 7; 143:1, 5.

poetic section in the Pentateuch, which draws together many key words and themes from the other poetic sections and from Genesis 1–3. I have also highlighted the song's special status of being remembered by future generations of Israelites, even rebellious ones. This implies that later prophetic authors would also remember the song and suggests that they could have easily alluded to it in their writings. These allusions often involve the Lord's eschatological judgment and salvation and, in the case of Habakkuk, patiently waiting in faith for the same. Just as the Lord "relented" (נחם, *niphal*) from the "calamity" (רָעָה) of wiping out Israel after the golden calf (Ex 32:12, 14), so he will "relent" (נחם, *hithpael*) concerning his "servants" (Deut 32:36; see Ex 32:13) by not wiping them out (Deut 32:26-27) through the "calamity" (רָעָה) of exile "in the last days" (Deut 31:29). Since the Lord relenting from the calamity of devastating judgment is also the hope of the nations (Jon 3:10; 4:2), Deuteronomy 32:1-43 is a sort of Old Testament gospel in song bearing witness to Israelites, and now to us. It says that he is faithful even when people are unfaithful and that human foolishness and impotence ultimately will manifest his wisdom and power.

6

2 SAMUEL 7

WHO IS THE SON WORTHY TO BUILD THE LORD'S HOUSE?

THE PREVIOUS CHAPTERS HAVE IDENTIFIED and analyzed four representative nexus passages from the Pentateuch. In general, nexus passages from the Pentateuch reverberate throughout the rest of the Old Testament, as seen through allusions to them in the Prophets and Writings. In addition to heightened intertextuality, we saw that nexus passages in the Pentateuch are often found at crucial junctures in its literary macrostructure and hence are compositionally strategic. Thus composition, literary strategy, and intertextuality frequently coincide. Stated differently, the literary and textual unity shown by nexus passages often drives the theological unity of Old Testament books and of the Old Testament itself. As we saw in chapter four, the high interconnectivity of Numbers 24 along with its synthesis of creation texts, Abrahamic covenant texts especially, and exodus texts to prophesy of the eschatological Messiah suggests that this savior is the center of the Pentateuch. If Genesis 3:15 is the climax of Genesis 1–3, then this messianic center is supported by that nexus passage as well. Moreover, if authors of later Old Testament books studied and understood the Pentateuch, then their own inspired writings would naturally reflect this center in various ways (see introduction).

As we consider our first nexus passage from the second division of the Hebrew canon, the Prophets, we will find that 2 Samuel 7 has significant intertextual connections to the Pentateuch, including its messianic aspects. These connections arise at points in the exegesis of 2 Samuel 7 below, which treats this text from different perspectives of the ark, night visions, and the quest for a son. Second Samuel 7 and its record of the institution of the Davidic covenant are central to 1–2 Samuel as a narrative climax as well as being the basis for the many texts in the Prophets and Writings that reflect on the Davidic covenant.[1] With its recounting of the Davidic covenant in 1 Chronicles 17 and focus on the Davidic house throughout, Chronicles is a book-length example of such a text. If Hendrik Koorevaar is right that this book "was written with the intention of closing and sealing the Old Testament canon," this Davidic focus has additional implications for the formation and meaning of the Tanak.[2] Texts that may be connected to 2 Samuel 7 and the Davidic covenant are numerous, and the discussion of nexus connections below will focus on Psalm 2 and Psalm 89 as two representative examples.[3]

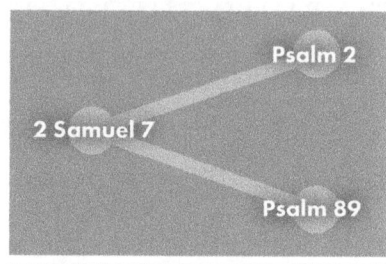

Figure 6.1. Two representative nexus connections to 2 Samuel 7

2 SAMUEL 7 AS A NARRATIVE CLIMAX IN 1–2 SAMUEL

Second Samuel 7 is a narrative climax in 1–2 Samuel and also in the Old Testament Historical books generally. At the beginning of 1 Samuel, Israel had not yet emerged from the dark era of the judges (1 Sam 3:1). Both Eli and Samuel are described as having "judged Israel" (1 Sam 4:18; 7:15; see 1 Sam 11:6; 2 Sam 7:11), like earlier judges (e.g., Judg 3:10; 4:4; 10:2-3).[4] Israel's request for a king displeased the Lord (1 Sam 8:5-9; 10:19; 12:17-20) and yielded their first king, Saul, who was a failure (1 Sam 13:8-14; 15:17-29, 35). Saul's rejection was coupled with the anointing of David to be Israel's next king (1 Sam 16:1-13). Since Saul was still in power, David had to wait

---

[1] See Walter Brueggemann, *First and Second Samuel*, Interpretation (Louisville: John Knox, 1990), 253. Daniel Block has drawn attention to the great amount of attention given to David in the OT. See Block, *Covenant: The Framework of God's Grand Plan of Redemption* (Grand Rapids, MI: Baker, 2021), 307.
[2] Hendrik Koorevaar, "Chronicles as the Intended Conclusion to the Old Testament Canon," in *The Shape of the Writings*, ed. Julius Steinberg and Timothy Stone (Winona Lake, IN: Eisenbrauns, 2015), 207.
[3] For other texts connected to 2 Sam 7, see Gary Edward Schnittjer, *Old Testament Use of the Old Testament* (Grand Rapids, MI: Zondervan, 2021), 879.
[4] Ralph Klein, *1 Samuel*, WBC (Waco, TX: Word, 1983), 44; Tony Cartledge, *1 & 2 Samuel*, SHBC (Macon, GA: Smyth & Helwys, 2001), 103.

until Saul died (1 Sam 31:1-6) before he became king first of Judah (2 Sam 2:4, 11) and then of all Israel (2 Sam 5:1-5).

Accordingly, the preceding context of 2 Samuel 7 says that David was getting "greater and greater, and the Lord God of hosts was with him" (2 Sam 5:10) and that he "knew that the Lord established him as king over Israel and that he exalted his kingdom for the sake of his people Israel" (2 Sam 5:12). David and his kingdom faced major challenges following his sins against Bathsheba and Uriah in 2 Samuel 11, so 2 Samuel 7 and its immediate context represent a high point in the narrative in which David is finally ruling Israel and enjoying the Lord's blessing. What distinguishes 2 Samuel 7 most from its context is the Lord's grand promise of an everlasting kingdom to David (2 Sam 7:16), which is explicitly called a "covenant" (בְּרִית) in 2 Samuel 23:5 (see 2 Sam 22:51). Reinforcing the importance of 2 Samuel 7, the references to an exalted king and a glorious house for the Lord's name in 2 Samuel 7:12-16 strategically align with similar emphases at the beginning and end of 1–2 Samuel (1 Sam 1:9; 2:10; 2 Sam 22:7, 51; 23:1-5).[5]

THE IMPORTANCE OF THE ARK IN 2 SAMUEL 7 AND 1–2 SAMUEL

As 2 Samuel 7 begins, the Lord has already given David rest from "all his enemies" (2 Sam 7:1), and he "sat [יָשַׁב] in his house" (2 Sam 7:1), "a house [בַּיִת] of cedar" (2 Sam 7:2).[6] Hiram king of Tyre had supplied this wood along with woodworkers and stonemasons, who "built a house for David" (וַיִּבְנוּ־בַיִת לְדָוִד, 2 Sam 5:11).[7] The construction of this house in conjunction with David's greatness and awareness of the Lord's blessing (2 Sam 5:10, 12) could have suggested to him that it was only fitting to likewise build a house for the Lord (2 Sam 7:5). Meanwhile, the ark had been moved from one "house" (בַּיִת) to another (2 Sam 6:3-4, 10-12) before being placed in a "tent" (אֹהֶל) in the city of David (2 Sam 6:12-17). David's self-consciousness

---

[5] This was pointed out to me by Jonathan Shelton.
[6] Proposals for how David's rest from "all his enemies" in 2 Sam 7:1 relates to his battles with additional enemies in 2 Sam 8 include taking the rest as temporary, taking 2 Sam 7 as not being in chronological order, or taking "all his enemies" as referring only to enemies within Israel's land. See David Toshio Tsumura, *The Second Book of Samuel*, NICOT (Grand Rapids, MI: Eerdmans, 2019), 127; Block, *Covenant*, 310.
[7] Tsumura, *Second Book of Samuel*, 127.

about living so comfortably when "the ark of God is dwelling in curtains [יֹשֵׁב בְּתוֹךְ הַיְרִיעָה]" in 2 Samuel 7:2 naturally follows from these recent events concerning his own house and the ark in 2 Samuel 5–6.

David's focus on "the ark of God" in 2 Samuel 7:2 ties not only to 2 Samuel 6 but also to ark passages elsewhere in 1–2 Samuel. These are concentrated in the ark narratives of 1 Samuel 4:1–7:1 and 2 Samuel 6 but can also be found in other strategic parts of 1–2 Samuel.[8] Yehoshua Gitay asserts, "The story of the Books of Samuel revolves around the ark."[9] Whether or not all readers will go this far, key moments in the narrative do indeed involve the ark. The calling of Samuel took place when he was "lying in the temple of the Lord, where the ark of God was" (1 Sam 3:3). Israel took the ark into battle with the Philistines as a sort of good-luck charm, with Eli's two sons Hophni and Phinehas accompanying it (1 Sam 4:3-4). This led to the capture of the ark by the Philistines, the deaths of Hophni and Phinehas (1 Sam 4:11), and Eli's own death upon hearing of the loss of the ark (1 Sam 4:17-18). This disaster induced Phinehas' wife to go into labor and die during childbirth, and she accordingly named her newborn son Ichabod (אִי־כָבוֹד, "no glory"), because "glory [i.e., the ark, Eli, Phinehas] has departed from Israel" (1 Sam 4:21-22). The references to the ark in 2 Samuel 6:2-17; 7:2; 11:11; 15:24, 25, 29 show its ongoing importance in 1–2 Samuel. Furthermore, when the close connection between the ark and the temple is recognized, this ark theme further relates to "temple" (הֵיכָל) references and themes that frame 1–2 Samuel (1 Sam 1:9; 2 Sam 22:7; see 1 Sam 1:7, 24; 2 Sam 24:16-25; 1 Chron 22:1; 2 Chron 3:1).[10]

Antony Campbell explains that the ark is "the symbol of God's presence to Israel."[11] Andy Stirrup adds that "glory or better, holiness" is the dominant

---

[8]For a helpful discussion of the history of interpretation of the ark narrative in 1 Sam 4:1–7:1, see Keith Bodner, "Ark-Eology: Shifting Emphases in 'Ark Narrative' Scholarship," *Currents in Biblical Research* 4, no. 2 (2006): 169-97.
[9]Yehoshua Gitay, "Reflections on the Poetics of the Samuel Narrative: The Question of the Ark Narrative," *CBQ* 54 (1992): 225.
[10]Interaction with Jonathan Shelton led to this point. See Joel Rosenberg, "1 and 2 Samuel," in *The Literary Guide to the Bible*, ed. Robert Alter and Frank Kermode (Cambridge, MA: Harvard University Press, 1987), 139. Rosenberg further points out the wordplay between "Araunah" (אֲרַוְנָה) in 2 Sam 24 and "ark" (אֲרוֹן).
[11]Antony Campbell, *1 Samuel*, FOTL (Grand Rapids, MI: Eerdmans, 2003), 60.

theme in the ark narrative of 1 Samuel 4:1–7:1.[12] Indeed, the Philistines' attempts to bring disgrace on the (ark of the) Lord brought judgment (1 Sam 5) until they gave "glory [כָּבוֹד] to the God of Israel" (1 Sam 6:5; see 1 Sam 15:29). After residents of Beth Shemesh died because they looked in the ark (1 Sam 6:19), they rightly asked, "Who can stand before the Lord, this holy [קָדוֹשׁ] God?" (1 Sam 6:20). As for the relationship between the Lord and the ark, he often identifies with the ark, such that mistreatment or mishandling of it brings judgment (1 Sam 5:1-6; 6:19; 2 Sam 6:3-7), and the opposite can bring blessing (2 Sam 6:11-12). On the other hand, he also transcends the ark and cannot be manipulated through it (1 Sam 4:3-4). Such associations of the ark with the Lord's holy presence fit the original construction of the ark as the centerpiece of the tabernacle in Exodus 25:10-22.

The themes of the ark and the Lord's glory, holiness, and transcendence are also found in 2 Samuel 6–7. The infamous "outbreak against Uzzah" (2 Sam 6:8) demonstrates the Lord's holiness yet again. David's fearful question shows that he got the point, "How will the ark of the Lord come to me?" (2 Sam 6:9), which resembles the earlier question asked in Beth Shemesh (1 Sam 6:20). After the ark brought blessing to Obed-Edom and his house (2 Sam 6:11-12), David had the ark carried properly to the city of David (2 Sam 6:12-13; see 1 Chron 15:11-15), rather than pulled on a cart (2 Sam 6:3).

In 2 Samuel 7, the Lord's rejection of David's plan to build a temple should be seen against this backdrop. Whereas David explicitly speaks only of building something better for "the ark of God" in 2 Samuel 7:2, the Lord treats David's intention as involving "build[ing] *me* a house to dwell in" (תִּבְנֶה־לִּי בַיִת לְשִׁבְתִּי) in 2 Samuel 7:5 (see Num 10:35-36). Continuing this identification between the ark and himself, the Lord explains, "I have not lived in a house" (לֹא יָשַׁבְתִּי בְּבַיִת) since Israel became a nation and never asked any of its ruling tribes, "Why did you not build me a house of cedar?" (2 Sam 7:6-7). Although the ark is only mentioned in 2 Samuel 7:2 (as "dwelling in the midst of curtains"), subsequent references to a house for

---

[12] Andy Stirrup, "'Why Has Yahweh Defeated Us Today Before the Philistines?' The Question of the Ark Narrative," *TynBul* 51, no. 1 (2000): 87.

the ark (i.e., a temple) and moving about "in a tent and in a tabernacle" show that the ark is still central to 2 Samuel 7:5-7.

The Lord's announcement that he will build David a house instead (2 Sam 7:11) reverses David's initial attempt to be the main actor, with the Lord/ark as passive recipient. Presumably, the house that the Lord builds for David will also vastly exceed the house Hiram had built for David in 2 Samuel 5:11. Thus, the Lord has been and always will be the glorious main actor, with David as a secondary recipient (see 2 Sam 7:8-10). To this effect, Kyle McCarter observes the emphatic use of personal pronouns, such as in 2 Samuel 7:5 ("Will *you* [אַתָּה] build *me* . . . ?") and 2 Samuel 7:8 ("*I* [אֲנִי] took you").[13] David's response, highlighting his own insignificance and the Lord's surpassing greatness, shows that the Lord's glory and transcendence are the focus yet again (2 Sam 7:18-23).[14] David's use of the title "Lord of hosts" (יְהוָה צְבָאוֹת) in 2 Samuel 7:26-27 also emphasizes the Lord's glory, in addition to echoing the Lord's own use of this title to introduce reminders of what he did for David (2 Sam 7:8). This title is also associated with the ark in 1 Samuel 4:4 ("ark of the covenant of the Lord of hosts") and 2 Samuel 6:2 ("the ark of God which is called by the name of the Lord of hosts"; see also 1 Sam 1:3, 11). Accordingly, David repeatedly refers to himself as "your servant" (2 Sam 7:19-21, 25-29), echoing the Lord calling him "my servant" in 2 Samuel 7:5, 8.

Although 2 Samuel 7:12-13 predicts that David's "seed" (זֶרַע) will "build a house for my name" (יִבְנֶה־בַיִת לִשְׁמִי), the reader is still left to wonder how this individual ("he" [הוּא]; see 1 Chron 17:11, where the seed is "from [i.e., one of] your sons") could be worthy to do so, since the reasons given by the Lord in 2 Samuel 7:5-7 still seem to apply (i.e., he never had and never wanted a house). Campbell explains, "It is not a matter of proposing to do the right thing at the wrong time; it is a matter of principle, the wrong thing, and the wrong idea of God."[15]

---

[13] P. Kyle McCarter Jr., *II Samuel*, AB (New York: Doubleday, 1984), 198.
[14] McCarter goes so far as refer to this as "a grandiose gesture of patronage toward Yahweh . . . [which] is taken as an affront" (*II Samuel*, 197).
[15] Antony Campbell, *2 Samuel*, FOTL (Grand Rapids, MI: Eerdmans, 2005), 73, commenting on 2 Sam 7:6.

Accordingly, many critical scholars note the theological discontinuity of 2 Samuel 7:13a with the surrounding context (which is also a syntactical disruption of a *weqatal* sequence) and see it as a late addition.[16] For the present purposes, I see 2 Samuel 7:13a as an interpretive crux (*crux interpretum*) for 1–2 Samuel, much like Isaiah 7:14 for Isaiah.[17] It raises the question: Who is this son/seed who will build a house for the Lord's name? The ark-related questions posed in 1 Samuel 6:20 ("Who can stand before the Lord, this holy God?") and 2 Samuel 6:9 ("How will the ark of the Lord come to me?") concerning the Lord's holiness and transcendence also generate suspense concerning the identity of the promised temple builder in 2 Samuel 7:12-13. As both the Philistines and Israelites learned the hard way, the ark/presence of the Lord can be dangerous.[18] Robert Polzin further points out that both the Philistines and the Israelites did not know how to treat the ark in 1 Samuel 4–6, and we have seen that 2 Samuel 6–7 shows that David on the two occasions of the Uzzah incident and the temple initiative did not know either.[19] However, in a way that strongly resembles "he will build a house for my name" (הוּא יִבְנֶה־בַּיִת לִשְׁמִי) in 2 Samuel 7:13a, Zechariah 6:12-13 predicts the coming of "a man, his name is 'Branch.' . . . He will build the temple of the Lord. And he will build the temple of the Lord [וְהוּא יִבְנֶה אֶת־הֵיכַל יְהוָה]. And he will bear honor and sit and rule on his throne." The postexilic prophet Zechariah thus declares that 2 Samuel 7:13a will be fulfilled by the Messiah. This one evidently can stand in the presence of a holy God without being destroyed (see Ps 15:1-5). Zechariah 6:12 even highlights "his name," "Branch" (see also 2 Sam 7:9), whereas 2 Samuel 7:13a only mentions the Lord's "name."

In addition to the question of who is worthy build such a house, an equally significant question that 2 Samuel 7:13a raises is: What kind of house will

---

[16]McCarter, *II Samuel*, 211; A. A. Anderson, *2 Samuel*, WBC (Dallas: Word, 1989), 118, 121. See also Cartledge, *1 & 2 Samuel*, 447-48, 453.
[17]See John Sailhamer, "The Messiah and the Hebrew Bible," *JETS* 44, no. 1 (2001): 17. He writes, "The rest of the book of Isaiah is intended as an exegesis of the prophet's tersely recorded vision in 7:14 and 15. Here we must not only understand the vision, but also the prophet's exegesis of that vision as it plays out in the remainder of the book."
[18]Campbell, *1 Samuel*, 81, 83.
[19]Robert Polzin, *Samuel and the Deuteronomist: 1 Samuel* (Bloomington: Indiana University Press, 1993), 57-58, 65. He notes Israel's "ill-advised rejoicing" in 1 Sam 6:13 (see also 1 Sam 4:5), which I note parallels David and Israel's in 2 Sam 6:5 before Uzzah is struck down.

this promised seed/son build? What kind of house could possibly be suitable for such a holy, transcendent God (1 Kings 8:27; Is 66:1; 2 Chron 2:6)? If this house can be said to be built by both the Messiah (2 Sam 7:13; Zech 6:12-13) and the Lord, the reference to a "sanctuary, O Lord, your hands established" (מִקְּדָשׁ אֲדֹנָי כּוֹנְנוּ יָדֶיךָ) in Exodus 15:17 is a promising candidate as a place "established" (כּוּן) and "made" (פָּעַל) by the Lord himself for his "dwelling" (לְשִׁבְתְּךָ; see 2 Sam 7:5, לְשִׁבְתִּי). Such divine establishment of a sanctuary in conjunction with the Lord's reign "forever" (עוֹלָם) in Exodus 15:18 matches the Lord "establishing" (כּוּן) the kingdom/house and throne of David's seed "forever" (עוֹלָם) in 2 Samuel 7:12-13, 16, 26.[20]

I thus suggest that the divinely established temple in Exodus 15:17 is manifested in conjunction with the divinely established messianic kingdom. Like the house in 2 Samuel 7:13a, the sanctuary in Exodus 15:17 often has been equated with Solomon's temple, but the ultimate destruction of this temple in contrast with the divine establishment and construction of the sanctuary in Exodus 15:17 (along with other considerations) suggest an eschatological temple instead. This would also cohere with the Messiah's involvement suggested by Zechariah 6:12-13. Evangelical consideration of an eschatological interpretation of Exodus 15:17 need not be constrained by some critical scholars assigning an early date for Exodus 15:1-18 but a late date for Israelite eschatology.[21]

Campbell observes the ark's departure from Israel and return to Israel in 1–2 Samuel, but not "to a central location of honor or to a major sanctuary in Israel" until it reaches Jerusalem.[22] Although Campbell seems content for the ark to have been brought to Jerusalem in 2 Samuel 6, that the prophesied "house for my name" (2 Sam 7:13) is not built by David's seed in 1–2 Samuel suggests that the ark has still not yet reached its final

---

[20]Kevin Chen, *Eschatological Sanctuary in Exodus 15:17 and Related Texts* (New York: Lang, 2013), 84-85.

[21]For Ex 15:1-18 as "one of the oldest compositions preserved by biblical sources," see Frank M. Cross, *Canaanite Myth and Hebrew Epic* (Cambridge, MA: Harvard University Press, 1973), 123. For Israelite eschatology arising in the postexilic period, see Sigmund Mowinckel, *He That Cometh*, trans. G. W. Anderson (New York: Abingdon, 1956), 3, 20, 130-33, 149-54, 261-63.

[22]Campbell, *1 Samuel*, 62, 81-83. Bodner calls Campbell "a distinguished savant of the Ark Narrative" ("Ark-Eology," 189).

home. Even after 2 Samuel 7, the ark is still in a tent in 2 Samuel 11:11 (see "house" in 2 Sam 11:8-11, 13) and is taken out of Jerusalem briefly before being brought back in 2 Samuel 15:24-29.[23] In 2 Samuel 11:11, the link to 2 Samuel 7 is particularly strong because of Uriah's feelings of guilt about going to his house when the ark and the army were dwelling in booths, which is an ironic parallel to what David once felt in 2 Samuel 7:2.

In any case, we may ask a slightly modified version of what Polzin calls "the primary question pervading the ark story," but on the scale of 1–2 Samuel as a whole: Who is to be the ark's/the Lord's proper caretaker?[24] Apparently it was not the Philistines, Israel, or even David himself (who "sinned"; see 2 Sam 12:13; 24:10, 17), but "he" who "will build a house for my name" (2 Sam 7:13). It would seem that only the Messiah will be qualified for all that this represents.[25] Unlike David's original plan, the Lord thus will build a house for David first and show himself to be David's forever caretaker, and subsequently a worthy seed will build a house befitting the holy and glorious Lord. David's silence concerning the temple in 2 Samuel 7:18-29 hints that he understands this order.[26]

THE DAVIDIC COVENANT AS A NIGHT VISION, LIKE THE ABRAHAMIC COVENANT

The prophetic message given by Nathan to stop David from carrying out his plan (2 Sam 7:2-3) is cast in terms of a night vision. This can be seen through the narrative framing of Nathan's message in 2 Samuel 7:4-17: "And *on that night* [בַּלַּיְלָה הַהוּא] *the word of the Lord* [דְּבַר־יְהוָה] came to Nathan, saying" (2 Sam 7:4), and "According to all these words and this whole *vision* [חִזָּיוֹן], so Nathan spoke to David" (2 Sam 7:17). Within 1–2 Samuel, this suggests

---

[23] Polzin points out that both 2 Sam 15 and 1 Sam 4–7 are about "the leaving and returning of the ark from and to its rightful place" (*Samuel and the Deuteronomist*, 62).

[24] Polzin asks, "Who is to be Israel's/the Lord's proper caretaker?" (*Samuel and the Deuteronomist*, 66). This is because he has just argued that the ark represents both Israel and the Lord's presence.

[25] Even in a postark world (Jer 3:16), this holy steward is uniquely qualified to build the temple and be in the Lord's presence.

[26] See Brian Kelly, *Retribution and Eschatology in Chronicles* (Sheffield: Sheffield Academic, 1996), 157. Kelly shows that the wording of 1 Chron 17:10b, 12a ("a house the Lord will build for you . . . he will build for me a house") brings this out even more clearly.

a connection to the calling of Samuel, which is introduced with the comment, "*The word of the Lord* [דְּבַר־יְהוָה] was rare in those days; there was no *vision* [חָזוֹן] breaking forth" (1 Sam 3:1). Samuel's calling also took place at night and involved a "vision" (מַרְאָה, 1 Sam 3:15). Whereas previously he did not know "the word of the Lord" (1 Sam 3:7), henceforth he would (1 Sam 3:19-21). The cognate terms for "vision" in 1 Samuel 3:1 (חָזוֹן) and 2 Samuel 7:17 (חִזָּיוֹן) appear only in these two texts in 1–2 Samuel, and the term used in 1 Samuel 3:15 (מַרְאָה) appears elsewhere in 1–2 Samuel but only here with this meaning. Although "the word of the Lord" is also found in a few other places in 1–2 Samuel (1 Sam 15:10, 13, 23, 26 [see "night" in 1 Sam 15:11, 16]; 2 Sam 12:9 [see 2 Sam 12:11-12; 11:2]; 24:11), the phrase remains a meaningful link between 1 Samuel 3 and 2 Samuel 7. The divine use of night visions in these two passages thus further emphasizes the importance of the calling of Samuel and especially the Davidic covenant in 1–2 Samuel. Whereas Samuel's call actually focused on the judgment of Eli's house (1 Sam 3:11-14), the prophetic message to David is mostly positive and promises him an everlasting kingdom/house (2 Sam 7:11-16).

Whereas night visions do appear elsewhere in the Old Testament (e.g., Dan 7:13; Zech 1:8; see 1 Kings 3:5), the one involving the Abrahamic covenant in Genesis 15 is especially relevant to 2 Samuel 7 because of additional verbal and thematic parallels linking the two covenants. The formal institution of the Abrahamic covenant in Genesis 15 through a prophetic night vision can be seen through "the word of the Lord came to Abram in a *vision*" (הָיָה דְבַר־יְהוָה אֶל־אַבְרָם בַּמַּחֲזֶה) in Genesis 15:1; Abram's looking to the stars (at night) in Genesis 15:5; and the sunset, Abram's "deep sleep" (תַּרְדֵּמָה), and darkness in Genesis 15:12 and 17. Thus, central texts of both the Abrahamic and Davidic covenants are cast as prophetic night visions. Both Genesis 15 and 2 Samuel 7 are also characterized by Abram and David's use of the divine title "Lord Yahweh" (אֲדֹנָי יֱהוִה; Gen 15:2, 8; 2 Sam 7:18-20, 22, 28-29), which appears elsewhere in the Pentateuch only in Deuteronomy 3:24; 9:26 and nowhere else in 1–2 Samuel.

Detailed comparison of Genesis 15 and 2 Samuel 7 reveals additional continuity between the two texts and covenants. The most important link is that the predictive elements focus on a "seed . . . who will go out from your loins" (אֲשֶׁר יֵצֵא מִמֵּעֶיךָ, Gen 15:3-4; 2 Sam 7:12).[27] Such a construction and accompanying terminology appear only in these two Old Testament texts. For Abram, the seed is his heir who will "possess" (יָרַשׁ) all his belongings as well as the Abrahamic covenant blessings (Gen 15:7-8). For David, the seed is also an heir and the one who will receive an everlasting kingdom in fulfillment of the Davidic covenant. Although Abram's seed in Genesis 15:3-4 could be taken as Isaac, the reuse of "possess" (יָרַשׁ) with respect to the fulfillment of Abrahamic covenant in Genesis 22:17 and especially in Genesis 24:60 of one of Isaac's descendants, suggests that this promise of an heir who will possess did not terminate with Isaac but was passed down through the generations.[28] When Genesis 15:3-4 is viewed within this network of passages in the Pentateuch (including Num 24:18), its connection to 2 Samuel 7:12 consists of not only an heir who fulfills a covenant but also the hope for the Messiah himself, the son of David and the son of Abraham (Mt 1:1), who fulfills both of these covenants. Both Genesis 15 and 2 Samuel 7 also predict Israel's dwelling in the land (Gen 15:7, 18; 2 Sam 7:10-11) and deliverance from those who "afflict" (עָנָה) them (Gen 15:13-14; 2 Sam 7:9, 11).

Table 6.1. Links between Genesis 15 and 2 Samuel 7

	Genesis 15 (Abrahamic covenant)	2 Samuel 7 (Davidic covenant)
"Vision" at night	Gen 15:1, 5, 12, 17	2 Sam 7:4, 17
"Lord Yahweh" (אֲדֹנָי יֱהוִה)	Gen 15:2, 8	2 Sam 7:18-20, 22, 28-29
"Seed . . . who will go out from your loins"	Gen 15:3-4	2 Sam 7:12
Israel will dwell in the land	Gen 15:7, 18	2 Sam 7:10-11
Deliverance from those who "afflict"	Gen 15:13-14	2 Sam 7:9, 11
Covenant heir(s) as servant(s)	Gen 15:13-14	2 Sam 7:5, 8, 19-21, 25-29

---

[27] For a grammatical and syntactical argument for interpreting *seed* in both passages as an individual, see Kevin Chen, *The Messianic Vision of the Pentateuch* (Downers Grove, IL: InterVarsity Press, 2019), 41-45.
[28] Chen, *Messianic Vision of the Pentateuch*, 45-46.

When connections between 2 Samuel 7 and additional Abrahamic covenant texts are considered, more parallels arise that further support the continuity of these two covenants.[29] The Lord's promise to David of a "great name [שֵׁם גָּדוֹל], like the name of the great ones in the land" (2 Sam 7:9), is very similar to his promise to Abraham, "I will make your name great" (וַאֲגַדְּלָה שְׁמֶךָ, Gen 12:2). Kingship, which is at the heart of 2 Samuel 7:11-16, is also promised to Abraham (Gen 17:6, 16). Although this could seem like a minor aspect among the promises to Abraham, the passing down of covenant blessings to Isaac, Jacob, and the twelves tribes sharpens the focus on not only kingship generally but also the fulfillment of the Abrahamic covenant through an individual king from the line of Judah who will rule Israel and the nations in the last days (Gen 27:27-29; 49:8-12; see Num 24:9, 14, 17-19).[30]

In 2 Samuel 7:13, 16, the promises to David, a Judahite, similarly find fulfillment in a king who reigns forever. Guided by the Spirit, David's last words in 2 Samuel 23:1-7 take on the flavor of both an aged patriarch and a prophet (like Jacob in Gen 49), link to Balaam's oracles in Numbers 24 (see chapter four), and describe an "eternal [עוֹלָם] covenant" and ideal king (2 Sam 23:3-5) who both fulfills 2 Samuel 7:11-16 (note עוֹלָם in 2 Sam 7:13, 16; see 2 Sam 7:24-26, 29) and brings blessing to creation in a way that recalls Genesis 27:27-29; 49:8-12.[31] Like the Abrahamic covenant, 2 Samuel 7 also involves receiving the Lord's blessing (2 Sam 7:29; see Gen 12:2-3). Thus, whether 2 Samuel 7 is considered in relation to Genesis 15 or Abrahamic covenant texts generally, the above evidence suggests that the Davidic covenant and the Abrahamic covenant are fulfilled by the same messianic individual.

THE QUEST FOR A SON

Suspense concerning the identity of the promised seed/son in 2 Samuel 7:12-13 is further heightened by the theme of the quest for a son

---

[29]See Chen, *Messianic Vision of the Pentateuch*, 45.
[30]Chen, *Messianic Vision of the Pentateuch*, 94-97, 114-16. See also T. Desmond Alexander, "Messianic Ideology in the Book of Genesis," in *The Lord's Anointed: Interpretation of Old Testament Messianic Texts*, ed. Philip Satterthwaite, Richard Hess, and Gordon Wenham (Grand Rapids, MI: Baker, 1995), 19-39.
[31]For 2 Sam 7 and 2 Sam 23, see David C. Mitchell, *The Message of the Psalter: An Eschatological Programme in the Book of Psalms* (Newton Mearns, UK: Campbell, 2003), 83.

(or sons) in 1–2 Samuel. Polzin highlights the connection between sons and Deuteronomistic kingship.[32] Indeed, the book opens with Hannah's prayer to have a son (1 Sam 1:8, 11), which is answered by the birth of Samuel (1 Sam 1:19-20; see 1 Sam 2:5), the future kingmaker. At the same time, her prayer of thanksgiving for Samuel climaxes with hope for another son, the Lord's "king/anointed one" (1 Sam 2:10).[33] Meanwhile, Eli's sons were introduced in 1 Samuel 1:3, and the description of their wickedness in 1 Samuel 2:12-17, 22-25 is juxtaposed with the better son, Samuel, in the surrounding context (1 Sam 2:11, 18-21, 26). In their respective ways, Eli's falling off his "throne" (כִּסֵּא; 1 Sam 4:13, 18; 1:9) and Hannah's declaration that the Lord causes the needy to inherit a "throne [כִּסֵּא] of glory" (1 Sam 2:8) artfully foreshadow the Davidic covenant promise that the "throne" (כִּסֵּא) of David and his seed will be established forever (2 Sam 7:13, 16).

Samuel becomes the replacement for Eli's sons (1 Sam 2:34-35).[34] Later, the wickedness of Samuel's own sons leads to Israel's request for a king (1 Sam 8:1-5). Thus, Saul in turn is a sort of replacement for Samuel's sons.[35] Saul's own failures result in his loss of the kingdom, which includes being replaced by "a man after [the Lord's] heart" who is "better than you" (1 Sam 13:14; 15:28). Since Saul's kingdom would have endured if he had been faithful to the Lord (1 Sam 13:13), the selection of David as Israel's next king also means that Saul's sons had been replaced. As Saul said to Jonathan, "As long as the son of Jesse is alive on this earth, you and your kingdom will not be established" (1 Sam 20:31; see 1 Sam 23:17). Accordingly, Saul's son Ish-Bosheth's reign was short and futile (2 Sam 2:8-10; 3:1; 4:5-8).

The Lord's promise of seed to David in 2 Samuel 7:12-16 should be seen against this background of the repeated failure and/or replacement of various sons in 1–2 Samuel, whether Eli's, Samuel's, or Saul's. It also recalls and continues in its own way the theme of "seed" in Genesis. The sequence in

---

[32]Polzin, *Samuel and the Deuteronomist*, 54, 63-64, 66-67; see also Bodner, "Ark-Eology," 177-78, 187-88.
[33]See Polzin, *Samuel and the Deuteronomist*, 63; Stephen Dempster, *Dominion and Dynasty: A Theology of the Hebrew Bible* (Downers Grove, IL: InterVarsity Press, 2003), 135.
[34]Gitay, "Reflections on the Poetics," 224. As a Nazirite (1 Sam 1:11), Samuel contrasts with and may also be a replacement for Samson (Judg 13:5; 16:17).
[35]Gitay, "Reflections on the Poetics," 225.

1–2 Samuel should in turn be seen against the background of Hannah's song, which longs for the Lord's chosen king (1 Sam 2:1-10). In the narrative subsequent to 2 Samuel 7, David's sons Amnon and Absalom are failures also (2 Sam 13–18), but the Lord promised never to replace David's house, even though he would discipline his sons as needed (2 Sam 7:14-15). Solomon's birth in 2 Samuel 12:24-25 is auspicious—"the Lord loved him," and his other name, Jedidiah, means "beloved of the Lord"—but 1–2 Samuel does not equate him with the promised seed in 2 Samuel 7:12-13. Instead, Solomon's failures in 1 Kings clash with the longing for a good son generated by 1–2 Samuel and perhaps assumed in 2 Samuel 7:12-13. Second Samuel 23:3-5 connects the Davidic covenant to a righteous ruler who rules in "the fear of God."

David's house would not be replaced, but the Davidic covenant would still have to be fulfilled in a worthy manner. Who else but a good son could have his kingdom established by the Lord forever? If Solomon was not as good as David (1 Kings 11:4), who was *not* permitted to build a house for the Lord/ark, Solomon's fulfillment of 2 Samuel 7:13 is not straightforward, even though he built a temple that housed the ark. Indeed, Solomon's doing "evil in the eyes of the Lord" in 1 Kings 11:6 and the subsequent "tearing away" (קָרַע) of almost all the kingdom from him in 1 Kings 11:1-13 recall Saul's doing "evil in the eyes of the Lord" (1 Sam 15:19) and having the kingdom "torn away" (קָרַע) in 1 Samuel 15:26-29. If anything, Solomon is more like one of David's sons who gets disciplined (2 Sam 7:14b) than one whose kingdom and throne is established forever (2 Sam 7:12-13).[36] At the same time, based on both text-critical (LXX) and intertextual evidence (Ps 89:30-32; 132:12), Brian Verrett argues that 2 Samuel 7:14b (MT: "when he commits wickedness") does not exclude a messianic interpretation because it leaves open the possibility that a Davidic king will not sin.[37]

Several scholars point out the negative or at least ambiguous portrait of Solomon in 1 Kings 1–11, which further weakens his connection to the

---

[36]Lissa Wray Beal, *1 & 2 Kings*, ApOTC (Downers Grove, IL: InterVarsity Press, 2014), 175.
[37]Verrett argues against the MT reading of 2 Sam 7:14b (*"when* he commits wickedness") for the LXX (*"if* his unrighteousness comes"). Brian Verrett, *The Serpent in Samuel: A Messianic Motif* (Eugene, OR: Resource, 2020), 127-29, 140-42. Unlike the MT, the LXX suggests that the Davidic king will not necessarily sin. See McCarter, *II Samuel*, 194.

promised son fulfilling 2 Samuel 7:12-13.[38] Such glory was always conditional on a Davidic king's obedience (1 Kings 9:4-5; see also 1 Kings 2:4; 3:14; 6:12). Thus, whether from the perspective of the books of Samuel or Kings, there are good reasons not to simply equate "he will build a house for my name" in 2 Samuel 7:13a with Solomon, whether as a prediction or as a later Deuteronomistic addition concerning him and the first temple.[39] We should also remember that the Judahite king promised in Genesis 49:8-12 will come "in the last days" (Gen 49:1), which is sometime after the exile (Deut 4:27-30; see Deut 31:29) and hence after all preexilic Davidic kings have come and gone.

Although the portrait of Solomon in Chronicles is far more positive than the portrait in Kings, this should be seen in light of the respective strategies of Kings and Chronicles, as well as Chronicles' likely use of Kings as a source.[40] Whereas Kings focuses on the decline of the Israelite monarchy from Solomon to the divided kingdom and then to exile, Chronicles presents both David and Solomon in a more positive light with a greater focus on the house of David and their work on the temple. The purpose of this focus is not nostalgia for the bygone era of David and Solomon but to give hope for a postexilic fulfillment of the Davidic covenant through a royal temple builder (1 Chron 17:11-14; 2 Chron 36:22-23), in lockstep with the hopes already set forth in Genesis 49:1, 8-12. To be sure, Chronicles still hints at Solomon's faults (2 Chron 1:3; 9:25, 28; 10:4, 10-11, 14) and also traces the decline and ultimate fall of David's house and the temple through the exile, while still ending with hope (2 Chron 36:22-23). In its own way, Kings likewise ends with a ray of hope through the favor shown to David's descendant Jehoiachin (2 Kings 25:27-30).[41]

Even though David equates Solomon with the fulfillment of the Davidic covenant in 1 Chronicles 22:5-10 and 28:5-7, David's own words in the same

---

[38]More negatively, see J. Daniel Hays, "Has the Narrator Come to Praise Solomon or to Bury Him? Narrative Subtlety in 1 Kings 1–11," *JSOT* 28, no. 3 (2003): 149-74; Jerome Walsh, *1 Kings*, Berit Olam (Collegeville, MN: Liturgical Press, 1996), 34, 65-68, 76-77, 89-90, 98-99, 115-16, 130-32, 137-38. More ambiguously, see Wray Beal, *1 & 2 Kings*, 57-58, 78-81.
[39]For the latter, see McCarter, *II Samuel*, 230.
[40]E.g., Brevard Childs, *Introduction to the Old Testament as Scripture* (Philadelphia: Fortress, 1979), 645.
[41]Stephen Dempster, "The End of History and the Last Man," in *The Seed of Promise: The Sufferings and Glory of the Messiah: Essays in Honor of T. Desmond Alexander*, ed. Paul Williamson and Rita Cefalu (Wilmore, KY: GlossaHouse, 2020), 113-41.

contexts (1 Chron 22:12-13; 28:7-9) and the Lord's words in 2 Chronicles 7:17-22 show that this fulfillment is still conditional on the Davidic king's faithfulness.[42] The mention of Ahijah's prophecy to Jeroboam concerning the division of the kingdom in 2 Chronicles 10:15 also assumes knowledge of the original prophecy in 1 Kings 11:29-39 and presumably of Solomon's idolatry recounted therein.[43] If this is the case, then it is yet another hint within Chronicles' overall positive portrait of Solomon that he did not actually fulfill the conditions for the fulfillment of the Davidic covenant.[44] As such, this covenant still awaits fulfillment from Chronicles' perspective. Solomon as Davidic temple builder is thus a picture of the Lion of Judah who will come "in the last days" (Gen 49:1, 8-12) but is not himself that king, who has yet to "go up" (2 Chron 36:23). In the end, the conditions of the Davidic covenant will be fulfilled by this Messiah in fulfillment of the Lord's ultimately unconditional promise.

2 SAMUEL 7 AND PSALM 2

If 2 Samuel 7 is foundational to the Davidic covenant, then other Old Testament references to this covenant should be understood in light of it. In some cases, such as Psalm 2 and Psalm 89, there seems to be sufficient textual evidence to see other Davidic covenant texts as specifically engaging 2 Samuel 7 *as a text*.[45] Psalm 2:7, "He said to me you are my son; today I have begotten you" (אָמַר אֵלַי בְּנִי אַתָּה אֲנִי הַיּוֹם יְלִדְתִּיךָ), has been

---

[42] John Sailhamer highlights the call to obedience in 1 Chron 22:13; 28:7 and that the author/chronicler, "contrary to David," is still waiting for the Davidic covenant to be fulfilled by a future son of David. Sailhamer, *First & Second Chronicles*, Everyman's Bible Commentary (Chicago: Moody, 1983), 55, 60. See also William Riley, who also cites 2 Chron 1:8-10 ("let your word with David my father be established"), 2 Chron 6:15-17 ("keep for your servant David my father what you spoke to him"), and 2 Chron 6:42 ("remember the mercies of David your servant"). Riley, *King and Cultus in Chronicles: Worship and the Reinterpretation of History* (Sheffield: JSOT Press, 1993), 88-92.

[43] Ralph Klein believes Chronicles emphasizes the fulfillment of the prophetic word here rather than Solomon's sins. Klein, *2 Chronicles*, Hermeneia (Minneapolis: Fortress, 2012), 161.

[44] Sara Japhet sees this as an unresolved tension between Chronicles' emphasis on retribution and its positive presentation of Solomon. See Japhet, *I & II Chronicles*, OTL (Louisville: Westminster John Knox, 1993), 657.

[45] This seems to be the simplest solution, rather than reversing the directionality of dependence. See Charles Augustus Briggs, *The Book of Psalms*, ICC (Edinburgh: T&T Clark, 1987), 1:15. Briggs writes that Ps 2:7 "is thinking of the covenant which Yahweh made with David through Nathan. . . . David himself speaks . . . quoting Yahweh's words to him by Nathan the prophet." For a more recent survey of critical dating of 2 Sam 7, see McCarter, *II Samuel*, 5, 210-11.

linked to 2 Samuel 7:14, "I will be a father to him and he will be a son to me" (אֲנִי אֶהְיֶה־לּוֹ לְאָב וְהוּא יִהְיֶה־לִּי לְבֵן; see Heb 1:5).[46] Robert Cole's observation that the speech in Psalm 2:7 is introduced as something "recounted" (piel סָפַר; see also Ps 44:1; 78:3; 79:13) strengthens the likelihood of dependence on a source, such as 2 Samuel 7:14.[47] Thus, Gerald Wilson explains, "Ps 2 introduces the idea of the Davidic covenant [to the Psalter]."[48]

Although Psalm 2:7 is very likely connected to 2 Samuel 7:14 and the Davidic covenant, the two texts still have differences that deserve attention. While a father-son relationship between the Lord and the king is common to both passages, Psalm 2:7 uses a simple verbless clause with just two Hebrew words, "You are my son" (בְּנִי אַתָּה), whereas 2 Samuel 7:14 has the verb הָיָה ("to be") and two *lamed*-prepositions, "he will be for me [לִּי] for a son [לְבֵן]." The construction in 2 Samuel 7:14 is commonly used to specify a relationship, such as in 2 Samuel 7:24, "You have established for yourself your people Israel *for yourself* [לְךָ] *for a people* [לְעָם] forever, and you, Lord, will be *for them* [לָהֶם] *for God* [לֵאלֹהִים]." This construction is probably best known through the promise, "You/they will be my people, and I will be your/their God" (Jer 24:7; 31:33; 32:38; see also Ex 6:7; Lev 26:12). Whereas this construction does not necessarily describe a relationship that always existed (Gen 20:12; 24:67; Ex 4:16), the verbless clause in Psalm 2:7, "You are my son," may suggest here a timelessness that gives it additional force. Perhaps this relates to Hebrews' citation of Psalm 2:7 twice but 2 Samuel 7:14 only once (Heb 1:5; 5:5; see also Acts 13:33) as well as the application of 2 Samuel 7:14 to believers in 2 Corinthians 6:18 and Revelation 21:7. In Genesis 27:21, Isaac's question to Jacob uses a verbless clause similar to Psalm 2:7, "Are you indeed my son [הַאַתָּה זֶה בְּנִי] Esau, or not?" The other construction probably would not have served the purpose.

Furthermore, in a way that "he will be for me for a son" (2 Sam 7:14) does not, "You are my son" in Psalm 2:7 connects with messianic prophecies in

---

[46]E.g., Gerald Wilson, *The Editing of the Hebrew Psalter* (Chico, CA: Scholars Press, 1981), 209. Wilson calls Ps 2:7 "clearly reminiscent of 2 Sam 7:14."
[47]Robert L. Cole, *Psalms 1–2: Gateway to the Psalter* (Sheffield: Sheffield Phoenix, 2012), 111-12, including n119.
[48]Wilson, *Editing of the Hebrew Psalter*, 209.

Genesis 27:27-29 and Genesis 49:8-12, both of which also speak of a king who will rule the nations as "my son" (בְּנִי).⁴⁹ Both texts also refer to this ruler in the second person (Gen 27:27-28, "See, the scent of *my son* [בְּנִי]. . . . May God give *to you* [לְךָ] dew"; Gen 49:8-9, "Judah are *you* [אַתָּה]. . . . Judah is a lion's whelp; from the prey, *my son* [בְּנִי], you go up"). Linking Psalm 2:7 to Genesis 49:8-12 is especially fitting because the prophecy of a Lion of *Judah* is the clearest connection to the Davidic covenant in the Pentateuch.⁵⁰

Additional aspects of Psalm 2 confirm its relationship to 2 Samuel 7 and the Davidic covenant. In Psalm 2:7, "You are my son" is called the "decree of the Lord" (חֹק יְהוָה), which Cole interprets as a reference to the Davidic covenant and parallel to David's reference to this covenant as "the law of the man/humanity" (תּוֹרַת הָאָדָם) in 2 Samuel 7:19.⁵¹ Both texts link the fulfillment of the Davidic covenant to some kind of decree/law, presumably distinct from Sinai/Deuteronomic law. The term "man/humanity" (אָדָם) in 2 Samuel 7:19 also suggests that the fulfillment of the Davidic covenant affects not only the house of David and Israel but also all humanity.⁵² This is not emphasized in 2 Samuel 7 (see 2 Sam 7:9-11, 23), but it is in Genesis 27:29 and 49:10. Furthermore, the reflection on the Davidic covenant in 2 Samuel 23:3 describes the righteous king as ruling "humanity" (אָדָם). Although not found in 2 Samuel 7, the term "M/messiah" (מָשִׁיחַ) is important to 1-2 Samuel and appears in Davidic covenant contexts in 2 Samuel 22:51 and 2 Samuel 23:1, as in Psalm 2:2. Both 2 Samuel 7 and Psalm 2 also contain direct speech by the Lord himself (2 Sam 7:5-16; Ps 2:6b, 7b-9).

The Davidic Messiah's rule over the whole earth is clear in Psalm 2. The nations and their kings rebel against the Lord and his Messiah (Ps 2:1-3), but the Lord ensures that the Messiah will rule them (Ps 2:6-9). They would be wise to submit (Ps 2:10-12). In particular, the Lord's offer to his

---

⁴⁹Chen, *Messianic Vision of the Pentateuch*, 99, 131.

⁵⁰The theme of the Lord "begetting" (יָלַד) in Ps 2:7 also parallels Deut 32:18, where he "begets" (יָלַד) Israel.

⁵¹Cole, *Psalms 1-2*, 113; see also Briggs, *Psalms* 1:15.

⁵²In this context, the term also appears in 2 Sam 7:14 ("beatings of the sons of men") and the same unpointed form as part of Obed-Edom's name (עֹבֵד אֱדֹם) in 2 Sam 6:10-12 (see also 2 Sam 8:14). His name, which means "servant of man/humanity," also links to the frequent use of the word "servant" (עֶבֶד) in 2 Sam 7 (2 Sam 7:5, 8, 19-21, 25-29).

king, "Ask [שְׁאַל] from me and I will give [וְאֶתְּנָה] the nations as your inheritance" (Ps 2:8), echoes his offer to Solomon to "Ask what I will give you" (שְׁאַל מָה אֶתֶּן־לָךְ) in 1 Kings 3:5, but one greater than Solomon is described in Psalm 2. David Mitchell characterizes this psalm as "of an intrinsically 'ultimate' character" since it uses "language [that] far exceeds the reality of any historical king or battle."[53] Though the present purpose is mainly to show the connection between 2 Samuel 7 and Psalm 2, Psalm 2 is also a nexus passage, with connections to Psalm 1 (its companion in the Psalter's introduction), other psalms (e.g., Ps 110), and still other Old Testament texts (e.g., Ps 2:9 and Gen 3:15/Gen 49:10/Ex 15:6/Num 24:17).[54]

2 SAMUEL 7 AND PSALM 89

Like Psalm 2, Psalm 89 is also located on one of the Psalter's seams (as the last psalm in Book III), has clear connections to 2 Samuel 7 and the Davidic covenant, and is itself a nexus passage.[55] As Psalm 89 begins, its focus on the Lord's love and faithfulness (Ps 89:1-2) is specifically directed to the "covenant . . . I swore to David my servant, 'I will *establish your seed forever* [עַד־עוֹלָם אָכִין זַרְעֶךָ], and I will *build your throne to all generations* [וּבָנִיתִי לְדֹר־וָדוֹר כִּסְאֲךָ]'" (Ps 89:3-4). Almost all of the terms in Psalm 89:4 can be traced to 2 Samuel 7 ("establish," 2 Sam 7:12-13, 16, 26; "your seed," 2 Sam 7:12; "forever," 2 Sam 7:13, 16, 24-26; "build," 2 Sam 7:27; "throne," 2 Sam 7:13, 16). Also, "David my servant" in Psalm 89:3, 20 recalls 2 Samuel 7:5, 8, 20, 26. Even the Lord's "steadfast love" (חֶסֶד) and "faithfulness" (אֱמוּנָה) from Psalm 89:1-2, 24, 49 parallel 2 Samuel 7:15-16 (חֶסֶד, נֶאֱמַן).

As Psalm 89 continues, more and more links to 2 Samuel 7 appear. In Psalm 89:8, "Lord God of hosts, who is like you?" (יְהוָה אֱלֹהֵי צְבָאוֹת מִי־כָמוֹךָ) resembles "Lord of hosts" (יְהוָה צְבָאוֹת) in 2 Samuel 7:8, 26-27 and "there is none like you" (אֵין כָּמוֹךָ) in 2 Samuel 7:22. Psalm 89:19 calls the prophetic word to David a "vision" (חָזוֹן), much like 2 Samuel 7:17. Included in the

---

[53]Mitchell, *Message of the Psalter*, 85.
[54]See Robert L. Cole, "An Integrated Reading of Psalms 1 and 2," *JSOT* 98 (2002): 75-88; Kevin Chen, "Psalm 110: A Nexus for Old Testament Theology," *CTR* 17, no. 2 (Spring 2020): 62-64. For discussion of Num 24 and its being braided with Gen 3:15 and Gen 49:8-12 in later OT texts, see chapter four above.
[55]See William C. Pohl IV, "A Messianic Reading of Psalm 89: A Canonical and Intertextual Study," *JETS* 58, no. 3 (2015): 507-25.

vision as recounted in Psalm 89:22 is victory over the "enemy" (אֹיֵב) and the promise that "the son of wickedness will not afflict him" (וּבֶן־עַוְלָה לֹא יְעַנֶּנּוּ), a striking parallel to 2 Samuel 7:9-11 ("all your enemies [אֹיְבֶיךָ] ... the sons of wickedness will not afflict him again [וְלֹא־יֹסִיפוּ בְנֵי־עַוְלָה לְעַנּוֹתוֹ] ... all your enemies [אֹיְבֶיךָ]").[56] Peter Craigie links "You are my father" (אָבִי אָתָּה) in Psalm 89:26 to 2 Samuel 7:14.[57] This verbless construction also nicely parallels "You are my son" (בְּנִי אַתָּה) in Psalm 2:7. Even the possibility of judgment on disobedient Davidic kings, along with reassurance of the Davidic covenant's endurance as given in 2 Samuel 7:14-16, has a parallel in Psalm 89:30-37.

Table 6.2. Links between 2 Samuel 7 and Psalm 89

	2 Samuel 7	Psalm 89
"Establish" David's "seed"/seed's kingdom "forever"	2 Sam 7:12-13	Ps 89:4
"Build" a "house" or "throne"	2 Sam 7:11	Ps 89:4
David as the Lord's "servant"	2 Sam 7:5, 8, 20, 26	Ps 89:3, 20
"Steadfast love" and "faithfulness"	2 Sam 7:15-16	Ps 89:1-2, 24, 49
None like "the Lord [God] of hosts"	2 Sam 7:8, 22, 26-27	Ps 89:8
Davidic covenant as "vision"	2 Sam 7:17	Ps 89:19
"Enemy"/"son[s] of wickedness will not afflict"	2 Sam 7:9-11	Ps 89:22
Father-son relationship	2 Sam 7:14	Ps 89:26
Disobedient kings to be disciplined	2 Sam 7:14-16	Ps 89:30-37

Like Psalm 2, Psalm 89 also highlights worldwide rule as part of the Messiah's fulfillment of the Davidic covenant. In Psalm 89:27, his father/the Lord makes him "most high among the kings of the earth." Indeed, just

---

[56] The phrase "son[s] of wickedness" appears elsewhere only in the parallel 1 Chron 17:9 and in 2 Sam 3:34. Pohl characterizes Ps 89:19-37 as an interpretation of an existing Davidic covenant tradition ("Messianic Reading of Psalm 89," 512).

[57] Peter Craigie, *Psalms 1–50*, WBC (Waco, TX: Word, 1983), 67.

as the Lord has power over the sea (Ps 89:9-10), so he has given this same power to his royal son (Ps 89:25).⁵⁸ However, unlike the realized (or about-to-be-realized) perspective on the Davidic covenant in Psalm 2, Psalm 89 wrestles with the apparent failure of the Davidic covenant (Ps 89:38-45).⁵⁹ The Davidic king has fallen (Ps 89:38-39), the land is in ruins (Ps 89:40-41), enemies triumph (Ps 89:42-43), and the throne is abased (Ps 89:44-45). Nevertheless, readers can be certain that the Lord will never break his covenant with David (see also Num 23:19). By lamenting, "Where are your former mercies [חֶסֶד], Lord, which you swore to David in your faithfulness [אֱמוּנָה]?" the psalmist seems to be asking the Lord to fulfill the Davidic covenant (Ps 89:49).

The concluding section (Ps 89:46-51) to Psalm 89 further seems to assume that the Lord fulfilling the Davidic covenant would bring blessing to all humanity by addressing the problems of futility and death (Ps 89:47-48).⁶⁰ In Psalm 89:47, the psalmist prays that the Lord "remember . . . for what futility [שָׁוְא] *you created all the sons of Adam* [בָּרָאתָ כָל־בְּנֵי־אָדָם]." He continues in Psalm 89:48 with a question, "Who is the man who will *live* [יִחְיֶה] and not see *death* [מָוֶת], and deliver his soul from the hand of Sheol?" Besides sounding like Ecclesiastes, these two verses draw on the teaching of Genesis 1–3 on creation and fall (see chapter two). Since Psalm 89:47-48 is preceded and followed by explicit references to the Davidic covenant (Ps 89:39, 49), the Davidic covenant in Psalm 89 seemingly effects not only the salvation of Israel through the house of David but also the salvation of humanity from the fall (see "the law of humanity," 2 Sam 7:19). Sure enough, Psalm 89 concludes with a prayer that the Lord regard the reproach that has landed on "the heels of your messiah" (עִקְּבוֹת מְשִׁיחֶךָ, Ps 89:51), which appears to borrow language and imagery from Genesis 3:15, "you will strike his heel" (אַתָּה תְּשׁוּפֶנּוּ עָקֵב).

---

⁵⁸For this and other parallels between the Lord and the king in Ps 89, see Jean-Bernard Dumortier, "Un rituel d'intronisation: le Ps. LXXXIX 2-38," *VT* 22 (1972): 185-89.

⁵⁹See Wilson, *Editing of the Hebrew Psalter*, 213-15.

⁶⁰See Frank-Lothar Hossfeld and Erich Zenger, *Psalms 2: A Commentary on Psalms 51–100*, trans. Linda Maloney, Hermeneia (Minneapolis: Fortress 2005), 412. Hossfeld and Zenger say this passage "expands the lament over the suffering of the anointed and his people to encompass the mortality of all humankind."

The psalmist's longing for the fulfillment of the Davidic covenant thus seems to be merged with an awareness of Genesis 3:15, which also promises that the enemy's head will be struck.[61] I will revisit Psalm 89 in chapter nine in relation to Psalm 72 and the composition of the Psalter. There are many more Old Testament texts that could be analyzed in relationship to such a highly connected passage as 2 Samuel 7, but the preceding illustrates the richness of these literary, textual, and theological relationships.

CONCLUSION

The account of the Davidic covenant in 2 Samuel 7 is one of the most important passages in the Prophets and in the Old Testament. Within the literary context of 1–2 Samuel, its promise of an eternal kingdom serves as a narrative and theological climax. This literary context also builds suspense concerning the quest for a son worthy to be the promised temple builder and eternal king. At the same time, the casting of the Davidic covenant as a night vision provides a significant link to the Abrahamic covenant in Genesis 15 that suggests the fulfillment of both covenants by the same heir, the Lion of Judah who comes "in the last days" of Genesis 49:1, 8-12. As the foundational Davidic covenant text, 2 Samuel 7 has connections to numerous other Davidic covenant texts in the Old Testament, such as Psalm 2 and Psalm 89. The longing for a great, even perfect, leader, still exists today, and 2 Samuel 7 and its nexus connections show us that this hope need not be in vain.

---

[61]There are also other ways to make this connection, such as tracing the seed of the woman to the seed of Abraham, and then to David's seed (see above for the connection between Gen 15:3-4 and 2 Sam 7:12). For David's defeat of Goliath as echoing Gen 3:15, see Dempster, *Dominion and Dynasty*, 139-40.

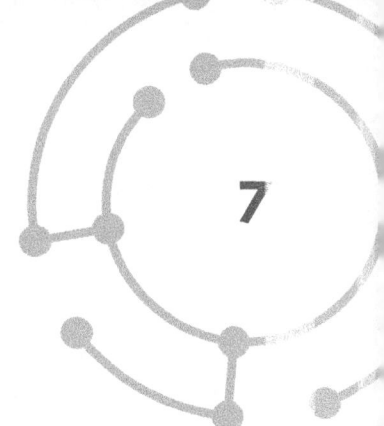

7

ISAIAH 52:13–53:12
THE SUFFERING SERVANT

ISAIAH 52:13–53:12 is one of the best-known passages in the Old Testament for its detailed prediction of a Suffering Servant, commonly interpreted by Christians as a prophecy of the suffering of Jesus Christ. Franz Delitzsch calls it "the most central, the deepest, and the loftiest thing" in Old Testament prophecy.[1] Isaiah 52:13–53:12 is indeed holy ground. Whereas messianic interpretation of this text can be traced to the New Testament itself (Mt 8:17; Lk 22:37; Jn 12:38; 1 Pet 2:22, 24-25) and some voices within Jewish interpretation, other influential Jewish voices (Rashi, ibn Ezra, Radak) have disputed this, arguing for a corporate interpretation of this servant as Israel.[2] Indeed, the question asked by the Ethiopian eunuch to Philip about Isaiah 53 is still relevant today: "Concerning whom does the prophet speak this? Concerning himself or someone else?" (Acts 8:34).

Like Philip, my answer sees the importance of "beginning from this Scripture" (Acts 8:35; see also Lk 24:27) but will naturally involve others as well. This is because in addition to being a classic Old Testament text, Isaiah 52:13–53:12 is also a nexus passage. As the fourth and final Servant Song, it has important textual links to the previous three Servant Songs

---

[1] C. F. Keil and Franz Delitzsch, *Isaiah*, trans. James Martin, Commentary on the Old Testament 7(repr., Peabody, MA: Hendrickson, 1996), 500.

[2] I rely here on the helpful work of Michael Brown, "Jewish Interpretations of Isaiah 53," in *The Gospel According to Isaiah 53: Encountering the Suffering Servant in Jewish and Christian Theology*, ed. Darrell Bock and Mitch Glaser (Grand Rapids, MI: Kregel, 2012), 61-83. Brown highlights Rashi, ibn Ezra, and Radak as the "big three" who argue for a corporate interpretation. For a comprehensive reference, see S. R. Driver and A. D. Neubauer, *The Fifty-Third Chapter of Isaiah According to the Jewish Interpreters* (Oxford: James Parker, 1877).

(Is 42:1-4; 49:1-6; 50:4-9), the immediate literary context of Isaiah 40–55, and the book of Isaiah as a whole.[3] It also has allusions to the Pentateuch and parallels with still other Old Testament books (e.g., Ps 22), though space prohibits me from exploring the latter here.[4] Due to the importance of the other Servant Songs and Isaiah 40–55 for understanding Isaiah 52:13–53:12, the discussion below offers an extended analysis of this context to bring out its meaning and some of its nexus connections. In the process, several significant connections to the Pentateuch will also be revealed. As we will see, Isaiah 52:13–53:12 is like a multifaceted diamond, which sparkles differently when looked at from different angles.[5]

THE SERVANT SONGS IN ISAIAH 40–55

The identification of the four Servant Songs in Isaiah 42:1-4; 49:1-6; 50:4-9; 52:13–53:12 is attributed to famed Isaiah scholar Bernard Duhm.[6]

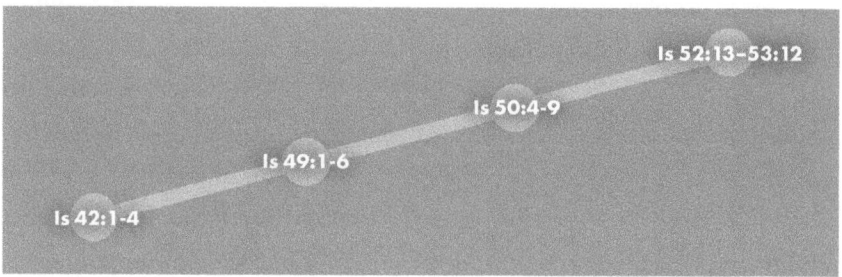

Figure 7.1. The four Servant Songs in Isaiah

---

[3] For the "confirmatory comment[s]" of Is 42:5-9; 49:7-13; 50:10-11; 54:1–55:13, see J. Alec Motyer, *The Prophecy of Isaiah* (Downers Grove, IL: InterVarsity Press, 1993), 321.

[4] Benjamin Sommer focuses on (what he believes to be) allusions to Jeremiah, Is 1–39, and Psalms. See Sommer, *A Prophet Reads Scripture: Allusion in Isaiah 40–66* (Stanford, CA: Stanford University Press, 1998), 3. Regarding Ps 22, it is difficult to know whether there is a dependence of one passage on the other or whether both draw from a common source such as the Pentateuch, but Ps 22 is in many ways like Is 53 except in the first person. Such a connection is passingly mentioned by Delitzsch, who calls Is 52:13–53:12 "the unravelling of Ps. 22 and Ps. 110" (*Isaiah*, 500). Both Ps 22 and Is 53 also have a sudden shift from death to life (Is 53:10-12; Ps 22:22). For the shift in Is 53, see Henning Graf Reventlow, "Basic Issues in the Interpretation of Isaiah 53," in *Jesus and the Suffering Servant: Isaiah 53 and Christian Origins*, ed. William Bellinger Jr. and William Farmer (Harrisburg, PA: Trinity Press International, 1998), 26-27.

[5] Sommer discusses how the presence of allusion affects interpretation of the alluding text (*Prophet Reads Scripture*, 12-13).

[6] See Christopher North, *The Suffering Servant in Deutero-Isaiah*, 2nd ed. (London: Oxford, 1956), 2, 47; Tryggve Mettinger, *A Farewell to the Servant Songs: A Critical Examination of an Exegetical Axiom* (Lund, Sweden: CWK Gleerup, 1983), 9.

However, because he believed they were postexilic in origin, he isolated them from the rest of Isaiah 40–55, which he took as exilic (ca. 540 BC).[7] Indeed, Duhm's classic "three Isaiahs" view of the authorship of Isaiah is that a preexilic Isaiah son of Amoz was behind Isaiah 1–39, an exilic Deutero-Isaiah behind Isaiah 40–55, and a postexilic Trito-Isaiah behind Isaiah 55–66. Whether separating the Servant Songs from their literary context or the bigger issue of seeing the book of Isaiah diachronically as the product of multiple authors and redaction, such fragmentation of this book drastically affects its meaning by undermining its literary and theological unity and radically redefining the proper context(s) of interpretation. Spurred on by Julius Wellhausen, the critical interpretation of the Pentateuch had also gone to a similar fate. Within critical frameworks like these, the literary relationship between the Pentateuch and Isaiah is very complicated, since both took centuries to reach their canonical form and were missing major blocks of material along the way, whether (postexilic) P, Trito-Isaiah, or otherwise.[8]

Without entering into this longstanding debate here, the analysis below follows the lead of those who emphasize the unity of Isaiah. Taking it a step further, I take Isaiah to be a thoroughly unified book whose various passages have the potential of being strategically related regardless of which "Isaiah" Duhm would have attributed them to or how far apart they may be in the canonical book of Isaiah. Duhm had a low regard for the literary unity of Isaiah, saying of Isaiah son of Amoz, "As much as Isaiah has written, he still is not a writer by calling. . . . We do not have the slightest reason to conclude that he has collected his speeches, poems, and reports himself and edited them as a whole."[9] Even with the relatively recent influences of redaction criticism and canonical criticism, which search for traces of literary unity in material formerly thought to be

---

[7] Bernard Duhm, *Das Buch Jesaia*, 4th ed. (Göttingen: Vandenhoeck & Ruprecht, 1968), 14, 18-19.
[8] Note the mediating position in Sommer that searches for allusions not to the Pentateuch but to its "texts in earlier literary settings" (*Prophet Reads Scripture*, 132; see also 149-51).
[9] Duhm, *Buch Jesaia*, 16-17. North discusses the widely accepted view that preexilic prophets were speaking prophets rather than writing prophets and the view that Is 40–55 is "a collection of short oracles" (*Suffering Servant*, 157-60).

disparate, the thoroughgoing unity of Isaiah is still not widely accepted or carried through exegetically as I attempt to do here.[10]

In contrast with Duhm's isolation of the Servant Songs from Isaiah 40-55, Christopher North argues that the Servant Songs appear to be written by the same author as Isaiah 40–55.[11] Either way, their content still legitimizes a distinction from other servant passages in Isaiah 40–55. Duhm himself was well aware that "the servant of the Lord" was common both to the Servant Songs and to their context in Isaiah 40–55 but saw the two perspectives as "entirely different." The surrounding passages in Isaiah 40–55 often identify the servant as corporate Israel (Is 41:8-9; 44:1-2, 21; 45:4; 48:20), concerning whom the Lord has great plans but who has become blind, deaf, and lacking understanding (Is 42:18-25; 43:8). As a blind people mired in sin (Is 43:24; 48:1; 50:1; see also Is 56:10; 59:10), they were in desperate need of salvation. They could not help themselves, much less the nations (Is 49:5-6; 51:18). On the other hand, argues Duhm, the Servant Songs depict a "hero" who is innocent, Yahweh's disciple, and faithful to his call to the people and the nations.[12] His ministry "to open the eyes of the blind" and "bring forth [hiphil יָצָא] the prisoner . . . those sitting in the darkness" (Is 42:7; see also Is 9:2) is exactly what blind, imprisoned Israel needs (see Is 42:22; 61:1). Though maintaining the connection between the Servant Songs and Isaiah 40–55, North also points out the general anonymity of the servant in these songs (Is 49:3 excepted) compared to frequent specification as Jacob-Israel elsewhere, the "heightened individualization" of this servant, and his active mission to Israel and the nations.[13] Thus, the Servant Songs have their own integrity without necessarily implying their isolation from Isaiah 40–55.

---

[10]See Paul Wegner, *Isaiah*, TOTC (Downers Grove, IL: InterVarsity Press, 2021), 32-34; Joseph Blenkinsopp, *Isaiah 1–39*, AB (New York: Doubleday, 2000), 73. One redaction critic who does emphasize the importance of a prophetic book compared to the mere byproduct of oral proclamation is Hans-Christoph Schmitt, "Prophetie und Schultheologie im Deuterojesajabuch: Beobachtungen zur Redaktionsgeschichte von Jes 40–55," *ZAW* 91 (1979): 43, 56.

[11]North, *Suffering Servant*, 186.

[12]Duhm, *Buch Jesaia*, 311. See also Gordon Hugenberger, "The Servant of the Lord in the 'Servant Songs' of Isaiah: A Second Moses Figure," in *The Lord's Anointed: Interpretation of Old Testament Messianic Texts*, ed. P. E. Satterthwaite, R. S. Hess, and G. J. Wenham (Grand Rapids, MI: Baker, 1995), 110. Hugenberger cites first-person plural pronouns (*we, our, us*) as "always the prophet speaking on behalf of the people of Israel with whom he identifies."

[13]North, *Suffering Servant*, 178-82, 205-7.

THE DAVIDIC COVENANT AND JUSTICE IN THE SERVANT SONGS

Let us consider the first Servant Song in Isaiah 42:1-4, which, like the other songs, will prove to have important links to the Davidic covenant and justice. Alec Motyer points out that "See [הֵן], my servant" in Isaiah 42:1 continues the pattern of "See [הֵן], you [false gods] are nothing" in Isaiah 41:24 and "See [הֵן], all of them [idolaters] are wicked" in Isaiah 41:29 (see also Is 41:11).[14] The silence and impotence of idols and idolaters in Isaiah 41:22-29 highlights not only the Lord's power and knowledge but also the servant's message of instruction/law in Isaiah 42:4. The Lord looked and "there was no man," "no counselor" (יוֹעֵץ; see the Davidic "wonderful counselor," Is 9:6-7), none to reply a word in Isaiah 41:28, but Isaiah 42:1 spotlights a chosen servant who will bring "justice [מִשְׁפָּט] to the nations." The presence of the Spirit on him in Isaiah 42:1 parallels the "shoot from the stump of Jesse" in Isaiah 11:1-4, who is also a wise man and righteous judge of the earth as well as a descendant of David. The islands waiting for his "instruction/law" (תּוֹרָה) in Isaiah 42:4 further resemble the nations going to Zion to hear the "law" (תּוֹרָה) of the Lord in the last days (Is 2:2-3). The law "goes forth" (יָצָא) from Zion in Isaiah 2:3, just as the servant "brings forth" (יוֹצִיא) justice to the nations in Isaiah 42:1, 3.

Within Isaiah 40–55 itself, "See [הֵן], my servant" in Isaiah 42:1 also links to "See [הִנֵּה], my servant" in Isaiah 52:13, and the Lord being "pleased" (רָצָה) with the servant in Isaiah 42:1 links him to the "pardon" (רָצָה) of Israel's guilt in Isaiah 40:2 (see Lev 26:41; רָצוֹן in Is 49:8; 61:2), a connection clarified in Isaiah 53:5, 10-12. The promise of "an everlasting covenant, the faithful [הַנֶּאֱמָנִים] mercies of David" in Isaiah 55:3 suggests that the messianic fulfillment of the Davidic covenant is within the purview of Isaiah 40–55, including the Servant Songs.[15] Duhm sees a dependence

---

[14] Motyer, *Isaiah*, 318.
[15] Contra Gerhard von Rad, *Old Testament Theology*, trans. D. M. G. Stalker (repr., Peabody, MA: Prince, 2005), 2:240. Von Rad sees the author of Is 55:3 (for him, Deutero-Isaiah) as unconcerned with the Davidic promises "in the traditional way, for he understands them to have been made not to David but to the whole nation," thus "democratising" the Davidic covenant, "robb[ing] it of its specific content," and leaving "no place" for "the Messianic hope." Jaap Dekker calls this "the now usual interpretation of this text." Dekker, "What Does David Have to Do with It? The Promise of a New Covenant in the Book of Isaiah," in *Covenant: A Vital Element of Reformed Theology: Biblical,*

of Isaiah 55:3-4 on 2 Samuel 7:8-16, pointing out the shared terms "faithful" (וְנֶאְמַן, 2 Sam 7:16; see Is 49:7) and "prince" (נָגִיד; 2 Sam 7:8).[16] "Steadfast love/mercy" (חֶסֶד; 2 Sam 7:15) and "forever/everlasting" (עוֹלָם; 2 Sam 7:13, 16) also link the two texts, as well as the theme of the nations (2 Sam 7:19; Is 55:4).

Table 7.1. Links between 2 Samuel 7 and Isaiah 55:3-4

	2 Samuel 7	**Isaiah 55:3-4**
David	passim	Is 55:3
"Everlasting/forever"	2 Sam 7:13, 16	Is 55:3, "everlasting *covenant*"
"Faithful"	2 Sam 7:16	Is 55:3
"Steadfast love/mercy"	2 Sam 7:15	Is 55:3
"Prince"	2 Sam 7:8	Is 55:4
"Nations" or "humanity"	2 Sam 7:19	Is 55:4

With the Lord's glory among the nations being such an important theme in Isaiah 40–55, it is no accident that Isaiah 36–39 has just shown that this glory in relation to Assyria and their idols is bound up with the success of Jerusalem and the house of David (Is 37:31, 35; 38:6). Since the Lord delivered Zion and Hezekiah from Assyria and vindicated himself from their blasphemies before "all the kingdoms of the earth" (Is 36:18-20; 37:10-13, 20, 36-38), this suggests that he will likewise save Zion and the house of David from Babylon despite their endurance of exile this time (Is 39:6-7).[17]

The Davidic house had faced threats before (Is 7:6; 37:35), but even the Babylonian shaming of the royal line and threat to the Davidic covenant by making eunuchs of some of Hezekiah's "sons who go out from [him]" (וּמִבָּנֶיךָ אֲשֶׁר יֵצְאוּ מִמְּךָ, Is 39:7; see 2 Sam 7:12, "your seed after you

---

Historical and Systematic-Theological Perspectives, ed. Hans Burger, Gert Kwakkel, and Michael Mulder (Leiden: Brill, 2021), 101. For a representative list of scholars holding this view, see Knut Heim, "The (God-)Forsaken King of Psalm 89: A Historical and Intertextual Enquiry," in *King and Messiah in Israel and the Ancient Near East*, ed. John Day (Sheffield: Sheffield Academic Press, 1998), 309n41. For reluctance to link the servant in Is 40–55 to the Davidic ruler of Is 1–39, see, e.g., Andrew Abernethy and Gregory Goswell, *God's Messiah in the Old Testament* (Grand Rapids, MI: Baker, 2020), 85-87.

[16]Duhm, *Buch Jesaia*, 414.

[17]In the important parallel passage in Is 7 in which the northern kingdom of Israel and Aram also try to topple the kingdom of Judah, the Lord apparently takes offense at their scheme (Is 7:4-6).

who will go out from your loins" [זַרְעֲךָ אַחֲרֶיךָ אֲשֶׁר יֵצֵא מִמֵּעֶיךָ]) could not stop the Lord's plan (see also Is 7:7; 37:3; 56:3).[18] He is "the God of David" (אֱלֹהֵי דָוִד) who on this basis extends Hezekiah's life in the face of death (Is 38:1, 5-6, 10) and should be trusted (Is 7:9; 36:4) to manifest his glory to the nations again (Is 40:5) through rescuing the house of David from its exilic deathbed in faithfulness to his promise of an everlasting Davidic kingdom (2 Sam 7:12-16; Is 55:3). His past salvation of Jerusalem "for my sake and for the sake of David *my servant*" (עַבְדִּי, Is 37:35; see 2 Sam 7:5) suggests that Zion's redemption from Babylon will be on the same basis (Is 40:2; 52:1; 55:3), a redemption that is accordingly accomplished in Isaiah 40–55 by a figure called "my servant."

As Motyer points out, justice is "the leading idea" of the first Servant Song in Isaiah 42:1-4.[19] Indeed, the servant's ministry of bringing forth or establishing "justice" (מִשְׁפָּט) is mentioned three times (Is 42:1, 3, 4). Whereas in this song the beneficiaries of this justice are the nations and the islands (Is 42:1, 4; see Is 41:1), the preceding context shows that Israel also longed for justice from the Lord. In Isaiah 40:27, the Lord refers to Israel's complaint that "my justice [מִשְׁפָּטִי] is disregarded by my God." In that context, the Lord responds that he is an everlasting God, Creator, and rewarder of those who "wait" (קָוָה) for him (Is 40:28-31). The islands also "wait" (יָחַל) in Isaiah 42:4. As in Isaiah 49:23 and Isaiah 51:5, this waiting seems to be specifically directed toward eschatological salvation.

Waiting, sometimes painfully, for the Lord to manifest his eschatological justice is also a core element of the Song of Moses in Deuteronomy 32:1-43 (see chapter five). Deuteronomy 32:4 declares that "all his ways are just" (מִשְׁפָּט), but the full manifestation of the Lord's justice and

---

[18] The Lord's use "signs" for the house of David in the past (Is 7:11, 14; 37:30; 38:7, 22) hints that he will do so again. Such would certainly fit the theme of second exodus (see below). The sign of Immanuel (Is 7:14) may be one such sign. Indeed, the signs in Is 37:30 and 38:7, 22 were for Hezekiah ("you" [singular]), but the sign in Is 7:14 is for "you" (plural), i.e., the (failed) house of David, which need not be limited to one Davidic king such as Ahaz. A sign in Is 7:11 was originally offered to Ahaz specifically ("you" [singular]), but his refusal of this opportunity resulted in the promised sign of Is 7:14. Regarding eunuchs, their lack of offspring resembles the servant in Is 53:8 (though see Is 53:10). Dan 1:3 also mentions "Ashpenaz, chief of his eunuchs," who brings Israelites, including some from the royal line, before the king.

[19] Motyer, *Isaiah*, 318.

"vengeance" (נָקָם) involves the use of godless nations to punish his people before justice is finally done (Deut 32:41; see also Deut 32:35, 43).[20] Like the "vengeance" (נָקָם) and "day of their calamity" (יוֹם אֵידָם) in Deuteronomy 32:35, an eschatological "day of vengeance" (יוֹם נָקָם) is likewise referenced in Isaiah 34:8; 61:2; 63:4. As in Deuteronomy 32:28-29, the manifestation of the Lord's justice is also linked to his wisdom in Isaiah 40:14, "[Who] taught him in the way of justice?" (see also Is 40:27). Furthermore, the Lord stopping the arrogant boasting of the enemy in Deuteronomy 32:27 ("lest they say, 'our hand is exalted'") is essentially what happens to Babylon, the primary instrument of Israel's exile, in Isaiah 47. The Lord was angry with his people, but Babylon was ruthless and boasted blasphemously in ways that contradicted the Lord's own words (Deut 32:39; Is 47:6-8, 10). Babylon would be destroyed like Assyria previously (Is 47:9, 11; see also Is 37:36-38).

Indeed, the relationship between the Song of Moses in Deuteronomy 32:1-43 and Isaiah was mentioned in chapter five. That discussion included a brief treatment of the Song of Moses and Isaiah 43. Thomas Keiser argues further for "a direct and conscious dependency between Isaiah xl–xlviii [Is 40–48] and the Song of Moses theologically, thematically and literarily."[21] In relation to Israel's failure, judgment, and ultimate salvation, Keiser insightfully points out that the perspective of Isaiah 40–48 is "a specific reference point from within the Song," that is, Deuteronomy 32:36, "the point in time when the Lord reverses the judgment."[22] Accordingly, the conclusion of the Song of Moses, which calls the nations to "shout for joy" because sin has been atoned for (Deut 32:43), has numerous parallels in Isaiah 40–55 to calling the nations, Israel, or creation to rejoice using the same verb (רָנַן; Is 42:11; 49:13; 52:8-9) or its

---

[20] See also "do/work" (פָּעַל/פְּעֻלָּה) in Deut 32:4, 27; Is 40:10; 41:4; 43:13; 45:11.
[21] Thomas Keiser, "The Song of Moses: A Basis for Isaiah's Prophecy," VT 55, no. 4 (2005): 487. On 488-98, he points out common language (rock, Eloah [uncommon term for "God"], Jeshurun, "I am he," El [an alternate term for "God"], and תֹהוּ ["formless," or better, "empty"]), theological parallels (e.g., Yahweh's incomparability, Israel's sin and failure, deliverance after judgment, and concern for the nations), and thematic parallels (e.g., Yahweh as Creator-Ruler, remembrance, wisdom, justice, and the Lord's servants).
[22] Keiser, "Song of Moses," 492.

cognate noun (רִנָּה; Is 44:23; 48:20; 51:11) related to the same reason of sin being put away (Is 40:2; 53:4-12).

Both "justice" (מִשְׁפָּט) and the pattern of the Lord's justice as set forth in Deuteronomy 32:1-43 are an important thread linking all four Servant Songs. The servant's primary task in Isaiah 42:1-4 is the ultimate establishment of justice for the nations, but Isaiah 49:4 shows that the servant must patiently entrust his own justice to the Lord prior to bringing salvation to the ends of the earth (Is 49:6).[23] Following a description of the servant's obedience in Isaiah 50:4-5, he endures mistreatment, humiliation, and condemnation involving a so-called "lord of my justice" (בַּעַל מִשְׁפָּטִי, Is 50:8). Isaiah 53:8 makes plain that his execution was a miscarriage of justice (see below). Nevertheless, the Lord's justice will prevail (Is 51:4; see also Is 54:17), and joyful shouts will resound (Is 54:1), just as in Deuteronomy 32:43.

DESERT AND SECOND EXODUS IN ISAIAH 40–55

Whereas Keiser's aforementioned treatment of Isaiah 40–48 in relation to the Song of Moses only briefly notes the desert theme in Deuteronomy 32:10-14 and Isaiah 41:17-20 and Isaiah 43:19-20, this theme deserves further attention since it contributes to the important theme of second exodus in Isaiah 40–55. As Deuteronomy 32:10-14 tells it, the beginning of the Lord's gracious dealings with Israel and the location of his continued provision is the desert (Deut 32:10, "He found him [Israel] in a desert [מִדְבָּר] land"). In the same way, the new era of "comfort" (נחם) for the Lord's people announced in Isaiah 40:1 (see also Deut 32:36) is followed by an announcement "in the desert" (מִדְבָּר) to prepare the way of the Lord in Isaiah 40:3, which has been identified as a second-exodus text (see below).

Deuteronomy 32:1-43 itself likely has second-exodus themes through its many links to the Song of the Sea (Ex 15:1-18): the Lord as divine

---

[23]Hans-Jürgen Hermisson points out a contrast between the servant's confidence regarding his justice in Is 49:4 and Israel's unbelief regarding theirs in Is 40:27. Hermisson, "The Fourth Servant Song in the Context of Second Isaiah," in *The Suffering Servant: Isaiah 53 in Jewish and Christian Sources*, ed. Bernd Janowski and Peter Stuhlmacher, trans. Daniel Bailey (Grand Rapids, MI: Eerdmans, 2004), 20-21.

warrior (Deut 32:41-42; see Ex 15:3), his incomparability with idols (Deut 32:31, 37-39; see Ex 15:11), the exaltation of the Lord's hand over human ones (Deut 32:27, 36, 39-41; see Ex 15:9, 17), the salvation of his people (Deut 32:36, 43; see Ex 15:13, 16), and the defeat of the enemy and "Pharaoh[s]" (Deut 32:27, 42; see Ex 15:4, 6, 9). The Song of the Sea (Ex 15:1-18) has similarly shaped Isaiah 43:14-21, which foretells the second exodus in connection with the provision of water in the desert and new creation (Is 43:19-20). Just as Exodus 15:13, 16 repeats a construction using the uncommon pronoun זוּ ("the people *whom* you redeemed" [עַם־זוּ גָּאָלְתָּ], "the people *whom* you acquired" [עַם־זוּ קָנִיתָ]), so Isaiah 43:21, the only other Old Testament passage with this construction, refers to "the people *whom* I formed for myself" (עַם־זוּ יָצַרְתִּי לִי). Isaiah 43:16-21 further shows that whereas the exodus was characterized by drying up land in the midst of the sea to make a path, the second exodus will be a "new thing" (חֲדָשָׁה) characterized by the preparation of a path in an already dry but desolate land (see Is 40:3) and the reverse act of bringing forth water in the desert (Is 43:18-20).[24] Thus, eschatological salvation will be like the exodus in some ways but will also differ from and surpass it in others (Is 43:19; see also Is 41:20; 42:9; 45:8; 48:6-7).

Whereas the second exodus is also emphasized earlier in Isaiah (e.g., Is 11:11-16; 12:2; 14:3, "harsh labor"), Bernard Anderson notes Isaiah 43:14-21 along with nine other texts in Isaiah 40–55 (Is 40:3-5; 41:17-20; 42:14-16; 43:1-3; 48:20-21; 49:8-12; 51:9-10; 52:11-12; 55:12-13) that show that the new exodus is "one of the dominant themes" in this section and presents "the meaning of the Exodus in an eschatological dimension."[25] The first and last of these ten passages form an *inclusio* emphasizing this theme (Is 40:3-5; 55:12-13). Gordon Hugenberger points out that numerous scholars see a second exodus as "the controlling

---

[24]See John Oswalt, *The Book of Isaiah: Chapters 40–66*, NICOT (Grand Rapids, MI: Eerdmans, 1998), 155; John McKenzie, *Second Isaiah*, AB (Garden City, NY: Doubleday, 1968), 57. Regarding "the way of the Lord" in the "desert" in Is 40:3 and "the way in the desert" in Is 43:19 being identical, see John Willis, *Images of Water in Isaiah* (Lanham, MD: Lexington, 2017), 98.

[25]Bernard Anderson, "Exodus Typology in Second Isaiah," in *Israel's Prophetic Heritage: Essays in Honor of James Muilenburg*, ed. Bernard Anderson and W. Harrelson (New York: Harper, 1962), 181-82.

and sustained theme" of Isaiah 40–55, calling it "almost omnipresent" and adding more passages to Anderson's list (e.g., Is 42:13; 44:27; 54:3, 13).[26] The centrality of the second exodus to Isaiah 40–55 suggests that still more texts actually connect to this broader strategy, such as the reference to soaring on wings like "eagles" (נְשָׁרִים) in Isaiah 40:31 (see Ex 19:4). Thus, Isaiah 40–55 appears to have been shaped by both the Song of Moses and the second exodus, the latter of which can be traced to the Pentateuch not only through the Song of the Sea and the Song of Moses but also Numbers 24:8; Deuteronomy 18:15-18; 34:10-12.

Given my belief in an early date for the (Mosaic) Pentateuch, such allusions to different parts of the Pentateuch are not surprising.[27] Isaiah 40–55 even appears to have numerous allusions to Genesis 1 through terms such as "create" (בָּרָא; Gen 1:1; Is 40:26, 28; 41:20; 42:5; passim), "empty" (תֹהוּ; Gen 1:2; Is 40:17, 23; 41:29; 44:9; 45:18-19; 49:4), and "light"/"darkness" (Gen 1:2-5; Is 42:6-7, 16; 45:7).[28] The creation reference in Isaiah 45:12 even includes references to "land" (אֶרֶץ), "humanity/Adam" (אָדָם), "heavens" (שָׁמַיִם), and "all their host" (כָּל־צְבָאָם; see Gen 2:1). Additional Genesis allusions are found in Isaiah 54:9 to Noah and in Isaiah 41:8; 48:19; and 51:2 to Abraham or the Abrahamic covenant (see Jacob in Is 41:8; 45:19). Isaiah 54:3 is particularly significant for the latter because "you will *break forth* [פָּרַץ] to the right and to the left" and "your seed will possess nations" (וְזַרְעֵךְ גּוֹיִם יִירָשׁ; see Ps 2:7-8) have apparently braided two Abrahamic covenant texts: Genesis 28:14, "you will *break forth* [פָּרַץ] to the west, east, north, and south" (see the land promise in Gen 28:13), and Genesis 22:17-18, "*may your seed possess* [וְיִרַשׁ זַרְעֲךָ] the gate of his enemies, and all the *nations* [גּוֹי] of the earth will be blessed in your seed [זֶרַע]."[29] Critical belief in a late date for the Pentateuch notwithstanding, a reference to the Pentateuch itself

---

[26]Hugenberger, "Servant of the Lord," 122-23.

[27]Sommer calls Is 40–66 "highly allusive" and its author "one of the most allusive ancient Israelite authors" (*Prophet Reads Scripture*, 3). The allusions are so extensive that "the use of older texts becomes a primary concern" (165).

[28]These allusions would not be permitted in a critical framework assigning Gen 1 to the postexilic Priestly source and Is 40–55 to exilic Deutero-Isaiah.

[29]Sommer calls the reverse dynamic of dividing a source phrase into two a "split up pattern" (*Prophet Reads Scripture*, 68-69, 159-60).

should also be considered in Isaiah 42:21, which says that the Lord "will magnify the law/*torah* and make it glorious."[30] Interpreting law/*torah* here as the Pentateuch also fits the subsequent verses, which characterize Israel being plundered as the Lord's doing because "they did not obey his law/*torah*" (Is 42:24). The use of rhetorical questions to emphasize the Lord's sovereign judgment of his people in Isaiah 42:24 mirrors Deuteronomy 32:30.

Presupposing the Pentateuch in Isaiah 40–55 could also help explain the problem of emphatic claims that the Lord had declared many things "from the beginning" (מֵרֹאשׁ; Is 40:21; 48:16; see also Is 41:4) or "from of old" (מֵאָז; Is 44:8; 45:21 [also מִקֶּדֶם]; Is 46:10), such as his greatness as Creator (Is 40:21, 28), his ultimate purposes (Is 45:21; 46:10), and his sending of a messenger and his Spirit (Is 48:16; see also Is 61:1).[31] Accordingly, these texts frequently refer to the "former things" (רִאשֹׁנוֹת; e.g., Is 41:22; 42:9; 43:18 [also קַדְמֹנִיּוֹת]; see also Is 9:1), "things to come"/"latter things"/"new things" (חֲדָשׁוֹת/אַחֲרֹנִים/אֹתִיּוֹת/בָּאוֹת; Is 41:4, 22-23; 42:9), "the beginning" (Is 41:4), and "the end" (Is 41:22; 47:7), asserting that it is the Lord himself who is the "beginning" (רִאשׁוֹן) and the "end" (אַחֲרוֹן; Is 44:6; 48:12).[32] This matches the Pentateuch's God-centered vision of

---

[30] My suggestion stands between Delitzsch, who says, "The reference is primarily and chiefly to the Sinaitic law," which seems to take it as referring to part of the Pentateuch, and Oswalt, who affirms its reference to the Pentateuch as well as to "God's revelation of the nature and meaning of life" more broadly (see Delitzsch, *Isaiah*, 422; Oswalt, *Isaiah: Chapters 40–66*, 132). Duhm sees the Deuteronomic flavor of this verse as conflicting with Deutero-Isaiah and attributes it and Is 42:24b to a third hand (neither Deutero-Isaiah nor the Deuteronomist; *Buch Jesaia*, 320).

[31] Even if other passages with the same terms do not clearly refer to the beginning of time (perhaps Is 41:26; 48:3, 5, 7), the respective contexts of the passages cited above also speak of creation and/or God's eternal nature, suggesting an absolute beginning. For Is 45:21, Motyer discusses the unresolved problem of finding these earlier prophecies when Is 45:20-21 is understood as narrowly referring to Cyrus (*Isaiah*, 365, including n1; see also 316-17). Instead, Motyer notes that "Cyrus has dropped into the background" in Is 45:9–46:13 and that the present concern is "to see the Cyrus-event in the context of the Lord's world-wide and eternal purposes." See also Campegius Vitringa, *Commentarius in Librum Prophetiarum Jesaiae* (Leeuwarden, Netherlands: Franciscus Halma, 1720), 2:507-8; Delitzsch, *Isaiah*, 449-50. None of these three scholars interpret the "fugitives of the nations" in Is 45:20 merely as Israelites who returned under Cyrus but rather link them to the salvation of the nations. This is solidly rooted in the Pentateuch and Abrahamic covenant. This is contra Oswalt, who thinks Is 45:21 is itself the prophecy that would be "from of old" by the time it was fulfilled (*Isaiah: Chapters 40–66*, 222). Also relevant is the interpretation of Is 41:2, 25; 46:11. See Vitringa, *Commentarius in Librum Prophetiarum Jesaiae* 2:393-96.

[32] Hugenberger believes that the "former things" refer "preeminently to the exodus redemption" ("Servant of the Lord," 124). Since the exodus is recorded at length in the Pentateuch, this does not contradict the overall point being made here.

reality, with God alone creating at the beginning in Genesis 1:1 and God on center stage "in the end of days" in Deuteronomy 32:35-43 (see Deut 31:29). The statement in Isaiah 46:10 that God "declares the end from the beginning [מֵרֵאשִׁית אַחֲרִית]" suggestively parallels the Pentateuch itself, from its "beginning" (רֵאשִׁית) in Genesis 1:1 to its prophetic vision for "the end [אַחֲרִית] of days" in Genesis 49:1; Numbers 24:14, 20; Deuteronomy 4:30; 31:29.

Back to the second exodus in Isaiah 40–55, the subthemes of desert, provision of water, and eschatological salvation play out in still more ways. In Isaiah 41:17-20, the provision of water in the desert for the thirsty not only brings new life and new creation but further results in people finally gaining wisdom (Is 41:19-20; see also Is 12:3; 35:1, 6). The combination of "see" (רָאָה), "know" (יָדַע), "understand" (שָׂכַל) in Isaiah 41:20 further contrasts not only with idolaters in Isaiah 44:18 but also with Eve in Genesis 3:5-7, suggesting a reversal of the fall. Water, wisdom, and new creation also appear together in Isaiah 43:18-20. The remark about the "new thing" in Isaiah 43:19 that "now it will *sprout*" (צָמַח) again recalls the Garden of Eden (Gen 2:5, 9; 3:18) as well as multiple messianic texts (2 Sam 23:5; Ps 132:17; see "branch"/צֶמַח in Is 4:2; Jer 23:5; Zech 3:8; 6:12). Similar plant imagery is found in Isaiah 53:2 (see below).

Moving in yet another direction, water for the thirsty represents the outpouring of the Spirit in Isaiah 44:3-4 ("I will pour out water . . . I will pour out my Spirit"; see also Is 32:15-16).[33] Joseph Blenkinsopp notes that water "aligns with the spirit . . . as the source of physical and psychic life (cf. 42:5) and serves as a powerful and polyvalent symbol throughout the book of Isaiah."[34] The equation of the provision of water with the outpouring of the Spirit in Isaiah 44:3 is in keeping with the new thing just mentioned in Isaiah 43:19. Indeed, Hugenberger points out that it is not only the second exodus in its general contours that has shaped Isaiah 40–55, but "a host of ancillary details connected with the original exodus are reapplied, with

---

[33]Willis refers to the outpouring of water as "metaphor" for the outpouring of the Spirit (*Images of Water in Isaiah*, 99). See also Duhm, *Buch Jesaja*, 331; Motyer, *Isaiah*, 342; Klaus Baltzer, *Deutero-Isaiah*, trans. Margaret Kohl, Hermeneia (Minneapolis: Fortress, 2001), 186.

[34]Joseph Blenkinsopp, *Isaiah 40–55*, AB (New York: Doubleday, 2002), 233.

appropriate escalation, to the second exodus."[35] Accordingly, Isaiah 44:3-4 proceeds to describe Israel's "seed" (זֶרַע) sprouting like well-nourished vegetation (see Num 24:6), where "seed" refers to Israel's descendants while taking advantage of the term *seed*'s other meaning as plant seed. Thus, the "new thing," like but transcending the original exodus, involves a path through the desert, abundant water in the desert, newfound wisdom, provision of the Spirit like water, and the flourishing of people like well-watered plants. The Spirit's life-giving work in Isaiah 44:3-4 coordinates with "the Spirit of the Lord" blowing on grass, representing "all flesh," and causing it to wither in Isaiah 40:6-7.

The themes of desert, provision of water, and second exodus continue to appear in Isaiah 49–55. Isaiah 49:9-11 describes freed captives traveling on "ways" with sufficient food and water. Isaiah 51:3 says again that the Lord will "comfort" (נָחַם) Zion in connection with making "her desert like Eden." In Isaiah 51:9-10, the "arm of the Lord" that dried up the sea in the exodus is called on again to win a maritime battle with the enemy (see Ex 15:4-10, 16; Ps 74:13-14). The Lord's people will go out from captivity again (Is 52:12). Isaiah 55 opens with an anonymous speaker calling "all who are thirsty to come to the waters [and drink]" (Is 55:1) and for them to "listen carefully to me and eat what is good. . . . Incline your ear and come to me and listen so that your soul will live" (Is 55:2-3; see also Is 6:9; 51:1, 7; Ex 19:5).[36] Motyer points out that "come to the waters" (לְכוּ לַמַּיִם) in Isaiah 55:1 is a metaphor for "come to me" (וּלְכוּ אֵלַי) in Isaiah 55:3.[37] Thus, whereas the Lord provides water in earlier passages without clearly specifying the means (Is 41:18; 43:19-20; 44:3), the speaker in Isaiah 55:1-3 is himself the water source.

We could simply take this speaker as the Lord and move on, but the suggestion that the Lord will "break forth" (בָּקַע) water from the rock (מַיִם מִצּוּר) for the returnees from Babylon in Isaiah 48:21 instead highlights a rock as the direct source of water (see Deut 32:13). Indeed, Campegius Vitringa (1659–1722) thinks that Isaiah 48:21 calls readers to

---

[35]Hugenberger, "Servant of the Lord," 124.
[36]Blenkinsopp draws a connection to the provision of water in the desert here, citing Is 48:21; 49:10 (*Isaiah 40–55*, 369).
[37]Motyer, *Isaiah*, 453.

consider "a more elevated [*sublimiore*] meaning of this pericope."[38] He argues that the miracle of water from the rock will be repeated but in a "spiritual sense" (*spirituali sensu*), since there was no historical fulfillment. Indeed, the breaking of the rock for the sake of others in Isaiah 48:21 has strong resonances with the striking of the servant in Isaiah 53. Thus, just as 1 Corinthians 10:4 says, a spiritual rock will produce a spiritual drink. Since the Lord is doing a new thing like but exceeding the exodus, a transformed water-from-the-rock miracle could be one of the "ancillary details" that reappears in the second exodus (Hugenberger).

Isaiah 48:21 LXX ("he *will* bring out [ἐξάξει] water from the rock") and some contemporary commentators also support some kind of repetition of a water-from-the-rock miracle in Isaiah 48:21.[39] Hans-Christoph Schmitt's assessment that Isaiah 48 is a "turning point" in Isaiah 40–55 supports paying special attention to its concluding emphasis on deliverance from Babylon (see Is 45–47) in connection with water from the rock (Is 48:20-21; see also Is 35:6; 63:12; Ex 17:6; Ps 78:15).[40] Both Isaiah 48:20-21 and Isaiah 12:3 especially link salvation with the provision of water. Isaiah 51:1 LXX also involves hewing a rock and "digging" (ὀρύσσω [נָקַר]) a "pit/well" (λάκκος [בּוֹר]; see Ex 17:6; 33:21; Num 21:18; Is 2:21; Jer 2:13).[41] Isaiah 55:3 connects such provision of water in Isaiah 55:1 with the fulfillment of the Davidic covenant (see Is 42:6; 49:8; 54:10).[42]

Given the use of water as a metaphor for the Spirit in Isaiah 44:3, it seems as though the second exodus and the provision of the water/Spirit can be linked to a future water-from-the-rock miracle and the Messiah who fulfills the Davidic covenant and ushers in a "new thing." This new thing

---

[38] Vitringa, *Commentarius in Librum Prophetiarum Jesaiae* 2:556. See the German translation: Anton Friderich Büsching, *Auslegung der Weissagung Jesaiae* (Halle: Johann Gottlob Bierwirths, 1751), 2:438.

[39] LXX: "he will bring out water from the rock for them, the rock will be split and water will flow" (ὕδωρ ἐκ πέτρας ἐξάξει αὐτοῖς σχισθήσεται πέτρα καὶ ῥυήσεται ὕδωρ). Hugenberger, "Servant of the Lord," 124-25; Oswalt, *Isaiah: Chapters 40–66*, 284; John Goldingay and David Payne, *Isaiah 40–55*, ICC (London: Bloomsbury, 2014), 2:149.

[40] Schmitt, "Prophetie und Schultheologie," 48. Motyer calls Is 48 "climactic" within Is 40–47 (*Isaiah*, 375). Baltzer emphasizes the Lord as "sole agent" in Is 48:21 (*Deutero-Isaiah*, 302).

[41] For an extended argument in favor of the LXX reading, see P. A. H. de Boer, *Second-Isaiah's Message* (Leiden: Brill, 1956), 58-67. See also Chen, *The Messianic Vision of the Pentateuch* (Downers Grove, IL: InterVarsity Press, 2019), 181-82, 208.

[42] See Brevard Childs, *Isaiah*, OTL (Louisville: Westminster John Knox, 2001), 434.

also includes superfood unlike "what is not bread" that can be bought with money in Isaiah 55:2.[43] Consistent with his comments above, Vitringa cites Jewish interpreters in support of taking Isaiah 55:1-2 as the words of the Messiah and referring to the beginning of messianic age.[44] When these references to water in Isaiah 44:3-4; 48:21 and 55:1 are viewed together, then there is a hint that the giving of the Spirit in the messianic age will involve the Messiah's suffering (see Is 32:15-16; 50:7; Jn 7:37-39).[45] Like Deuteronomy 32:4, 13, 15, 18, Isaiah 44:8 refers to the Lord as "rock" (צוּר; see Is 8:14; 26:4), and Isaiah 48:21 uses the same term.[46]

Space prohibits extensive further analysis of Isaiah 40–55, but a final point is that these second-exodus themes are tied in with all four Servant Songs. Isaiah 42:4 describes the islands waiting for the servant's "instruction" (תּוֹרָה), reminiscent of but exceeding Moses (see Deut 32:1-2), who is also called "my servant" (Num 12:7-8; Josh 1:2, 7; see Is 42:1). The preceding context has already introduced the second exodus (Is 40:3-5; 41:17-20). For the latter three Servant Songs (Is 49:1-6; 50:4-9; 52:13–53:12), each is immediately preceded by an overt second-exodus passage (Is 48:20-21, "Go out from Babylon, flee the Chaldeans"; Is 50:2-3, "Is my hand surely too short to redeem? With my rebuke I dry up the sea"; Is 52:11-12, "Depart, depart, go out from there"). This pattern suggests that the servant in these songs is a central figure in the second exodus, such as the prophet like Moses (Deut 18:15, 18).[47] Though he does not raise his

---

[43] Delitzsch, *Isaiah*, 532.
[44] Vitringa, *Commentarius in Librum Prophetiarum Jesaiae* 2:704. The call to "all who are thirsty" to "buy" (שָׁבַר) "bread" (לֶחֶם) and water "without silver" (בְּלוֹא־כֶסֶף) from an individual recalls Egyptians and surrounding peoples using "silver" to "buy" "bread" from Joseph (Gen 41:54-57; 42:25; passim) and hints that the speaker in Is 55:1-2 is an eschatological Joseph. Other interesting connections to Joseph are the Lord causing something to "prosper" in the "hand" of a "servant" (Gen 39:3, 17; Is 53:10) and, more faintly, "comfort[ing]" and "speak[ing] kindly" to the guilty (Gen 50:21; Is 40:1-2).
[45] E.g., Marjo Korpel connects the water as Spirit imagery in Is 44:3 to Is 55:1, 3. Korpel, "Metaphors in Isaiah LV," *VT* 46 (1996): 50-52.
[46] Sommer points out parallels between Is 48:20-21 and the first part of the Song of Moses in Deut 32:1-5 (*Prophet Reads Scripture*, 273-74n8), and although he sees a mere echo rather than a strategic allusion, Keiser's aforementioned article and my own analysis of the Song of Moses suggest otherwise (see chapter five).
[47] Gerhard von Rad, *Old Testament Theology* (Peabody, MA: Hendrickson, 1965), 2:261; Hugenberger makes this point but distinguishes the prophet like Moses from the Messiah ("Servant of the Lord," 106, 119-39).

voice (Is 42:2) and is silent at a crisis moment (Is 53:7; but note "his mouth" here and in Is 53:9), his speech is highlighted in Isaiah 42:4 ("instruction"), Isaiah 49:2 ("he made my mouth like a sharp sword"; see also Is 11:4), and Isaiah 50:4 ("the Lord God gave me a trained tongue"). Accordingly, those who fear the Lord are characterized by "listening to the voice of his servant" in Isaiah 50:10, which is exactly what Deuteronomy 18:19 commands concerning the prophet like Moses. As in the Lord's previous victory over Assyria equally "for my sake and for the sake of David my servant" (Is 37:35), there is no conflict between the exaltation of this servant (Is 52:13) and the Lord's glory, as emphasized in Isaiah 41:28; 42:8; 43:11, 25; 48:11; 50:2 (see also Deut 32:39).

THE SUFFERING SERVANT OF ISAIAH 52:13-53:12

The preceding discussion of Isaiah 40–55 provides evidence and a framework for understanding the fourth and climactic Servant Song in Isaiah 52:13–53:12 as likewise alluding to the exodus, the Song of Moses (Deut 32:1-43), and creation (Gen 1–3). As noted above, Isaiah 52:13–53:12, like the previous two Servant Songs, is immediately preceded by strong second-exodus themes. Closer examination reveals that Isaiah 52:11-12 references the exodus in a way that recalls the key elements of Passover and the Red Sea. In the original exodus, the striking of Egyptian firstborns finally compelled Pharaoh to send away the Israelites. After the Passover, he commanded, "Arise, *go out from the midst of my people*" (צְאוּ מִתּוֹךְ עַמִּי) in Exodus 12:31. Likewise, Isaiah 52:11 cries, "Depart, depart, *go out* [צְאוּ] from there! . . . *Go out from her midst*" (צְאוּ מִתּוֹכָהּ; see also Is 48:20, "Go out [צְאוּ] from Babylon"). The urgency of Israel's departure from Egypt (Ex 12:33) is reflected in repeated commands to leave in Isaiah 52:11 (see also Is 48:20/Ex 14:5, "flee"). Yet transcending the Passover, this time the Lord's people will not go "in haste" (בְחִפָּזוֹן, Is 52:12; see Ex 12:11). They will again have "the Lord going before them/you" (וַיהוָה הֹלֵךְ לִפְנֵיהֶם, Ex 13:21; הֹלֵךְ לִפְנֵיכֶם יְהוָה, Is 52:12) and protecting them just as at the Red Sea through the pillar of cloud/fire (see Ex 14:19-20, 24).

This combined allusion to Passover and Red Sea (braiding), which is the climax of the exodus narrative (Ex 1–15), even the exodus itself, matches the climactic nature of the fourth Servant Song. It also hints to the reader that Isaiah 52:13–53:12 will focus on the decisive salvific act of the second exodus, which resembles but also transcends the Passover sacrifice and Red Sea deliverance. Accordingly, Isaiah 53:4-7 describes the substitutionary sacrifice of one "like a lamb" (כַּשֶׂה) who saves people who "like a flock of sheep [כַּצֹּאן] . . . went astray" (Is 53:4-7; see also Is 43:3-4, 23). Isaiah 53:10 calls "his life" (נַפְשׁ) a "guilt offering" (אָשָׁם; see Lev 5:1-7, 15), which has a categorically different value from silver (Is 52:3; see Is 48:10; 55:1-2). Anthony Ceresko notes the servant's experience of "pre-exodus sufferings" associated with Egyptian enslavement through terms such as "taken away" (לָקַח, Is 53:8a; see Is 52:5), "afflicted" (עָנָה, Is 53:4, 7; see Ex 1:11-12), "bearing [a heavy load]" (סָבַל, Is 53:4, 11; see Ex 1:11; 2:11), "servant/slave" (עבד, Is 52:13; 53:11; see Ex 1:13-14), "sickness" (חֳלִי, Is 53:4; see Ex 15:26; Deut 7:15), and "struck" (נָכָה, Is 53:4; see Deut 28:61), further extending the servant's experience of exodus to parallel Israel's suffering in Egypt also.[48]

Whereas Israel's enslavement in Egypt was not punishment for sin, Isaiah 40–55 begins by framing the second exodus in terms of the problem of sin, which is an enemy older and more fundamental than Babylon (Gen 4:7; 11:4; Is 6:5; 13:9; Mic 7:19).[49] The opening call to comfort the Lord's people in Isaiah 40:1 is followed by a reason, "for her guilt [עָוֹן] is pardoned" and "She has received from the hand of the Lord double for all her sins [חַטָּאת]" (Is 40:2). Indeed, the Lord "sold" Israel into exile because of her "iniquities" and "transgressions" (Is 50:1; see Is 42:24; Deut 32:30).

Whereas the previous Servant Songs did not directly address this sin problem, they are part of a crescendo building toward Isaiah 52:13–53:12 that explains the servant's redemptive suffering for transgressions, iniquities, and sin (Is 53:5, 11-12). The first two Servant Songs describe the end

---

[48]Anthony Ceresko, "The Rhetorical Strategy of the Fourth Servant Song (Isaiah 52:13–53:12): Poetry and the Exodus-New Exodus," *CBQ* 56 (1994): 47-50, though he interprets the servant as the prophetic author of Is 40–55 (p. 43).
[49]See Chen, *Messianic Vision of the Pentateuch*, 157, 166-67.

result of salvation for the nations, whereas the last two Servant Songs show how the servant's redemptive suffering accomplishes this salvation by dealing with sin.[50] These sins are serious, having "wearied" (יָגַע) the One who does not grow weary (Is 43:24; see Is 7:13; 40:28) and having been committed since Israel's birth (Is 48:8). Fittingly, Isaiah 40–55 closes with a call to the wicked to repent because the Lord "will abundantly forgive" (סָלַח, Is 55:7; see also Is 48:22; 53:9). If there is a connection between "atonement" (כִּפֶּר) and forgiveness (see Ex 32:30, 32), Isaiah 53 corresponds to the last statement of the Song of Moses, "he will atone [כִּפֶּר] for his land and his people" (Deut 32:43). Isaiah 6:7 relatedly describes an atonement (כִּפֶּר) that follows "touching/striking" (נָגַע; see Is 53:4, 8, 10).[51]

The first statement of the fourth Servant Song, "Behold, my servant will *act wisely*" (שָׂכַל, Is 52:13), shows that he is not only a Suffering Servant but also a wise man. Isaiah 42:1, 4 already referred to the Spirit being on him and "his instruction," and Isaiah 50:4 to his "trained tongue" (see Is 11:1-2). As in Isaiah 50:10, those who recognize him in Isaiah 52:15 are also wise ("understand," בִּין). The servant's being "high and lifted up and very exalted" (יָרוּם וְנִשָּׂא וְגָבַהּ מְאֹד) in Isaiah 52:13 strongly connects this figure with the Lord himself, who "alone will be exalted" over everything else that is "high" (רוּם) and "lifted up" (נָשָׂא) on the day of the Lord (Is 2:11-12, 14) and whose throne is "high and lifted up" (רָם וְנִשָּׂא, Is 6:1; see also Is 57:15). Accordingly, Mount Zion will be "lifted up" (וְנִשָּׂא) above all other mountains "in the last days" (Is 2:2), and the Lord will teach the nations peace from there (Is 2:3-4).[52] Thus, the servant's status as servant and temporary humiliation belie his imminent exaltation, which will equal the Lord's own exaltation ("*very* [מְאֹד] exalted" in Is 52:13). It also masks the Lord's delight in him (Is 42:1), the glory he will bring to the Lord (Is 49:3), the Lord's vindication of him (Is 50:7-9; 53:12), and his own status as light of

---

[50]Hermisson describes the last Servant Song as "show[ing] for the first time that his suffering was not only the unavoidable consequence but also a functional part of his office" ("Fourth Servant Song," 34).

[51]See Sommer, *Prophet Reads Scripture*, 93-95.

[52]Regarding the importance of Is 2:2-4 to the whole book of Isaiah, see H. G. M. Williamson, *Isaiah 1–5*, ICC (London: Bloomsbury, 2014), 172; Blenkinsopp, *Isaiah 1–39*, 191.

the nations and covenant for the people (Is 42:6; 49:6, 8; see also Is 9:2).[53] Like a priest-king, he will "sprinkle many nations" and be respected by kings (Is 52:15; see Is 2:2-4; 49:7; Lev 4:6). These messianic indicators are confirmed in Numbers 24:7, which describes the Messiah and his kingdom as "high" (רוּם) and "lifted up" (נָשָׂא).

The focus of the fourth Servant Song, however, is on the servant's humiliation and suffering. His extreme ugliness is mentioned several times in the early part of the song (Is 52:14; 53:2-3). This part of the song also draws in the second-exodus subtheme of new life in the (undesirable) desert: "He went up like a *young plant* before him, and like a *root* [שֹׁרֶשׁ] from *dry ground*" (Is 53:2). Isaiah 41:18 refers to "dry ground" (אֶרֶץ צִיָּה) becoming a place of springs of water (see also Is 12:3), and many other passages in Isaiah 40–55 do likewise (e.g., Is 43:19-20; 44:3; 51:3). Even earlier, in Isaiah 11:1, 10, the (messianic) new growth that comes from Jesse's stump or "root[s]" (שֹׁרֶשׁ) also matches the picture in Isaiah 53:2 (see also Is 40:24). For the "dry ground" that becomes well-watered in Isaiah 41:18, the result is multiple instances of new plant life in Isaiah 41:19 and people gaining wisdom in Isaiah 41:20. Since the new growth and wisdom in Isaiah 41:18-20 involves a perfected eschatological age and the fourth Servant Song does not (at least not immediately), this suggests that the Messiah comes first and that the second exodus has a humble beginning. His sprouting and his wisdom (Is 52:13; 53:2) lead the way to his people's sprouting and wisdom (Is 41:20; 42:9; 43:19).

This process, however, involves rejection, shame, and great suffering. Although ultimately "the glory of the Lord will be revealed [גָּלָה], and all flesh will see it together" (Is 40:5) and "all the ends of the earth will see the salvation of our God" (Is 52:10), the perspective of the fourth Servant

---

[53]The phrase "covenant for the people" (בְּרִית עָם) is difficult but in both contexts is linked to being the source of worldwide salvation ("light of the nations," Is 49:6; see Gen 12:3; 18:18; 22:18). This can be interpreted as the servant fulfilling the Abrahamic and Davidic covenants and mediating covenant blessings to all. The phrase itself somewhat resembles another unclear but important phrase, "the instruction of humanity" (תּוֹרַת הָאָדָם), in 2 Sam 7:19. Covenant and instruction/law are linked in Ps 78:10; Hos 8:1. For "people" in Is 42:6 as referring to humanity as in Is 40:7 and Is 42:5, see Wong Yee-cheung, *A Text-Centered Approach to Old Testament Exegesis and Theology and Its Application to the Book of Isaiah* (Hong Kong: Alliance Bible Seminary, 2001), 337-38. See also Vitringa, *Commentarius in Librum Prophetiarum Jesaiae* 2:428; Duhm, *Buch Jesaia*, 314.

Song is instead, "Who has believed our report, and to whom has the arm of the Lord been revealed [גָּלָה]?" (Is 53:1). Whereas Isaiah 49:7 already said that the servant would be "despised" (בָּזֹה) and "abhorred" (תָּעֵב), Isaiah 52:14 and Isaiah 53:2-3 are emphatic about his ugliness and rejection, referring to his terrible "appearance" (תֹּאַר/מַרְאֶה) several times and to the fact that "we did not regard/see [רָאָה] him" or "desire [חָמַד] him."

When combined with the servant's comparison to a plant in Isaiah 53:2 and his wisdom in Isaiah 52:13, there arises a surprising reversal of the fall and the tree of the knowledge of good and evil in Genesis 2–3. Whereas humanity plunged itself into ruin and death because Eve "saw [רָאָה] that the tree [עֵץ] was good for food and pleasing to the eyes [תַאֲוָה־הוּא לָעֵינַיִם] and desirable for gaining wisdom [וְנֶחְמָד הָעֵץ לְהַשְׂכִּיל]" (Gen 3:6), the eschatological second exodus takes place through someone "like a root [שֹׁרֶשׁ] out of dry ground" (not well-watered Eden), an ugly person whom we neither "see/regard" (רָאָה) nor "desire" (חָמַד) but who is in fact full of wisdom and "acts wisely" (שָׂכַל, Is 52:13; 53:2).

Table 7.2. Contrast between tree of knowledge of good and evil and "root" in Isaiah 53:2

	Tree of knowledge (Gen 2–3)	Root out of dry ground (Is 53:2)
Location	Garden of Eden	"dry ground"
Maturity	fruit-bearing tree	"young plant," "root"
Appearance	attractive (Gen 3:6)	unattractive (Is 52:14; 53:2-3)
Association with wisdom	falsely promises wisdom (Gen 3:6)	has true wisdom (Is 52:13)
Impact	death	atonement and life through his death

This is the one whom Israel and all humanity needs (Deut 32:29; Is 44:18) to restore Edenic blessing and teach us wisdom (Is 41:18-20). The language of Isaiah 43:10 further connects such wisdom with faith, "so that you may know and *believe* [אָמַן] in me and discern [בִּין]." Isaiah 52:15–53:1 seem to do the same ("understand," "believe"), while suggesting that readers ought to "believe" in the Suffering Servant (see Is 7:9; 28:16).[54]

---

[54]For a discussion of faith in Isaiah, see Wong, *Text-Centered Approach*, 313-44.

The servant's endurance of shame and humiliation (Is 50:6-7) ultimately delivers Zion from the same (Is 54:4; note בּוֹשׁ, כָּלַם).

The physical suffering of the servant in Isaiah 53 emphasizes his being struck. Todd Hibbard notes a "discourse" about striking in the book of Isaiah and points out that it primarily describes "judgment against a nation or person." Unexpectedly, he claims, "The texts which participate in this discourse all occur in so-called First and Third Isaiah."[55] While granting the value of his analysis of these two parts of Isaiah, Isaiah 53 fits smoothly and even significantly into this conversation.[56] Isaiah 53:4 says that the servant is considered "struck" (נָגוּעַ), even "struck by God" (מֻכֵּה אֱלֹהִים) and "afflicted" (מְעֻנֶּה). Isaiah 53:5 describes his being "pierced" (חָלָל) and "crushed" (דָּכָא), as well as his endurance of "punishment" (מוּסָר) and an injurious "blow" (חַבּוּרָה). Such language and themes repeat in Isaiah 53:7 ("oppressed" [נָגַשׂ], "afflicted" [עָנָה], "slaughter" [טֶבַח]), Isaiah 53:8 ("cut off" [גָּזַר], "stricken" [נֶגַע]), and Isaiah 53:10 ("crush," [דָּכָא]). The third Servant Song had already described the servant giving his "back" (גֵּו) to those who "strike" [נָכָה] him (Is 50:6; see also Is 51:23) and setting his face "like flint" (Is 50:7; see also Is 48:21, "he broke a rock"; Is 51:1).[57] In both the third and fourth Servant Songs, the servant's obedience to the Lord thus is not simply a private matter but also involves the endurance of violence and humiliation. This opposition, though fierce, is also fleeting (Is 50:9), a fact that is used to encourage the Lord's persecuted people in Isaiah 51:6-8. The servant's being considered struck by God in Isaiah 53:4 but struck by men in Isaiah 50:6 suggests the Lord's sovereign, mysterious work.

In the intervening context between the third and fourth Servant Songs, there are other references to the theme of striking, but these are

---

[55] J. Todd Hibbard, "Isaiah XXVII 7 and Intertextual Discourse About 'Striking' in the Book of Isaiah," VT 55, no. 4 (2005): 463-64.

[56] For discussion of the Lord striking Israel, Assyria striking Israel, God striking Assyria, and God restoring instead of striking Israel, see Hibbard, "Isaiah XXVII 7 and Intertextual Discourse," 464-73.

[57] Regarding Is 48:21, see Vitringa's comments above. Goldingay and Payne do not take the rock in Is 51:1 as the Lord on the grounds that "pit" in the parallel line never describes the Lord (*Isaiah 40–55*, 223). Along with others, they prefer understanding the rock here as Abraham, even as they concede that this is (also) unprecedented. For references to the Lord as rock in Isaiah, see Is 8:14; 26:4; 30:29; 44:8 (see also Is 28:16).

recollections of the Lord "hewing" (חָצֵב) Rahab and "piercing" (חָלַל) the sea monster (תַּנִּין) in the exodus (Is 51:9; see Ps 74:13-14). To be precise, the actor in Isaiah 51:9-10 is called "the arm of the Lord" (זְרוֹעַ יְהוָה), which the preceding context has described as ruling for the Lord (Is 40:10), gathering the flock (Is 40:11), judging the nations (Is 48:14; 51:5), and being revealed to the nations (Is 52:10).[58] The flow of thought from Isaiah 51:9-10 to Zion's redemption in Isaiah 51:11 implies that the arm of the Lord will again strike the enemy (see Is 27:1).

Isaiah 53:1 also highlights "the arm of the Lord" but evidently during a phase of the divine plan in which this arm has not yet been "revealed" (גָּלָה) to many (see Is 40:5; 52:10).[59] Motyer equates the Lord's arm with the servant, and there is at least a natural connection between the work of this arm and the servant's ministry.[60] When Isaiah 51:9 and Isaiah 53:5 are viewed together, the result is that the work of the arm of the Lord involves both "piercing" (חָלַל) the enemy and the servant being "pierced" (חָלַל) himself (see Is 53:10; 1QIsa^a). Since the word translated "sea monster" in Isaiah 51:9 can also mean "snake" in some contexts (Ex 7:9-12), the piercing in Isaiah 51:9 already has strong resonances with Genesis 3:15, but adding Isaiah 53:5 to the mix yields a suggestive parallel between the bidirectional "piercing" (חָלַל) in Isaiah 51:9/53:5 and "He will *strike* [שׁוּף] your head, and you will *strike* [שׁוּף] his heel" in Genesis 3:15. It would appear that the "he" (הוּא) in Genesis 3:15 is the same "he" (הוּא) as emphasized in Isaiah 53:4-5, 7, 11-12.[61]

Though not part of a Servant Song, Isaiah 51 has additional connections to these songs. Isaiah 51:4 reads, "For law will go out from me, and I will set my justice as a light for the peoples" (כִּי תוֹרָה מֵאִתִּי תֵצֵא וּמִשְׁפָּטִי לְאוֹר עַמִּים אַרְגִּיעַ). The reference to the law/justice pair picks up on the servant's "law" (תּוֹרָה) and divine "justice" (מִשְׁפָּט) in Isaiah 42:4, and likewise "light for the

---

[58] See Motyer, *Isaiah*, 427.
[59] Regarding Is 53:1, Hermann Spieckermann notes its "skeptical overtone" and that the servant's success "is expected in the future." Spieckermann, "The Conception and Prehistory of the Idea of Vicarious Suffering in the Old Testament," in Janowski and Stuhlmacher, *Suffering Servant*, 15.
[60] Motyer, *Isaiah*, 427.
[61] Chen, *Messianic Vision of the Pentateuch*, 44-45, 152, 203.

peoples" (אוֹר עַמִּים) on the servant's role as "light to the nations" (אוֹר גּוֹיִם) in Is 42:6/49:6.[62] Furthermore, the prediction that "law will go out" (יֵצֵא) from the Lord in Isaiah 51:4 connects to Isaiah 2:3, "For the law will go out from Zion" (כִּי מִצִּיּוֹן תֵּצֵא תוֹרָה; see Is 37:32; Hab 1:4).[63] Viewed together, this suggests that the law/instruction going forth from the Lord/Zion and the establishment of justice for the nations as foretold in Isaiah 2:3 and Isaiah 51:4 is achieved by the servant, the embodiment of justice (i.e., "my justice"). Yet the servant's work in the third and fourth Servant Songs involves his endurance of a travesty of justice (Is 50:8-9; 53:8).[64] Thus, the voluntary endurance of injustice for the salvation of others by the light of the nations/peoples allows him to embody a greater justice and ultimately establish the Lord's justice on earth. As shown above, a mysterious process leading to such eschatological justice suggests that the extended allusion to the Song of Moses in Isaiah 40–55 also involves and even relies on Isaiah 53.

Maybe it is only this kind of incarnational instruction accompanied by example (see Is 50:4-6) that will cause the nations to lay down their arms willingly, cease from war, and bring peace as predicted in Isaiah 2:4 (see Is 53:5). Indeed, it is one who has himself toiled to the point of exhaustion (Is 49:4) who knows how to speak a word that helps the "weary" (Is 50:4; see Is 40:29). He whose "mouth" (פֶּה) was made like a "sharp sword" (Is 49:2) first had an open ear (Is 50:4-5) and knew how and when to "not open his mouth" (Is 53:7). We might call this teaching "Jesus Christ and him crucified" (1 Cor 2:2) and consider why Martin Luther declares, "The cross alone is our theology."[65]

Another significant element of Isaiah 53 is the servant's work of bearing sin. Isaiah 53:4 says that he "bore" (נָשָׂא) our sicknesses and "carried" (סָבַל) our sorrows. Similarly, Isaiah 53:5 says, "The punishment that brought us

---

[62] See Childs, *Isaiah*, 402.
[63] See Sommer, *Prophet Reads Scripture*, 78-80.
[64] Reventlow sees "clear indications in content that the fourth Song looks back to the third" (Is 50:6/ Is 53:7) and concludes, "Isaiah 53 is, in a way, a commentary, especially on the third Song" ("Basic Issues in the Interpretation," 25-26).
[65] Martin Luther, *D. Martin Luthers Werke: Kritische Gesamtausgabe*, vol. 5, *Operationes in Psalmos. 1519–1521* (Weimar: Hermann Böhlau, 1981), 176.32. He is commenting on Ps 5:12.

peace was *upon him*" (עָלָיו), and Isaiah 53:6 adds, "The Lord laid *on him* [בּוֹ] the iniquity of us all." Isaiah 53:11-12 concludes, "He will carry [סָבַל] their iniquities . . . he bore [נָשָׂא] the sin of many." Such language and themes recall Isaiah 46:1-4, which describes idols as a "burden [מַשָּׂא] to the weary" (Is 46:1), whereas the Lord "carries" (נָשָׂא, סָבַל) his people from birth to old age (Is 46:3-4).[66] This connection not only closely associates the sin-bearing servant with the Lord again (see Is 52:13) but also depicts the servant's ministry of bearing with respect to the people's deepest need, slavery to sin.[67] The promised forgiveness and justification from the Lord (Is 43:25; 44:22; 45:25) is thus accomplished by the servant (Is 53:11).

Furthermore, his sin-bearing ministry appears to allude to the scapegoat in Leviticus 16:21-22, which first has "all the iniquities" (כָּל־עֲוֹנֹת) of Israel and "all their transgressions in all their sins" (כָּל־פִּשְׁעֵיהֶם לְכָל־חַטֹּאתָם) placed on its head and then "*bear*[s] [נָשָׂא] all their iniquities to a *cut-off land*" (אֶרֶץ גְּזֵרָה), that is, "the desert" (מִדְבָּר).[68] Isaiah 53:6 even refers to "the iniquity of all of us" (עֲוֹן כֻּלָּנוּ) and Isaiah 53:8 to the servant being "*cut off* from the *land* of the living" (נִגְזַר מֵאֶרֶץ חַיִּים). This connection supports the importance of vicarious suffering to Isaiah 52:13–53:12, which interpreters have seen in the song itself and has already been noted above with reference to the Passover lamb.[69] Hermann Spieckermann further connects the servant's bearing of sin (Is 53:4, 12) to his exaltation in Isaiah 52:13 ("lifted up") through repetition of the verb נָשָׂא.[70]

The servant's ministry of sin bearing is intertwined with his ministry of healing. Isaiah 53:4 says that he bore "our sicknesses" (חֳלָיֵנוּ), and Isaiah

---

[66] Paul Hanson, "The World of the Servant of the Lord in Isaiah 40–55," in Bellinger and Farmer, *Jesus and the Suffering Servant*, 17. See Is 9:6, "The government was/will be *on his shoulder*."

[67] These associations are thought-provoking because of other texts that emphasize the Lord's incomparability (Is 40:18, 25; 46:5).

[68] See Chen, *Messianic Vision of the Pentateuch*, 194, 196.

[69] E.g., Spieckermann, "Conception and Prehistory," 5-8 (though note his rejection of Lev 16:22 for reasons of its later date, p. 3); Reventlow, "Basic Issues in the Interpretation," 27-28; Bernd Janowski, "He Bore Our Sins: Isaiah 53 and the Drama of Taking Another's Place," in Bellinger and Farmer, *Jesus and the Suffering Servant*, 48-74; Hermisson, "Fourth Servant Song," 30.

[70] Spieckermann, "Conception and Prehistory," 7. This sounds like Jesus being "lifted up" or "glorified" in John (e.g., Jn 3:14; 7:39; 8:28; 12:16, 23, 32, 34).

53:5 adds that his suffering an injurious blow results in our being "healed" (רָפָא). Israel's need for healing was implied at the beginning of Isaiah (Is 1:5-6) and made explicit in Isaiah's call to be a prophet (Is 6:10). Significantly, the need for healing in Isaiah 6:9-10 is not physical but results from Israel's deafness, blindness, and hardheartedness to the Lord, matching the servant's solution of the sin problem in Isaiah 52:13–53:12 and his opening the eyes of the blind in Isaiah 42:7, even blind and deaf Israel (Is 42:18-20; see Deut 32:39). Hezekiah's "sickness" (חֳלִי, Is 38:9; see Is 38:1; 39:1) might have been related to his sins (Is 38:17), and either way the servant's sin bearing should be understood as including the guilt of the house of David as well (Is 7:13). It is this humiliating bearing of sin unto death that is emphasized at the end of this final Servant Song (Is 53:11-12), results in great reward and victory (Is 53:12; see Is 9:3), and is the decisive salvific act in the second exodus that brings salvation to the nations.[71]

CONCLUSION

As the final Servant Song, Isaiah 52:13–53:12 is climactic with respect to both the Servant Songs and the second exodus in Isaiah 40–55. There is an abundance of nexus connections for Isaiah 52:13–53:12 based on these relationships alone. Yet the study of these texts reveals still more connections to other parts of Isaiah and to the Pentateuch. The second exodus itself can be traced to the Pentateuch, and we also saw above the suggestive coherence between the Song of Moses in Deuteronomy 32:1-43 and Isaiah 40–55 as well as several significant links to creation and fall in Genesis 1–3. Isaiah 52:13–53:12 itself is part of this rich network and makes its own contributions to these multiple extended allusions.

While careful attention to Isaiah 52:13–53:12 itself is essential, such attention reveals intertextual relationships that cause it to sparkle in new ways when viewed from the different angles provided by these allusions.[72]

---

[71] Hermisson observes how the fourth Servant Song reveals that the servant's success and reward take place after his death ("Fourth Servant Song," 21-22). This reward is "the success of Yahweh's saving will or plan" (41).

[72] These angles can also be thought of as synchronic "allusive layers" in a richly layered text. The use of the term *layers* here assumes authorial intent and is distinct from redaction or other diachronic uses.

This process of exegesis has also suggested that the Suffering Servant is indeed the Messiah, who is both the seed of the woman (Gen 3:15) and David's promised seed (2 Sam 7:12). Through him, the Lord demonstrates his commitment to reveal his glory to the nations through the house of David (Is 37:35; 38:5; 55:3). Isaiah 53 accordingly continues to question readers whether we have believed this message: "Who has believed our report?" (Is 53:1). It also sets forth the example of one who endured injustice and now embodies the Lord's perfect justice for the world to see.

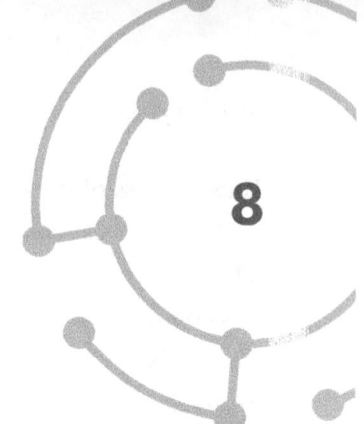

8

JONAH 2
EXODUS 1.5

My last representative example of a nexus passage from the Prophets comes from the Minor Prophets: Jonah's poetic prayer in Jonah 2. Although this passage is not as well-known as many other nexus passages, close examination reveals its importance not only to the book of Jonah but also to the Twelve (i.e., the Minor Prophets considered as a literary unity). Jonah 2 also alludes extensively to the crossing of the Red Sea in Exodus 14–15 and so has strong links to a nexus passage in the Pentateuch (Ex 15:1-18), which suggests Jonah experienced an exodus of his own. Furthermore, the poetic form and content of Jonah 2 have numerous links to the Psalter, often to Davidic psalms. The most notable of these links is to Psalm 18, which involves the parallel text in 2 Samuel 22 and its context in 1–2 Samuel. Such a high level of intertextuality suggests that the book of Jonah and Jonah 2 in particular is a nexus passage "striving to situate itself in relation to other biblical texts, drawing biblical elements into itself with the goal of being drawn into the tradition of biblical literature."[1]

JONAH'S PRAYER IN THE BOOK OF JONAH AND IN RELATION TO EXODUS 15

The book of Jonah begins with the prophet disobeying the Lord's command for him to go and preach against Nineveh (Jon 1:1-3). Rather than take a land journey to Nineveh, Jonah instead boards a boat at Joppa for Tarshish,

---

[1]Steven Weitzman, *Song and Story in Biblical Narrative: The History of a Literary Convention in Ancient Israel* (Bloomington: Indiana University Press, 1997), 113.

"away from the presence of the Lord" (Jon 1:3). However, the Lord sends a "great wind" (רוּחַ־גְּדוֹלָה) that threatens to wreck the ship (Jon 1:4). The sailors eventually find out that this is Jonah's fault (Jon 1:5-10). Although initially trying to spare his life, they ultimately throw him overboard so that the sea will be stilled (Jon 1:11-15). Afterward, the sailors fear the Lord and sacrifice to him (Jon 1:16). Meanwhile, the Lord sends a "large fish" (דָּג גָּדוֹל) to swallow Jonah, and he remains inside it for three days and three nights (Jon 1:17).

While inside the fish (Jon 2:1), Jonah prays (Jon 2:2-9). Like a psalmist, the prophet prays for deliverance from his distress (Jon 2:2-5), and the Lord hears from his temple and responds (Jon 2:6-7). The prayer closes with a description of the futility of idolatry (Jon 2:8) and a personal commitment to worship the Lord in response to his salvation (Jon 2:9). The perspective of this psalm in Jonah 2:2-9 differs from the narrative's perspective in Jonah 1 and Jonah 3–4.[2] The pious Jonah of the prayer contrasts with the rebellious, stubborn Jonah of the narrative, and the prayer says that, rather than the sailors (Jon 1:15), the Lord cast Jonah into the sea (Jon 2:3), a "theocentric emphasis" that also appears in other poems such as Exodus 15:1-18.[3] At the same time, Jonah makes orthodox statements about the Lord in the narrative as well despite his rebellion (Jon 1:9; 4:2).[4]

Commentators further observe that his declaration of the Lord's salvation (Jon 2:9) curiously comes when he is still inside the fish. Resolving issues of plot coherence and the characterization of Jonah is important, but so is recognizing the importance of the poetic prayer in

---

[2]Scholars have long wrestled with this incongruity. E.g., George Landes, "The Kerygma of the Book of Jonah: The Contextual Interpretation of the Jonah Psalm," *Int* 21 (1967): 3-31; Ray Lubeck, "Prophetic Sabotage: A Look at Jonah 3:2-4," *TJ* 9 NS (1988): 41-42. For a more recent survey of proposals, see Hugh Pyper, "Swallowed by a Song: Jonah and the Jonah-Psalm Through the Looking-Glass," in *Reflection and Refraction: Studies in Biblical Historiography in Honour of A. Graeme Auld*, ed. Timothy Lim et al. (Leiden: Brill, 2007), 337-39. While agreeing with Pyper's emphasis on the poem, I focus on the final composition of the book of Jonah and the intertextual relationship of Jon 2 to other passages in the OT.

[3]James W. Watts, *Psalm and Story: Inset Hymns in Hebrew Narrative* (Sheffield: Sheffield Academic Press, 1992), 190.

[4]Watts, *Psalm and Story*, 138.

the compositional strategy of Jonah and its intertextual connections to other passages in the Twelve and beyond. Thus, reading Jonah's psalm in terms of the narrative and reckoning with Jonah's stubbornness is necessary for constructing a coherent characterization of Jonah, but allowing the poem to stand without explaining parts of it away can highlight theological significance that is difficult to see otherwise.[5] James Nogalski argues that "the function of the psalm can only be properly understood" if it is "not harmonized with the narrative."[6] In terms of the plot, he sees Jonah's turning to the Lord in the psalm as properly preceding Jonah's return to land.[7] Even if Jonah 3–4 shows that the prophet still has much to learn, his prayer is still true as far as it goes and maintains its potential for additional significance in the Twelve and the Tanak. As for his still being in the fish while celebrating salvation, Jonah has indeed been delivered from drowning, and his return to land is imminent.

Within the book of Jonah, Jonah 2:2-9 plays a key role also because of its poetic contribution to what is otherwise a narrative book. Nogalski explains that Jonah is "unique in prophetic literature" not only for its positive portrayal of foreigners compared to a prophet but also because it "so extensively consists of prophetic narrative."[8] Thus, Jonah 2 as an embedded poem in a narrative book is also unique in prophetic literature. Yet the embedding of poems in narrative books is a common macrostructural device in other Old Testament books and a key part of the compositional strategy of such books (Pentateuch, Judges, 1–2 Samuel).[9] John Sailhamer points out that the Pentateuch is a narrative whose literary macrostructure relies on its four major poetic sections (Gen 49:1-27; Ex 15:1-18;

---

[5] For critical scholars, this issue can be intertwined with the relative dating of the narrative and the poem.
[6] James Nogalski, *Redactional Processes in the Book of the Twelve* (Berlin: de Gruyter, 1993), 266. Nogalski also cites "catchword associations" between Jon 2 and Mic 1:2-7 (e.g., "your/his holy temple," Jon 2:4, 7/Mic 1:2; "water," Jon 2:5/Mic 1:4; "descend," Jon 2:6/Mic 1:3). Other catchwords listed (249n2) are "mountains" (Jon 2:6/Mic 1:4), "earth" (Jon 2:6; Mic 1:2, 3), and idols (Jon 2:8/Mic 1:7).
[7] Nogalski, *Redactional Processes in the Book of the Twelve*, 266.
[8] Nogalski, *Redactional Processes in the Book of the Twelve*, 248.
[9] See Watts, though he treats Deut 32:1-43 more as concluding Deuteronomy than the Pentateuch (*Psalm and Story*, 80-81).

Num 23–24; Deut 32–33), which set forth the Pentateuch's central message of messianic eschatology (Gen 49:1, 8-12; Num 24:14, 17-19; Deut 31:29).[10] The poems in 1 Samuel 2:1-10 and 2 Samuel 22:1–23:7 also play a key role in the literary macrostructure of 1–2 Samuel, with these poems likewise emphasizing the Messiah but as the fulfillment of the Davidic covenant (1 Sam 2:10; 2 Sam 22:51; 23:3-4). By matching the literary macrostructure of the Pentateuch and 1–2 Samuel but on a smaller scale, the composition of the book of Jonah generates expectations that the poem in Jonah 2 likewise has special importance, despite Jonah's complexity as an individual and his not yet having gone to Nineveh.[11] Textual links to Exodus 15:1-18 and 2 Samuel 22:1-51 reinforce this connection.

In the case of the Pentateuch and its second major poem, Exodus 15:1-18, these expectations are strengthened by a broader connection between Exodus 14–15 and Jonah 1–2. The narratives of Exodus 14 and Jonah 1 have numerous parallels: Israel/Jonah "flee" (Ex 14:5/Jon 1:3), the Lord sends strong "wind" on the "sea" (Ex 14:21/Jon 1:4), Israel/sailors "fear" and later "fear the Lord" (Ex 14:10, 31/Jon 1:10, 16), and the Lord saves Israel/sailors but drowns Jonah/Egyptians (Ex 14:28-30; Jon 1:15-16).[12] Jacques Vermeylen conservatively concludes that the author of Jonah was "inspired consciously or unconsciously" by the exodus story and further

---

[10] John Sailhamer, *The Pentateuch as Narrative* (Grand Rapids, MI: Zondervan, 1992), 34-37.
[11] Watts sees the function of Jon 2 in light of these plot and character tensions, which "subvert" readers' expectations (*Psalm and Story*, 189). He believes the date of the book of Jonah is sufficiently late to assume that its earliest readers were familiar with the literary device of embedding psalms in narrative (144). See also Steven Weitzman, *Song and Story in Biblical Narrative: The History of a Literary Convention in Ancient Israel* (Bloomington, IN: Indiana University Press, 1997), 59-63, 94, 122, 127-28. Weitzman grants the influence of the Pentateuch especially "as a model of literary expression" (65, 127) on a few late biblical compositions that are supported by textual evidence (Dan 3:24-68 LXX; Is 38:9-20 [see also 2 Kings 20]; 1 Chron 16:7-36 [see also 2 Sam 6]) and on many postbiblical compositions, a development that coincided with the rise of canon consciousness. At the same time, on the basis of narrative setting (without the textual evidence other passages involve), he includes Jon 2, along with Is 38; 1 Sam 2; and 2 Sam 22, as an earlier example of "scripturalizing revisionism" during an "age of emergent canon-consciousness" (105). Weitzman believes in the influences of Ex 15 and Deut 32 (pp. 93-94, 121) but does not consider how the Pentateuch's four poetic sections function together as a model literary and theological expression.
[12] For a helpful chart with additional parallels, see Jacques Vermeylen, "La prière de Jonas (Jon 2) et le cantique de Moïse (Ex 15)," in *Écritures et réécritures: la reprise interprétative des traditions fondatrices par la littérature biblique et extra-biblique*, ed. Claire Clivaz et al. (Leuven: Peeters, 2012), 188. He ultimately rejects an allusion, opting instead for production from a common Persian milieu (187, 193-95).

points out that both salvation narratives are punctuated by a poem, Exodus 15 and Jonah 2.[13] Despite Vermeylen's hesitance, these similarities in literary structure, terminology, and themes begin to suggest the conscious use of Exodus 14–15 by Jonah 1–2.

A closer look at Jonah 2 will naturally lead to its relationship to Exodus 15:1-18. One thing that stands out about Jonah 2:2-9 is that there is no mention of the "large fish [דָּג גָּדוֹל]" of Jonah 1:17. George Landes remarks, "Quite obviously the conditions to which the psalm refers have nothing to do with a distress experienced in a fish's viscera."[14] Furthermore, the "belly of the fish [מְעֵי הַדָּגָה]" (Jon 1:17–2:1) in the narrative becomes "the belly of Sheol [בֶּטֶן שְׁאוֹל]" (Jon 2:2) in the poem. Although the two words for "belly" are different (מֵעָה, בֶּטֶן), other passages that contain both words suggest significant semantic overlap (Gen 25:23; Num 5:22; Ps 71:6; Is 49:1; Ezek 3:3). It is as though the large fish that "swallowed [בָּלַע]" Jonah (Jon 1:17) has been recast as Sheol or the grave. This fits the characterization of Sheol elsewhere as being able to "swallow [בָּלַע]" up the living (Prov 1:12; see also Num 16:30; Hab 2:5) but never being satisfied (Prov 27:20; 30:16). Accordingly, Jonah's "descent" (note יָרַד), which began in the preceding narrative (Jon 1:3, 5), does not end in the fish's belly but "at the bases of the mountains," even "the pit" (Jon 2:6; see also Ps 16:10). On the other hand, what is consistent between the narrative and poetry in Jonah 1–2 is the key role of the waters. The problems at sea narrated in Jonah 1:4-5, 11-15 are carried over into Jonah 2, as can be seen by the terms "depth [מְצוּלָה]," "seas [יַמִּים]," "river [נָהָר]," "breakers [מִשְׁבָּר]," "waves [גַּל]," "waters [מַיִם]," and "deep [תְּהוֹם]" (Jon 2:3, 5). From the midst of these waters and of Sheol, Jonah looks to the temple (Jon 2:4), prays (Jon 2:7), and is delivered from death (Jon 2:6, 9).

The poetic recounting of the crossing of the Red Sea in Exodus 15:1-18 also differs from the preceding narrative account in Exodus 14 in several ways. One difference is the poem's emphasis on the Lord's direct

---

[13]Vermeylen, "La prière de Jonas," 189.
[14]Landes, "Kerygma of the Book," 4. See also 10: "The affliction to which the psalm refers is clearly not that of being imprisoned within a large marine creature."

intervention compared to the narrative's inclusion of Moses' role in the deliverance (Ex 14:16, 21, 26-27). This parallels the theocentric emphasis in Jonah 2:2-9, which does not mention the fish or sailors. Silence concerning the fish here allows this poem to focus on the Lord's deliverance from Sheol and the waters, even as some other texts portray sea monsters as representing evil and/or enemies (Is 27:1; Ezek 29:3-4), including with reference to the exodus (Ps 74:13-14).[15] If a partially positive role for the fish in Jonah 2 is insisted on, even this can be understood as death and Sheol being an occasion for and intermediate step toward Jonah's deliverance from death to new life.[16]

The recasting of this fish (as Sheol) is further paralleled by the recasting of Israel's enemies in Exodus 15:1-18. Although Pharaoh and his army are still mentioned in Exodus 15:1, 4, other parts of the song generalize them with the terms "enemy [אוֹיֵב]" (Ex 15:6, 9) and "those who rise up against you [קָמֶיךָ]" (Ex 15:7). The parallel between Exodus 15 and Jonah 2 is even more notable because both involve the Lord's "salvation" (יְשׁוּעָה; Ex 15:2; Jon 2:9) accomplished through his power over mighty waters, and both poems play key structural and strategic roles in their respective books, as mentioned above.

Exodus 15 and Jonah 2 share water-related terminology (יָם, תְּהוֹם, מְצוּלָה, מַיִם; Ex 15:1, 4-5, 8, 10; Jon 2:3, 5). Still more shared

---

[15] See Scott Noegel, "Jonah and Leviathan: Inner-Biblical Allusions and the Problem with Dragons," HENOCH: Studies in Judaism and Christianity from Second Temple to Late Antiquity 37, no. 2 (2015): 238-42. Noegel argues that the LXX translation of "[large] fish" with κῆτος ("sea monster") instead of ἰχθύς ("fish," Jon 1:17) identifies the creature in Jonah with the "great sea creatures" in Gen 1:21 (LXX: κῆτος), such as Leviathan (see also κῆτος in LXX translation of Job 3:8; 9:13; 26:12). Citing Jon 1:4; Ps 89:9-10; and Job 26:12-13, he further points out the connection between Leviathan and a raging sea (243-44). Tova Forti writes, "Thus the fish in Jonah is associated with such marvelous creatures as Behemoth, Leviathan, Tanin, Rahab, and Tehom." Forti, "Of Ships and Seas, and Fish and Beasts: Viewing the Concept of Universal Providence in the Book of Jonah Through the Prism of Psalms," JSOT 35 (2011): 372. Timothy Stone writes, "The raging of the sea's water is associated in the OT with the forces of evil." Stone, "Following the Church Fathers: An Intertextual Path from Psalm 107 to Isaiah, Jonah, and Matthew 8:23-27," Journal of Theological Interpretation 7 (2013): 52.

[16] See Marvin Sweeney, The Twelve Prophets (Collegeville, MN: Liturgical Press, 2000), 1:317. He writes, "Jonah's presence in the belly of the fish suggests the imagery of pregnancy for the fish and new birth or new creation for Jonah." Constantin Oancea points out the paradoxical nature of the phrase "womb of Sheol" as bringing together both life and death. Oancea, "Water and Death as Metaphors in Jonah's Psalm," Revue Biblique 128 (2021): 182.

terminology includes "reed [סוּף]" (Ex 15:4; Jon 2:6), "holiness [קֹדֶשׁ]" (Ex 15:11, 13; Jon 2:4, 8), "descend [יָרַד]" (Ex 15:5; Jon 2:6), and "in the heart of the sea[s]" (Ex 15:8; Jon 2:3).[17] When the surrounding narrative contexts are also considered, even more common terms include "swallow [בָּלַע]" (Ex 15:12; Jon 1:17), "dry land [יַבָּשָׁה]" (Ex 14:29; 15:19; Jon 2:10), and "spirit/wind [רוּחַ]" (Ex 15:8, 10; Jon 1:4). Enrique Sanz Giménez-Rico highlights the "sea–dry land" pair, which ties together Jonah's "great confession" in Jonah 1:9 ("I fear the Lord . . . who made the sea and the dry land"), his being cast into the sea in Jonah 1:15 and his return to "dry land" in Jonah 2:10, the crossing of the Red Sea (Ex 14:16, 22, 29; 15:19), and even creation (Gen 1:10).[18] Furthermore, themes of being thrown into waters (Ex 15:1, 4; Jon 2:3), the temple (Ex 15:13, 17; Jon 2:4, 7), and the nations (Ex 15:4, 14-16; Jon 1:2-3; 3:2) are common to both contexts. Alastair Hunter accordingly refers to the "strong bonds" between Exodus 15 and Jonah 2.[19]

Table 8.1. Shared terms and themes between Exodus 15 and Jonah 2

	Exodus 15	Jonah 2
"In the heart of the sea[s]," "depth," "deep," "waters"	Ex 15:1, 4-5, 8, 10	Jon 2:3, 5
"Reed"	Ex 15:4	Jon 2:6
"Holiness"	Ex 15:11	Jon 2:4, 7
"Descend"	Ex 15:5	Jon 2:6
"Swallow"	Ex 15:12	Jon 1:17
"Dry land"	Ex 14:29; 15:19	Jon 2:10
Thrown into the waters	Ex 15:1, 4	Jon 2:3
Temple	Ex 15:13, 17	Jon 2:4, 7

These extensive similarities suggest not only an allusion to Exodus 15 in Jonah 2 but also that Jonah's deliverance from the waters has been

---

[17]See Alastair Hunter, "Jonah from the Whale: Exodus Motifs in Jonah 2," in *The Elusive Prophet: The Prophet as a Historical Person, Literary Character and Anonymous Artist*, ed. Johannes C. de Moor (Leiden: Brill, 2001), 147-50.
[18]Enrique Sanz Giménez-Rico, "La mediación y petición en el libro de Joel y su relación con Jonás," *Scripta Theologica* 50 (2018): 576.
[19]Hunter, "Jonah from the Whale," 150.

intentionally cast in terms of the paradigmatic deliverance of the Israelites at the Red Sea. Yet Jonah's distress of being thrown into the sea (Jon 2:4, 6-7) does not match the Israelites' experience but that of their enemies (Ex 15:1, 4-5, 10). Thus, the prophet is like both the Israelites and the Egyptians, but in different ways: like the Israelites because he was saved from the waters to dry land, but like the Egyptians because he was thrown into the sea.[20] This complex relationship falls under the category of what Jonathan Grossman refers to as "dynamic analogies," which are analogies that are not one-to-one.[21] Jonah experiences both the depths of the sea and the safety of dry land, that is, death and life, as well as the truth of his earlier confession of the Lord's sovereignty over both (Jon 1:9).

To be sure, the differences between Jonah 1–2 and Exodus 14–15 are real, and some see the book of Jonah as a parody.[22] Indeed, Jonah's experience does not truly mirror the exodus in the sense of an exact or close replication but is like a funhouse mirror that takes the original object and transforms it in certain ways. Yet from the broader perspective of Old Testament theology and the foundational role of the Pentateuch's major poems, the exodus is not ultimate anyway since it too is a partial reflection of eschatological reality (see chapter seven), and mirroring the exodus closely is not always necessary. So, even if Jonah is a sort of funhouse mirror, it transforms the exodus in some ways that more closely resemble the real thing, the messianic second exodus.

Whereas Nogalski argues that Jonah in Jonah 2 represents exiled Israel as cut off from the temple (see Jon 2:4, 7), his discussion does not account sufficiently for the complex allusion to Exodus 15:1-18, that Israel is not *cast* into the waters in the exodus or second exodus (see Is 11:15-16; 43:2;

---

[20]Hunter, "Jonah from the Whale," 150: "There is a very strong case for the thesis that at the heart of Jonah lies a commentary albeit a very off-beat one—on the cherished exodus myth."

[21]Jonathan Grossman, "'Dynamic Analogies' in the Book of Esther," VT 59 (2009): 395: "In some cases the analogy between narratives encourages the presentation of a certain character from one narrative as paralleling more than one character in the other. . . . This phenomenon, assuming that it is intentional, may be called 'dynamic analogy.'"

[22]John A. Miles Jr., "Laughing at the Bible: Jonah as Parody," *Jewish Quarterly Review* 65 (1975): 168-81; Arnold Band, "Swallowing Jonah: The Eclipse of Parody," *Prooftexts* 10 (1990): 177-95; Will Kynes, "Beat Your Parodies into Swords, and Your Parodied Books into Spears: A New Paradigm for Parody in the Hebrew Bible," *BibInt* 19 (2011): 300-303.

Mic 7:19; Zech 10:10-11), or Gentile salvation in the book of Jonah.[23] Instead, Jonah should be seen as an *individual* who was thrown into the waters and "driven out" (גָּרַשׁ) by the Lord from his presence (Jon 2:3-4; see Gen 3:24; Hos 9:15) and yet whose prayer is ultimately heard by the Lord (Jon 2:6-7) so that he declares the Lord's salvation (Jon 2:9). Additional investigation will sharpen this intriguing picture.

JONAH'S PRAYER AND THE SECOND EXODUS IN THE TWELVE

Scholars such as Nogalski and others show extensive external and internal evidence for the unity of the Minor Prophets, or the Twelve.[24] Within this corpus, Jonah provides examples of Gentile inclusion in the Lord's kingdom through the sailors and the Ninevites. This theme traces back to the "possession of Edom" in Amos 9:12 and Obadiah 19 (see Num 24:18; Joel 3:19; "Tarshish" in Is 60:9; Ps 72:10) and anticipates the pilgrimage of all peoples to Zion in Micah 4:1-3 and Zechariah 9–14.[25] Lena-Sofia Tiemeyer also points out the connection between the sailors' worship in Jonah 1:16 and Malachi 1:11 ("From the rising of the sun to its setting my name will be great among the nations. . . . Incense and clean offering will be brought").[26] Indeed, the Ninevites' faith and repentance "from the greatest to the least of them" (מִגְּדוֹלָם וְעַד־קְטַנָּם, Jon 3:5) makes it look like new-covenant blessings reach them before Israel (Jer 31:34, "all of them will know me from the least to the greatest of them"). Nogalski notes catchwords between Jonah 2 and Micah 1, and we can pursue further how Jonah 2 and its particular account of Jonah's deliverance from the waters and from Sheol (Jon 2:2) might relate to still other passages in the Twelve.[27]

---

[23]Nogalski, *Redactional Processes in the Book of the Twelve*, 266-67.

[24]James Nogalski, *Literary Precursors to the Book of the Twelve* (Berlin: de Grutyer, 1993); Nogalski, *Redactional Processes in the Book of the Twelve*; Sweeney, *Twelve Prophets* 1:xv-xxxix; Paul House, *The Unity of the Twelve* (Sheffield: Sheffield Academic Press, 1990).

[25]See Michael Shepherd, "Compositional Analysis of the Twelve," *ZAW* 120 (2008): 187-88; Sanz Giménez-Rico, "La mediación y petición," 562.

[26]Lena-Sofia Tiemeyer, "Attitudes to the Cult in Jonah: In the Book of Jonah, the Book of the Twelve, and Beyond," in *Priests and Cults in the Book of the Twelve*, ed. Lena-Sofia Tiemeyer (Atlanta: SBL Press, 2016), 122.

[27]Nogalski, *Literary Precursors to the Book of the Twelve*, 266.

Second exodus in Hosea 1–3. Given the extensive allusions to the Song of the Sea (Ex 15:1-18) in Jonah 2:2-9, a natural step would be to situate Jonah's poetic prayer in relation to themes of exodus and especially second exodus within the Twelve. The importance of the second exodus is seen immediately in the opening chapters of the Twelve, Hosea 1–3. In the first major salvation passage of the book (Hos 1:10–2:1; see esp. Hos 1:7), the Lord says, "The sons of Judah and the sons of Israel will be gathered together and will set for themselves one head [רֹאשׁ אֶחָד], and *they will go up from the land* [וְעָלוּ מִן־הָאָרֶץ]" (Hos 1:11; see Jer 3:18; Jon 2:6, descent to/ascent from a "land"). This promise of regathering and reunification involves a leaving, a "going up" (עָלָה), from the "land" (אֶרֶץ), just as the exodus did (Ex 1:10; 3:8, 17; 13:18).[28]

The next major salvation passage in Hosea has even stronger second exodus themes (Hos 2:14-23). It begins, "Therefore, behold, I will allure her, and I will lead her in the *desert* [מִדְבָּר], and *I will speak kindly to her* [וְדִבַּרְתִּי עַל לִבָּהּ]" (Hos 2:14; see Deut 32:10). This combination of a new work of the Lord in the desert and his speaking kindly to his people (דָּבָר עַל־לֵב) matches Isaiah 40:1-3 and the second-exodus themes of Isaiah 40–55 (see chapter seven). While also drawing on the Achan incident in Joshua 7, Hosea 2:15 likens Israel's response to the Lord's future salvation to "the days of her youth and the day she *went up from the land of Egypt*." Accordingly, this salvation also involves a "covenant" (Hos 2:18) that brings Edenic restoration, including the Lord "sowing" Israel in the land (Hos 2:23; see Ex 15:17; Amos 9:13-15).

Although second-exodus themes are not found in the third salvation passage in Hosea 1–3, Hosea 3 draws on the previous two passages that do. Hosea 3:5 concludes with a climactic prediction of Israel's repentance, "Afterwards the sons of Israel will turn [שׁוּב] and seek [בָּקַשׁ] the Lord their God and David their king, and they will tremble before the Lord and his goodness in the last days [בְּאַחֲרִית הַיָּמִים]" (see also Hos 5:6; 7:10). The reference not only to "the Lord their God" but also to "David

---

[28]Yair Hoffman calls this "a clear analogy." Hoffman, "A North Israelite Typological Myth and a Judaean Historical Tradition: The Exodus in Hosea and Amos," *VT* 39 (1989): 173.

their king" suggests that the "one head" who leads reunified Israel out of the land in Hosea 1:11 is both prophet like Moses and Messiah (see Hos 12:13). The combination of marriage themes and the reversal of devastation in Hosea 3 matches Hosea 2:2-23, which alludes to the exodus, as shown above. Moreover, exiled Israel's "turning" and "seeking" "the Lord their God . . . in the last days" alludes to Deuteronomy 4:29-30 ("You will seek from there the Lord your God. . . . In the last days you will turn to the Lord your God"). Michael Shepherd also points out the allusion to Jeremiah 30:8-9 ("In that day . . . they will not serve [עָבַד] foreigners anymore, and they will serve *the Lord their God and David their king* [וְעָבְדוּ אֵת יְהוָה אֱלֹהֵיהֶם וְאֵת דָּוִד מַלְכָּם]"), a text also having second-exodus themes (see Jer 30:24; 31:1-14).[29]

Exodus and second-exodus themes continue in Hosea (e.g., Hos 8:13; 9:3; 11:1, 11), including at a high frequency in its final chapters (Hos 12:9, 13; 13:4, 14; 14:5-7). Its last verse calls the wise to "understand these things" (Hos 14:9) and is part of a compositional seam within the Twelve. The result is that Hosea 1–3, programmatically for both the book of the Hosea and the Twelve, sets forth eschatological salvation in terms of the second exodus while also linking this with the messianic David (Hos 3:5).[30] In addition to the mention of Egypt at the end of Joel (Joel 3:19), several exodus references can be found in Amos (Amos 2:10; 3:1; 4:10), including at its conclusion, which, like Hosea 1–3, combines exodus/second exodus with messianic prophecy (Amos 9:7, 11-15).

Along with these two seams in Joel 3 and Amos 9, the last chapter of Micah (Mic 7) also has strong second-exodus themes. More references include Haggai 2:5-6 and Zechariah 10:10-11, with Malachi 4:4 concluding the Twelve and the Prophets with a broadly encompassing command to

---

[29]Michael Shepherd, "The New Exodus in the Composition of the Twelve," in *Text and Canon: Essays in Honor of John H. Sailhamer*, ed. Robert L. Cole and Paul J. Kissling (Eugene, OR: Pickwick, 2017), 122-23. Hos 3:5 is thus another instance of braiding.

[30]Though arguing for the use of exodus mythology against state religion in the Northern Kingdom, see Mark Leuchter, "Hosea's Exodus Mythology and the Book of the Twelve," in Tiemeyer, ed., *Priests and Cults in the Book of the Twelve*, 43, 48-49. Hoffman refers to "the central position" of the exodus in Hosea and its "typological character" but sees the latter as an "innovation" by Hosea ("North Israelite Typological Myth," 170, 175-77).

"remember the law of my servant Moses" (Mal 4:4), that is, the Pentateuch, which includes its self-evident exodus themes and second-exodus prophecies. Thus, the Twelve provides a substantial exodus/second-exodus framework into which Jonah 2 and its own exodus themes fit. Particularly relevant to Jonah 2 are Hosea 13:14 and Micah 7:19.

Figure 8.1. Jonah 2 links to Hosea 13:14 and Micah 7:19

Second exodus in Hosea 13:14. Although its connection to the second-exodus motif is disputed, Hosea 13:14 is an important second-exodus passage: "From the hand of Sheol I will redeem [פָּדָה] them; from death I will redeem [גָּאַל] them; where are your plagues, Death? Where is your sting, Sheol?" Some interpret this as a rhetorical question that accords with the context of judgment ("Will I redeem them . . . ?" answer: no), but rapid topic switches in prophetic literature are common (e.g., Hos 1:7), and this part of Hosea 13:14 can still be read as a brief reference to salvation that contrasts with the surrounding emphasis on Ephraim's death (Hos 13:1, 7-9, 13, 16).[31] Using the same language as Hosea 13:14, Psalm 49:15 declares similarly, "God will redeem [פָּדָה] my soul from the hand of Sheol [מִיַּד־שְׁאוֹל], for he will take me" (see Gen 5:24; Ps 89:48).

The two terms for "redeem" (פָּדָה, גָּאַל) in Hosea 13:14 are used elsewhere in relation to the exodus (פָּדָה in Deut 7:8; 13:6; 15:15; גָּאַל in Ex 6:6; 15:13) and the second exodus (Is 35:9-10; Jer 31:11), including in the Twelve (e.g., Hos 7:13; Mic 4:10; 6:4; Zech 10:8).[32] The "redemption" (גָּאַל/פָּדָה) promised in Hosea 13:14 thus fits and contributes to the

---

[31] See Sweeney, *Twelve Prophets* 1:130, 134.
[32] Zech 10:8 promises that the Lord will "gather" (קָבַץ; Hos 1:11) Israel, "for I have redeemed [פָּדָה] them." The return from exile (Zech 10:8-10) is even linked to passing "through the sea of distress [בַּיָּם צָרָה]" and the defeat of "waves [גַּלִּים]" and "depths [מְצוּלוֹת]" (Zech 10:11). All four of these words in Zech 10:11 also appear in Jon 2:2-3 and connect Jonah's deliverance to Israel's eschatological return from exile, both of which fit the paradigmatic deliverance at the Red Sea.

Twelve's second-exodus framework. Although connecting Sheol and "death" (מָוֶת) to the Canaanite god of death Mot and Samaria, Mark Leuchter includes Hosea 13:14 in his study of exodus themes in Hosea. He further argues that the defeat of an enemy followed by the Lord leading his people and planting them in the land in Hosea 13:14–14:8 shares the same plot structure as Exodus 15:3-17 in the Song of the Sea.[33] Without denying implications for Mot, a more straightforward reading of Hosea 13:14 is that it is about redemption from death/Sheol itself, just as Jonah experienced (note "die" in Jon 4:3, 8-9).

Exile and death. To solidify the connection between Jonah's deliverance from Sheol and second-exodus redemption, we can consider additional passages besides Hosea 13:14 that suggest that the deliverance from exile in the second exodus is also a deliverance from death. A fundamental connection between exile and death is rooted in the Garden of Eden because the fall resulted in death and exile from the presence of the Lord (Gen 3:19, 22-24). Covenant warnings to Israel against disobedience likewise involve both exile and death (Deut 4:26-27; 28:20-26, 32, 36-37). The need to be delivered from death, which is because of Israel's sins, is implied by the repeated references to death in the context of Hosea 13:14 (Hos 13:1, 7-9, 13, 16). The same context reminds Israel of the Lord's salvation in the exodus (Hos 13:4-5). In addition to the punishment of exile (Hos 3:4; 9:17; 11:5), several other passages in Hosea describe Israel's death, such as Hosea 2:3 ("I will kill her [וַהֲמִתִּיהָ] with thirst"; see also Hos 6:5); Hosea 9:6 ("Memphis will bury them [תְּקַבְּרֵם]"); Hosea 9:13 ("Ephraim will bring out his sons to a slayer [אֶל־הֹרֵג]").

In Hosea 5:13-14, Israel's punishment (see Hos 5:9-11) is accordingly described as an illness that cannot be "healed" (רָפָא) and as being "torn to pieces" (טָרַף) by the Lord ("I, I [אֲנִי אֲנִי]") so that "there is none to deliver" (וְאֵין מַצִּיל). In response to the need to seek the Lord "in their distress" (Hos 5:15; see Deut 4:29-30), the prayer of repentance in Hosea 6:1-3 expresses hope not only that "[the Lord] will heal us" (וְיִרְפָּאֵנוּ) but also that

---

[33] Leuchter, "Hosea's Exodus Mythology," 41-42.

"he will revive us [יְחַיֵּנוּ] after two days, on the third day *he will raise us up* [יְקִמֵנוּ] that *we may live* [וְנִחְיֶה] before him." The theme of deliverance from death parallels Hosea 13:14 as well as Deuteronomy 32:39 ("I, I [אֲנִי אֲנִי] am he. . . . I put to death, and then I make alive [וַאֲחַיֶּה]; I strike, and I will heal [אֶרְפָּא], and no one delivers from my hand [וְאֵין מִיָּדִי מַצִּיל]"). Resembling the emphasis on the Lord's sovereignty over life and death in Deuteronomy 32:39, the lion that kills Israel in Hosea 5:14 and Hosea 13:7-8 is also the lion whose roar calls them home out of exile in Hosea 11:10-11.

Uncannily aligning with the prayer in Hosea 6:1-2 ("let us turn to the Lord . . . he struck [us] . . . on the third day he will raise us up"), Jonah is also punished by the Lord, and his turn to the Lord in prayer is similarly followed by deliverance after "three days and three nights" (Jon 1:17). Nogalski notes the parallels of the Lord's "departure causing Israel[/Jonah] distress" (Hos 5:15; Jon 2:4), salvation after two or three days (Hos 6:2; Jon 1:17), and prayer (Hos 6:1-3; Jon 2:2-9), but he interprets this in terms of his aforementioned belief that Jonah represents Israel.[34] In contrast, I take Jonah 1:17–2:10 as alluding to Hosea 6:1-2 and applying it to Jonah as an individual who is part of but not equivalent to Israel. The childbirth and womb imagery in Hosea 13:13 (see also Hos 12:4) followed by redemption from Sheol in Hosea 13:14 also map to Jonah's being in the "belly/womb" (בֶּטֶן) of the fish/"Sheol" (Jon 2:1-2) and his subsequent deliverance from the same (Jon 2:6, 9-10), raising the possibility of yet another connection between Jonah and Hosea.[35]

The connection between exile and death is reinforced elsewhere in the Twelve. In the only other passage in this corpus besides Hosea 13:14 that uses the terms "Sheol" (שְׁאוֹל) and "death" (מָוֶת), Habakkuk 2:5 describes a "proud man" (גֶּבֶר יָהִיר; see Hab 2:4, "his soul is puffed up"), probably the king of Babylon (see Hab 1:6), as having "enlarged his soul like Sheol [כִּשְׁאוֹל] . . . he is like death [כַּמָּוֶת] and will not be satisfied." Both this enemy and death are greedy, gluttons for human life. Accordingly, the

---

[34]Nogalski, *Redactional Processes in the Book of the Twelve*, 268-69, which also extends the connection to Hos 6:4-6 and Israel's/Jonah's fickleness.
[35]See Sweeney, *Twelve Prophets* 1:134, 317; Hans Walter Wolff, *Hosea*, trans. Gary Stansell, Hermeneia (Philadelphia: Fortress, 1974), 228.

Chaldeans going "through the breadth of the land to possess dwellings not theirs" (Hab 1:6) and "gather [אָסַף] captives like sand" (Hab 1:9; see also Hab 1:15) refers to the impending Babylonian invasion.[36] Thus, the comparison of the king of Babylon to Sheol and death in Habakkuk 2:5 connects the exile to death itself and in turn the king of Babylon to the large fish in Jonah, which is also likened to Sheol in Jonah 2:1-2. The "swallowing" (בָּלַע) of Jonah by the fish in Jonah 1:17 even accords with Habakkuk 1:13, "The wicked swallows up [בָּלַע] the one more righteous than he" (note also the fish theme in Habakkuk 1:14-17). The only other instances of "swallow" in the Twelve also involve exile (Hos 8:7-8). Consistent with this, Zion says in Jeremiah 51:34 that Nebuchadnezzar king of Babylon "swallowed me like a sea monster [בְּלָעַנִי כַּתַּנִּין], filled his stomach with my delicacies."

Whereas deliverance from death is subordinated to the broader theme of deliverance from historical Babylon in some passages (e.g., Ezek 37:12), the nature of the second exodus itself suggests that this relationship in reality is reversed. As eschatological salvation, the second exodus is first and foremost concerned with deliverance from sin and death, of which the Babylonian exile is an instance. As suggested above, the first exile was that of Adam and Eve from the garden because of their sin and was connected to their death sentence (Gen 3:19, 22-24). The second exodus was always about more than returning from just Babylon (e.g., Hos 11:10-11; Is 11:11), and even the partial return of exiles in Ezra-Nehemiah fell far short of what was promised (e.g., Neh 9:36, "We are slaves today, and the land which you gave to our fathers . . . we are slaves on it"). Hosea itself looks all the way to "the last days" (Hos 3:5), and the Edenic betrothal of Israel to the Lord forever (Hos 2:19) seems to assume salvation from death itself. Within such a second-exodus framework in the Twelve that includes deliverance from death itself, Jonah's deliverance from Sheol (Jon 2:2) provides a foretaste of the eschatological redemption promised in Hosea 13:14.

---

[36]Similarly, his "gather[ing] for himself all nations" conflicts with the Lord's ultimate purpose to gather the nations to himself (Joel 3:2; Mic 2:12; 4:6).

Second exodus in Micah 7. As the conclusion to Micah and a seam in the Twelve, Micah 7 likewise shows that the second exodus is not merely about deliverance from historical Babylon but about the defeat of ultimate enemies. Micah 7:15 sets the stage with the Lord's promise of the second exodus, "As in the days you went out from the land of Egypt, I will show them wonders" (נִפְלָאוֹת; see Ex 3:20; 15:11; Judg 6:13). Nations will look on and be silent (Mic 7:16), just as in Exodus 15:14-16. The humiliation of enemies so that they "lick dust like the serpent [יְלַחֲכוּ עָפָר כַּנָּחָשׁ], like those things that crawl on the earth" (Mic 7:17; see Gen 3:14; Deut 32:24; Ps 72:9) hints that an ultimate enemy, the serpent, has been defeated and that by the messianic seed of the woman (Gen 3:15).[37] Like Hosea 3:5, Micah also looks forward to "the last days" (Mic 4:1) in connection with the Messiah's rule (Mic 5:2). Like the second exodus, he also has his origin in "days of old/eternity" (עוֹלָם/מִימֵי קֶדֶם; Mic 5:2; 7:20).

But it is not only enemy nations and presumably the serpent who will be defeated in the eschatological second exodus. Micah 7:18-20 presents sin as another ultimate enemy that will be defeated also. Like Hosea 14:2 ("Forgive all iniquity" [כָּל־תִּשָּׂא עָוֹן]), Micah 7:18 mentions the Lord "forgiving iniquity" (נֹשֵׂא עָוֹן), just as part of the classic statement in Exodus 34:7 says. For Micah 7:18-20, the allusions to the Lord's self-revelation in Exodus 34:6-7 abound: "transgression" (פֶּשַׁע), mitigation of "anger" (אַף), "have compassion"/"compassionate" (רָחַם/רַחוּם), "sin" (חַטָּאָה), "steadfast love" and "truth" (חֶסֶד, אֱמֶת), and when the broader context of Exodus 34:6-7 is considered, "pass over" (עָבַר, Ex 34:6/Mic 7:18), "inheritance" (נַחֲלָה, Mic 7:18; see "inherit us" [וּנְחַלְתָּנוּ], Ex 34:9), "turn" (שׁוּב, Ex 32:12), and "Jacob"/"Abraham" (Ex 32:13; 33:1).[38] Thus, the second exodus is also a climactic manifestation of the Lord's character. Allusions to Exodus 34:6-7 also appear in the Twelve in Joel 2:13; Jonah 4:2; Nahum 1:3.

Furthermore, the promise that the Lord will "*subdue* [כָּבַשׁ] our iniquities" in Micah 7:19 seems to allude to the creation mandate in

---

[37]Note how Mic 7:17 braids Deut 32:24 ("things that crawl" [זֹחֵל]) and Gen 3:14 ("serpent," "dust"), supporting the connection argued for in chapter five between snake themes in both passages.

[38]See James Nogalski, *The Book of the Twelve: Micah–Malachi*, SHBC (Macon, GA: Smyth & Helwys, 2011), 591; Sweeney, *Twelve Prophets* 2:413.

Genesis 1:28 ("fill the earth and *subdue* [כָּבַשׁ] it") as well as personify iniquities as enemies, just as Genesis 4:7 does with reference to Cain ("Sin is lying at your door.... You must rule over it"). Even more to the point, Micah 7:19 continues with a clear allusion to the Song of the Sea that again personifies sin as an enemy, likening sin to the Egyptian army: "You will cast [שָׁלַךְ] all their sins into the depths [מְצוּלָה] of the sea." Whereas the narrative in Exodus 14:27 says, "The Lord *shook off* [נָעַר] the Egyptians in the midst of the sea," only the Song of the Sea uses the imagery of him *casting* (יָרָה, רָמָה; different words from Mic 7:19) them into the sea (Ex 15:1, 4). The song in Exodus 15:5 also uses the uncommon term "depth" (מְצוּלָה) as part of the very similar form "in the depths" (בִמְצוֹלֹת), which is also found in Micah 7:19 (בִּמְצֻלוֹת). Both passages ask, "Who is like you?" (Ex 15:11) or "Who is a God like you?" (Mic 7:18) Accordingly, Lesley DiFransico points out the numerous allusions to Exodus 15:1-18 in Micah 7:7-20 and sees in the latter "the personification of sin as a military enemy."[39]

Thus, Micah 7:15-20 shows again that the concept of second exodus within the Twelve is not limited to deliverance from historical Babylon but focuses on salvation from ultimate enemies such as sin, the serpent, and the serpent's seed (e.g., hostile nations). Given that all these enemies can be traced to Genesis 3, the redemption from death in Hosea 13:14 can also be understood as part of this eschatological salvation from ultimate enemies. An Edenic restoration was already mentioned in relation to Hosea 2:18-23 and can also be found outside the Twelve (e.g., Is 11:1-9). Based on Genesis 3:22-24, such restoration would involve access to the tree of life. Death, being a consequence of sin, is itself also an enemy that the Lord will "swallow up [בָּלַע]" on eschatological Mount Zion (Is 25:6-8; see Rom 5:14; 8:2; 1 Cor 15:26).

Furthermore, Nogalski notes the rare construction in Micah 7:19, "You will cast in the depths" (וְתַשְׁלִיךְ בִּמְצֻלוֹת) with the Lord as subject,

---

[39]Lesley DiFransico, "'He Will Cast Their Sins into the Depths of the Sea...': Exodus Allusions and the Personification of Sin in Micah 7:7-20," *VT* 67 (2017): 187-203. For interaction with DiFransico's article, see Kevin Chen, *The Messianic Vision of the Pentateuch* (Downers Grove, IL: InterVarsity Press, 2019), 157, 166-67.

and argues for an allusion to Jonah 2:3, "You cast me in the depth" (וַתַּשְׁלִיכֵנִי מְצוּלָה; see Neh 9:11).[40] He also views this allusion as helping integrate the book of Jonah into the Twelve by drawing a parallel between Jonah's salvation and the congregation in Micah 7:19b (consistent with his view that Jonah represents Israel) and hence as significant to the compositional unity of the Twelve.[41] While granting the value of Nogalski's move to relate these two texts, the parallel between Jonah 2:3 and Micah 7:19, regardless of the direction of dependence, more directly suggests a connection between Jonah and iniquities, since both are cast into the sea for the salvation of (other) people. This relationship is logically prior to determining whom Jonah may or may not represent (*pace* Nogalski). Significantly, it is Israel's *iniquities*, not Israel itself, that are cast in the sea in Micah 7:19. Thus, just as the Lord casting Jonah into the sea in Jonah 2:3 means salvation for the Gentile sailors (and his deliverance resulted in the salvation of the Ninevites), so the Lord casting Israel's sins into the sea in Micah 7:19 means salvation for Israel. This accords with the fact that eschatological salvation in the Twelve is for both a remnant of Israel and a remnant of the nations (Amos 9:12; Mic 7:18). Since the Twelve affirms that this salvation is secured by the Messiah (Hos 3:5; Amos 9:11; Mic 5:2-4), even a suffering Messiah (Zech 12:10), and in view of the second-exodus emphasis in the Twelve, it is within the realm of possibility that Jonah's undergoing an exodus of his own for the well-being of others faintly echoes expectations that the Messiah will suffer and die as a substitute for sinners (Gen 3:15; 49:11-12; Ex 12:12-13; Lev 16:21-22).[42]

The connection between Micah 7:15-20 and the book of Jonah has even more dimensions. The prediction in Micah 7:16-17 that, as a result of the Lord's "wonders" (נִפְלָאוֹת), "nations" (גּוֹיִם) will *"tremble [פָּחַד]* before the

---

[40]Nogalski, *Literary Precursors to the Book of the Twelve*, 153; Nogalski, *Book of the Twelve: Micah–Malachi*, 592. Like Jon 2, Neh 9:11 also links to Ex 15:1-18.

[41]Nogalski says Mic 7:19b was "likely inserted into Micah [i.e., late] when Jonah was added to the corpus of the Twelve" (*Book of the Twelve: Micah–Malachi*, 592). For Nogalski, this construal of redaction and dating allows Mic 7:19b to allude to Jonah, the supposedly later book.

[42]Chen, *Messianic Vision of the Pentateuch*, 55, 134-35. See also Stone, who discusses this allusion but interprets Jonah as representing Israel in exile and thus Israel's exile as atoning for Israel's sins ("Following the Church Fathers," 46-48).

Lord our God and *be afraid* [יָרֵא] of you" recalls the sailors' fear in Jonah 1:10, 16 (יָרֵא; see Jon 3:5; Ex 14:31). At the same time, the nations' "trembling" (פַּחַד) before the Lord in Micah 7:17 matches eschatological Israel's in Hosea 3:5, and the nations' seeing, being ashamed, and silence here matches Exodus 15:14-16 and Isaiah 52:15. Thus, without being eschatological itself, the book of Jonah gives a foretaste of the eschatological salvation of the Gentiles and maybe also a passing glimpse of its means.

Related to the original exodus and Exodus 15:1-18, the observation by Hunter that "the national experience of the exodus" has been made "personal and individual" in Jonah can be rooted in the message of the Pentateuch itself.[43] In Balaam's second and third speeches, Israel's exodus from Egypt (Num 23:22, "God brought them [מוֹצִיאָם] out of Egypt") is used as a picture of the second exodus, led by an individual messianic king (Num 24:8, "God brought him [מוֹצִיאוֹ] out of Egypt"), which will take place "in the last days" (Num 24:14).[44] The distinction between these two exoduses allows for Jonah 2 to resemble Israel in some ways while still maintaining its own status as an individual encounter with Sheol and exile (Jon 2:2, 4).[45] Thus, Jonah's unique experience of both being cast into the waters *and* delivered from them, distinct from the first exodus and the second exodus and yet with resemblances to both, stands in between them as a sort of Exodus 1.5. Like David in Psalm 18:16 (see below), Jonah experiences an individual exodus, a "bringing up" (עָלָה, Jon 2:6; see also Hos 1:11) after having repeatedly "gone down" (יָרַד, Jon 1:3, 5; 2:6; see also Gen 37:35; 39:1; Ex 3:8).[46]

---

[43] Hunter, "Jonah from the Whale," 154. Recall Nogalski's belief that Jonah represents Israel and see likewise Landes, "Kerygma of the Book," 23: "When Jonah finds himself in the watery Deep, he joins that company of Israelites who have experienced the threat and terror of an untimely death and cried to Yahweh for deliverance." Similarly, Stone takes Jon 2 as "a figure of Israel in exile" ("Following the Church Fathers," 46). Although Israel was indeed "swallowed up" through the exile (Jer 51:34; Hos 8:8; Hab 1:13), their safe passage during the second exodus and the drowning of their *sins* (rather than themselves) in Mic 7:19 suggests otherwise.

[44] Sailhamer, *Pentateuch as Narrative*, 408; John Sailhamer, *The Meaning of the Pentateuch* (Downers Grove, IL: InterVarsity Press, 2009), 519-20.

[45] Landes, "Kerygma of the Book," 24-25: "Through his experience in the Deep, Jonah is made vividly conscious of a fundamental truth in the Israelite conception of death: death means radical separation from God."

[46] Hunter notes the interplay between Egypt and Sheol related to these two verbs ("Jonah from the Whale," 155). We may further note associations between the exodus and deliverance from death (Ex 1:12, 16, 22; 12:30, 33; 14:30; Deut 4:20; 28:60-61).

Unlike the Egyptians in Exodus 14–15 and "sins" in Micah 7:19, Jonah is not only cast into the waters but also delivered from them. As such, the results of his experience of a sort of death by drowning are unique too: the salvation of Gentiles (contra the Egyptians) and even himself. This part of his profile fits that of the messianic seed of the woman who suffers death, puts away sin, defeats the enemy, and saves the nations (Gen 3:15). He will also be raised to rule these nations forever (Gen 49:8-10; Num 24:9).[47] Unlike the Israelites who passed through the Red Sea via the safety of dry land (Ex 14:16, 22, 29; 15:19) and come out safely from the nations in the second exodus (Hos 1:11; 11:10-11; Mic 7:15; Zech 10:11), the Messiah will be drowned in the waters of death, taking sin down with him, before being saved himself and leading Israel and the nations to safety. As we will see below, these associations can be traced in another direction through the Psalms.

JONAH'S PRAYER AS A PSALM AND IN RELATION TO 2 SAMUEL 22/PSALM 18

Interpreters have long recognized that Jonah's poetic prayer is essentially a psalm.[48] For example, note the opening line in Jonah 2:2 compared to Psalm 3:4 and Psalm 120:1:

קָרָאתִי מִצָּרָה לִי אֶל־יְהוָה וַיַּעֲנֵנִי
I called from my distress to the Lord, and he answered me. (Jon 2:2)
קוֹלִי אֶל־יְהוָה אֶקְרָא וַיַּעֲנֵנִי מֵהַר קָדְשׁוֹ
I called with my voice to the Lord, and he answered me from his holy hill. (Ps 3:4)
אֶל־יְהוָה בַּצָּרָתָה לִי קָרָאתִי וַיַּעֲנֵנִי
To the Lord I called in my distress, and he answered me. (Ps 120:1)

Claude Lichtert provides a thorough but not exhaustive list, which I adapt table 8.2 for English versification.[49]

---

[47] Chen, *Messianic Vision of the Pentateuch*, 124-30.
[48] Hermann Gunkel and Joachim Begrich, *Introduction to Psalms*, trans. James Nogalski (Macon, GA: Mercer University Press, 1998), 199-206; Claus Westermann, *Praise and Lament in the Psalms*, trans. Keith Crim and Richard Soulen (Atlanta: John Knox, 1981), 102-4.
[49] Claude Lichtert, "La Prière de Jonas (Jon 2)," *Studia Rhetorica Biblica et Semitica* 15 (2007): 15. See also Jonathan Magonet, *Form and Meaning: Studies in the Literary Techniques of the Book of Jonah* (Frankfurt: Lang, 1976), 44-49.

Table 8.2. Parallels between Jonah 2 and various psalms

Jon 2:2	Ps 18:6; 30:8; 31:22; 69:17; 86:6; 116:1; 118:5; 120:1; 130:2
Jon 2:3	Ps 42:7; 88:7, 17
Jon 2:4	Ps 5:7; 31:22; 138:2a
Jon 2:5a	Ps 18:4-5; 69:1b
Jon 2:5b-6b	
Jon 2:6c	Ps 16:10; 30:3; 71:20; 103:4
Jon 2:7	Ps 18:6; 42:6; 77:3, 11; 88:2a; 107:5; 143:5
Jon 2:8	Ps 31:6
Jon 2:9	Ps 3:8a; 22:25; 50:14, 23; 56:12; 66:13; 107:22; 116:17-18

Table 8.2 shows that almost all of Jonah 2:2-9 has a close parallel in the Psalms. For the blank concerning Jonah 2:5b-6b, I propose Psalm 18:7 ("the foundations of the mountains tremble") as a parallel to Jonah 2:6a ("I went down to the bases of the mountains"). Either way, it easier to understand Jonah 2 as dependent on these psalms, like 1 Chronicles 16:7-36, than the other way around.

A closer look at this list reveals that several psalms appear more than once. In particular, parts of Psalm 18:4-6 appear three times, paralleling Jonah 2:2, 5a, 7. Indeed, this Davidic psalm describes David being "surrounded" (סָבַב/אָפַף) by "cords of Sheol" (חֶבְלֵי שְׁאוֹל; Ps 18:4-5; see Jon 2:2 ["belly of Sheol"], 5 ["surrounded" by waters]) and "calling out" (קָרָא) to the Lord "in my distress" (בַּצַּר־לִי, Ps 18:6; see Jon 2:2), as well as the Lord hearing from "his temple" (Ps 18:6; see Jon 2:7) and bringing him out from "many waters" (Ps 18:15-16; see Jon 2:3, 5) to a "broad place"/"dry land" (Ps 18:19; see Jon 2:10). As in Jonah 2, death and the waters are closely intertwined in Psalm 18 (see "torrents of Belial," Ps 18:4; 2 Sam 22:5 also has "waves [מִשְׁבָּר] of death"; see "all your waves," Jon 2:3).[50] The form וַיֹּאמֶר ("and he said") appears in Jonah 2:2 and 2 Samuel 22:2/Psalm 18:1, where Psalm 18 is the only instance in the Psalter of "and he said" to introduce a psalm. Working with his own shorter list of parallels between

---

[50] P. Kyle McCarter Jr. takes "Belial" (בְּלִיַּעַל) as a "composite word" meaning "(place of) not-coming-up," which would reinforce the death/Sheol theme. McCarter, *II Samuel*, AB (New York: Doubleday, 1984), 373, 465. Regarding these themes in Jon 2, see Oancea, "Water and Death as Metaphors," 173-89.

Jonah 2 and the Psalms, Frank Cross sees the imagery in Jonah's psalm accordingly as "most closely" resembling 2 Samuel 22:5-7/Psalm 18:4-6.[51]

On the other hand, there are differences between Jonah 2 and Psalm 18, which include Jonah's actual rather than metaphorical drowning, different ordering of material, the absence of war imagery in Jonah 2 (see Ps 18:7-14), and Jonah's guilt (see David's innocence in Ps 18:20-25).[52] But a complete match is not necessary for intentionality, nor could it be coherently implemented in Jonah 2. Instead, strong resonances between the texts result in Jonah 2 taking on Davidic overtones in its canonical context, flanked on the one side by 2 Samuel 22 earlier in the Tanak and on the other side by Psalm 18 later in the Tanak. This gives Jonah 2 not only a psalmic feel but a specifically Davidic one. In 2 Samuel 22/Psalm 18, this Davidic element is even tied to the Davidic covenant through "David and his seed" and a "m/Messiah" at the end of each poem (2 Sam 22:51/Ps 18:50).

Jonah is of course a far cry from David, but his experience echoes David's, and he prays like David in 2 Samuel 22/Psalm 18 in one of the few poems in which David explicitly reflects on the Lord's faithfulness to the Davidic covenant and to his word (2 Sam 22:31/Ps 18:30, "the word of the Lord proves true"). Thus, for a reader attuned to 2 Samuel 22/Psalm 18, Jonah 2, though obviously not a Davidic psalm, still reads like one, such that the Exodus 1.5 of Jonah 2 also features a David-like voice.

Like Jonah 2, 2 Samuel 22/Psalm 18 also has links to the Song of the Sea, some of which concern deliverance from the waters while others concern war (e.g., "sea," "breath of his/your nostril[s]," "waters," "enemy," 2 Sam 22:16-18/Ps 18:15-17; see Ex 15:8-9). In addition to these, David speaking "to the Lord [לַיהוָה] the words of *this song*" (הַשִּׁירָה הַזֹּאת) in 2 Samuel 22:1 and the title of Psalm 18 connects to Moses and Israel

---

[51] Frank M. Cross, "Studies in the Structure of Hebrew Verse: The Prosody of the Psalm of Jonah," in *The Quest for the Kingdom of God: Studies in Honor of George Mendenhall*, ed. H. B. Huffmon, F. A. Spina, and A. R. W. Green (Winona Lake, IN: Eisenbrauns, 1983), 160. See also Jack Sasson, *Jonah*, AB (New York: Doubleday, 1990), 168-201 (under "Illustrative Passages").

[52] See Lichtert, "La Prière de Jonas," 15-16. Thomas Bolin notes parallels between Ps 18:4-7 and Jon 2:3-7 but ultimately emphasizes the different ordering of the cry for help and the description of threatening waters. Bolin, *Freedom Beyond Forgiveness: The Book of Jonah Re-Examined* (Sheffield: Sheffield Academic Press, 1997), 114. Hunter recognizes that the "river ordeal" is "particularly strong" in Ps 18; Ps 69; and Jon 2 but does not pursue it further ("Jonah from the Whale," 154).

singing "this song to the Lord" (הַשִּׁירָה הַזֹּאת לַיהוָה) in Exodus 15:1. Like Jonah, David speaks as though he were engulfed in the waters of death (2 Sam 22:5/Ps 18:4), and his being "drawn out" (מָשָׁה) of these "many waters" (מִמַּיִם רַבִּים) strongly links him to baby Moses being "drawn out" (מָשָׁה) by Pharaoh's daughter "from the waters" (מִן־הַמַּיִם) in Exodus 2:10. These are the only texts in the Old Testament with these characteristics, and David's connection to Moses is reinforced by his being called "the servant of the Lord" in the title of Psalm 18. Like Jonah and baby Moses (note "reed" [סוּף], in Ex 2:3, 5; 15:4; Jon 2:5), David's water experience was an individual experience with both similarities and differences to the exodus.

Several of the other psalms that appear more than once in Lichtert's list are also Davidic (Ps 30–31; 69). These receive attention as well from scholars in relation to Jonah 2.[53] Psalm 69 in particular emphasizes David's deliverance from waters (Ps 69:1-2, 14-15), and Kyle McCarter considers Psalm 69; Psalm 18; and Jonah 2 as "parade example[s]" of divine deliverance from the waters.[54] This gives additional support to the connection between Jonah 2 and Psalm 18. Resembling Jonah 2:2-9 in other ways, Psalm 3, the first Davidic psalm in the Psalter, has a call to the Lord, an answer from the temple, and dangers surrounding, and concludes with "salvation belongs to the Lord" (Ps 3:4, 6, 8). Other psalms, some Davidic and some not, have also been investigated by scholars.[55] Without denying connections to non-Davidic psalms, the evidence still supports Davidic

---

[53]For Ps 30, see Magonet, *Form and Meaning*, 45-46; Amanda Benckhuysen, "Revisiting the Psalm of Jonah," *Calvin Theological Journal* 47 (2012): 15-16. For Ps 31, see J. Henk Potgieter, "David in Consultation with the Prophets: The Intertextual Relationship of Psalm 31 with the Books of Jonah and Jeremiah," in *"My Spirit at Rest in the North Country" (Zechariah 6.8)*, ed. Hermann Michael Niemann and Matthias Augustin (Frankfurt: Lang, 2011), 159-61. Hunter deals with Ps 55 (Davidic); Ps 69; 107 (non-Davidic), among other OT texts ("Jonah from the Whale," 145-47, 157-58).

[54]P. Kyle McCarter, "The River Ordeal in Israelite Literature," *Harvard Theological Review* 66 (1973): 404. See also Stuart Lasine, who lists Ps 18; 22; 69; 88 as "the Psalms most often cited" with reference to Jon 2. Lasine, *Jonah and the Human Condition: Life and Death in Yahweh's World* (London: T&T Clark, 2020), 50.

[55]See Forti, who deals with Ps 8 (Davidic), Ps 104 (non-Davidic), and Ps 107 (non-Davidic; "Of Ships and Seas," 359-74); Stone, "Following the Church Fathers," 40-48. Oancea focuses on Ps 42; 69; and 88 because of his interest in water and death imagery ("Water and Death as Metaphors," 184-85).

overtones for Jonah 2. Though beyond the scope of the present argument, we could further inquire into the theme of deliverance from the waters in the Psalter (see Ps 38:4; 42:7; 107:23-30).[56]

The special connection between Jonah 2 and 2 Samuel 22/Psalm 18 leads to further reflection on these three texts. As mentioned above, 2 Samuel 22 and Jonah 2 both function strategically in the literary macro-structure of their respective books as poems embedded in narrative books. None of the parallels to other psalms feature this. Furthermore, like Jonah in Jonah 2, David in 2 Samuel 22 is presented in a much more positive light (2 Sam 22:21-25) than the preceding narrative (e.g., 2 Sam 11), and in the case of Psalm 18, than other psalms that refer to David's sins (e.g., Ps 32; 51). The idealization of Jonah and David in these two poems opens the door to their heightened theological significance. An ideal Davidic seed is the hope of the Davidic covenant and 1–2 Samuel (2 Sam 7:12-14; 2 Sam 23:3-5; Jer 30:9; Hos 3:5; see chapter six). Within 1–2 Samuel, the reference to the Lord's "faithfulness to his Messiah, to David and to his seed forever" (חֶסֶד לִמְשִׁיחוֹ לְדָוִד וּלְזַרְעוֹ עַד־עוֹלָם) in 2 Samuel 22:51 has the important function of tying the guiding light of Hannah's hope for the Lord's Messiah in 1 Samuel 2:10 to the Davidic covenant near the end of 1–2 Samuel (see "the Lord thunders [יַרְעֵם] from/in heaven," 2 Sam 22:14/Ps 18:13; 1 Sam 2:10; see also "you shatter them" [תְּרֹעֵם], Ps 2:9). In a similar way, the same phrase in Psalm 18:50 strategically reiterates themes of Messiah and Davidic covenant in Psalm 2:2, 7 set forth in the Psalter's introduction.[57]

Not only are Jonah and David presented differently in Jonah 2 and 2 Samuel 22, but so are hostile figures who were present in the preceding narrative. Just as the large fish in the preceding context of Jonah 2 is absent from the poem and recast as Sheol (Jon 2:1-2), so Saul, who is the enemy who provides the occasion for 2 Samuel 22 (2 Sam 22:1; see Ps 18 title), does

---

[56]Following those who study the Psalter as a book as in the seminal work by Gerald Wilson, *The Editing of the Hebrew Psalter* (Chico, CA: Scholars Press, 1985).

[57]For Ps 1–2 as introduction (not just Ps 1), see Robert L. Cole, *Psalms 1–2: Gateway to the Psalter* (Sheffield: Sheffield Phoenix Press, 2012), especially the bibliography on 1n1. Also see David Mitchell, *The Message of the Psalter: An Eschatological Programme in the Book of Psalms* (Newton Mearns, UK: Campbell, 2003), 73n19.

not appear in the poem, which refers to "enemies" (2 Sam 22:4; see 2 Sam 22:38, 41, 49), a vague "strong enemy" (2 Sam 22:18), "cords of death" (2 Sam 22:5-6), and threatening waters (2 Sam 22:5, 17). Moreover, "Saul" (שָׁאוּל) in 2 Samuel 22:1 and the title of Psalm 18 has the same consonantal form as "Sheol" (שְׁאוֹל) in 2 Samuel 22:6/Psalm 18:5 (שאול), raising the possibility of a wordplay that blurs the lines between Saul and Sheol, similar to the interplay between the large fish and Sheol in Jonah 2. Mitchell Dahood notices that the construction "from the hand of Saul" (מִיַּד שָׁאוּל) in the title of Psalm 18 ("palm of Saul" in 2 Sam 22:1) can be repointed as "from the hand of Sheol" (מִיַּד שְׁאוֹל), which is the same construction found in Hosea 13:14 discussed above.[58] Whereas Dahood actually advocates for this repointing and sees it as fitting the context of Psalm 18, I am content with the suitability of a wordplay here, especially in an unpointed text (see 1 Sam 1:28/1 Sam 2:6).

The result is that the Lord's historical deliverance of David from Saul in the title of 2 Samuel 22/Psalm 18 becomes linked to a perfect David's deliverance from death itself and the waters (see Jon 2). Given the overt reference to the Lord's faithfulness "to his Messiah, to David and his seed forever" in 2 Samuel 22:51/Psalm 18:50, the blamelessness of "David" in 2 Samuel 22:21-25/Psalm 18:20-24, and the messianic connections to 1 Samuel 2:10 and Psalm 2, 2 Samuel 22/Psalm 18 themselves at least have messianic overtones, if not being directly messianic. By extension, the similarity of Jonah 2 to 2 Samuel 22/Psalm 18 thus involves not only Davidic overtones but also messianic ones related to the deliverance of a perfect David from the waters.

CONCLUSION

In view of its intertextual relationships, the seemingly innocuous poem in Jonah 2 is revealed to be a nexus passage whose meaning is enhanced by

---

[58]Mitchell Dahood, *Psalms I: 1–50*, AB (Garden City, NY: Doubleday, 1966), 104: "The poet's delivery from Sheol forms the subject matter of vss. 4-7. In fact, rescue from the grasp of all his enemies and from the hand of Sheol fairly summarizes the contents of the entire poem." The ambiguity of שאול has also been discussed (and resolved) concerning a Second Temple ossuary lid inscription. See Philip Johnston, *Shades of Sheol: Death and the Afterlife in the Old Testament* (Downers Grove, IL: InterVarsity Press, 2002), 77. This wordplay on שאול was initially made known to me independently by Chris Chen.

these connections. This recalls how transfer stations are important parts of multiple subway lines (see introduction). In addition to playing a significant role in its own book, Jonah 2 is strongly linked to the Song of the Sea in Exodus 15:1-18, which suggests Jonah's experience of a sort of individual exodus. Furthermore, Jonah 2 fits into a broader second-exodus framework in the Twelve. Viewed in relation to the second-exodus promise in Hosea 13:14 of eschatological redemption "from the hand of Sheol," Jonah's deliverance from Sheol in Jonah 2:2, 10 provides an individualized, historical foretaste of this redemption. Moreover, the parallel between the Lord casting Jonah into the depth in Jonah 2:3 and the Lord casting Israel's iniquities into the depths in Micah 7:19, both times with salvific results, associates the drowning prophet with the eschatological putting away of sin. In the context of the Tanak, the many parallels between Jonah 2:2-9 and various psalms, especially Davidic psalms such as Psalm 18/2 Samuel 22, further result in Jonah's prayer taking on Davidic, even messianic, overtones.

Taken together, these considerations suggest Jonah 2 involves a Davidish figure whose casting into the waters is a sort of Exodus 1.5 that has intriguing parallels to the Messiah, who also experiences an exodus (Num 24:8) and gives himself up for the salvation of others (Gen 3:15).

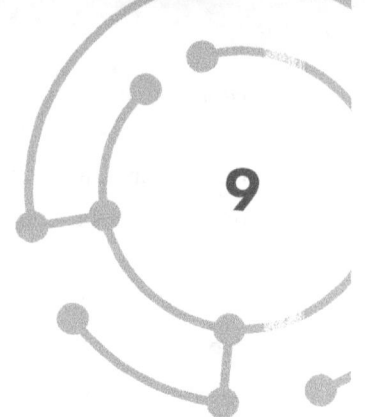

9

PSALM 72

A MESSIANIC PEAK IN THE MIDDLE OF THE PSALTER

THE PRECEDING REPRESENTATIVE NEXUS PASSAGES from the Law and the Prophets show how such texts exhibit the literary, textual, and theological, even Christocentric, unity of the Old Testament. As the last major section in the Tanak, the Writings has nexus passages of its own, especially in the Psalter. This should not be surprising given its manifold connections to the rest of the Old Testament, as poignantly captured by Martin Luther's characterization of it as "a little Bible," since "in it is comprehended most beautifully and briefly everything that is in the entire Bible."[1] Indeed, there are multiple nexus passages in the Psalter (e.g., Ps 1; 2; 18; 89), and I have already dealt with one elsewhere (Ps 110).[2]

Led by Gerald Wilson and carried forward in various ways by others, the study of the Psalter as a book seeks meaning in its five-book structure, arrangement of individual psalms, and internal relationships between psalms.[3] In the case of Psalm 72, this approach is particularly meaningful because Psalm 72 concludes Book II (Ps 42–72) as a seam psalm and is even punctuated by the macrostructural comment, "The prayers of David son of Jesse are concluded" (Ps 72:20). As Wilson points out, royal and

---

[1] Martin Luther, "Preface to the Psalter," in *Luther's Works* (Philadelphia: Fortress, 1960), 35:254.
[2] Kevin Chen, "Psalm 110: A Nexus for Old Testament Theology," *CTR* 17, no. 2 (2020): 49-65.
[3] Gerald Wilson, *The Editing of the Hebrew Psalter* (Chico, CA: Scholars Press, 1985). For a recent survey of this broader approach, see David Howard Jr., and Michael Snearly, "Reading the Psalter as a Unified Book: Recent Trends," in *Reading the Psalms Theologically*, ed. David Howard Jr. and Andrew Schmutzer (Bellingham, WA: Lexham, 2023), 1-35.

Davidic covenant themes link Psalm 72 with Psalm 2 and Psalm 89, which are also strategically located at the Psalter's seams.[4] Unlike Wilson, my interpretation of Psalm 72, which involves allusions to the Pentateuch and 2 Samuel, is that this psalm, in itself and in the context of the final form of the Psalter, expresses the hope that the Abrahamic and Davidic covenants as well as the creation ideal will be fulfilled in the Messiah.

ENGAGING GERALD WILSON'S VIEW OF PSALM 72 IN THE PSALTER

Besides the status of Psalm 72 as a seam psalm, Wilson's understanding of its role in the Psalter flows out of his views of the Psalter's compositional history, the meaning of Psalm 89, and the introduction to the Psalter being Psalm 1 alone.[5] For Wilson, Psalms 2 and 89 "bracket the whole of Books One–Three at beginning and end." At the same time, Psalm 72:20 "suggests that Books One and Two may have combined to form an earlier collection introduced and concluded by 'Royal' pss [i.e., Ps 2; 72]." The reference to "the prayers of David" in this verse is in keeping with the predominance of Davidic psalms in Books I-II. The frequent mention of David, the reference to Solomon in the title of Psalm 72, and optimism concerning the Davidic covenant leads Wilson to see Psalms 2–72 as "a celebration of YHWH's faithfulness to the covenant which found its fullest expression during the united monarchy under these two kings." In particular, Psalm 2 begins Book I by proclaiming the Davidic covenant (Ps 2:7), Psalm 41 closes Book I with David being assured of the Lord's protection (Ps 41:1-2, 11-12), and Psalm 72 involves the Davidic covenant being passed to David's descendants, specifically Solomon.[6]

For Wilson, there is an important "progression in thought" and a "new perspective" with Psalm 89, the conclusion of Book III (Ps 73–89). Namely, "The Davidic covenant introduced in Ps 2 has come to nothing and the combination of three books [Books I–III] concludes with the anguished

---
[4]Wilson, *Editing of the Hebrew Psalter*, 207-14.
[5]For Ps 1 as introduction, see Wilson, *Editing of the Hebrew Psalter*, 204-7.
[6]Wilson, *Editing of the Hebrew Psalter*, 208-11. For a different explanation of Ps 72:20, see Mitchell, *Message of the Psalter*, 66-70.

cry of the Davidic descendants."⁷ Books I–III thus involve "the institution (Psalm 2), the transmission (Psalm 72), and the failure (Psalm 89) of the Davidic covenant."⁸ Book IV (Ps 90–106), which Wilson sees as "the editorial 'center' of the final form of the Hebrew Psalter," answers Psalm 89 and Books I–III by declaring the kingship of Yahweh, his being Israel's refuge before the monarchy, his continuing availability as a refuge, and the blessedness of those who take refuge in him.⁹ Drawing on manuscript evidence from Qumran, he argues that Books I–III and Books IV–V are "two segments of the Psalter . . . representing two significantly different periods of redaction."¹⁰

The key psalm for Wilson in Books I–III is thus Psalm 89, which gives the last word for this part of the Psalter (Ps 2–89). Whereas Psalms 2; 41; 72 celebrate the Lord's faithfulness to the Davidic covenant during the reigns of David and Solomon, Psalm 89 views this covenant "as established in the dim past" and "as broken, failed."¹¹ In other words, times have changed. In Wilson's understanding of the Psalter, Psalm 89 has effectively canceled out Psalms 2; 41; 72 with their hope that the Davidic covenant will be fulfilled. Their declarations, confidence, and prayers have been largely left behind as historical records of hopes once held in the "progression in thought" that Psalm 89 represents.

Several issues arise with such a construal. If Psalm 2 is also part of the introduction to the Psalter, as many believe, then its strong affirmation of the Davidic covenant is part of the central message of the entire Psalter, not just Books I–II.¹² As such, the Lord's declaration that his "son" need only ask and he will receive "the nations" and "the ends of the earth" as his

---

⁷Wilson, *Editing of the Hebrew Psalter*, 209, 212-13.
⁸Gerald Wilson, "Shaping the Psalter: A Consideration of Editorial Linkage in the Book of Psalms," in *Shape and Shaping of the Psalter*, ed. J. Clinton McCann (Sheffield: Sheffield Academic Press, 1993), 78.
⁹Wilson, *Editing of the Hebrew Psalter*, 215.
¹⁰Gerald Wilson, "King, Messiah, and the Reign of God: Revisiting the Royal Psalms and the Shape of the Psalter," in *The Book of Psalms: Composition and Reception*, ed. Peter Flint and Patrick Miller (Leiden: Brill, 2005), 393.
¹¹Wilson, *Editing of the Hebrew Psalter*, 212-13.
¹²E.g., Robert Cole, "An Integrated Reading of Psalms 1 and 2," *JSOT* 26 (2002): 75-88; Cole, *Psalms 1–2: Gateway to the Psalter* (Sheffield: Sheffield Phoenix Press, 2013), 79-141.

possession (Ps 2:2, 7-8) is a divine promise that cannot be overridden, not even by Wilson's proposed interpretation of Psalm 89. Furthermore, since this promised rule far exceeds that of any preexilic Davidic king, Psalm 2 can rightfully be interpreted as a messianic psalm.[13] Brevard Childs further points out that at the time the Psalter came together as a book, "when the institution of kingship had long since been destroyed, what earthly king would have come [to] mind other than God's Messiah?"[14] The crucial role of Psalm 2 as part of the Psalter's introduction and its assumption that the Davidic covenant endures elevates the standing of Psalm 72 along with it. Rather than being overridden, Psalm 72 stands alongside Psalm 2 as a significant exposition of the Psalter's messianic theology. Whether viewed in itself or in the final form of the Psalter, its prayers for the fulfillment of the Davidic covenant will be answered and thus inform our understanding of the glory of the messianic kingdom.

The enduring validity of the Davidic covenant also mitigates the progression in thought Wilson proposes in connection with Psalm 89. Likewise, even if Books I–II were once an earlier collection, the continuance of the Davidic covenant prevents a strong disjuncture with Book III based on differing perceptions of this covenant, even granting the crisis of exile in Psalm 89. Clinton McCann relatedly shows that the problems of exile and dispersion, which Wilson sees Books IV and V as answering, are already being faced in Psalms 2; 42–44; and 73–74 (the beginnings of Books I–III).[15]

Whereas McCann builds on Wilson's proposal and accordingly sees these beginnings of Books I–III as achieving a "reorientation beyond the traditional grounds of hope, that is, beyond the Davidic/Zion covenant theology," Psalm 2 reads more like a synthesis that affirms the traditional Davidic covenant in spite of serious opposition from the nations.[16] Thus,

---

[13]See David C. Mitchell, *The Message of the Psalter: An Eschatological Programme in the Book of the Psalms* (Newton Mearns, UK: Campbell, 2003), 85-86.
[14]Brevard Childs, *Introduction to the Old Testament as Scripture* (Philadelphia: Fortress, 1979), 516.
[15]J. Clinton McCann, "Books I–III and the Editorial Purpose of the Hebrew Psalter," in McCann, *Shape and Shaping of the Psalter*, 93-107.
[16]McCann, "Books I–III and the Editorial Purpose," 95.

Psalm 2 and its guiding vision of the reign of the Lord and his Messiah over the nations is more of a hermeneutical key to the Psalter than Psalm 89, as important as Psalm 89 still is. The nations' challenge to the Davidic covenant and their ultimate failure are already depicted in Psalm 2 such that the destruction and reproach they bring in Psalm 89 (Ps 89:40-43, 50-51; see Deut 32:27, 30) fit within this broader framework that upholds the Davidic covenant.[17] Even though the rendition of the Davidic covenant in Psalm 2 involving worldwide Gentile resistance cannot be grounded fully in 2 Samuel 7 in isolation, it does accord with the Pentateuch's seminal prediction of the messianic Lion of Judah's coming "in the last days" (Gen 49:1, 8-12; Num 24:14, 17-19; Deut 4:30 [exile]; 31:29 [exile]). Second Samuel 7 should be set within this foundational framework also, such that its prediction of an everlasting kingdom for a future Davidic king is the outgrowth of the earlier promise concerning David's tribe, Judah, in Genesis 49:1, 8-12.

Furthermore, if Psalm 2 is part of the introduction to the Psalter along with Psalm 1, then the Psalter has a wisdom-Messiah frame, not simply a "wisdom frame" that Wilson roots in Psalm 1 and other key wisdom psalms/texts (Ps 73; 90:11-12; 107:42-43; 145:19-20) and that wins out over a "royal covenantal frame" in the final form of the Psalter.[18] As Jamie Grant points out, the combination of a Torah psalm with one or more royal psalms is set forth in Psalms 1–2; 18–21; 118–119.[19] He sees this combination as rooted in the law of the king in Deuteronomy 17:14-20, which calls for the king's devotion to Scripture. When the combination of these two psalm types is considered as a *wisdom* psalm with a royal/messianic psalm, another result is that it also appears in Psalms 72–73 and Psalms 89–90 (with lament elements also appearing in both types of psalms), thus fully constituting two macrostructural seams in the Psalter and binding Books II and III together as well as Books III and IV.[20]

---

[17]Robert Cole, *The Shape and Message of Book III (Psalms 73–89)* (Sheffield: Sheffield Academic Press, 2000), 208; see also Mitchell, *Message of the Psalter*, 87.
[18]Wilson, "Shaping the Psalter," 79-81.
[19]Jamie Grant, *The King as Exemplar: The Function of Deuteronomy's Kingship Law in the Shaping of the Book of Psalms* (Atlanta: Society of Biblical Literature, 2004), 1-5.
[20]See David Howard Jr., *The Structure of Psalms 93–100* (Winona Lake, IN: Eisenbrauns, 1997), 203.

Since Psalms 18–21 are in Book I and Psalms 118–119 are in Book V, the wisdom-Messiah frame of the Psalter's introduction has thus shaped all five books of the Psalter and is central to its compositional and theological unity through its presence in the introduction (leading directly into Book I) and seams spanning Books II–IV. The wisdom-royal/messianic psalm combination also appears in Psalms 144–145 (Book V), and Michael Snearly further points out links between Psalms 1–2 and the Psalter's conclusion in Psalms 146–150 (untitled psalms, movement from individual to communal, and lexical and thematic connections, e.g., king and Zion [Ps 2:6; 146:10; 149:2], final judgment [Ps 1:4-6; 2:9, 12; 146:4; 147:6; 149:7-9]).[21]

On the canonical level, another significant result is that the wisdom-Messiah frame in the Psalter is the same kind of frame that John Sailhamer argues for in the seams of the Tanak (Deut 34:10/Josh 1:8; Mal 4:4-6/ Ps 1:2; see also 2 Chron 36:23).[22] Maybe Psalm 2 should also be considered as part of the canonical seam involving Psalm 1 (since the Psalter's introduction is not just Ps 1), but either way, this matched framing gives us a uniquely compositional way of seeing the Psalter as a "little [Hebrew] Bible." This raises questions about the relationship between the final authors of the Psalter and the Tanak, but I will not pursue this here.

A related issue is Wilson's claim Psalm 89 that describes a "broken, failed" Davidic covenant. David Howard and Michael Snearly further link Wilson's view here to subsequent wisdom or democratizing approaches (e.g., Erich Zenger) that claim that "all the roles, actions, and functions attributed to the royal figure in the Psalms ultimately are applied to the people of God at large," such that they, not the Messiah, usher in God's kingdom.[23] While granting the importance of the Lord's reign (e.g., Ps 93–100; 145), wisdom (e.g., Ps 1), and similarities between king and people in the Psalter, I find this kind of democratization of the Davidic covenant problematic theologically, whether proposed for the Psalter or

---

[21] Michael Snearly, *The Return of the King: Messianic Expectation in Book V of the Psalter* (New York: T&T Clark, 2016), 178-81; see also Cole, *Psalms 1–2*, 82.
[22] John Sailhamer, "The Messiah and the Hebrew Bible," *JETS* 44 (2001): 12; Sailhamer, *Introduction to Old Testament Theology: A Canonical Approach* (Grand Rapids, MI: Zondervan, 1995), 239-49.
[23] Howard and Snearly, "Reading the Psalter," 5-6.

Isaiah 40–55 (see chapter seven). This kind of democratization is in fact a substantive change to the expected fulfillment of the Davidic covenant as originally instituted (2 Sam 7:12-16). As such, it impugns the Lord's faithfulness to his word and the reliability of his word. As Numbers 23:19 says, "God is not a man that he would lie, nor a son of man that he would change his mind. Will he speak and not act? Will he speak and not establish it?"

Contra Wilson, McCann, and others, Howard insists that "the Davidic kingdom and YHWH's kingdom coexist in complementary roles throughout the Psalter." He continues, "The placement of royal psalms, along with other considerations, are evidence in the Psalter of a continuing hope that is focused on both Zion and the Davidic covenant, despite the many flaws of the kings and people who were heirs of that covenant." As for Psalm 89, he explains that the people failed, not the Davidic covenant, and "thus the Davidic Covenant has of necessity taken a back seat historically (and in the Psalter) for a time . . . but it does not completely disappear."[24] William Pohl IV similarly explains that the failure of the Davidic covenant is only apparent, pertaining to the temporary fall of the Davidic dynasty through exile.[25]

Psalm 89 itself celebrates the Lord's "steadfast love" and "faithfulness" (Ps 89:1-2) with respect to the Davidic covenant (Ps 89:3-4), which will stand even if Davidic kings rebel (Ps 89:33-37).[26] Even though the fall of the Davidic dynasty was all too real (Ps 89:38-45), the prayer, "Where are your former mercies, Lord, which you swore to David in faithfulness?" (Ps 89:49), seems to assume the continuing validity of the Davidic covenant in appealing for its fulfillment.[27] Moreover, "your enemies" (אוֹיְבֶיךָ) reproaching "the heels of your messiah" (עִקְּבוֹת מְשִׁיחֶךָ) at the end of the psalm

---

[24]Howard, *Structure of Psalms 93–100*, 201-2, 205; see also Grant, *King as Exemplar*, 26, 34.
[25]William Pohl IV, "A Messianic Reading of Psalm 89: A Canonical and Intertextual Study," *JETS* 58 (2015): 507-25.
[26]Knut Heim, "The (God-)Forsaken King of Psalm 89: A Historical and Intertextual Enquiry," in *King and Messiah in Israel and the Ancient Near East*, ed. John Day (Sheffield: Sheffield Academic Press, 1998), 300: "In Psalm 89 the Davidic promise/covenant remains *unconditional*, and it introduces legal covenant terminology to emphasize the *immutable certainty* of this unconditional and perpetual promise [Ps 89:30-34]."
[27]See Heim, "(God-)Forsaken King of Psalm 89," 303, 305-6; Pohl, "Messianic Reading of Psalm 89," 514-15.

(Ps 89:51) has strong resonances with "enmity," "seed," and "strike his heel" in Genesis 3:15 (see divine wrath, Adam/humanity, death, and exile[/fall] in Ps 89:46-48). Psalm 89:51 thus seems to draw together the sufferings of the Davidic house and those of the seed of the woman in pleading for the messianic seed to come (see 2 Sam 7:12-16; Ps 2:6-9). In addition to the Davidic covenant, there is the even older promise in which it is rooted, Genesis 3:15. In any case, if the Davidic covenant has not really failed in Psalm 89, then the manner in which Books IV–V answer Books I–III cannot be exactly what Wilson believes it to be. Books IV–V still encourage readers with the Lord's kingship unto wise living but all the while maintaining hope in the Davidic covenant and its messianic fulfillment.

THE MESSIANIC KINGDOM IN PSALM 72

Although Psalm 72 has its own literary unity, its dense intertextuality suggests that it cannot be understood properly in isolation from other texts.[28] In response to Zenger's view that concentrated intertextuality can be found only in Psalm 72:8-11, 15, 17cd, Gianni Barbiero shows that intertextuality is actually "a characteristic of every verse of Psalm 72."[29] Many of the texts Barbiero cites come from other psalms, Isaiah, and the Pentateuch, with a few other important ones coming from Samuel, Micah, and Zechariah. The discussion below treats what I believe to be the most important examples.

The first matter that deserves attention is the title of Psalm 72, "Of/For Solomon" (לִשְׁלֹמֹה). Along with Psalm 127, it is one of two Solomonic psalms and explicit references to Solomon in the Psalter. The prayer for "the son of a king" in Psalm 72:1 and "the prayers of David" in Psalm 72:20 could suggest a prayer by David on behalf of Solomon (see LXX title; 1 Kings 2:2-4; 1 Chron 22:13; 28:7-9). Another possibility is that Solomon

---

[28]See Knut Heim, "The Perfect King of Psalm 72: An 'Intertextual' Inquiry," in *The Lord's Anointed: Interpretation of Old Testament Messianic Texts*, ed. P. E. Satterthwaite et al. (Grand Rapids, MI: Baker, 1995), 231-33.

[29]Gianni Barbiero, "The Risks of a Fragmented Reading of the Psalms: Psalm 72 as a Case in Point," ZAW 120 (2008): 71, 81-82, which includes helpful tables. See also Erich Zenger and Frank-Lothar Hossfeld, *Psalms 2: A Commentary on Psalms 51–100*, trans. Linda Maloney (Minneapolis: Fortress, 2005), 208.

is the author of the psalm. Either way, the prayers for the glorious fulfillment of the Davidic covenant suggest a messianic fulfillment, especially in the final form of the Psalter, when the Davidic dynasty was no more.[30]

The opening request that God give "your judgments" (מִשְׁפָּטֶיךָ) and "your righteousness" (צִדְקָתְךָ) to this king (Ps 72:1), and the prayer that this king judge "with righteousness" and "with justice" (Ps 72:2), associate the Lord's perfectly just rule with this king (Ps 89:14; 99:4; 103:6). Whereas the earlier part of David's rule was characterized by justice and righteousness (2 Sam 8:15) and Solomon's entire reign should have been also (1 Kings 10:9; see 1 Kings 3:9), this standard will be met only by the messianic king who brings a "peace" (שָׁלוֹם) with "no end" (אֵין־קֵץ) and sits on David's throne "with justice and with righteousness from now until forever" (Is 9:7; see also Jer 23:5-6). The pairing of justice and righteousness can be traced back to the Abrahamic covenant in Genesis 18:18-19, which links the nations being "blessed in him" (see Ps 72:17) to Abraham "command[ing] his sons and his house . . . to do righteousness and justice." As for peace, Psalm 72:3 continues accordingly with a prayer that "the mountains bear *peace* [שָׁלוֹם] for the people" as a result of the king's righteous rule, and Psalm 72:7 with a prayer that there be "great *peace* [שָׁלוֹם] until the moon is no more" (see the association of "Solomon" and "peace" in 1 Chron 22:9).

As many note, the king's just rule in Psalm 72 is repeatedly shown through his treatment of the poor. At the same time, the first reference to this group is simply "your people" in Psalm 72:2a (עַמְּךָ), an important parallel descriptor. Psalm 72:2b prays that the king will "judge your poor/afflicted [עֲנִיֶּיךָ] with justice," and Psalm 72:4 likewise, "May he judge the poor/afflicted of the people [עֲנִיֵּי־עָם], may he save the children of the needy [אֶבְיוֹן], and crush the oppressor." The homage that he receives in Psalm 72:9-11 is because he "delivers the needy [אֶבְיוֹן] who cries out and the poor/afflicted [עָנִי] who has no one helping him" (Ps 72:12). He "takes pity" (חוּס) on the "weak" (דַּל) and "redeems" (גָּאַל) them from "violence"

---

[30]Heim, "Perfect King of Psalm 72," 235.

(חָמָס) since he sees them and values their lives (Ps 72:13-14). In Psalm 41:1, David had pronounced a blessing on "the one who considers the weak" (דָּל). Noting the connection between Psalm 72:2-4, 8 and Zion's future king in Zechariah 9:9-10, Zenger and Hossfeld explain that this figure "can become the judge = savior of the poor of YHWH because he himself is poor [עָנִי], and he can rescue because he himself has experienced rescue."[31] Isaiah 11:4 and 61:1 also describe the Messiah's salvation of the poor.[32]

Although several psalms characterize David as "poor/afflicted" and "needy" (עָנִי וְאֶבְיוֹן, Ps 40:17; see also Ps 9:13; 22:24; 35:10), this David only partially represents the historical David. The prophet Nathan's parable in 2 Samuel 12:1-7 about David's sins against Bathsheba and Uriah equates David instead with a rich man who oppresses a poor man. The just rule and deliverance of the needy depicted in Psalm 72 also contrasts with Solomon, who laid "hard service" (עֲבֹדָה קָשָׁה) and a "heavy [כָּבֵד] yoke" on the people (1 Kings 12:4) and used "forced labor" (מַס; 1 Kings 4:6; 5:13-14; 9:15, 21; 12:18). Unlike the liberator of Psalm 72:2, 4, 12-14, Solomon in 1 Kings is instead like Pharaoh who enslaved Israel long ago (Ex 1:11, 14; 5:9; 6:9).[33]

When seen against the background of the Davidic covenant, the prayer in Psalm 72:5, "May they fear you with the sun [שֶׁמֶשׁ] and before the moon [יָרֵחַ], throughout all generations," need not be taken as hyperbole or a generic wish for a king's long life but instead the fulfillment of the specific promise of an eternal king and kingdom (2 Sam 7:12-16; see "until the moon [יָרֵחַ] is no more," Ps 72:7; Gen 1:16).[34] Knut Heim points out the parallel descriptions of the Davidic covenant in Psalm 89:29, 36-37, "I will establish his seed forever and his throne *like the days of the heavens*. . . .

---

[31]Zenger and Hossfeld, *Psalms 2*, 214-15.
[32]Barbiero also lists Prov 31:1-9, a suggestive example at the conclusion of Proverbs ("Risks of a Fragmented Reading," 82).
[33]For negative appraisals of Solomon in 1 Kings, see Jerome Walsh, *1 Kings*, Berit Olam (Collegeville, MN: Liturgical Press, 1996), 65-68, 76-77, 89-90, 98-99, 115-16, 130-32, 137-38; J. Daniel Hays, "Has the Narrator Come to Praise Solomon or to Bury Him? Narrative Subtlety in 1 Kings 1–11," *JSOT* 28 (2003): 149-74.
[34]See Cole, *Shape and Message of Book III*, 17n5. For the translation difficulty concerning "with the sun and before the moon," see Zenger and Hossfeld, *Psalms 2*, 203.

His throne will be *like the sun* [שֶׁמֶשׁ] before me. *Like the moon* [יָרֵחַ] it will be established forever."[35]

The fear of this king in Psalm 72:5 echoes the call to kings to "serve the Lord with fear" and "kiss the son" in Psalm 2:11-12. The continuous reverence for this messianic king in terms of sun and moon in Psalm 72:5 further recalls the righteous person's meditation on Scripture "day and night" in Psalm 1:2. Robert Cole points out additional links between Psalms 1–2 and Psalm 72 (e.g., "ends of the earth," Ps 2:8/Ps 72:8; "kings"/"nations," Ps 2:1-2/Ps 72:11; "his fruit," Ps 1:3/Ps 72:16; "blessed," Ps 1:1/Ps 2:12/Ps 72:17; "in him," Ps 2:12/Ps 72:17) and explains, "Psalm 72 reiterates and confirms the eventual fulfillment of promises and commands made in Psalm 2." Furthermore, these parallels "reveal a predominant focus on the Davidic covenant and through it the restoration of creation."[36]

Related to this restoration, the prayer in Psalm 72:6 that this king "descend like rain [כְּמָטָר] on mown grass, like showers that water the earth [אָרֶץ]" alludes to the messianic imagery in 2 Samuel 23:3-4.[37] This poetic "oracle of David" (2 Sam 23:1) on the one hand combines with the poems in 1 Samuel 2:1-10 and 2 Samuel 22:1-51 in the macrostructure of 1–2 Samuel, and on the other hand harks back to Balaam's messianic oracles beginning in Numbers 24:3, 15 ("oracle of *x* son of *y*, and the oracle of the man"). Peter Ho also draws a connection between "the last words of David . . . son of Jesse" in 2 Samuel 23:1 and "The prayers of David son of Jesse have ended" in Psalm 72:20.[38] Speaking by "the Spirit of the Lord" (2 Sam 23:2; see also Num 24:2), the aged king David speaks of a "righteous" (צַדִּיק) ruler over "humanity" (אָדָם) who "rules in the fear of God" (מוֹשֵׁל יִרְאַת אֱלֹהִים) and how this person is like a sunrise on a clear day "after *rain* that brings *grass* from the *earth*" (מִמָּטָר דֶּשֶׁא מֵאָרֶץ, 2 Sam 23:3-4; see also Deut 32:2; Hos 6:3). As in Psalm 72:6, the imagery of rain nourishing grass depicts the blessings of the messianic kingdom. That this king "descends" (יָרַד) in Psalm 72:6 ("may

---

[35] Heim, "Perfect King of Psalm 72," 240n39. Similarly, Cole, *Shape and Message of Book III*, 179, 202.
[36] Cole, *Psalms 1–2*, 85-86.
[37] See Barbiero, "Risks of a Fragmented Reading," 82.
[38] Peter C. W. Ho, *The Design of the Psalter: A Macrostructural Analysis* (Eugene, OR: Pickwick, 2019), 227-28.

he descend [יֵרֵד] like rain," not "may he be [יְהִי] like rain that descends"; see 1 Sam 25:26; Job 27:7), presumably from above, hints at his heavenly origin, as in Psalm 2:7 and Psalm 109:3 LXX (=110:3 MT)("I have begotten you"). There also seems to be an echo of the messianic precipitation in Genesis 27:28 ("may God give you dew from heaven") and a parallel to the Lord's saving word in Isaiah 55:10-11 that descends like rain and does its work.

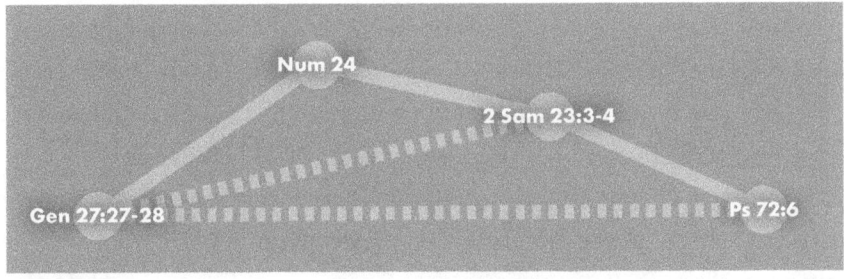

Figure 9.1. Nexus connections to Psalm 72:6 (dotted line indicates echo)

After referring to the Davidic covenant as "an everlasting covenant," 2 Samuel 23:5-7 continues with agrarian language reminiscent of the themes of Eden and the fall ("sprout" [צֶמַח], 2 Sam 23:5; "thorns [קוֹץ]," 2 Sam 23:6; see Gen 2:9; 3:18). Accordingly, in contrast with the "ground" once cursed and so affecting "all the days of your [= Adam's] life" (Gen 3:17), Psalm 72:7 follows the prayer for messianic rainfall with a prayer for its result, "May the righteous flourish in his days, and abundant peace [רֹב שָׁלוֹם] until the moon is no more." The term for "flourish" (פָּרַח) is often used of plant life sprouting (Is 35:1-2) and is applied metaphorically here (see Ps 92:7, 12-13; Is 27:6). Unlike the temporary "peace" (שָׁלוֹם) that Solomon (שְׁלֹמֹה) brought (see "peace" in Hezekiah's "days," 2 Kings 20:19/Is 39:8), the Messiah brings great peace "in his days" (Ps 72:7), that is, forevermore (see Is 9:6-7; Jer 23:5-6).

As Zenger and Hossfeld emphasize, Psalm 72:5-7 depicts the king as mediator of divine blessing whose reign brings life both to his people (especially the oppressed) and to creation itself.[39] Bernard Renaud also

---

[39]Zenger and Hossfeld, *Psalms 2*, 215.

points out the four instances of "bless" (בָּרַךְ) in this psalm (Ps 72:15, 17-19), which include both people blessing the king (Ps 72:15) and being blessed by the king (Ps 72:17).[40] To this already high number can be added the related term for "bless" (אָשַׁר) in Psalm 72:17 ("they will bless him"; see Ps 41:3). The line "Let them be blessed in him; all nations will bless him" (וְיִתְבָּרְכוּ בוֹ כָּל־גּוֹיִם יְאַשְּׁרוּהוּ) in Psalm 72:17 has been recognized as a strong link to the Abrahamic covenant in Genesis 22:18, "All the nations of the earth will be blessed in your seed" (וְהִתְבָּרְכוּ בְזַרְעֲךָ כֹּל גּוֹיֵי הָאָרֶץ; see also Gen 18:18).[41] This bond is strengthened further by people also blessing the king in Psalm 72:15, since the Abrahamic covenant regularly mentions the bidirectionality of humanity blessing Abraham/his seed and being blessed as a result (Gen 12:3; 27:29; Num 24:9).

I argued in chapter four that these Abrahamic covenant texts concern a messianic king "in the last days" (Gen 49:1; Num 24:14) from the perspective of the Pentateuch itself, and Psalm 72 confirms this while also drawing in the messianic fulfillment of the Davidic covenant. From the perspective of Psalm 72, the "him" who is being blessed in Psalm 72:15 and by whom the nations are blessed in Psalm 72:17 is the righteous Davidic king who fulfills the Abrahamic and the Davidic covenants. From its inception in 2 Samuel 7, the Davidic covenant was rooted in the Abrahamic covenant (see chapter six), and one common element carries over into Psalm 72. Just as Abraham and David were promised a great "name" (שֵׁם; Gen 12:2; 2 Sam 7:9), so Psalm 72:17 prays concerning the perfect king, "Let his name endure forever." Even the corresponding praise of the Lord's name in Psalm 72:19 aligns with 2 Samuel 7:26 (see 2 Sam 7:13, 23). The convergence of these major Old Testament themes of Abrahamic covenant, Davidic covenant, and Messiah in these texts (Ps 72 has creation themes also) demonstrates again how nexus passages leverage literary and textual unity for theological unity centered on the eschatological Messiah. It also shows again how nexus passages themselves are often interconnected.

---

[40]Bernard Renaud, "De la bénédiction du roi à la bénédiction de Dieu (Ps 72)," *Biblica* 70 (1989): 305-6. Ps 72:15 is difficult, but translations and commentators tend to understand the prayers and blessings in Ps 72:15b as offered for/to the king as object of these verbs, not as subject.

[41]E.g., Zenger and Hossfeld, *Psalms 2*, 218; Sailhamer, *Meaning of the Pentateuch*, 499, 502.

The prayer in Psalm 72:8 continues with additional significant allusions, "May he rule from sea to sea, and from the river to the ends of the earth" (וְיֵרְדְּ מִיָּם עַד־יָם וּמִנָּהָר עַד־אַפְסֵי־אָרֶץ). The verb "rule" (רָדָה) in this form (וְיֵרְדְּ) is found in only one other Old Testament text, Numbers 24:19, which says of the eschatological, royal "star from Jacob" (Num 24:14, 17), "May he rule from Jacob" (וְיֵרְדְּ מִיַּעֲקֹב). As pointed out in chapter four, "rule" (רָדָה) in Numbers 24:19 itself alludes to the same verb in Genesis 1:26, 28 such that the star fulfills God's command at creation that humanity rule. The king's worldwide rule in Psalm 72:8 also matches the star's rule over Israel and other peoples in Numbers 24:17-18. Edom and Seir in Numbers 24:18 ("Edom will be a possession, and Seir, his enemies will be a possession") not only refer to an ancient people but could even represent the nations in the original context of Balaam's oracle. As argued in chapter four, "Edom" (אֱדוֹם) here represents "humanity" (אָדָם; see Amos 9:12; Obadiah; "sons of Seth" in Num 24:17), and "Seir, his enemies" plays off "the gate of his enemies" in Genesis 22:17 (who could be from anywhere). Thus, the king's worldwide rule in Psalm 72:8 matches Numbers 24:18, and Psalm 72:8 seems to skillfully draw on Numbers 24:17-19.

At the same time, Heim notes the parallels between the king's rule "from sea to sea, and from the river to the ends of the earth" in Psalm 72:8 and the description of the borders of the Promised Land in Exodus 23:31, "I will set your border from the Sea of Reeds [מִיַּם־סוּף] to the Sea of the Philistines [וְעַד־יָם פְּלִשְׁתִּים], and from the wilderness to the river [עַד־הַנָּהָר]."[42] Although Heim interprets Psalm 72:8 in its original preexilic setting as "hyperbolic poetic imagery" based on Exodus 23:31, some texts within the Pentateuch itself hint that the land promise potentially included the whole world (Gen 13:14-18; 26:3). Zenger and Hossfeld mention Genesis 15:18, "To your seed I give this land, from the river of Egypt to the great river, the Euphrates," in connection with Psalm 72:17 ("let [the nations] be blessed in him") and its allusion to Abrahamic covenant texts involving the nations (Gen 12:1-3; 22:18; 28:14).[43] Thus, in

---
[42]Heim, "Perfect King of Psalm 72," 244-46.
[43]Zenger and Hossfeld, *Psalms 2*, 215.

addition to drawing on Numbers 24:17-19, Psalm 72:8 seems to use the language of Genesis 15:18 and/or Exodus 23:31.

The clearest nexus connection to Psalm 72:8 is to Zechariah 9:10, "His rule will be from sea to sea and from the river to the ends of the earth," which differs from the corresponding line in Psalm 72:8 by only one word ("his rule" [וּמָשְׁלוֹ] instead of "may he rule" [וְיֵרְדְּ]). Coming from a postexilic book, the prophecy of Jerusalem's coming king riding on a donkey in Zechariah 9:9-10 is a messianic prophecy that seems to have cited Psalm 72:8. Thus, these interconnected texts from the Law, Prophets, and Writings (Num 24:17-19; Zech 9:9-10; Ps 72:8) predict with one voice the worldwide rule of the Messiah.

The theme of the Messiah's worldwide rule continues with additional imagery and accompanying allusions in Psalm 72:9-11. In Psalm 72:9a, he receives homage from "desert animals/tribes" (צִיִּים is difficult here; see Num 24:24?). "His enemies will lick dust" (וְאֹיְבָיו עָפָר יְלַחֵכוּ) in Psalm 72:9b which alludes to the Lord's judgment against the serpent in Genesis 3:14, "you will eat dust" (וְעָפָר תֹּאכַל). Genesis 3:15 relatedly mentions "enmity" (אֵיבָה) and the serpent's "seed" (זֶרַע). In Psalm 72:9, the king's enemies licking dust suggests that he is the seed of the woman of Genesis 3:15 in addition to being the fulfillment of the Abrahamic and Davidic covenants. "May he crush the oppressor" (וִידַכֵּא עוֹשֵׁק) in Psalm 72:4 reinforces this connection through its similarity to "he will crush your head" (הוּא יְשׁוּפְךָ רֹאשׁ) in Genesis 3:15 (see Ps 89:10). Thus, the creation themes already noted in Psalm 72 are not limited to a return to Edenic abundance (Ps 72:6, 16) but also include the salvation promised in Genesis 3:15 that secures this return (see Gen 1:26, 28/Num 24:18). The climactic second-exodus passage in Micah 7:15-20 (see chapter eight) also alludes to Genesis 3:15, like Psalm 72:9, by saying of the nations, "They will lick dust like the serpent" (יְלַחֲכוּ עָפָר כַּנָּחָשׁ, Mic 7:17; see also Is 49:23; 65:25). If a protocanonical Psalm 72 was accessible then, Micah 7:17 could be citing it also. Either way, there is likely a direct dependence between Psalm 72:9 and Micah 7:17. Like Psalm 72:5, 9, 17, Malachi 4:1-3 draws together eschatological sun imagery ("the sun of righteousness will dawn") with an allusion to Genesis 3:15 ("you will crush the wicked, for they will be ashes under the soles of your feet").[44]

Barbiero argues further that the nations' pilgrimage to Jerusalem in Psalm 72:9-11 alludes to Isaiah 2:1-5 and 60:1-22.[45] Whatever the direction of dependence, the bringing of gifts by "the kings of Tarshish and of the islands" and "the kings of Sheba and Seba" (Ps 72:10), even homage from "all kings" and "all nations" (Ps 72:11), exceeds Solomon's grandeur (1 Kings 10:1, 22) and matches the eschatological picture of the nations traveling to Zion to learn from the Lord in Isaiah 2:2-3. Significantly, the one they are coming to see in Psalm 72 is specifically the messianic king, suggesting his close relationship and possible identification with the Lord in Isaiah 2:2-3.

Similarly, Isaiah 60, which names "Sheba" (Is 60:6), "islands" (Is 60:9), and "ships of Tarshish" (Is 60:9) among the gift-bearing pilgrims coming to Zion, declares, "The darkness [חֹשֶׁךְ] covers the earth ... but the Lord will dawn [זָרַח] on you, and his glory will be seen [רָאָה] upon you. Nations will come to your light [אוֹר] and kings to the shining [נֹגַהּ] of your dawning [זָרַח]" (Is 60:2-3; see also Deut 33:2; "sun," Ps 72:5, 17). The same imagery is used in Isaiah 9:2, "The people walking in the darkness [חֹשֶׁךְ] have seen [רָאָה] a great light [אוֹר גָּדוֹל]; those dwelling in the shadow of death, upon them light has shone [אוֹר נָגַהּ]," where this "great light" is the messianic king of Isaiah 9:6-7. Thus, whether the book of Isaiah or Psalm 72, the nations bring offerings to the messianic king, the "light of the nations" (Is 42:6; 49:6). Such messianic language and imagery is consistent with Numbers 24:17, "I see [רָאָה] him but not now, I behold him [אֲשׁוּרֶנּוּ]; LXX: "bless"/ μακαρίζω from אָשַׁר] but not near, a star [כּוֹכָב] marches [LXX: "dawn"/ ἀνατελεῖ from זָרַח; see Syriac; Vulgate] from Jacob," and 2 Samuel 23:4, which characterizes the righteous king as being "like the light of the morning [וּכְאוֹר בֹּקֶר], the sun dawns [יִזְרַח־שָׁמֶשׁ], a morning without clouds."

---

[44]Mal 4:1-3 is also part of a seam (or near a seam, Mal 4:4-6) in the Tanak, since it closes the Prophets corpus. As such, allusions to Gen 3:15 seem to strategically appear in or near the Tanak's seams also in Deut 32:42 and Ps 2:9. Gen 3:15 itself is close to the beginning of the Tanak. 2 Chron 36:23 does not allude to Gen 3:15 directly but still links to it via the Davidic covenant.

[45]Barbiero, "Risks of a Fragmented Reading," 73. In n24, he notes Ps 72:5/Is 60:19-20; Ps 72:7/Is 61:11; Ps 72:10/Is 60:5-9; Ps 72:11/Is 60:14; Ps 72:12/Is 61:1-3.

The glorious picture of the Messiah's rule over the nations in Psalm 72:8-11 climaxes in Psalm 72:11. The possible identification between the king and the Lord becomes more likely because "all kings" and "all nations" are called to worship him: "May all kings bow down to him, all nations serve him" (וְיִשְׁתַּחֲווּ־לוֹ כָל־מְלָכִים כָּל־גּוֹיִם יַעַבְדוּהוּ). As I have pointed out previously, the combination of verbs "bow down" (הִשְׁתַּחֲוָה) and "serve" (עָבַד) is consistently used of worship, especially of idols (e.g., Ex 23:24; Deut 4:19).[46] In the Ten Commandments, Israel is not to make a graven image (Ex 20:4/Deut 5:8) and is neither to "bow down to them" (תִשְׁתַּחְוֶה לָהֶם) or "serve them" (תָעָבְדֵם; Ex 20:5/Deut 5:9). The obvious reason is, "You shall have no other gods before me" (Ex 20:3/Deut 5:7). In Deuteronomy 8:19, to "serve" (עָבַד) other gods and "bow down" (הִשְׁתַּחֲוָה) to them is equivalent to "forgetting" (שָׁכַח) the Lord. In Deuteronomy 11:16, these same idolatrous acts mean that Israel's heart has been "enticed" (פָּתָה) so that they "turn aside" (סוּר). Both of these texts describe the fierce divine wrath that would ensue (Deut 8:19; 11:17). Deuteronomy 17:2-4 calls the same two acts "evil" (רַע), "transgressing [the Lord's] covenant" (עֲבֹר בְּרִיתוֹ), and an "abomination" (תּוֹעֵבָה; Deut 17:2-4).

Against this background of heinous sin, divine wrath, and destruction, the call to all kings and all nations in Psalm 72:11 to bow down to and serve a human king who reigns in glory stands out as a striking exception.[47] But are the bowing down and serving in Psalm 72:11 idolatry? Not if this king is also divine, even the Lord himself. This way of depicting worship of the Messiah by the world is not an innovation but is rooted in the Pentateuch's messianic vision. In Genesis 27:29, Isaac's blessing of Jacob, which is no mere family matter but transfers to Jacob the blessings of the Abrahamic covenant, including its messianic elements, declares, "May the peoples serve [עָבַד] you and may the nations bow down [הִשְׁתַּחֲוָה] to you." In

---

[46] Kevin Chen, *The Messianic Vision of the Pentateuch* (Downers Grove, IL: InterVarsity Press, 2019), 96-97. Many of such texts are translated with προσκυνέω and λατρεύω in the LXX, a pairing also found on the lips of Jesus in Mt 4:10; Lk 4:8. Perhaps sensing the theological difficulty, both Gen 27:29 and Ps 72:11 use δουλεύω instead of λατρεύω.

[47] In the context of prohibiting specific forms of idolatry, Deut 4:19; 17:3 use the terms "sun" (שֶׁמֶשׁ) and "moon" (יָרֵחַ), which also appear in Ps 72:5, 7.

addition to the aforementioned echo of Genesis 27:28 in Psalm 72:6, Psalm 72:11 is thus a second, even stronger link to Genesis 27:27-29.

If Psalm 72:11 indeed implies worship of the Messiah, then this would suggest that the call to nations and kings of Psalm 2 (Ps 2:1-2, 10) to "kiss the son" in Psalm 2:12 is also an act of worship parallel to the call to "serve the Lord with fear" in Psalm 2:11 (see 1 Kings 19:18; Hos 13:2; Job 31:27). Such equal treatment of the Lord and king fits the special father-son relationship between the Lord and the Messiah in Psalm 2:7 ("You are my son; today I have begotten you"). Psalm 89 likewise describes an "idealized David" who calls the Lord "my father" (Ps 89:26), is his "firstborn" and "Most High [עֶלְיוֹן] to the kings of the earth" (Ps 89:27; see Ps 47:2; Gen 14:18-20), and has divine power (e.g., Ps 89:9-10, 25).[48]

Table 9.1. Particularly important allusions involving Psalm 72

Psalm 72	Intertext (directionality varies)
"May he rule" the world (Ps 72:8)	"May he rule [the nations] from Jacob" (Num 24:19)
"May he rule from sea to sea and from the river to the ends of the earth" (Ps 72:8)	"His rule will be from sea to sea and from the river to the ends of the earth" (Zech 9:10)
"His enemies will lick dust" (Ps 72:9); see also "May he crush the oppressor" (Ps 72:4)	"You will eat dust" (Gen 3:14; see also "He will crush your head," Gen 3:15); "They will lick dust like the serpent" (Mic 7:17)
"May all kings bow down to him, all nations serve him" (Ps 72:11)	"May the peoples serve you and may the nations bow down to you" (Gen 27:29)
"Let them be blessed in him; all nations will bless him" (Ps 72:17)	"All the nations of the earth will be blessed in your seed" (Gen 22:18)

Psalm 72:12-14 returns to the theme of the king's care for the poor by giving this as the reason for his glorious reign in the preceding context (Ps 72:12, "For he delivers the needy"). Whereas most of the earlier description in Psalm 72:2-4 concerns justice for the poor ("judge" [דִּין / שָׁפַט], "righteousness" [צְדָקָה/צֶדֶק], "justice" [מִשְׁפָּט]; see also "save" [יָשַׁע], Ps 72:4), language of salvation and mercy dominate Psalm 72:12-14 ("deliver" [נָצַל], "the poor when he has no helper" [אֵין־עֹזֵר לוֹ], "takes pity" [חוּס], "saves" [יָשַׁע], "redeems" [גָּאַל], "their blood is precious in his eyes"). The judgment and salvation described in Psalm 72:2-4, 12-14 has suggestive lexical and thematic links to the

---
[48]Heim, "(God-)Forsaken King of Psalm 89," 314-15.

eschatological predictions of Deuteronomy 32:35-38, 43 ("vengeance," "judge" [דִּין], "people" [עַם], "have mercy" [*hithpael* נחם], "no strength" [אָזְלַת יָד], "help" [עָזַר], "the blood of his servants" [דַּם־עֲבָדָיו]) and Isaiah 63:1-5 ("righteousness" [צְדָקָה], "save" [יָשַׁע], "blood" [נֵצַח], "redemption" [גְּאוּלִים], "vengeance" [נָקָם], "there is no helper" [אֵין עֹזֵר]). Related to the apparent worship he receives in Psalm 72:11, the prayer, "May he judge your people" (יָדִין עַמְּךָ) in Psalm 72:2 depicts the king doing what the Lord does in Deuteronomy 32:36/Psalm 135:14, "The Lord will judge his people" (יָדִין יְהוָה עַמּוֹ).

As noted above, the description of the messianic king concludes in Psalm 72:15-17 with prayers for his long life and eternal renown (Ps 72:15, 17), a return to Edenic flourishing (Ps 72:16), and both the king's reception of people's blessing and his causing "all nations" to "be blessed in him" (Ps 72:15, 17) in fulfillment of the Abrahamic covenant. Psalm 72 thus begins with the Davidic covenant theme of a Davidic "son" (Ps 72:1) and concludes with a strong tie to Abraham's "seed" (Gen 22:18). The references in Psalm 72:18-19 to the Lord "doing wonders" (עֹשֵׂה נִפְלָאוֹת) and his "glory" (כְּבוֹדוֹ) recall the celebration of the exodus in Exodus 15:11 (see Ps 77:14; 78:4; Neh 9:17) and further cast the preceding description of the Messiah's glorious reign as a new wonder and deliverance for his afflicted people (see Ps 98:1). Allusions to the Pentateuch here and earlier in Psalm 72 are not unusual given the prominence of Moses in the Psalter (Ps 90 title; Ps 99:6; 103:7; 105:26; 106:16, 23, 32) and other allusions to the Pentateuch elsewhere in the Psalter (e.g., Ps 33:6; 86:15; 103:18; 145:18).

PSALMS 72–73 AND NONLINEARITY IN THE PSALTER

As many have noted, Psalm 73 reverses Psalm 72 in many ways. The "wicked" (רְשָׁעִים) prosper, enjoy "peace" (שָׁלוֹם), and advance "violence" (חָמָס) and "oppression" (עֹשֶׁק; Ps 73:3, 6, 8), in stark contrast with justice for the poor, deliverance from "the oppressor" and "violence," and "peace" that comes from righteous rule in Psalm 72:2-4, 7, 12-14. Yet the harsh realities of life in a fallen world as voiced in Psalm 73 do not necessarily mean that Psalm 72 is naive or that its hopes have been dashed. Psalm 72 is based on the Davidic covenant, which from its inception both predicted a messianic kingdom and accounted for sin and divine discipline along the way (2 Sam 7:12-16), just like the Pentateuch's eschatology does (Gen 49:1, 8-12; Num 24:14, 17-19; Deut 4:30; 31:29). As the messianic half of the Psalter's guiding framework in Psalm 1–2, Psalm 2 is rooted in a view of the Davidic covenant that includes both the Messiah's glorious rule to the ends of the earth and the realism of the nations' present rebellion. Thus, the extended messianic vision of Psalm 72 is challenged but not shattered by Psalm 73.

In fact, both Psalm 72 and Psalm 73 are eschatological in outlook but from different perspectives. Whereas Psalm 72 prays for the coming of an eschatological messianic kingdom, the eschatological outlook of Psalm 73 arises from the psalmist's struggle with the prosperity of the wicked. The turning point in Psalm 73 comes when the psalmist enters "the sanctuaries of God" and realizes (or perhaps was reminded of) the Lord's eschatological judgment: "I discerned into *their end*" (אָבִינָה לְאַחֲרִיתָם; Ps 73:17). This construction expressing discerning into someone's end appears elsewhere in the Old Testament only in Deuteronomy 32:29, where it concerns foolish Israel's inability to "discern into their end" (יָבִינוּ לְאַחֲרִיתָם; see also Deut 32:20; Jer 23:20; 30:24).[49] Unlike Israel, the psalmist is able to discern this before it is too late.

Although the Song of Moses in Deuteronomy 32:1-43 is also differentiated from Psalm 73 because it describes the judgment of both Israel and the nations in respective ways, the underlying theology of judgment is essentially the same. Deuteronomy 32:35 says of the wicked, "At the appointed time their foot will slip." Psalm 73:18 likewise declares, "You set them in slippery places." In his classic sermon, "Sinners in the Hands of an Angry God," Jonathan Edwards begins by arguing from these same two texts that, despite appearances, the wicked are actually "always exposed to sudden unexpected destruction."[50] Both Deuteronomy 32:1-43 and Psalm 73 also describe how the temporary success of the wicked causes the Lord's people to be "jealous" (קָנָא, Deut 32:21; Ps 73:3). Furthermore, both poems have strong wisdom themes, which include concern for future

---

[49] Cole further notes the related use of "this" (זֹאת) in both Deut 32:29 and in Ps 73:16 (*Shape and Message of Book III*, 29, including n2).

[50] This sermon was preached on July 8, 1741 and is in the public domain. For one recent edition, see Jonathan Edwards, *Sinners in the Hands of an Angry God* (Phillipsburg, NJ: P&R, 1992).

generations (Deut 31:19-21; Ps 73:15), represent the pride of the wicked by their fatness (Deut 32:15; Ps 73:7), and ultimately exalt the Lord as "Rock" (צוּר; Deut 32:4; Ps 73:26) for his "work[s]" (מַלְאֲכוֹתָיךָ/פֹּעַל; Deut 32:4; Ps 73:28). These extensive parallels suggest allusions to Deuteronomy 32:1-43 in Psalm 73 and hence that the turning point for the psalmist was both experiential ("I entered the sanctuaries of God," Ps 73:17) and rooted in Scripture, in this case involving a text that was remembered for generations (Deut 31:19-21; see chapter five).

In both Deuteronomy 32:1-43 and Psalm 73, the pride of the wicked is also connected with language expressing height and results (or could easily result) in blasphemous boasting. Deuteronomy 32:27 says, "Our hand is high [רָמָה]; the Lord has not done all this," and Psalm 73:8-9, 11 reads, "They speak from *on high* [מִמָּרוֹם]. They set their mouth *in the heavens* [בַּשָּׁמַיִם]. . . . They say, 'How does God know [יָדַע], and is there knowledge in the Most High?'"[51] The arrogance of Psalm 73:8-9, 11 further contradicts key statements in the Psalter's introduction: "The Lord *knows* [יָדַע] the way of the righteous" (Ps 1:6) and "The one [= the Lord] who sits *in the heavens* laughs" (Ps 2:4). The "setting" (שִׁית) of boastful mouths in the heavens in Psalm 73:9 further clashes with the exaltation of the Messiah to the right hand of the Lord (in heaven) and the "setting" of the Messiah's enemies as his footstool in Psalm 110:1 (see also Ps 8:3).

Allusions to Deuteronomy 32 in Psalm 72 have already been noted in the previous section, and allusions to the Song of Moses continue to appear in Book III (e.g., "foolish people/nation," Ps 74:18/Deut 32:6, 21; "They provoked him/me. . . . They made him/me jealous," Ps 78:58/Deut 32:16, 21; "vengeance of the blood of your servants," Ps 79:10/Deut 32:43), thus suggesting a broader influence of the Song of Moses on Psalm 72 and Book III.[52] The prominence of themes of exile and

---

[51] See Num 24:16 for the collocation of these terms for "God," "know/knowledge," and "Most High," where this knowledge is connected to messianic eschatology (Num 24:14, 17).

[52] Also, "days of old/everlasting" and "years everlasting/of many generations," Ps 77:5/Deut 32:7; "give ear . . . incline your ear/listen," Ps 78:1/Deut 32:1 (as well as the content of both poems recounting exodus, wilderness, rebellion, and exile); "fat of wheat" and "honey from the rock," Ps 81:16/Deut 32:13-14. Additional suggestive parallels include Ps 75:7/Deut 32:39b; Ps 76:8-9/

dispersion in Book III also supports the plausibility of allusions to Deuteronomy 32:1-43.[53]

If Psalm 72 and Psalm 73 are thus both eschatological in outlook, then these two psalms at the seam of Books II–III do not compete with each other but are complementary, similar to the major poems of the Pentateuch (see Num 24:15-19 and Deut 32:1-43). Moreover, rather than being muted by Psalm 73, Psalm 89, Book III generally, or Books IV–V, Psalm 72 stands as a towering messianic peak in the middle of the Psalter, on par with Psalm 2 and Psalm 110. Thus, the attention that Psalm 73 receives for its central position structurally and theologically within the Psalter should be shared equally with Psalm 72, which energizes its eschatological hope in the canonical Psalter.[54]

Besides treating Psalm 72 merely as a wish or unfulfilled prayer, a related factor that has sometimes resulted in downplaying its messianic hope is the search for linear development from the Psalter's beginning to end, as exemplified by Wilson's aforementioned belief in a progression in thought in Psalm 89.[55] Although such searches are often helpful and nuanced, it should be remembered that the Psalter's linear elements do not eliminate its nonlinear (e.g., cyclical or repetitive) elements.[56] Claus Westermann notes both the (nonlinear) alternation of songs of lament and songs of thanks (or praise) in the Psalter and the predominance of lament psalms in the first half of the Psalter and of praise psalms in the second half (i.e., a

---

Deut 32:36; Ps 81:1/Deut 32:43; Ps 81:13-14/Deut 32:29-30. Allusions to the Song of the Sea could also be mentioned here (e.g., Ps 74:12-14; 77:13-20).

[53] For these themes, see McCann, "Books I–III and the Editorial Purpose," 98.

[54] Regarding Ps 73, see Walter Brueggemann, "Bounded by Obedience and Praise: The Psalms as Canon," *JSOT* 50 (1991): 80-88; Walter Brueggemann and Patrick Miller, "Psalm 73 as a Canonical Marker," *JSOT* 72 (1996): 45-56. Though it does not mention the place of Ps 73 within the Psalter, see J. Clinton McCann, "Psalm 73: A Microcosm of Old Testament Theology," in *The Listening Heart: Essays in Wisdom and the Psalms in Honor of Roland O. Murphy, O. Carm*, ed. Kenneth Hoglund et al. (Sheffield: JSOT Press, 1987), 247-57.

[55] Other examples include John Walton, "Psalms: A Cantata About the Davidic Covenant," *JETS* 34 (1991): 21-31; O. Palmer Robertson, *The Flow of the Psalms: Discovering Their Structure and Theology* (Phillipsburg, NJ: P&R, 2015); and David "Gunner" Gundersen, "A Story in the Psalms? Narrative Structure at the 'Seams' of the Psalter's Five Books," in *Reading the Psalms Theologically*, ed. David M. Howard Jr. and Andrew J. Schmutzer (Bellingham, WA: Lexham Academic, 2023), 79-95.

[56] E.g., Ps 2 (Davidic covenant triumphant) and Ps 3 (David fleeing from Absalom). For Book II, see McCann, "Books I–III and the Editorial Purpose," 97.

linear arrangement).⁵⁷ On a more detailed level, Ho argues for both linear and concentric (i.e., nonlinear) elements in the macrostructure of the Psalter.⁵⁸ The coexistence of linear and nonlinear elements along with messianic prophecy characterizes not only the Psalter but also the book of Isaiah. Such interplay can be complex, but messianic texts such as Psalm 72 are a stabilizing force as a constant in such high-flux environments. Rather than allowing this psalm to get lost in the shuffle, the endurance of the Davidic covenant by the faithfulness of God means that neither existential crisis nor exile can diminish the message of messianic hope in Psalm 72.⁵⁹ This psalm directs our gaze away from both David and Solomon to the perfect Davidic king, whose promised coming is an anchor amid the ups and downs of the Psalter.

CONCLUSION

With its numerous textual links to the Davidic covenant, the Pentateuch, and several other Old Testament books, Psalm 72 is a clear example of a nexus passage. At the same time, its status as a seam psalm at the conclusion of Book II in the Psalter indicates its importance in the compositional strategy of the Psalter. This strategic role especially relates to other structurally and theologically significant psalms such as Psalms 2; 73; 89. As for its content, Psalm 72 repeatedly draws on both Davidic covenant and pentateuchal promises of an eschatological messianic king. Given this literary-historical background, the prayers of Psalm 72 are best understood as informed prayers that the Lord fulfill his word, rather than as hyperbole or wishes that will ultimately be disappointed. As such, this messianic peak in the middle of the Psalter casts an expansive vision of the Messiah's worldwide rule that can still give hope today.

---

[57] Claus Westermann, *Praise and Lament in the Psalms*, trans. Keith Crim and Richard Soulen (Atlanta: John Knox, 1981), 24-25, 75, 80-81, 152-55, 254-58.

[58] Ho, *Design of the Psalter*, 134-92, 333-34.

[59] The brief treatment in Walton treats Ps 72 in terms of the transfer of rule from David to Solomon ("Psalms: A Cantata," 24, 26-27). Ho also emphasizes the transfer of power at the end of David's reign, though he also refers to the "idealized manner" in which the Solomonic king is described and his messianic significance (*Design of the Psalter*, 228-29; see also 95-97, 153, 227, 232, 335-36). Similarly, Gundersen seems to juggle transfer of rule, the disappointment of Ps 73, and the messianic potential of Ps 72 ("Story in the Psalms?," 81, 86-87).

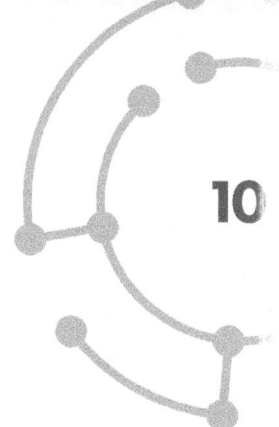

10

PROVERBS 8:22-31

WISDOM, THE BEGINNING OF THE LORD'S WAY

WE CONTINUE OUR INVESTIGATION of nexus passages in the Writings with the book of Proverbs. This book was discussed earlier (chapter two) in relation to Genesis 1–3 and its foundational role especially for Wisdom literature (Proverbs, Ecclesiastes, and Job). The earlier discussion focused on showing how the language, themes, and theology of Proverbs 1–3, as representative of Proverbs 1–9 and the book of Proverbs, are rooted in Genesis 1–3. Working again within Proverbs 1–9, this time I consider Proverbs 8:22-31, a classic passage involving the personification of wisdom, "the beginning of his [i.e., the Lord's] way" (Prov 8:22). This personification focuses on wisdom's presence at and involvement in creation. As such, it has a rich history of christological interpretation, which bears on the proposed messianic center of the Old Testament.[1] This issue will naturally arise in the analysis below, showing that Proverbs 8:22-31 is intricately connected to other texts within Proverbs (especially Prov 1–9; 30:4) as well as to the Pentateuch, Psalms, and Job.

PROVERBS 8:22-31 IN CONNECTION TO PROVERBS 1–9

Wisdom speeches in Proverbs 1–9. As noted in chapter two, Proverbs 1–9 is the first major section in Proverbs and serves as a long introduction and

---

[1]See the helpful excursus, "Proverbs 8, Wisdom, Christology, and the Arian Controversy," in Andrew Steinmann, *Proverbs*, Concordia Commentary (St. Louis: Concordia, 2009), 219-29. See also J. Robert Wright, ed., *Proverbs, Ecclesiastes, Song of Solomon*, Ancient Christian Commentary on Scripture 9 (Downers Grove, IL: InterVarsity Press, 2005), 60-70.

guiding framework for the rest of the book.² I also cited Raymond Van Leeuwen's view that the primary message of Proverbs 1–9 involves a created world where wisdom, good, and life contrast with folly, evil, and death.³ Within this section, Bálint Károly Zabán gives special attention to the three wisdom speeches in Proverbs 1:20-33; 8:1-36; 9:1-6, which he believes are "framing pillars in . . . the poetic structure of Prov 1–9 as a whole."⁴ Since the present nexus passage, Proverbs 8:22-31, is part of one of these speeches, his research highlights the importance of Proverbs 8:22-31 in Proverbs 1–9 and its connection to other wisdom speeches.

Wisdom is personified in these speeches, often involving Lady Wisdom appealing to passersby in the street to respond to her (Prov 1:20-33; 8:1-10; 9:1-6) rather than to Lady Folly (Prov 9:13-18). At the same time, William Brown remarks that Proverbs 8:22-31 "marks the pinnacle of Wisdom's discourse in Proverbs . . . [and] the culmination of her self-presentation, in which she establishes her preeminent place within the cosmic sweep of creation's genesis."⁵ In other words, the earthy imagery of a woman calling out in the streets is augmented in Proverbs 8:22-31 to cosmic proportions with personified wisdom testifying about being at the Lord's side before and during creation. Roland Murphy notes that wisdom's testimony in Proverbs 8:30 is marked by two appearances of the form וָאֶהְיֶה ("and I was"), resembling the repetition of אֶהְיֶה ("I am") in Exodus 3:14.⁶ Thus, several scholars see Proverbs 8 and especially Proverbs 8:22-31 as climactic in Proverbs 1–9.⁷

In this way, Proverbs 8:22-31 especially establishes the authority of (personified) wisdom. The first wisdom speech in Proverbs 1:20-33 began

---

²Roland Murphy calls Prov 1–9 "a kind of 'introduction' to chapters 10–31." Murphy, *Proverbs*, WBC (Nashville: Thomas Nelson, 1998), xix.
³Raymond Van Leeuwen, "Liminality and Worldview in Proverbs 1–9," *Semeia* 50 (1990): 111, 116, 130.
⁴Bálint Károly Zabán, *The Pillar Function of the Speeches of Wisdom: Proverbs 1:20-33, 8:1-36 and 9:1-6 in the Structural Framework of Proverbs 1–9* (Berlin: de Gruyter, 2012), 4. His point is a good one without necessarily taking it as far as he does (see 36, 40, 51; wisdom's house in Prov 9:1 as concerning the literary features of Prov 1–9).
⁵William P. Brown, "Proverbs 8:22-31," *Int* 63, no. 3 (2009): 286. See also Brevard Childs, *Introduction to the Old Testament as Scripture* (Philadelphia: Fortress, 1979), 554.
⁶Murphy, *Proverbs*, 52-53.
⁷For a survey of literature, see Zabán, *Pillar Function of the Speeches*, 299-300, 315, even though Zabán himself believes that Prov 9 surpasses Prov 8.

to do this through wisdom's confrontation and mockery of those who habitually ignored her (Prov 1:22-28). Commenting on the complementary nature of the two speeches in Proverbs 1:20-33 and Proverbs 8:1-36, Zabán remarks, "The author [in the first speech] recontextualizes in the mouth of Wisdom the prophetic judgment proclamation and recall[s] with it the history of Israel. . . . From Prov 8 it is clear that here one deals with someone who is more than a prophet."[8] From my perspective, relating personified wisdom to the prophets, even "someone who is more than a prophet," suggests parallels to "the prophet like Moses" in Deuteronomy 18:15-19.[9] Both figures seem to possess divine authority because of their special relationship with God (Deut 34:10) and as such must be obeyed or else (Deut 18:15-16, 19; Prov 1:23-27, 30-33; 8:6, 10). Daniel Treier further points out wisdom's mediatorial role between God and the world, especially humanity, in Proverbs 8:22-31 (which begins with "the Lord" and ends with "humanity") and in the preceding context.[10] An echo of Moses' repeated ascending and descending Mount Sinai is likewise found in Proverbs 30:4 ("Who has ascended to heaven and descended?"), which I will discuss in relation to Proverbs 8:22-31 in due course.

Parental instruction in Proverbs 1–9. Another major element in Proverbs 1–9 is fatherly instruction to "my son" (e.g., Prov 1:8; 2:1; 3:1; passim; "sons" in Prov 4:1; 5:7; 7:24), which runs throughout Proverbs 1–7 (see the dominance of wisdom speeches in Prov 8–9). R. N. Whybray observes that these parental instructions call the son (or sons) to "hear" (שְׁמַע) or the like (e.g., Prov 1:8; 4:1, 10).[11] Such themes and language are frequent in Deuteronomy (e.g., Deut 4:10; 6:4-7, 20-25; 11:19) but are equally important in the major poems of the Pentateuch (e.g., Gen 49:2; Num 23:18; 24:4, 16; Deut 32:1; 33:7). In Genesis 49:1-2, the aged patriarch and father Jacob calls his sons to hear what will happen to them "in

---

[8]Zabán, *Pillar Function of the Speeches*, 114-15.
[9]See my discussion of the prophet like Moses in Kevin Chen, *The Messianic Vision of the Pentateuch* (Downers Grove, IL: InterVarsity Press, 2019), 224-46.
[10]Daniel Treier, *Proverbs and Ecclesiastes*, Brazos Theological Commentary on the Bible (Grand Rapids, MI: Brazos, 2011), 50.
[11]R. N. Whybray, *Wisdom in Proverbs* (Naperville, IL: Allenson, 1965), 34.

the last days." Likewise, the aged Moses warns Israel, who are the Lord's "sons" (Deut 32:5-6, 18-20; see also Deut 14:1), about their future rebellion and ensuing calamity "in the last days" (Deut 31:29; see also Moses' father-like blessing in Deut 33). Thus, from the Pentateuch's perspective, parental wisdom includes not only lessons learned from a lifetime of walking with the Lord (e.g., Gen 22:8; 48:15) but also those that specifically concern the eschatological, messianic future (Gen 49:8-12; see also Deut 32:34-43).

Returning to Proverbs 1–9, the parental instructions have a close relationship to the wisdom speeches and thus to Proverbs 8:22-31. This is clearest in the parental instructions' frequent warnings against the adulteress (Prov 2:16-19; 5:3-8, 20; 6:23-32; 7:5, 10-27), who is the polar opposite of Lady Wisdom (see Prov 5:1-2; 7:4). In its own way, Proverbs 8:22-31 also links parent-child (even father-son) themes with a wisdom speech. Unlike wisdom's more frequent personification as a woman, sometimes Proverbs 8:22-31 personifies wisdom instead as the child/son of the Lord (who in turn instructs other "sons" in Prov 8:31-32), and the feminine nature of wisdom, though present in Proverbs 8:30b-31a (see feminine participles), is otherwise in the background and probably not sustained in Proverbs 8:22, 30a (see below).

Wisdom builds a house. Another consideration that concerns both the wisdom speeches and Proverbs 1–9 is Van Leeuwen's influential work on house building and house filling as it relates to creation, temple, and wisdom. Drawing on research into ancient Mesopotamia and Israel, he argues that these societies saw "temples and ordinary houses . . . as microcosms" of the cosmos, a "macrocosmic 'house,'" each of which were not only wisely built but also filled (or provisioned). For my purposes, his analysis of biblical data is especially relevant. Van Leeuwen sees the building-filling pattern in Solomon's temple (1 Kings 10:4-8, 23-24; see also Eccles 2:4), creation (Gen 1:1–2:3), and elsewhere (e.g., Is 6:1-4; Ps 104:24; Job 3:14-15; 38).[12] Other scholars' observations concerning

---

[12]Raymond Van Leeuwen, "Cosmos, Temple, House: Building and Wisdom in Ancient Mesopotamia and Israel," in *From the Foundations to the Crenellations: Essays on Temple Building in the Ancient Near East and Hebrew Bible*, ed. Mark Boda and Jamie Novotny (Münster: Ugarit-Verlag, 2010), 399, 407-9.

parallels between creation and the tabernacle, which was built with wisdom, furnished, and filled with glory (Ex 28:3; 31:3; 40:34-35), reinforce Van Leeuwen's point.[13] Concerning Proverbs 3:19-20, which presents creation in terms of wise building (e.g., "The Lord founded the earth with wisdom"), Van Leeuwen points out a close parallel in Proverbs 24:3-4 that also mentions filling: "With wisdom a house is built, and with discernment it is established. And with knowledge, its rooms are *filled* with all wealth, precious and pleasant."[14] Within Proverbs 1–9, he further notes sinners' enticement using several common terms: "*All precious wealth* we will find, we will *fill our houses* with spoil" (Prov 1:13).[15]

Zabán points out that this building-filling pattern can also be found in the wisdom speeches of Proverbs 8:1-35 and Proverbs 9:1-6.[16] Personified wisdom in Proverbs 8 says, "I will *fill* their treasuries" (Prov 8:21) and concludes with a call to "keep watch" at "my doors" and "the doorposts of my doorways" (Prov 8:34).[17] This is continued explicitly in Proverbs 9:1-2 with personified wisdom, who "builds her house" (בָּנְתָה בֵיתָהּ), "hews her seven pillars" (חָצְבָה עַמּוּדֶיהָ שִׁבְעָה), and prepares a sumptuous meal (Prov 9:1-2). Although Zabán is interested in wisdom's house as referring to Proverbs 1–9 itself as a work of literature, I suggest that there are resonances with the Davidic covenant, which also involves building a figurative house, or dynasty (2 Sam 7:11, 27; 1 Chron 17:10, 25), and the Messiah's fame filling the earth (Ps 72:8, 17).

Furthermore, whereas Van Leeuwen focuses on a broader pattern that encompasses Solomon's temple and wisdom's house in Proverbs 9:1, the strong link between Proverbs and Solomon (Prov 1:1; 10:1; 25:1) simultaneously hints at a contrast between wisdom's house and the house that

---

[13]For parallels, see John Sailhamer, *The Pentateuch as Narrative* (Grand Rapids, MI: Zondervan, 1992), 298-99.
[14]Van Leeuwen, "Cosmos, Temple, House," 409-12. Though form critics make a sharp distinction between Prov 1–9 and Prov 10–29, Van Leeuwen argues that "fundamental worldview concepts [e.g., like the one he is arguing for] are not bound to a genre" (411).
[15]Van Leeuwen, "Cosmos, Temple, House," 412.
[16]Zabán, *Pillar Function of the Speeches*, 36.
[17]The language here parallels the "keeping" of the Passover, which involved "doorposts" and not going out the "doorway" until morning (Ex 12:22-25), though Prov 8:34 seems to involve keeping watch *outside* wisdom's house.

Solomon built (1 Kings 6:12; 9:3), which was eventually destroyed because of the sins of him and his "sons" (1 Kings 9:6-8).[18] It is as though Solomon, who in 1 Kings 5:5 equates himself with the promised son who "will build a house for my name" (2 Sam 7:13-14), against the backdrop of repeated warnings to avoid the house of the adulteress (Prov 2:18; 5:8; 7:8, 27; 9:14), climactically points instead to the house that wisdom builds in Proverbs 9:1. Greater than any house Solomon ever built is wisdom's house, and the important thing is to respond to her invitation to dine there (Prov 9:1-6). Unlike Solomon's temple, wisdom's house endures (see Ps 127:1), being established with "seven pillars" (Prov 9:1) by one who was involved with creation itself (Prov 8:22-31; see also Prov 12:7; 14:1; 15:6; 24:3-4). Wisdom's role in creation in Proverbs 8:22-31 thus leads directly to the description of wisdom building her house in Proverbs 9:1 and gives greater force to her invitation in Proverbs 9:4-6.

In this regard, Solomon's love for "many foreign women" (נָשִׁים נָכְרִיּוֹת רַבּוֹת; 1 Kings 11:1) falls far short of obedience to Proverbs 9:1-6, the preceding warnings against "the foreign woman" (e.g., Prov 2:16; 5:20; 6:24; 7:5), and the requirements for the king given in Deuteronomy 17:17. This failure factored in both his and the temple's demise (1 Kings 9:6-8). Solomon thus ultimately failed to live in "the fear of the Lord" (1 Kings 11:4-8) so often commended in Proverbs and Wisdom literature (e.g., Prov 1:7; 2:5; 3:7; 8:13; 9:10). Deuteronomy likewise calls both people and king to "learn to fear the Lord" (Deut 4:10; 17:19). On the other hand, the Davidic covenant will be fulfilled by a perfectly wise heir (Is 11:1-3; 52:13; Jer 23:5), even one who "rules in the fear of God" (2 Sam 23:3), who will both ensure the everlasting reign of the house of David and build an enduring temple for the Lord (Zech 6:12-13).

Scholars also observe a close connection between Proverbs 3:19-20 and Proverbs 8:22-31, since both texts describe the Lord creating the universe with "wisdom" (חָכְמָה; Prov 3:19; 8:22, 27, 30). Both Proverbs 3:19-20 and Proverbs 8:22-31 describe this as an act of building. The terms "found"

---

[18] Steinmann points out the common terminology of "wisdom" and "house" in Prov 9:1 and 1 Kings 10:4/2 Chron 9:3 (*Proverbs*, 234).

(יָסַד) and "establish" (כּוּן) appear in Proverbs 3:19, parallel to "establish" (כּוּן) in Proverbs 8:27 and the cognate "foundation" (מוֹסָד) in Proverbs 8:29. Though Proverbs 3:19-20 is not a wisdom speech, additional links further show that these verses are closely connected to Proverbs 8:22-31. The terms "earth" (אֶרֶץ), "heavens" (שָׁמַיִם), "depths" (תְּהוֹמוֹת), and "clouds" (שְׁחָקִים) are also common to both passages (Prov 3:19-20; 8:23-24, 26-29, 31). Both Proverbs 3:19 and Proverbs 8:22 begin with "the Lord" (יְהוָה, uncommon in Proverbs; see Prov 20:12) and place the focus on him. Both contexts also involve the only statements of blessing involving the word אַשְׁרֵי ("blessed") in Proverbs 1–9 (Prov 3:13; 8:32, 34; note also "man" [אָדָם]). Jewish tradition also links both Proverbs 3:19 and Proverbs 8:22-31 to Genesis 1:1 (e.g., Bereshit Rabbah 1.1, 1.4).

Just as chapter two showed that Proverbs 3:19-20 has strong ties to Genesis, so the discussion below will show that Proverbs 8:22-31 does too. In fact, the discussion in chapter two concerning links to Genesis 1–3 in Proverbs 1–3 increases the likelihood that Proverbs 8:22-31 also has such links, just as the discussion below further supports the broader point in chapter two that Wisdom literature is rooted in Genesis 1–3.

Figure 10.1. Proverbs 8:22-31 is linked to Proverbs 3:19-20 and Proverbs 30:4

WISDOM AS "BEGINNING" OR "FIRSTFRUITS" (PROV 8:22) IN RELATION TO GENESIS 1:1 AND PROVERBS 30:4

Turning to Proverbs 8:22-31 itself, the reader is immediately confronted with an interpretive crux in Proverbs 8:22a (יְהוָה קָנָנִי רֵאשִׁית דַּרְכּוֹ). Translations of this clause reveal both its difficulty and its theological significance. For example, the KJV reads, "The LORD possessed me in the beginning of his way," whereas the NIV reads, "The LORD brought me forth as the first of his works." So was wisdom "possessed," "brought forth," or even "created" (RSV)? Furthermore, did this happen "in the beginning" (KJV), or is wisdom itself the "first"/"beginning" of the Lord's way/work in creation (NIV)? The underlying issues concern the meaning of the verb קָנָה ("possess," "brought forth") as well as the term רֵאשִׁית ("beginning," "first").

Based on its usage, the verb קָנָה has the basic meaning of "acquire" or "possess" in a broad sense.[19] This can explain much of the variation in its translation. If money secures such an acquisition, קָנָה is naturally translated as "buy" but remains a subcategory of "acquiring" (e.g., Gen 25:10). That money need not be involved is shown through the use of קָנָה in connection with the Lord's redemption of Israel (e.g., Ex 15:16; Ps 74:2). Although the LXX translates this term as "create" (κτίζω) in Proverbs 8:22, this meaning remains insufficiently attested.[20] The meaning "brought forth" or "beget" can also be subsumed under the broader meaning of "acquire" or "possess" (i.e., through the birth of a child). This subcategory is attested in Deuteronomy 32:6, "Is he not *your father, who acquired/begot you* [אָבִיךָ קָּנֶךָ]?" (see also Deut 32:18, "the rock who begot you [יְלָדְךָ] . . . the God who brought you forth [מְחֹלְלֶךָ]") and Eve's words in Genesis 4:1, "I have acquired/begotten a man" (קָנִיתִי אִישׁ).

In Proverbs 8:22, the evidence suggests that the broader meaning of "acquire" with the subcategory involving the birth of a child fit here. In Proverbs 1:5 and Proverbs 4:5, 7, קָנָה is also used in the broader sense of "acquiring" discernment and wisdom, and Andrew Steinmann suggests that Proverbs 8:22 depicts God as having done "from eternity past what humans are urged to do in 1:5 and 4:5, 7."[21] At the same time, the usage and context in Proverbs 8:22 involving the Lord "acquiring" a person (i.e., wisdom personified) who is also said to be "brought forth" (חוּל, Prov 8:24-25) suggest that the birth of a child and a parent-child relationship are also in view here, just as in Genesis 4:1 and Deuteronomy 32:6, cited above.

This leads to a closer look at the term רֵאשִׁית, commonly translated "beginning" (Gen 1:1). As seen above, some modern translations treat the

---

[19]See Michael V. Fox, *Proverbs 1–9*, AB (New York: Doubleday, 2000), 279.
[20]In Gen 14:19, 22, קָנָה could just as easily mean "possess." Steinmann argues that in Ps 139:13 "acquire" fits the context (see LXX, Vulgate, Peshitta; *Proverbs*, 208).
[21]Steinmann, *Proverbs*, 206.

Hebrew text as though it read "in the beginning" (בְּרֵאשִׁית) even though the preposition "in" (בְּ) is absent in Proverbs 8:22. If we take רֵאשִׁית as it stands, it is more accurately understood as being in apposition to "me" (i.e., wisdom itself), resulting in a translation like, "The Lord acquired me, the beginning of his way." This is how the LXX treats רֵאשִׁית, by translating it in the same case as the immediately preceding "me" (i.e., accusative: με ἀρχήν; Vulgate: *me initium*). In other words, Proverbs 8:22 is not saying that the Lord acquired wisdom *in* the beginning but that he acquired wisdom, which *is* the "beginning" (רֵאשִׁית) in some sense yet to be determined. Of course, the subsequent context also implies that wisdom was there *in* the beginning, but that is not what the words of Proverbs 8:22 are saying.

Due to the frequent usage of רֵאשִׁית with a temporal meaning (Gen 1:1), it may seem natural to understand this term in the same way in Proverbs 8:22. Indeed, the related term תְּחִלָּה in Proverbs 9:10 ("the fear of the Lord is the *beginning* of wisdom") does mean "beginning" or "first" in the temporal sense. However, this is not the only attested meaning of רֵאשִׁית, including in Proverbs 1–9 itself (Prov 1:7; 3:9; 4:7; 8:22). For example, Proverbs 3:9 uses רֵאשִׁית with the meaning of "firstfruits," which are meant to honor the Lord (see Lev 2:12). Likewise, in the midst of a fatherly exhortation to "acquire wisdom" (קְנֵה חָכְמָה), Proverbs 4:7 adds, "Wisdom is the firstfruits/ principal thing" (רֵאשִׁית חָכְמָה; see KJV). Although most translations render this instead as "the beginning of wisdom" (see Ps 111:10), this is more disruptive to the grammar and flow of the verse (i.e., "The beginning of wisdom: acquire wisdom"). In contrast, if the phrase is understood as "wisdom is the firstfruits," then the subsequent command to "acquire wisdom" follows more naturally.[22] This reading of the grammar of Proverbs 4:7 also agrees

---

[22] Though Delitzsch himself does not adopt this view of the syntax, he lists Hitzig, Mercier, De Dieu, Döderlein, and Zöckler, who do. See C. F. Keil and Franz Delitzsch, *Proverbs, Ecclesiastes, Song of Solomon*, Commentary on the Old Testament 6 (repr., Peabody, MA: Hendrickson, 1996), 78; Ferdinand Hitzig, *Die Sprüche Salomos's* (Zürich: Orell, Füssli, 1858), 31-32. Bruce Waltke believes that the different meanings of רֵאשִׁית all fit Prov 4:7, "suggesting that it may be deliberately polysemous." Waltke, *The Book of Proverbs: Chapters 1–15*, NICOT (Grand Rapids, MI: Eerdmans, 2004), 281. If so, then this opens the possibility of another layer of intended meaning in the controlling statement for the whole book of Proverbs, "the fear of the Lord is the beginning of knowledge, but fools despise wisdom and discipline" (Prov 1:7).

with the grammar of Proverbs 8:22, that is, that wisdom is the "beginning/firstfruits" (רֵאשִׁית). Thus, the simple temporal meaning of רֵאשִׁית (e.g., Gen 1:1) does not necessarily characterize its use in Proverbs 1–9.

Furthermore, רֵאשִׁית can refer to a firstborn son as a type of "firstfruits." Jacob calls Reuben "the firstfruits of my strength" (רֵאשִׁית אוֹנִי) in Genesis 49:3, and parallel uses of this phrase likewise refer to the firstborn son of an unloved wife (Deut 21:17) and the firstborn sons of the Egyptians (Ps 78:51; 105:36). Genesis 49:3 also refers to Reuben using the more common term for "firstborn" (בְּכוֹר), which suggestively appears in relation to the Davidic covenant in Psalm 89:27. In view of the varied use of רֵאשִׁית, including in Proverbs 1–9, and the use of קָנָה ("acquire") and חוּל ("brought forth") in Proverbs 8:22, 24-25 concerning the birth of a child, Proverbs 8:22 can be understood as the Lord begetting wisdom as his child, even his "firstfruits" or firstborn son.[23]

From a different angle, Treier argues that "Wisdom clearly is beyond just another created reality . . . while not solely identifiable with God either," and hence a christological interpretation provides "the resolution of a mystery latent in the text, though not always clearly recognized."[24] Perhaps also reflecting the flexible use of רֵאשִׁית, Colossians 1:18 suggestively refers to Christ as "the beginning, the firstborn" (ἀρχή, πρωτότοκος).[25] Though grammatically feminine, רֵאשִׁית when referring to a firstborn child always refers to a son, not a daughter. Thus, the feminine personification of wisdom is not strictly maintained here. Steinmann likewise points out that wisdom's role as "master craftsman" (אָמוֹן) in Proverbs 8:30 is also masculine both grammatically and in meaning.[26]

---

[23]See note 1 for bibliography regarding the history of a christological interpretation of this verse. See also Seth Postell, "Proverbs 8: The Messiah: Personification of Divine Wisdom," in *The Moody Handbook of Messianic Prophecy*, ed. Michael Rydelnik and Edwin Blum (Chicago: Moody, 2019), 739-46. More recently, he has changed his view of wisdom in Prov 8:22-31 to refer to the Spirit. See Postell, "Messianism in Light of Literary Strategy," *BSac* 177 (2020): 344-45. As Steinmann points out, this was the view of Irenaeus (*Against Heresies* 4.20.3; *Proverbs*, 221-22). Treier also mentions Theophilus of Antioch (*Proverbs and Ecclesiastes*, 54).

[24]Treier, *Proverbs and Ecclesiastes*, 49, 51, respectively. He takes the perspective of early Jewish Christians who had messianic hopes, which is not a purely exegetical consideration.

[25]For discussion of Gen 1:1 and Col 1, see John Sailhamer, *NIV Compact Bible Commentary* (Grand Rapids, MI: Zondervan, 1994), 552-53.

[26]Steinmann, *Proverbs*, 217. In support of this meaning, he cites its only other appearance, in Jer 52:15, and a cognate, אֹמֶן, in Song 7:1 (p. 212). The form also matches the root אמן, "to be faithful."

The casting of wisdom as the Lord's firstfruits, even firstborn son, in Proverbs 8:22 provides another link to the Davidic covenant (2 Sam 7:14; Ps 89:27) in addition to the aforementioned one in Proverbs 9:1 ("wisdom builds her house"). This firstborn son in turn delights in the "sons" of Adam and calls "sons" to listen (Prov 8:31-32). It seems no accident that the final section of Proverbs (Prov 30–31) attributes wisdom and creation to the Lord and "his son" in Proverbs 30:4 (see Ps 2:7, 11-12).[27] Reminiscent of both Exodus 3:13 ("What is his name?") and Deuteronomy 30:12 ("Who will ascend for us to heaven?"), Proverbs 30:4 asks what some have called a riddle: "Who ascended the heavens and came down? Who gathered the wind in his fists? Who bound up the waters in a garment? Who established all the ends of the earth? What is his name, and what is the name of his son?"[28] These rhetorical questions not only attribute creation and perfect wisdom to the Lord and his son equally but simultaneously call the reader to ponder who this son is. His profile as involved with creation matches that of wisdom in Proverbs 8:22-31. In the context of the book of Proverbs, we would also expect that he would fulfill the ideal of the wise son in Proverbs 1–9 and elsewhere in Proverbs (e.g., Prov 10:1, 5; 13:1).[29]

Along these lines, Zabán remarks, "One might have the impression as if the rhetorical questions that belch forth from Augur's [sic] mouth (Prov 30:2-4) here would all be answered."[30] In other words, personified wisdom's involvement with creation in Proverbs 8:22-31 is part of the answer to the questions in Proverbs 30:4, such that the identity of the Lord's son in Proverbs 30:4 has already been given as personified wisdom in Proverbs 8:22-31. The plausibility of an intended link between these two

---

[27]Tracy McKenzie and Jonathan Shelton links Prov 30:4 to 2 Sam 7:14 (and in turn to 2 Sam 23; Num 24; Is 9:6-7; Ps 89; 2; Dan 7) and the Davidic covenant. See McKenzie and Shelton, "From Proverb to Prophecy: Textual Production and Theology in Proverbs 30:1-6," *Southeastern Theological Review* 11, no. 1 (Spring 2020): 3, 9-10, 23-26.
[28]McKenzie and Shelton, "From Proverb to Prophecy," 19-21; Roland Murphy, *The Tree of Life: An Exploration of Biblical Wisdom Literature*, 2nd ed. (Grand Rapids, MI: Eerdmans, 1996), 25; Eva Rydelnik, "Proverbs 30:4: The Riddle of the Son," in Rydelnik and Blum, *Moody Handbook of Messianic Prophecy*, 747-56. McKenzie and Shelton also note the common terms *heavens*, *earth*, *spirit*, and *waters* between Prov 30:4 and Gen 1:1-2.
[29]Steinmann, *Proverbs*, 595-96. See also the discussion of sonship in chapter 6.
[30]Zabán, *Pillar Function of the Speeches*, 159.

texts is further increased by a probable link between Proverbs 30:3 and Proverbs 9:10 (noting the proximity of Prov 8:22-31 and Prov 9:10) through the uncommon pairing "wisdom" (חָכְמָה) and "knowledge of the holy ones" (דַּעַת קְדֹשִׁים).[31] Tracy McKenzie and Jonathan Shelton takes the "holy ones" in Proverbs 30:3 as referring to the Lord and his son in Proverbs 30:4.[32] Proverbs 30:2-4 was discussed in chapter four in relation to the oracles in Numbers 24, but we can see that its association of the Lord, his son, wisdom, and creation also provides a strong link to Proverbs 8:22-31.

The interconnectivity of these passages along with the above discussion suggests that wisdom's personification as a "firstfruits" (רֵאשִׁית) begotten by the Lord may be interconnected with additional messianic texts in the Old Testament, such as Psalm 2. As I argued in chapter two, Proverbs 3:19 appears to be part of a wisdom-inspired poetic reworking of Genesis 1:1 in which the word רֵאשִׁית ("beginning") has been substituted for חָכְמָה ("wisdom"). Based on the above discussion, Proverbs 1–9 and Proverbs 8:22 may actually be playing on the word רֵאשִׁית, a riddle in itself (see Prov 1:6). Again interchanged with wisdom (see Prov 8:12), רֵאשִׁית in Proverbs 8:22 refers to a person (wisdom), not to a time as in Genesis 1:1. Yet this wisdom figure is also "beside" (אֵצֶל) God at creation in Proverbs 8:30 (see Jn 1:1-2). Thus, Proverbs 8:22-31 still implies that God created the universe "with the firstborn/רֵאשִׁית," or, circling back to Genesis 1:1 yet again, בְּרֵאשִׁית.[33]

WISDOM'S PREEXISTENCE IN PROVERBS 8:22-31 AND CONNECTIONS TO PSALM 2

After establishing the relationship between the Lord and wisdom in Proverbs 8:22a, most of Proverbs 8:22b-31 is occupied with poetically describing wisdom's preexistence as well as presence at creation

---

[31] McKenzie and Shelton, "From Proverb to Prophecy," 12-13.
[32] McKenzie and Shelton, "From Proverb to Prophecy," 13.
[33] Rashi's comments on Gen 1:1 show his awareness that רֵאשִׁית is pregnant with meaning (i.e., the words בְּרֵאשִׁית בָּרָא are telling the reader, "Interpret me" [דרשני]). The specific play I am proposing fits the use of the בְּ preposition in Prov 8 both temporally (Prov 8:24-25, 27-29) and to indicate accompaniment or instrumentality (Prov 8:15-16). For discussion of Targum Neofiti on Gen 1:1 ("In the beginning, with wisdom, the Son of Yahweh created the heavens and the earth"), see Michael Shepherd, "Targums, the New Testament, and Biblical Theology of the Messiah," *JETS* 51, no. 1 (2008): 51-52. See also Sailhamer, *NIV Compact Bible Commentary*, 552-53.

(Prov 8:22b-30a). Though not referring to time, רֵאשִׁית in Proverbs 8:22a already hinted at this. The preexistence of wisdom becomes explicit in Proverbs 8:22b-23. Wisdom is "before his works from of old" (Prov 8:22b) and "installed from everlasting, from the beginning, from the earliest times of the earth" (Prov 8:23). The various terms used ("ancient times" [קֶדֶם], "of old" [מָאָז], "everlasting" [עוֹלָם], "beginning" [רֹאשׁ]), make plain the preexistence of wisdom, which should be expected given the eternal nature of God, including his perfect wisdom.[34]

These terms can refer to primeval times elsewhere in the Old Testament. For example, the Lord asks regarding idols in Isaiah 45:21, "Who declared this from *ancient times* [מִקֶּדֶם], told it *from of old* [מֵאָז]?" Likewise, the Lord says in Isaiah 41:4 that he, who is both "first" (רִאשׁוֹן) and "last" (אַחֲרֹנִים), "calls the generations *from the beginning* [מֵרֹאשׁ]." Again, Psalm 93:2 reads, "Your throne is established *from of old* [מֵאָז]; you are *from everlasting* [מֵעוֹלָם]." Although there certainly are examples in which these terms refer merely to the past or distant past and not to eternity past, the Lord's possession of wisdom in creation in Proverbs 8:22-31 strongly suggests that eternity past is in view here. Steinmann further notes a connection to the messianic prophecy in Micah 5:2, which describes the Messiah's origins or "going forth" (יָצָא, מוֹצָאָה) on the one hand as being from Bethlehem and on the other as being "from ancient times, from days of everlasting" (מִקֶּדֶם מִימֵי עוֹלָם).[35] In the context of the Davidic covenant, which is likely part of the assumed background of Micah 5:2, the language used here for the Messiah's "going forth" ("from you will *go forth* for me" [מִמְּךָ לִי יֵצֵא]) also hints at his birth (2 Sam 7:12, "your seed ... who will *go forth* from your loins" [זַרְעֲךָ ... אֲשֶׁר יֵצֵא מִמֵּעֶיךָ]; see Gen 15:5).

This messianic thread is strengthened by significant parallels with Psalm 2. Just as wisdom declares, "I was *installed* from everlasting" (מֵעוֹלָם נִסַּכְתִּי) in Proverbs 8:23, so the Lord says of "his anointed one" (מְשִׁיחוֹ, Ps 2:2) in Psalm 2:6, "I have *installed* [נָסַכְתִּי] my king on Zion, my holy mountain."

---

[34]See Athanasius, *Defence of the Nicene Definition* 4.15, NPNF[2] 4:159: "Let them [i.e., Arians] dare to say openly what they think in secret that God was once wordless and wisdomless."
[35]Steinmann, *Proverbs*, 209.

The verb נָסַךְ when meaning "install" is rare and only appears in these two passages and in the same consonantal form (נסכתי; with the MT inflecting it in Ps 2:6 as *qal* but in Prov 8:23 as *niphal*). The LXX has even translated the unpointed ואני נסכתי in Psalm 2:6 as "I have *been* installed" (*niphal*), such that it has the Messiah speaking like wisdom does in Proverbs 8:23 MT (though not LXX). Either way, both wisdom and the Messiah were installed to prominent positions.

The parallels between the two texts continue with the Lord's "decree" (חֹק) in Psalm 2:7, "You are my son; today I have begotten you" (בְּנִי אַתָּה אֲנִי הַיּוֹם יְלִדְתִּיךָ). Just as Psalm 2:7 uses the terminology of "son" (בֵּן) and "beget" (יָלַד), Proverbs 8:22-31 uses the language of "acquire" (קָנָה), "firstfruits" (רֵאשִׁית), and "bring forth" (חוּל) to express the same themes of childbirth and a father-son relationship. Furthermore, the Lord's "decree" (חֹק) in Psalm 2:7 in relation to enemy kings and nations parallels his "decree" (חֹק) for the sea in Proverbs 8:29 and the cognate acts of decreeing (חָקַק) in Proverbs 8:27, 29 (see also Prov 8:15).[36] The decrees in both texts set in place a divine order limiting powerful forces, whether concerning creation or kingdom. Of course, creation and kingdom overlap significantly, since both are under the Lord's authority and concern the domain of heavens and earth (Ps 2:2, 4, 8, 10; Prov 8:23, 26-27, 29). Other notable common terms (sometimes cognates) between the two texts are "gather together"/"foundation" (יָסַד/מוֹסָד; Ps 2:2; Prov 8:29), "laugh" (שָׂחַק; Ps 2:4; Prov 8:30-31), and "way" (דֶּרֶךְ; Ps 2:12; Prov 8:22).[37] On the thematic level, rebellious kings are urged to "be wise" (הַשְׂכִּילוּ) in Psalm 2:10 and "kiss the son" lest they be destroyed (Ps 2:12), which parallels the frequent call to heed wisdom in the wisdom speeches in Proverbs 1–9 (e.g., Prov 1:20-33; 8:1-21, 32-36; 9:4-6). Submitting to the son and listening to Lady Wisdom are thus both cast as preeminently wise acts and would seem to be related.

---

[36]Within Proverbs, these cognates are concentrated in Prov 8; see also Prov 30:8; 31:5, 15.
[37]Still more repeated terms exist but are common in the OT and sometimes used differently in the two passages, i.e., "I" (אֲנִי; Ps 2:6; Prov 8:27), "mountain" (הַר; Ps 2:6; Prov 8:25), "son" (בֵּן; Ps 2:7; Prov 8:31), and "day" (יוֹם; Ps 2:7; Prov 8:30).

Table 10.1. Wisdom in Proverbs 8:22-31 and the son in Psalm 2

	Proverbs 8:22-31	Psalm 2
"Installed" to important positions, most likely by God	"I was installed from everlasting" (Prov 8:23)	"I have installed my king on Zion" (Ps 2:6)
Father-son relationship	"The Lord acquired me, the firstfruits" (Prov 8:22); "I was brought forth" (Prov 8:25)	"You are my son; today I have begotten you" (Ps 2:7)
"Decree"	"When he set his decree for the sea" (Prov 8:29)	"Let me recount the decree of the Lord" (Ps 2:7)
"Gather together," "foundation"	Prov 8:29	Ps 2:2
"Laugh"	Prov 8:30-31	Ps 2:4
"Way"	Prov 8:22	Ps 2:12
Wisdom	passim	"Be wise" (Ps 2:10)

One apparent difference between the two passages is the timing of the messianic son's birth in Psalm 2:7. Whereas wisdom's "begetting" and origins are clearly from eternity past in Proverbs 8:22-31, the Lord says in Psalm 2:7 that he has begotten his son "today" (הַיּוֹם). But when is this "today"? Many modern scholars believe that this today refers to the Davidic king's coronation day, in which the Davidic covenant was reaffirmed.[38] The interpretation of this detail is affected by the broader issue of whether Psalm 2 is taken as concerning each Davidic (and preexilic) king or only the eschatological Messiah. While debate on this issue will likely continue, I believe that his exalted position over the kings of the earth (Ps 2:2, 10-11), the Lord's strong support of him (Ps 2:6), the intimate father-son relationship he enjoys with the Lord (Ps 2:7), his right to rule the "ends of the earth" (Ps 2:8-9), and the call for all to take refuge in him are best interpreted as referring to the Messiah alone (Ps 2:12).[39] A messianic

---

[38] E.g., Peter Craigie, *Psalms 1–50*, WBC (Waco, TX: Word, 1983), 67.

[39] Many scholars interpret Ps 2 as concerning the Messiah, at least when interpreted in the Psalter's (postexilic) final form. E.g., Brevard Childs, *Introduction to the Old Testament as Scripture* (Philadelphia: Fortress, 1979), 515-16; David C. Mitchell, *The Message of the Psalter: An Eschatological Programme in the Book of Psalms* (Newton Mearns, UK: Campbell, 2003), 82-87; Robert L. Cole, *Psalms 1–2: Gateway to the Psalter* (Sheffield: Sheffield Phoenix Press, 2013), 93-94; Peter C. W. Ho, *The Design of the Psalter: A Macrostructural Analysis* (Eugene, OR: Pickwick, 2019), 205-7. Even Andrew T. Abernethy and Gregory Goswell, who see very few OT texts as concerning an eschatological Messiah ("full-blown messianism"), see Ps 2 as an exception (see their "fully eschatological reading" of Hos 3:5. Abernethy and Goswell, *God's Messiah in the Old Testament* (Grand

interpretation of Psalm 2, when combined with other messianic texts that testify to the Messiah's preexistence (Mic 5:2; see above) and even divinity (Is 9:6, "Mighty God"), suggests that both the begetting and the father-son relationship in Psalm 2:7 are eternal, just as the Nicene and Athanasian creeds affirm.[40] Even so, modern evangelical scholars who affirm an orthodox doctrine of the Trinity and a messianic meaning of Psalm 2 sometimes have still interpreted "today" with reference to the installation of the king, or specifically the resurrection (Acts 13:33; Rom 1:4).[41] Thus, it is instructive to consider the evidence for taking "today" in Psalm 2:7 as meaning eternity.

In response to the Arian controversy, trinitarian scholars interpreted Psalm 2:7 in light of Psalm 110:4, taking both psalms as messianic.[42] Indeed, the New Testament had already similarly linked these two psalms in Hebrews 5:5-6 (see also Heb 1:3, 5, 13). Moreover, in the LXX translation of Psalm 110:3, that is, Psalm 109:3 LXX (the LXX being the primary OT text used by the early church), the Lord describes the birth of the one exalted to his right hand: "From the womb before the morning star I begot you" (ἐκ γαστρὸς πρὸ ἑωσφόρου ἐξεγέννησά σε). If "before the morning star" means before creation and hence eternity past, the begetting of the Messiah in Psalm 109:3 LXX depicts an eternal relationship, which can then inform the meaning of the begetting of the son "today" in Psalm 2:7.[43] Naturally,

---

Rapids, MI: Baker Academic, 2020) 184, 135. For a representative explanation of how some of the above scholars believe the meaning of Ps 2 changed from its original setting to its canonical one (which is not my view), see Gerald Wilson, *Psalms*, New International Version Application Commentary (Grand Rapids, MI: Zondervan, 2002), 1:114-17.

[40] For an argument for the Messiah's divinity based on Gen 27:27-29, see Chen, *Messianic Vision of the Pentateuch*, 96-97.

[41] For the former, see Cole, who further agrees with Amos Hakham that "today" probably means "from this day and forward" (*Psalms 1-2*, 114). Cole also argues that the preceding nominal clause, "You are my son," indicates "a condition or state" that precedes his begetting "today." For the latter, see Gert Steyn, "Psalm 2 in Hebrews," *Neotestamentica* 37, no. 2 (2003): 269-70, who also points out the differing uses of Ps 2:7 in Heb 1:5 and Heb 5:5 with reference to sonship and priesthood, respectively, unrelated to the resurrection.

[42] E.g., Athanasius, *Defence of the Nicene Definition* 3.13, *NPNF*[2] 4:158. See also Theodoret of Cyr in *Psalms 1-50*, ed. Craig Blaising and Carmen Hardin, Ancient Christian Commentary on Scripture 7 (Downers Grove, IL: InterVarsity Press, 2008), 14.

[43] Steinmann explains that some of the church fathers argue that the creation of the son in Prov 8:22 refers only to Christ's human nature (*Proverbs*, 227). This was also applied to "today" in Ps 2:7 as referring to his human birth (see Cyril of Alexandria in Blaising and Hardin, *Psalms 1-50*, 14). But Steinmann points out that Prov 8:22-31 does not distinguish between his two natures (*Proverbs*,

Psalm 109:3 LXX accords with Micah 5:2 concerning the Messiah's origins "from eternity" and Proverbs 8:23 concerning wisdom being "installed from eternity."

Modern scholars working with the Hebrew text also make a connection between Psalm 2 and Psalm 110, including Psalm 2:7 and Psalm 110:3 specifically.[44] Both psalms focus on the Lord and his chosen king who rules from Zion over enemies, especially enemy kings.[45] Although Psalm 110:3 MT does not mention birth, the consonantal form of "your youth" (יַלְדֻתֶיךָ) is identical to "I have begotten you" (יְלִדְתִּיךָ) in Psalm 2:7, the only two places in the Old Testament where this form appears. This explains the LXX translation of the unpointed form as "I begot you" (ἐξεγέννησά σε) in Psalm 109:3 LXX, very similar to Psalm 2:7 (γεγέννηκά σε).[46] This reading is also found in many Hebrew manuscripts (*BHS*: "mlt Mss"), Syriac manuscripts (see *BHS*), and the Vulgate (*ex utero ante luciferum genui te*). Thus, linking Psalm 2:7 and Psalm 110:3 via the form ילדתיך is supported not only by LXX but by broader manuscript evidence, and the begetting of the son "today" in Psalm 2:7 does not necessarily break the connection to the bringing forth of wisdom from eternity past in Proverbs 8:24-25.[47]

On both the lexical and the thematic levels, the Lord's begetting of his son in Psalm 2 is analogous in significant ways to his bringing forth of wisdom, his "firstfruits," in Proverbs 8:22-31. In both cases, the father-son relationship suggests the son's sharing in divine nature, which distinguishes

---

228). It also emphasizes wisdom's preexistence, which does not apply to his human nature. As for Ps 2, speaking of his human birth and hence his infancy does not fit his characterization as a ruling monarch in the psalm.

[44]E.g., Frank-Lothar Hossfeld and Erich Zenger, *Psalms 3: A Commentary on Psalms 101–150*, trans. Linda Maloney, Hermeneia (Minneapolis: Fortress, 2011), 145-49.

[45]For further links between Ps 2 and Ps 110, see Kevin Chen, "Psalm 110: A Nexus for Old Testament Theology," *CTR* 17, no. 2 (2020): 62-64.

[46]The immediately preceding "yours is dew" (לְךָ טַל) in the MT is not reflected in the LXX or Vulgate (see *BHS* apparatus), as though their Hebrew sources read מרחם משחר ילדתיך. For further discussion, see Hossfeld and Zenger, *Psalms 3*, 142.

[47]Although Ps 110:3 MT is notoriously difficult, it is interesting that both the LXX and Vulgate contain respective terms (ἀρχὴ, *principium*) that are often used to translate רֵאשִׁית, which was discussed at length in Prov 8:22 above. These terms correspond to the term יָלְדֻת in the MT, which is not translated similarly elsewhere in the LXX or Vulgate. Also, the phrase "in the day of your strength" (בְּיוֹם חֵילֶךָ) has led the *BHS* editors to propose that חֵיל is actually derived from the verb חִיל ("to give birth"), resulting in the meaning "in the day of your birth." This reading is uncertain, though it does recall the use of this verb in Prov 8:24-25.

the son from creation. The Nicene Creed famously affirms that God the Son was "begotten, not made," and Athanasius further explains the corresponding difference between a son and a creature, "If then son, therefore not creature; if creature, not son; for great is the difference between them, and son and creature cannot be the same, unless his essence be considered to be at once from God and external to God."[48] These historic statements of the Christian faith can be grounded in a responsible exegesis of Proverbs 8:22-31 and Psalm 2 viewed in light of each other. Even if we are not sure which text came first (Acts 4:25 suggests Ps 2), the lexical and thematic connections are sufficient to see a dependence between the two texts.

WISDOM'S PRESENCE AND INVOLVEMENT WITH CREATION IN RELATION TO JOB 38

As mentioned above, most of Proverbs 8:22-31 concerns wisdom's presence at and even before creation. This can already be seen from the analysis of Proverbs 8:22-23 above ("before his works from of old," "installed from everlasting, from the beginning, from the earliest times of the earth"). The passage continues with more references to creation, Genesis 1, and other creation texts. Wisdom was brought forth "when there were no depths" (תְּהֹמוֹת) or "springs [מַעְיָנוֹת] full of water" (Prov 8:24). This is an allusion to the "deep" (תְּהוֹם) in Genesis 1:2 and to the "springs of the deep" (מַעְיְנֹת תְּהוֹם) in Genesis 7:11 and 8:2, which presumably originate from creation. As discussed in chapter two, Proverbs 3:19-20 also has links to both the creation and flood narratives. The bringing forth of wisdom was also "before the mountains were sunk" (Prov 8:25). Using similar language to Proverbs 8:24-25, Psalm 90:2 describes the eternal nature of God as "before the mountains were born [בְּטֶרֶם הָרִים יֻלָּדוּ] and you brought forth [וַתְּחוֹלֵל] the earth and the world." Wisdom was there when the Lord had not yet "made the earth" (Prov 8:26) and also while he "established the heavens," "inscribed a circle on the face of the deep," set up the "clouds," and set a boundary for the sea (Prov 8:27-29). The

---

[48] Athanasius, *Defence of the Nicene Definition* 3.13, NPNF[2] 4:158.

terminology "make" (עָשָׂה), "earth" (אֶרֶץ), "heavens" (שָׁמַיִם), "on the face of the deep" (עַל־פְּנֵי תְהוֹם), and "sea" (יָם) in these verses reinforces what is already a strong connection to creation in Genesis 1.

An equally strong connection can be made to Job 38:4-11, as scholars observe.[49] Though this is not as familiar a passage as Genesis 1, careful comparison of Proverbs 8:22-31 to Job 38:4-11 reveals extensive similarities. Following the Lord's confrontation of Job for speaking "words without knowledge" (Job 38:2), the Lord proceeds to emphasize Job's absence at and ignorance of creation in Job 38:4-11. This of course is the opposite of wisdom in Proverbs 8:22-31, who was present and active at creation. Whereas the Lord asks Job, "Where were you *when I laid the foundation of the earth* [בְּיָסְדִי־אֶרֶץ]?" (Job 38:4), wisdom was present "when he inscribed the foundations of the earth" (בְּחוּקוֹ מוֹסְדֵי אֶרֶץ, Prov 8:29). Job did not "set its measures" or "stretch out a measuring line over it" like a master architect (Job 38:5), but wisdom was "there" (שָׁם) when the Lord was creating (Prov 8:27-29) and was even by his side assisting as a "master craftsman" (Prov 8:30). Job did not know on what the earth's bases were "sunk" (טָבַע, Job 38:6), but wisdom was with God before the mountains were "sunk" (טָבַע) and presumably knew such things (Prov 8:25). Both passages even give special attention to the Lord setting a "decree" (חֹק) for the sea preventing it from transgressing the divine will (Prov 8:29; Job 38:8-11).

Although it is difficult to determine which text influenced the other, these numerous parallels between Proverbs 8:22-31 and Job 38:4-11 suggest their interdependence and in turn a contrast between Job and personified wisdom. Job was absent and uninvolved with creation, but wisdom was there as a participant. Concerning this same contrast, Bruce Waltke remarks, "Wisdom speaks authoritatively because she possessed the prerequisite comprehensive knowledge he [i.e., Job] lacked."[50]

---

[49]See Tremper Longman, *Job*, Baker Commentary on the Old Testament Wisdom and Psalms (Grand Rapids, MI: Baker Academic, 2012), 428; Waltke observes several connections between Prov 8:22-31 and Job 38 (*Proverbs: Chapters 1–15*, 413, 416-17, 422).
[50]Waltke, *Proverbs: Chapters 1–15*, 417.

As mentioned in chapter two, Job's finitude is also highlighted in Job 15:7 when Eliphaz asks, "Were you the first man born?" His following question, "Were you brought forth before the hills [וְלִפְנֵי גְבָעוֹת חוֹלָלְתָּ]?" reinforces the point that Job's birth was relatively recent. For the present purposes, this question is a striking parallel to wisdom's testimony in Proverbs 8:25, which uses the same three terms, "Before the hills I was brought forth" (לִפְנֵי גְבָעוֹת חוֹלָלְתִּי). Similar to the above, the result is a contrast between Job, who was neither preexistent nor brought forth before creation, and wisdom, who was.[51] Job was not the first man born, either (Job 15:7), but Proverbs 8:22 calls wisdom the Lord's firstfruits in a way that suggests that wisdom is the Lord's firstborn son. Taken together with Job 38:4-11, Job's finitude and nonparticipation in creation appears to be a foil for personified wisdom in Proverbs 8:22-31. In its own way, contrasting Job and personified wisdom in Proverbs 8:22-31 also hints that the latter's personification of wisdom may not be purely figurative.

CONCLUSION

Proverbs 8:22-31 has a long and rich history of interpretation related to its christological interpretation, though often based on the LXX. Nevertheless, the Hebrew text of this passage also contains significant support for such interpretation, most notably language and themes concerning the birth of a child and a father-son relationship (i.e., "acquired," "firstfruits," "brought forth"). As Treier argues, wisdom in Proverbs 8:22-31 is more than a divine attribute, since it makes "no sense . . . to claim that God gave birth to God's own character."[52] As Proverbs 8:22-31 is a nexus passage, such an interpretation is further supported by interconnected texts. On the one hand contributing to the wisdom speeches in Proverbs 1-9, Proverbs 8:22-31 also connects to the Lord's wise son in Proverbs 30:4, who was involved with creation. Furthermore, the installation of wisdom, who is the Lord's firstfruits, to a position of prominence parallels that of the messianic son on Mount Zion in Psalm 2:6-7. While having clear connections to creation in

---

[51]See Waltke, *Proverbs: Chapters 1–15*, 412.
[52]Treier, *Proverbs and Ecclesiastes*, 49.

Genesis 1, Proverbs 8:22-31 also has extensive lexical and thematic links to Job 38:4-11, suggesting a contrast between personified wisdom and Job, who was absent from and uninvolved with creation.

Taken together, these connections at least suggest that personified wisdom in Proverbs 8:22-31 is like the Lord's son (Prov 30:4; Ps 2:6-7) and unlike Job (or any other typical human being). I assert that personified wisdom indeed is the Lord's messianic son, his firstfruits. No wonder Paul refers to Christ Jesus as "the wisdom of God" (1 Cor 1:24, 30), and Jesus speaks of himself as "the wisdom of God" in Luke 11:49-51 (see also Mt 23:34-36) and as "wisdom" (Mt 11:19; Lk 7:34-35).[53]

---

[53]Steinmann, *Proverbs*, 216-17.

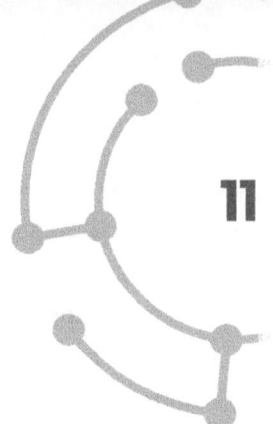

DANIEL 9
DANIEL, STUDENT OF SCRIPTURE

NOT ONLY IS THE LAST NEXUS PASSAGE treated in this book another example of a highly connected text that displays the literary, textual, and theological unity of the Old Testament, but also it sets forth Daniel as an example to imitate in our own study of Scripture. Daniel 9:2 describes him studying "the word of the Lord to Jeremiah" concerning Jerusalem's desolation for seventy years (see Jer 25:11-12; 29:10). Daniel's interest in Jeremiah's prophecy arose from having "discerned [it] in the books" (סְפָרִים, Dan 9:2), which further places the book of Jeremiah among other books, probably biblical books. Accordingly, John Collins interprets "books" here as referring "presumably to the books of the Prophets," without implying canonization at this time.[1] Moreover, the two references to "what is written in the law of Moses" in Daniel's subsequent prayer (Dan 9:11, 13) would suggest that these books included the Pentateuch as well. Furthermore, the many connections between Jeremiah and Deuteronomy, which involve the passages containing the seventy-year prophecies themselves (Deut 31:29/Jer 25:6-7; Deut 28:37/Jer 25:9, 11; Deut 4:29/Jer 29:13), suggest in turn that Jeremiah also knew the Pentateuch.[2]

---

[1] See John Collins, *Daniel*, Hermeneia (Minneapolis: Fortress, 1993), 348.
[2] For a sampling of these connections but without drawing this conclusion, see Moshe Weinfeld, *Deuteronomy and the Deuteronomic School* (Winona Lake, IN: Eisenbrauns, 1992), 359-61.

Thus, Daniel joined a preexisting conversation between Jeremiah and Moses, and we get to listen in on this conversation that now includes Daniel as well.³

Figure 11.1. Daniel 9 depends on Jeremiah, which depends on Deuteronomy

Allusions to additional Old Testament books in Daniel 9 suggest that this conversation involves still more Old Testament authors. Given the book of Daniel's late date relative to other Old Testament books (by any accounting), I agree with Matthias Henze's assessment that "to inquire into the use of Scripture in Daniel is thus an exercise in inner-biblical interpretation," even "a *locus classicus* of inner-biblical exegesis."⁴ Michael Fishbane specifically calls Daniel 9 "a skilful exegetical ensemble."⁵

Like that of Michael Shepherd, my analysis below situates the book of Daniel primarily within its native context of the Hebrew Bible, not world history or apocalyptic literature.⁶ By such prioritization of the text of Daniel and its *textual* context in the Tanak, I aim to avoid what Christopher Seitz calls, in a nod to Hans Frei, "the eclipse of biblical prophecy," in which historical reconstruction (e.g., of the life and setting of each prophet) overshadows the prophetic books themselves in their canonical form and order, unity (for Seitz, redactional), and often transtemporal messages.⁷ But

---

³For a prophetic "conversation with an echo," see John Sailhamer, *The Meaning of the Pentateuch* (Downers Grove, IL: InterVarsity Press, 2009), 224.
⁴Matthias Henze, "The Use of Scripture in the Book of Daniel," in *A Companion to Biblical Interpretation in Early Judaism*, ed. Matthias Henze (Grand Rapids, MI: Eerdmans, 2012), 279-80. However, Henze sees obvious "reworking of earlier Scripture" (280) and an "ease to adopt and reshape generously what [the authors of Daniel] had received" (285).
⁵Michael Fishbane, *Biblical Interpretation in Ancient Israel* (Oxford: Clarendon, 1985), 489.
⁶Michael Shepherd, *Daniel in the Context of the Hebrew Bible* (New York: Lang, 2009), 1-2.
⁷Christopher Seitz, *Prophecy and Hermeneutics: Toward a New Introduction to the Prophets* (Grand Rapids, MI: Baker, 2007), 75-92. He describes this in terms of "an interest in the personality of the prophet and the historical setting in which he lived and worked . . . rather than being concerned for the literary deposit of the prophets and the way this was said to find correspondence [to the NT]" (81; see also 82, 87). This is because "the prophets have seemed easiest to deal with on the basis of historical-critical concern for authorship, setting, audience, and historical background"

first, let us consider the example of Daniel as a student of Scripture with an eye toward personal application as our consideration of nexus passages nears its end.

DANIEL, MAN OF LEARNING AND INSIGHT

Although Daniel is rightly known as a prophet, he should also be known as a man of learning, linguist, and student of Scripture. As the book of Daniel begins, the reader is introduced to Daniel as one of the promising Israelite youths who were excellent in appearance, intelligence, and physical health (Dan 1:3-6). Along with the others, he was to learn "the literature [lit. "book"; סֵפֶר] and language [לָשׁוֹן] of the Chaldeans" (Dan 1:4). With the blessing of God, Daniel and his three friends indeed gained "knowledge and understanding *in all literature* [בְּכָל־סֵפֶר] and wisdom" (Dan 1:17). Indeed, Daniel 5:7-8, 15-17, 25-28 show Daniel reading (קְרָא) and giving the "interpretation" (פְּשַׁר) of the "writing" (כְּתָב) on the wall (a text!). Thus, Daniel apparently had natural ability, but God gave him additional grace to become a man skilled in interpreting texts as well as visions and dreams (Dan 1:17). Daniel himself declares that "wisdom," "knowledge," and revelation (גְּלָה) of "deep and hidden things"/"mysteries" comes from God (Dan 2:21-22, 28-29). Yet Daniel's study of literature was not limited to Babylonian works or obscure messages, as his study of Jeremiah in Hebrew among other presumably biblical books shows (Dan 9:2). Even Darius's officials knew Daniel for his devotion to "the law of his God" (דָּת אֱלָהּ, Dan 6:5). Over time, he gained a reputation for wide-ranging wisdom that encompassed "all mysteries" (כָּל־רָז; Dan 4:9), "riddles," and "problems" (Dan 5:12).

Ron Haydon argues that the Law and the Prophets (i.e., the first two parts of the tripartite Hebrew canon) have had a formative influence on

---

(77). Seitz also notes that the Documentary Hypothesis and late dating of the Pentateuch meant that the prophets were the "founders of Israel's religion" (80), "the main joist in Old Testament religion" (82; see discussion of von Rad, 62-63, 86-87). For their transtemporal message, see 36-37, 44, 65-67, 80, 82. Seitz notes that the rejection of predictive prophecy (an eclipse in itself, I would add) made prophetic experience crucial (66). Thus, the "canonical portrayal" is "bypassed" (85) because "historical redescription virtually requires instability, for the past is constantly requiring fresh reconstructions of it" (68).

Daniel 9:3-19.[8] Further support will be provided below, but for now I highlight his observations concerning Daniel 9:3-19 and the seams, or boundary passages, of the tripartite Tanak.[9] Haydon points out that "the conclusions to both the Law (Deut 34:10-12) and the Prophets (Mal 4:4-6)" have "a family resemblance with Dan 9:3-19" through terms such as "prophet[s]" (נָבִיא; Deut 34:10; Mal 4:5; Dan 9:2, 6, 10, 24), "Moses" (Deut 34:1, 5, 7-10, 12) or "the law of Moses [God's 'servant']" (Mal 4:4; Dan 9:11, 13; see also Josh 1:2, 7-8), "awesome and great" or vice versa (Deut 34:12; Mal 4:5; Dan 9:4), and "all Israel" (Deut 34:12; Mal 4:4; Dan 9:7, 11).[10]

Whereas Haydon's discussion of canonical seams also cites "Moses my servant" in Joshua 1:2, 7 as a link to references to Moses in Deuteronomy 34 and Malachi 4, further consideration of Joshua 1 (the beginning of the Prophets) and Psalm 1 (in some orderings, the beginning of the Writings; see also Lk 24:44; 4QMMT) not only strengthens the connection to Daniel 9 but also suggests that Daniel himself is being presented as an ideal reader of Tanak.[11] As John Sailhamer points out, Joshua 1 and Psalm 1 both commend "meditat[ing]" (הָגָה) "day and night" (יוֹמָם וָלַיְלָה) on divine "instruction" (תּוֹרָה, Josh 1:8; Ps 1:2).[12] For Joshua, the "book" (סֵפֶר) on which he was to meditate was necessarily "the law of Moses" only (Josh 1:7-8), whereas Psalm 1 describes the blessed man meditating on "the law of the Lord" more generally (Ps 1:2). Like the latter, Daniel "discerned in the books" (Dan 9:2), that is, presumably the Law and the Prophets if not more, and his study of Scripture suggests that he is an example of the kind of reader that Joshua 1:8 and Psalm 1:2 commend.

---

[8]Ron Haydon, *"Seventy Sevens Are Decreed": A Canonical Approach to Daniel 9:24-27* (Winona Lake, IN: Eisenbrauns, 2016), 34-35, 38-50; Haydon, "'The Law and the Prophets' in MT Daniel 9:3-19," *BBR* 24, no. 1 (2014): 15-26.
[9]Haydon, *Canonical Approach to Daniel 9:24-27*, 58-61; Haydon, "'Law and the Prophets,'" 23-24.
[10]Haydon, "'Law and the Prophets,'" 23.
[11]For the place of the Psalter in the Writings, see Roger Beckwith, "Formation of the Hebrew Bible," in *Mikra: Text, Translation, Reading and Interpretation of the Hebrew Bible in Ancient Judaism and Early Christianity*, ed. Martin Jan Mulder (Minneapolis: Fortress, 1990), 52-55.
[12]John Sailhamer also places other "nameless prophets" among those who study Scripture "day and night." Sailhamer, *The Meaning of the Pentateuch* (Downers Grove, IL: InterVarsity Press, 2019), 205, 152, 217; John Sailhamer, "The Messiah and the Hebrew Bible," *JETS* 44, no. 1 (2001): 11-12.

Moreover, like the blessed man of Psalm 1:1, Daniel lived a holy life set apart from evildoers (e.g., Dan 1:8), and like Joshua 1:7-8, he obeyed God's commands and prospered (e.g., Dan 6:28; see also Dan 1:19-21; 3:30). Daniel was no mere intellectual but combined his study of Scripture with prayer and repentance (Dan 9:2-4; see also Dan 6:11), as he lived a life of faith and faithfulness (אֱמַן) even to the point of risking his life (Dan 6:5, 23). The expectation of an eschatological work of God in the Tanak's seams (Deut 34:10 [implying the prophet like Moses is yet to come]; Mal 4:5, "Elijah") also matches Daniel's focus on the seventy years of Jerusalem's desolation (Dan 9:2), his daily prayers while facing Jerusalem (Dan 6:10), and the theme of God's everlasting kingdom (e.g., Dan 2:44; 4:3; 7:14). Although Daniel could not have read the canonical Tanak (Esther, Chronicles), his appearance near the end of the Tanak sets forth a suggestive example for later readers, including us, who likewise await eschatological salvation while in exile (1 Pet 2:11). His study of Jeremiah in Daniel 9 also fits the special emphasis on Jeremiah at the end of the Tanak (Ezra 1:1; 2 Chron 36:12, 21-22).

Whereas Daniel's visions and dreams do mark him as a prophet (Dan 7:1; 8:1; see Num 12:6), the book of Daniel itself more frequently casts him as a wise man (see Josh 1:7-8; Ps 1:2-3). As Brevard Childs observes, "Never once does Daniel address his hearers in the traditional idiom of the prophet: 'hear the word of Yahweh.'"[13] Indeed, he is often described as possessing wisdom and/or as a chief wise man/magician (Dan 1:4, 17, 20; 2:48; 4:9). Time and time again, Daniel's wisdom is shown through his interpretation of both visions (including dreams) and texts. In the book of Daniel, both are means of divine revelation, and several times dreams are specifically tied to a "word/thing" (מִלָּה), further blurring the lines between the two (see Gen 37:11). Daniel thanks God for revealing Nebuchadnezzar's dream and its interpretation, referring to it as "the word/matter of the king" (Dan 2:23). In Daniel 7:1, he "wrote" down his own dream (presumably with words) and then spoke of it with "words" (see

---

[13] Brevard Childs, *Introduction to the Old Testament as Scripture* (Philadelphia: Fortress, 1979), 614.

Hab 2:2).[14] Later, he learns the interpretation of these "words/things" (Dan 7:16) and ultimately keeps this "word/thing" in his heart (Dan 7:28), resembling what the psalmist does with Scripture in Psalm 119:11 (see Josh 1:8; Ps 1:2). In Daniel 9:21-23, Gabriel gives Daniel understanding into "the vision" (מַרְאֶה) and "the word" (דָּבָר), a combination also found in Daniel 10:1.[15]

Whether a vision or a text, Daniel is able to understand and interpret them not through his own intellectual powers (Dan 2:27-28) but often through asking (בעה) the Lord or an angel for help (Dan 2:18, 23; 7:16). Indeed, there are several occasions when Daniel does not understand (Dan 7:15-16, 19; 8:15-17, 27; 9:22-23), but God repeatedly gives Daniel understanding, whether through an undescribed means, an angel, or Scripture (Dan 9:2, "I discerned in the books"). Reminiscent of Pharaoh's assessment of Joseph, Gentile rulers recognize Daniel as one in whom is the "s/Spirit" (Dan 4:8-9, 18; 5:11, 14; see Gen 41:38).[16]

Daniel's wisdom in the Babylonian era and into the Persian era fits Sailhamer's belief that there is a transition from prophecy to wisdom in the late stages of the writing and formation of the Hebrew Bible.[17] Whereas his visions and angelic encounters may not be normative, Daniel's faithful life and study of Scripture map very closely to the seams of the Tanak.[18] This prophet–wise man shows us that despite the real authority of a king's "word" (מִלָּה; e.g., Dan 2:5; 3:22), "law" (דָּת; e.g., Dan 2:9), "decree" (טְעֵם; e.g., Dan 3:10; 6:13), or "injunction" (אֱסָר; e.g., Dan 6:7-9), only the Lord's word and law have absolute authority (Dan 4:33; 9:11-13) and truly cannot be "changed" (עֲדָה/שְׁנָא; see Dan 2:21, 45; 6:8; 7:14). As such, it is the Lord and his word that deserve our utmost devotion as we await the fulfillment of his sure and faithful promises.

---

[14] Sailhamer sees Habakkuk as representative of prophets who "recorded their vision along with its explanation" (*Meaning of the Pentateuch*, 239).
[15] See Collins, *Daniel*, 352.
[16] For discussion of many parallels to Joseph, see Henze, "Use of Scripture," 281-86.
[17] Sailhamer, *Meaning of the Pentateuch*, 202-3, 217-18.
[18] See Stephen Chapman, *The Law and the Prophets* (Grand Rapids, MI: Baker, 2020), 240. Chapman notes in this connection, "The abiding authority of *scripture* is never questioned, only its proper interpretation (Dan 9:20-27)."

DANIEL 9 AND JEREMIAH'S PROPHECY OF THE SEVENTY YEARS

The reference to King Darius the Mede in Daniel 9:1 indicates that the Babylonian Empire has passed and sets the stage for Daniel to consider Jeremiah's prophecies of the seventy-year desolation of Jerusalem. Despite some uncertainty regarding Darius and his relationship to Cyrus (Dan 1:21; 10:1), the revelation of "seventy sevens" (Dan 9:24) demonstrates not only that final salvation was still future but also that Cyrus's decree, though also an important fulfillment of prophecy (Ezra 1:1; 2 Chron 36:22), was a step along the way to this final salvation and not equivalent to it (see Is 44:28–45:1).[19] Unlike other chapters in Daniel that begin with a dream or vision, Daniel 9 is distinctive, as Collins points out, because "another biblical text serves explicitly as the point of departure for the revelation."[20]

Daniel testifies in Daniel 9:2 that he "discerned in the books the number of years, according to the word of the Lord which came to Jeremiah the prophet, that were necessary to fulfill the desolations of Jerusalem to be seventy years." The key passages are Jeremiah 25:11-12 and Jeremiah 29:10, with both texts referring explicitly to "seventy years" of desolation or punishment, though the flow of thought differs in each context. The message in Jeremiah 25 was given in the "first year of Nebuchadnezzar" (Jer 25:1) in 605 BC, whereas the letter from Jeremiah 29 was addressed to those later exiled in 597 BC (Jer 29:1-2; 2 Kings 24:12-15). These relatively recent prophetic messages would have been particularly relevant to the exile Daniel.[21] Jeremiah 25:3-10 focuses on Judah's persistent rejection of Jeremiah and "[the Lord's] servants the prophets" (Jer 25:3-5; see also Jer 29:19; Dan 9:6, 10) with the result that judgment from the "north" was imminent (Jer 25:9). The land would be a "desolation" (חָרְבָּה) and the people would "serve" (עָבַד) foreigners for "seventy years" until the Lord "visits" (פָּקַד) the sins of the captors (Jer 25:11-12), which is reminiscent of the exodus (Gen 15:13-16; 50:24-25).

---

[19]Contra Collins, who sees the seventy sevens as contradicting the interpretations of the seventy years in 2 Chron 36:20-22 and Zech 1:12 (*Daniel*, 349, 352).
[20]Collins, *Daniel*, 347.
[21]Tremper Longman points out that Daniel may not have been reading a canonical version of Jeremiah. Longman, *How to Read Daniel* (Downers Grove, IL: InterVarsity Press, 2020), 110.

In contrast, Jeremiah 29:10 is part of a letter Jeremiah wrote to those already in exile about how they would stay there for a long time (Jer 29:5-7), contrary to the claims of false prophets (Jer 27:16; 28:3, 11). Jeremiah paints a picture of flourishing in exile (Jer 29:5-7): building (בָּנָה; see Jer 1:10), planting (נָטַע; see Jer 1:10), eating, marrying, multiplying (רָבָה; see Gen 1:28), and seeking "peace" (שָׁלוֹם) for the Gentile city of their residence and enjoying this peace along with Gentiles (see Jer 4:2; Gen 12:3; 18:18; 22:18). It is as though salvation, creation blessing, and Abrahamic covenant blessing are supposed to be experienced while still in exile. Yet when "seventy years" are "fulfilled" (מָלֵא; see Jer 25:12; Dan 9:2) for Babylon/Babel (בָּבֶל), the Lord "will visit [פָּקַד] you" and bring his people back home (Jer 29:10). The relationship between the blessings experienced in exile and those after the return is another question, but for Daniel the more pressing question was whether the passing of seventy calendar years would bring an end to "the desolations of Jerusalem" (Dan 9:2; see Is 52:9) and a return to the land. Were the Lord's "plans of peace" (שָׁלוֹם) for his people to give them a blessed "end" (אַחֲרִית) and "hope" (תִּקְוָה) imminent (Jer 29:11; see Jer 31:17)?

The respective contexts of Jeremiah 25:11-12 and Jeremiah 29:10 emphasize the Lord's fulfillment of "all my words" (כָּל־דְּבָרַי; Jer 25:13) or "my good word" (דְּבָרִי הַטּוֹב; Jer 29:10; see also Jer 25:3, 8; 29:19). Both also highlight the *written* word (of Jeremiah: "all that is written in this book," Jer 25:13; "these are the words of the book," Jer 29:1), such that the content of these texts could have reinforced for Daniel the importance of the written Word of God.[22] Certainly the fulfillment of these words of judgment against the enemy and the "good word" to bring the exiles home is exactly what the seventy-years prophecies are about. Another text that Daniel seems to have been aware of, Solomon's prayer for the temple in 1 Kings 8 (see below), also highlights the Lord's "word" (1 Kings 8:20, 26), including the written word of Scripture (1 Kings 8:53, 56).

---

[22]See Gerald Wilson, who connects the "books" in Dan 9:2 to Jer 29:1, 24-32. Wilson, "The Prayer of Daniel 9: Reflection on Jeremiah 29," *JSOT* 48 (1990): 93.

When Gabriel comes to give Daniel insight (Dan 9:21-22), it becomes clear that "seventy years" refers not to seventy calendar years but figuratively to a longer period of "seventy sevens" (Dan 9:24).[23] Special significance also accompanies the number seventy elsewhere in the Old Testament, such as Lamech's boast in Genesis 4:24, the table of seventy nations in Genesis 10, the seventy members of Jacob's family (Gen 46:27; Ex 1:5; Deut 10:22), and seventy of Israel's elders (Ex 24:1; Num 11:24-25). Symbolic numbers appear frequently in Daniel (e.g., four: Dan 1:17; 2:40; 3:25; 7:2-3, 7, 19, 23; seven: Dan 3:19; 4:16, 23, 25, 32; ten: Dan 1:12, 20; 7:7, 20, 24). As Gabriel explains, "seventy sevens" must pass before final salvation comes for "your people" and "your holy city" (i.e., Jerusalem); "transgression," "sin," and "iniquity" are put away; everlasting righteousness comes; all prophecy is fulfilled; and the temple is restored (Dan 9:24). The final drama will center on Jerusalem, a certain "m/Messiah," the temple, and a final enemy (Dan 9:25-27), to which we will return momentarily.

DANIEL'S PRAYER (DAN 9:3-19) AND ITS NEXUS CONNECTIONS

Having discussed nexus connections between Daniel's prayer of confession in Daniel 9:3-19 and the seams of the Tanak above, more connections to this prayer can be added. For example, his response of prayer and repentance in Daniel 9:3-19 suggests that he understood the role of prayer in the completion of the seventy years in Jeremiah 29:12-14 ("You will call on me. . . . You will pray to me. . . . You will seek me and find when you search with all your heart"; see Deut 4:29-30).[24] Just as Jeremiah 29:14 speaks of answered prayer and the return from exile ("I will be found by you. . . . I will bring back your captives"), Daniel's prayer concludes with a suggestive reference to the exodus (Dan 9:15) and a plea for the salvation of "your city Jerusalem" (Dan 9:16), "your sanctuary that is desolate" (Dan 9:17), and "your people" (Dan 9:19). Thus, Gerald Wilson sees Daniel as

---

[23]Sailhamer observes that this interpretation fits LXX Jeremiah, which focuses on a more open-ended enemy from the "north" (Jer 25:9; see "that nation," Jer 25:12) rather than Nebuchadnezzar specifically, as in the MT (*Meaning of the Pentateuch*, 165-66).

[24]Wilson sees the setting in Jer 29:1-3 as "compatible in all points with that of Daniel 9" ("Prayer of Daniel 9," 94).

fulfilling the "conditions for restoration" in Jeremiah 29:12-14, but the takeaway for Daniel ends up being the same as for the exiles who received Jeremiah's original letter in Jeremiah 29:1-23—be prepared for a long delay.[25] Are there then similar implications for today's readers who can look *back* at seventy times seven years as though it (or, most of it) has already passed? If the seventy years were not what they seemed, perhaps the seventy sevens are not either, with both encouraging faithful expectancy rather than calculation of precise dates (see Acts 1:7).

Commentators also observe Daniel's likely awareness of Solomon's prayer in 1 Kings 8, especially 1 Kings 8:46-51.[26] Solomon speaks of the situation in which Israel has been taken captive because of sin (1 Kings 8:46) but "make[s] supplication [חָנַן] . . . saying, 'We have sinned, and we have committed iniquity, we have acted wickedly [חָטָאנוּ וְהֶעֱוִינוּ רָשָׁעְנוּ],' and turn[s] to [the Lord] with all their heart . . . and pray [פָּלַל] to [the Lord]" (1 Kings 8:47-48; see also Deut 4:29; Jer 29:13). As Daniel "seek[s]" (בָּקַשׁ) the Lord, he likewise makes "supplications" (תַּחֲנוּן), "pray[s]" (פָּלַל), and confesses, "We have sinned, and we have committed iniquity, we have acted wickedly" (חָטָאנוּ וְעָוִינוּ הִרְשָׁעְנוּ; Dan 9:3-5). His closing appeal that the Lord "hear" (שָׁמַע), "open [his] eyes" (פְּקַח עֵינֶיךָ), show his "mercies" (רַחֲמִים), and "forgive" (סָלַח) for the sake of his own glory in Daniel 9:17-19 likewise follows 1 Kings 8:48-52. Praying in the direction of Israel, Jerusalem, and the temple while in exile as mentioned in 1 Kings 8:48 (see 1 Kings 8:29-30, 35, 38, 42, 44) also strongly resembles Daniel opening his windows toward Jerusalem and praying in Daniel 6:10.

Daniel's request in Daniel 9:17 for the Lord's grace ("supplications," תַּחֲנוּן) and request that he "shine [his] face [וְהָאֵר פָּנֶיךָ] on [his] sanctuary" further uses Numbers 6:25 from the priestly benediction in Numbers 6:24-27, "May the Lord *shine his face* towards you and *be gracious to you*" (יָאֵר יְהוָה פָּנָיו אֵלֶיךָ וִיחֻנֶּךָּ).[27] James Hamilton sees Daniel as praying this way because "he saw himself living out the realities with which

---

[25] Wilson, "Prayer of Daniel 9," 97-98.
[26] E.g., Longman, *How to Read Daniel*, 111.
[27] See John E. Goldingay, *Daniel*, WBC (Dallas: Word, 1989), 254.

Solomon's prayer was concerned... and sought the restoration for which Solomon pleaded."[28]

Scholars also observe the relationship between Daniel 9 and Leviticus 25–26.[29] Like 1 Kings 8:46-51, Leviticus 26:27-39 describes a situation in which Israel's persistent rebellion leads to the Lord punishing them through exile (Lev 26:33, 38), among other terrible things. Yet this solemn threat is followed by a promise that if they "confess their iniquity and the iniquity of their fathers concerning their unfaithfulness in acting unfaithfully against me" (וְהִתְוַדּוּ אֶת־עֲוֹנָם וְאֶת־עֲוֹן אֲבֹתָם בְּמַעֲלָם אֲשֶׁר מָעֲלוּ־בִי; Lev 26:40), the Lord will "remember" his "covenant" and the "land" in connection with the exodus (Lev 26:42, 45; see 1 Kings 8:51; Dan 9:15). Daniel likewise "confessed" (*hithpael* יָדָה; Dan 9:4, 20) the sins and "iniquities" (עָוֹן) of his own generation and those of their "fathers" (אָב; Dan 9:5-6, 8, 16), which resulted in exile "because of their unfaithfulness in acting unfaithfully against you" (בְּמַעֲלָם אֲשֶׁר מָעֲלוּ־בָךְ; Dan 9:7). Hamilton accordingly sees Daniel as purposely doing "exactly what Moses spoke of" in Leviticus 26:40.[30]

Leviticus 26:27-45 also ties the devastation of the land and Israel's exile to the land "enjoy[ing] its Sabbaths" (רָצָה; Lev 26:34, 43). This in turn connects to Israel "mak[ing] amends for their iniquity" (יִרְצוּ אֶת־עֲוֹנָם) while in exile (Lev 26:41, 43; see also Is 40:2). Leviticus 25:2-4 commands a Sabbath year for the land every seven years, and Leviticus 25:8-12 a Jubilee Year every fifty years after "seven Sabbath years, or seven years seven times" (שֶׁבַע שַׁבְּתֹת שָׁנִים שֶׁבַע שָׁנִים שֶׁבַע פְּעָמִים). Second Chronicles 36:20-21 explicitly links Jeremiah's prophecy of the seventy years to "the land enjoy[ing] its Sabbaths," and some accordingly see the seventy sevens of Daniel 9:24 in terms of seventy *Sabbath* years, or 490 years, as though the seventy-year punishment has been multiplied by seven, resembling the "sevenfold" (שֶׁבַע) punishments in Leviticus 26:18, 21, 24, 28.[31]

---

[28] James Hamilton, *With the Clouds of Heaven: The Book of Daniel in Biblical Theology* (Downers Grove, IL: InterVarsity Press, 2014), 107.
[29] Collins, *Daniel*, 352; Goldingay, *Daniel*, 232.
[30] Hamilton, *With the Clouds of Heaven*, 106.
[31] G. Brooke Lester, *Daniel Evokes Isaiah: Allusive Characterization of Foreign Rule in the Hebrew-Aramaic Book of Daniel* (London: T&T Clark, 2015), 37-38; Collins, *Daniel*, 352; Goldingay,

Fishbane argues that "their iniquity" (עֲוֺנָם) and "everlasting desolations" (שִׁמְמוֹת עוֹלָם) in Jeremiah 25:12 show a "Jeremiah-Leviticus connection" (see Lev 26:32-35, 38-40), and Haydon believes that Jeremiah 25–29 has Leviticus 25–26 in view.[32]

For the term "sevens/weeks," the use of a masculine plural ending (שָׁבֻעִים) in Daniel 9:24-26 and Daniel 10:2-3 instead of a feminine plural ending, as elsewhere in the Old Testament (שָׁבֻעוֹת), results in a puzzle of a phrase, especially in an unpointed text (שבעים שבעים), whose difficulty and duplication recalls the likewise mysterious *"mene mene teqel uparsin"* (מְנֵא מְנֵא תְּקֵל וּפַרְסִין) in Daniel 5:25 MT.[33] Both revelations require and receive divine interpretation in Daniel 5:25-28 and Daniel 9:24-27.[34] To better to understand specifics of the seventy sevens in Daniel 9:24-27, it should be seen in relation to other key eschatological texts within Daniel, especially Daniel 2.

A STONE IN THE LAST DAYS, THE SON OF MAN, AND THE MESSIAH WHO IS CUT OFF

The unfolding of the eschatological vision of the book of Daniel begins with Nebuchadnezzar's dream in Daniel 2. With execution looming if he does not find out what this dream was and interpret it, Daniel calls his three friends together to pray to the Lord for mercy and revelation (Dan 2:17-18). God answers and reveals the "mystery" (רָז) to Daniel in another night vision (Dan 2:19; see chapter six). His praise to God, who "changes times and seasons, removing kings and setting up kings" (Dan 2:21), is a central theme of the dream itself and the rest of the book

---

Daniel, 232. See the "oath" (הַשְּׁבֻעָה) coming on Israel in Dan 9:11, this form quite close to "seven" (שֶׁבַע).

[32]Fishbane, *Biblical Interpretation in Ancient Israel*, 489; Haydon, *Canonical Approach to Daniel 9:24-27*, 50-52.

[33]For discussion of this masculine ending but coming to a different conclusion, see Gerhard Hasel, "The Hebrew Masculine Plural for 'Weeks' in the Expression 'Seventy Weeks' in Daniel 9:24," *Andrews University Seminary Studies* 31, no. 2 (1993): 105-18. Regarding Dan 5:25, many scholars prefer the shorter Greek reading with only one *mene*, but see Goldingay, *Daniel*, 102, 110-11.

[34]The use of wordplay to decipher in Dan 5:25-28 would seem to raise the same possibility for "seventy sevens" in Dan 9:24. "Seventy" could play off not only "oath" in Dan 9:11, as noted above, but also the root שׂבע ("plenty, satisfaction"), as it does in Gen 41:29-31, 34, 37, 53.

of Daniel (e.g., Dan 2:44, 47; 4:17; 5:20-21). In Daniel's opening comments to Nebuchadnezzar, he emphasizes that what Nebuchadnezzar had asked was humanly impossible (Dan 2:27), but "there is a God in heaven who reveals secrets and has made known to King Nebuchadnezzar what will be *in the last days*" (Dan 2:28).

Besides indicating the eschatological significance of the dream, the Aramaic phrase "in the last days" (בְּאַחֲרִית יוֹמַיָּא) provides a strong link to the parallel Hebrew phrase in the Pentateuch and the Prophets (בְּאַחֲרִית הַיָּמִים). Given Daniel's knowledge of the Pentateuch and the Prophets (see above), this would further suggest that his use of this key phrase connects the eschatology of Nebuchadnezzar's dream to the eschatology of the Pentateuch (see Gen 49:1; Num 24:14; Deut 4:30; 31:29) and the Prophets (see Is 2:2; Jer 23:20; 30:24; 48:47; 49:39; Ezek 38:16; Hos 3:5; Mic 4:1). Daniel 2:28 and Daniel 10:14 are the only appearances of this phrase in the Writings and demonstrate its importance in all three sections of the Tanak as well as remind readers of this importance toward the end of the Tanak.[35] Furthermore, somewhat reminiscent of Balaam, a revelation of "the last days" is given to a pagan Gentile, Nebuchadnezzar. But unlike Balaam, on whom the Spirit descended so as to give him insight (Num 24:2-4, 15-16), the Babylonian king needs Daniel's help to understand his dream.

As Daniel explains, the dream was not merely of a static image of a statue but culminates in this statue being crushed to bits by a "rock" (אֶבֶן) and blown away by the wind (see Ps 1:4), while that rock becomes a giant mountain that fills the earth (Dan 2:34-35, 44-45). Since I am ultimately interested in how this helps clarify the eschatology of Daniel 9:24-27, I focus here on this action sequence. Scholars note the similarity between the giant mountain in Daniel 2:35 and Zion in Isaiah 2:2, which becomes the highest mountain in the world.[36] Though Henze ultimately discounts this connection, Shepherd's observation that both passages begin with "in

---

[35]See Shepherd, *Daniel in the Context*, 73: "The author has brought the eschatological and messianic weight of the entire Hebrew Bible to bear on the stories and visions of the book."
[36]E.g., Collins, *Daniel*, 165; Goldingay, *Daniel*, 49.

the last days" (Is 2:2; Dan 2:28) reinforces it.[37] Both texts also involve God's perfect rule over all the nations of the earth (Is 2:2-4; Dan 2:35). The "great mountain" (טוּר רַב) in Daniel 2:35 "fill[ing] all the earth" (וּמְלָת כָּל־אַרְעָא) further alludes to Genesis 1:28 ("fill the earth and subdue it and rule" [וּמִלְאוּ אֶת־הָאָרֶץ וְכִבְשֻׁהָ וּרְדוּ]) and suggests that this rock-turned-mountain not only establishes God's kingdom but also somehow fulfills the creation command that *humanity* rule. Such blending of human and divine rule appears again in the rule of "one like a son of man" in Daniel 7:13 and relates to the Davidic covenant (Ps 2:6-9; 1 Chron 17:11, 14).[38]

Table 11.1. Giant mountains in Daniel 2 and Isaiah 2

	Daniel 2	Isaiah 2
"In the last days"	Dan 2:28	Is 2:2
Large mountain	Dan 2:35	Is 2:2
God's rule over the world	Dan 2:35	Is 2:2-4

Although Nebuchadnezzar may not have understood, allusions to Genesis and Isaiah should not be seen as unusual or irrelevant to the reader of the *book* of Daniel. A distinction should be maintained here between the historical event involving Daniel and Nebuchadnezzar and the biblical text in a canonical book intended for a reader.[39] Regarding Genesis, scholars recognize additional parallels between Daniel's interpretation of Nebuchadnezzar's dream and Joseph's interpretation of dreams in Genesis 40–41.[40] Daewoong Kim also points out allusions to Genesis 10–11 in Daniel 1–2, including going east (Gen 11:2), "Babel/Babylon" (בָּבֶל; Gen 10:10; 11:9; Dan 1:1), "the land of Shinar" (אֶרֶץ־שִׁנְעָר; Gen 10:10; 11:2; Dan 1:2), language (Gen 11:1, 7, 9; Dan 1:4, 7; see also Dan 2:4), and a structure of

---

[37]Shepherd, *Daniel in the Context*, 75. Henze sees it as a reappropriation of "the promise once given to the exiles" in Is 41:15-16 that they would thresh mountains (enemies) and crush them like chaff, which is then blown away by the wind ("Use of Scripture," 285). This is a fascinating connection also but takes nothing away from the stronger connection of a giant eschatological mountain with Is 2:2-3.

[38]This creational scope along with the pagan environment may help explain the lack of explicit reference to David.

[39]The same point applies to the sign of Immanuel in Is 7 and Ahaz, concerning whom it is often insisted that the sign must be fully intelligible to him.

[40]See note 16 above.

human pride that is brought to an end by God (Tower of Babel, statue in Nebuchadnezzar's dream; see Dan 3:1; 4:10-14; 5:23).[41] He also mentions the desire not to "scatter on the face of all the earth" (Gen 11:4, 9) in connection with "fill the earth" in Genesis 9:1, which leads back to the point above about Genesis 1:28 and Daniel 2:35.[42] The stone "striking" (מְחָא) the statue in Daniel 2:34-35 further recalls the Messiah "striking" (שׁוּף) the serpent's head (Gen 3:15) and especially his "striking" (מָחַץ) enemy nations in Numbers 24:17 (note the similarity of the Aramaic מְחָא and the Hebrew מָחַץ).[43]

As for Isaiah, Jewish tradition further connects the opening verses of Daniel to Isaiah's prophecy to Hezekiah in Isaiah 39:1-7.[44] Having recovered from illness, Hezekiah received Babylonian guests (bearing "letters [סְפָרִים] and a gift," Is 39:1; "literature," Dan 1:4) and showed them "all the house of his vessels [כָּל־בֵּית כֵּלָיו] and all which was found in his treasures [אוֹצָר]" (Is 39:2; see also Is 39:4). Isaiah then predicted that one day everything in Hezekiah's "house" (בַּיִת) and what his fathers "stored up as treasure" (אָצַר) would be taken to "Babylon" (בָּבֶל), and some royal descendants of Hezekiah would be "eunuchs [סָרִיס] in the palace/temple of the king of Babylon [בְּהֵיכַל מֶלֶךְ בָּבֶל]" (Is 39:6-7). In Daniel 1, Nebuchadnezzar, "king of Babylon" (מֶלֶךְ־בָּבֶל; Dan 1:1), defeats Jerusalem as part of the divine plan (Dan 1:2, "the Lord gave Jehoiakim king of Judah into his hand"). Taking "vessels" (כְּלִי) from the temple, he puts them in "the house of the treasury [בֵּית אוֹצַר] of his god" (Dan 1:2). Nebuchadnezzar then commands "the chief of his eunuchs" (רַב סָרִיסָיו) to bring from the Israelites "royal offspring" (וּמִזֶּרַע הַמְּלוּכָה) and nobility, excellent young men fit to serve "in the palace of the king" (בְּהֵיכַל הַמֶּלֶךְ; Dan 1:3-4).

Daniel 1 thus reads as though it specifically fulfills Isaiah 39:1-7, in addition to prophecies of exile generally. Accordingly, Jewish interpreters

---

[41]Daewoong Kim, "Biblical Interpretation in the Book of Daniel: Literary Allusions in Daniel to Genesis and Ezekiel" (PhD diss., Rice University, 2013), 50-51, 74-80.
[42]Kim, "Biblical Interpretation in the Book," 54.
[43]See *HALOT*; Targum Onqelos Deut 32:39; Targum Psalms Ps 110:5-6. The precise etymological relationship is uncertain, but an allusion can still be considered. For allusions to a Hebrew text in an Aramaic text, see Lester, *Daniel Evokes Isaiah*, 111-12.
[44]For sources and discussion, see Collins, *Daniel*, 135.

often have seen Daniel as a eunuch (Dan 1:7-11). Collins questions whether סָרִיס means "eunuch" here and seems to discount the connection to Isaiah 39:1-7, but even if Daniel were not a eunuch, the other links between Isaiah 39 and Daniel 1 still sustain an allusive and historical link (see Jer 29:2).[45] Thus, Jennie Grillo argues that Daniel 1 situates the book of Daniel in the "narrative gap" that exists in the Old Testament concerning life in Babylonian exile and the temporal gap in the macrostructure of the book of Isaiah between its prediction of Babylonian exile in Isaiah 39 and the implied setting of Babylonian exile in Isaiah 40–55.[46] Indeed, scholars have been pointing out the influence of Isaiah on Daniel for some time already (e.g., Is 10; see below).[47]

Furthermore, if the author of Daniel has engaged the book of Isaiah carefully and not in piecemeal fashion, as Grillo and others argue, we would expect to see not only more Isaianic allusions in Daniel but also coordinated ones that strategically draw out Isaianic theology.[48] This is precisely what was found with the giant mountain in Daniel 2:35 alluding to Isaiah 2:2. The same applies for the "stone ... cut without hands" (אִתְגְּזֶרֶת/הִתְגְּזֶרֶת אֶבֶן דִּי־לָא בִידַיִן), which "strikes" the image and not only becomes this "mountain" (טוּר) but was first cut out "from the mountain" (מִטּוּרָא; Dan 2:34-35, 45). The book of Isaiah uses terms for "stone/rock" (צוּר, אֶבֶן) in strategic ways that are drawn together in Daniel 2:34-35, 45. In both books, the identity of the stone is crucial for interpretation.

The stone that strikes in Daniel 2:34-35 resembles the "stone of striking" (אֶבֶן נֶגֶף) for Israel in Isaiah 8:14, where this stone is the Lord himself. He is relatedly called "rock" (צוּר) in this verse and Isaiah 17:10; 26:4; 44:8 (see also Deut 32:4). Yet the stone in Daniel 2 is distinct from the Lord, for this text suggests that the Lord "cut" it from the mountain

---

[45]Collins, *Daniel*, 134-35.
[46]Jennie Grillo, "From a Far Country: Daniel in Isaiah's Babylon," *JBL* 136 (2017): 363-80.
[47]Fishbane, *Biblical Interpretation in Ancient Israel*, 489-91, 494; Lester, *Daniel Evokes Isaiah*, 2-3; Grillo, "From a Far Country," 365-67.
[48]Grillo, "From a Far Country," 378-79; Lester, *Daniel Evokes Isaiah*, 91; Fishbane, *Biblical Interpretation in Ancient Israel*, 490; Andrew Teeter, "Isaiah and the King of As/Syria in Daniel's Final Vision: On the Rhetoric of Inner-Scriptural Allusions and the Hermeneutics of 'Mantological Exegesis,'" in *A Teacher for All Generations: Essays in Honor of James C. VanderKam*, ed. Eric Mason (Leiden: Brill, 2012), 169-99.

and set it up as an everlasting kingdom (Dan 2:35, 44-45). Accordingly, Isaiah 28:16 describes the Lord having "laid a foundation in Zion a stone [אֶבֶן], a tested stone [אֶבֶן בֹּחַן], a precious cornerstone [פִּנַּת יִקְרַת] laid as a foundation" (see Ps 118:22), which closely parallels the implicit divine selection and preparation of a stone and its becoming an everlasting kingdom in Daniel 2. Andrew Teeter further observes that Isaiah 8 and Isaiah 28 are themselves related within the book of Isaiah and have influenced the book of Daniel. Along with Isaiah 10, these two texts are also messianic hotspots in Isaiah (see Immanuel in Is 8:8, 10; "a remnant will return to mighty God" in Is 10:21; see also Is 7:3; 9:6), and Isaiah 8:14 and Isaiah 28:16 are cited messianically in the New Testament (Rom 9:33; 1 Pet 2:6, 8).[49]

A stone that is "tested" (בֹּחַן) in Isaiah 28:16 further suggests the refining of gold or silver (Ps 66:10; Job 23:10; Prov 17:3), just as Israel itself undergoes in Isaiah 1:25 through exile, and "precious" (יָקָר) recalls the foundation of Solomon's temple (1 Kings 5:31 MT; 7:9-11) while also suggesting a gemstone (2 Sam 12:30; 1 Kings 10:2; Ezek 28:13; Prov 3:15). To illustrate divine wisdom, Job 28 describes gems, "stone," and "every precious thing [יָקָר]" being hewn out of "mountains" (הָרִים) and "stone/flint/rock" (צוּר/חַלָּמִישׁ/אֶבֶן; Job 28:2-3, 6, 9-10). Whereas Job 28 emphasizes the value of wisdom and the difficulty of finding it, we are also left to ponder whether Nebuchadnezzar's dream and its interpretation, which equally highlights divine wisdom, also involves a mined jewel even though Daniel 2 merely refers to a stone cut from a mountain.

In his work on Daniel's allusions to Isaiah, Brooke Lester does not relate Isaiah 28:16 to Daniel 2, but he does cite Isaiah 51:1-2, "Look to the rock [from which] you [= Israel] were hewn. . . . Look to Abraham your father and Sarah."[50] Lester sees Isaiah 51:1-2 as implying that Israel is itself a rock that has been quarried and interprets the stone in Daniel 2 as Israel, which proceeds to grow and crush its enemies in accordance with Isaiah 41:15-16

---

[49]Teeter, "Isaiah and the King," 172-83; Fishbane, *Biblical Interpretation in Ancient Israel*, 489-91; Lester, *Daniel Evokes Isaiah*, 89-92.

[50]Lester, *Daniel Evokes Isaiah*, 109-10. He does, however, relate Is 28:16 to Is 10:22-25 as background for Dan 8-12 on 137-39.

and Daniel 2:34-35, 44-45. Recognizing the importance of Isaiah 51:1-2 and allusions to Isaiah, I suggest that the connections to Isaiah 2:2 and Isaiah 28:16 ("in the last days," giant mountain, divine rule over the earth, important stone) are stronger than to Isaiah 41:15-16, which does involve crushing enemies to bits who are then blown away (see Dan 2:35) but does not mention an important stone or giant mountain.

Furthermore, Isaiah 51:1 LXX appears to use the same consonantal text as Isaiah 51:1 MT (הביטו אל צור חצבתם) and reads more smoothly in the LXX than the MT: "Look to the rock you hewed [qal]" (LXX) versus "Look to the rock [from which] you were hewn [$pual$]."[51] Unlike the MT, which has Israel being hewn from a rock, the LXX states that *Israel* hewed a rock and hence does not suggest that Israel is also a rock. Furthermore, the rock in Isaiah 51:1b can just as easily be understood as the Lord (Is 51:1a, "Listen to me") instead of Abraham (Is 51:2a, "Look to Abraham"), which would balance the proportion and meaning of Isaiah 51:1 and Isaiah 51:2 better.[52] As seen in chapter seven, the rock hewing in Isaiah 51:1 is preceded by messianic instances of a rock or rock-like thing being struck (Is 48:21; 50:7). Thus, I understand Isaianic rock allusions in Daniel 2 to bring together the foundation stone of Isaiah 28:16, the giant mountain of Isaiah 2:2, and the suggestive hewing of a rock in Isaiah 51:1.

Table 11.2. Stone/rock in Daniel 2 and Isaiah

	Daniel 2	Isaiah
Stone or rock	Dan 2:34-35, 45	Is 8:14; 17:10; 26:4; 28:16; 44:8
Divine origin	"cut without hands" (Dan 2:34, 45)	"I lay a foundation stone in Zion" (Is 28:16)
Rock that is hewed	Dan 2:45	Is 51:1

---

[51]For an extended argument in favor of the LXX reading, see P. A. H. de Boer, *Second-Isaiah's Message* (Leiden: Brill, 1956), 58-67. See also Chen, *The Messianic Vision of the Pentateuch* (Downers Grove, IL: InterVarsity Press, 2019), 181-82, 208.

[52]See Klaus Baltzer, *Deutero-Isaiah*, trans. Margaret Kohl, Hermeneia (Minneapolis: Fortress, 2001), 345-46. Baltzer further notes that both *rock* and *well* in Is 51:1 provided water in the wilderness (note the well in Num 21:16-18) and that *rock* connects to Deut 32. For an extreme separation of Is 51:1a from Is 51:1b-2, see Claus Westermann, *Isaiah 40–66*, OTL (Philadelphia: Westminster, 1969), 232-37.

The stone "*cut* [גְּזַר] without hands" in Daniel 2:34, 45 could also echo the messianic Suffering Servant, who "was *cut off* [נִגְזַר] from the land of the living" in Isaiah 53:8 (see chapter seven). Although "cut" in Daniel 2:34, 45 seems to imply origin rather than death, the triconsonantal roots of the Aramaic and Hebrew verbs are the same (גזר), and both verbs are passive. At the same time, the cut stone in Daniel 2:34, 45 also coordinates with an eschatological "m/Messiah" (מָשִׁיחַ) who "will be cut off" (יִכָּרֵת) in Daniel 9:26. The fit between Daniel 9:26 and Isaiah 53:8 is actually closer, and Daniel 9:26 deserves consideration as an early, individual, messianic interpretation of Isaiah 53, rivaling Daniel 12:3 and its proposed corporate interpretation of the same ("those who justify the many [will shine] like the stars," where "those who justify" [= "the wise"/*maskilim* in Dan 12:3a] are equated with the Suffering Servant).[53] Daniel 12:3 still echoes Isaiah 53 but need not imply a corporate interpretation, since the exegesis of Isaiah 53 itself and Daniel 9:26 suggest otherwise.

The form יִכָּרֵת ("will be cut off") in Daniel 9:26 has additional fascinating resonances. On the one hand, it recalls the lawbreaker being "cut off [*niphal* כָּרֵת] from his people" so frequently mentioned in the Pentateuch (e.g., Ex 30:33, 38; 31:14; Lev 7:20-21, 25, 27). On the other hand, when considered messianically, it also recalls the Lord's promise to David, "A man will not be *cut off* [יִכָּרֵת] from being upon the throne of Israel for you" (1 Kings 2:4; 8:25; 9:5; 2 Chron 6:16; 7:18; see also Jer 33:17). Of course, this promise was conditional on the obedience of the Davidic house, and their disobedience resulted in their being cut off in exile (1 Kings 9:7). The Messiah's being cut off in Daniel 9:26 is not because of his sins or lawbreaking (see Is 50:8-9), but neither is the Servant's in Isaiah 53, who was innocent and suffered vicariously for the sins of the people (see Dan 9:24, "atone for iniquity"). The Servant's being cut off is also temporary (Is 53:10-12), since the Lord will fulfill the Davidic covenant through him. Antti Laato also points out parallels between Daniel 9:24-26 and the striking of the good shepherd in Zechariah 13:7-9.[54]

---

[53] H. L. Ginsberg, "The Oldest Interpretation of the Suffering Servant," *VT* 3 (1953): 402-3.

[54] Antti Laato, "The Seventy Yearweeks in the Book of Daniel," *ZAW* 102 (1990): 222-23. Laato, however, interprets the shepherd's death "as the rejection of the Messianic programme." He also discusses eschatological conflict in Jerusalem with reference to Zech 12; 14, Joel 3; Ezek 38–39.

Although the book of Daniel does not explicitly refer to David or the Davidic covenant, in many places Daniel refers to things that are only one very small step away from these central Old Testament realities. In the opening lines of Daniel, "Jehoiakim king of Judah" (Dan 1:1-2) is obviously a Davidic king, and his defeat by Nebuchadnezzar represents the fall of the house of David and the apparent failure of the Lord himself to uphold the Davidic covenant (see Dan 5:2-4). Relatedly, the group of promising Israelite captives includes those "from the seed of the *kingdom*" (הַמְּלוּכָה; Dan 1:3), and Daniel is accordingly described as "from the sons of [the exile of] *Judah*" (Dan 1:6; 2:25; 5:13; 6:13). Daniel's concern for Jerusalem and the temple is based on the Lord's own concern for the same (Dan 9:2, 16-20, 24-26; Jer 3:17), which passages such as 2 Samuel 7:13; Isaiah 37:35; 38:5-6; and Psalm 132:13-17 show is rooted in the Davidic covenant. His corporate prayer of confession includes "our kings" (מְלָכֵינוּ; Dan 9:6, 8; see also Jer 2:26; 25:18), naturally understood as Davidic kings, and "we have committed iniquity" (וְהֶעֱוִינוּ)" in Daniel 9:5 not only follows 1 Kings 8:47 but also uses the same key term in 2 Samuel 7:14 ("when he commits iniquity" [עָוָה]), which concerns the possibility that Davidic kings sin. The terms "m/Messiah" (מָשִׁיחַ) and "prince" (נָגִיד) in Daniel 9:25-26 can also be linked to the Davidic covenant (1 Sam 2:10; 2 Sam 7:8; 22:51; Is 55:4).

Based on such considerations and scholars' recognition that Daniel is highly interconnected to the rest of the Old Testament, the Davidic covenant and its key texts should be allowed to inform our understanding of Daniel. The location of Chronicles also at the end of the Tanak and its obvious emphasis on David and the Davidic covenant reinforce this (e.g., 1 Chron 17:1-15). In this way, the messianic meaning of Daniel emerges with full force. This is because the prediction in Daniel 2:44, "The God of the heavens will establish [יָקִים] a kingdom [מַלְכוּ; on earth, Dan 2:35] which will never be destroyed [לְעָלְמִין לָא תִתְחַבַּל] . . . and it will stand forever" (וְהִיא תְּקוּם לְעָלְמַיָּא), is then best understood as a reaffirmation of the Davidic covenant, which had famously promised David, "I will raise up [וַהֲקִימֹתִי] your seed after you. . . . I will establish the throne of his kingdom forever [וְכֹנַנְתִּי אֶת־כִּסֵּא מַמְלַכְתּוֹ עַד־עוֹלָם]. . . . Your house and your kingdom [וּמַמְלַכְתְּךָ] will endure forever [עַד־עוֹלָם] before you; your throne will be established forever" (2 Sam 7:12-13, 16; see also 1 Kings 9:5; 1 Chron 17:11).[55] Even Daniel's closing statement that "the dream is true and the interpretation *trustworthy*" (מְהֵימַן, Dan 2:45) matches "will endure/be faithful" (וְנֶאְמַן) in 2 Samuel 7:16. Both texts coordinate well with faith (אָמַן) in the divine word of deliverance in Isaiah 7:7-9 and Isaiah 28:16 (note David/Zion themes), as well as the faith theme in the Pentateuch (see chapter three).

Whereas Daniel 2 explicitly predicts only the divine establishment of an everlasting *kingdom*, the strategically parallel vision in Daniel 7 sharpens the focus on the *king* who will rule this kingdom, as already suggested to the sensitive reader by the stone. Like Daniel 2, Daniel 7 also involves four successive earthly kingdoms followed by a triumphant, divinely established, everlasting kingdom. This time, however, this kingdom is specifically given to "one like a son of man" (כְּבַר אֱנָשׁ; Dan 7:13), that is, an individual human king. Coming with "the clouds of heaven," he reaches the "Ancient of days" (Dan 7:13) and is given "dominion and honor and a kingdom" (Dan 7:14). This dominion is "his dominion [i.e., the son of man's]," "an everlasting dominion that will not be taken away" (שָׁלְטָן עָלַם דִּי־לָא יֶעְדֵּה), and the kingdom is "his kingdom, which will not be destroyed" (מַלְכוּתֵהּ דִּי־לָא תִתְחַבַּל; Dan 7:14). The everlasting rule of the son of man is identical to that promised to David's messianic seed, "the only one to whom God gives the world's kingdoms permanently in the Old Testament."[56] Evidently, it is this king who, like God (Dan 4:34; 6:20, 26), will actually "live forever" (לְעָלְמִין חֱיִי), not Nebuchadnezzar, Belshazzar, Darius, or any other human king (Dan 2:4; 3:9; 5:10; 6:6, 21). The rock-turned-mountain kingdom "which will not be destroyed forever" (לְעָלְמִין לָא תִתְחַבַּל) in Daniel 2:44 is thus the kingdom of "one like a son of man" (see Is 11:1, 9). In this way, viewing Daniel 2 in relation to Daniel 7 clarifies that Daniel 2 does not simply involve the kingdom of God in a

---

[55] See Shepherd, *Daniel in the Context*, 29, 75.
[56] Paul House, *Daniel*, TOTC (Downers Grove, IL: InterVarsity Press, 2018), 131.

general sense but specifically as ruled by this "one like a son of man," the Davidic Messiah (see Ps 2; 110).

Yet his reception of worship (פְּלַח) by "all peoples, nations, and tongues" (וְכֹל עַמְמַיָּא אֻמַיָּא וְלִשָּׁנַיָּא) demonstrates that this is no ordinary human king (Dan 7:14). The preceding context showed Daniel and his three friends on separate occasions refusing to "worship" (פְּלַח) anything or anyone besides the one true God (Dan 3:12, 17-18; 6:16, 20). Nebuchadnezzar's attempt to force "all peoples, nations, and tongues" (Dan 3:7) to worship the golden image was ultimately a failure because such worship belongs to God alone (Dan 3:28). But God's rightful reception of worship is apparently shared with "one like a son of man." It is as though he is both God and man. Indeed, he comes with "the clouds of heaven" (Dan 7:13; see "stone cut without hands"), unlike other human beings, who dwell "on the earth" (Dan 2:10-11, 38). Nebuchadnezzar was allowed to rule "all peoples, nations, and tongues" for a time (Dan 5:19), but "one like a son of man" will do so forever and be worshiped by them. Such a picture of the Messiah not only ruling the world but also receiving its worship has reused the picture found in the messianic text Genesis 27:29, "Let the peoples serve you and the nations bow down to you" (יַעַבְדוּךָ עַמִּים וְיִשְׁתַּחֲוּוּ לְךָ לְאֻמִּים; see discussion of Ps 72:11 in chapter nine).[57]

As Shepherd observes, Daniel 9 links the visions of the four kingdoms in Daniel 2 and Daniel 7 to Jeremiah's prophecy of Jerusalem's redemption after seventy years.[58] The first three kingdoms have been identified (Dan 2:38; 8:20-21), and Daniel 9 passingly references the second (Dan 9:25, a "word to restore and build Jerusalem"; Ezra 1:2-3) before focusing on the fourth (Dan 9:26-27; see also Dan 7:21, 25).[59] Since Daniel 2 and Daniel 7 are so strongly eschatological and messianic especially in relation to this fourth kingdom, landing the final stages of the

---

[57] Chen, *Messianic Vision of the Pentateuch*, 96-97. For reuse of such textual pictures, see Kevin Chen, "The 'Deuteroevangelium' in Numbers 21–24," Cateclesia Institute, December 13, 2021, https://cateclesia.com/2021/12/13/the-deuteroevangelium-in-numbers-21-24/.

[58] Shepherd, *Daniel in the Context*, 67.

[59] Shepherd, *Daniel in the Context*, 95. Contra House, who sees all four kingdoms in Dan 9:24-27 with the fourth kingdom only present in Dan 9:27b, the second half of the last seven (*Daniel*, 157-63).

seventy sevens and its "m/Messiah" in any other era (e.g., the Maccabean) falls flat. Not only would Daniel 9:24-27 have little to do with the rock-turned-mountain, son of man, and everlasting kingdom that will not be destroyed, but such an interpretation would gut the meaning of Jeremiah's prophecies of the seventy years that it is supposed to be explaining. In some cases, critical rejection of predictive prophecy seems to have led to seeking past referents in Daniel 9:24-27 with respect to a second-century BC date for the book of Daniel.[60] But Jeremiah's prophecy, it should be remembered, is an eschatological prophecy of judgment on Babylon (Jer 25:11-14) and the hopeful "end" (אַחֲרִית) of Israel (Jer 29:10-14; see Num 23:10; Deut 4:29-31).

The restoration of Israel and the temple, the final dealing with sin, the bringing of "everlasting righteousness" (צֶדֶק עֹלָמִים), and the sealing of prophecy in Daniel 9:24 should be seen as nothing less (see Jer 3:16-17; 23:5-6; 31:31-34). The cutting off the Messiah after the sixty-ninth week in Daniel 9:26 should likewise be understood as reaffirming Isaiah 53 while placing the Suffering Servant's coming late but not at the very end of the divine timetable for world history. His death does not bring peace immediately, for the final enemy ("the coming prince") subsequently destroys the city and the sanctuary, and "war" (מִלְחָמָה) continues (Dan 9:26; see 7:21; Is 2:4). The references to "desolations are decreed" (נֶחֱרֶצֶת שֹׁמֵמוֹת), "flood" imagery (שֶׁטֶף), and a "decreed consumption" (כָּלָה וְנֶחֱרָצָה) in Daniel 9:26-27 cast this enemy in terms of Assyria in Isaiah 8:7-8 (flood/שֶׁטֶף); Isaiah 10:22-23 ("decreed destruction overflowing with righteousness" [כִּלָּיוֹן חָרוּץ שׁוֹטֵף צְדָקָה]; "decreed consumption" [כָּלָה וְנֶחֱרָצָה]); and Isaiah 28:15, 17-18, 22 (flood/שֶׁטֶף; "decreed consumption" [כָּלָה וְנֶחֱרָצָה]).[61] Suggestively, these same passages present Immanuel

---

[60]For discussion of this, see Richard Hess, "The Seventy Sevens of Daniel 9: A Timetable for the Future?," *BBR* 21, no. 3 (2011): 328. Laato references scholarly agreement that the last and seventieth seven is "referring to the Maccabean period from the time of the murder of Onias III (at the end of the 170's B. C.) to the time of the purification of the Temple (in 164 B. C.)" ("Seventy Yearweeks in the Book," 213). He adds, "There is good reason to suppose that Dan 9,24–27 in its present form refers to the murder of Onias III [i.e., the 'messiah']" (217).

[61]I adapt the work of Fishbane, Lester, and Teeter here. See Fishbane, *Biblical Interpretation in Ancient Israel*, 489-91; Lester, *Daniel Evokes Isaiah*, 90-93; Teeter, "Isaiah and the King," 172-74, 176-78, 180-83.

(Is 8:8; see also Is 7:14), the remnant's repentance toward "mighty God" (Is 10:21; see also Is 9:6), and the laying of a foundation stone in Zion (Is 28:16) in relation to deliverance from this same enemy. It is as though from Daniel's perspective, "the great Isaianic oracles against Assyria had *not yet* been fulfilled."[62]

We must leave further study of the final enemy for another time, but the important thing is that he will meet his "end" (קֵץ, Dan 9:26), whereas the dominion of the son of man is "an everlasting dominion" (Dan 7:14) with "no end" (אֵין־קֵץ, Is 9:7).

CONCLUSION

Daniel 9 is a clear example of a nexus passage, with its explicit reference to Jeremiah and his prophecy of the seventy years. The above analysis also showed its reliance on the law of Moses and the prophets more broadly. These prophets include Isaiah, which is especially important in the book of Daniel, including for Nebuchadnezzar's eschatological dream in Daniel 2. This dream interlocks with the son of man in Daniel 7 as well as the seventy sevens in Daniel 9. Since Daniel 9 is the last nexus passage in this book, I have also paid special attention to the presentation of Daniel as an ideal reader of the Tanak as an example for us to imitate of faithful living in a difficult world. Like him, we await the fulfillment of prophecy and the Lord's everlasting kingdom.

---

[62]Fishbane, *Biblical Interpretation in Ancient Israel*, 491, emphasis original. "By quoting the Isaianic oracle from the age of Assyrian domination, the author of Dan. 9:26-7 meant to suggest that the old prophetic text was spoken for his day, when Israel still anticipated the decreed destruction and revival in glory" (490).

CONCLUSION

In *The Shape of Difficulty: A Fan Letter to Unruly Objects*, Bret Rothstein introduces readers to the fascinating world of three-dimensional puzzles (mechanical puzzles), including their history, designers, and accompanying subculture. One special case he mentions is a puzzle that actually cannot be solved and as such is "ontologically difficult." Relatedly, he explains how a particular designer has played on the doubts of users (or "aspirants") by alternately suggesting that a puzzle is impossible to assemble while also hinting that it can be assembled. Although we have little reason to believe that the Old Testament was intentionally written to confuse, we are still left with the question whether its constituent texts can be assembled into a textual unity. Is such a textual assembly possible? Or is the Old Testament really just a collection of various pieces that are, strictly speaking, unassembleable as meaning-bearing texts? These are important questions, for the way one answers dictates whether an intrinsic unity is pursued or abandoned. At the same time, one's answer to these questions can be more reflective of an overall attitude toward the Old Testament (even if having some empirical basis) than the result of rigorous proof. As Rothstein points out, "Interpretability is an attitude we bring to an object."[1]

A historical example from biblical studies that illustrates the truth of Rothstein's statement is Julius Wellhausen. Within the opening pages of his classic *Prolegomena to the History of Israel*, Wellhausen provides a brief autobiographical insight into his intellectual journey and the development of his Documentary Hypothesis. He recounts how he enjoyed Old Testament historical and prophetic books but struggled with the Law (i.e., the

---

[1] Bret Rothstein, *The Shape of Difficulty: A Fan Letter to Unruly Objects* (University Park: Pennsylvania State University Press, 2019), 13, 136-38, 146; see also 29, 40-44.

Pentateuch), even seeing them as "two wholly distinct worlds." Subsequently, when Wellhausen heard of Karl Heinrich Graf's idea of dating the Law after the Prophets, "almost without knowing his reasons for his hypothesis, I was prepared to accept it."[2] In other words, he intuitively believed it to be true without detailed proof. Based on his own experiences and existing knowledge, Wellhausen already held a particular attitude toward the interpretability, or perhaps uninterpretability, of the Old Testament that influenced his study of it.

In the introduction to this book, I used the illustration of a subway network mainly because of the analogy between transfer stations and nexus passages in the Old Testament. What it oversimplifies is the complexity of even a single Old Testament book. An Old Testament book is far more complex than a single subway line in a metro transit network, no matter how complicated a path that line might take. With Rothstein in mind, a better analogy for a single biblical book is a puzzle. The literary macrostructure of the book parallels the edge pieces of a puzzle, which serve as its framework. Ideally, these pieces should be identified and put in place first, and then the other pieces afterward in this context. Longer books are like puzzles with more pieces—they generally take more time and effort to complete. Each passage is like a single puzzle piece, which fits into its immediate context (the pieces directly connecting with or touching it) and the context of the whole book (the whole puzzle and the picture it displays).

The puzzles that are most familiar to us are two-dimensional, rectangular jigsaw puzzles. If we were to follow this analogy all the way, however, we would be left with a conception of the Old Testament in which each book is a discrete puzzle but with no clear way to link one to another. We can imagine a situation in which the puzzles of every book in the Old Testament have been completed and laid out across the floor but with each puzzle still remaining largely independent of the others. Indeed, this result is not far off from the current state of biblical studies, which has emphasized specialization but often with an additional result of

---

[2]Julius Wellhausen, *Prolegomena to the History of Israel*, trans. J. Sutherland Black and Allan Menzies (Edinburgh: Adam & Charles Black, 1885), 3.

fragmentation. While specialization itself is not necessarily the root problem, the discovery and exploration of nexus passages can provide a counterbalance to the tendency toward fragmentation.

If the preceding puzzle analogy is to more closely approximate our conception of the Old Testament, the discrete, two-dimensional puzzles must be transformed into interlocking, interdependent puzzles within three-dimensional space. Indeed, Rothstein analyzes many types of three-dimensional puzzles, and though not all of them challenge the user to assemble them, some do (e.g., burrs).[3] The type of three-dimensional puzzle I have in mind for the Old Testament is necessarily a hypothetical one. Each Old Testament book is no longer represented by a flat, rectangular puzzle but a three-dimensional, nonplanar puzzle. The shapes of such puzzles could resemble anything from a ribbon that twists and turns in three-dimensional space to a finite, curved surface, and more. If we imagine many of these three-dimensional surfaces mutually enfolding and sometimes interlocking (compare protein structure in molecular biology), then nexus passages are these points at which one puzzle connects to another. These nexus points are shared between multiple surfaces/puzzles and simultaneously support the cohesion of each puzzle involved. In this sense, it is as though nexus passages are parts of multiple puzzles, just as transfer stations are part of multiple transit lines.

Yet if the Old Testament as a whole really is a literary, textual, and theological unity, then not only must these three-dimensional surfaces be coherent individually, occupy the same general space, and interlock, but the way in which they interlock and the resultant three-dimensional composite object must also exhibit an overarching design. A reader may rightfully expect intentionality, even beauty, in the literary and textual cohesion of the Old Testament text, whether on the level of passages, sections of books, whole books, groups of books, or the entire Old Testament, especially the Tanak (Law, Prophets, Writings). To this end, nexus passages are a powerful way to perceive the interconnectivity, overarching design, and beauty of the Old Testament text.

---

[3]Rothstein, *Shape of Difficulty*, 58, 60, 133-34.

By bringing out these features, nexus passages show that the Hebrew Bible is itself a literary, textual, and theological wonder. Like a carefully designed, extensive subway system, key texts and their interrelationships are depicted in the simplified diagram below, which includes all ten nexus passages in this book and several other key passages but even so shows only a few connections for each text. More links and more passages could easily be added for the sake of accuracy, but at a certain point the (heuristic) diagram becomes very difficult to draw.

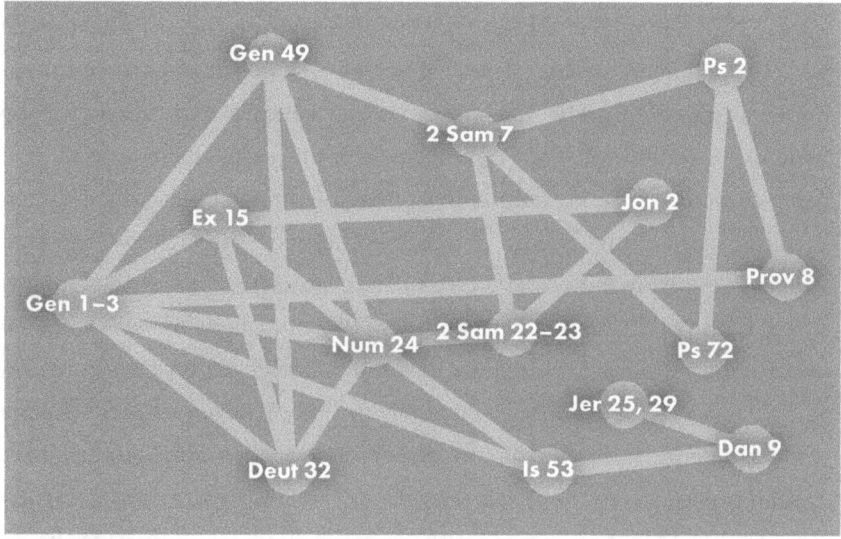

Figure 12.1. Simplified diagram of nexus passages and the interconnectivity of the Old Testament

Those today who do not believe in a thoroughly textual unity of the Old Testament may feel that they have tried everything and see no way forward. Gerhard von Rad, for example, questions whether "understand[ing] the Old Testament as a unity" is a "legitimate demand," declaring, "I very much doubt whether the main task of an Old Testament theology is the understanding of Israel's literary legacy as a unity."[4] With all due respect to such giants as von Rad and Wellhausen, Rothstein pertinently points

---

[4]Gerhard von Rad, *Old Testament Theology*, trans. D. M. G. Stalker (Peabody, MA: Hendrickson, 2005), 2:427.

out that difficult puzzles challenge the belief that we really have tried everything and lead us to try something else. Surely it would be a mistake to assume that just because some do not see how a particular task can be accomplished that this task is therefore impossible. Indeed, Rothstein urges us not to reach premature conclusions regarding what is possible and impossible, especially if there are outstanding issues that we do not yet fully understand. The way forward could be right in front of us, waiting to be discovered. Neither should we uncritically rely on common sense (e.g., consensus), which, Rothstein points out, "depends entirely on local knowledge."[5]

This book is evidence that I believe in the interpretability of the Old Testament as a textual, literary, and ultimately theological unity and that one helpful way forward is nexus passages. These highly interconnected texts have a special depth of meaning and an ability to draw the vast Old Testament material together.[6] The analogies from the physical world of mechanical puzzles and of subway systems are intended to help us imagine and envision the Old Testament in new and constructive ways. If the Old Testament is really this interconnected, there are significant implications for Old Testament exegesis in general. First, although close attention to a particular text is fundamental, we should avoid an atomistic view of individual passages and as much as possible try to understand each text in relationship to the book of which it is a part. This includes not only its immediately preceding and following context but also the book as a whole, even in longer books. Second, we should be aware of the possibility of a significant connection to a passage in another book altogether. Of course not every passage has these connections, but those that truly do are illuminated by these other texts. To be sure, it takes time and practice to discern and interpret these connections, but fortunately there is more and more helpful material today that can provide guidance and examples. Third,

---

[5]Rothstein, *Shape of Difficulty*, 47, 94-95, 44. He cites Clifford Geertz, "Common Sense as a Cultural System," *Antioch Review* 33, no. 1 (1975): 22: "The really important facts of life lie scattered openly along its surface."

[6]Borrowing insights from mathematician G. H. Hardy, Rothstein also sees a relationship between depth and interconnectivity for puzzles (*Shape of Difficulty*, 56-57).

knowledge of Biblical Hebrew is very useful for identifying these links because we often begin by looking for shared language. That is to say, "wonders from your law" (Ps 119:18) are best seen and enjoyed in the original language.

I hope that, in my own imperfect and limited way, I have helped readers see these wonders for themselves. I further pray that readers will discover more such wonders on their own, share and refine them with others, and be increasingly convinced that the Old Testament bears the marks of divine genius working through deeply thoughtful human authors, who set forth the eschatological Messiah for us to behold. The story of Old Testament theology will no doubt continue, with new characters and plot turns yet to come, but what will remain are the Scriptures themselves and the wonders therein, awaiting our discovery.

BIBLIOGRAPHY

Abernethy, Andrew, and Gregory Goswell. *God's Messiah in the Old Testament*. Grand Rapids, MI: Baker, 2020.

Alexander, T. Desmond. "Further Observations on the Term 'Seed' in Genesis." *TynBul* 48, no. 2 (1997): 363-67.

———. "Messianic Ideology in the Book of Genesis." In *The Lord's Anointed: Interpretation of Old Testament Messianic Texts*, edited by Philip Satterthwaite, Richard Hess, and Gordon Wenham, 19-39. Grand Rapids, MI: Baker, 1995.

Anderson, A. A. *2 Samuel*. WBC. Dallas: Word, 1989.

Anderson, Bernard. "Exodus Typology in Second Isaiah." In *Israel's Prophetic Heritage: Essays in Honor of James Muilenburg*, edited by Bernard Anderson and W. Harrelson, 177-95. New York: Harper, 1962.

Anderson, William. "The Curse of Work in Qoheleth: An Exposé of Genesis 3:17-19 in Ecclesiastes." *EvQ* 70, no. 2 (1998): 99-113.

Ansberry, Christopher. "Arbors Among Aphorisms: The Anatomy of the Tree in the Book of Proverbs." In *Networks of Metaphors in the Hebrew Bible*, edited by Danilo Verde and Antje Labahn, 263-79. Leuven: Peeters, 2020.

Ashley, Timothy. *The Book of Numbers*. NICOT. Grand Rapids, MI: Eerdmans, 1993.

Athanasius. *Defence of the Nicene Definition*. NPNF^2 4:150-72.

Bailey, Randall. "The Redemption of YHWH: A Literary Critical Function of the Songs of Hannah and David." *BibInt* 3, no. 2 (1995): 213-31.

Baker, David L. *Two Testaments, One Bible*. Downers Grove, IL: InterVarsity Press, 1976.

———. *Two Testaments, One Bible*. 3rd ed. Downers Grove, IL: InterVarsity Press, 2010.

Baltzer, Klaus. *Deutero-Isaiah*. Translated by Margaret Kohl. Hermeneia. Minneapolis: Fortress, 2001.

Band, Arnold. "Swallowing Jonah: The Eclipse of Parody." *Prooftexts* 10 (1990): 177-95.

Barbiero, Gianni. "The Risks of a Fragmented Reading of the Psalms: Psalm 72 as a Case in Point." *ZAW* 120 (2008): 67-91.

Bartholomew, Craig. "Biblical Theology and Biblical Interpretation: Introduction." In *Out of Egypt: Biblical Theology and Biblical Interpretation*, edited by Craig Bartholomew et al., 1-19. Grand Rapids, MI: Zondervan, 2004.

———. "Qohelet as a Master of and Mastered by Metaphor." In *Networks of Metaphors in the Hebrew Bible*, edited by Danilo Verde and Antje Labahn, 329-46. Leuven: Peeters, 2020.

Bartholomew, Craig, and Ryan O'Dowd. *Old Testament Wisdom Literature: A Theological Introduction*. Downers Grove, IL: InterVarsity Press, 2011.

Bates, Matthew. *The Birth of the Trinity*. Oxford: Oxford University Press, 2016.
Batto, Bernard. "The Reed Sea: *Requiescat in Pace*." *JBL* 102, no. 1 (1983): 27-35.
Beale, G. K. *A New Testament Biblical Theology: The Unfolding of the Old Testament in the New*. Grand Rapids, MI: Baker Academic, 2011.
Beckwith, Roger. "Formation of the Hebrew Bible." In *Mikra: Text, Translation, Reading and Interpretation of the Hebrew Bible in Ancient Judaism and Early Christianity*, edited by Martin Jan Mulder, 39-86. Minneapolis: Fortress, 1990.
Belcher, Richard, Jr. *Finding Favour in the Sight of God: A Theology of Wisdom Literature*. New Studies in Biblical Theology 46. Downers Grove, IL: InterVarsity Press, 2018.
Benckhuysen, Amanda. "Revisiting the Psalm of Jonah." *Calvin Theological Journal* 47 (2012): 5-31.
Bengel, Johann Alberti. *Ordo Temporum*. Stuttgart: J. B. Mezler, 1770.
———. *Sechzig erbauliche Reden über die Offenbarung Johannis*. 2nd ed. Stuttgart: J. C. Erhard, 1758.
Benz, Ernst. *The Mystical Sources of German Romantic Philosophy*. Translated by Blair Reynolds and Eunice Paul. Allison Park, PA: Pickwick, 1983.
Bergey, Ronald. "The Song of Moses (Deuteronomy 32.1-43) and Isaianic Prophecies: A Case of Early Intertextuality?" *JSOT* 28, no. 1 (2003): 33-54.
"Biblical Theology." The Gospel Coalition. www.thegospelcoalition.org/topics/biblical-theology/.
Blaising, Craig, and Carmen Hardin, eds. *Psalms 1–50*. Ancient Christian Commentary on Scripture 7. Downers Grove, IL: InterVarsity Press, 2008.
Blenkinsopp, Joseph. *Isaiah 1–39*. AB. New York: Doubleday, 2000.
———. *Isaiah 40–55*. AB. New York: Doubleday, 2002.
———. *The Pentateuch*. New York: Doubleday, 1992.
———. *Prophecy and Canon*. Notre Dame, IN: Notre Dame University Press, 1977.
Block, Daniel. *Covenant: The Framework of God's Plan of Redemption*. Grand Rapids, MI: Baker, 2021.
———. *Obadiah: The Kingship Belongs to Yahweh*. Hearing the Message of Scripture. Grand Rapids, MI: Zondervan, 2013.
Boda, Mark, Russell Meek, and William Osborne, eds. *Riddles and Revelations: Explorations into the Relationship Between Wisdom and Prophecy in the Hebrew Bible*. New York: T&T Clark, 2018.
Bodner, Keith. "Ark-Eology: Shifting Emphases in 'Ark Narrative' Scholarship." *Currents in Biblical Research* 4, no. 2 (2006): 169-97.
Bolin, Thomas. *Freedom Beyond Forgiveness: The Book of Jonah Re-Examined*. Sheffield: Sheffield Academic Press, 1997.
Boston, James R. "The Wisdom Influence upon the Song of Moses." *JBL* 87, no. 2 (1968): 198-202.
Brecht, Martin. "Johann Albrecht Bengels Theologie der Schrift." *ZTK* 64, no. 1 (1967): 99-120.
Briggs, Charles Augustus. *The Book of Psalms*. ICC. Edinburgh: T&T Clark, 1987.
Bright, John. *Jeremiah*. AB. Garden City, NY: Doubleday, 1965.

Brown, Michael. "Jewish Interpretations of Isaiah 53." In *The Gospel According to Isaiah 53: Encountering the Suffering Servant in Jewish and Christian Theology*, edited by Darrell Bock and Mitch Glaser, 61-83. Grand Rapids, MI: Kregel, 2012.

Brown, William P. "Proverbs 8:22-31." *Int* 63, no. 3 (2009): 286-88.

Brueggemann, Walter. "Bounded by Obedience and Praise: The Psalms as Canon." *JSOT* 50 (1991): 63-92.

———. *First and Second Samuel*. Interpretation. Louisville: John Knox, 1990.

Brueggemann, Walter, and Patrick Miller. "Psalm 73 as a Canonical Marker." *JSOT* 72 (1996): 45-56.

Bruno, Chris. "10 Things You Should Know About Biblical Theology." Crossway, February 10, 2017. www.crossway.org/articles/10-things-you-should-know-about-biblical-theology/.

Brunson, Andrew. *Psalm 118 in the Gospel of John: An Intertextual Study on the New Exodus Pattern in the Theology of John*. WUNT 2.158 Tübingen: Mohr Siebeck, 2003.

Büsching, Anton Friderich. *Auslegung der Weissagung Jesaiae*. Halle: Johann Gottlob Bierwirths, 1751.

Campbell, Antony. *1 Samuel*. FOTL. Grand Rapids, MI: Eerdmans, 2003.

———. *2 Samuel*. FOTL. Grand Rapids, MI: Eerdmans, 2005.

Cartledge, Tony. *1 & 2 Samuel*. SHBC. Macon, GA: Smyth & Helwys, 2001.

Ceresko, Anthony. "The Rhetorical Strategy of the Fourth Servant Song (Isaiah 52:13–53:12): Poetry and the Exodus-New Exodus." *CBQ* 56 (1994): 42-55.

Chapman, Stephen B. *The Law and the Prophets: A Study in Old Testament Canon Formation*. Grand Rapids, MI: Baker Academic, 2020.

Cheek, Jonathan. "Recent Developments in the Interpretation of the Seed of the Woman in Genesis 3:15." *JETS* 64 (2021): 215-36.

Chen, Kevin. "The 'Deuteroevangelium' in Numbers 21–24." Cateclesia Institute, December 13, 2021. https://cateclesia.com/2021/12/13/the-deuteroevangelium-in-numbers-21-24/.

———. *Eschatological Sanctuary in Exodus 15:17 and Related Texts*. New York: Lang, 2013.

———. "Gleanings from the John H. Sailhamer Papers at Southeastern Baptist Theological Seminary." *Southeastern Theological Review* 9, no. 1 (2018): 93-112.

———. *The Messianic Vision of the Pentateuch*. Downers Grove, IL: InterVarsity Press, 2019.

———. "(Mis)Understanding Sailhamer." *Journal for the Evangelical Study of the Old Testament* 7, no. 1 (2021): 27-59.

———. "Psalm 110: A Nexus for Old Testament Theology." *CTR* 17, no. 2 (Spring 2020): 49-65.

Childs, Brevard. *Biblical Theology: A Proposal*. Minneapolis: Fortress, 1993.

———. *Biblical Theology in Crisis*. Philadelphia: Westminster, 1970.

———. *Biblical Theology of the Old and New Testaments*. Minneapolis: Fortress, 1993.

———. *The Book of Exodus*. OTL. Louisville: Westminster, 1974.

———. *Introduction to the Old Testament as Scripture*. Philadelphia: Fortress, 1979.

———. *Isaiah*. OTL. Louisville: Westminster John Knox, 2001.

———. "The Sensus Literalis of Scripture: An Ancient and Modern Problem." In *Beiträge zur Alttestamentlichen Theologie. Festschrift für Walther Zimmerli zum 70. Geburtstag*, edited by H. Donner, 80-93. Göttingen: Vandenhoeck & Ruprecht, 1977.

Clemens, David. "The Law of Sin and Death: Ecclesiastes and Genesis 1–3." *Themelios* 19, no. 3 (1994): 5-8.

Clines, David. *Job 1–20*. WBC. Dallas: Word, 1989.

Cole, R. Alan. *Exodus*. TOTC. Downers Grove, IL: InterVarsity Press, 1973.

Cole, Robert L. "An Integrated Reading of Psalms 1 and 2." *JSOT* 98 (2002): 75-88.

———. *Psalms 1–2: Gateway to the Psalter*. Sheffield: Sheffield Phoenix, 2012.

———. *The Shape and Message of Book III (Psalms 73–89)*. Sheffield: Sheffield Academic Press, 2000.

Collins, John. *Daniel*. Hermeneia. Minneapolis: Fortress, 1993.

Cooper, Alan. "The Song of Moses (Deuteronomy 32:1-43) as the Plan of Jewish History." In *Ve-'Ed Ya'aleh (Gen 2:6): Essays in Biblical and Ancient Near Eastern Studies Presented to Edward L. Greenstein*, edited by Peter Machinist et al., 2:989-1005. Atlanta: SBL Press, 2021.

Cornhill, Carl Heinrich. *Einleitung in das Alte Testament*. Freiburg: Mohr, 1891.

Craigie, Peter. *Psalms 1–50*. WBC. Waco, TX: Word, 1983.

Cross, Frank M. *Canaanite Myth and Hebrew Epic*. Cambridge, MA: Harvard University Press, 1973.

———. "Studies in the Structure of Hebrew Verse: The Prosody of the Psalm of Jonah." In *The Quest for the Kingdom of God: Studies in Honor of George Mendenhall*, edited by H. B. Huffmon, F. A. Spina, and A. R. W. Green, 159-67. Winona Lake, IN: Eisenbrauns, 1983.

Curtis, John Briggs. "Word Play in the Speeches of Elihu (Job 32–37)." *Proceedings of the Eastern Great Lakes and Midwest Bible Societies* 12 (1992): 23-30.

Dahood, Mitchell. *Psalms I: 1–50*. AB. Garden City, NY: Doubleday, 1966.

Davidson, Richard M. "Back to the Beginning: Genesis 1–3 and the Theological Center of Scripture." In *Christ, Salvation, and the Eschaton: Essays in Honor of Hans K. LaRondelle*, edited by Daniel Heinz, Jiří Moskala, and Peter M. van Bemmelen, 5-29. Berrien Springs, MI: Old Testament Dept., Seventh-day Adventist Theological Seminary, Andrews University, 2009.

Davies, John A. "'Discerning Between Good and Evil': Solomon as a New Adam in 1 Kings." *WTJ* 73 (2011): 39-57.

Day, John. "God and Leviathan in Isaiah 27:1." *BSac* 155 (1998): 423-36.

De Beaugrande, Robert, and Wolfgang Dressler. *Introduction to Text Linguistics*. New York: Longman, 1981.

De Boer, P. A. H. *Second-Isaiah's Message*. Leiden: Brill, 1956.

Dekker, Jaap. "What Does David Have to Do with It? The Promise of a New Covenant in the Book of Isaiah." In *Covenant: A Vital Element of Reformed Theology: Biblical, Historical and Systematic-Theological Perspectives*, edited by Hans Burger, Gert Kwakkel, and Michael Mulder, 101-23. Leiden: Brill, 2021.

Delitzsch, Franz. *Messianic Prophecies in Historical Succession*. Translated by Samuel Ives Curtiss. Reprint, Eugene, OR: Wipf & Stock, 1997.

Dell, Katharine J. "Exploring Intertextual Links Between Ecclesiastes and Genesis 1–11." In *Reading Ecclesiastes Intertextually*, edited by Katharine J. Dell and Will Kynes, 3-14. London: Bloomsbury, 2014.

Dempster, Stephen. "'At the End of the Days' (בְּאַחֲרִית הַיָּמִים)—An Eschatological Technical Term? The Intersection of Context, Linguistics and Theology." In *The Unfolding of Your Words Gives Light: Studies on Biblical Hebrew in Honor of George L. Klein*, edited by Ethan Jones, 118-41. University Park, PA: Eisenbrauns, 2018.

———. *Dominion and Dynasty: A Theology of the Hebrew Bible*. Downers Grove, IL: InterVarsity Press, 2003.

———. "The End of History and the Last Man." In *The Seed of Promise: The Sufferings and Glory of the Messiah: Essays in Honor of T. Desmond Alexander*, edited by Paul Williamson and Rita Cefalu, 113-41. Wilmore, KY: GlossaHouse, 2020.

Diestel, Ludwig. *Geschichte des Alten Testamentes in der christlichen Kirche*. Jena: Mauke, 1869.

DiFransico, Lesley. "'He Will Cast Their Sins into the Depths of the Sea . . .': Exodus Allusions and the Personification of Sin in Micah 7:7-20." *VT* 67 (2017): 187-203.

Driver, S. R. *Deuteronomy*. ICC. Reprint, Edinburgh: T&T Clark, 1986.

Driver, S. R., and A. D. Neubauer. *The Fifty-Third Chapter of Isaiah According to the Jewish Interpreters*. Oxford: James Parker, 1877.

Duhm, Bernard. *Das Buch Jesaia*. 4th ed. Göttingen: Vandenhoeck & Ruprecht, 1968.

Dumortier, Jean-Bernard. "Un rituel d'intronisation: le Ps. LXXXIX 2-38." *VT* 22 (1972): 176-96.

Durham, John. *Exodus*. WBC. Waco, TX: Word, 1987.

Duvall, J. Scott, and J. Daniel Hays. *God's Relational Presence: The Cohesive Center of Biblical Theology*. Grand Rapids, MI: Baker, 2019.

Ebeling, Gerhard. "Die Anfänge von Luthers Hermeneutik." *ZTK* 48, no. 2 (1951): 172-230.

———. "The Meaning of 'Biblical Theology.'" *Journal of Theological Studies* 6, no. 2 (1955): 210-25.

Edwards, Jonathan. *Sinners in the Hands of an Angry God*. Phillipsburg, NJ: P&R, 1992.

Ehlen, Arlis John. "Old Testament Theology as Heilsgeschichte." *Concordia Theological Monthly* 35, no. 9 (1964): 517-44.

Eichrodt, Walter. *Theology of the Old Testament*. Translated by J. A. Baker. Philadelphia: Westminster, 1961.

Estelle, Bryan. *Echoes of Exodus: Tracing a Biblical Motif*. Downers Grove, IL: InterVarsity Press, 2018.

Faro, Ingrid. *Evil in Genesis: A Contextual Analysis of Hebrew Lexemes for Evil in the Book of Genesis*. Bellingham, WA: Lexham, 2021.

Fishbane, Michael. *Biblical Interpretation in Ancient Israel*. Oxford: Clarendon, 1985.

———. "Jeremiah IV 23-26 and Job III 3-13: A Recovered Use of the Creation Pattern." *VT* 21 (1971): 151-67.

———. *Text and Texture*. New York: Schocken, 1979.

Fohrer, Georg. "Das Alte Testament und das Thema 'Christologie.'" *Evangelische Theologie* 30, no. 6 (1970): 281-98.

Forman, Charles. "Koheleth's Use of Genesis." *Journal of Semitic Studies* 5, no. 3 (1960): 256-63.

Forti, Tova. "Of Ships and Seas, and Fish and Beasts: Viewing the Concept of Universal Providence in the Book of Jonah Through the Prism of Psalms." *JSOT* 35 (2011): 359-74.

Fox, Michael V. *Proverbs 1–9*. AB. New York: Doubleday, 2000.

Fox, R. Michael, ed. *Reverberations of the Exodus in Scripture*. Eugene, OR: Wipf & Stock, 2014.

Frei, Hans. *The Eclipse of Biblical Narrative*. New Haven, CT: Yale University Press, 1974.

Fritsch, Charles. "Bengel, the Student of Scripture." *Int* 5, no. 2 (1951): 203-15.

Gaffin, Richard. "The Redemptive-Historical View." In *Biblical Hermeneutics: Five Views*, edited by Stanley Porter and Beth Stovell, 89-110. Downers Grove, IL: InterVarsity Press, 2012.

Garrett, Duane. *Proverbs, Ecclesiastes, Song of Songs*. New American Commentary. Nashville: Broadman, 1993.

Geertz, Clifford. "Common Sense as a Cultural System." *Antioch Review* 33, no. 1 (1975): 5-26.

Geiger, Abraham. *Urschrift und Übersetzungen der Bibel in ihrer Abhängigkeit von der innern Entwicklung des Judentums*. Breslau: Julius Hainauer, 1857.

Gentry, Peter, and Stephen Wellum. *Kingdom Through Covenant: A Biblical-Theological Understanding of Covenants*. Wheaton, IL: Crossway, 2012.

Gilbert, George. "Biblical Theology: Its History and Its Mission. II." *The Biblical World* 6 (1895): 358-66.

Ginsberg, H. L. "The Oldest Interpretation of the Suffering Servant." *VT* 3 (1953): 400-404.

Gitay, Yehoshua. "Reflections on the Poetics of the Samuel Narrative: The Question of the Ark Narrative." *CBQ* 54 (1992): 221-30.

Gladd, Benjamin. "Series Preface." In *Exodus Old and New: A Biblical Theology of Redemption*, by L. Michael Morales, ix-x. Downers Grove, IL: InterVarsity Press, 2020.

Goldingay, John E. *Daniel*. WBC. Dallas: Word, 1989.

———. "The 'Salvation History' Perspective and the 'Wisdom' Perspective Within the Context of Biblical Theology." *EvQ* 51 (1979): 194-207.

Goldingay, John, and David Payne. *Isaiah 40–55*. ICC. London: Bloomsbury, 2014.

Goldsworthy, Graeme. *Christ-Centered Biblical Theology*. Downers Grove, IL: InterVarsity Press, 2012.

———. *Gospel-Centered Hermeneutics*. Downers Grove, IL: InterVarsity Press, 2006.

———. *The Tree of Life: Reading Proverbs Today*. Sydney: Anglican Information Office Press, 1993.

———. "What Is the Discipline of Biblical Theology." 9Marks, February 26, 2010. www.9marks.org/article/what-discipline-biblical-theology/.

Grant, Jamie. *The King as Exemplar: The Function of Deuteronomy's Kingship Law in the Shaping of the Book of Psalms*. Atlanta: Society of Biblical Literature, 2004.

Gray, George Buchanan. *A Critical and Exegetical Commentary on Numbers*. ICC. Edinburgh: T&T Clark, 1986.

Grillo, Jennie. "From a Far Country: Daniel in Isaiah's Babylon." *JBL* 136 (2017): 363-80.

Grossman, Jonathan. "'Dynamic Analogies' in the Book of Esther." *VT* 59 (2009): 394-414.

Gundersen, David "Gunner." "A Story in the Psalms? Narrative Structure at the 'Seams' of the Psalter's Five Books." In *Reading the Psalms Theologically*, edited by David M. Howard Jr. and Andrew J. Schmutzer, 79-95. Bellingham, WA: Lexham Academic, 2023.

Gunkel, Hermann, and Joachim Begrich. *Introduction to Psalms*. Translated by James Nogalski. Macon, GA: Mercer University Press, 1998.

Hamilton, James. *God's Glory in Salvation Through Judgment: A Biblical Theology*. Wheaton, IL: Crossway, 2010.

———. "The Skull Crushing Seed of the Woman: Inner-Biblical Interpretation of Genesis 3:15." *Southern Baptist Journal of Theology* 10, no. 2 (2006): 30-54.

———. *With the Clouds of Heaven: The Book of Daniel in Biblical Theology*. Downers Grove, IL: InterVarsity Press, 2014.

Hanson, Paul. "The World of the Servant of the Lord in Isaiah 40–55." In *Jesus and the Suffering Servant: Isaiah 53 and Christian Origins*, edited by William Bellinger Jr. and William Farmer, 9-22. Harrisburg, PA: Trinity Press International, 1998.

Harman, Allan. *Isaiah*. Fearn, UK: Christian Focus, 2005.

Harris, Scott. *Proverbs 1–9: A Study of Inner-Biblical Interpretation*. Atlanta: Scholars Press, 1996.

Hasel, Gerhard. "The Hebrew Masculine Plural for 'Weeks' in the Expression 'Seventy Weeks' in Daniel 9:24." *Andrews University Seminary Studies* 31, no. 2 (1993): 105-18.

———. *Old Testament Theology: Basic Issues in the Current Debate*. 4th ed. Grand Rapids, MI: Eerdmans, 1991.

Haydon, Ron. "'The Law and the Prophets' in MT Daniel 9:3-19." *BBR* 24, no. 1 (2014): 15-26.

———. *"Seventy Sevens Are Decreed": A Canonical Approach to Daniel 9:24-27*. Winona Lake, IN: Eisenbrauns, 2016.

Hayes, John, and Frederick Prussner. *Old Testament Theology: Its History and Development*. Atlanta: John Knox, 1985.

Hays, J. Daniel. "Has the Narrator Come to Praise Solomon or to Bury Him? Narrative Subtlety in 1 Kings 1–11." *JSOT* 28, no. 3 (2003): 149-74.

Heim, Knut. "The (God-)Forsaken King of Psalm 89: A Historical and Intertextual Enquiry." In *King and Messiah in Israel and the Ancient Near East*, edited by John Day, 296-322. Sheffield: Sheffield Academic Press, 1998.

———. "The Perfect King of Psalm 72: An 'Intertextual' Inquiry." In *The Lord's Anointed: Interpretation of Old Testament Messianic Texts*, edited by Philip Satterthwaite, Richard Hess, and Gordon Wenham, 223-48. Grand Rapids, MI: Baker, 1995.

Helmbold, Andrew. "J. A. Bengel:—'Full of Light.'" *Bulletin of the Evangelical Theological Society* 6, no. 3 (1963): 73-81.

Henze, Matthias. "The Use of Scripture in the Book of Daniel." In *A Companion to Biblical Interpretation in Early Judaism*, edited by Matthias Henze, 279-307. Grand Rapids, MI: Eerdmans, 2012.

Hermisson, Hans-Jürgen. "The Fourth Servant Song in the Context of Second Isaiah." Translated by Daniel Bailey. In *The Suffering Servant: Isaiah 53 in Jewish and Christian Sources*, edited by Bernd Janowski and Peter Stuhlmacher, 16-47. Grand Rapids, MI: Eerdmans, 2004.

———. "Observations on the Creation Theology in Wisdom." Translated by Barbara Howard. In *Israelite Wisdom: Theological and Literary Essays in Honor of Samuel Terrien*, edited by John Gammie, 43-57. Missoula, MT: Scholars Press, 1978.

Hertzberg, Hans Wilhelm. *I & II Samuel*. Translated by John Bowden. OTL. Philadelphia: Westminster, 1964.

Hess, Richard. "The Seventy Sevens of Daniel 9: A Timetable for the Future?" *BBR* 21, no. 3 (2011): 315-30.

Hibbard, J. Todd. "Isaiah XXVII 7 and Intertextual Discourse About 'Striking' in the Book of Isaiah." *VT* 55, no. 4 (2005): 461-76.

Hitzig, Ferdinand. *Die Sprüche Salomos's*. Zürich: Orell, Füssli, 1858.

Ho, Peter C. W. *The Design of the Psalter: A Macrostructural Analysis*. Eugene, OR: Pickwick, 2019.

Hoffman, Yair. "A North Israelite Typological Myth and a Judaean Historical Tradition: The Exodus in Hosea and Amos." *VT* 39 (1989): 169-82.

Hossfeld, Frank-Lothar, and Erich Zenger. *Psalms 2: A Commentary on Psalms 51–100*. Translated by Linda Maloney. Hermeneia. Minneapolis: Fortress, 2005.

———. *Psalms 3: A Commentary on Psalms 101–150*. Hermeneia. Translated by Linda Maloney. Minneapolis: Fortress, 2011.

House, Paul. *Daniel*. TOTC. Downers Grove, IL: InterVarsity Press, 2018.

———. *Old Testament Theology*. Downers Grove, IL: InterVarsity Press, 1998.

———. *The Unity of the Twelve*. Sheffield: Sheffield Academic Press, 1990.

Howard, David, Jr. *The Structure of Psalms 93–100*. Winona Lake, IN: Eisenbrauns, 1997.

Howard, David, Jr., and Michael Snearly. "Reading the Psalter as a Unified Book: Recent Trends." In *Reading the Psalms Theologically*, edited by David Howard Jr. and Andrew Schmutzer, 1-35. Bellingham, WA: Lexham, 2023.

Hübner, Eberhard. *Schrift und Theologie: Eine Untersuchung zur Theologie Joh. Chr. K. von Hofmanns*. Munich: Chr. Kaiser, 1956.

Hugenberger, Gordon. "The Servant of the Lord in the 'Servant Songs' of Isaiah: A Second Moses Figure." In *The Lord's Anointed: Interpretation of Old Testament Messianic Texts*, edited by Philip Satterthwaite, Richard Hess, and Gordon Wenham, 105-40. Grand Rapids, MI: Baker, 1995.

Hunter, Alastair. "Jonah from the Whale: Exodus Motifs in Jonah 2." In *The Elusive Prophet: The Prophet as a Historical Person, Literary Character and Anonymous Artist*, edited by Johannes C. de Moor, 142-58. Leiden: Brill, 2001.

Janowski, Bernd. "He Bore Our Sins: Isaiah 53 and the Drama of Taking Another's Place." In *Jesus and the Suffering Servant: Isaiah 53 and Christian Origins*, edited by William Bellinger Jr. and William Farmer, 48-74. Harrisburg, PA: Trinity Press International, 1998.

Japhet, Sara. *I & II Chronicles*. OTL. Louisville: Westminster John Knox, 1993.

Jefferson, Helen. "Psalm LXXVII." *VT* 13, no. 1 (1963): 87-91.

Jobes, Karen, and Moisés Silva. *Invitation to the Septuagint*. 2nd ed. Grand Rapids, MI: Baker, 2015.

Johnston, Philip. *Shades of Sheol: Death and the Afterlife in the Old Testament*. Downers Grove, IL: InterVarsity Press, 2002.

Jones, Ethan. "1 Samuel 2:6: Time and *Wayyiqtol* in Hannah's Song." *VT* 72, no. 1 (2022): 26-46.

Josephus. *The New Complete Works of Josephus*. Translated by William Whiston. Grand Rapids, MI: Kregel, 1999.

Kaiser, Walter. "The Davidic Promise and the Inclusion of the Gentiles (Amos 9:9-15 and Acts 15:13-18): A Test Passage for Theological Systems." *JETS* 20, no. 2 (1977): 97-111.

Kamphausen, Adolf. *Das Lied Moses. Deut. 32, 1–43*. Leipzig: F. A. Brockhaus, 1862.

Keil, C. F., and Franz Delitzsch. *Isaiah*. Commentary on the Old Testament 7. Reprint, Peabody, MA: Hendrickson, 1996.

———. *The Minor Prophets*. Commentary on the Old Testament 10. Reprint, Peabody, MA: Hendrickson, 1996.

———. *The Pentateuch*. Commentary on the Old Testament 1. Reprint, Peabody, MA: Hendrickson, 1996.

———. *Proverbs, Ecclesiastes, Song of Solomon*. Commentary on the Old Testament 6. Reprint, Peabody, MA: Hendrickson, 1996.

Keiser, Thomas. "The Song of Moses: A Basis for Isaiah's Prophecy." *VT* 55, no. 4 (2005): 486-500.

Kelly, Brian. *Retribution and Eschatology in Chronicles*. Sheffield: Sheffield Academic Press, 1996.

Kidner, Derek. *Psalms 73–150*. TOTC. Downers Grove, IL: InterVarsity Press, 1975.

Kim, Brittany, and Charlie Trimm. *Understanding Old Testament Theology*. Grand Rapids, MI: Zondervan, 2020.

Kim, Daewoong. "Biblical Interpretation in the Book of Daniel: Literary Allusions in Daniel to Genesis and Ezekiel." PhD diss., Rice University, 2013.

Klein, Ralph. *1 Samuel*. WBC. Waco, TX: Word, 1983.

———. *2 Chronicles*. Hermeneia. Minneapolis: Fortress, 2012.

———. "The Last Words of David." *Currents in Theology and Mission* 31, no. 1 (2004): 15-23.

Klingbeil, Gerald, ed. *The Genesis Creation Account and Its Reverberations in the Old Testament*. Berrien Springs, MI: Andrews University Press, 2015.

Knight, George A. F. *The Song of Moses: A Theological Quarry*. Grand Rapids, MI: Eerdmans, 1995.

Koorevaar, Hendrik. "Chronicles as the Intended Conclusion to the Old Testament Canon." In *The Shape of the Writings*, edited by Julius Steinberg and Timothy Stone, 207-35. Winona Lake, IN: Eisenbrauns, 2015.

Korpel, Marjo. "Metaphors in Isaiah LV." *VT* 46 (1996): 43-55.

Kraus, Hans-Joachim. *Geschichte der historisch-kritischen Erforschung des Alten Testaments*. 3rd ed. Neukirchen-Vluyn: Neukirchener, 1982.

Kselman, John. "Psalm 77 and the Book of Exodus." *Journal of the Ancient Near Eastern Society* 15 (1983): 51-58.

Kugel, James. *The Idea of Biblical Poetry: Parallelism and Its History*. New Haven, CT: Yale University Press, 1981.

Kynes, Will. "Beat Your Parodies into Swords, and Your Parodied Books into Spears: A New Paradigm for Parody in the Hebrew Bible." *BibInt* 19 (2011): 276-310.

———. *An Obituary for "Wisdom Literature": The Birth, Death, and Intertextual Reintegration of a Biblical Corpus*. Oxford: Oxford University Press, 2019.

Laato, Antti. "The Seventy Yearweeks in the Book of Daniel." *ZAW* 102 (1990): 212-25.

Lambinet, Julien. "Les principes de la méthode exégétique de J. A. Bengel (1687–1752), piétiste du Württemberg." *Ephemerides Theologicae Lovanienses* 89, no. 4 (2013): 253-78.

Landes, George. "The Kerygma of the Book of Jonah: The Contextual Interpretation of the Jonah Psalm." *Int* 21 (1967): 3-31.

Lasine, Stuart. *Jonah and the Human Condition: Life and Death in Yahweh's World*. London: T&T Clark, 2020.

Leithart, Peter. *Deep Exegesis: The Mystery of Reading Scripture*. Waco, TX: Baylor University Press, 2009.

Leonard, Jeffery M. "Identifying Inner-Biblical Allusions: Psalm 78 as a Test Case." *JBL* 127, no. 2 (2008): 241-65.

Lester, G. Brooke. *Daniel Evokes Isaiah: Allusive Characterization of Foreign Rule in the Hebrew-Aramaic Book of Daniel*. London: T&T Clark, 2015.

Leuchter, Mark. "Hosea's Exodus Mythology and the Book of the Twelve." In *Priests and Cults in the Book of the Twelve*, edited by Lena-Sofia Tiemeyer, 31-49. Atlanta: SBL Press, 2016.

Levine, Baruch. *Numbers 21–36*. AB. New York: Doubleday, 2000.

Lichtert, Claude. "La Prière de Jonas (Jon 2)." *Studia Rhetorica Biblica et Semitica* 15 (2007): 1-17.

Lindars, Barnabas. *New Testament Apologetic: The Doctrinal Significance of the Old Testament Quotations*. London: SCM Press, 1961.

Loewenstamm, Samuel E. *The Evolution of the Exodus Tradition*. Translated by Baruch Schwartz. Jerusalem: Magnes, 1992.

Lohfink, Norbert. *The Christian Meaning of the Old Testament*. Translated by R. A. Wilson. Milwaukee: Bruce, 1968.

Longman, Tremper. *The Fear of the Lord Is Wisdom: A Theological Introduction to Wisdom in Israel*. Grand Rapids, MI: Baker Academic, 2017.

———. *How to Read Daniel*. Downers Grove, IL: InterVarsity Press, 2020.

———. *Job*. Baker Commentary on the Old Testament Wisdom and Psalms. Grand Rapids, MI: Baker Academic, 2012.

López, René A. "The Meaning of 'Behemoth' and 'Leviathan' in Job." *BSac* 173 (2016): 401-24.

Lubeck, Ray. "Prophetic Sabotage: A Look at Jonah 3:2-4." *TJ* 9 NS (1988): 37-46.

Luther, Martin D. *Martin Luthers Werke: Kritische Gesamtausgabe*. Vol. 5, *Operationes in Psalmos. 1519–1521*. Weimar: Hermann Böhlau, 1981.

———. "Preface to the Psalter." In *Luther's Works*. Vol. 35. Philadelphia: Fortress, 1960.

Magonet, Jonathan. *Form and Meaning: Studies in the Literary Techniques of the Book of Jonah*. Frankfurt: Lang, 1976.

Martens, Elmer. "Old Testament Theology Since Walter C. Kaiser, Jr." *JETS* 50, no. 4 (2007): 673-91.

Mathys, Hans-Peter. *Dichter und Beter: Theologen aus spätalttestamentlichere Zeit*. Göttingen: Vandenhoeck & Ruprecht, 1994.

McCann, J. Clinton. "Books I–III and the Editorial Purpose of the Hebrew Psalter." In *Shape and Shaping of the Psalter*, edited by J. Clinton McCann, 93-107. Sheffield: Sheffield Academic Press, 1993.

———. "Psalm 73: A Microcosm of Old Testament Theology." In *The Listening Heart: Essays in Wisdom and the Psalms in Honor of Roland O. Murphy, O. Carm*, edited by Kenneth Hoglund et al., 247-57. Sheffield: JSOT Press, 1987.

McCarter, P. Kyle, Jr. *I Samuel*. AB. New York: Doubleday, 1980.

———. *II Samuel*. AB. New York: Doubleday, 1984.

———. "The River Ordeal in Israelite Literature." *Harvard Theological Review* 66 (1973): 403-12.

McCartney, Dan, and Peter Enns. "Matthew and Hosea: A Response to John Sailhamer." *WTJ* 63 (2001): 97-105.

McConville, J. Gordon. *Deuteronomy*. ApOTC. Downers Grove, IL: InterVarsity Press, 2002.

McKenzie, John. *Second Isaiah*. AB. Garden City, NY: Doubleday, 1968.

McKenzie, Tracy, with Jonathan Shelton. "From Proverb to Prophecy: Textual Production and Theology in Proverbs 30:1-6." *Southeastern Theological Review* 11, no. 1 (Spring 2020): 3-30.

Meier, Sam. "Job I–II: A Reflection of Genesis I–III." *VT* 39, no. 2 (1989): 183-93.

Mettinger, Tryggve. *A Farewell to the Servant Songs: A Critical Examination of an Exegetical Axiom*. Lund, Sweden: CWK Gleerup, 1983.

Michel, Diethelm. *Tempora und Satzstellung in den Psalmen*. Bonn: H. Bouvier, 1960.

Miles, John A., Jr. "Laughing at the Bible: Jonah as Parody." *Jewish Quarterly Review* 65 (1975): 168-81.

Milgrom, Jacob. *Numbers*. JPS Torah Commentary. Philadelphia: Jewish Publication Society, 1990.

Mitchell, David C. *The Message of the Psalter: An Eschatological Programme in the Book of Psalms*. Newton Mearns, UK: Campbell, 2003.

Moore, George. *A Critical and Exegetical Commentary on Judges*. ICC. Edinburgh, T&T Clark, 1989.

Morales, L. Michael. *Exodus Old and New: A Biblical Theology of Redemption*. Downers Grove, IL: InterVarsity Press, 2020.

Morgan, Robert. "Gabler's Bicentenary." *Expository Times* 98, no. 6 (1987): 164-68.

———. "New Testament Theology as Implicit Theological Interpretation of Christian Scripture." *Int* 70, no. 4 (2016): 383-98.

Motyer, J. Alec. *The Prophecy of Isaiah*. Downers Grove, IL: InterVarsity Press, 1993.

Mowinckel, Sigmund. *He That Cometh*. Translated by G. W. Anderson. New York: Abingdon, 1956.

Moyer, Clinton. "Who Is the Prophet, and Who the Ass? Role-Reversing Interludes and the Unity of the Balaam Narrative (Numbers 22–24)." *JSOT* 37, no. 2 (2012): 167-83.

Murphy, Roland. *Proverbs*. WBC. Nashville: Thomas Nelson, 1998.

———. *The Tree of Life: An Exploration of Biblical Wisdom Literature*. 2nd ed. Grand Rapids, MI: Eerdmans, 1996.

Nilsen, Tina Dykesteen. *The Origins of Deuteronomy 32: Intertextuality, Memory, Identity*. New York: Lang, 2018.

Noegel, Scott. *Janus Parallelism in the Book of Job*. Sheffield: Sheffield Academic Press, 1996.

———. "Jonah and Leviathan: Inner-Biblical Allusions and the Problem with Dragons." *HENOCH: Studies in Judaism and Christianity from Second Temple to Late Antiquity* 37, no. 2 (2015): 236-60.

Nogalski, James. *The Book of the Twelve: Micah–Malachi*. SHBC. Macon, GA: Smyth & Helwys, 2011.

———. *Literary Precursors to the Book of the Twelve*. Berlin: de Grutyer, 1993.

———. *Redactional Processes in the Book of the Twelve*. Berlin: de Gruyter, 1993.

North, Christopher. *The Suffering Servant in Deutero-Isaiah*. 2nd ed. London: Oxford, 1956.

Oancea, Constantin. "Water and Death as Metaphors in Jonah's Psalm." *Revue Biblique* 128 (2021): 173-89.

Oehler, Gustav Friedrich. *Theology of the Old Testament*. Revised translation by George Day. New York: Funk & Wagnalls, 1883.

Oeming, Manfred. "To Be Adam or Not to Be Adam: The Hidden Fundamental Anthropological Discourse Revealed in an Intertextual Reading of אדם in Job and Genesis." In *Reading Job Intertextually*, edited by Katharine J. Dell and Will Kynes, 19-29. New York: Bloomsbury, 2013.

Ortlund, Dane. "Is Jeremiah 33:14-26 a 'Centre' to the Bible? A Test Case in Inter-canonical Hermeneutics." *EvQ* 84, no. 2 (April 2012): 119-38.

Ortlund, Eric. "The Identity of Leviathan and the Meaning of the Book of Job." *TJ* 34 (2013): 17-30.

Osborne, William R. "The Tree of Life in Proverbs and Psalms." In *The Tree of Life*, edited by Douglas Estes, 100-121. Leiden: Brill, 2020.

Oswalt, John. *The Book of Isaiah: Chapters 1–39*. NICOT. Grand Rapids, MI: Eerdmans, 1986.

———. *The Book of Isaiah: Chapters 40–66*. NICOT. Grand Rapids, MI: Eerdmans, 1998.

Pao, David. *Acts and the Isaianic New Exodus*. Tübingen: Mohr Siebeck, 2000.

Paulsen, Henning. "Traditionsgeschichtliche Methode und religionsgeschichtliche Schule." *ZTK* 75, no. 1 (1978): 20-55.

Phillips, Elaine. "Serpent Intertexts: Tantalizing Twists in the Tales." *BBR* 10, no. 2 (2000): 233-45.

Pohl, William C., IV. "A Messianic Reading of Psalm 89: A Canonical and Intertextual Study." *JETS* 58, no. 3 (2015): 507-25.

Polzin, Robert. *Samuel and the Deuteronomist: 1 Samuel*. Bloomington: Indiana University Press, 1993.

Postell, Seth. *Adam as Israel: Genesis 1–3 as the Introduction to the Torah and Tanakh*. Eugene, OR: Wipf & Stock, 2011.

———. "Messianism in Light of Literary Strategy." *BSac* 177 (2020): 329-50.

———. "Numbers 24:5-9: The Distant Star." In *The Moody Handbook of Messianic Prophecy: Studies and Expositions of the Messiah in the Old Testament*, edited by Michael Rydelnik and Edwin Blum, 285-308. Chicago: Moody, 2019.

———. "Proverbs 8: The Messiah: Personification of Divine Wisdom." In *The Moody Handbook of Messianic Prophecy*, edited by Michael Rydelnik and Edwin Blum, 739-46. Chicago: Moody, 2019.

———. "Reading Genesis, Seeing Moses: Narrative Analogies with Moses in the Book of Genesis." *JETS* 65, no. 3 (2022): 437-55.

Postell, Seth, Eitan Bar, and Erez Soref. *Reading Moses, Seeing Jesus: How the Torah Fulfills Its Goal in Yeshua*. 2nd ed. Wooster, OH: Weaver, 2017.

Potgieter, J. Henk. "David in Consultation with the Prophets: The Intertextual Relationship of Psalm 31 with the Books of Jonah and Jeremiah." In *"My Spirit at Rest in the North Country" (Zechariah 6.8)*, edited by Hermann Michael Niemann and Matthias Augustin, 153-63. Frankfurt: Lang, 2011.

Provan, Iain. "The Messiah in the Books of Kings." In *The Lord's Anointed: Interpretation of Old Testament Messianic Texts*, edited by Philip Satterthwaite, Richard Hess, and Gordon Wenham, 67-85. Grand Rapids, MI: Baker, 1995.

Pyper, Hugh. "Swallowed by a Song: Jonah and the Jonah-Psalm Through the Looking-Glass." In *Reflection and Refraction: Studies in Biblical Historiography in Honour of A. Graeme Auld*, edited by Timothy Lim et al., 337-58. Leiden: Brill, 2007.

Rad, Gerhard von. *Deuteronomy*. Translated by Dorothea Barton. OTL. Philadelphia: Westminster, 1966.

———. *Old Testament Theology*. Translated by D. M. G. Stalker. Peabody, MA: Hendrickson, 2005.

———. *Wisdom in Israel*. Translated by James D. Martin. Nashville: Abingdon, 1972.

Renaud, Bernard. "De la bénédiction du roi à la bénédiction de Dieu (Ps 72)." *Biblica* 70 (1989): 305-26.

Rendsburg, Gary. "The Northern Origin of 'The Last Words of David' (2 Sam 23,1-7)." *Biblica* 69, no. 1 (1988): 113-21.

Rendtorff, Rolf. "Gerhard von Rad und Religionsgeschichte." In *Theologie in Israel und in den Nachbarkulturen*, edited by Manfred Oeming et al., 17-24. Münster: LIT, 2004.

Reventlow, Henning Graf. "Basic Issues in the Interpretation of Isaiah 53." In *Jesus and the Suffering Servant: Isaiah 53 and Christian Origins*, edited by William Bellinger Jr. and William Farmer, 23-38. Harrisburg, PA: Trinity Press International, 1998.

Riley, William. *King and Cultus in Chronicles: Worship and the Reinterpretation of History*. Sheffield: JSOT Press, 1993.

Robertson, O. Palmer. *The Flow of the Psalms: Discovering Their Structure and Theology*. Phillipsburg, NJ: P&R, 2015.

Rogerson, John. *Old Testament Criticism in the Nineteenth Century*. Philadelphia: Fortress, 1985.

Rosenberg, Joel. "1 and 2 Samuel." In *The Literary Guide to the Bible*, edited by Robert Alter and Frank Kermode, 122-45. Cambridge, MA: Harvard University Press, 1987.

Rosner, Brian. "Biblical Theology." In *New Dictionary of Biblical Theology*, edited by T. Desmond Alexander and Brian Rosner, 3-11. Downers Grove, IL: InterVarsity Press, 2000.

Rothstein, Bret. *The Shape of Difficulty: A Fan Letter to Unruly Objects*. University Park: Pennsylvania State University Press, 2019.

Rouillard, Hedwige. *Le Pericope de Balaam (Nombres 22–24): La Prose et les "Oracles."* Paris: J. Gabalda et Cie, 1985.

Rowold, Henry. "לְי־הוּא? מִי הוּא! Leviathan and Job in Job 41:2-3." *JBL* 105 (1986): 104-9.

Rydelnik, Eva. "Proverbs 30:4: The Riddle of the Son." In *The Moody Handbook of Messianic Prophecy*, edited Michael Rydelnik and Edwin Blum, 747-56. Chicago: Moody, 2019.

Ryrie, Charles. *Dispensationalism Today*. Chicago: Moody, 1965.

Saebø, Magne. "Johann Philipp Gablers Bedeutung für die Biblische Theologie." *ZAW* 99, no. 1 (1987): 1-16.

Sailhamer, John. *First & Second Chronicles*. Everyman's Bible Commentary. Chicago: Moody, 1983.

———. *Genesis Unbound*. Reprint, Eugene, OR: Wipf & Stock, 2001.

———. "Hosea 11:1 and Matthew 2:15." *WTJ* 63 (2001): 87-96.

———. *Introduction to Old Testament Theology: A Canonical Approach*. Grand Rapids, MI: Zondervan, 1995.

———. "Johann August Ernesti: The Role of History in Biblical Interpretation." *JETS* 44 (2001): 193-206.

———. *The Meaning of the Pentateuch: Revelation, Composition, and Interpretation*. Downers Grove, IL: InterVarsity Press, 2009.

———. "The Messiah and the Hebrew Bible." *JETS* 44, no. 1 (2001): 5-23.

———. *NIV Compact Bible Commentary*. Grand Rapids, MI: Zondervan, 1994.

———. *The Pentateuch as Narrative*. Grand Rapids, MI: Zondervan, 1992.

Sandys-Wunsch, John. "G. T. Zachariae's Contribution to Biblical Theology." *ZAW* 92, no. 1 (1980): 1-23.

Sandys-Wunsch, John, and Laurence Eldredge. "J. P. Gabler and the Distinction Between Biblical and Dogmatic Theology: Translation, Commentary, and Discussion of His Originality." *SJT* 33 (1980): 133-58.

Sanz Giménez-Rico, Enrique. "La mediación y petición en el libro de Joel y su relación con Jonás." *Scripta Theologica* 50 (2018): 561-88.

Sasson, Jack. *Jonah*. AB. New York: Doubleday, 1990.

Schaper, Joachim. "The Question of a 'Biblical Theology' and the Growing Tension Between 'Biblical Theology' and a 'History of the Religion of Israel': From Johann Philipp Gabler to Rudolf Smend, Sen." In *Hebrew Bible/Old Testament: The History of Its Interpretation*, edited by Magne Saebø, 3.1:628-35. Göttingen: Vandenhoeck & Ruprecht, 2013.

Schipper, Bernd. "'Teach Them Diligently to Your Son!': The Book of Proverbs and Deuteronomy." In *Reading Proverbs Intertextually*, edited by Katharine Dell and Will Kynes, 21-34. London: T&T Clark, 2019.

Schmitt, Hans-Christoph. "Prophetie und Schultheologie im Deuterojesajabuch: Beobachtungen zur Redaktionsgeschichte von Jes 40–55." *ZAW* 91 (1979): 43-61.

———. "Redaktion des Pentateuch im Geiste der Prophetie." *VT* 32 (1982): 170-89.

Schnittjer, Gary Edward. *Old Testament Use of the Old Testament*. Grand Rapids, MI: Zondervan, 2021.

Scobie, Charles. "The History of Biblical Theology." In *New Dictionary of Biblical Theology*, edited by T. Desmond Alexander and Brian Rosner, 11-20. Downers Grove, IL: InterVarsity Press, 2000.

———. *The Ways of Our God: An Approach to Biblical Theology*. Grand Rapids, MI: Eerdmans, 2003.

Seitz, Christopher R. *Prophecy and Hermeneutics: Toward a New Introduction to the Prophets*. Studies in Theological Interpretation. Grand Rapids, MI: Baker Academic, 2007.

Seufert, Matthew. "The Presence of Genesis in Ecclesiastes." *WTJ* 78 (2016): 75-92.

Shepherd, Michael. *A Commentary on the Book of the Twelve*. Grand Rapids, MI: Kregel, 2018.

———. "Compositional Analysis of the Twelve." *ZAW* 120 (2008): 184-93.

———. *Daniel in the Context of the Hebrew Bible*. New York: Lang, 2009.

———. "The New Exodus in the Composition of the Twelve." In *Text and Canon: Essays in Honor of John H. Sailhamer*, edited by Robert L. Cole and Paul J. Kissling, 120-36. Eugene, OR: Pickwick, 2017.

———. "Targums, the New Testament, and Biblical Theology of the Messiah." *JETS* 51, no. 1 (2008): 45-58.

———. *The Twelve Prophets in the New Testament*. New York: Lang, 2011.

Smend, Rudolf. *Die Mitte des Alten Testaments: Exegetische Aufsätze*. Tübingen: Mohr Siebeck, 2002.

Smith, Henry Preserved. *The Books of Samuel*. ICC. Edinburgh: T&T Clark, 1977.

Snearly, Michael. "Psalm 118: The Rejected Stone." In *The Moody Handbook of Messianic Prophecy*, edited by Michael Rydelnik and Edwin Blum, 693-700. Chicago: Moody, 2019.

———. *The Return of the King: Messianic Expectation in Book V of the Psalter*. New York: T&T Clark, 2016.

Sommer, Benjamin. *A Prophet Reads Scripture: Allusion in Isaiah 40–66*. Stanford, CA: Stanford University Press, 1998.

Spieckermann, Hermann. "The Conception and Prehistory of the Idea of Vicarious Suffering in the Old Testament." Translated by Daniel Bailey. In *The Suffering Servant: Isaiah 53 in Jewish and Christian Sources*, edited by Bernd Janowski and Peter Stuhlmacher, 1-15. Grand Rapids, MI: Eerdmans, 2004.

Steinmann, Andrew. *Proverbs*. Concordia Commentary. St. Louis: Concordia, 2009.

Sternberg, Meir. *The Poetics of Biblical Narrative*. Bloomington: Indiana University Press, 1985.

Steyn, Gert. "Psalm 2 in Hebrews." *Neotestamentica* 37, no. 2 (2003): 262-82.

Stirrup, Andy. "'Why Has Yahweh Defeated Us Today Before the Philistines?' The Question of the Ark Narrative." *TynBul* 51, no. 1 (2000): 81-100.

Stone, Timothy. "Following the Church Fathers: An Intertextual Path from Psalm 107 to Isaiah, Jonah, and Matthew 8:23-27." *Journal of Theological Interpretation* 7 (2013): 37-55.

Stuckenbruck, Loren. "Johann Philipp Gabler and the Delineation of Biblical Theology." *SJT* 52 (1999): 139-57.

Sweeney, Marvin. *The Twelve Prophets*. Collegeville, MN: Liturgical Press, 2000.

Tate, Marvin. *Psalms 51–100*. WBC. Dallas: Word, 1990.

Teeter, Andrew. "Isaiah and the King of As/Syria in Daniel's Final Vision: On the Rhetoric of Inner-Scriptural Allusions and the Hermeneutics of 'Mantological Exegesis.'" In *A Teacher for All Generations: Essays in Honor of James C. VanderKam*, edited by Eric Mason, 169-99. Leiden: Brill, 2012.

Thompson, Benjamin. "Pride and Kingship: A Literary Reading of 1 and 2 Samuel Considering the Role of the Poetry in the Characterisation of the Kings." PhD diss., Queen's University, 2021.

Thompson, John A. *The Book of Jeremiah*. NICOT. Grand Rapids, MI: Eerdmans, 1980.

Tiemeyer, Lena-Sofia. "Attitudes to the Cult in Jonah: In the Book of Jonah, the Book of the Twelve, and Beyond." In *Priests and Cults in the Book of the Twelve*, edited by Lena-Sofia Tiemeyer, 115-29. Atlanta: SBL Press, 2016.

Tigay, Jeffrey. *Deuteronomy*. JPS Torah Commentary. Philadelphia: JPS, 1996.

Treier, Daniel. *Proverbs and Ecclesiastes*. Brazos Theological Commentary on the Bible. Grand Rapids, MI: Brazos, 2011.

Trublet, Jacques. "Approche canonique des Psaumes du Hallel." In *The Composition of the Book of Psalms*, edited by Erich Zenger, 339-76. Leuven: Peeters, 2010.

Tsumura, David Toshio. *The First Book of Samuel*. NICOT. Grand Rapids, MI: Eerdmans, 2007.

———. *The Second Book of Samuel*. NICOT. Grand Rapids, MI: Eerdmans, 2019.

Vaillancourt, Ian. *The Multifaceted Saviour of Psalms 110 and 118: A Canonical Exegesis*. Sheffield: Sheffield Phoenix, 2019.

Van Leeuwen, Raymond. "Cosmos, Temple, House: Building and Wisdom in Ancient Mesopotamia and Israel." In *From the Foundations to the Crenellations: Essays on Temple Building in the Ancient Near East and Hebrew Bible*, edited by Mark Boda and Jamie Novotny, 399-421. Münster: Ugarit-Verlag, 2010.

———. "Liminality and Worldview in Proverbs 1–9." *Semeia* 50 (1990): 111-44.

Verde, Danilo. "'Who Is Like You Among the Gods, O YHWH?' (Exod 15,11): The Interweaving of Metaphors in the Song of the Sea." In *Networks of Metaphors in the Hebrew Bible*, edited by Danilo Verde and Antje Labahn, 13-30. Leuven: Peeters, 2020.

Vermeylen, Jacques. "La prière de Jonas (Jon 2) et le cantique de Moïse (Ex 15)." In *Écritures et réécritures: la reprise interprétative des traditions fondatrices par la littérature biblique et extrabiblique*, edited by Claire Clivaz et al., 185-95. Leuven: Peeters, 2012.

Verrett, Brian. *The Serpent in Samuel: A Messianic Motif*. Eugene, OR: Resource, 2020.

Vitringa, Campegius. *Commentarius in Librum Prophetiarum Jesaiae*. Leeuwarden, Netherlands: Franciscus Halma, 1720.

Von Hofmann, J. C. K. *Weissagung und Erfüllung im alten and im neuen Testamente*. Nördlingen: Beck, 1841.

Vos, Geerhardus. *Biblical Theology: Old and New Testaments*. Edinburgh: Banner of Truth, 1948.

———. "The Idea of Biblical Theology as a Science and as a Theological Discipline." In *Redemptive History and Biblical Interpretation: The Shorter Writings of Geerhardus Vos*, edited by Richard Gaffin, 3-24. Phillipsburg, NJ: Presbyterian and Reformed, 1980.

Walsh, Jerome. *1 Kings*. Berit Olam. Collegeville, MN: Liturgical Press, 1996.

Waltke, Bruce. *An Old Testament Theology*. Grand Rapids, MI: Zondervan, 2007.

———. *The Book of Proverbs: Chapters 1-15*. NICOT. Grand Rapids, MI: Eerdmans, 2004.

Walton, John. "Psalms: A Cantata About the Davidic Covenant." *JETS* 34 (1991): 21-31.

Watts, James W. *Psalm and Story: Inset Hymns in Hebrew Narrative*. Sheffield: JSOT Press, 1992.

Watts, Rikki E. *Isaiah's New Exodus in Mark*. Biblical Studies Library. Grand Rapids, MI: Baker Academic, 2000.

Webb, Barry. *The Message of Isaiah*. Bible Speaks Today. Downers Grove, IL: InterVarsity Press, 1996.

Webb, William. *Returning Home: New Covenant and Second Exodus as the Context for 2 Corinthians 6.14-7.1*. Sheffield: JSOT Press, 1993.

Wegner, Paul. *Isaiah*. TOTC. Downers Grove, IL: InterVarsity Press, 2021.

Weinfeld, Moshe. *Deuteronomy and the Deuteronomic School*. Winona Lake, IN: Eisenbrauns, 1992.

Weitzman, Steven. *Song and Story in Biblical Narrative: The History of a Literary Convention in Ancient Israel*. Bloomington: Indiana University Press, 1997.

Wellhausen, Julius. *Prolegomena to the History of Israel*. Translated by J. Sutherland Black and Allan Menzies. Edinburg: Adam & Charles Black, 1885.

Wendebourg, Ernst-Wilhelm. "Die Heilsgeschichtliche Theologie J. Chr. K. v. Hofmanns in ihrem Verhältnis zur romantischen Weltanschauung." *ZTK* 52, no. 1 (1955): 64-104.

Wenham, Gordon. *Genesis 1-15*. WBC. Waco, TX: Word, 1987.

———. *Numbers*. TOTC. Downers Grove, IL: InterVarsity Press, 1981.

———. "Sanctuary Symbolism in the Garden of Eden Story." In *Proceedings of the Ninth World Congress of Jewish Studies, Division A: The Period of the Bible*, 19-25. Jerusalem: World Union of Jewish Studies, 1986.

Westermann, Claus. *Isaiah 40–66*. OTL. Philadelphia: Westminster, 1969.

———. *Praise and Lament in the Psalms*. Translated by Keith Crim and Richard Soulen. Atlanta: John Knox, 1981.

Weth, Gustav. *Die Heilsgeschichte: Ihr universeller und ihr individueller Sinn in der offenbarungsgeschichtlichen Theologie des 19. Jahrhunderts*. Munich: Chr. Kaiser, 1931.

Whybray, R. N. *Wisdom in Proverbs*. Naperville, IL: Allenson, 1965.

Wifall, Walter. "The Sea of Reeds as Sheol." *ZAW* 92, no. 3 (1980): 325-32.

Wilcock, Michael. *The Message of Psalms 73–150*. Downers Grove, IL: InterVarsity Press, 2001.

Williamson, H. G. M. *Isaiah 1–5*. ICC. London: Bloomsbury, 2014.

Willis, John. *Images of Water in Isaiah*. Lanham, MD: Lexington, 2017.

Wilson, Gerald. *The Editing of the Hebrew Psalter*. Chico, CA: Scholars Press, 1985.

———. "King, Messiah, and the Reign of God: Revisiting the Royal Psalms and the Shape of the Psalter." In *The Book of Psalms: Composition and Reception*, edited by Peter Flint and Patrick Miller, 391-406. Leiden: Brill, 2005.

———. "The Prayer of Daniel 9: Reflection on Jeremiah 29." *JSOT* 48 (1990): 91-99.

———. *Psalms*. New International Version Application Commentary. Grand Rapids, MI: Zondervan, 2002.

———. "Shaping the Psalter: A Consideration of Editorial Linkage in the Book of Psalms." In *Shape and Shaping of the Psalter*, edited by J. Clinton McCann, 72-82. Sheffield: Sheffield Academic Press, 1993.

Wilson, Lindsay. *Proverbs*. TOTC. Downers Grove, IL: InterVarsity Press, 2018.

Wolff, Hans Walter. *Hosea*. Translated by Gary Stansell. Hermeneia. Philadelphia: Fortress, 1974.

Wong Yee-cheung. *A Text-Centered Approach to Old Testament Exegesis and Theology and Its Application to the Book of Isaiah*. Hong Kong: Alliance Bible Seminary, 2001.

Wray Beal, Lissa. *1 & 2 Kings*. ApOTC. Downers Grove, IL: InterVarsity Press, 2014.

Wright, Christopher J. H. "Mission as Matrix for Hermeneutics and Biblical Theology." In *Out of Egypt: Biblical Theology and Biblical Interpretation*, edited by Craig Bartholomew et al., 102-43. Grand Rapids, MI: Zondervan, 2004.

Wright, G. Ernest. "The Lawsuit of God: A Form-Critical Study of Deuteronomy 32." In *Israel's Prophetic Heritage*, edited by Bernhard Anderson and Walter Harrelson, 26-67. New York: Harper, 1962.

Wright, J. Robert, ed. *Proverbs, Ecclesiastes, Song of Solomon*. Ancient Christian Commentary on Scripture 9. Downers Grove, IL: InterVarsity Press, 2005.

Wright, N. T. *Paul and the Faithfulness of God*. Minneapolis: Fortress, 2013.

Yoder, Christine Roy. "Wisdom Is the Tree of Life: A Study of Proverbs 3:13-20 and Genesis 2–3." In *Reading Proverbs Intertextually*, edited by Katharine Dell and Will Kynes, 11-19. London: T&T Clark, 2019.

Zabán, Bálint Károly. *The Pillar Function of the Speeches of Wisdom: Proverbs 1:20-33, 8:1-36 and 9:1-6 in the Structural Framework of Proverbs 1–9*. Berlin: de Gruyter, 2012.

Zakovitch, Yair. *"And You Shall Tell Your Son . . .": The Concept of the Exodus in the Bible.* Jerusalem: Magnes, 1991.

———. "Through the Looking Glass: Reflections/Inversions of Genesis Stories in the Bible." *BibInt* 1 (1993): 139-52.

Zimmerli, Walther. "The Place and Limit of the Wisdom in the Framework of the Old Testament Theology." *SJT* 17, no. 2 (1964): 146-58.

GENERAL INDEX

Abernethy, Andrew, 26, 95, 194, 279
Abra(ha)m, 8, 80, 115-16, 124, 176-78, 199, 231, 250, 254, 302-3
Abrahamic covenant. *See* covenant, Abrahamic
Adam, 51-54, 56-57, 59-61, 66-67, 69-70, 75, 108-9, 116, 153, 187, 199, 230, 249, 275
Alexander, T. Desmond, 90, 128-29, 178
allusion, xv, 132, 134, 141, 155, 199-201, 219-20, 222, 231, 252, 255, 287, 299
    coordinated, 124-25, 165
    directionality, xxiv-xxvi
    disassembly (or split-up pattern) and, 159, 199
    various purposes of, xxvi
    See also braiding, intertextuality
Anderson, A. A., 133, 173
Anderson, Bernard, 198-99
Anderson, William, 67
Ansberry, Christopher, 58
ark of the covenant, 169-75
    can be dangerous, 173
    relation to glory and holiness, 170-1
Ashley, Timothy, 106-7
Athanasius, 277, 280, 282
atonement, 152, 193
author
    divine authorship of Scripture and inspiration, xvi-xvii
    dual authorship, xx
    genius of, xx, 316
    later OT authors' knowledge of the Pentateuch, xxiv-xxvi, 50, 133, 141, 167
    purpose of, in nexus passages, xviii-xix, 140-1
    strategy of. *See* composition and compositional strategy
author's intent
    divine, xxi
    dual authorship and, xxi
    expressed through the text, xx, xxxviii
    expressed through the whole book, 5
    Gabler's emphasis on and confusion regarding, 2-5
    human, xxii
Babel/Babylon, 70, 81, 194-96, 202-6, 229-32, 288, 291-93, 299-301, 308

Bailey, Randall, 160
Baker, David L., 30-31
Balaam
    blindness and seeing of, 114-16, 122, 124-25
    his donkey and, 107
    "proverbs" of, 106, 113-14, 135
Baltzer, Klaus, 201, 203, 303
Band, Arnold, 223
Bar, Eitan, 137
Barbiero, Gianni, 249, 251-52, 257
Bartholomew, Craig, xvi, 6, 24, 50, 55, 58, 68-69
Bates, Matthew, 123
Batto, Bernard, 78
Bauer, Georg Lorenz, 7-9
Beale, Gregory, 22, 37
Beckwith, Roger, 289
Begrich, Joachim, 235
Belcher, Richard, Jr., 48, 50-51
Benckhuysen, Amanda, 238
Bengel, Johann Alberti, 13, 15-16, 18, 22, 38-39
Benz, Ernst, 15
Bergey, Ronald, 160-61
Bezalel, 62
biblical theology
    authorial intent and, 2
    distinction from dogmatic theology, 2
    Gabler's formative influence on, 2
    "historical" origin of, 2
    irony of seeking historical meaning but undermining it through unifying frameworks, 11-12
    parent discipline of OT theology, 1
    study of history and, 22, 24-25, 34
    use as a term, 7
Blenkinsopp, Joseph, 39, 192, 201-2, 207
bless(ing), 86-87, 109-11, 178, 253-54
Block, Daniel, 46, 130-31, 168-69
Boda, Mark, 106
Bodner, Keith, 170, 174, 179
Bolin, Thomas, 237
Boston, James R., 142-43, 146-47
braiding, xi, xxii, 120-21, 126-30, 138, 140, 159, 185, 199, 206, 226, 231, 301-3

of Gen 3:15, Gen 49:8-12, and Num 24:17-19, 138-140
Brecht, Martin, 16, 18
Briggs, Charles Augustus, 182, 184
Bright, John, 131-32
bronze snake, 108-9
    relationship to omens, 108-9
Brown, Michael, 189
Brown, William, 266
Brueggemann, Walter, 168, 263
Bruno, Chris, 13
Brunson, Andrew, 77
Büsching, Anton Friderich, 203
Campbell, Antony, 170, 172-74
canon (or Tanak)
    Daniel as ideal reader of Tanak, 289
    emphasis on Jeremiah at end of Tanak, 290
    not organized chronologically, 20-21
    tripartite canon of the Hebrew Bible (Tanak), xvi, xxiii, xxvi, 27, 32-33, 46, 144, 168, 218, 237, 242, 247, 288-91, 298, 305, 313
    within a canon, 6
Cartledge, Tony, 136, 168, 173
Ceresko, Anthony, 206
Chapman, Stephen, xxiii, 142, 291
Cheek, Jonathan, 46
Chen, Chris, 240
Chen, Kevin, xix, xxi, 31-32, 39-41, 46, 81, 83, 85-87, 90-91, 94, 98, 104-5, 108-9, 112, 117, 123, 125, 128, 133, 138-40, 151-52, 154-56, 159, 163, 174, 177-78, 184-85, 203, 206, 211, 213, 232-33, 235, 242, 258, 267, 280-81, 303, 307
Christology, 90, 155, 205, 253, 258-60, 278-82, 299, 307
center of the OT, xxvii, 1
    different conceptions of, 27-33
    exegetical-compositional, integrative, 27, 31-33, 43, 45, 104, 126, 129-30, 141, 153
    many proposals for, 26
    Messiah as, xvi, xx, xxvii, 27, 31-32, 43, 45, 104, 126, 130, 141, 153, 167, 254
    single or multiple, 26
    See also unity of OT and Scripture
Childs, Brevard, 7, 11-12, 19-20, 24, 41, 85, 88, 92, 181, 203, 212, 245, 266, 279, 290
Clemens, David, 66-67
Clines, David, 71
Cocceius, Johannes, 10, 13
Cole, R. Alan, 83
Cole, Robert L., 99-100, 183-85, 239, 244, 246-47, 251-52, 261, 279-80
Collins, John, 286, 291-92, 296, 298, 300-301

composition and compositional strategy, xvii, xx-xxii, 27, 31, 33, 41, 43, 45, 49, 78, 104, 113, 116, 131, 133, 135-36, 138, 140, 157, 164, 167, 188, 218-19, 226, 233, 243, 247, 264
    literary macrostructure and, xxi-xxiii, 86-88, 91-94, 113, 131, 135-36, 138, 140-41, 144-45, 218-19, 239, 242, 252, 264, 301, 312
Cooper, Alan, 143
Cornhill, Carl Heinrich, 142
covenant, 225
    Abrahamic, xi, 81-82, 89, 109-11, 122, 176-78, 199, 250, 254-56, 258, 260
    Davidic, xi, 32-33, 137, 168, 175-87, 193-95, 203, 237, 239, 243-54, 264, 269, 277, 279, 299, 304-7
    new, xxiv, 32, 68, 114, 224
Craigie, Peter, 186, 279
creation, 47-51, 61-65, 69-71, 75, 80, 91, 109, 126-27, 148, 178, 187, 199, 205, 231, 243, 252-56, 266, 268-70, 275-78, 282-84, 293, 299
    de-creation, 71
    Eden, 46, 57-59, 61, 69, 90-91, 95, 103, 116-17, 120, 127, 157, 201-2, 209, 225, 228, 230, 232, 253, 256, 260
    new creation, 91, 198, 201, 221
Cross, Frank M., 174, 237
Curtis, John Briggs, 70
Dahood, Mitchell, 240
David, xxv, 32, 102, 126, 130, 134-36, 159, 168-73, 175-81, 184-85, 225-26, 237-41
    self-consciousness regarding his house, 169, 175-78
Davidson, Richard M., 26, 29, 31
Davies, John A., 56
Day, John, 72
De Beaugrande, Robert, xxii
De Boer, P. A. H., 203, 303
De Wette, W. M. L., 10-11
death, 52-53, 66-68, 101, 108, 158, 187, 195, 209, 220-21, 223, 227-30, 232, 235-36, 238, 240, 249, 304, 308
    See also Sheol
Dekker, Jaap, 193
Delitzsch, Franz, 15, 17, 56, 189-90, 200, 204, 273
Dell, Katharine J., 64, 67
Dempster, Stephen, ix-xi, 21, 37, 40, 86, 123, 137, 179, 181, 188
democratization (of the Davidic covenant), 193, 247-48
desert (or wilderness), 83, 92, 96, 148, 153, 197-98, 201-2, 208, 213, 225
"deuteroevangelium," 108, 126, 141

General Index 339

Diestel, Ludwig, 7-11, 13-14, 16-17, 36
DiFransico, Lesley, 232
divinity of the Messiah, 155, 258-59, 280, 307
    See also Christology
Dressler, Wolfgang, xxii
Driver, S. R., 142, 189
Duhm, Bernard, 190-94, 200-201, 208
Dumortier, Jean-Bernard, 187
Durham, John, 78, 83
Duvall, J. Scott, 31
dynamic analogy, 223
Ebeling, Gerhard, 9, 36
eclipse of biblical prophecy, 287
Eden. *See* creation, Eden
Edom/Esau/Seir, 139
    Edom wordplay on Adam/humanity, 128
    Seir wordplay on "gate," 128
Edwards, Jonathan, 261
Ehlen, Arlis John, 17, 36
Eichrodt, Walter, 22-23, 25
Eldredge, Laurence, 2-4, 6-7, 9, 12, 35
Emmaus road, ix
Enns, Peter, 133
Ernesti, Johann August, 35
eschatology, xvi, xx, xxiii, xxv, 27, 33, 45, 77, 86-88, 98, 105, 109, 111, 113, 116-20, 122-26, 128-30, 132, 135, 139-41, 144-47, 153, 155, 157, 164-67, 174, 195-96, 198, 201, 208-9, 212, 219, 223, 226, 230-34, 241, 254-57, 261-64, 268, 279, 290, 297-99, 304, 307-9, 316
Estelle, Bryan, 78
eunuch(s), 194, 300-301
event (historical). *See* text
exile, xxv, 33, 46, 103, 113, 143-45, 166, 181, 194-96, 206, 227-30, 234, 245-46, 248-49, 262, 264, 290, 293-96, 300-302, 304
exodus
    Balaam narrative and, 111-12
    glory of the Lord and, 78
    individual, 216, 223-24, 233-35
    narrative alludes to creation, enmity, and Abrahamic covenant, 79-82
    paradigmatic example of salvation, 77
    Promised Land and, 112
    second, 77, 95, 101, 103, 122, 197-99, 201-5, 208, 209, 214, 223-28, 230-32, 234-35, 241, 256
Fall, 19, 46, 53, 65, 67, 70-71, 157, 187, 201, 209, 214, 228, 249, 253
Faro, Ingrid, 54, 116
Fishbane, Michael, 71-72, 77-78, 94, 103, 287, 297, 301-2, 308-9

Fohrer, Georg, 30
food/bread, 204
Forman, Charles, 64-66
Forti, Tova, 221, 238
Fox, Michael, 272
Fox, R. Michael, 78
fragmentation in biblical studies, ix, xvi, 19, 191, 313
Frei, Hans, 10, 15, 287
Fries, Jakob Friedrich, 11
Fritsch, Charles, 15
funhouse mirror, 223
Gabler, Johann Phillip, xxvii, 1-12, 14, 16-17, 21-22, 34-38, 42, 44
Gaffin, Richard, 18
Garrett, Duane, 57, 65
Geertz, Clifford, 315
Geiger, Abraham, 118
genre (literary), xv, xxii
Gentry, Peter, 12, 36-37
Gilbert, George, 12
Ginsberg, H. L., 304
Gitay, Yehoshua, 170, 179
Gladd, Benjamin, 13
Gog, 118-19, 133
Goldingay, John, 24, 49, 203, 210, 295-98
Goldsworthy, Graeme, 11, 13-14, 37, 58
Goswell, Gregory, 26, 95, 194, 279
Gramberg, C. P. W., 10
Grant, Jamie, 246, 248
Gray, George Buchanan, 106, 109, 132
Grillo, Jennie, 301
Grossman, Jonathan, 223
Gundersen, David "Gunner," 263-64
Gunkel, Hermann, 23, 235
Hamilton, James, 13, 22, 26, 32, 36-37, 40, 126, 137, 295-96
Hanson, Paul, 213
Harman, Allan, 94, 96
Harris, Scott, 76
Hasel, Gerhard, 8, 22, 26-31, 297
Haydon, Ron, 121, 288-89, 297
Hayes, John, 8
Hays, J. Daniel, 31, 181, 251
he (Hebrew pronoun), strategic use of, 211
Heilsgeschichte. *See* salvation history
Heim, Knut, 194, 248-52, 255, 259
Heir. *See* inheritance/possession
Helmbold, Andrew, 22
Henze, Matthias, 287, 291, 298-99
Hermisson, Hans-Jürgen, 51, 197, 207, 213-14
Hertzberg, Hans Wilhelm, 135-36

Hess, Richard, 308
Hibbard, J. Todd, 210
historical, different meanings of, xix, 1, 34-36, 40
    as referring to author's intent, 2, 6
historical reconstruction, xxi
Hitzig, Ferdinand, 273
Ho, Peter C. W., 252, 264, 279
Hoffman, Yair, 225-26
Hofmann, J. C. K. von, xxvii, 1, 7, 12-22, 24-25, 29, 36-37, 42
Hossfeld, Frank-Lothar, 187, 281
House, Paul, 37, 224, 306-7
Howard, David, Jr., 242, 246-48
Hübner, Eberhard, 14, 19-20, 24
Hugenberger, Gordon, 192, 198-204
Hunter, Alastair, 222-23, 234, 237-38
imagery (or picture), xv, xxii, 68, 117, 125-26, 139, 148, 155, 187, 201, 208, 229, 232, 252, 256-57, 266, 307
inheritance/possession, 91, 105, 130, 132, 177
inspiration of Scripture, xvii, xx, 6
    Gabler's lower view of, 6
    von Hofmann's non-traditional broadened view of, 16
intentional foreshadowing, 33
intertextuality, xxv, 33, 49-50, 58, 79, 94, 96, 99, 103-4, 120, 132, 139, 141, 167, 180, 214, 216, 218, 240, 249, 259
    authorially intended, xv, xxii
    criteria for. See nexus passages, criteria for identifying
    directionality, xxiv-xxvi
    OT theology and, xvi-xvii
    See also allusion, braiding, nexus passages
"in the last days," xxv, 33, 86-87, 89, 93, 113, 123, 127, 132, 144, 146-47, 151, 155, 166, 178, 181-82, 188, 193, 201, 207, 225-26, 230-31, 234, 246, 254, 268, 297-99, 303
Isaac, 80, 121-22, 128, 134, 177-78, 183, 258
Israel, eschatological, 117
Jacob (patriarch), 79, 81, 86-87, 121-23, 125, 134, 144, 147, 178, 183, 199, 258, 267, 274
Janowski, Bernd, 213
Japhet, Sara, 182
Jefferson, Helen, 100
Jeremiah (prophet), xxiv
Jesus' belief that the OT is about him, ix-x
Jobes, Karen, 118
Johnston, Philip, 240
Jonah (prophet)
    characterization of, 217-19
    comparison to Israelites and Egyptians at Red Sea, 223-24, 233-35
    makes orthodox statements, 217
Jones, Ethan, 158
Joseph, 80, 107, 139, 163, 204, 291, 299
    dreams of, 124-26
Josephus, 143, 153
Joshua, 98, 114, 145, 289
Judah, 87, 122, 124, 159, 178, 184, 246, 305
jussive verbs, 159
justice. See Song of Moses, justice in; servant of the Lord in Isaiah, justice and,
    for the poor, 250-1, 259-60
Kaiser, Gottlob Philipp Christian Kaiser, 8, 10-11
Kaiser, Walter, 24, 130
Kamphausen, Adolf, 144
Keil, C. F., 56, 130-31
Keiser, Thomas, 161, 196-97, 204
Kelly, Brian, 175
Kidner, Derek, 144
Kim, Brittany, 25
Kim, Daewoong, 299-300
Klein, Ralph, 135, 168, 182
Klingbeil, Gerald, 46
Knight, George A. F., 143-45, 148-49, 151, 153
Koorevaar, Hendrik, 168
Korpel, Marjo, 204
Kraus, Hans-Joachim, 13-14, 19-20, 36
Kristeva, Julia, xxii
Kselman, John, 100
Kugel, James, 119
Kynes, Will, 49-50, 63, 223
Laato, Antti, 304, 308
Lambinet, Julien, 15
Landes, George, 217, 220, 234
Lasine, Stuart, 238
Leithart, Peter, xxii
Leonard, Jeffery, xxii, xxvi
Lester, G. Brooke, 296, 300-302, 308
Leuchter, Mark, 226, 228
Leviathan. See sea monsters
Levine, Baruch, 105, 107, 109, 114, 124, 136
lexical repetition, xxii
Lichtert, Claude, 235, 237-38
Lindars, Barnabas, 119, 133
Loewenstamm, Samuel E., 78
Lohfink, Norbert, 98, 100
Longman, Tremper, 47-52, 55, 283, 292, 295
López, René A., 73
Lubeck, Ray, 217
Luther, Martin, 36, 212, 242
Magonet, Jonathan, 235, 238

General Index

Martens, Elmer, 24-26, 37, 40
Mathys, Hans-Peter, 94
McCann, J. Clinton, 245, 248, 263
McCarter, P. Kyle, Jr., 135, 158, 160, 172-73, 180-82, 236, 238
McCartney, Dan, 133
McConville, J. Gordon, 111, 142, 149, 153
McKenzie, John, 198
McKenzie, Tracy, 275-76
Meier, Sam, 69-71
Messiah in the OT, xvi, xxvii, 18, 27, 31-33, 38, 43, 87-89, 95, 101-4, 113, 116, 124-30, 137, 140-41, 147, 155-57, 159-60, 165, 173-75, 177-78, 184-86, 193, 201, 203-4, 208, 219, 226, 233-35, 239-41, 245-47, 249-61, 263-64, 276-79, 294, 300, 302, 304-8
Mettinger, Tryggve, 190
Michel, Diethelm, 158
Miles, John A., Jr., 223
Milgrom, Jacob, 106-7, 109, 111, 115, 130, 137
Miller, Patrick, 263
Mitchell, David C., 178, 185, 239, 245-46, 279
Moore, George, 138
Morales, L. Michael, 13, 78, 81-83, 103
Morgan, Robert, 4-5, 11
Morus, Samuel, 3-4
Moses, 73, 81-82, 84-86, 89, 92, 96, 114, 145-46, 148-51, 204, 221, 227, 237-38, 260, 267-68, 286-87, 289, 296
    as author of the Pentateuch, xxiv, 5, 38-39
    See also prophet like Moses
Motyer, J. Alec, 94-97, 190, 193, 195, 200-203, 211
Mowinckel, Sigmund, 174
Moyer, Clinton, 107
Murphy, Roland, 49, 55, 64, 133, 266, 275
Neubauer, A. D., 189
nexus passages
    ability to integrate OT material, xv, xix-xx, xxviii, 42, 122, 126-30, 153-57, 167, 216, 254-56, 313
    analysis of, based on Pentateuchal priority, xxiv-xxvi, 50, 199-200
    criteria for identifying, xv, xxii-xxiii
    description of, xv, xxii
    Messiah and, xvi, xx, xxvii-xxviii, 18, 27, 31-32, 137, 140-41, 155-57, 254, 260
    Pentateuch's reverberate in the rest of the OT, 167
    rationale for choosing the ones in this book, xxvii
    seams and, xxiii, 131

themselves often interconnected, xix, 79, 254, 276, 314
    transfer stations in a subway system as an illustration of, xvi-xx
new covenant. See covenant, new
Nilsen, Tina Dykesteen, 145, 160
Noah, 80, 127, 199
Noegel, Scott, 70, 221
Nogalski, James, 218, 223-24, 229, 231-35
North, Christopher, 190-92
Oancea, Constantin, 221, 236, 238
O'Dowd, Ryan, 50, 55, 58, 69
Oehler, Gustav Friedrich, 15, 22
Oeming, Manfred, 70
Old Testament, intrinsic meaning of, xv
Old Testament theology
    canonical approaches to, 24-25, 40-41
    comparative methodology and extrabiblical sources for, 8-9, 22-24
    external frameworks used for, 8-11, 18-19
    evangelical approaches to in recent decades, 24-25
    evangelical presuppositions for, x, xvi-xvii, 1, 34, 40, 42
    first treatment distinct from biblical theology, 7
    history of interpretation as story, 1, 316
    history of religions and, 9-10, 22-24, 34
    multiple definitions of, xv
    narrative approaches to, 24-25
    periodization and, 10
    subfield of biblical theology, 1, 7
    working definition of, xv
Ortlund, Dane, 26, 29
Ortlund, Eric, 74
Osborne, William R., 58
Oswalt, John, 95-96, 198, 200, 203
Pao, David, 78
parallelism, 61, 73, 119, 125
Passover, 82-84, 205-6, 213
Paulsen, Henning, 23
Payne, David, 203, 210
Pentateuch
    as one book, 86
    canonical form, xxiv
    later OT authors' knowledge of and engagement with, xxiv-xxvi, 130, 136, 141
    Mosaic authorship of, xxiv-xxv
    faith-theme in, 92-93, 164, 306
    major poetic sections in, 85-88, 218
    Messianic meaning of, 32-33, 87-89, 104, 113, 116

priority of, xxiv-xxvi, 50, 199-200
structure of, 85-88, 113
theology of, 86-87
Pharaoh, 78, 80-84, 90, 112, 205, 221, 251
Balak's parallels to, 112
as seed of serpent, 81-82, 90
wordplay on "locks/leaders," 150, 154, 198
Phillips, Elaine, 73
plot structure, xv, xxii, 121-22, 228
poetry
Christocentrism or theocentrism of, 85, 88, 141, 217, 221
embedded in narrative, 85-88, 113, 135-38, 217-18, 239
in the structure of the Pentateuch, 85-88, 113
Pohl, William C., IV, 185-86, 248
Polysemy. *See* wordplay
Polzin, Robert, xxi, 173, 175, 179
Possession. *See* inheritance/possession
Postell, Seth, xxvi, 46, 103, 107, 111, 115, 119, 128, 131, 135, 137, 274
Potgieter, J. Henk, 238
priest-king, 208
progressive revelation, 14-15, 24, 38-39
prophet like Moses, 204-5, 226, 267, 290
Provan, Iain, xxvi
Prussner, Frederick, 8
Psalter
Davidic covenant in, 243-45, 247-49
introduction as Ps 1 or Ps 1–2, 243-45
linear and nonlinear aspects, 260-64
as a "little Bible," 242, 247
Messiah in, 243, 245-46
multiple nexus passages in, 242
study of as a book, 242-49, 262-64
wisdom-Messiah frame of, 246-47
puzzles (as a metaphor for the OT and its books), 311-13, 315
Pyper, Hugh, 217
qatal verb form, 138, 158
Rad, Gerhard von, 22-24, 28-29, 33, 47-49, 51, 77, 142, 158, 193, 204, 288, 314
Radak, 123, 189
Rambam, 107
Ramban, 63, 118, 123-24, 143
Rashi, 63, 118-20, 123, 126-27, 189, 276
Red Sea, 78, 80, 84, 92, 94, 96, 98, 205, 206, 216, 220, 222-23, 235
redaction, xxi, xxv
Renaud, Bernard, 253-54
Rendsburg, Gary, 134
Rendtorff, Rolf, 23-24

resurrection
Messiah's, 235
Reventlow, Henning Graf, 190, 212-13
Riley, William, 182
Robertson, O. Palmer, 263
rock (or stone)
Lord as, 153, 158-59, 163, 165, 204, 262, 272, 301
striking the statue, 298-301, 303, 306, 308
water from, 163, 202-3
Rogerson, John, 329
Rosenberg, Joel, 170
Rosner, Brian, 11
Rothstein, Bret, 311-15
Rouillard, Hedwige, 112
Rowold, Henry, 75
Rydelnik, Eva, 275
Ryrie, Charles, 10
Sabbath, 84, 296
Saebø, Magne, 4-5, 7
Sailhamer, John, xxi-xxiii, xxvi, 1, 8, 12, 15, 17-18, 20-21, 31-32, 34-37, 40-41, 57, 79, 86-91, 106, 112-13, 118-20, 122, 125-26, 129, 131, 133, 136, 139, 148, 157, 173, 182, 218-19, 234, 247, 254, 269, 274, 276, 287, 289, 291, 294
salvation history (or *Heilsgeschichte*),
act-revelation, word-revelation, broader definition of prophecy and, 14, 16, 37
cannot be disproven, 19
as chronological framework, 18-20
conflicts with canonical form and order, 20-21
history as prophecy, 14, 16
not driven by author's intent, 17-19, 21
not the only evangelical approach to biblical theology, 36-38
periodization and precursors of, 10, 15
progressive revelation and, 14-15
as reality versus unifying framework, 21, 40
romantic and idealistic influences on, 13-14
sometimes treated as axiomatic, 12-13
typology and, 14, 17
use as a framework versus one aspect among many, 12, 22
von Hofmann a key representative of, 12
von Hofmann as mediating figure between conservative and critical scholarship, 17
von Hofmann's non-traditional broadened view of inspiration and, 16
Vos an influential evangelical example of, 12-13
Vos dependent on Gabler and von Hofmann, 36-37

General Index 343

Sandys-Wunsch, John, 2-4, 6-7, 9, 11-12, 35, 43
Sanz Giménez-Rico, Enrique, 222, 224
Sasson, Jack, 237
Saul, 118, 120, 168-69, 179-80, 239-40
scapegoat, 213
Schaper, Joachim, 2, 8-9
Schipper, Bernd, 64, 76
Schmitt, Hans-Christoph, 92, 164, 192, 203
Schnittjer, Gary Edward, 121, 133, 168
Scobie, Charles, 2, 9, 19, 21, 27, 29, 31, 36, 39, 50
sea monsters (e.g., Leviathan), 72-75
seams, xxiii, 32-33, 113, 125, 131, 136, 185, 226, 231, 242-43, 246-47, 257, 263-64, 289-91, 294
Second Exodus. *See* exodus, second
seed, 117-19, 202, 305
    of Abraham, 115, 128, 177, 199, 254-55, 260
    of David, 172-75, 177-80, 185-86, 194, 215, 237, 239-40, 251, 277, 305-6
    of the serpent, 79, 81-82, 90, 126, 153-54, 232, 256
    "son" and, 173-74, 178-80
    of the woman, 45-46, 79, 90, 104, 108-9, 126-27, 139, 153, 157, 215, 231, 235, 249, 256
Seitz, Christopher, xix, 20-21, 287-88
sensus plenior, 14.
    See also author's intent
serpent (snake)
    bronze. *See* bronze snake
    in Eden, 52-54, 56, 70-75, 90, 116, 126, 139, 152-56, 231-32, 256, 300
    poisonous, 108
    sea creatures and, 72-75
servant of the Lord in Isaiah
    justice and, 195, 197, 212
    servant as Israel, 192
    Servant Songs, 189-97, 204-11
    Suffering Servant, 189, 205-14
Servant Songs. *See* servant of the Lord in Isaiah
seventy-sevens, meaning of, 295, 307-8
Seufert, Matthew, 64, 67-68
Shelton, Jonathan, 135, 159, 169-70, 275-76
Sheol, 78, 158, 187, 220-21, 224, 227-30, 234, 236, 239-41.
    See also death
Shepherd, Michael, 130, 133, 224, 226, 276, 287, 298-99, 306-7
Silva, Moisés, 118
sin, 66-68, 146, 180, 192, 196-97, 206-7, 212-14, 230-32, 235, 241, 258, 261, 294-95, 305, 308
Sinai/Deuteronomic law, 184
Smend, Rudolf, 30
Smith, Henry Preserved, 160

Snearly, Michael, 101-2, 242, 247
Solomon, 9, 11, 48, 56, 118, 137, 174, 180-82, 185, 243-44, 249-51, 253, 257, 264, 268-70, 293, 295-96, 302
Sommer, Benjamin, 190-91, 199, 204, 207, 212
son, 178-84
Song of Hannah, 157-60
    death-to-life sequence in, 158
    integration of poetic sections in the Pentateuch, 159-60
Song of Moses
    allusions to Gen 1–3, 147-48, 153-56
    allusions to in the Psalms, 144, 261-63
    allusions to in Isaiah, 160-62, 196, 212
    atonement in, 152
    Christology and, 155-57, 259-60
    emphatic use of "I," 162
    eschatological, 146-47, 153-57
    exile and, 145, 153, 162
    faithfulness theme in, 164
    focuses on idolatry, 145
    food theme in, 151-53
    integration of material from previous poetic sections, 151, 153, 155-56, 166
    joy in, 156
    justice in, 162, 195-97
    the Lord's "hand" in, 150
    the Lord's perfect "work" in, 148-50
    the Lord's restraint in, 161
    memorization of, 143-44, 166, 262
    parallels with flood account, 146, 148
    parallels with golden calf/Ex 32, 146
    as part of last major poetic section in the Pentateuch, 144-45
    plan of Jewish history, 143
    prophetic literature and, 142
    snakes, poison, crushing enemy, and 153-56
    wisdom, Wisdom literature and, 142-43, 146-47
Song of the Sea
    as corporate response of faith, 92-93
    climax of Ex 1-15, 78-79
    creation themes, 90-91
    everlasting kingdom and, 89
    faith-theme and, 91-93
    Jonah 2 and, 219-23
    predicts fulfillment of Abrahamic covenant, 89
    relation to second exodus, 197-98
    uniqueness as major poetic section in the Pentateuch, 88-89
Soref, Erez, 137

Spieckermann, Hermann, 211, 213
Spirit, xxiv, 16, 42, 71, 84, 95, 114-16, 127, 134-35, 178, 193, 200-204, 207, 252, 291, 298
Stanfield, Yohanan, 152, 160
Steinmann, Andrew, 265, 270, 272, 274-75, 277, 280, 285
Sternberg, Meir, xix
Steyn, Gert, 280
Stirrup, Andy, 170-71
Stone. *See* rock (stone)
Stone, Timothy, 221, 233-34, 238
Stuckenbruck, Loren, 4, 6-7
subway system and transfer stations
    complexity and design of, xvii-xviii
    high connectivity of transfer stations, xviii, 241
    as metaphors, x-xi, xvi-xx, xxii, 312, 314
    necessity of transfer stations, xviii
    nexus passages and, xviii
    as thought experiment, xvi
Suffering Servant. *See* servant of the Lord in Isaiah
Sweeney, Marvin, 221, 224, 227, 229, 231
syntax, xv, xxii, 62, 82, 100, 134, 136, 156, 158, 173, 177, 273
targum(s), 63, 107, 117-18, 127, 137, 276, 300
Tate, Marvin, 9
Teeter, Andrew, 301-2, 308
temple, 169-175
    Solomon's dedicatory prayer for, 295
    Solomon's versus eschatological, 174
    Solomon's versus wisdom's, 269-70
text and event, xx-xxi, 5, 299
    act-revelation, word-revelation and, 14, 16, 37
    historical reliability and, xxi
themes
    integration of, xx, 27, 31, 122, 126-27, 140-41, 153, 156-57, 159-60, 188, 249, 254-57, 260
    proposed as center of the OT, 26-27
    some nexus passages characterized by single theme, xxvii
Thompson, Benjamin, 135
Thompson, John A., 132
three days, 229
Tiemeyer, Lena-Sofia, 224
Tigay, Jeffrey, 143, 149, 160
tradition history, 23-24
transfer stations. *See* subway system and transfer stations
Treier, Daniel, 267, 274, 284
Trimm, Charlie, 25
Trublet, Jacques, 100-101
Tsumura, David Toshio, 136, 158, 160, 169

type/typology, 14, 17
    See also intentional foreshadowing
ugliness, 208-9
unity of OT and Scripture, ix-x,
    as a wonder, xix-xx
    Christocentric, xvi, xxviii, 20, 43, 104, 140-41, 242, 254
    Gabler's sharp distinction between the Testaments, 3, 8-9
    Gabler's use of universal ideas to achieve, 3-6
    models and theories for, xvi-xvii
    nexus passages as achieving literary, textual, and theological, xv-xvi, xviii, xx, xxv-xxvi, xxviii, 27, 41-42, 141, 153, 156-57, 167, 242, 254, 313, 315
    on literary, textual, and theological grounds, 7, 41, 50
    salvation history as weak unity, xviii, 18-19, 21
    thematic conceptions of, xviii
    See also center of the OT
"universal ideas" (Gabler), 3-6
Vaillancourt, Ian, 101-2
Van Leeuwen, Raymond, 55, 62, 266, 268-69
Verde, Danilo, 93
Vermeylen, Jacques, 219-20
Verrett, Brian, 180
Vitringa, Campegius, 200, 202-4, 208, 210
Vos, Geerhardus, 10, 12-14, 36-37, 39
Walsh, Jerome, 181, 251
Waltke, Bruce, 22, 40, 273, 283-84
Walton, John, 263-64
water, 48, 52, 72, 79, 81, 84, 90-91, 93, 95-96, 99-100, 117, 198, 201-4, 208, 218, 220-24, 234-41, 275, 282
Watts, James W., 79, 85-86, 88, 217-19
Watts, Rikki, 78
wayyiqtol verb form, 158
Webb, Barry, 95-96, 98
Webb, William, 78
Wegner, Paul, 192
Weinfeld, Moshe, 142, 286
Weitzman, Steven, 88, 216, 219
Wellhausen, Julius, 22, 51, 191, 311-12, 314
Wellum, Stephen, 12, 36-37
Wendebourg, Ernst-Wilhelm, 13, 20, 24
Wenham, Gordon, 46, 71, 127, 131-2
weqatal verb form, 125, 173
Westermann, Claus, 235, 263-64, 303
Weth, Gustav, 17, 36
weyiqtol verb form, 158
Whybray, R. N., 267
Wifall, Walter, 78

Wilcock, Michael, 99-100
Williamson, H. G. M., 207
Willis, John, 198, 201
Wilson, Gerald, xxiii, 183, 187, 239, 242-49, 263, 280, 293-95
Wilson, Lindsay, 134
wisdom
    in the Balaam narrative, 106-7, 116
    as "beginning," 271-76
    builds a house, 268-71
    contest, 53, 82
    fear of the Lord and, 49, 55
    in Gen 1–3, 52-55
    Messiah's, 207-8, 270
    parental instruction and, 56, 267-68
    personified in Proverbs, 265-67
    poetic seams in the Pentateuch and, 87, 136, 267-68
    preexistence of, 276-77
    prophecy and, 106-7, 226, 290-91
    second exodus and, 201-2
    speeches in the structure of Prov 1–9, 266
    as tree of life, 57-61
    two ways and, 52, 56-57

Wisdom Literature, xxvii, 33, 45-51, 142, 265, 272
    diachronic issues concerning, 48-49, 51, 64, 69
    difficulty of integrating into OT theology, 47-48
    relationship to creation, 47-49
    rooted in Gen 1–3, 45, 49-51, 265, 272
Wolff, Hans Walter, 229
Wong Yee-cheung, 208-9
wordplay (including polysemy), 70, 78, 128, 137, 154, 170, 240, 273, 297
    clause-level, 128
Wray Beal, Lissa, 180-81
Wright, Christopher J. H., 31
Wright, G. Ernest, 142, 157-58
Wright, N. T., 153, 165
Yeast. *See* Feast of Unleavened Bread
yiqtol verb form, 156, 158
Yoder, Christine Roy, 58-61, 63
Zabán, Bálint Károly, 266-67, 269, 275
Zacharia, G. T., 7, 9, 11, 43
Zakovitch, Yair, xxvi, 77, 79, 83
Zenger, Erich, 101-2, 187, 247, 249, 251, 253-55, 281
Zimmerli, Walther, 47-48, 64

SCRIPTURE INDEX

OLD TESTAMENT

Genesis
1, 49, 51, 52, 54, 58, 62, 64, 65, 69, 71, 80, 199, 282, 283
1–2, 91
1–3, 26, 29, 31, 45, 46, 47, 49, 50, 51, 52, 53, 55, 56, 57, 58, 59, 61, 63, 64, 65, 66, 67, 68, 69, 70, 71, 72, 73, 75, 76, 79, 81, 87, 90, 103, 104, 106, 147, 166, 167, 187, 205, 214, 265, 271, 314
1–11, 64
1–15, 71
1:1, 52, 56, 61, 62, 63, 64, 83, 147, 199, 201, 271, 272, 273, 274, 276
1:1-2, 63, 275
1:1–2:3, 52, 268
1:1–2:4, 51, 71, 72
1:2, 52, 63, 71, 114, 148, 199, 282
1:2-5, 199
1:2-31, 57
1:3-5, 52
1:4, 52
1:5, 52
1:6-7, 52
1:8, 52
1:10, 52, 222
1:11-12, 52, 148
1:14, 52
1:16, 251
1:18, 52
1:20-21, 80
1:21, 52, 64, 72, 73, 154, 221
1:22, 69
1:24-25, 52
1:26, 65, 128, 129, 148, 255, 256
1:26-27, 53, 58, 128
1:26-28, 52, 129
1:27, 64
1:28, 67, 69, 75, 80, 128, 129, 255, 256, 293, 299, 300
1:31, 65, 68, 117
2, 70
2–3, 52, 55, 56, 58, 59, 60, 65, 66, 70, 209
2:1, 147, 199
2:3, 64, 70
2:4, 48, 51, 147
2:5, 67, 201
2:5-6, 63
2:6, 143
2:7, 66
2:8, 69, 90, 91, 117
2:8-14, 117
2:9, 52, 53, 54, 55, 56, 57, 60, 69, 201, 253
2:10, 91
2:11-12, 59, 60
2:15, 69, 90
2:16-17, 53
2:17, 52, 53, 55, 60, 61, 72, 116
2:23, 71
2:25, 54, 70, 71
3, 49, 59, 60, 63, 65, 70, 71, 73, 74, 75, 107, 108, 116, 148, 151, 153, 154, 156, 232
3:1, 53, 56, 60, 72, 74
3:1-2, 108, 156
3:1-6, 108
3:2-3, 56
3:4, 53, 72, 108, 156
3:5, 52, 53, 54, 55, 116
3:5-7, 201
3:6, 54, 56, 59, 60, 69, 116, 209
3:7, 54, 55, 60, 71, 116
3:7-8, 60
3:7-11, 54
3:8, 70
3:10, 56
3:10-11, 60, 71
3:13-14, 108
3:13-15, 156
3:14, 59, 60, 70, 74, 231, 256, 259
3:14-15, 108
3:15, 15, 45, 46, 70, 74, 75, 79, 81, 86, 87, 90, 104, 108, 114, 116, 126, 128, 129, 137, 138, 139, 141, 152, 153, 154, 155, 156, 157, 160, 167, 185, 187, 188, 211, 215, 231, 233, 235, 241, 249, 256, 257, 259, 300
3:15-17, 60
3:16, 67
3:16-17, 67
3:16-19, 56
3:17, 59, 60, 67, 70, 253
3:17-19, 67, 68
3:18, 67, 201, 253
3:19, 66, 68, 71, 228, 230
3:21, 60
3:22, 52, 53, 54, 55, 57, 59, 60, 67
3:22-23, 116
3:22-24, 228, 230, 232
3:23-24, 56
3:24, 57, 60, 157, 224
4, 65
4:1, 272
4:7, 206, 232
4:12, 103
4:14, 103
4:16, 103
4:24, 294
4:25, 127
5:1, 65
5:1-2, 57
5:6-8, 127
5:24, 227
5:28-29, 127
6:5, 54, 65, 148
6:11-12, 146, 148
6:11-14, 152
7:11, 63, 282
8:2, 282
8:17, 80
8:21, 54, 148
9:1, 80, 300
9:6, 65

9:7, *80*
10, *127, 294*
10–11, *299*
10:1, *127*
10:10, *299*
10:23, *69*
11, *70*
11:1, *299*
11:2, *299*
11:3-4, *81*
11:4, *103, 206, 300*
11:4-5, *84*
11:7, *84, 299*
11:8, *103*
11:9, *103, 299, 300*
12, *51*
12:1-3, *255*
12:2, *80, 178, 254*
12:2-3, *110, 178*
12:3, *110, 132, 149, 208, 254, 293*
12:10-20, *79*
13:14-18, *255*
13:16, *80, 110*
14:18-20, *149, 259*
14:19, *147, 148, 272*
14:20, *155*
14:22, *147, 148, 272*
15, *176, 177, 178, 188*
15:1, *115, 124, 176, 177*
15:2, *176, 177*
15:3-4, *115, 177, 188*
15:4, *91*
15:5, *80, 110, 115, 124, 176, 177, 277*
15:6, *14, 92, 164*
15:7, *81, 177*
15:7-8, *177*
15:7-21, *81, 110, 116*
15:8, *176, 177*
15:12, *176, 177*
15:13, *81*
15:13-14, *177*
15:13-16, *292*
15:14, *81*
15:17, *176, 177*
15:18, *177, 255, 256*
17:6, *178*
17:16, *178*
18:18, *80, 132, 208, 254, 293*
18:18-19, *250*
20:12, *183*

22:8, *56, 268*
22:12, *56*
22:14, *56*
22:17, *80, 90, 91, 110, 114, 124, 128, 129, 149, 156, 177, 255*
22:17-18, *110, 199*
22:18, *128, 132, 156, 208, 254, 255, 259, 260, 293*
22:21, *69*
24:60, *91, 128, 129, 149, 177*
24:67, *183*
25:10, *272*
25:23, *123, 220*
26:3, *255*
26:4, *110, 124*
26:16, *80*
27:1, *122*
27:21, *183*
27:27, *137*
27:27-28, *184, 253*
27:27-29, *121, 122, 126, 129, 134, 178, 259, 280*
27:28, *148, 253, 259*
27:29, *91, 110, 111, 114, 120, 121, 122, 123, 124, 126, 129, 155, 184, 253, 254, 258, 259, 307*
28:13, *199*
28:14, *81, 110, 132, 199, 255*
32:12, *110*
36:28, *69*
37–50, *80*
37:1-3, *125*
37:6-10, *125, 126, 128, 129*
37:7, *124, 125*
37:9, *124, 125*
37:9-10, *124, 125*
37:11, *290*
37:13, *125*
37:31-33, *139*
37:33, *125*
37:35, *234*
39:1, *234*
39:3, *204*
39:17, *204*
40–41, *299*
40:5, *107*
40:8, *107*
40:12, *107*
40:16, *107*
40:18, *107*
40:22, *107*
41:8, *107*

41:11, *107*
41:12-13, *107*
41:15, *107*
41:29-31, *297*
41:34, *297*
41:37, *297*
41:38, *291*
41:39, *107*
41:53, *297*
41:54-57, *204*
42:6, *115*
42:25, *204*
44:14, *115*
45:5-8, *163*
46:2, *116*
46:27, *294*
47:27, *80*
48:10, *122*
48:15, *268*
49, *125, 144, 147, 151, 153, 159, 178, 314*
49:1, *33, 86, 87, 89, 113, 123, 134, 144, 147, 151, 181, 182, 188, 201, 219, 246, 254, 261, 298*
49:1-2, *86, 87, 147, 267*
49:1-27, *86, 87, 88, 89, 113, 121, 124, 144, 148, 218*
49:2, *147, 151, 267*
49:3, *274*
49:3-7, *124*
49:8, *90, 115, 122, 124, 125*
49:8-9, *184*
49:8-10, *122, 235*
49:8-12, *33, 39, 87, 89, 113, 122, 124, 126, 129, 134, 137, 138, 152, 157, 159, 178, 181, 182, 184, 188, 219, 246, 261, 268*
49:9, *120, 121, 122, 124, 125, 126, 137, 138, 159*
49:9-10, *114, 138*
49:10, *91, 122, 124, 126, 128, 129, 138, 184, 185*
49:11, *139, 152*
49:11-12, *117, 139, 140, 152, 233*
49:12, *138, 152*
49:18, *151, 156, 159*
49:21, *147*
49:23, *155*
49:24, *158*
49:25-26, *86*
49:28, *86*
50:20, *163*

Scripture Index

50:21, *204*
50:24-25, *292*
50:26, *80*

Exodus
1, *112, 234, 237, 241*
1–2, *112*
1–14, *78, 79, 85, 91, 92, 93, 94, 103*
1–15, *82, 85, 99, 206*
1–15:21, *79*
1:1-5, *80*
1:5, *80, 294*
1:6, *80*
1:7, *80*
1:7-12, *80*
1:9, *80, 112*
1:10, *80, 82, 225*
1:11, *81, 83, 206, 251*
1:11-12, *81, 206*
1:11-14, *81, 112*
1:12, *80, 112, 234*
1:13-14, *81, 206*
1:14, *81, 83, 251*
1:15-21, *112*
1:16, *82, 234*
1:17, *82*
1:20, *80*
1:21, *82*
1:22, *112, 234*
2:3, *238*
2:5, *238*
2:10, *238*
2:11, *83, 206*
2:23, *103*
2:23-24, *83*
2:24, *81*
3:1–4:17, *114*
3:6, *81*
3:6-8, *89*
3:8, *151, 225, 234*
3:9, *103*
3:13, *275*
3:13-15, *149*
3:14, *266*
3:15-16, *81*
3:15-17, *89*
3:16-17, *112*
3:17, *151, 225*
3:18, *83*
3:20, *85, 231*
4:2, *85*

4:3, *73*
4:4, *85*
4:5, *81*
4:6-7, *85*
4:16, *183*
4:23, *82*
4:31, *92*
5:1, *83*
5:2, *78*
5:3, *83*
5:4-5, *83*
5:5, *83, 84*
5:8, *103*
5:9, *82, 251*
5:9-14, *83*
5:12, *103*
5:15, *83, 103*
6:6, *83, 227*
6:6-7, *83*
6:6-8, *112*
6:7, *183*
6:8, *81*
6:9, *83, 251*
7:4-5, *85*
7:5, *78*
7:9-10, *73, 154*
7:9-12, *211*
7:11, *81, 82, 112*
7:12, *73, 154*
7:15, *73, 81*
7:22, *81, 112*
8:1, *82*
8:3, *80*
8:7, *81*
8:10, *78, 82*
8:18, *81*
8:18-19, *82*
8:19, *82*
8:20, *81, 82*
8:22, *78*
8:27, *83*
9:1, *82*
9:3, *85*
9:11, *82*
9:13, *82*
9:14, *82*
9:15, *85*
9:16, *78*
9:18, *78*
9:24, *78*
10:2, *78*
10:3, *82*

10:5, *112*
10:9, *83*
10:14, *78*
10:15, *112*
10:26, *83*
11:6, *78*
12:2, *83*
12:11, *205*
12:12-13, *233*
12:14, *83*
12:22-25, *269*
12:25-26, *83*
12:25-27, *83*
12:27, *83*
12:30, *234*
12:31, *205*
12:31-32, *82, 84*
12:33, *205, 234*
13:3, *83*
13:5-6, *83*
13:8, *78*
13:9, *84*
13:14, *78, 83*
13:18, *225*
13:21, *205*
14, *80, 84, 85, 111, 219, 220*
14–15, *84, 100, 216, 219, 220, 223, 235*
14:2, *84*
14:4, *78, 84*
14:5, *82, 84, 205, 219*
14:6-7, *84*
14:7, *84*
14:8, *84*
14:9, *84*
14:10, *84, 92, 219*
14:13, *84, 92, 96, 97, 103, 151*
14:14, *85*
14:16, *84, 85, 221, 222, 235*
14:17, *84*
14:17-18, *78, 84*
14:18, *78*
14:19-20, *205*
14:21, *84, 85, 219, 221*
14:22, *84, 85, 222, 235*
14:23, *84*
14:24, *84, 205*
14:25, *84, 85*
14:26, *84*
14:26-27, *85, 221*
14:27, *232*
14:28, *84*

14:28-30, *219*
14:29, *84, 85, 222, 235*
14:30, *84, 97, 103, 234*
14:30-31, *85*
14:31, *56, 82, 84, 92, 93, 100, 164, 219, 234*
15, *79, 85, 88, 90, 91, 101, 104, 151, 219, 220, 221, 222, 314*
15:1, *84, 89, 92, 93, 97, 99, 100, 101, 151, 221, 222, 223, 232, 238*
15:1-2, *97, 159*
15:1-12, *89*
15:1-18, *78, 79, 81, 83, 84, 85, 86, 87, 88, 89, 91, 92, 93, 94, 95, 96, 97, 98, 99, 100, 101, 103, 157, 174, 197, 198, 216, 217, 218, 219, 220, 221, 223, 225, 232, 233, 234, 241*
15:2, *84, 93, 96, 97, 99, 100, 101, 150, 151, 159, 221*
15:2-3, *97*
15:3, *89, 97, 198*
15:3-17, *228*
15:4, *84, 93, 150, 198, 221, 222, 232, 238*
15:4-5, *221, 222, 223*
15:4-10, *202*
15:5, *93, 99, 150, 222, 232*
15:6, *89, 90, 93, 99, 101, 150, 151, 155, 156, 185, 198, 221*
15:6-7, *74*
15:7, *93, 97, 221*
15:8, *85, 99, 221, 222*
15:8-9, *237*
15:8-10, *100*
15:9, *89, 91, 150, 198, 221*
15:9-10, *101*
15:10, *85, 93, 99, 221, 222, 223*
15:11, *78, 82, 93, 96, 97, 99, 100, 101, 198, 222, 231, 232, 260*
15:11-18, *100*
15:12, *85, 99, 101, 150, 151, 222*
15:12-17, *100*
15:13, *89, 90, 99, 119, 150, 159, 198, 222, 227*
15:13-18, *89, 94, 103, 151*
15:14, *78, 91, 97, 98, 99, 100*
15:14-15, *96, 150*
15:14-16, *98, 101, 222, 231, 234*
15:16, *90, 91, 96, 98, 99, 148, 150, 159, 198, 202, 272*

15:16-17, *150, 151*
15:17, *85, 89, 90, 91, 94, 97, 98, 99, 101, 117, 150, 151, 174, 198, 222, 225*
15:17-18, *103*
15:18, *89, 93, 174*
15:19, *84, 85, 99, 222, 235*
15:20, *97, 101*
15:20-21, *89, 97*
15:21, *84, 93, 96, 97, 99*
15:22-27, *96*
15:26, *147, 206*
16:1, *111*
16:3, *111*
16:6, *111*
16:30, *84*
16:32, *111*
17:1-7, *96*
17:6, *203*
17:16, *100*
18:1, *111*
18:21, *116*
19:1, *111*
19:3-6, *114*
19:4, *148, 199*
19:5, *202*
19:9, *92*
19:20-24, *114*
20:2, *81, 83, 111*
20:3, *258*
20:4, *258*
20:5, *149, 258*
23:12, *84*
23:14-17, *83*
23:24, *258*
23:31, *255, 256*
24:1, *294*
24:5, *83*
24:9-11, *83*
24:11, *116*
25:10-22, *171*
25:26, *125*
26:18, *125*
28:3, *269*
30, *152*
30:33, *304*
30:38, *304*
31:3, *269*
31:14, *304*
32:7, *146, 152*
32:12, *166, 231*
32:13, *166, 231*
32:14, *166*

32:30, *207*
32:32, *207*
33:1, *231*
33:7-11, *114*
33:21, *203*
34:5-7, *149*
34:6, *231*
34:6-7, *231*
34:7, *231*
34:9, *231*
34:21, *84*
40:34-35, *269*

Leviticus
2:12, *273*
4:6, *208*
5:1-7, *206*
5:15, *206*
7:20-21, *304*
7:25, *304*
7:27, *304*
13:41, *125*
16:21-22, *213, 233*
16:22, *213*
19:9, *125*
19:13, *150*
19:27, *125*
20:24, *151*
25–26, *296, 297*
25:2-4, *296*
25:8-12, *296*
25:43, *128*
25:46, *128*
25:53, *128*
26:12, *183*
26:17, *128*
26:18, *296*
26:21, *296*
26:24, *296*
26:27-39, *296*
26:27-45, *296*
26:28, *296*
26:32-35, *297*
26:33, *296*
26:34, *296*
26:38, *296*
26:38-40, *297*
26:40, *296*
26:41, *193, 296*
26:42, *296*
26:43, *296*
26:45, *296*

Scripture Index

Numbers
5:22, *220*
6:24-27, *295*
6:25, *295*
9:1-5, *83*
10:9, *155*
10:35-36, *171*
11:17, *114*
11:24-25, *294*
11:25-27, *114*
11:29, *114*
12:6, *116, 290*
12:6-8, *39*
12:7-8, *204*
14:8, *151*
14:11, *92, 164*
15–24, *87*
16:1-10, *124*
16:30, *220*
20:2-13, *163*
20:3-5, *117*
20:12, *92, 124, 164*
20:14-17, *112*
20:14-21, *105, 127*
21, *105, 108, 109*
21–24, *104, 108, 109, 116, 126, 141, 155, 159, 307*
21–36, *105, 107, 109, 114, 124, 136*
21:4-9, *108, 126, 154, 163*
21:5, *117, 163*
21:6, *108, 109, 156*
21:6-7, *108*
21:6-9, *127*
21:7, *108*
21:7-9, *108*
21:8-9, *95, 108, 109*
21:9, *108*
21:11, *105*
21:13, *105*
21:14-15, *105*
21:15, *105*
21:16-18, *303*
21:17-18, *92, 105*
21:18, *203*
21:20, *105, 117*
21:21-35, *105, 112*
21:23-25, *105*
21:24, *105*
21:26, *105*
21:26-29, *105*
21:27, *106*
21:28, *132*
21:28-29, *132*
21:29, *132*
21:32, *105*
21:35, *105*
22–24, *105, 106, 107, 108, 109, 111, 112, 127*
22:3, *112*
22:3-4, *127*
22:5, *107, 111, 112*
22:6, *86, 109, 111, 112*
22:7, *112*
22:7-8, *127*
22:10, *127*
22:11, *110, 111, 112*
22:12, *110*
22:17, *110*
22:21-30, *122*
22:21-35, *107*
22:22, *115*
22:23, *107*
22:24, *115*
22:26, *115*
22:28, *107, 115*
22:29, *107*
22:30, *107*
22:31, *107, 109, 115, 116, 122*
22:33, *107*
22:34, *107, 116*
22:35, *106, 123*
22:38, *106, 123*
22:41, *115*
23–24, *88, 89, 106, 113, 125, 147, 151*
23:1, *106*
23:5, *106*
23:7, *87, 106, 110*
23:7-10, *86, 87, 113*
23:8, *110*
23:9, *109, 156*
23:9-10, *117*
23:10, *110, 156, 308*
23:11, *110*
23:12, *106*
23:13, *110, 115*
23:14, *105, 106*
23:16, *106*
23:18, *106, 147, 151, 267*
23:18-24, *86, 87, 113*
23:19, *109, 110, 156, 187, 248*
23:19-20, *149*
23:20, *110, 156, 162*
23:21, *117, 119*
23:21-22, *119*
23:22, *111, 117, 119, 120, 127, 234*
23:23, *108, 109, 112, 127, 150, 151*
23:24, *156*
23:25, *110*
23:26, *106*
23:27, *110*
23:28, *105, 117*
23:29, *106*
24, *45, 91, 104, 105, 107, 109, 111, 112, 113, 114, 115, 116, 117, 119, 121, 123, 124, 125, 127, 129, 130, 131, 132, 133, 134, 135, 136, 137, 139, 140, 141, 144, 147, 151, 153, 155, 156, 159, 167, 178, 185, 253, 275, 276, 314*
24:1, *108, 127, 156*
24:1-2, *114*
24:2, *106, 115, 116, 127, 135, 252*
24:2-4, *88, 298*
24:3, *106, 134, 136, 252*
24:3-4, *114, 115, 122*
24:3-9, *86, 87, 105, 113, 144*
24:4, *115, 138, 147, 267*
24:5, *91*
24:5-6, *117, 120*
24:5-9, *107, 111, 115, 119, 128*
24:6, *90, 91, 117, 127, 202*
24:6-7, *117*
24:7, *88, 91, 117, 118, 119, 120, 122, 133, 135, 159, 208*
24:7-8, *133*
24:7-9, *87, 117*
24:8, *90, 91, 103, 111, 119, 120, 121, 122, 127, 130, 133, 138, 155, 156, 199, 234, 241*
24:8-9, *120, 122, 138*
24:9, *110, 111, 120, 121, 122, 124, 126, 127, 129, 135, 138, 159, 178, 235, 253, 254*
24:10, *110, 112*
24:10-11, *111, 123*
24:12-13, *123*
24:13, *106*
24:14, *86, 87, 89, 105, 108, 113, 123, 124, 127, 132, 134, 144, 147, 151, 155, 156, 178, 201,*

219, 234, 246, 254, 255, 261, 262, 298
24:14-17, 87
24:14-19, 33, 87, 144
24:15, 106, 134, 136, 252
24:15-16, 88, 114, 115, 122, 298
24:15-19, 132, 263
24:15-24, 86, 113
24:16, 115, 116, 124, 138, 147, 262, 267
24:16-17, 115, 116
24:16-19, 122
24:17, 105, 108, 109, 110, 115, 117, 124, 125, 126, 127, 128, 131, 132, 137, 138, 139, 153, 155, 156, 157, 185, 255, 257, 262, 300
24:17-18, 120, 135, 140, 255
24:17-19, 39, 87, 89, 90, 104, 105, 113, 123, 127, 128, 129, 133, 135, 178, 219, 246, 255, 256, 261
24:17-1947, 129
24:18, 91, 105, 115, 127, 128, 130, 132, 139, 177, 224, 255, 256
24:18-19, 131
24:19, 105, 120, 128, 129, 130, 255, 259
24:20, 91, 113, 156, 201
24:20-21, 106
24:22, 109
24:23, 106, 118
24:24, 132, 256
25:1, 117
25:14, 124
27:18, 114

Deuteronomy
3, 287
3:21, 112
3:24, 176
4:10, 267, 270
4:19, 258
4:20, 234
4:25, 152
4:25-28, 33, 145
4:26-27, 228
4:27, 103
4:27-30, 181
4:28, 150
4:29, 286, 295
4:29-30, 226, 228, 294

4:29-31, 113, 308
4:30, 86, 113, 123, 144, 146, 246, 261, 298
5:6, 81
5:7, 258
5:8, 258
5:9, 149, 258
6:1, 146
6:3, 151
6:4-7, 267
6:4-9, 56
6:6-9, 56
6:11-12, 151
6:12, 143
6:18, 146
6:20-25, 267
7:8, 227
7:9, 110
7:9-10, 164
7:10, 163
7:15, 206
7:24, 75
8:10-14, 151
8:15, 163
8:15-16, 163
8:19, 258
9:2, 75
9:7, 146
9:24, 146
9:26, 176
10:22, 294
11:15-16, 151
11:16, 258
11:17, 258
11:19, 146, 267
11:25, 75
11:31, 57
12:28, 146
13:6, 227
14:1, 268
14:29, 151
15:4, 110
15:15, 227
17:2-4, 258
17:3, 258
17:17, 270
17:19, 270
18:15, 204
18:15-16, 267
18:15-18, 32, 199
18:18, 146, 204
18:19, 205, 267

21:17, 274
23:3-6, 111
23:4, 111
23:24, 151
26:12, 151
27:15, 150
28:20-26, 228
28:32, 228
28:36-37, 228
28:37, 106, 286
28:60-61, 234
28:61, 206
28:64, 103
29:4, 54, 115
30:3, 103
30:12, 275
30:14, 146
30:15, 52, 61, 146
30:19, 147
31–32, 145
31:1-8, 145
31:4, 105, 112
31:13-15, 145
31:16, 145, 146
31:16-18, 145
31:16-29, 33
31:16-30, 153
31:18, 148
31:19, 87, 146, 161
31:19-21, 143, 262
31:19-22, 92
31:20, 151, 161
31:20-21, 146
31:21, 144, 148, 160, 161
31:21-22, 146
31:22, 87, 146
31:26, 161
31:27, 146
31:28, 86, 146, 147
31:29, 86, 87, 113, 143, 144, 146, 147, 148, 150, 151, 152, 155, 156, 166, 181, 201, 219, 261, 268, 286, 298
31:30, 92, 143, 146, 151
32, 88, 142, 143, 145, 147, 149, 151, 153, 155, 157, 159, 160, 161, 163, 164, 165, 219, 262, 303, 314
32–33, 86, 88, 89, 134, 144, 147, 150, 219
32:1, 144, 146, 147, 150, 151, 160, 262, 267

Scripture Index 353

32:1-2, *87, 146, 148, 204*
32:1-3, *143*
32:1-5, *204*
32:1-18, *160*
32:1-43, *87, 88, 92, 113, 142, 143, 144, 145, 146, 147, 151, 152, 156, 157, 160, 161, 162, 164, 165, 166, 197, 205, 214, 218, 261, 262, 263*
32:2, *148, 252*
32:3-4, *148*
32:4, *92, 149, 150, 151, 153, 156, 160, 161, 162, 163, 164, 195, 196, 204, 262, 301*
32:4-6, *149*
32:5, *146, 148, 152*
32:5-6, *147, 149, 161, 268*
32:6, *62, 96, 143, 148, 150, 161, 262, 272*
32:6-7, *150*
32:7, *143, 262*
32:8, *150*
32:8-9, *150*
32:9, *142*
32:10, *117, 148, 153, 197, 225*
32:10-11, *148*
32:10-14, *197*
32:10-19, *163*
32:12, *144, 150*
32:13, *163, 202, 204*
32:13-14, *152, 153, 262*
32:14, *144, 152*
32:15, *143, 151, 152, 159, 161, 204, 262*
32:15-18, *164*
32:16, *159, 262*
32:17, *150*
32:18, *143, 184, 204, 272*
32:18-20, *147, 161, 268*
32:19, *159*
32:20, *92, 143, 156, 161, 164, 261*
32:21, *143, 149, 159, 162, 163, 261, 262*
32:22, *142, 158*
32:22-25, *158*
32:23, *155*
32:24, *148, 152, 153, 154, 156, 231*
32:25, *149, 163*
32:26, *156*
32:26-27, *153, 166*
32:27, *149, 150, 155, 159, 161, 163, 165, 196, 198, 246, 262*
32:28, *143*
32:28-29, *161, 196*
32:29, *143, 156, 161, 209, 261*
32:29-30, *263*
32:30, *149, 200, 206, 246*
32:31, *158, 198*
32:31-33, *153*
32:32, *154, 161*
32:32-33, *154, 156*
32:33, *73, 117, 148, 150, 154*
32:34-43, *149, 151, 268*
32:35, *149, 161, 162, 196, 261*
32:35-36, *164*
32:35-38, *260*
32:35-43, *201*
32:36, *144, 150, 156, 165, 166, 196, 197, 198, 263, 302*
32:36-38, *159*
32:37, *158*
32:37-38, *142, 153*
32:37-39, *162, 198*
32:38, *150, 153*
32:39, *150, 155, 156, 158, 159, 161, 162, 165, 196, 205, 214, 229, 262, 300, 302*
32:39-41, *151, 198*
32:39-42, *157, 164, 165*
32:39-43, *155, 165*
32:40, *143, 150*
32:40-41, *161*
32:41, *144, 149, 150, 156, 161, 162, 165, 196*
32:41-42, *150, 198*
32:41-43, *149, 155, 156, 165*
32:42, *117, 148, 150, 152, 154, 155, 156, 161, 165, 198, 257*
32:42-43, *152*
32:43, *91, 144, 149, 151, 152, 156, 161, 164, 196, 197, 198, 207, 260, 262, 263*
33, *268*
33:1, *87*
33:1-27, *87*
33:1-29, *157*
33:2, *257*
33:2-29, *113*
33:3, *91*
33:7, *87, 90, 113, 155, 267*
33:11, *150, 156*
33:12, *57*
33:17, *91*
33:19, *91*
33:28, *57, 117*
33:29, *150*
34, *32, 289*
34:1, *289*
34:1-9, *145*
34:5, *289*
34:7-10, *289*
34:10, *39, 247, 267, 289, 290*
34:10-12, *32, 78, 199, 289*
34:12, *289*

Joshua
1, *32, 289*
1:2, *204, 289*
1:5, *75*
1:7, *204, 289*
1:7-8, *289, 290*
1:8, *32, 100, 136, 247, 289, 291*
2:10-11, *112*
3–4, *94*
4:23-24, *94*
7, *225*
9:9-10, *112*
24:2-13, *112*
24:9-10, *133*
24:9-11, *112*

Judges
3:10, *168*
4–5, *137*
4:4, *168*
5, *33, 88, 137, 138*
5:3, *147*
5:24, *138*
5:25, *138*
5:26, *137, 138*
5:26-27, *137, 138, 139, 140, 141*
5:27, *138*
6:13, *231*
10:2-3, *168*
11:25, *133, 138*
13:5, *179*
14:6, *16*
16:17, *179*

1 Samuel
1:1-16, *158*
1:3, *172, 179*
1:6, *159*
1:6-7, *159*

1:7, *170*
1:8, *179*
1:9, *169, 170, 179*
1:11, *172, 179*
1:16, *159*
1:19-20, *179*
1:24, *170*
1:28, *240*
2, *88, 219*
2:1, *159*
2:1-10, *135, 157, 158, 160, 165, 180, 219, 252*
2:2, *158*
2:3-9, *159*
2:5, *179*
2:6, *158, 240*
2:7, *159*
2:8, *159, 179*
2:9, *159*
2:10, *88, 135, 159, 160, 165, 169, 179, 219, 239, 240, 305*
2:11, *179*
2:12-17, *179*
2:18-21, *179*
2:22-25, *179*
2:26, *179*
2:34-35, *179*
3, *176*
3:1, *168, 176*
3:3, *170*
3:7, *176*
3:11-14, *176*
3:15, *176*
3:19-21, *176*
4–6, *173*
4–7, *175*
4:1–7:1, *170, 171*
4:3-4, *170, 171*
4:4, *172*
4:5, *173*
4:11, *170*
4:13, *179*
4:17-18, *170*
4:18, *168, 179*
4:21-22, *170*
5, *171*
5:1-6, *171*
6:5, *171*
6:13, *173*
6:19, *171*
6:20, *171, 173*
7:15, *168*

8:1-5, *179*
8:5-9, *168*
10:12, *106*
10:19, *168*
11:6, *168*
12:17-20, *168*
13:8-14, *168*
13:13, *179*
13:14, *179*
15:10, *176*
15:11, *176*
15:13, *176*
15:16, *176*
15:17-29, *168*
15:19, *180*
15:23, *176*
15:26, *176*
15:26-29, *180*
15:28, *179*
15:29, *171*
15:35, *168*
16:1-13, *168*
17:45, *102*
20:31, *179*
23:17, *179*
25:26, *253*
31:1-6, *169*

2 Samuel
1–7, *134*
1:18-27, *135*
1:22, *156*
2:4, *169*
2:8-10, *179*
2:11, *169*
3:1, *179*
3:34, *186*
4:5-8, *179*
5–6, *170*
5:1-5, *169*
5:10, *169*
5:11, *169, 172*
5:12, *169*
6, *170, 174, 219*
6–7, *171, 173*
6:2, *172*
6:2-17, *170*
6:3, *171*
6:3-4, *169*
6:3-7, *171*
6:5, *173*
6:8, *171*

6:9, *171, 173*
6:10-12, *169, 184*
6:11-12, *171*
6:12-13, *171*
6:12-17, *169*
7, *167, 168, 169, 171, 173, 175, 176, 177, 178, 179, 180, 181, 182, 183, 184, 185, 186, 187, 188, 194, 246, 254, 314*
7:1, *169*
7:2, *169, 170, 171, 175*
7:2-3, *175*
7:4, *175, 177*
7:4-17, *175*
7:5, *169, 171, 172, 174, 177, 184, 185, 186, 195*
7:5-7, *172*
7:5-16, *184*
7:6, *172*
7:6-7, *171*
7:8, *172, 177, 184, 185, 186, 194, 305*
7:8-10, *172*
7:8-16, *194*
7:9, *173, 177, 178, 254*
7:9-11, *184, 186*
7:10-11, *177*
7:10-13, *91*
7:11, *168, 172, 177, 186, 269*
7:11-16, *176, 178*
7:12, *177, 185, 188, 194, 215, 277*
7:12-13, *172, 173, 174, 178, 180, 181, 185, 186, 306*
7:12-14, *239*
7:12-16, *169, 179, 195, 248, 249, 251, 261*
7:13, *150, 173, 174, 175, 178, 179, 180, 181, 185, 194, 254, 305*
7:13-14, *270*
7:14, *137, 180, 183, 184, 186, 275, 305*
7:14-15, *180*
7:14-16, *186*
7:15, *194*
7:15-16, *185, 186*
7:16, *169, 174, 178, 179, 185, 194, 306*
7:17, *175, 176, 177, 185, 186, 187*
7:18-20, *176, 177*
7:18-23, *172*
7:18-29, *175*
7:19, *184, 194, 208*

7:19-21, *172, 177, 184*
7:20, *185, 186*
7:22, *176, 177, 185, 186*
7:23, *184, 254*
7:24, *150, 183*
7:24-26, *178, 185*
7:25-29, *172, 184*
7:25-2927, *177*
7:26, *174, 185, 186, 254*
7:26-27, *172, 185, 186*
7:27, *185, 269*
7:28-29, *176, 177*
7:29, *178*
8, *169*
8:14, *184*
8:15, *250*
11, *169, 239*
11:2, *176*
11:8-11, *175*
11:11, *170, 175*
11:13, *175*
12:1-7, *251*
12:9, *176*
12:11-12, *176*
12:13, *175*
12:24-25, *180*
12:30, *302*
13–18, *180*
15, *175*
15:24, *170*
15:24-29, *175*
15:25, *170*
15:29, *170*
22, *88, 163, 216, 219, 237, 239, 240, 241*
22–23, *88, 135, 314*
22–23:7, *135*
22:1, *237, 239, 240*
22:1-51, *219, 252*
22:1–23:7, *219*
22:2, *236*
22:3, *158*
22:4, *240*
22:5, *236, 238, 240*
22:5-6, *240*
22:5-7, *237*
22:6, *240*
22:7, *169, 170*
22:14, *239*
22:16-18, *237*
22:17, *240*
22:18, *240*

22:21-25, *239, 240*
22:31, *160, 237*
22:32, *158*
22:38, *240*
22:41, *240*
22:47, *88, 135, 158*
22:49, *240*
22:51, *160, 169, 184, 219, 237, 239, 240, 305*
23, *134, 178, 275*
23:1, *133, 134, 136, 184, 252*
23:1-2, *88*
23:1-5, *133, 134, 136, 169*
23:1-7, *88, 134, 135, 136, 178*
23:2, *135, 252*
23:3, *135, 158, 184, 270*
23:3-4, *135, 141, 219, 252, 253*
23:3-5, *178, 180, 239*
23:4, *148, 257*
23:5, *135, 169, 201, 253*
23:5-7, *253*
23:6, *253*
24, *170*
24:10, *175*
24:16-25, *170*
24:17, *175*

1 Kings
1–11, *180, 181, 251*
2:2-4, *249*
2:4, *181, 304*
3:5, *176, 185*
3:9, *55, 250*
3:14, *181*
4:6, *251*
4:30, *50*
4:34, *50*
5:5, *270*
5:13-14, *251*
5:31 (MT), *302*
6:12, *181, 270*
7:14, *63*
8, *293, 295*
8:20, *293*
8:25, *304*
8:26, *293*
8:27, *174*
8:29-30, *295*
8:35, *295*
8:38, *295*
8:42, *295*
8:44, *295*

8:46, *295*
8:46-51, *295, 296*
8:47, *305*
8:47-48, *295*
8:48, *295*
8:48-52, *295*
8:51, *296*
8:53, *293*
8:56, *293*
9:3, *270*
9:4-5, *181*
9:5, *304, 306*
9:6-8, *270*
9:7, *304*
9:15, *251*
9:21, *251*
10:1, *257*
10:1-3, *50*
10:2, *302*
10:4, *270*
10:4-8, *268*
10:9, *250*
10:22, *257*
10:23-24, *268*
11:1, *270*
11:1-13, *180*
11:4, *180*
11:4-8, *270*
11:6, *180*
11:29-39, *182*
12:4, *251*
12:18, *251*
19:18, *259*

2 Kings
19:18, *150*
20, *219*
20:19, *253*
22:17, *150*
24:12-15, *292*
25:27-30, *181*

1 Chronicles
5:4, *118*
15:11-15, *171*
16:7-36, *88, 219, 236*
17:1-15, *305*
17:9, *186*
17:10, *175, 269*
17:11, *172, 299, 306*
17:11-14, *181*
17:14, *299*

17:25, 269
22:1, 170
22:5-10, 181
22:9, 250
22:10-11, 32
22:12-13, 182
22:13, 182, 249
28:5-7, 181
28:7, 182
28:7-9, 182, 249

2 Chronicles
1:3, 181
1:8-10, 182
2:6, 174
3:1, 170
6:15-17, 182
6:16, 304
6:42, 182
7:18, 304
9:3, 270
9:25, 181
9:28, 181
10:4, 181
10:10-11, 181
10:14, 181
10:15, 182
25:4, 86
36, 32
36:12, 290
36:20-21, 296
36:20-22, 292
36:21-22, 290
36:22, 292
36:22-23, 181
36:23, 32, 182, 247, 257

Ezra
1:1, 290, 292
1:2-3, 307

Nehemiah
1:8, 103
9:11, 233
9:17, 260
9:36, 230
13:2, 133

Job
1–2, 68, 69, 71, 72, 73, 74, 75
1–3, 70
1–20, 71

1:1, 56, 69
1:2-3, 69
1:3, 69
1:5, 70
1:6, 72, 75
1:8, 69
1:10, 70
1:11, 70, 72
1:12, 75
1:14-17, 71
1:18-19, 71
1:19, 71
1:20, 71
1:21, 70, 71
2:1, 75
2:3, 69, 71
2:5, 70, 71, 72
2:6, 75
2:9, 69, 70, 71
3–37, 68
3:1, 70
3:1-13, 71, 72
3:4, 71
3:8, 72, 74, 221
3:14-15, 268
5:7, 71
5:23, 75
7:12, 72, 74, 75
9:13, 72, 221
11:3, 74
12:4, 158
12:12, 59
15:5, 70
15:7, 70, 284
20:4-7, 70
20:14, 73
20:16, 73
23:10, 302
26:12, 72, 221
26:12-13, 73, 74, 75, 221
26:13, 72, 73
27:1, 106
27:7, 253
28, 302
28:2-3, 302
28:6, 302
28:8, 74
28:9-10, 302
28:14, 74
28:15-19, 59
28:28, 55
31:15, 62

31:27, 259
31:33, 70
32–37, 70
32:6, 70
32:17, 70
37:4, 70
38, 268, 283
38–39, 74
38–41, 51, 75
38–42, 68, 69
38:2, 283
38:4, 62, 283
38:4-7, 70
38:4-11, 283, 284, 285
38:5, 283
38:6, 283
38:8-11, 75, 283
38:13-15, 74
38:21, 70
38:41, 74
39:7, 74
39:18, 74
39:22, 74
39:25, 74
40–41, 74
40:9-13, 75
40:9-14, 74
40:11-12, 74
41, 74, 75
41:1, 74
41:1-34, 72
41:2-3, 75
41:3, 74
41:4, 75
41:7-8, 75
41:10, 75
41:11, 74
41:12, 74
41:13, 75
41:15-17, 74
41:19, 75
41:21, 75
41:30, 74
41:33, 74
41:34, 74

Psalms
1, 32, 52, 100, 185, 239, 242, 243, 244, 246, 247, 289
1–2, 133, 183, 184, 239, 244, 246, 247, 252, 261, 279, 280
1–50, 186, 279, 280

Scripture Index

1:1, *252, 290*
1:2, *100, 136, 247, 252, 289, 291*
1:2-3, *32, 290*
1:3, *91, 252*
1:4, *298*
1:4-6, *247*
1:6, *262*
2, *102, 132, 133, 168, 182, 183, 184, 185, 186, 187, 188, 240, 242, 243, 244, 245, 246, 247, 249, 251, 252, 253, 254, 255, 259, 261, 263, 264, 275, 276, 277, 279, 280, 281, 282, 307, 314*
2–72, *243*
2–89, *244*
2:1-2, *252, 259*
2:1-3, *102, 184*
2:2, *184, 239, 245, 277, 278, 279*
2:4, *262, 278, 279*
2:5, *98*
2:6, *184, 247, 277, 278, 279*
2:6-7, *284, 285*
2:6-9, *184, 249, 299*
2:7, *182, 183, 184, 186, 239, 243, 253, 259, 275, 278, 279, 280, 281*
2:7-8, *199, 245*
2:8, *185, 252, 278*
2:8-9, *102, 133, 279*
2:9, *185, 239, 247, 257*
2:10, *259, 278, 279*
2:10-11, *279*
2:10-12, *147, 185*
2:11, *98, 259*
2:11-12, *252, 275*
2:12, *247, 252, 259, 278, 279*
3, *101, 102, 238, 263, 281*
3:4, *235, 238*
3:6, *238*
3:8, *236, 238*
5:7, *236*
5:12, *212*
8, *238*
8:3, *62, 262*
9:13, *251*
14, *280*
15:1-5, *173*
16:10, *220, 236*
18, *216, 236, 237, 238, 239, 240, 241, 242*
18–21, *246, 247*

18:1, *236*
18:4, *236, 238*
18:4-5, *236*
18:4-6, *236, 237*
18:4-7, *237*
18:5, *240*
18:6, *236*
18:7, *236*
18:7-14, *237*
18:7-17, *99*
18:13, *239*
18:15-16, *236*
18:15-17, *237*
18:16, *234*
18:19, *236*
18:20-24, *240*
18:20-25, *237*
18:30, *237*
18:33, *158*
18:48, *158*
18:50, *237, 239, 240*
21:4, *59*
22, *190*
22:1, *102*
22:6-8, *102*
22:22, *190*
22:24, *251*
23:6, *59*
24:2, *62*
30, *238*
30–31, *238*
30:3, *236*
30:8, *236*
31, *238*
31:6, *236*
31:22, *236*
32, *239*
32:9, *107*
33:6, *260*
35:10, *251*
36:1, *134*
38:4, *239*
40:3, *56*
40:17, *251*
41, *243, 244*
41:1, *251*
41:1-2, *243*
41:3, *254*
41:11-12, *243*
42, *238*
42–44, *245*
42–72, *242*

42:6, *236*
42:7, *236, 239*
44:1, *183*
47:2, *259*
48:5-6, *98*
49:15, *227*
51, *239*
51–100, *99, 187, 249*
54:2, *146*
55, *238*
66:10, *302*
69, *237, 238*
69:1, *236*
69:1-2, *238*
69:14-15, *238*
69:17, *236*
71:6, *220*
71:20, *236*
72, *188, 242, 243, 244, 245, 249, 250, 251, 252, 254, 255, 256, 257, 259, 260, 261, 262, 263, 264, 314*
72–73, *246*
72:1, *249, 250, 260*
72:2, *250, 251, 260*
72:2-4, *251, 259, 260*
72:3, *250*
72:4, *250, 251, 256, 259*
72:5, *251, 252, 256, 257, 258*
72:5-7, *253*
72:6, *148, 252, 253, 256, 259*
72:7, *250, 251, 253, 257, 258, 260*
72:8, *128, 251, 252, 255, 256, 259, 269*
72:8-11, *249, 258*
72:9, *231, 256, 259*
72:9-11, *250, 256, 257*
72:10, *224, 257*
72:11, *252, 257, 258, 259, 260, 307*
72:12, *250, 257, 259*
72:12-14, *251, 259, 260*
72:13-14, *251*
72:15, *249, 254, 260*
72:15-17, *260*
72:16, *252, 256, 260*
72:17, *249, 250, 252, 254, 255, 256, 257, 259, 260, 269*
72:17-19, *254*
72:18-19, *260*
72:19, *254*

72:20, 242, 243, 245, 249, 252
73, 246, 260, 261, 262, 263, 264
73–74, 245
73–89, 99, 243, 246
73–150, 99, 144
73:3, 260, 261
73:6, 260
73:7, 262
73:8, 260
73:8-9, 262
73:9, 262
73:11, 262
73:15, 262
73:16, 261
73:17, 261, 262
73:18, 261
73:22, 137
73:26, 262
73:28, 262
74:2, 272
74:12-14, 75, 263
74:13, 90
74:13-14, 72, 202, 211, 221
74:18, 262
75:7, 262
76, 99
76:6, 99
76:8-9, 262
77, 94, 98, 99, 100, 103
77:1-4, 98
77:3, 236
77:5, 262
77:5-6, 98
77:7-9, 98
77:10, 99, 100
77:10-20, 98, 99
77:11, 99, 100, 236
77:12, 99, 100
77:13, 99
77:13-15, 100
77:13-20, 263
77:14, 92, 99, 260
77:15, 99
77:15-20, 98
77:16, 92, 99, 100
77:16-19, 99
77:18, 99
77:19, 99
77:19-20, 100
77:20, 100
78:1, 146, 164, 262
78:3, 183

78:4, 260
78:8, 164
78:10, 208
78:12, 99
78:15, 203
78:22, 164
78:32, 164
78:37, 164
78:51, 274
78:58, 262
78:69, 62
79:10, 262
79:13, 183
81, 144
81:1, 144, 263
81:7, 83
81:8, 144
81:9, 144
81:13-14, 263
81:14-15, 144
81:16, 144, 262
82, 247
85–86, 252
86:6, 236
86:15, 260
88, 238
88:2, 236
88:7, 236
88:17, 236
89, 51, 102, 168, 182, 185, 186,
    187, 188, 194, 242, 243, 244,
    245, 246, 247, 248, 249, 259,
    263, 264, 275
89–90, 246
89:1-2, 185, 186, 248
89:3, 185, 186
89:3-4, 185, 248
89:4, 185, 186
89:8, 185, 186
89:9-10, 187, 221, 259
89:10, 256
89:11, 62
89:14, 250
89:14-15, 92
89:19, 185, 186
89:19-37, 186
89:20, 185, 186
89:22, 186
89:24, 185, 186
89:25, 187, 259
89:26, 186, 259
89:27, 186, 259, 274, 275

89:29, 110, 251
89:30-32, 180
89:30-34, 248
89:30-37, 186
89:33-34, 110
89:33-37, 248
89:36-37, 251
89:37, 62
89:38-39, 187
89:38-45, 187, 248
89:39, 187
89:40-41, 187
89:40-43, 246
89:42-43, 187
89:44-45, 187
89:46-48, 249
89:46-51, 187
89:47, 187
89:47-48, 187
89:48, 187, 227
89:49, 185, 186, 187, 248
89:50-51, 246
89:51, 187, 249
90, 260
90–106, 244
90:2, 282
90:11-12, 246
90:13, 144
91:13, 73
91:16, 59
92:2, 165
92:4, 165
92:6, 137
92:7, 253
92:12-13, 253
93, 51
93–100, 92, 246, 247, 248
93:1-2, 92
93:2, 277
93:5, 59
95:3, 92
96:1, 98, 157
96:5, 92
98:1, 98, 260
98:1-2, 157
98:2, 92
99:1, 98
99:4, 250
99:6, 260
101–150, 101, 281
103:4, 236
103:6, 250

Scripture Index   359

103:7, 260
103:18, 260
104, 51, 238
104:5, 62
104:24, 268
104:26, 72
105:26, 260
105:36, 274
106:12, 92, 100
106:16, 260
106:23, 260
106:32, 260
107, 221, 238
107:1, 102
107:23-30, 239
107:40, 158
107:42-43, 246
109:3, 253, 280, 281
110, 32, 101, 102, 132, 133, 140, 141, 152, 185, 242, 263, 281, 307
110:1, 262
110:3, 280, 281
110:4, 280
110:5-6, 102, 300
110:118, 101
111:3, 165
111:7, 165
111:10, 62, 273
113–118, 101
113:5, 101
114, 280
115:11, 56
115:18, 93
116:1, 236
118, 77, 94, 100, 101, 102, 103
118–119, 246, 247
118:1-4, 101, 102
118:5, 100, 101, 236
118:6, 102
118:7, 100, 102
118:8, 102
118:10, 102
118:10-12, 102
118:10-16, 101
118:14, 100, 101
118:14-15, 101
118:15, 101, 102
118:15-16, 101
118:17-18, 101
118:17-19, 100
118:18, 102

118:21, 100, 101
118:22, 101, 102, 103, 302
118:23-24, 102
118:24, 101
118:25, 101
118:26, 102
118:26-27, 101, 102
118:28, 100
118:29, 101
119:11, 291
119:15, 100
119:18, 316
119:23, 100
119:27, 100
119:48, 100
119:52, 100
119:78, 100
119:148, 100
120:1, 235, 236
127, 249
127:1, 270
130:2, 236
132:12, 180
132:13-17, 305
132:17, 201
133:3, 59
135, 144
135:5, 144
135:14, 144, 260
135:15-18, 144
136:10-11, 158
138:2, 236
139:13, 272
142, 281
143:1, 165
143:5, 165
144–145, 247
145, 247
145:1-2, 93
145:18, 260
145:19-20, 246
146–150, 247
146:4, 247
146:10, 89, 247
147:6, 247
149:2, 247
149:7-9, 247

Proverbs
1, 56
1–3, 55, 57, 61, 63, 265, 271
1–7, 267

1–9, 55, 58, 63, 64, 76, 265, 266, 267, 268, 269, 271, 272, 273, 274, 275, 276, 278, 284
1:1, 48, 55, 269
1:1-7, 55
1:2, 55, 56
1:3, 56, 59
1:4, 56
1:5, 272
1:6, 276
1:7, 52, 56, 62, 270, 273
1:7–9:18, 56
1:8, 147, 267
1:8-9, 56
1:10, 56, 147
1:10-33, 56
1:12, 220
1:13, 269
1:15, 147
1:16, 61
1:20-33, 57, 266, 267, 278
1:22, 56
1:22-28, 267
1:23-27, 267
1:29, 56
1:30-33, 267
1:31, 56
1:33, 57
2, 57
2:1, 147, 267
2:4, 59, 60
2:5, 270
2:5-6, 56
2:6, 63
2:9, 61
2:10, 56
2:11, 57
2:12, 61
2:12-15, 57
2:14, 61
2:16, 270
2:16-19, 57, 268
2:18, 270
2:20, 61
2:21, 57
2:21-22, 57
3, 57
3:1, 267
3:2, 59
3:4, 58, 60, 61
3:5, 57
3:5-6, 55

3:5-7, 56
3:7, 56, 57, 61, 270
3:9, 57, 273
3:11-12, 57
3:13, 58, 59, 60, 61, 271
3:13-18, 57, 58, 59, 60, 61
3:13-20, 58, 63
3:14, 61
3:14-15, 59, 60
3:14-16, 60
3:15, 59, 60, 302
3:16, 59, 60
3:17, 60
3:18, 57, 58, 59, 60, 61, 63
3:19, 61, 62, 63, 91, 270, 271, 276
3:19-20, 62, 63, 269, 270, 271, 282
3:20, 63
3:30, 58
3:35, 57
4:1, 267
4:5, 146, 272
4:7, 62, 272, 273
4:10, 267
5:1-2, 268
5:3-8, 268
5:7, 267
5:8, 270
5:20, 268, 270
6:2, 146
6:16, 106
6:23-32, 268
6:24, 270
7:4, 268
7:5, 268, 270
7:8, 270
7:10-27, 268
7:24, 267
7:27, 270
8, 55, 62, 265, 266, 267, 269, 274, 276, 278, 314
8–9, 267
8:1-10, 266
8:1-21, 278
8:1-35, 269
8:1-36, 266, 267
8:6, 267
8:8, 146
8:10, 267
8:12, 62, 276
8:13, 61, 270

8:15, 278
8:15-16, 276
8:19, 59
8:21, 269
8:22, 62, 265, 268, 270, 271, 272, 273, 274, 275, 276, 277, 278, 279, 280, 281, 284
8:22-23, 282
8:22-31, 58, 265, 266, 267, 268, 269, 270, 271, 273, 274, 275, 276, 277, 278, 279, 280, 281, 282, 283, 284, 285
8:23, 277, 278, 279, 281
8:23-24, 271
8:24, 282
8:24-25, 272, 274, 276, 281, 282
8:25, 278, 279, 282, 283, 284
8:26, 282
8:26-27, 278
8:26-29, 91, 271
8:27, 270, 271, 278
8:27-29, 276, 282, 283
8:29, 271, 278, 279, 283
8:30, 266, 268, 270, 274, 276, 278, 283
8:30-31, 278, 279
8:31, 271, 278
8:31-32, 268, 275
8:32, 271
8:32-36, 278
8:34, 269, 271
9, 266
9:1, 106, 266, 269, 270, 275
9:1-2, 269
9:1-6, 52, 266, 269, 270
9:4-6, 270, 278
9:10, 55, 270, 273, 276
9:13-18, 52, 266
9:14, 270
10–29, 63, 269
10–31, 63, 64
10:1, 269, 275
10:2, 59
10:5, 275
10:11, 58
10:30, 59
11:4, 59
11:28, 59
11:30, 58
11:31, 59
12:1, 137
12:3, 59

12:7, 59, 270
12:19, 59
12:28, 59
13:1, 275
13:12, 58
13:14, 58
13:23, 63
14:1, 270
14:12, 55
14:20, 63
14:27, 58
14:31, 63
15:4, 58
15:6, 270
15:33, 55
16:22, 58
16:25, 55
17:3, 302
17:5, 63
17:8, 63
20:12, 63, 271
20:26, 158
22:2, 63
24:3-4, 62, 269, 270
24:16, 106
25:1, 269
26:16, 106
26:25, 106
27:20, 220
29:13, 63
30, 136
30–31, 136, 275
30:1, 133, 134, 136
30:1-2, 136
30:1-4, 133, 134, 137
30:1-6, 275
30:2, 137
30:2-4, 275, 276
30:3, 137, 276
30:4, 137, 265, 267, 271, 275, 276, 284, 285
30:8, 278
30:16, 220
31:1-9, 251
31:5, 278
31:15, 278

Ecclesiastes
1:1, 48
1:1-11, 66
1:2, 68
1:3, 67, 71

Scripture Index

1:4, 66
1:9, 68
1:13, 67
1:14, 68
1:15, 68
2:1-13, 66
2:4, 268
2:14, 66
2:15, 66
2:16, 66
2:17, 67
2:17-18, 66
2:26, 67
3:2, 66
3:10, 67
3:11, 64, 67
3:14, 64
3:17, 67
3:19-21, 66
3:20, 66
4:2, 66
4:8, 67
5:15, 66
6:3-6, 66
6:12, 66
7:1-2, 66
7:13, 67, 68
7:15, 68
7:15-17, 66
7:20, 65
7:29, 65, 67
8:8, 66
8:14, 68
8:16, 67
9:2-5, 66
9:3, 65
9:10, 66
11:7–12:14, 66
11:9, 67
12:1, 64
12:1-7, 66
12:7, 66
12:13, 55, 63, 82
12:14, 63, 67

Song of Solomon
7:1, 274

Isaiah
1, 160, 165, 211
1–5, 207
1–12, 94
1–36, 160
1–39, 190, 191, 192, 194, 207
1:1, 160, 164
1:2, 147, 160, 161
1:2-4, 160
1:3, 107, 161
1:4, 161
1:5-6, 214
1:7-9, 161
1:9-10, 161
1:18, 161
1:21, 161
1:24, 161
1:25, 161, 302
1:25-26, 161
1:26, 94
1:26–2:6, 94
1:27, 161
2, 299
2:1-5, 257
2:2, 123, 207, 298, 299, 301, 303
2:2-3, 193, 257, 299
2:2-4, 95, 207, 208, 299
2:2-437, 299
2:3, 193, 212
2:3-4, 207
2:4, 212, 308
2:8-22, 96
2:11-12, 207
2:14, 207
2:21, 203
3, 190
4:2, 95, 201
5, 160
6–8, 94
6–12, 94
6:1, 207
6:1-4, 268
6:1-7, 97
6:5, 206
6:7, 207
6:9, 54, 202
6:9-10, 214
6:10, 214
7, 194, 299
7:3, 95, 302
7:4-6, 194
7:6, 194
7:7, 195
7:7-9, 306
7:9, 195, 209

7:11, 195
7:13, 207, 214
7:14, 173, 195, 309
7:15, 152
7:22, 152
8, 302
8:7-8, 308
8:8, 302, 309
8:10, 302
8:14, 204, 210, 301, 302, 303
9:1, 200
9:2, 192, 208, 257
9:3, 83, 214
9:6, 213, 280, 302, 309
9:6-7, 95, 160, 193, 253, 257, 275
9:7, 89, 250, 309
10, 301, 302
10:20, 94
10:20-22, 95
10:21, 302, 309
10:22-23, 308
10:22-25, 302
10:27, 83, 94
11–12, 94
11:1, 95, 208, 306
11:1-2, 207
11:1-3, 270
11:1-4, 193
11:1-9, 95, 232
11:1-10, 95
11:2, 95
11:3-5, 95
11:4, 205, 251
11:6-8, 95
11:9, 95, 306
11:10, 94, 95, 103, 208
11:10–12:6, 94
11:11, 94, 95, 96, 230
11:11-12, 96
11:11-16, 77, 95, 96, 198
11:12, 95, 103
11:14, 96
11:15-16, 95, 98, 223
12, 94, 95, 96, 97, 98, 103
12:1, 94, 96, 97
12:1-2, 97
12:2, 96, 97, 100, 198
12:2-3, 96, 97
12:3, 96, 97, 201, 203, 208
12:4, 94, 96, 97
12:5, 96, 97, 100
12:5-6, 97

12:6, *97*
13:7-8, *98*
13:9, *206*
14:3, *198*
14:4, *106*
14:25, *83*
17:10, *301, 303*
19:19-25, *103*
19:20, *103*
25:6-8, *232*
26:1, *100*
26:2, *165*
26:4, *100, 204, 210, 301, 303*
26:10, *100*
27:1, *72, 73, 75, 154, 211, 221*
27:6, *253*
28, *160, 302*
28:15, *308*
28:16, *91, 102, 209, 210, 302, 303, 306, 309*
28:17-18, *308*
28:21, *163*
28:22, *308*
30, *160*
30:27, *102*
30:29, *210*
32:15-16, *201, 204*
33:14, *98*
34:8, *196*
35:1, *201*
35:1-2, *253*
35:6, *201, 203*
35:9-10, *227*
36–39, *194*
36:4, *195*
36:18-20, *194*
37:3, *195*
37:10-13, *194*
37:20, *194*
37:30, *195*
37:31, *194*
37:32, *212*
37:35, *194, 195, 205, 215, 305*
37:36-38, *194, 196*
38, *219*
38:1, *195, 214*
38:5, *215*
38:5-6, *195, 305*
38:6, *194*
38:7, *195*
38:9, *214*
38:9-20, *88, 219*

38:10, *195*
38:11, *100*
38:17, *214*
38:22, *195*
39, *301*
39:1, *214, 300*
39:1-7, *300, 301*
39:2, *300*
39:4, *300*
39:6-7, *194, 300*
39:7, *194*
39:8, *253*
40–47, *203*
40–48, *196, 197*
40–55, *162, 190, 191, 192, 193, 194, 195, 196, 197, 198, 199, 200, 201, 202, 203, 204, 205, 206, 207, 208, 210, 212, 213, 214, 225, 301*
40–66, *190, 199, 303*
40:1, *197, 206*
40:1-2, *204*
40:1-3, *225*
40:2, *193, 195, 197, 206, 296*
40:3, *197, 198*
40:3-5, *198, 204*
40:5, *195, 208, 211*
40:6-7, *202*
40:7, *208*
40:10, *196, 211*
40:11, *211*
40:14, *196*
40:17, *199*
40:18, *213*
40:21, *200*
40:23, *199*
40:24, *208*
40:25, *213*
40:26, *199*
40:27, *195, 196, 197*
40:28, *199, 200, 207*
40:28-31, *195*
40:29, *212*
40:31, *199*
41:1, *195*
41:2, *200*
41:4, *196, 200, 277*
41:8, *199*
41:8-9, *192*
41:11, *193*
41:15-16, *299, 302, 303*
41:17-20, *197, 198, 201, 204*

41:18, *202, 208*
41:18-20, *208, 209*
41:19, *208*
41:19-20, *201*
41:20, *198, 199, 201, 208*
41:22, *200*
41:22-23, *200*
41:22-29, *193*
41:24, *193*
41:25, *200*
41:26, *200*
41:28, *193, 205*
41:29, *193, 199*
42:1, *193, 195, 204, 207*
42:1-4, *190, 193, 195, 197*
42:2, *205*
42:3, *193, 195*
42:4, *193, 195, 204, 205, 207, 211*
42:5, *199, 208*
42:5-9, *190*
42:6, *203, 208, 212, 257*
42:6-7, *199*
42:7, *192, 214*
42:8, *205*
42:9, *198, 200, 208*
42:11, *196*
42:13, *199*
42:14-16, *198*
42:16, *199*
42:18-20, *214*
42:18-25, *192*
42:21, *200*
42:22, *192*
42:24, *200, 206*
43, *161, 165, 196*
43:1-3, *198*
43:2, *223*
43:3-4, *206*
43:3-5, *162*
43:8, *161, 192*
43:9, *161*
43:10, *161, 165, 209*
43:10-13, *162*
43:11, *205*
43:13, *165, 196*
43:14-21, *198*
43:15, *162*
43:16-21, *198*
43:18, *200*
43:18-20, *198, 201*
43:19, *198, 201, 208*

Scripture Index

43:19-20, *197, 198, 202, 208*
43:21, *198*
43:23, *206*
43:24, *192, 207*
43:25, *205, 213*
44, *161*
44:1-2, *192*
44:3, *201, 202, 203, 204, 208*
44:3-4, *201, 202, 204*
44:6, *200*
44:8, *200, 204, 210, 301, 303*
44:9, *199*
44:18, *201, 209*
44:21, *192*
44:22, *213*
44:23, *197*
44:27, *199*
44:28–45:1, *292*
45–47, *203*
45:4, *192*
45:7, *199*
45:8, *198*
45:9–46:13, *200*
45:11, *196*
45:12, *199*
45:18-19, *199*
45:19, *199*
45:20, *200*
45:20-21, *200*
45:21, *200, 277*
45:25, *213*
46:1, *213*
46:1-4, *213*
46:1-7, *96*
46:3-4, *213*
46:5, *213*
46:10, *200, 201*
46:11, *200*
47, *196*
47:6-8, *196*
47:7, *200*
47:9, *196*
47:10, *196*
47:11, *196*
48, *203*
48:1, *192*
48:3, *200*
48:5, *200*
48:6-7, *198*
48:7, *200*
48:8, *207*
48:10, *206*

48:11, *205*
48:12, *200*
48:14, *211*
48:16, *200*
48:19, *199*
48:20, *192, 197, 205*
48:20-21, *198, 203, 204*
48:21, *202, 203, 204, 210, 303*
48:22, *207*
49–55, *202*
49:1, *220*
49:1-6, *190, 204*
49:2, *205, 212*
49:3, *192, 207*
49:4, *197, 199, 212*
49:5-6, *192*
49:6, *197, 208, 257*
49:7, *194, 208, 209*
49:7-13, *190*
49:8, *193, 203, 208*
49:8-12, *198*
49:9-11, *202*
49:10, *202*
49:13, *196*
49:23, *195, 199, 256*
50:1, *192, 206*
50:2, *205*
50:2-3, *204*
50:4, *205, 207, 212*
50:4-5, *197, 212*
50:4-6, *212*
50:4-9, *190, 204*
50:6, *210, 212*
50:6-7, *210*
50:7, *204, 210, 303*
50:7-9, *207*
50:8, *197*
50:8-9, *212, 304*
50:9, *210*
50:10, *205, 207*
50:10-11, *190*
51, *211*
51:1, *202, 203, 210, 303*
51:1-2, *302, 303*
51:2, *199, 303*
51:3, *202, 208*
51:4, *197, 211, 212*
51:5, *195, 199, 211*
51:6-8, *210*
51:7, *202*
51:9, *74, 211*
51:9-10, *198, 202, 211*

51:11, *197, 211*
51:18, *192*
51:23, *210*
52:1, *195*
52:3, *206*
52:5, *206*
52:8-9, *196*
52:9, *293*
52:10, *208, 211*
52:11, *205*
52:11-12, *198, 204, 205*
52:12, *202, 205*
52:13, *102, 193, 205, 206, 207, 208, 209, 213, 270*
52:13–53:12, *39, 189, 190, 191, 193, 195, 197, 199, 201, 203, 204, 205, 206, 207, 209, 211, 213, 214, 215*
52:14, *208, 209*
52:15, *207, 208, 234*
52:15–53:1, *209*
53, *162, 189, 190, 197, 203, 207, 210, 212, 213, 215, 304, 308, 314*
53:1, *209, 211, 215*
53:2, *201, 208, 209*
53:2-3, *208, 209*
53:3, *102*
53:3-5, *102*
53:4, *206, 207, 210, 212, 213*
53:4-5, *211*
53:4-7, *206*
53:4-12, *197*
53:5, *193, 206, 210, 211, 212*
53:6, *213*
53:7, *205, 206, 210, 211, 212*
53:8, *195, 197, 206, 207, 210, 212, 213, 304*
53:9, *205, 207*
53:10, *195, 204, 206, 207, 210, 211*
53:10-12, *190, 193, 304*
53:11, *206, 213*
53:11-12, *206, 211, 213, 214*
53:12, *102, 207, 213, 214*
54:1, *197*
54:1–55:13, *190*
54:3, *199*
54:4, *210*
54:9, *199*
54:10, *203*
54:13, *199*

54:17, *197*
55, *202*
55–66, *191*
55:1, *202, 203, 204*
55:1-2, *204, 206*
55:1-3, *202*
55:2, *204*
55:2-3, *202*
55:3, *193, 194, 195, 202, 203, 204, 215*
55:3-4, *194*
55:4, *194, 305*
55:7, *207*
55:10-11, *253*
55:12-13, *198*
56:3, *195*
56:10, *192*
57:17, *207*
59:10, *192*
60, *257*
60:1-22, *257*
60:2-3, *257*
60:5-9, *257*
60:6, *257*
60:9, *224, 257*
60:14, *257*
60:19-20, *257*
61:1, *192, 200, 251*
61:1-3, *257*
61:2, *193, 196*
61:11, *257*
63:1, *139*
63:1-3, *139, 141*
63:1-5, *260*
63:2, *139*
63:4, *196*
63:12, *203*
64:1, *98*
65:9, *128*
65:17, *68*
65:25, *256*
66:1, *174*

Jeremiah
1:10, *91, 293*
2:13, *203*
2:26, *305*
2:28, *142*
3:16, *175*
3:16-17, *308*
3:17, *305*
3:18, *225*

4:2, *293*
10:16, *142*
15:14, *142*
16:14-15, *77*
17:4, *142*
23:5, *201, 270*
23:5-6, *250, 253, 308*
23:6, *57*
23:20, *261, 298*
24:7, *183*
25, *292, 314*
25–29, *297*
25:1, *292*
25:3, *293*
25:3-5, *292*
25:3-10, *292*
25:6-7, *286*
25:8, *293*
25:9, *286, 292, 294*
25:11, *286*
25:11-12, *286, 292, 293*
25:11-14, *308*
25:12, *293, 294, 297*
25:13, *293*
25:18, *305*
27:16, *293*
28:3, *293*
28:11, *293*
29, *292, 293, 314*
29:1, *293*
29:1-2, *292*
29:1-3, *294*
29:1-23, *295*
29:2, *301*
29:5-7, *293*
29:10, *286, 292, 293*
29:10-14, *308*
29:11, *293*
29:12-14, *294, 295*
29:13, *286, 295*
29:14, *294*
29:19, *292, 293*
29:24-32, *293*
30:8-9, *226*
30:9, *239*
30:11, *103*
30:24, *226, 261, 298*
31:1-14, *226*
31:11, *227*
31:17, *293*
31:31, *68*
31:31-34, *308*

31:33, *183*
31:34, *224*
32:38, *183*
33:14-26, *26, 29*
33:16, *57*
33:17, *304*
46:21, *163*
48, *132*
48:44, *131*
48:45, *126, 131, 132*
48:45-47, *105, 132*
48:46, *132*
48:47, *123, 132, 298*
49:39, *123, 298*
51:34, *230, 234*
52:15, *274*

Lamentations
5:20, *59*

Ezekiel
3:3, *220*
16:47, *152*
16:63, *152*
17:2, *107*
28:13, *59, 302*
28:13-14, *90*
29:3, *81, 90*
29:3-4, *221*
32:2, *81, 90*
34:25, *75*
36:19, *103*
36:26, *68*
37:12, *230*
38–39, *118, 304*
38:16, *123, 298*
38:17, *118, 132*
38:18, *133*

Daniel
1, *300, 301*
1–2, *299*
1:1, *299, 300*
1:1-2, *305*
1:2, *299, 300*
1:3, *195, 305*
1:3-4, *300*
1:3-6, *288*
1:4, *288, 290, 299, 300*
1:6, *305*
1:7, *299*
1:7-11, *301*

Scripture Index

1:8, *290*
1:12, *294*
1:17, *288, 290, 294*
1:19-21, *290*
1:20, *290, 294*
1:21, *292*
2, *297, 299, 301, 302, 303, 306, 307, 309*
2:4, *299, 306*
2:5, *291*
2:9, *291*
2:10-11, *307*
2:17-18, *297*
2:18, *291*
2:19, *297*
2:21, *291, 297*
2:21-22, *288*
2:23, *290, 291*
2:25, *305*
2:27, *298*
2:27-28, *291*
2:28, *123, 298, 299*
2:28-29, *288*
2:34, *303, 304*
2:34-35, *298, 300, 301, 303*
2:35, *298, 299, 300, 301, 302, 303, 305*
2:38, *307*
2:40, *294*
2:44, *290, 298, 305, 306*
2:44-45, *89, 298, 302, 303*
2:45, *291, 301, 303, 304, 306*
2:47, *298*
2:48, *290*
3, *88*
3:1, *300*
3:7, *307*
3:9, *306*
3:10, *291*
3:12, *307*
3:17-18, *307*
3:19, *294*
3:22, *291*
3:24-68, *219*
3:25, *294*
3:28, *307*
3:30, *290*
4:3, *290*
4:8-9, *291*
4:9, *288, 290*
4:10-14, *300*
4:16, *294*

4:17, *298*
4:18, *291*
4:23, *294*
4:24, *302*
4:25, *294*
4:32, *294*
4:33, *291*
4:34, *306*
5:2-4, *305*
5:7-8, *288*
5:10, *306*
5:11, *291*
5:12, *288*
5:13, *305*
5:14, *291*
5:15-17, *288*
5:19, *307*
5:20-21, *298*
5:23, *300*
5:25, *297*
5:25-28, *288, 297*
6:5, *288, 290*
6:6, *306*
6:7-9, *291*
6:8, *291*
6:10, *290, 295*
6:11, *290*
6:13, *291, 305*
6:16, *307*
6:20, *306, 307*
6:21, *306*
6:23, *290*
6:26, *306*
6:28, *290*
7, *275, 306, 307, 309*
7:1, *290*
7:2-3, *294*
7:7, *294*
7:13, *176, 299, 306, 307*
7:13-14, *89*
7:14, *290, 291, 306, 307, 309*
7:15-16, *291*
7:16, *291*
7:19, *291, 294*
7:20, *294*
7:21, *307*
7:23, *294*
7:24, *294*
7:25, *307*
7:28, *291*
8–12, *302*
8:1, *290*

8:15-17, *291*
8:20-21, *307*
8:27, *291*
9, *287, 289, 290, 291, 292, 293, 294, 295, 296, 297, 299, 301, 303, 305, 307, 308, 309, 314*
9:1, *292*
9:2, *286, 288, 289, 290, 291, 292, 293, 305*
9:2-4, *290*
9:3-5, *295*
9:3-19, *121, 289, 294*
9:4, *289, 296*
9:5, *305*
9:5-6, *296*
9:6, *289, 292, 305*
9:7, *289, 296*
9:8, *296, 305*
9:10, *289, 292*
9:11, *286, 289, 297*
9:11-13, *291*
9:13, *286, 289*
9:15, *294, 296*
9:16, *294, 296*
9:16-20, *305*
9:17, *294, 295*
9:17-19, *295*
9:19, *294*
9:20, *296*
9:20-27, *291*
9:21-22, *294*
9:21-23, *291*
9:22-23, *291*
9:24, *289, 292, 294, 296, 297, 304, 308*
9:24-26, *297, 304, 305*
9:24-27, *289, 297, 298, 307, 308*
9:25, *307*
9:25-26, *305*
9:25-27, *294*
9:26, *304, 308, 309*
9:26-27, *307, 308*
9:27, *307*
10:1, *291, 292*
10:2-3, *297*
10:14, *298*
11:30, *132*
12:3, *304*

Hosea
1–3, *225, 226*
1:7, *225, 227*

1:10–2:1, 225
1:11, 225, 226, 227, 234, 235
2:2-23, 226
2:3, 225, 228
2:9, 225
2:12, 225
2:14, 225
2:14-23, 225
2:15, 225
2:18, 75, 225
2:18-23, 232
2:19, 230
2:22, 225
2:23, 225
3, 225, 226
3:4, 228
3:5, 123, 225, 226, 230, 231, 233, 234, 239, 279, 298
5:6, 225
5:9-11, 228
5:13-14, 228
5:14, 229
5:15, 228, 229
6:1-2, 229
6:1-3, 228, 229
6:2, 229
6:3, 252
6:4-6, 229
6:5, 228
7:10, 225
7:13, 227
8:7-8, 230
8:8, 234
8:10, 208
8:13, 226
9:3, 226
9:6, 228
9:13, 228
9:15, 224
9:17, 228
11:1, 132, 133, 226
11:5, 228
11:10-11, 229, 230, 235
11:11, 226
12:4, 229
12:9, 226
12:10, 107
12:13, 226
13:1, 227, 228
13:2, 259
13:4, 226
13:4-5, 228

13:7-8, 229
13:7-9, 227, 228
13:13, 227, 228, 229
13:14, 226, 227, 228, 229, 230, 232, 240, 241
13:14–14:8, 228
13:16, 227, 228
14:2, 231
14:5-7, 226
14:9, 106, 226

Joel
2:13, 231
3, 226, 304
3:2, 230
3:18, 225
3:19, 224, 226

Amos
2:10, 226
3:1, 226
4:10, 226
7:1, 118
9, 226
9:3, 73
9:5, 158
9:7, 226
9:9-15, 130
9:11, 233
9:11-12, 130, 141
9:11-15, 226
9:12, 103, 128, 130, 131, 132, 224, 233, 255
9:12-13, 139
9:13-15, 225

Obadiah
12–15, 163
17–21, 130, 131
18–19, 130
19, 224
21, 130

Jonah
1, 217, 219
1–2, 219, 220, 223
1:1-3, 216
1:2-3, 222
1:3, 217, 219, 220, 234
1:4, 217, 219, 221, 222
1:4-5, 220
1:5, 220, 234

1:5-10, 217
1:9, 217, 222, 223
1:10, 219, 234
1:11-15, 217, 220
1:15, 217, 222
1:15-16, 219
1:16, 217, 219, 224, 234
1:17, 217, 220, 221, 222, 229, 230
1:17–2:1, 220
1:17–2:10, 229
2, 98, 216, 217, 218, 219, 220, 221, 222, 223, 224, 225, 227, 229, 231, 233, 234, 235, 236, 237, 238, 239, 240, 241, 314
2:1, 217
2:1-2, 229, 230, 239
2:2, 220, 224, 230, 234, 235, 236, 241
2:2-3, 227
2:2-5, 217
2:2-9, 217, 218, 220, 221, 225, 229, 236, 238, 241
2:3, 217, 220, 221, 222, 233, 236, 241
2:3-4, 224
2:3-7, 237
2:4, 218, 220, 222, 223, 229, 234, 236
2:5, 218, 220, 221, 222, 236, 238
2:6, 218, 220, 222, 225, 229, 234, 236
2:6-7, 217, 223, 224
2:7, 218, 220, 222, 223, 236
2:8, 217, 218, 222, 236
2:9, 217, 220, 221, 224, 236
2:9-10, 229
2:10, 222, 236, 241
3–4, 217, 218
3:2, 222
3:2-4, 217
3:5, 224, 234
3:10, 166
4:2, 166, 217, 231
4:3, 228
4:8-9, 228

Micah
1, 224
1:2, 218
1:2-7, 218
1:3, 218

Scripture Index

1:4, *218*
1:7, *218*
2:12, *230*
4:1, *123, 231, 298*
4:1-3, *224*
4:6, *230*
4:10, *227*
5:2, *231, 277, 280, 281*
5:2-4, *233*
6:4, *227*
6:5, *133*
7, *98, 226, 231*
7:7-20, *232*
7:15, *231, 235*
7:15-20, *77, 232, 233, 256*
7:16, *231*
7:16-17, *233*
7:17, *153, 231, 234, 256, 259*
7:18, *231, 232, 233*
7:18-20, *231*
7:19, *206, 227, 231, 232, 233, 234, 235, 241*
7:20, *231*

Nahum
1:3, *231*

Habakkuk
1–2, *164*
1:4, *162, 163, 212*
1:5, *163, 164*
1:6, *164, 229, 230*
1:6-11, *163*
1:7, *162*
1:9, *230*
1:12, *162, 165*
1:12–2:4, *162*
1:13, *234*
1:14-17, *230*
1:15, *230*
2:2-3, *164*
2:2-20, *162, 164*
2:3, *102, 162, 164*
2:4, *162, 164, 165, 229*
2:5, *220, 229, 230*
2:13, *163*
2:13-14, *163*
2:16, *163*
3, *164*
3:2, *163, 164*
3:2-15, *164*
3:7, *98*

3:10-12, *99*
3:11, *165*
3:12-13, *165*
3:13, *154, 165*
3:13-14, *165*
3:16, *164*
3:16-17, *164*
3:16-19, *164*
3:18-19, *164*
3:19, *163*

Zephaniah
1:15, *163*

Haggai
2:5-6, *226*

Zechariah
1:8, *176*
1:12, *292*
3:8, *201*
6, *238*
6:12, *173, 201*
6:12-13, *173, 174, 270*
9–14, *224*
9:9-10, *251, 256*
9:10, *256, 259*
10:8, *227*
10:8-10, *227*
10:10-11, *224, 226*
10:11, *227, 235*
12, *304*
12:10, *233*
13:7-9, *304*
14, *304*

Malachi
1:11, *224*
4, *32, 289*
4:1-3, *256, 257*
4:4, *32, 226, 227, 289*
4:4-6, *247, 257, 289*
4:5, *32, 289, 290*

NEW TESTAMENT

Matthew
1:1, *177*
2:15, *133*
4:10, *258*
8:17, *189*
8:23-27, *221*

11:19, *285*
11:28-30, *83*
21:42, *101*
23:34-36, *285*

Mark
12:10, *101*

Luke
4, *289*
4:8, *258*
7:34-35, *285*
11:49-51, *285*
22:37, *189*
24:27, *189*
24:44, *289*

John
1:1, *38*
1:1-2, *276*
1:14, *38*
3:14, *213*
5:21, *158*
7:37-39, *204*
7:39, *213*
8:28, *213*
12:16, *213*
12:23, *213*
12:32, *213*
12:34, *213*
12:38, *189*

Acts
1:7, *295*
2:30, *135*
4:11, *102*
4:25, *282*
8:34, *189*
8:35, *189*
13:33, *183, 280*
13:41, *164*
15:13-18, *130*

Romans
1:4, *280*
5:14, *232*
8:2, *232*
9:33, *302*

1 Corinthians
1:24, *285*
1:30, *285*

2:2, *212*
10:4, *203*
15:26, *232*

2 Corinthians
6, *78*
6:18, *183*

Galatians
4:9, *3*

Ephesians
1:10, *14*

Colossians
1, *274*
1:15-16, *43*
1:17, *43*
1:18, *274*

1 Timothy
6:20, *61*

2 Timothy
3:16, *6*

Hebrews
1:1-2, *38*
1:3, *280*
1:5, *183, 280*

1:13, *280*
5:5, *183, 280*

James
2:23, *14*
3:15, *61*

1 Peter
2:6, *302*
2:6-7, *103*
2:7, *101*
2:8, *302*
2:11, *290*
2:22, *189*
2:24-25, *189*

ALSO BY KEVIN S. CHEN

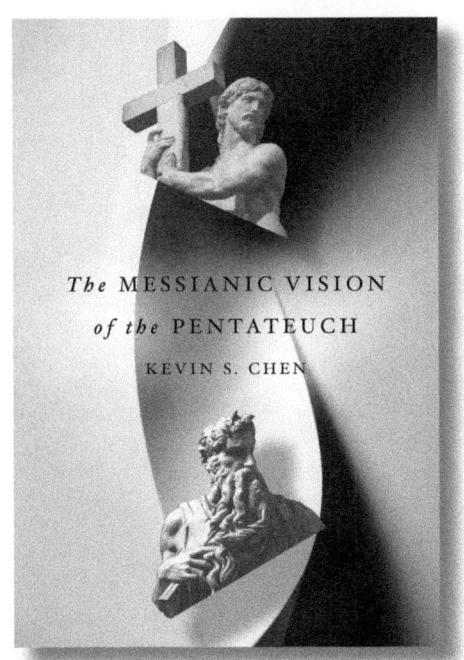

The Messianic Vision of the Pentateuch
978-0-8308-5264-2